The SAGE
Handbook of
# Organizational
# Behavior

## Volume II

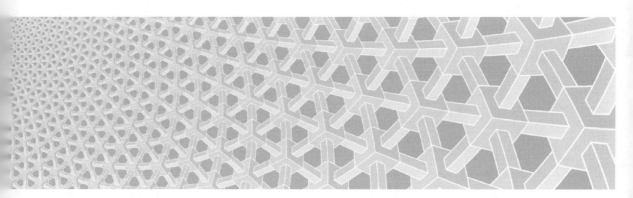

# The SAGE Handbook of

# Organizational Behavior

## Volume II
## Macro Approaches

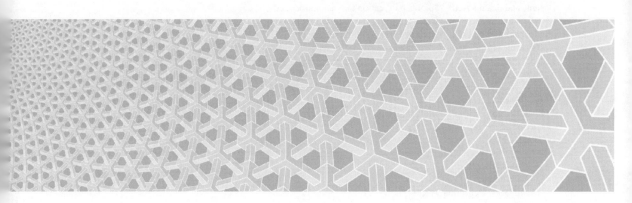

Edited by

# Stewart R. Clegg
# and Cary L. Cooper

Los Angeles • London • New Delhi • Singapore • Washington DC

SAGE Publications Ltd
1 Oliver's Yard
55 City Road
London EC1Y 1SP

SAGE Publications Inc.
2455 Teller Road
Thousand Oaks, California 91320

SAGE Publications India Pvt Ltd
B 1/I 1 Mohan Cooperative Industrial Area
Mathura Road, Post Bag 7
New Delhi 110 044

SAGE Publications Asia-Pacific Pte Ltd
33 Pekin Street #02-01
Far East Square
Singapore 048763

**Library of Congress Control Number: 2008922918**

**British Library Cataloguing in Publication data**

A catalogue record for this book is available from the British Library

ISBN 978-1-4129-3427-5

Typeset by CEPHA Imaging Pvt. Ltd., Bangalore, India
Printed in Great Britain by The Cromwell Press, Trowbridge, Wiltshire
Printed on paper from sustainable resources

# Contents

# About the Editors

**Stewart R. Clegg** is Professor at the University of Technology, Sydney and Research Director of the Centre for Management and Organization Studies; a Visiting Professor of Organizational Change Management, Maastricht University Faculty of Business; a Visiting Professor to the EM-Lyon Doctoral Program, and Visiting Professor and International Fellow in Discourse and Management Theory, Centre of Comparative Social Studies, Vrije Universiteit, Amsterdam, and also at Copenhagen Business School. He is a prolific publisher in leading academic journals in management and organization theory, who has published a large number of papers and chapters and is the author and editor of over 40 monographs, textbooks, encyclopedia, and handbooks. He is a Fellow of the Academy of the Social Sciences in Australia and a Distinguished Fellow of the Australian and New Zealand Academy of Management. He is also an International Fellow of the Advanced Institute of Management Research. To his surprise he has been researched as one of the top 200 business guru's in the world (*What's the Big Idea? Creating and Capitalizing on the Best New Management Thinking* by Thomas H. Davenport, Lawrence Prusak and H. James Wilson, 2003). His current empirical research is on project work and on business coaching.

**Cary L. Cooper** is Professor of Organizational Psychology and Health, and Pro Vice Chancellor at Lancaster University. He is the author/editor of over 100 books (on occupational stress, women at work and industrial and organizational psychology), has written over 400 scholarly articles for academic journals, and is a frequent contributor to national newspapers, TV and radio. He is currently Founding Editor of the *Journal of Organizational Behavior* and Co-Editor of the medical journal *Stress & Health*. He is a Fellow of the British Psychological Society, The Royal Society of Arts, The Royal Society of Medicine, The Royal Society of Health, British Academy of Management and an Academician of the Academy for the Social Sciences. Professor Cooper is past President of the British Academy of Management, is a Companion of the Chartered Management Institute and one of the first UK-based Fellows of the (American) Academy of Management (having also won the 1998 Distinguished Service Award for his contribution to management science from the Academy of Management). In 2001, Cary was awarded a CBE in the Queen's Birthday Honours List for his contribution to occupational safety and health. He holds Honorary Doctorates from Aston University (DSc), Heriot-Watt University (DLitt), Middlesex University (Doc. Univ) and Wolverhampton University (DBA); an Honorary Fellowship of the Faculty of Occupational Medicine, in 2006 was awarded an Honorary Fellowship of the Royal College of Physicians (Hon FRCP), and in 2007 a Life Time Achievement Award from the Division of Occupational Psychology of the British Psychological Society.

# About the Contributors

**Stephen Ackroyd** is Professor of Organizational Analysis at Lancaster University Management School. The main themes of his research work concern the effects of the mediation of social and economic power by organizations and occupations. His early research was into organizational misbehaviour, which was completed whilst he was a consultant in the British engineering industry. After spending much time subsequently researching the professions and public sector organizations, his current work is concerned with the activities and strategies of the largest British companies still involved in manufacturing, and the current transformation of British capitalism. His recent books include: *Realist Perspectives on Management and Organisation* (2000) and *Critical Realist Applications in Organisation and Management Studies* (2004) (both written and edited with S. Fleetwood), *The Organisation of Business* (2002), *The New Managerialism and the Public Service Professions* (2005 with Ian Kirkpatrick). Recently, he has co-edited and co-authored with R. Batt and others *The Oxford Handbook of Work and Organisations* (2006) and with D. Muzio and J.-F. Chanlat *Redirections in the Study of Expert Labour* (2007).

**Elena Antonacopoulou** is Professor of Organizational Behaviour at the University of Liverpool Management School and founder of GNOSIS, a research initiative advancing Practice Relevant Scholarship. Her principal research interests include change and learning practices in organizations and the development of new methodologies for studying social complexity. She is currently undertaking a series of research projects in Organizational Learning, Social Practice and Dynamic Capabilities working collaboratively with leading researchers internationally and with practitioners and policy-makers in co-creating knowledge for action. She writes on all the above areas and her work is published in international journals such as *Organization Studies, Journal of Management Studies, Academy of Management Review*. She is currently Subject Editor for Organizational Learning and Knowledge for the *Emergence: Complexity and Organizational Journal* and has recently completed a five-year term as joint Editor-in-chief of the international journal *Management Learning*. She serves on the editorial board of *Organization Science, Academy of Management Learning and Education Journal* and *Society, Business and Organization Journal, Irish Journal of Management*. She has recently completed a four-year prestigious Senior Research Fellowship as part of the Advanced Institute of Management Research. She has served on the EGOS Board for two terms (6 years) and has been elected to several positions at Board and Executive levels at the Academy of Management (USA) where she has now been appointed to lead the Practice Theme Committee.

**Yehuda Baruch** is a Professor of Management at Norwich Business School, UEA Norwich UK and formerly a Visiting Professor at the University of Texas at Arlington, USA and a Visiting Research Fellow at London Business School. He holds a BSc in Electronic Engineering (Ben Gurion, Israel), MSc and DSc in Management and Behavioral Sciences (The Technion, Israel). After being a project manager in the high technology industry he embraced a career in academia.

He teaches graduate and undergraduate courses in the areas of organizational behaviour and human resource management. His research interests are Global and Strategic HRM, Careers, and Technology Impact on Management. He has published over 80 refereed papers in a number of journals, including *Human Resource Management, Organizational Dynamics, Journal of Vocational Behavior, Human Relations*, and *Organization Studies*. The author of *Managing Career: Theory and Practice* and co-editor of *Winning Reviews: A Guide for Evaluating Scholarly Writing* and *Opening the Black Box of Editorship*, as well as over 20 book chapters. Professor Baruch is the Editor of *Group & Organization Management*, former editor of *Career Development International* and served as the Chair for the Careers Division of the Academy of Management.

**Rosemary Beckham** co-founded Triarchy Press with Gerard Fairtlough, a press that exists to promote high-level new thinking about organization and organizations. Rosie believes that trust, openness and critique are the key to organizational success. She is interested in the dynamic process of people working together to get things done, especially without a dominant hierarchy. This necessarily includes: an exploration of the distinction between 'managing' (the processes used to get things done) and 'hierarchy' (control over people); an understanding of the role of learning in knowledge; and an understanding of the role of shared culture and communication in innovation and change. Rosie studied business management at the South Bank University and after an early career in HR development, moved into sales and marketing, since when she has worked for several start-up companies where her creativity, flexibility and generalist skills have been most useful. Rosie also has a first-class degree from the University of Exeter and is a fluent French speaker.

**Suzanne Benn** is a Professor at Macquarie University, Sydney. She has a background in the sciences and social sciences and currently researches and teaches in the area of sustainability and corporate social responsibility. Her recent publications include *Organisational Change for Corporate Sustainability* (Second edition, Routledge, 2007 with Dexter Dunphy and Andrew Griffiths) and *Corporate Governance and Sustainability* (Routledge, 2007 edited with Dexter Dunphy). Suzanne is currently working on *Key Concepts of CSR* (for Sage) and *Leadership for Global Sustainability* (for Edward Elgar).

**René ten Bos** is Professor of Philosophy and Organizational Theory at Radboud University, The Netherlands. He has published on strategy, ethics, poststructuralism, management fashion, and many other topics. His work has appeared in journals such as *Organization, Organization Studies, Journal of Organizational Change Management, Social Epistemology, Culture & Organization, Theory, Culture & Society, Business Ethics: A European Review*, and *Journal of Management Studies*. He is the (co-)author of *Fashion in Utopia in Management Thinking* (2000) and *For Business Ethics* (2006) and co-editor of *Philosophy and Organization* (2007). He has also published 12 books and numerous articles in his native language. ten Bos is member of the editorial board of *Organization* and associate editor of *Culture & Organization*. His current research interests are in animals and in water.

**Andrew D. Brown** took his MA at Christ Church, Oxford, and his MSc and PhD degrees at the University of Sheffield. He held faculty positions at Manchester Business School, the University of Nottingham and the University of Cambridge, before taking up a Chair in Organization Studies at the University of Bath. He sits on the editorial boards of *Human Relations* and *Journal of Management Studies* and is a Senior Editor of *Organization Studies*. His principal research interests are centred on issues of discourse and identity. He has published work in a range of scholarly journals, including *Academy of Management Review*, *Journal of Management Studies*, *Human Relations* and *Organization Studies*.

**Kim S. Cameron** is Professor of Management and Organizations at the Michigan University Ross School of Business. He has researched organizational downsizing, organizational effectiveness, corporate quality culture and the development of leadership excellence, which have been published in more than 100 articles and 10 books: *Coffin Nails and Corporate Strategies* (Prentice Hall), *Developing Management Skills* (Prentice Hall), *Diagnosing and Changing Organizational Culture* (Jossey Bass), *Organizational Decline* (Ballinger), *Organizational Effectiveness* (Academic Press), *Paradox and Transformation* (Ballinger), *Positive Organizational Scholarship* (Berrett-Koehler), *Leading with Values* (Cambridge University Press), *Competing Values Leadership* (Edward Elgar), and *Making the Impossible Possible* (Berrett Koehler). His current research focuses on virtuousness in and of organizations – such as forgiveness, gratitude, kindness, and compassion – and their relationship to performance. He is one of the co-founders of the Center for Positive Organizational Scholarship at the University of Michigan, whose work was recognized as one of the 20 highest impact ideas of 2004 by the *Harvard Business Review*.

**Arne Carlsen** is a Senior Scientist at SINTEF Technology and Management in Norway and affiliated with the Center for Research on Radical Organizational Change at the Norwegian University of Science and Technology. Much of his research has been linked to practical development processes in and with professional service organizations. Articles from his PhD on organizational becoming and enactment of drama have recently appeared in *Organization Science* and *Journal of Positive Psychology*. Arne has contributed to many books and was the editor (with Roger Klev and Georg Von Krogh) of *Living Knowledge: The Dynamics of Professional Service Work* (2004).

**Chris Carter's** is Professor of Management at the University of St Andrews in Scotland, where he is also Co-Director of Research in the Management School. His principal research themes revolve around trying to understand managerialism, the changing nature of professions in society, and the sociology of strategy. Chris was born and raised in Cornwall, his first degree was in Accounting and Finance (Bournemouth University) before taking a Masters and PhD in Organization Theory (Aston Business School).

**Arran Caza** is an Assistant Professor of Business Administration at the University of Illinois at Urbana-Champaign and a Fellow of the New Zealand Leadership Institute. His research focuses on leadership and management discretion. He has published in *Journal of Management Inquiry, Journal of Business Ethics, American Behavioral Scientist* and *Academy of Management Review.*

**David Collinson** is Professor of Leadership and Organization at Lancaster University Management School, UK. He is currently seconded as the National Research Director to the Centre for Excellence in Leadership. Previously at the Universities of Warwick, Manchester, St. Andrews and South Florida, David is the founding co-editor of the journal *Leadership* published by Sage (www.sagepub.co.uk/resources/leadership.htm), and founding co-organizer of the International Conference in Leadership Research. He has published five books including *Managing the Shopfloor* (1992), *Managing to Discriminate* (1990) and *Men as Managers, Managers as Men,* and over 100 journal articles, book chapters and research reports that develop a critical approach to organization, management and leadership studies. His work on power, identity, management, gender, masculinity, safety, resistance and humour has been widely cited. David's current research focuses on the development of critical approaches to leadership and followership. Recent publications include: *Dialectics of Leadership*, *Re-thinking Followership*, *Questions of Leadership Distance*, *Identities and Insecurities*, *Critical Studies on Men, Masculinities and Management*, *Humour and Leadership*, and *Conformist, Resistant and Disguised Selves*.

**Ian Colville** is Senior Lecturer in Organizational Change at the School of Management, University of Bath. He has a first class degree in psychology from Cardiff University, and an MPhil and PhD in management from Bath University. He is director of *The Change Management Forum* at the University of Bath which aims to provide a place where thinking practitioners and academics interested in doing practice meet to exchange perspectives and 'make sense of change and leadership', which also lies at the heart of his research. He has published with Karl Weick and Bob Waterman in the journal *Organization*. Previous publications appeared in such places as *Public Administration*, *Organization*, *Long Range Planning*, and *Accounting Organization & Society*. He is on the editorial board of *Organization Studies*.

**Jay Conger** holds the Henry Kravis Research Chair Professorship of Leadership at Claremont McKenna College in Claremont, California. Author of over 90 articles and book chapters and 13 books, he researches leadership, organizational change, boards of directors, and the training and development of leaders and managers. His articles have appeared in the *Harvard Business Review*, *Organizational Dynamics*, *Business & Strategy*, the *Leadership Quarterly*, the *Academy of Management Review* and the *Journal of Organizational Behavior*. His most recent books include *The Practice of Leadership* (2006), *Growing Your Company's Leaders* (2003), *Shared Leadership* (2002), *Corporate Boards: New Strategies for Adding Value at the Top* (2001), *The Leader's Change Handbook* (1999), *Building Leaders* (1999), *Winning 'Em Over: A New Model for Management in the Age of Persuasion* (1998). He has taught at the Harvard Business School, INSEAD (France), the London Business School, McGill University, and the University of Southern California. He received his BA from Dartmouth College, his MBA from the University of Virginia, and his DBA from the Harvard Business School.

**David Courpasson** is Professor of Sociology at EM LYON Business School, France. He is also a Visiting Professor at Lancaster University, the Management School. The main themes of his research work concern the effects of organizational and political dynamics on power structures and regimes, and new forms of resistance in the workplace. His recent books include *Power and Organizations* (Sage, 2006, with Stewart Clegg and Nelson Phillips), and *Soft Constraint: Liberal Organizations and Domination* (CBS Press/Liber, 2006). He is also editor in chief of *Organization Studies* and sits on the editorial board of *Organization Science*.

**Gerard Fairtlough**[†] trained as a biochemist, graduating from Cambridge University in 1953. He worked in the Royal Dutch/Shell group for 25 years, the last five as CEO of Shell Chemicals UK. In 1980 he founded the leading biopharmaceuticals company Celltech and was its CEO until 1990. He was involved in the start-up of several high-technology businesses as a non-executive director or 'business angel'. In 2005 he founded Triarchy Press, a publishing house that specializes in short, rigorous books on organizational design and adaptation. He was an adviser to various government and academic institutions, including Specialist Adviser to the House of Commons Select Committee on Science and Technology, a member of the Science and

---

[†]Deceased.

Engineering Research Council and Chair of the Advisory Panel, Science Policy Research Unit at Sussex University. His publications include *Creative Compartments: A Design for Future Organization* (London: Adamantine Press, 1994), *The Power of the Tale: Using Narratives for Organisational Success* (with Julie Allan and Barbara Heinzen, Chichester: Wiley 2001), *New York Changed My Life: A Memoir of the 1960s* (2004), and *The Three Ways of Getting Things Done*: *Hierarchy, Heterarchy & Responsible Autonomy in Organizations* (Triarchy Press, 2005).

**Raymond Gordon** is the Head of the School of Business and the Associate Dean of Research for the Faculty of Business, Technology and Sustainable Development at Bond University. His research interests include power in organizations, leadership, ethics and social control systems. He is an ethnographer and employs discourse analysis, narrative and story telling methods. He has published extensively in internationally recognized academic journals such as the *Leadership Quarterly*, *Organization Studies*, *the Journal of Public Administration* and the *Organization Management Journal*. He authored the book entitled *Power, Knowledge and Domination*, which was published in 2007 by Liber/Copenhagen Business School Press as part of its Advances in Organizations Studies series.

**Anne-Marie Greene** is Reader in Industrial Relations at the University of Warwick Business School and Research Scholar of the ESRC's Advanced Institute of Management (AIM). She is a member of the editorial boards of *Gender, Work and Organization and Equal Opportunities International*. Her research interests include the theory and practice of diversity and equality; equality and diversity issues within trade unions; and e-collectivism, particularly the use of ICTs by trade unions. She has published widely on these subjects in leading journals including *Work, Employment and Society*; *European Journal of Industrial Relations*; *Gender, Work and Organization*; *Industrial Relations Journal*; *International Journal of Human Resource Management*; and *Economic and Industrial Democracy*. She is co-author of *The Dynamics of Managing Diversity: A Critical Approach* (Elsevier, 2005) and author of *Voices from the Shopfloor: Dramas of the Employment Relationship* (Ashgate, 2001).

**Mary Jo Hatch** is Professor Emerita, McIntire School of Commerce, University of Virginia (USA) and Adjunct and Visiting Professor at the Copenhagen Business School (Denmark). Her research interests include organizational culture, identity and corporate branding; and aesthetic approaches to organizing, leadership and epistemological and methodological issues in organization theory. You will find her work on these topics in *Academy of Management Review, Administrative Science Quarterly, European Journal of Marketing, Harvard Business Review, Human Relations, Journal of Brand Management, Organization, Organization Science* and *Organization Studies*. Her most recent books are *The Three Faces of Leadership: Manager, Artist, Priest* (with Monika Kostera and Andrzej Koźmiński, 2005); *Organization Theory: Modern, Symbolic and Postmodern Perspecitves*, Second edition (with Ann Cunliffe, Oxford University Press 2006) and *Taking Brand Initiative: How Companies Can Align Strategy, Culture and Identity Through Corporate Branding* (with Majken Schultz, Jossey-Boss 2008). Mary Jo is a former European Editor of *JMI* and sits on the editorial boards of *Academy of Management Review, Human Relations, Corporate Reputation Review, Organization Studies* and *Scandinavian Journal of Management*.

**Stefan Heusinkveld** is an Assistant Professor at the Nijmegen School of Management, Radboud University, Nijmegen, The Netherlands. In 2004 he obtained his PhD from the Radboud University, Nijmegen with a dissertation on transience and persistence in management thinking.

After his PhD he visited Durham University, and the Stockholm School of Economics. His current research concentrates on management consultants and the evolution of management ideas in the managerial discourse and organizational praxis.

**Kerr Inkson** is semi-retired. He is Adjunct Professor of Management at the University of Waikato, New Zealand, and Honorary Professor at the University of Auckland. He has a Masters degree in Occupational Psychology from the University of London and a PhD from the University of Otago. He has previously held chairs in New Zealand at the University of Auckland, the University of Otago, and at Massey University. An expert in general management, organizational behaviour and career development, Kerr has published over 60 refereed journal articles, over 30 book chapters, and 12 books. In 1997 he won the Award for Best International Paper at the Academy of Management. His latest books are *Cultural Intelligence* (co-authored with David C. Thomas, Berrett-Koehler, 2004), *Understanding Careers: The Metaphors of Working Lives*, (Sage Publications, 2007), and *Working on the Edge: A Portrait of Business in Dunedin* (co-edited with Victoria Browning and Jodyanne Kirkwood, Otago University Press, 2007). He is a Fellow of the New Zealand Psychological Society and the New Zealand Institute of Management, a Distinguished Member of the Australian and New Zealand Academy of Management, and a former Chair of the Careers Division, Academy of Management.

**Gill Kirton** is Reader in Employment Relations at the Centre for Research in Equality and Diversity, School of Business and Management, Queen Mary, University of London. Her research interests lie in the area of equality and diversity in employment and organizations. Her recent work includes studies of gendered careers, strategies and practices within trade unions; stakeholder involvement in organizational diversity management. Gill's work is published in a number of leading journals including, *Work, Employment and Society, British Journal of Industrial Relations, Industrial Relations Journal, International Journal of Human Resource Management, Gender, Work and Organization*. In addition, she is the author of three books: *The Dynamics of Managing Diversity: A Critical Approach* (2005, Elsevier, with Anne-Marie Greene); *Women, Employment and Organizations* (2006, Routledge, with Judith Glover Routledge); *The Making of Women Trade Unionists* (2006, Ashgate). Gill is a member of the editorial boards of *Gender, Work and Organization* and *Equal Opportunities International*.

**Alison M. Konrad** joined the Richard Ivey School of Business, University of Western Ontario in 2003 as a Professor of Organizational Behavior and holder of the Corus Entertainment Chair in Women in Management. Professor Konrad was Chair of the Academy of Management's Gender and Diversity in Organizations Division in 1996–97 and received the Division's Sage Scholarship Award for contributions to the field of gender and diversity in organizations in 1998. She was President of the Eastern Academy of Management in 1997–98 and was named a Fellow of that organization in 2004. She is past Editor of *Group and Organization Management*, a ranked journal in the fields of management and applied psychology. She is a past Associate Editor of the journal, *Gender, Work and Organization* and a past editorial board member for the *Academy of Management Review*. She has published over 50 articles and chapters on topics relating to workplace diversity in outlets such as the *Academy of Management Journal, Administrative Science Quarterly, Gender, Work and Organization, Group and Organization Management, Human Relations, Journal of Organizational Behavior, Psychological Bulletin, Sex Roles*, and the *Strategic Management Journal*. Professor Konrad's current work focuses on gender and diversity in organizations, with a special focus on organizational diversity and inclusiveness initiatives and the diversity of social networks.

**Miguel Martínez Lucio** is a Professor at Manchester Business School, University of Manchester. He was also a Professor at Bradford University. His research is concerned with the changing patterns of rights and regulation within employment relations and human resource management. Much of this work has a comparative and international perspective. He has also led and participated in a range of research projects regarding the impact of deregulation, privatization and marketization in terms of work, employment and management in the public sector and privatized industries across various countries (financed by the ESRC and the Leverhulme Trust). He has also studied the development of European Works Councils and transnational labour networks in their response to globalization and marketization (Anglo-German Foundation, DFG Germany). The political dimension has been developed in terms of research on the changing nature of collectivism at work, trade union renewal/modernization, and the changing composition of collective voice mechanisms in terms of race and ethnicity. The central concern of much of this work is the position and role of regulation and institutions in the context of globalization, increasing managerialism, and socio-economic uncertainty.

**Sarah MacCurtain** is Co-Director of the Health Services Performance Research Group. She received her PhD from Aston Business School. She teaches Organizational Behaviour at the University of Limerick. Continuing research interests include top management team effectiveness, trust and organizational performance, employee stress and wellbeing in the health services, organizational climate and innovation. She has co-authored publications inclusive of books, monographs, book chapters, journal articles and conference papers. Her books and monographs include *High Performance Work Systems: The Economic Evidence* (2005, National Centre for Partnership and Performance); *Principles of Organisational Behaviour, An Irish Text* (2004); *Managing Knowledge Based Organizations: Top Management Teams and Innovation* (2002); *Effective Top Management Teams: An International Perspective* (2001). Her articles have been published in journals such as *Management Revue, Personnel Review, International Journal of Human Resource Management* and *Irish Journal of Management*.

**Woody Van Olffen** is an Associate Professor of Organization Theory at the Strategy and Business Environment Department of RSM Erasmus University in Rotterdam, The Netherlands. He likes to think of himself as a generalist. Topics he has published about include team composition, team dynamics and turnover, manager's personality and organizational commitment. His current academic interests are in professionalism, professional development and the dynamics of professional industries, in particular inter-organizational migration. He also works as a personal coach, especially to academics.

**Martin Parker** is Professor of Organization and Culture at the University of Leicester School of Management. His current interests are in cultural representations of organization, so he is writing about pirates, spaceships and skyscrapers. Relevant books for this chapter are *Against Management* (Polity, 2002), and *The Dictionary of Alternatives* (with Fournier and Reedy, Zed Books, 2007).

**Tyrone Pitsis** is Senior Lecturer at the University of Technology, Sydney. He teaches organizational behaviour and leadership in the Executive MBA programme at UTS. He has co-authored or authored papers in leading academic journals (such as *Organization Science, Organization Studies, International Journal of Project Management, Management Learning* etc), books and book chapters, and international conferences where he has also been recipient of best paper awards. Tyrone's academic interests are in leadership in project-based organizations, pragmatic phenomenology and positive psychology. He is co-director of the Centre for Management and Organizations at UTS. His most recent book is Clegg, Kornberger and Pitsis (2008) *Managing and Organizations: An Introduction to Theory and Practice.* London: Sage.

**Judith K. Pringle** is Professor of Organization Studies at Auckland University of Technology. Her research has focused on women's experiences in organizations, gendered organizational identities, workplace diversity, intersections of social identities (gender/ethnicity/sexuality/age) and reframing career theory. She is a co-investigator of a recently funded large project aimed at theorizing careers within the film industry that take into account aspects of gender, age and ethnicity. Judith is co-editor of the Sage *Handbook of Workplace Diversity* (2006) and has published numerous book chapters, and in scholarly journals such as *British Journal of Management, Journal of World Business, International Journal of HRM, British Journal of Management, Women in Management Review, Career Development International* and *Asia Pacific Journal of HR.*

**Alison Pullen** is an Associate Professor of Organization Studies at the University of Technology, Sydney's School of Management having formerly held posts at the Universities of York, Durham, Essex and Leicester in the UK. Her work can be read in major international journals and edited collections. Alison is author of *Managing Identity* (Palgrave, 2006) and co-editor of *Organization and Identity* (Routledge, 2005), *Thinking Organization* (Routledge, 2005), and *Exploring Identity: Concepts and Methods* (Palgrave, 2007). She is currently co-editing a collection called *Bits of Organization* (Liber, 2008) which presents some of the most avant-garde work in the field of organization studies. Some of Alison's current research projects involve exploring the relationship between women's bodies, space and performativity; the gendered nature of change, and corporeality and ethics.

**Tim Ray** works on knowledge and innovation at the UK's Open University Business School. Before joining the Open University in 1999, he spent seven years working in Japan for Japanese organizations. His earlier experience includes positions at the University of Manchester and Manchester Metropolitan University.

**Carl Rhodes** is Professor of Organization Studies in the School of Management at the University of Technology Sydney (UTS). He researches and writes on issues related to ethics in organizations, knowledge and identity in organizations, and popular culture and organizations. His most recent books are *Critical Representations of Work and Organization in Popular Culture* (Routledge, 2008 – co-authored with Robert Westwood), *Humour, Work and Organization* (Routledge, 2007, co-edited with Robert Westwood) and *Management Ethics – Contemporary Contexts* (Routledge, 2006, co-edited with Stewart Clegg). His work can also be found in journals such as *Organization, Organization Studies, The Leadership Quarterly,* and *Qualitative Inquiry.* Carl is currently editing a volume entitled *Bits of Organization* (Liber, 2008) with Alison Pullen.

**Robert Roe** is Professor of Organisational Theory and Organisational Behaviour at the University of Maastricht, The Netherlands. He has been Professor of Work & Organisational Psychology at the Dutch universities of Delft, Tilburg and Nijmegen, director of the Work and Organization Research Center in Tilburg and of the Netherlands Aeromedical Institute, and organizational consultant. He was also founding president of the European Association of Work & Organisational Psychology (1991). His publications cover books, book chapters and journal articles on human resources management, organizational behaviour, work performance, and research methodology. In his current work the emphasis is on temporal facets of behavioural and organizational phenomena.

**Majken Schultz** is Professor of Management at Copenhagen Business School. She is also partner at the The Reputation Institute. Her research interests are located at the interface between culture, identity and image, corporate branding and reputation management. She has published more than 50 articles in international journals, among others in *Harvard Business Review, California Management Review, Academy of Management Review, Academy of Management Journal, Human Relations, Organization Studies, Journal of Marketing Communication, Journal of Management Inquiry, European Journal of Marketing*. Among her books (together with Mary Jo Hatch) are *The Expressive Organization* and *Organizational Identity: A reader* with Oxford University Press. Her most recent book also with Hatch is *Taking Brand Initiative: How Companies Can Align Their Strategy, Culture and Identity Through Corporate Branding* with Jossey Bass. She serves on several company boards, including Danske Bank and COWI. She is very active in the public debate on issues related to identity and corporate branding and is a regular columnist in the leading business newspaper *Boersen*.

**Alan Scott** is Professor of Sociology at the University of Innsbruck, Austria and convenor of the School of Political Science and Sociology's Contemporary Europe: Governance and Civil Society research programme. His research and teaching interests cover political and organizational sociology, and social theory. Recent publications include a co-translation of Georg Simmel's *Rembrandt* (Routledge, 2005) and, as co-editor, a collection on universities and regional development, *Bright Satanic Mills* (Ashgate, 2007).

**Graham Sewell** is Professor of Organization Studies and Human Resource Management in the Department of Management and Marketing, University of Melbourne, Australia. Prior to this appointment, Graham was professor and chair in organizational behaviour at the Tanaka Business School, Imperial College London. From August 2004–July 2005 he was the Spanish Ministry of Science and Education visiting professor at the Universitat Pompeu Fabra, Barcelona. He has also held visiting appointments at the University of South Florida, the University of California Santa Cruz, and the University of California Berkeley. He gained his PhD in urban planning from Cardiff University in 1994. Graham has been researching the effects of workplace surveillance since the late 1980s and has published extensively on this topic in journals such as the *Academy of Management Review*, the *Administrative Science Quarterly*, and *Sociology*. His article with James R. Barker, 'Neither good, nor bad, but dangerous: Workplace surveillance as an ethical paradox', was recently reprinted in *The Surveillance Studies Reader* (McGraw-Hill/OUP, 2007).

**Omar Solinger** started as a PhD candidate in October, 2004, on 'The dynamics of commitment' at Maastricht University, The Netherlands. His conceptual work on the organizational commitment phenomenon is published in the *Journal of Applied Psychology* (2008). Besides 'organizational commitment', topics of his interest are longitudinal research methodology and change (i.e., dynamics, transitions, learning, growth, sense-making, and change management). He wrote his master's thesis for Royal Dutch Airlines on 'HRM and outsourcing: Making sense of change'. A summary of his theoretical work on psychological processes during outsourcing was published by the Human Talent Trophy Foundation. He studied Work and Organizational Psychology at the Radboud University, Nijmegen. In his private life he is an active pianist (performer, teacher, and composer), dancer (salsa) and socializer.

**André Spicer** is an Associate Professor of Organization Studies at Warwick Business School. He holds a PhD from the University of Melbourne, Australia. His work focuses on political dynamics of organizations. He has conducted research in numerous settings including social movements, public broadcasters, ports and libraries. His work has appeared in journals such as *Organization Studies*, *Organization*, *Human Relations*, and *Journal of Management Studies*.

Recently he published a monograph with Cambridge University Press entitled *Contesting the Corporation* (with Peter Fleming).

**Robert Watson** is a Professor at The University of Durham Business School. His research interests include corporate governance, executive pay, organizational design, SME performance, regulation, and entrepreneurship. In addition to publishing many articles in management, finance and accounting journals on these topics, he has also co-authored three research monographs and has obtained research funding from a wide variety of sources, including the Economic and Social Research Council (ESRC), Department of Employment, Leverhulme Trust, National Westminster Bank plc, and several of the major accountancy firms. Currently he is undertaking ESRC-funded research into Remuneration Committee decision.

**Richard Weiskopf** is an Associate Professor at the School of Management at the University of Innsbruck (Austria). His research focuses on the problematization of organizational and managerial practices. He is particularly interested in poststructuralist philosophies and their potential for critical analysis and rethinking of organizations and organizing. He is editor of *Menschenregierungskünste. Anwendungen poststrukturalistischer Analyse auf Management und Organisation* (Wiesbaden, Westdeutscher Verlag). A co-written book (with G. Krell) on strategies of organizing passion appeared in 2006 (*Die Anordnung der Leidenschaften*, Wien: Passagen). Currently he is working on an empirical and theoretical project on ethical and aesthetic practices of organizing work in the so called 'Creative Industries'.

**Michael West** is Executive Dean of Aston Business School. He graduated from the University of Wales in 1973 and received his PhD in 1977. He has authored, edited or co-edited 16 books and has published over 150 articles for scientific and practitioner publications, as well as chapters in scholarly books. He is a Fellow of the British Psychological Society, the American Psychological Association (APA), the APA Society for Industrial/Organizational Psychology, the Royal Society for the Encouragement of Arts, Manufactures and Commerce, the International Association of Applied Psychologists, the British Academy of Management and a Chartered Fellow of the Chartered Institute of Personnel and Development. His areas of research interest are team and organizational innovation and effectiveness, particularly in relation to the organization of health services. He lectures widely both nationally and internationally about the results of his research and his ideas for developing effective and innovative organizations.

**David C. Wilson** is Professor of Strategy and Organization in the University of Warwick where he is also Deputy Dean of the Business School. He is the author of eight books and over 70 journal articles. He was Chairman of the British Academy of Management (1994–1997) where he served for over 10 years as an Executive member. He is a Fellow of the Academy, elected in 1994. He is listed in *Who's Who in Social Science*, a list of leading international scholars in their field, published by Edward Elgar (2000). He was Chairman of the scholarly society, the European Group for Organisation Studies (EGOS) from 2002 to 2006. He has had a long association with the journal *Organization Studies*, beginning as Editorial Assistant (1981–1996), becoming Co-Editor (1992–1996), Deputy Editor (1996–1999) and finally Editor-in-Chief (1999–2003). He is currently Chair of the Editorial Advisory Board for *Organization Studies*. He has been a member of EGOS for over 20 years and has served on the Board for the last six years.

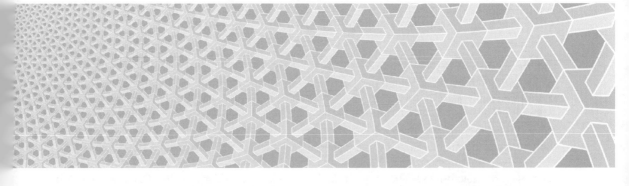

# Introduction: Why a Handbook of Macro-organizational Behavior?

Stewart Clegg

## INTRODUCTION

Most research in organizational behavior is micro in focus, betraying the deep embeddedness of the discourse in psychology, the study of individuals. Thus, the distinctive feature of micro-organizational behavior is that it is the study of the behavior of individuals and groups in the organization, as seen from a psychological perspective. If there are similar disciplinary auspices for macro-organizational behavior they relate to sociology, strategy and economics.

Is macro-organizational behavior the same thing as organization studies, organization theory or organization analysis? Well, if it is not the same thing it is very similar: there are strong family resemblances; they are cousins, at least. Perhaps the major difference is that macro-organizational behavior has a focus on the person and group, even where the effects that are inscribed in them are quite macro whereas one is as likely to find that the phenomena of interest in the close cousins may well be the population of organizations, the organization's form, or the effects of macro-systemic and macro-societal forces on organization level phenomena (Clegg *et al.*, 2006).

The present collection is a first; although other resources exist in the general area of macro-organization behavior, that claim to be 'handbooks', notably Viber's (2004) *Theories of Macro-organizational Behavior: A Handbook of Ideas and Explanations,* one should note that Viber's (2004) text is not a Handbook in the way that the present text is. Viber's 'handbook' is a sole-authored textbook that addresses many different 'perspectives' on the field, ranging from a large number of 'functional economic theories of the firm', 'functionalist organization theories', 'interpretive and social constructivist perspectives', through to 'humanist and structuralist perspectives', 35 different perspectives in total. It is all rather exhausting and, for the student, perhaps a little confusing, as the question must arise, which perspective should I be using now, and why?

The present Handbook is nothing like the Viber text; instead, we decided what we thought were the major *issues* in rather than *perspectives* on organizational behavior as seen with a macro-lens. Then, we asked people drawn from the front ranks of research-based scholars whom we knew to have done exemplary work in these fields to write for us. Where we were not sure whom to invite we sought advice from our illustrious Editorial Board. Each author or authorial team received detailed feedback on the draft chapters that they had produced and then we thought about the structuring of the volume.

Readers might think that one would have worked out the precise structure of a volume such as this in advance; my experience, and that of Cary, which is pretty expansive, is that this is rarely the case. Strategy does not determine structure; nor does the structure get chosen in advance and determine the strategy. The process is more emergent, more organic, and more grounded in the material actually produced. Thus, we had elicited a number of contributions that addressed some substantial, central, key questions; these clearly played a framing role in the volume as a whole. The contributors were chosen because of their expertise in the area that they had been asked to contribute to and were not subject to any prescribed framing by the editors in terms of either approach or methods. Having chosen outstanding contributors we felt confident that we could get exemplary contributions.

## FRAMING THE FIELD: INTRODUCING SOME BIG ISSUES

The question 'what do organization behavior tools actually do?' is at first glance innocuous, a mere seeking for information about why people might develop and use such tools. However, as André Spicer suggests, such a question can be deeply problematic. Posing it can be deeply divisive of the community of OB scholars. Issues of relevance, style, and audience, not to mention ethics and practice, immediately jostle for attention when what OB does is considered.

For Spicer, there are a number of dimensions to the question. First, there is the status of theory: OB claims to be a theoretical discipline – what ideas of theory does it work with? Second, given that OB does develop theories, what does it matter? What is the impact of the theories produced by researchers on what managers do in practice? Third, given that these theories might frame much of what goes on in organizational life, how is this knowledge used? Addressing the last of these questions takes us into consideration of matters of prediction, understanding, and critique of, as well as innovation in, organizational behavior.

Theory in organizational behavior is established, in dominant versions, as being abstract in its representations; ideally, these representations connect conceptual ideas causally; they do so by means of argumentation that connects different theoretical elements whether logically or, by means of data, with empirical tendencies in the real world. All of this must be seen in terms of context: the limiting condition for theoretical applicability.

The auspices of the aforementioned conception of theory are quite clear: they derive, essentially, from a modern, scientifically framed view of the universe of knowledge. For the majority of practitioners of OB this would be the appropriate context within which to view their disciplinary work; they do science when they do OB. The science may be a little different from pure physics, in that it is less definitely deterministic in its specification of relations and somewhat more probabilistic, but it indubitably bears a family resemblance to the other sciences. Essentially, it tests out propositions that are derived either deductively from empirical clues or inductively from conceptual frameworks.

There are other views of theory that Spicer also discusses, in which the theorist does not take for granted either the way that conceptual relations appear to correspond to the empirical world or the necessary correctness of the conceptual scaffolding in use. Instead, the theorist is profoundly suspicious of the sense data that provides their information about this world, in part because any understanding of the social world is already mediated by some kind of theory. We do not observe 'raw' sense data but data that has already been made sense of through the interpretive lenses that we find natural to use. In this view, theory is a way of approaching the world based on constant questioning of immediate sense data and its interpretation. Theory breeds suspicion of what we think we apprehend, empirically. It constantly invites new ways of seeing.

Considered either as propositional or suspicious science, what is the point of theory? Well, it helps us manage the worlds through which we move. Take the example of organizations conceived as routines, for instance. Routines emerge around recurrent activities, such as hiring staff. These activities then become the focus of many different organizational behavior approaches that address the consequence and corollaries of different ways of doing this activity. Over time, these routines become understood through the wisdom embedded in these organization behavior approaches as something to which various theories of selection apply. As members of many different organizations in many different places come to understand the process of selection through these theories – often taught in higher education – and apply these theories in practice then they become a constitutive part of common sense used in practice. Subsequently, common sense provides an implicitly theoretical template for the conduct of everyday life. Thus, one important effect of OB theories is the creation of tacit-and-taken-for-granted knowledge. Smart people, realizing this, act to create discontinuous markets in common sense by developing consultancy and intellectual products that periodically remodel its assumptions, creating fashions in ideas.

To the extent that a market in management ideas is captured by particular theories these theories can become, if widely adopted in practice, what Spicer refers to as ideologies – strict and appealing normative schemes for making sense of the world of sense data. He uses the idea of leadership as one example and, as another, the very ubiquity of 'management' in the contemporary world where there is hardly any situation, practice or process to which the tag 'management' cannot be applied. Of course, any sophisticated market has many claims to small differentia among products so that not all products compete directly with each other. Canny investors in ideas will seek out those ideas that seem to have the highest status in the market; thus, one factor driving the adoption of management practices will be the cultural capital that attaches to them, how high a cultural value they seem to have. So another thing that organization behavior ideas do is to shape conformity in the design and conduct of behavior; not necessarily because of functional efficiencies attached to the use of specific theories but because they become, for a time, highly valued.

Organization behavior tools that become widely used, such as particular selection instruments, personality tests, or behavioral profiling, become technologies of management. It is not so much that managers use the tools but the tools use managers, they operate through managers, to produce categorically coherent knowledge about work and organization. The knowledge that these theories encode becomes a constitutive part of almost everyone's ways of making sense and performing their work. Theories become performative tools.

What kind of performance particular theories can produce depends on the type of theory that they are, categorically. Conventionally, following the work of the German sociologist Habermas, the categorical work that theory performs has been classified as one or other of explaining causal relations, understanding and interpreting, and critiquing the world. It is the former activity – the explanation of causal relations – that most often preoccupies academic practitioners of theory. The reason is simple: academics circulate their ideas in a milieu in which prediction has an especial cachet – that of the modern university – in which the sciences enjoy poll position. Of course, most of the objects that most modern science attends to do not have theories about their own behavior, as do people. Moreover, in organization behavior the picture is even more complicated – it is not just that theorizing occurs about what people do but it also occurs through the terms with which people speak about what they do. At every point, theory is embedded in everyday language and understandings; it is, in part, the everyday assumptions about the world that already reflect pre-existing theories that shape how the theorist will understand phenomena of and from that world. As Spicer suggests, this can have perverse effects: 'we develop a one-dimensional and rather unsupple understanding of the social world. At times we can end up in a situation where our law-like generalizations act as mechanisms that reproduce existing patterns of domination and subjection. This means our theories can act as a break on social change and enforce a single dominant version of how things should be'.

It is this first way of approaching theory that is most popular in academic circles. The reason is obvious: academics make stellar careers through publishing their ideas in the most reputable journals; the most reputable journals, by and large, adopt a natural science view of the world, even when dealing with social rather than natural reality. There is a premium attached to explaining things in causal terms. The more abstracted these terms are from the terms of everyday life that they draw on the more refined the theory. However, no matter the extent to which theory is refined it can never escape its necessary embeddedness in the common sense understandings of everyday life if it contains empirical points of reference – because these empirical points are always tied up in and made sensible by these understandings.

Focusing on understanding gives rise to the second way of thinking about theory in which the purpose is to seek to interpret how it is that the world is understood in particular ways. The task of an organizational behavior theory in this perspective is to try and communicate how other people interpret and understand the social world by recovering the assumptions, meaning and frames of reference that they find conventional to use. Thus, such an approach to theory is less concerned with providing tools for use and application in everyday life so much as in understanding how the tools in use and application in everyday life shape mundane organizational life and its understandings. The approach is inherently conservative in terms of what exists because it seeks to uncover the meanings that inhere in particular situations and chart their effects. It is not trying to suggest new ways of understanding phenomena but merely to chart, in all their complexity and subtlety, the effects of ideas in use. It is an approach to theorizing that is much favored by anthropologists because it sheds light on strange and different ways of being in the world; applied by organizational behaviorists it seeks to make the everyday life of the organization 'strange' by bracketing the assumptions shared by theory with ordinary ways of thinking and reflecting. From the perspective of those whose knowledge is being bracketed the exercise can seem a little pointless; even though they may not be able to say in so many words what they know they know, they know it, and its reiteration by theorists may seem curiously unedifying and unilluminating – especially as it comes back to them tricked out with words and phrases that belong more to the theorists' world than their own. Moreover, if all understandings belong to a specific context it is hard to accumulate knowledge if all knowledge has its character determined by the ways in which it is used in specific contexts.

The third way that Habermas thinks theory can be used is as a tool for critique, as a calling into question of existing social relations and ways of organizing. From this perspective the organizational behaviorist neither produces predictive theory of what already exists nor attempts to excavate a deep understanding of how what already exists is possible.

Instead, they seek to deconstruct, destabilize and disinter those self-evident 'truths' that people ordinarily hold dear. The reason that this is attempted is because critical theorists, as adherents of this perspective are known, believe that knowledge is best advanced by continually asking questions in order to create some kind of radical or emancipatory social change. They seek not only to understand the world but to change it. In doing so, as Spicer wryly notes, they can become rather egotistical, sure in the certainty of their own critique simultaneously as they seek to expose the uncertainties of everyone else's understandings.

The three positions discussed exhaust Habermas' ways of thinking about the relation of theories to the world; however, there is one other approach that Spicer commends, which involves theoretical work as a process of creative innovation, one that involves creating new concepts that allow us to think about organizations in a different way. The aim is to tell us something that we did not already know, to show us something that enables us see the world in different terms, ways of seeing which create new possibilities for organizing and living. There are risks associated with this view of what organization behavior theories might do and these risks are those that attach to any unbridled innovation programme: much which will be created might be interesting but curious; attractive in itself but useless when applied in the existing contexts of understanding.

Whichever of these approaches to theory are used by organization behaviorists there will be consequences. Some theorists seek to limit these by either corralling their theories within specific paradigms – or models – of research, thus concentrating merely on the internal coherence of their approach, or by adopting an activist orientation towards their favored theory, building alliances and an intellectual movement around it as they seek to extend its influence. Beyond either paradigms or politics, suggests Spicer, there may be a more modulated practical stance. When we apply and use theory we are doing something in the world. What we should consider when we observe something in the world is what its effects are likely to be. Taking this approach involves asking why I am doing this something with this theory, for what purpose; it entails considering who will benefit, and what might be the best way of ensuring these benefits. In answering these questions the theorists may well find that no one of the previously outlined perspectives is entirely adequate; instead the theorists will need to move between different positions, experimenting with ideas here, seeking predictable effects there, and seeking to understand deeply elsewhere, perhaps throwing some critical elements into the mix elsewhere in order to see what conversations are sparked. Indeed, from this perspective good research should be like good conversation, it should not merely affirm but also inform, occasionally unsettle, and sometimes take off in entirely unpredictable and innovative directions.

Organizational behavior spawns innovation. New fields emerge to be charted, debated, critiqued, and reformed. We shall meet many such fields in this Handbook. However, in recent years few have been as influential as the idea of 'knowledge work'. The idea that there was something distinctive called 'knowledge work' was first enunciated by Peter Drucker, as Tim Ray suggests at the outset of asking what it is that knowledge work does. He uses an amusing story to make the point that, if knowledge work largely involves thinking, someone may be doing knowledge work even as they cannot be seen to be doing so. No one ever knows what is going on in the head of the other except in those terms with which the other tells it.

If knowledge work is hard to see it is also hard to define. Ray suggests we should focus less on the abstract noun of knowledge and more on the active verb processes of knowing. That there is such a thing as abstract knowledge is largely due to the prestige with which modern science has become regarded in recent centuries. It is science that produces abstract knowledge.

Science is one of those words that can be attached to almost any practice: sports science, domestic science, computer science, management science. However, as Ray suggests, calling something a science does not necessarily make it a science much as other sciences are already constituted to be. To make this point clear he cites a British philosopher, Simon Blackburn, for whom the idea of a management science seems as preposterous as Feng Shui or Flying Saucers. (Such views are very entertaining and go down very well in élite circles, such as the University of Cambridge, which employs Professor Blackburn to do his knowledge work.) As Ray suggests:

> During the second half of the 1990s, Anglophone management science became bewitched by a curious departure from its realist roots, as oriental oracular mystique shaped the rise of new nostrums. According to Japanese academics, Ikujiro Nonaka and Hirotaka Takeuchi, what the Hungarian-born scientist and Michael Polanyi (1891–1976) called tacit knowledge, which is in the heads of persons and entirely subjective, could be converted into universally comprehensible explicit knowledge objects that can be managed (see Tsoukas, 2003; Ray, 2008a).

Ray excoriates the views advanced by these eminent Japanese professors. He does so because he believes that they let a relativist cat out of the conceptual knowledge bag. He suggests that the tacit-explicit knowledge-conversion process that forms the basis for Knowledge Management (KM) is promulgated not on the foundations that Polanyi laid down, but goes right against the grain of his argument. Tacit knowledge is tacit precisely because one cannot provide an explicit account of it.

Traditionally, economics has dealt with three commodity sources of value: land, labor and capital. To these in recent times, probably after Drucker, and certainly after Nonaka and Takeuchi, has been added knowledge – on the basis of the alchemical tacit-explicit knowledge-conversion process. As Ray suggests, when what a person knows as knowledge is coded as information it is possible to treat their personal knowledge as a scarce commodity that could be priced according to the laws of supply and demand. Yet, if one sells another their land, labor

or capital one alienates oneself from that which is sold – literally – one severs the tie between one's possession of the thing and one's disposition to do with it whatever one will. One passes control of its disposition into the hands of the other: landowner, or investment manager of a bank, for instance. Information is different. If one sells some information that one knows to some other party one still knows it and has the ability to dispose of it after the sale. If you sell information, you still have the thing that you sold. And today, as Ray argues, most knowledge that is sold as information is produced organizationally by a multiplicity of knowers rather than by a solitary thinker. Increasingly, such knowledge became identified in the 1990s as 'mode 2' knowledge – not pure scientific knowledge embedded in a relatively closed disciplinary context but knowledge that is transdisciplinary, relying on informal cooperation among practitioners and users from a variety of backgrounds. Such mode 2 knowledge seemed precisely to be the type of knowledge that Nonaka and Takeuchi felt could flow from tacit-explicit knowledge-conversion processes. Commodified personal knowledge can emerge from ineffable personal knowledge and be shared with the personal knowing of others to create explicit knowledge.

Ray believes that, to the extent that this process of conversion does occur, it occurs in Japanese companies because of some very specific contextual features. Such organizations can take the long-term loyalty of knowledge workers for granted because of deeply embedded institutional expectations about the role of 'company as family' workplace organizations in Japanese society. Employees will 'give up' what they know because they know the company is committed to them and their future is linked to the organization's success. Cooperation among colleagues is natural and easy where insiders form a cohort that sees things in an aligned way, without the necessity for extensive managerial coordination. The normal practices of power and discipline in Japanese organizations made possible what Nonaka and Takeuchi took for granted. Elsewhere, however, in different institutional contexts, one could not rely on the ease of knowledge disposal and sharing, and in these other cases the project of KM's construction would be sown on far less fertile soil.

Only under certain organizational conditions of power relations, which Japanese organizations approximate, will subjects feel eager to share what they know. Knowledge resides in the heads of persons and no knowing subject can construct what they know other than through their experience. Knowledge is actively constructed by the cognizing subject; it does not consist of the 'discovery' of an ontological reality, so much as reside in a subject's cognitive capacity to organize their experiential world. Hence, science, much as any other knowledge-oriented endeavor, is not premised on an ever more perfect approximation of an unchanging reality – both because reality is always changing – think of global warming – and because whatever we learn new changes what we already knew. Scientific knowledge is produced where the constraints under which a phenomenon is observed have been carefully specified; where an explanation of something that is interesting or surprising about the phenomenon under review is noted; where, on this basis, one can make future predictions about the nature of the phenomenon in question, and create standing conditions that should lead to the observation of the predicted phenomenon. Of course, as Spicer suggests in the previous chapter, there are other conceptions of theory that bear less family resemblance to this conception of scientific knowledge that should not be dismissed out of hand because they do not create predictions. Rather than treat knowledge as a part of an object world, it might be more helpful to address the processes by which people learn how to 'do things' in concert with others, where concertation is based on what they know, and specific standing conditions that enable them to share what they know with others. From this perspective KM looks to be a lot less objectivistic and to be a lot more concerned with the construction of conditions

under which knowing can and will be shared. From this perspective, much of KM misses the mark: the focus should be less on what is produced as objective knowledge and much more on the processes whereby knowing becomes – or does not – become shared knowledge.

KM gained its enormous popularity in the West at a time when neo-economic liberalism was very much in the ascendancy. The finest economic historian of the emergence of the liberal market economy from the bonds of feudalism remains Karl Polanyi, who was, incidentally, Michael Polanyi's elder brother. As Scott and Weiskopf elaborate, central to the elder Polanyi's account was the notion of a 'double movement': that as a market emerged in genuine commodities it also emerged in commodities that were fictitious. The fiction most deeply held and widely entertained was that of labor as a commodity on the labor market. In fact, labor only became a commodity through the destruction of a dense institutional fabric of feudal bondage. The market did not so much emerge spontaneously but was created by distinct legislation and regulation, such as the various Poor Laws of nineteenth century Britain, which fixed the status of wage earner as a desirable category at the same time that they stigmatized the categories of destitution (see Clegg et al., 2006: 43–4). Thus the economic subject as a person in a market for labor was one of the first constructions that market society objectified. That the construction took such thorough root, suggest Scott and Weiskopf, is in part because the conditions of its existence represented a tangible freedom denied to those who labored under feudal bondage. More recently, they suggest, the promise of release and freedom from the bondage of bureaucracy that came, with the growth of the market economy, to characterize the mature state of organized capitalism, has increasingly been promulgated. The chief promulgator is the enormously influential Tom Peters (2003), whose project seems to be one of re-enchanting economic activity by fusing the passions and the interests, and in the process overthrowing the barriers that have traditionally marked off civil from market society, public from private life, and the employee role from the many roles that the self might play. It seeks to demarcate the organizational role as primary; to reconstitute this role as entrepreneurial, and to infuse it with passion.

These conditions of existence are both novel and specific. Their novelty develops from the 1980s onwards, with the political programmes of Thatcherism and Reaganism, and the intellectual work of characters such as Tom Peters. Their specificity is given, in the first instance, by the economically liberal Anglo-economies of the UK, US, New Zealand and Australia. In this new order, as Scott and Weiskopf suggest, passion is not an option; it is demanded by the new forms of post-bureaucratic organization that Peters endorses. Those who cannot commit utterly to the passions unleashed are not welcome. While the bureaucratic subject was dominated by the rules of the bureau the new post-bureaucratic subject's organizational behavior will be dominated by no one but their self. However, the freedom is somewhat illusory because only those subjects who willingly constitute themselves as freely entrepreneurial, as subjects able to conduct their own conduct as (self-) responsible entrepreneurs, who are, in a word, *enterprising*, can be allowed to be free. The freedom allowed is, in fact, an obligation. We have to manage ourselves and our career as a series of projects in which we can only blame ourselves for any failure or disappointments. Where all life takes place in a market – from schools, through dating, to job-seeking, employment, insurance, and including all general life-chances, the market and marketization becomes a governing principle that structures life itself. Foucault's (1979) neologism of 'governmentality' (a combination of government and rationality, which becomes fused in the mentality of the subject) comprises the complex of notions, calculations and strategies through which diverse authorities act upon the lives and conduct of others by constituting these subjects as their own arbiters of the degrees of freedom

and unfreedom that they will tolerate in their day-to-day life. Life becomes a project in which the chief investor is the person whose life supports the many projects in which they engage. At all points in these projects, the expertise of the behaviorist is applicable: the autonomous subject is governed at work by organizational behavioral technologies that allow them to reflect on possibilities and opportunities in terms of the discursive categories provided by behavioral experts just as much as they are governed in sport by or dating by coaches or life-style trainers.

Organizationally, choice frees organizational oligarchies from responsibility for the success or failure of projects in which subaltern teams, set in competition with and against each other within the internal market, are made free to make their own strategic decisions but are made also to bear a correspondingly greater responsibility for their own fate. The oligarchs can simply set the efficiency benchmarks that freedom must aspire to by simultaneously lowering costs and raising the level of activity. The post-bureaucratic organization becomes a network of nodal points connecting different projects and project teams in which audit and activity-based cost accounting are the central steering mechanism. For Scott and Weiskopf the exemplar industry for their location are the new creative industries.

The new creative industries represent the shock troops of the new organizational behavior: their workers are both highly qualified and underemployed, often on short-term contracts and project-based work. Above all, flexibility in all things is demanded and self-organization and self-management are seen as the mechanisms that will deliver this flexibility, as projects are bid for, worked on, and negotiated and shared with others who are similarly highly organizationally mobile, flexible in their work times and habits, working always on temporary assignments with high levels of self-responsibility, unclear boundaries and insecure incomes. And on top of everything, the subject is expected, in their organizational behavior, to embrace these new conditions with passion, to invest emotional commitment into their projects, to revitalize the organizational life worlds that they traverse with charismatic conviction and enthusiasm. The recent enthusiasms of empowerment, spirituality and teams take on a very different appearance viewed through the lens of this chapter.

What links Ray's, Scott and Wesikopf's and the following chapter on managerialism by Martin Parker is a similar concern with the much-vaunted end of bureaucracy and the emergence of a post-bureaucratic space, peopled by autonomous creative knowledge workers. Bureaucracy conceived on a rational-legal basis was a revolutionary project, attacking aristocratic privilege and instilling liberal norms everywhere it touched. Left critics railed against the illiberality of its liberalism at the apex of power – where the military-industrial complex meant that technocrats could move freely from one sphere of influence to another. As we have seen in Scott and Weiskopf's discussion of Tom Peters, bureaucracy has come under attack as too slow and too hierarchical. Running through all these critiques and those of the new 'new left' – the ecologists, feminists, and contemporary syndicalists – is a strong anti-managerialism, where managerialism is defined as a fusion of bureaucracy and a belief in the power of reason as the vehicle for delivering more scientifically efficient solutions to whatever problems presented themselves. Saint-Simon is its earliest figure but in contemporary times, the criticism of managerialism proceeds on at least four fronts, which broadly cover complaints rooted in nostalgia, modernization, everyday cultural experience, and anti-authoritarianism.

Nostalgia isn't what it is cracked up to be when viewed historically because it often appears as an infinite regress as each generation displays nostalgia for the world that they believe they have lost. Thus, themes that appear distinctly modern when read in the twenty-first century can be seen to be but echoes of concerns that have rattled the iron cages of bureaucracy and industrialism almost from their inception. Such critiques

are often those of élites who feel themselves by-passed by the rationalization they abhor. More contemporary critiques come from the radical utopians, the modernizers, whom Scott and Weiskopf associated with Tom Peters. For Parker, the criticisms are associated with consultants who sell ideas about culture, re-engineering, spirit, networks and transformational leadership. When associated with reform of state organizations and the public sector the criticisms are not as full-bloodedly marketizing but offer instead various simulacra for markets. The sphere in which most people will be familiar with criticisms of managerialism is cultural, as it is regularly exhibited in shows such as *The Simpsons* and *Futurama*, and strip-cartoons such as *Dilbert*. These are critiques that resonate with the sympathies of those who toil under authority figures who, on the whole, they have little respect for. However, as with the nostalgic, the critiques just keep on coming – at least since the days of mid-nineteenth century critics such as Dickens, through early twentieth century critics such as Kafka. They were differentially developed in different markets: in the US community and common virtue were opposed as wholesome alternatives to big business whilst in Europe opposition to bureaucratic rationalization more often than not was expressed through workers councils, and a general commitment to socialism. From Dickens' Gradgrind to *The Office*'s David Brent, suggests Parker, managers are figures of unease, objects of derision, and ill-regard. The best-developed critique of managerialism derive from anarchist tendencies, suggests Parker, and stretch back at least to the cooperative ideas of the early nineteenth century, and have spread into not only anarchist but also workerist, feminist, and environmentalist criticisms of organization and management. On the whole, these are criticisms from the margins of modernity, from various groups who feel unrepresented or marginalized by modernity. What is remarkable, suggests Parker, is that there are deep traditions from each of these tendencies that are highly critical of managerialism as the dominant expression of organizational behavior yet which are rarely articulated within the field of organizational behavior itself, other than in the somewhat closed and unreflective project of a Critical Management Studies that largely fails to connect with what most organizational behaviorists do. There is a history; it is worth retrieving, and it has much to teach us about the general and pervasive sense of the dark side of organizational behavior.

If Parker dwells on the dark side, the final chapter in Part One of the Handbook by Arran Caza and Kim Cameron seeks to develop positive lessons for organizational behavior. The authors are advocates of Positive Organizational Scholarship (POS). While these authors do not search the historical depths noted by Martin Parker they characterize traditional organization behavior in terms of a hypothetical world of greed, manipulation, and distrust to which they seek, positively, to oppose appreciation, collaboration, and meaningfulness. As they explain it, 'positive' is meant to signal an affirmative attitude to life-enhancing rather than negative experiences, 'organizational' is meant to stress the emphasis on organized contexts, as opposed to purely individual phenomena, while 'scholarship' indexes the importance of research and theory. What is positive, they suggest, are elevating processes, excellence, human strength, resilience, vitality, and meaningfulness. Intellectually, POS draws on positive psychology, community psychology, positive organizational behavior, prosocial organizational behavior, organization development, and corporate social performance. While these are all reasonably well-developed fields, there is, of course, always the matter of interpretation – one person's excellence can be another person's nightmare, as the three previous chapters have been at pains to elaborate.

The major assumption that is made by POS is that people desire positive, happy experiences and that the desire to improve the human condition is universal and the capacity to do so is latent in most systems. Perhaps it could only be in a nation whose constitution establishes a right to human

happiness that such a sanguine view could flourish. It is certainly a long way from the gloomy view of human neuroses that Freud developed at the start of modern psychology; or from a Hobbesian view of human nature and social order as nasty, poor, brutish and short, or from the anti-foundational biases of much contemporary and post-modern thinking, in philosophers such as Richard Rorty. Behind the affirmative assumptions is a commitment to a heliotropic principle which sees living systems as seeking that which is life-giving and avoiding that which is life-depleting. Various studies – from psychology and from linguistics – are cited to support the existence of the heliotropic principle in social life, as well as noting its existence in the biological sciences. The chapter then explains its categorical principles and, using these, proceeds to discuss 21 recent empirical papers that elaborate the POS agenda. These are discussed in terms of six themes – Individual Virtue and Social Concern, Leadership, Organizational Virtue, Positive Relationships and Performance, Psychological Capital and Absence of Negativity – that can be found in the research literature. Taken together, they provide a significant set of signposts for those who want to develop more positive theories and studies.

Caza and Cameron do not simply elaborate the usefulness of POS in research terms, however; they also look at its applications in practice, including case studies that document especially positive organizational performance, specific tools and techniques for generating positive effects, and instructional programmes centred on POS knowledge. With all this positiveness in evidence it would be encouraging if the posited eudemonic nature of individuals and their organizations did lead to positive behavior, create positive dynamics, and produce positive results, but, this is not the case. The empirical evidence suggests more complex relationships where positive emotions can produce negative behaviors, negative emotions can produce positive behaviors and positive behaviors may produce negative results. These findings, once again, suggest that what is positive must be considered more complex than the heliotropic orientation suggested. If human conflict, travail and misery can produce positive outcomes does this mean that we should encourage such phenomena because, in the long run, they can facilitate positive outcomes? Some solutions to the definition of positive are suggested: being positive is better than a median point in a normal distribution or being positive could be defined in contextual terms. The latter would seem to be fraught with the difficulties identified earlier by Spicer: how does one aggregate a general theory from the specificities of local contexts? Moreover, there is a more general issue of cultural specificity – thus far the majority of studies come from developed Western societies, although there are some few exceptions. In these exceptions there appear to be counter-factual tendencies to those observed in the US, suggesting that, not surprisingly, what is positive is culturally contingent. Nonetheless, with all the careful caveats that Caza and Cameron articulate, it is evident from the extensive literature reviewed that POS has already made a significant impact on the field and should continue to do so.

## MACRO ORGANIZATIONAL BEHAVIOR AND IMMANENT PROCESSES

The most fundamental human capacity is the capability of learning, one which is, of course, shared with other primates, but in a far less developed way. By extension, organization behavior has increasingly talked of the capacity of organizations to learn. When organizations learn they change, it is assumed but Antonacopoulou argues that this is too simple: organizations that learn might learn in such a way that the social, emotional and political forces at play lead not to change and transformation but to a degree of stability. Learning reinforces the status quo through a focus on what is known rather than a drive towards the unknown. One reason why

learning is so often equated with effective change is that learning and changing has so often been conceptualized in terms of stable patterns of routines and practices. Hence, if one changes the independent variable, learning, then one knows that it has been effective by the changes displayed in the dependent variables of routines and practices. The latter changes stand as ciphers for the effectiveness of the former interventions.

A part of the issue with restricted approaches to learning is that they often betray their disciplinary auspices in one or other of the social sciences; Antonacopoulou calls for a more trans-disciplinary approach, learning from approaches to complexity theory and process approaches to becoming, which she terms trialectical, focusing on the unfolding of phenomena in time and space. From complexity theory three key principles are employed: *inter-connectivity, diversity* and *self-organization*, to which she adds a fourth element neglected by both complexity and learning debates – *politics*. Greater inter-connectivity, diversity and self-organization are all conducive to more complex learning, but all learning takes place in a political world that might equally hinder or facilitate certain privileged and less-privileged forms of learning.

Learning is a practice – in a double sense: it is both something done and something honed through practice. Conceptualizing learning as practice enables us to focus on the co-existence of multiple adjoining and interlocking practices as they co-evolve. Unlike institutional theory that tends to see learning as dominated by the end of that which is institutionally valued, the approach that Antonacopoulou develops sees learning as a much more open, less reductive practice – one that is captured in the notion of practising. While practice and practicing refer to the institutionalization of activities and routines, practise and practising focus on the holistic and emergent nature of practice. There are, she suggests, significant epistemological and ontological implications of the shift in focus that she recommends. Epistemologically the focus moves to the gerund, to practices of learning and working in different contexts, paying attention to dynamic relations between individual agency, social structures and systems surrounding complex tasks. Ontologically, the focus shifts to the study of process, to research into how practice is practised or rehearsed in performance. Although influenced by the initial US literature on learning, from major figures such as Schon and Argyris, Antonacopoulou's chapter also draws heavily on more European sources.

That there are quite distinct emphases between the two sides of the Atlantic is further reinforced in the chapter by Robert Roe, Omar Solinger and Woody Van Olffen. This chapter offers a critical discussion of the background, meaning and operational significance of the concept of organizational commitment in organizational research. The notion of organizational commitment had its roots in the contract-based labor relations that are prevalent in North America, and gained popularity as a conceptual counterweight to the deteriorating labor relations that resulted from the 1980s wave of industrial restructuring. To a large degree, commitment expresses a concern about unwanted employee turnover. Since most studies have been cross-sectional, little is known about the way in which commitment emerges and how it develops over time. A temporal perspective would provide a better understanding of what commitment actually is and how it affects the way in which people in organizations behave. While much of the literature addresses the 'best' level of commitment the authors show that the idea of 'the more the better' is untenable. They discuss the question of 'what can be done to shape commitment', a question that they see as a managerial paradox. The more commitment is under pressure because of threat of job loss or poor employment conditions, the less managers can do to prevent it from falling – let alone raise it. In as far as commitment can be shaped it is at the start of the employment relationship.

The need for commitment parallels the exercise of power; the more power has to be exercised in order to restore control the less strong the power relations that precipitated the need for its exercise. In such situations, the exercise of power is a sign of relational weakness. Similarly, while commitment is often seen as diametrically opposed to power, the structural and relational situation is very similar. The greater the need for commitment to be present, the less likely it is to be evident. If commitment is the central currency of soft domination and power (Courpasson, 2006), efforts to increase it signal a currency deficit just as much as do attempts to reassert domination through the exercise of power. Neither soft power gloved in commitment, nor its harder exercise without the protective covering, can be exercised without advertising, precisely, the deficit of that which is desired: a settled order. Maintaining commitment seems to be a matter of keeping promises and striking a balance between organizational and employee interests, and interests, as we shall see, have been seen to be central to power.

Power is precisely the topic of the next chapter by Raymond Gordon. The chapter begins by making a distinction between two distinct streams of literature: one with an idealist orientation, the other with an orientation that is pragmatist. Standard organizational behavioral approaches to power are, Gordon suggests, idealist, as are critical theory approaches, because both operate with a normative model of what power relations should be like. The lineages of these approaches derive from Weber and Marx respectively and a major point of passage was the debate generated in American political science about the nature of community power, which developed from the late 1950s. Many of the definitions and ideas about power generated therein, which were remarkably behaviorist and mechanical in their conception, were to influence notable organization contributions. By contrast, the pragmatists owe a debt to Nietzsche and Machiavelli, and the main point of passage in their debates has been the work of Foucault. On the whole, while this work has been enormously influential in some of the most significant contributions to the organizational literature, it has hardly defined the normal science of power – that has been much closer to the behavioral models developed within what Lukes (1974; 2005) termed the one-dimensional view of power, conceived as an A getting a B to do something that they would not otherwise do. Additionally, in the organizations literature, there is usually a tacit acceptance that power is something that is exercised illegitimately; power is counter-posed to authority – which is the name for power when exercised by management. Hence, power is something that is done by less legitimate and marginal actors, who are seen to generate conflict in organizations – usually because of a lack of commitment to the normative order of the organization.

The Community Power Debate gave rise to what became known as the second face of power; the kind of power that occurs without conflict, without an explicit clash of polarities. From these perspectives derives the idea that all organizations have a certain mobilization of bias inherent to them; that some issues never materialize and remain regarded as non-issues because the balance of power relations is against making them issues. That some issues are not raised as problematic and thus do not generate conflict does not mean that they do not exist; they do exist, but in the under-life of the organization, rather than being on the formal agendas and in policy directions.

A decade after the political scientists Morton Bartaz and Peter Bachrach first artic-ulated the second face of power, an Oxford don, named Steven Lukes, a major-league social theorist, published a slim little book on power. In this text he introduced the idea that there was a third dimension to power: power could be exercised through the management of meaning in such a way that people – members of organizations, for instance – were unable to formulate an independent account of where their interests lay. They could think about and see the world only through subaltern concepts that already positioned them as subjected, and subjects of, a power that had no need to exercise itself crudely through one-dimensional manoeuvres. In fact, he saw power as operating much more insidiously through the way in which the categories of consciousness were already pervaded by the taken-for-granted world views and categories of the powerful – a conception that he related to the idea of hegemony as promulgated by the noted Italian political theorist, Antonio Gramsci (1971).

What makes the aforementioned streams idealist is that each of the accounts proffered has a normative view of what power is and should be. For the one-dimensional theorists the ideal is clearly a world of plural power relations; for the two-dimensional theorists the ideal is clearly a world in which those things that are issues for those who feel the yoke of power relations are not regarded as so hot to handle that they languish as unspoken and unarticulated but barely repressed non-issues. Theorists of ethnicity, gender, and of intersectional issues that fuse with these, have, not surprisingly, been attracted to this perspective.

Contributors to the 'pragmatist stream' are not concerned with telling people how power 'ought' to be in organizations, rather they are concerned with studying 'how' power comes to be exercised in the way that it is, says Gordon. Here the impulse is resolutely empirical and descriptive, and is often regarded as dangerously amoral because of the emphasis on the workings of power irrespective of the niceties of its actual deployment. The description, Machiavellian, named after the founding father of this stream, is often applied to such analysis as if it were a term of opprobrium. Rather, for theorists of this persuasion, it should be considered a compliment, a way of capturing a determined anthropological desire to follow the actors and the action wherever it takes one. Moreover, there is a strong resistance to subscribing to the idealism of other accounts in which certain positions, practices, authorities are *a priori* positioned as legitimate and others as illegitimate. Such matters are a question of empirics, not principle: not surprisingly then, Nietzsche is also a major influence on this stream, often through the influence of Foucault. With few exceptions, much of the work influenced by this stream has hardly been a significant influence on the OB field; of the major post-Foucauldian figures that Gordon addresses, Haugaard and Flyvbjerg have largely influenced cognate fields such as political theory and planning, while only Clegg is a recognized contributor to the organization's literature.

Gordon's sympathies are clearly with the more pragmatist orientation rather than the more idealist, despite the good work that has been done under its auspices. The pragmatist accounts stress the interpenetration of power with knowledge as socially constructed and thus culturally significant and context dependent, used as resources in strategic local games of politics. For these theorists, ultimately, all politics is local.

At the core of Gordon's conception of pragmatic politics is the centrality of the ways that people make sense. Surprisingly, politics has not been central to the development of the sensemaking perspective on organizations. Nor does it feature in Colville's insightful chapter on organizational change and sensemaking. That this is the case is hardly surprising because the progenitor of sensemaking as a perspective, Karl Weick, has also had very little to say about how the politics of power/knowledge are tied up with those of sensemaking. There is a connection to be made here and a gap to be filled.

The main focus of Colville's chapter is on how organizational change episodes can be illuminated by a sensemaking perspective. The status of sensemaking as a perspective is contested, in part because of the enormous signature that attaches to Karl Weick's writings, a signature that a number of commentators have noted as poetic. The writing – for those familiar with Weick – stands out from the run of the mill organizational behavior literature because he is one of the few people working in the area whose clear and deep care about the prose that he writes results in writing that, much as another maverick, Jim March, stands out for its authentic voice and quality – what Van Maanen refers to as presence – but, as Colville says, for sensemaking to have a future after Weick others will have to step up to the mark. Weick's writing is in part a response to the 'double dialectic' identified by Davis: briefly, what specialists find interesting is often unfathomable to laypersons; what laypersons find interesting is often a bore for specialists. Translated into management terms there is every chance that management theory and management practice will fail to connect. The competitive advantage of sensemaking theory, according to Colville, is that it stands a better chance of resolving the dilemma of the double dialectic because it takes as its point of departure the everyday world of practice. In this respect, it demonstrates its origins in Schutz's (1967) phenomenology and Garfinkel's (1967) ethnomethodology, both of which start from the premise that the proper object of a social science should be the ways in which the social world is a profound achievement of practical action and practical rationality, and show its affinity with the work of Erving Goffman (1959) as an investigation of the practical strategies of everyday life.

Weick abhors nouns and prefers verbs. Hence, it is not surprising to find Colville rejecting the study of organizational change in favor of organizational changing. Uniquely, amongst our authors thus far, Colville demonstrates the utility of the sensemaking perspective as he has developed it by addressing an empirical case – a short story about banking – a story with, as befits a Weickian tale, much presence and a great many twists. We won't spoil it by abridging it here.

As Colville makes sense of the banking story he notes that sensemaking can act *both* as a resource *and* a topic. That is, sensemaking theory as a resource can be applied to the ways in which people make sense as a topic. If the topic in hand is of immediate relevance to managers then the chances of solving the dilemma of the double dialectic also increase. Provocatively, Colville uses this probability to make a nuanced plea for more 'claptrap' in theory – by which he means writing that wins applause from its audience. Clearly, he says, the way to do this is to engage with what the audience want and enjoy rather than treating them as benighted, indifferent, intellectually untutored spectators. Elitism in the arts rarely sustains an audience outwith public subsidy; Colville seems to be suggesting something similar about the élitism of the sciences, in this case organizational behavior. If the audience is the élite that read the specialist journals then don't be surprised if those who are the ostensive consumers of the knowledge produced, the lumpen intellectuals one finds in practice, turn off rather than tune in. In other words, Weick rocks because he connects all ways.

Ian Colville works at the University of Bath as does Andrew Brown the author of the next chapter. Was it chance or some other mechanism that assigned them adjacency as a pair? The reader may care to speculate. Certainly, it allowed a nice transition for the writer of this prose. Colville's focus on sensemaking is not too far removed from Brown's attention to identity: before we make sense of the world, for many people, it is first necessary to make sense of their self – or should we say selves? The management of multiple identities and identifications is *the* key issue for modern organizations, suggests Brown, emerging from the broad social sciences and humanities interest in identity issues as well as a focus on the cultures of organizations. Further, there is the postmodern fascination for fragmentation, discontinuity and difference, which encourages scholars to see any and all conceptions of identity as sites of struggle, conflict and ambiguity.

Organizationally, identity is most often regarded as an internalized cognitive structure that defines what an organization stands for, and what it wants to become. It is this view that one finds in what has probably been the most influential of the organizational contributions to the literature on identity: Albert and Whetten's (1985) statement of organization identity as representing a distinctive, continuous essence of an organization. As Brown elaborates there are good foundations for such a view in predecessor work, especially in sociology and social psychology.

Contemporary work on identity is differentiated, in ideal type terms, as 'functionalist', 'interpretive', 'psychodynamic' and 'postmodern'. Functionalist accounts of identity

see it in terms of clear branding, often tagged as corporate identity, with objective properties, something essential about it. Interpretive perspectives look at the ways that members and stakeholders of organizations interpret it – the sense they share and the sense that they do not share, with different sorts of actors seeing the organization, interpretively, in different ways. Psychodynamic perspectives build on the work of Freud in seeing conceptions of identity as a bulwark against the vagaries of a world that is indifferent or hostile; organizational identity is a 'defensive solution' to psychological threats to members which may or may not be articulated at the level of consciousness. Organizations are means for regulating collective self-esteem through individual, group, and organizational defensive mechanisms that seek to ameliorate anxieties. Where psychodynamics work at their best organizations are able to learn, develop and to adapt through critical self-reflexivity, sophisticated dialogues, and a willingness to explore sources of anxiety. Postmodern conceptions of identity see it as provisional, discursively and textually produced and represented, sometimes almost mythically, in so far as it is represented in any stable articulation. At its core it is a narrative without end, or at least for as long as the organization endures and people in and around it tell others about it, through whatever media.

The chapter concludes with some directions for future research oriented around five key questions, which at present are more arenas for debate than questions to which agreed answers will likely be found. Is organizational identity a construct, a question or a metaphor? Do organizations have one or multiple identities? Do these identities endure or are they mutable? What's the relation between organizational identity and cognate terms such as 'reputation' and 'image'? How does organizational identity relate to processes of identification? The discussion of these issues is sufficient to launch any number of future research projects, most of which would seem more likely to explore the concept as 'essentially contested' rather than as one or other of the ways in which the four ideal types posit it as being, and to realize that any questions of identity are necessarily suffused with power.

Although we have been careful to argue that power relations in organizations need not necessarily be accompanied by conflict, in many cases they will be, if only because, in situations of neither hegemonic domination by one party over others or gross inequalities of access to relational resources, the most likely form of action by parties that perceive themselves as weaker is to attack and create conflict that disrupts normalcy: think of classical industrial relations scenarios in which unions strike – the balance of power relations will always reside with those who own and control means of production, administration, and distribution, yet they may be vulnerable to disruptions of normalcy, and so the strike weapon becomes a tool of power. Of course, conversely, employers can use the lockout as a form of counter-attack when they perceive that the balance of industrial relations power has shifted against the terms of trade that they want to normalize on the labor market.

Stephen Ackroyd discusses some of the major approaches to organizational conflict. The basic proposition with which he works is that the development of numerous organizations significantly increases the number and variety of relationships in which people are tangled up; the more lives become tangled together the more difficult it is to sustain clear lines of cleavage and allegiance. Thus, modern social life rests on a complicated gradation of indifferences, aversions and antipathies. However, to the extent that conflicts do occur, organizations are amongst the most significant sites for its expression because they act to channel conflict.

The basic organizing principles of the chapter are quite clear and simple: to divide discussion of organizational conflict into intra- and inter-organizational instances, and then to interrogate these instances through some classical resources of social theory. In terms of intra-organizational conflict the key

dimensions are the degree of intensity and duration of conflict, which, in a $2 \times 2$ table, serve to categorize much of the substantive particularity of the field. A great many of the conflicts so categorised arise from the structuring of antagonisms characteristic of a market economy, with a labor market, that typifies private capitalism. However, as Ackroyd notes, a great deal of the work on conflict displays its functionalist presuppositions. The similarities with the standard OB literature on power that Gordon reviews are remarkably close. Conflict is regarded as a bad thing, a case of organizational misbehavior, or a sign of deviance. These assumptions were built into the earliest management theories from F. W. Taylor onwards.

In the post-World War II era a number of anthropologically influenced studies of workplaces discovered that employees and employers were often acting rationally by their own lights but that these were specific – and often conflicting – rationalities. Such conflicting rationalities need not merely be the effect of vertical stratification between employees and employers but can occur horizontally, between different types of employees as well as horizontally between different units of capital (see Clegg, 1981 for a systematic elaboration of these points). Any of the conflicts that occur in organizations may be decisive; organizations are not fixed entities but continuously renegotiated entities in which conflicts – and their decisions and non-decisions – figure heavily in the negotiation of the order.

Looking at the employer/employee axis, alternate rationalities may be constructed around what are taken to be (often diverging) interests, the negotiation of whose meaning is often expressed in terms of the amount of effort employees are prepared to expend: what the British industrial sociologist Baldamus (1961) called the 'effort bargain'. Where the assumptions of one parties' rationality are violated then organizational conflict ensues over issues such as the duration and intensity of work effort, the use of tools and technologies, the assignment of tasks, teams and colleagues, recognition of status, membership of key committees, boards, etc. Such conflict varies on a continuum for spontaneous and informal resistance to more formal and organized resistance.

Much of the focus, historically, in studies of conflict has focused on the labor process. However, organizational conflict is not something confined merely to divergent interests over the pace, duration, organization, and remuneration of employment relations. It can also occur at much more senior level in organizations, as a cursory acquaintance with the financial press, animated by accounts of boardroom struggles, take-over attempts, managerial coups, and stakeholder revolts indicates. Categories of member such as shareholders, senior managers, and directors are by no means homogenous in their interests or placid in their behaviors, nor do the interests and behaviors of the different categories necessarily align with each other. Substantial business school discourses, such as principal-agency theory and transaction costs economics have developed around these routine antagonisms.

Additionally, there is a rich and fertile field of inter-organizational research topics ripe for cultivation. Changes in populations of organizations, as charted through population ecology perspectives, and organizational fields, seen in terms of institutional theory, can also reflect struggles that find expression in inter-organizational conflicts that are often encoded as competing strategies, whose effects may range anywhere from being mild and ephemeral to acute and temporally long term. These occur not only in terms of conventional competitive strategies or the periodic creative destruction that bunches around clusters of innovations that punctuate long waves in economic development, but can also relate to other, non-competitor organizations, such as regulatory authorities, the state, the judiciary and criminal justice system, where strategy entails suspected malfeasance. One case that Ackroyd discusses that meets all these criteria is the extensive period of transformation of US industry in the 1980s that was created by new organizations of financial capital.

Historically, of course, the major organizational conflicts have been between collective workers and specific units of capital embedded in specific organizations confronted with particular trade unions that fought these organizations over specific issues of remuneration, organization, acknowledgement, entitlement and so on. The incidence of such conflicts has varied comparatively and historically anywhere from riotous assembly, through insurrection, to full-blown revolutionary struggle but has most often been normalized in terms of trade union activities, notably the withdrawal of labor through the mechanism of the strike and associated picketing. Just as with conflict about the nature of capitalism itself, in terms of the legality of new forms of financial organization, these conflicts have often been moderated by regulatory authorities, the state, the judiciary and criminal justice system, as the state has changed the parameters of what are construed as legal methods of mobilization. In this perspective, the strike is but one of the repertoires of collective action available to disgruntled employees, and one which only developed its acuity in the latter part of the nineteenth century. In the latter part of the twentieth century and into the twenty-first, it is a device that, judging by comparative statistics from bodies such as the International Labor Organization (ILO), may well have peaked in the strike waves of the 1970s, although some authorities argue that such a commonly held view may be in part a statistical artefact (Gall, 1999).

If Marx was the first theorists to systematically address the nature of organizational conflict in a theory of history it is fair to say that the times have not been kind either to the theory that he advanced or those ideas that many subsequent political proponents argued that he advanced. Conflicts do not necessarily lead to contradictions and contradictions need not be cataclysmic for system reproduction where they occur; as Simmel (1902) suggested, conflict is both constitutive of organizational and social systems and a major source of their reproduction as such. Conflicts can persist, endure, be channelled, change shape, become more or less latent, and often not be resolved at all. Even though traditional forms of industrial conflict may have declined in recent times this should not be regarded, normatively, as some regression to a more ideal mean: conflict is normal, endemic and constitutive of organizations albeit that its structuration varies comparatively and historically. Despite the emphasis given to employee satisfaction and effective organizations there is no reason to assume that an organization bereft of conflict is either possible or desirable.

Once upon a time organizational careers were what many employees aspired to, seeking employment with organizations that seemed blue-chip, whether private or public, which offered many opportunities for promotion, training, and development. The notion of a career is a construct that only makes sense in societies organized around status-achievement rather than status-ascription principles. Where statuses are ascribed, the notion of a career is, by definition, highly unlikely, as the determinations of caste, status and other sources of social ascription, such as gender or tribe, are determinant in shaping one's life-chances. Even in early modern society in Western Europe for most people the notion of career, if held at all, was tied up in a parallel system of task and status structure administered through guilds as custodians of traditional knowledge. Few organizational careers existed outside of the Church, Navy, and Army, except with the major trading companies, such as the Dutch East India Company, and these were often systematically skewed towards those with wealth and privilege.

In more contemporary times the idea that one has a career has become a major constituent part of the way that one organizes and accounts for one's life. The classical definition of a career is of a series of progressions through the offices of an organization or organizations. The development of powerful internal labor markets and organizational careers, particularly for staff in technical, professional and managerial roles, became part of a powerful recipe for organizational

success in the post-war era as Inkson and Baruch note in their chapter on organizational careers. Even as late as the 1980s, the normalcy of large organizations with stable and progressive organizational careers was a staple of thinking about management and organizations, and even in these more flexible times, oligarchs require some means of reproducing themselves as the strategic élites of organizations, and thus need some form of organizational career management system that organizations for managing organizational succession.

The authors introduce the *Career Active System Triad* (the CAST), as a multi-level conceptual framework developed to help understand the human side of career management. The CAST comprises values, approaches, and behaviors as three levels of analysis. Values are the basis from which the others emerge. Management approaches are meant to transform and translate values into third-level behaviors shaping action and practice. Inkson and Baruch regard the key managerial question as how to fit the person to the organization and how to provide organizational support for the fit. Ideally, values shape individual aspirations and strategy and percolate into individual attitudes and organizational policies. The process of alignment is always dynamic and ongoing; responding to the external environment of structured labor markets shaping demand and supply of particular types of occupations as well as internal organizational politics dynamics. Typically, top management teams will strive to make the alignment strategic. Career management strategies will be subordinated to organizational strategies in this view.

Sociologically, organizational careers can be seen as largely structurally determined by class, education, race, and gender, while educationalists, psychologists and career counsellors see occupational careers as the result of personal choices, rational decision making, and personal maturation. Both sociological and psychological perspectives focus on the individual whose career is seen as more or less the repository of social forces or social choices rather than as something organizationally managed. The latter perspective is developed in perspectives on Organizational Career Management (OCM).

Organizational Career Management (OCM) strategies involve activities relevant to career development, such as selection, training, employee development, appraisal and compensation practices, as well as the design of formal career paths, career planning and development exercises, mentoring and career counselling. Such strategies may entail significant investment of organizational personnel's time and resources and should be calibrated according to the available disposition of these rather than ideal strategy. Not all careers will be organizational in a conventional sense of personal advancement and status; careers may be organized in terms of professions, developing specialist skills, or entrepreneurial, oriented towards value creation rather than personal or professional development.

From an integrationist perspective that strives to combine sociological, psychological and organizational perspectives on careers four significant issues for future research are identified. The first of these is a tension between a focus on structure and a focus on action, which is a sign of the lack of resolution between more sociological and psychological approaches. The second question addresses the tension between stasis and adaptation in careers: are careers relatively stable or do they change over time? The third question addresses whether or not careers can only be studied in their particularity or whether or not there are generalizations that can be made universally. As the authors note, there is little or no consensus on this issue in the field. Attempts at generalization seem to generate many exceptions. Finally, the authors suggest that the question of knowledge in relation to careers needs to be posed: where does career knowledge reside? In individuals or in institutions related to their careers?

There will be organizational careers to manage the more that these careers are determined by structure rather than action; are stable rather than adaptive; are not structured according to idiosyncratic behavior and change, and are based on institutional rather than individual knowledge. The assumptions of vocational areas such as Human Resource Management are based on these precepts. The individual's career is considered to be at the disposal of the organization's planning, performance evaluation, employee development, and succession planning to extract maximum value from each unit of labor under management's control. Organizational careers are of particular value, because they maximize opportunities to develop human assets to company advantage.

These conditions have been in decline over the past 25 years in the developed world, as organizations have grown leaner and meaner, specialized on core competencies and outsourced other areas of activity, such that is appropriate to speak of the decline of organizational careers. Consequently, new models of career have developed as something that the individual manages as a project in external labor markets, between rather than within organizations. Careers become increasingly boundaryless, traversing organizations, laced through specific projects. People invest their careers in organizations and organizations invest in their careers; however, some investments may turn out, on either side, to have been duds. In the dynamics of labor markets in which one will participate for 40 or more years it is always going to be difficult to make successful investments.

Changing circumstances mean that the concept of the organizational career may mean a commitment that lasts organizations a lifetime as a precious resource, or it may be something that they partake of fleetingly, as the individual manages a portfolio of career-related projects. The challenge for future organizations will be to find forms of engagement and relationships that adequately reflect the range of employees' career objectives and strategies.

Successful management careers take one to the top; increasingly the heights of organizations are explored through the burgeoning literature on top management teams (TMT). Sarah MacCurtain and Michael West guide us through the TMT literature of the past 20 years or so. The literature suggests that TMT dynamics can enhance creativity and decision making but do not always do so; hence, it is important to identify the factors that enhance or impede effective top team working and performance.

Although the terminology of the TMT is relatively new, the idea clearly has auspices in Cyert and March's (1963) notion of the dominant coalition – the powerful people who span the boundary between the organization and the external environment and make decisions that have a significant impact on the organization's future. Who these individuals might be is not agreed upon. Some researchers suggest job titles hold the key; others focus on board membership, while still others propose that it is the decision-making circles to which they belong that are important. Whomsoever they are designated as being, one thing is for sure: TMTs comprise senior players in power games in and around organizations, people who have high levels of education, well-developed expertise, who are able to command significant organizational and professional resources, and who are paid to have firm views on many things. Moreover, if the organizations in question follow the lead of research, and compose these teams on the basis of functional, if not social diversity, then these teams are likely to be more creative and innovative. Not surprisingly, in Ackroyd's terms, TMTs are likely repositories of organizational conflict. A dilemma faces top management teams: task conflict is necessary in order to discuss problems in an open and critical manner but it is vital that such conflict does not trigger affective conflict that may potentially destroy the team's commitment to implementing the decision.

Conflict will be specially prevalent when an oligarchic élite has clung on to the seats of power so long that there is a considerable age difference in the successor cohort: research on age diversity suggests that dysfunctional conflict, lack of consensus and ineffective communication will occur when the development of a shared language between individuals that results from similar background and experiences is lacking. Obviously, from this perspective, élite reproduction is a matter to be constantly attending to rather than something to be left until the patriarchs have almost quit the scene. Difference in age is associated with difference in world views.

Too much diversity may be as dangerous as too much homogeneity: the relationship between tenure heterogeneity and outcomes is curvilinear, the literature suggests. Diversity has different effects on different aspects of team performance: high diversity has negative effects on social integration but is positive for cognitive outcomes, such as producing a more polyphonic culture. However, it is likely to be polyphony within bounded rationality: despite demographic diversity there is likely to be similarity in world views and beliefs, certain behaviors, values and experiences expressed through such as loyalty, commitment, dedication, and success, which all serve to facilitate membership of the top team. These are the types of phenomena that students of power usually discuss in terms of hegemony, and some sociologists refer to as anticipatory socialization – a propensity to assume élite views if one presumes to aspire to the élite. Shared views are insufficient in themselves: the processes that make them especially effective will be contingently specific to the situation at hand, MacCurtain and West argue. A certain amount of debate is necessary but there needs to be a degree of consensus in order to achieve decision. Consensus involves both shared understanding and shared commitment, yet if there is too much consensus, creativity and innovation may suffer.

Top teams have to be reflexive, have to be able to learn from their reflection of what they do and have done, in order to inform what they will do. What is necessary is an entwined process of reflection (retrospective reflection), planning (prospective reflection) and doing (immersion in action). There must be delicate balancing of power relations within the TMT. Leaders should not dominate but they must lead through conscientiousness, and emotional stability. Dysfunctional leaders, such as the narcissist, the paranoid, and the controlling, encourage irrational and unconscious processes more than rational consideration of the issues at hand; indeed, as MacCurtain and West observe, there is considerable empirical evidence suggesting that the top management team in general, as well as the leader, influence organizational climate as a direct behavioral manifestation of organizational culture. Central to the climate in the organization is the management of emotions at work. Demographics have a significant relation with TMT characteristics that have an impact on a firm's global strategy: TMTs with lower average age, higher average tenure, higher average education, higher average international experience, and higher tenure heterogeneity lead to a climate in which organizations become more internationally diversified.

Top management teams have complex psychodynamics. Often we glimpse these in snatches of insight into political leaders' lives provided by diaries, memoirs, and leaks. Often these relationships are driven by intense emotions: Alan Clarke's (1993) diaries of the Thatcher years provide a good case in point, signifying a diminishingly consistent or homogenous affective reaction within the Tory TMT – the Cabinet – towards the end of Mrs Thatcher's ascendancy as Prime Minister. There is a sense in which the hubris of TMTs that have been successful for some time can lead them to overstep the limits of what they can achieve and in doing so sow the seeds of their own decline and fall.

One of the crucial issues in TMTs, as we have seen, is their composition in terms of the balance between oligarchical reproduction and renewal. If the issue has been important in the past it can only become even more critical in the immediate future, because, as Conger argues in his chapter on succession management, as a result of the imminent demographic retirement of the baby boomer generation, most organizations will have to replace a considerable number of TMT members at the same time, to the extent that their teams have been fairly homogenous in age terms. Moreover, as the boomers retire and

Gen X and Y move into TMT positions, they bring with them quite different attitudes and dispositions from those formed in the 1940s and 1950s. Witness to the massive downsizing initiatives of large corporations in the late 1980s and 1990s, cynical about the world that the boomers enjoyed and whose rules they then changed for the next generation (fees for universities rather than state support, for instance), younger generations have little commitment to traditional notions of organizational commitment, having a strong sense that they have to manage their careers because they cannot rely on external authorities – whether state or private sector – to do it for them. The Internet and the easy availability of comparative information and opportunities make it easier for the web-savvy generation to be managers of their own careers.

In the past, says Conger, succession management's primary purpose was to identify replacements for senior executives who would eventually depart the organization. Often dead men's shoes or retirees seats were filled in a mechanical lock-step progression up the list of seniority. The possibility that career succession might be used to develop or retain talent remained largely unrealized. By the late 1980s things began to change a little, suggests Conger. Succession management came to be deployed as a mechanism for identifying and cultivating leadership talent across the different organizational generations. The shift in focus was from replacing those exiting to developing all those who entered. In doing so, the focus became much more transparently developmental; members are aware they are on potential career tracks in competition with others and senior managers realize that developing those who report to them is an important part of their leadership portfolio.

Highly effective succession management systems provide a continuous stream of talent capable of meeting the changing circumstances with which organizations must cope. In doing so they serve to keep members challenged and motivated and thus retain them within the organization, rather than seeing them flit to greener pastures and greater opportunities elsewhere. Such systems should be easy to use by executives and line managers and easy for members to access and understand, as well as being evidently developmental of opportunities tailored to particular individuals. Moreover, they are dynamic systems, constantly being revised in the light of experience and changing situations. Nonetheless, the contours of a best practice model are elaborated by Conger in terms of a number of characteristics that the chapter goes on to elaborate:

- Alignment of the succession strategy to the organization's overarching strategy
- Senior level sponsorship and HR 'process' ownership
- Identification and effective deployment of key linchpin positions
- Rigorous talent identification processes
- Strong developmental linkages that accompany talent identification
- Multiple stakeholders assessments with developmental feedback
- Rigorous tracking and feedback metrics.

The TMT must be focused on talent recruitment, training, development, retention and succession in this mode and must feel comfortable addressing both high flyers and low achievers. The former should be rewarded with opportunities and assignments that stretch and develop their capabilities while low achievers must be led to greater heights, rather than being tolerated, with the effect of lowering performance and the attractiveness of the organization to high achievers. If that means speaking truth to power – and to weakness – so be it.

Much of the remit of the good advice and sound research results that have been covered in the chapters to present can only be delivered by highly effective leadership and, as Collinson addresses in his contribution, leadership requires followership. Although leadership is one of the topics most widely discussed and researched in macro-organizational behavior, the conditions of its existence and generation have been

remarkably homogenous because the vast bulk of research has been done using US assumptions and models, with a tacit model of society that corresponds to the US, suggests Collinson, even when these models are applied elsewhere. Thus, highly individualist models of leadership have flourished as the norm – even when there are large parts of the globe where their cultural fit cannot easily be assumed. One consequence of these dominant US models has been an underplaying of issues of power. To illuminate a power perspective on leadership and followership, Collinson draws on critical, post-structuralist and feminist insights.

Leadership studies are usually informed by a desire to describe in some way what makes an effective leader, a question to which the literature provides no clear answer. It all depends on the type of leadership theory one elects to follow! There are several approaches that have flourished in the mainstream of leadership research that Collinson reviews. He concludes that, irrespective of which of these approaches one chooses, followers are often taken for granted and the dynamics of power that relate leaders and followers underspecified. Moreover, leaders are often romanticized and lionized as if they were solitary and extraordinary individuals. More realistically, the relations between leaders and followers should be considered in terms of dialectics of control characterized by interdependencies and power asymmetries. Power relations between leaders and followers are likely to be interdependent, asymmetrical, and contested. Reciprocal resistance of either to the actions of the other is to be expected as a normal feature of organizational life; its pervasiveness depends on contextual factors that leadership can shape: followers value leaders who exercise control and take responsibility and do so in clear, fair and transparent ways while, when leaders exercise control in unfair, dictatorial, coercive, nepotistic, narcissistic and/or self-interested ways, resistance is much more likely; when views have not been considered, leaders are seen as 'out of touch' and there are discrepancies between leaders' policies and practices.

In such situations, which Collinson's research suggests are quite common, members who feel relatively marginalized or excluded will tend to withdraw psychologically from the organization, operating subtly but cynically through small acts of resistance and subversion that are hardly starkly confrontational and thus difficult for leaders to detect, and will project their dissent and dissatisfaction outside into the broader community. Vicious circles can be enacted as leaders find their leadership failing and tighten their surveillance and control of subordinates in order to try and deliver better results, which merely exacerbates the behavior that they seek to rectify by demonstrating more of the same behavior that is occasioning the withdrawal responses.

Conventional approaches to leadership are not good at addressing the more covert, subtle dialectics relating leaders to followers, which is why Collinson draws on feminist post-structuralist analyses that seem better able to address these dynamics, which are often a constitutive part of gender relations. The gender aspects of leadership – as a mostly masculine activity – also need to be addressed as Collinson demonstrates. What are often taken for granted as gender neutral attributes of leadership are, in fact, highly masculine gender-specific characteristics. Organizations and their leadership are riddled through with the biases of masculinity, as Collinson argues. The traditional dualism of leader and follower in many respects resembles and draws from the patriarchal dualism of superordinate males and subordinate females.

## MACRO ORGANIZATIONAL BEHAVIOR AND KEY PRACTICES

The 'Labor Process' as a familiar term in industrial sociology and related disciplines, would be well known in European and Australasian organization theory, but is not really a mainstream term in organizational behavior. The origins of the term are usually attributed to Marx's (1976) *Capital*, where he analyses what he terms the labor process.

For Marx, what was important about the work done in organizations – the labor process – was that it was done under conditions of control by Capitalists in order to reproduce Capital – which he discussed in terms such as 'surplus value'. Basically, he argued that unless the labor employed was exploited – that is, created more value for the capital that employed it than it was rewarded with in terms of wages – the labor process would not be productive and the organization would be inefficient. Efficient capital exploited the labor process. In his chapter Graham Sewell recognizes that this view might be somewhat limited as a useful basis for contemporary discussion, given the assumptions of 'naked' and 'rampant' exploitation that Marx saw in Victorian English factories. Nonetheless, the value of labor process analysis has been the ability to link what happens inside organizations at the point of intersection of organization control and production with the changing macro-economic and societal circumstances in which these encounters occur, as Sewell recognizes.

The core of employee relations and labor process theory is the notion of a contract between a fictional entity – the organization in question – and a real individual, monitored and implemented by other real individuals, often and usually in the organization's employ. The employment relationship is normally constituted by a written contract that places certain expectations on employers and employees in terms of their conduct towards each other. Such explicit contract and implicit reciprocity as it contains is a relatively recent historical phenomenon, when set aside the many great achievements of antiquity founded on coerced, involuntary and slave labor. It was an emergent nexus of relations among a changing balance of feudal power, as free men and women began to emerge, changing conceptions of property and of the rights of man, tied up with the transition from feudalism to capitalism, the Reformation, and the development of civil society that signalled a shift towards a widespread contractual basis for employment relations. The expenditure of effort, the reward of that effort, and the creation of value through employment of organized labor became increasingly related in formal organizations. As these changes took place the traditional patterns of work relations, holidays and holy days broke down and working life intensified, a fact noted by many early commentators, as well as Marx. Marx's innovation was to note that the labor nominally employed – measured in time – and that actually deployed, would usually differ and the difference was an object of struggle between the labor employed and the employee. Laborers sought to minimize the amount of time and effort expended in work, often for very long hours indeed, in order to preserve what energies they could – for the little of life that occurred outside work. Bear in mind that working class people started work as children and that the length of the working day was typically twice as long as we would think normal today, with the work taking place often in conditions that were dark, dangerous, extremely physically demanding and with little labor-saving technology. Thus, the individual employee had an interest in minimizing their individual labor effort while the individual employer had an interest in maximizing it. The scene was set for what Marx believed would be the central struggle in society – between individual employees who came to realize the commonality of their collective situation as mere labor power, against the employers who were well aware of their common interest, one based on their ownership of the means of production, in using this labor power as much as they were able. Thus, in the labor process approach, the effective organization of the labor power employed, in order to produce useful value for employers, will be the central problem for employers and analysts alike, regardless of the social conditions under which the contractual exchange takes place. As Sewell remarks, provided we can still observe a separation of mental supervisory and managerial from manual labor that is supervised and managed then Marx's fundamental observations apropos the subordination of labor to capital through management's monopoly of the conception of work are still as valid

today as they were in 1867 when he first published them.

Sewell argues that the labor process approach is still useful today for understanding subordination and work intensification but it requires a shift from an exclusive focus on the separation of conception and execution in labor and a focus on instances where employees exercise a formally acknowledged degree of discretion, not only over *what* work is done but also *how* it is done. By doing this, he argues, labor process theory can be related to contemporary social theory that places surveillance, superordinate or lateral vision of the person at the heart of its conceptualization of social order and cohesion. In particular, it connects the theory of the employee in organizations with the central focus on some of the influential work of Michel Foucault (1977) on discipline, surveillance, and control, a literature that Sewell explores with reference to an interesting historical context and cast of characters.

In contemporary terms, the task that Sewell sees as central for labor process analysis is to be able to provide a plausible account of contemporary – rather than nineteenth century – forms of the organization of work. Above all, he argues, this means an appreciation of the role that enhanced autonomy at work through team membership, delegation and empowerment, for example, can play in ensuring, seemingly paradoxically, that there is a greater intensification of work and exploitation, and the creation of increased levels of surplus and thus profits, from the labor deployed. From this tack there are many points of affinity with some of the contemporary and past classics of organization theory and behavior, with the work of Alvin Gouldner providing key contributions. The implementation of totalizing systems of control is seen as a frequent corollary of many forms of organization. Whether these are pursued through the physical sequestration of an individual in time and space, through bureaucratic means, or through electronic surveillance, is immaterial. From this perspective, a great deal of organizational behavior, in as much as it consists of relations between subordinates and superordinates (and sometimes fellow team workers) should be recast as a discourse of coercion focused on two main roles: the activities of managers who wish to guarantee the constant visibility of employees in order to maximize their effort and the activities of employees who wish to avoid this scrutiny in order to minimize their subordination to managers. Thus, managers become seen as agents of oppression and, in this respect, the discourse of coercion concentrates on how surveillance allows the more powerful to dominate the less powerful. Sewell characterizes the work that flows from this perspective as a 'radical' research programme. By contrast, there is a 'liberal' research programme that is closely related. Here, the person is problematized as an individual who has the potential to indulge in self-interested behavior left to their own devices. Thus, organizational surveillance (usually in the guise of individual performance monitoring) is deemed to be legitimate so long as it protects the organization and fellow employee interests as judged by the watchful eyes of impartial managers, where all members recognize that organizational surveillance is reasonable and where they trust in the impartiality of those responsible for its operation. However, as Sewell suggests in his conclusion, the dream (or nightmare) of total control will always be unachievable. People's ingenuity in resistance and the unanticipated opportunities offered by all technological advancement will see to that. The failure of present surveillance projects merely becomes the sufficient and necessary cause for the pursuit of further ones. As the indeterminacy of labor has moved to incorporate a cognitive as well as corporeal element in contemporary work, the labor process can be characterized as a problem of the 'indeterminacy of knowledge' where surveillance is implicated in a process of expropriating cognitive faculties including imagination, ingenuity, problem-solving skills, and other forms of embodied knowledge. These can be exercised in ways that managers applaud – but they can also be used in projects that they would not approve of if they knew of them, projects

that may be deeply corrosive of existing authority relations and discipline. As Sewell concludes, the analyst – whether consultant or researcher – is irremediably caught up in the ethics of workplace surveillance as questions of whose control and whose autonomy, whose privacy and whose rights, will always intrude into any analysis of actual organization practice.

There are some immediate echoes between Sewell's chapter and that which follows it. Notably, Judith Pringle, Alison Konrad, and Anne-Marie Greene argue that organizational behavior requires a 'new structuralism' that looks at how society shapes organizations, more in line with what has typically been normal practice in European rather than North American work. More multi-level approaches are required that combine what is usually thought of as the micro, macro and meso. One would expect this to be especially the case from a perspective that focuses on practical aspects of organizational behavior and lived experience – as their focus on gender does. One's experience of gender does not come bundled up in levels of analysis but is experienced as all of a piece in various situated actions and practices, especially where, as they remark, gender equality in the workplace remains a distant goal and where the division of unpaid household labor continues to be unequally skewed against women, and women are routinely the subjects of representational practices that are sexually exploitative. In this environment – which they see as characteristic of contemporary times – it is unlikely that women's equality will be well served by organizational behavior.

Women still occupy a small minority of élite organizational positions, they establish, even in those societies where symbolically important positions have been or are occupied by women. Norway is in the vanguard, with nearly 30% of top management positions being filled by women; the figures rapidly decline as one considers the southern European countries. Elsewhere, of course, outside the OECD nations, in the Middle East, Africa and Asia, the numbers would be even lower.

In the household sphere research consistently establishes that women take responsibility for two-thirds or more of caretaking and household labor in almost every country researched. For many women in contemporary industrialized societies full-time or part-time employment is combined with demanding family responsibilities and employers are finding that they need to provide work-life flexibility benefits to retain female workers, which are associated with positive outcomes for women's careers, where the organization has a supportive work-family culture. This is rarely the case for those who make it to the top, whether men or women, although most of the men will have a wife supplying that two thirds of domestic work which women do.

Women do not fit the stereotypes of successful business leaders as dominant, aggressive, achievement-oriented, autonomous, exhibitionist, and with high levels of endurance: these are represented not as female but male characteristics. Gender stereotypes prescribe as well as describe, and in doing so affect how people are judged by others as gendered entities. Leadership is still viewed cross-culturally as more consistent with masculinity than with femininity; organization is taken for granted as it is and the assumption is often that it is individual women who have to change if they desire to advance in their careers, rather than the organizations that employ them. The default position of many organizations is that masculinity is normal. Amongst other reasons more widely distributed in societal practice, such as representational norms, this is one explanation of why women are often treated as objectified sexual objects, defined by their bodies and dress rather than their professionalism or accomplishments. To the extent that organizations themselves endorse or practise such representational norms they are hardly being sincere in any professed commitment that they might make to the equality of opportunity on a gendered basis, even where they offer work-life flexibility, women's networks, and sexual harassment training programmes as positive organizational programmes.

There are various ways of gauging the progress of organizational programmes to counter discrimination and the extent of negatively gendered practices. For instance, one can look at the overall demographics of female participation rates, where, just about everywhere, patriarchy trumps equality of demographic representation; of course, when intersectional concerns of ethnicity and sexual identity are factored in the situation is even more skewed. These vary with historical context although, even in those contexts where women's issues have been raised they have often been somewhat neglected in the ways that they intersect with other non-gendered bases of identity. Often the formal rituals of nations assure everyone of equality in terms of legislation although almost everywhere the practice may lag behind the legislation; one should not be surprised for if there were no gap there would be no need for legislation. While legislation can shape labor market conditions it is most likely to do so where practice is less problematic, in public sector and corporate organizations, rather than in the very large number of small and medium enterprises which often escape the legislative framework.

Of course, organizational behavior as a discourse has a role to play in the gendering of organizations. Equal opportunity and diversity practitioners are often employed to implement policies that redress gender inequities – does the continuance of these mean that such people are ineffective? Not really, the authors suggest: these practitioners often operate with limited resources and difficult role conflicts that make positive outcomes harder to achieve. Moreover, as they elaborate, such practitioners operate in an area of conceptual confusion about what constitutes 'equality' and 'diversity', which can have a potential impact on the efficacy of policies.

What is referred to in the literature as the 'business case' strategy has provided the keystone for policy making and regulation in most countries in the equity area in recent times. Taking this approach, each organization is expected to move to a less gendered set of practices because it enables them to make best use of their human resources. The strategy is opposed to those top-down legislative approaches that mandate practices. Proponents of the business case argue that as it is in the interests of organizations to make the best use of their talents it is only rational to allow them to do so as they know best how to do so. Legal compulsion forces a one-best way on a wide variety of different, contingent contexts. Of course, there is a degree of circular logic to this: if organizations did what the business case strategy suggests, the problem that legislation strives to address would hardly exist.

Within many organizations Equal Opportunity offices have been constructed largely as institutional responses to a legislative demand. One consequence is that they are often institutionally isolated from the wider concerns of the business and there is often little organizational commitment amongst managerial and other ranks for the policies and practices that they espouse. Where a social or joint regulatory approach that provides a significant role for representatives of lower-level, non-managerial employees, and in particular for trade unions, is used, then it tends to build more commitment and espousal.

Gender equity is just one aspect of diversity in organizations, as Pringle and her colleagues are at pains to articulate. Diversity has been identified as an area of organizational behavior that typically offers prescriptive techniques and tools for managing 'difference'. Of course, in the early days of research this 'difference' was constituted in terms of being other than a national, as well as someone white, male and middle class. As Gill Kirton establishes in her chapter on 'Managing multi-culturally in organizations in a diverse society' the diversity literature is now far richer and is influenced by a variety of (sometimes overlapping) theoretical perspectives, including post-colonial theory, feminism, postmodernism, critical approaches, and social identity theory. Increased academic interest in diversity reflects the rapid growth in organizational policies seeking

to 'manage' diversity. Such management is seen as a corollary of employing people from increasingly hybrid and multicultural societies, requiring that systematic attention is paid to recruiting and retaining employees from diverse demographic backgrounds, and not merely recruiting people who look like those who are already *in situ*. The practice of diversity management arose initially in the United States where the legacy of slavery and the multiplicity of immigrations meant that there were very obvious and ostensive differences between potential applicants for positions as well as legislative programmes designed to ensure that organizations did not systematically discriminate. In such a context many of the more progressive organizations decided it was not enough just not to be caught being discriminatory but that they should take positive steps to see that they were actively managing both multiculturally, as a form of practice, and multiculturalism, as a phenomenon. As in the previous chapter, we see that there is a common business case for doing this which has to do with utilizing *all* the talents – not just those that fit the look of the present management team.

Diversity is a highly problematic term, suggests Kirton. In part this is because it emerged from the specificities of American experience and has been globally exported – often to contexts that have very different peoples and histories. Diversity can be understood in various ways: it can be used as a descriptor of employee differences (workforce diversity); it can be used as an organizational policy approach explicitly focused on utilizing and valuing employee differences – usually referred to as diversity management or managing diversity; it can be seen as a conceptual construct, or even as a discourse or set of discursive practises. Seeing it in each of these different ways has specific consequences for organizational behavior as Kirton elaborates and deconstructs.

One of the reasons why there is often a gap between the rhetoric and reality of diversity management is that most organizations propose generic business case arguments, often based on some espousal of multiculturalism as a generically good thing. However, in some organizations, differences might be seen as a potential problem hindering, rather than assisting, effective service delivery. Think of the religious edicts of some faiths, such as Islam, where there are strict rules about gendered dress and who can do what with whom in normal social interaction. A concern with diversity can extend from managing differences in the workforce or responding appropriately to differences in a customer or client base. In the Islamic example, for instance, there would often be a customer case for non-difference rather than difference in a public sector field such as health care that might sit ill with broader commitments to equity. As Kirton explains the field of managing diversity can be highly problematic for managers. Some groups and individuals, from a variety of motives, may well be opposed to diversity in specific organizations. Others, who have been denied power and opportunities in organizations, may seize the opportunity to use the rhetoric of diversity to pursue sectional rather than business goals, in a Trojan horse strategy. Managers who assume that they will be doing the right thing by promoting diversity may well ferment troubles that they had barely imagined.

Being 'for diversity' is no guarantee of more equal opportunity. The rhetoric of diversity can also be used to argue that, as everyone is different and has different needs, aspirations etc., different outcomes are to be expected and do not need to be addressed. The celebration of diversity can be used to deny the existence of injustice, inequalities, discrimination and exploitation or become so inclusive as to become meaningless, both as a concept and as a policy approach. It can also undercut other approaches to equity such as those based on gender. Diversity management is not the simple managerial recipe that it initially appears to be.

Issues of equity and diversity often fall under the sway of human resource management (HRM) practices. What role does human resource management play in the organizational structures and strategies of organizations? Miguel Martínez Lucio

identifies what he terms five projects of HRM in recent times, each of which enables one to answer this question in a slightly different way. First, there was the attempt to relocate HRM and 'push it down the line' in a context of decentralized organizations. Second, HRM was to be a link between internal and external providers and sub-units in network organizations. Third, the focus on ethics and corporate social responsibility positioned HRM departments at the core of organizational value systems. Fourth, training and human resource development remained core HRM issues. Finally, HRM has had a key role in achieving the effectiveness and quality of 'high performance' organizational outputs.

HRM as a label effectively re-badged many personnel managers and industrial relations specialists from the 1980s onwards, not always happily, in academic departments in which the industrial relations specialist often saw themselves as more pro-worker than the personnel specialists who were sometimes seen as more likely to be pro-management. As HRM developed it often split into binaries: the Harvard versus the Michigan School, hard versus soft HRM, and so on. Overlain on this was a search for universalistic 'best practices', a search that many colleagues who were committed to contingency theory might have thought strangely universalistic and inappropriate. Contingently, evident differences of emphasis between European and US approaches began to coalesce. European approaches were more attuned to political contexts and realities and less intra-organizational in focus than those that were identified as US-centric. HRM became rhetorically intensive with the rhetoric often connecting new HRM paradigms to performance, strategy, and core business. The rhetoric often exceeded the limits of practice. HRM increasingly took on the contours of a professional and profession-alizing project which sought to re-position its practitioners, with only limited success, in the top management team. Competing interests, changing environmental factors, particularly in the political/industrial relations arena, and changing professional strategies saw HRM attempt to legitimate the role of people management in the core of business, much as finance or accounting. The neo-liberal climate that has prevailed in most Western nations from the 1980s onwards saw this struggle expressed in terms of HRM's promise to offer more flexible employment solutions, individually tailored, to replace the collectivism of an earlier age. HRM allied itself implicitly with the 'new right' against the 'old left'.

The alignment was usually expressed as a shift towards a more strategic emphasis for HRM, often captured as Strategic Human Resource Management (SHRM), representing the de-bureaucratization of people management. However, the 1980s also began to see a greater emphasis on the local, the immediate and the tangible in terms of how workers and local managers engaged with the challenge of change; consultancies began to deal with this more directly; for example, this was especially the case in terms of teamworking, and the idea that every manager had to become something of a people manager – not just leave it to a distant personnel department – but become do-it-yourself HRM managers. The strength of the shift to de-centralization somewhat undercut the SHRM project.

What began to emerge within the narratives of HRM was an alternative view of the organization based on changing organizational boundaries, greater subcontracting, and increased interest in the relations between organizational units. The emergence of *networking* or the *network firm* became a more mature version of the decentralization thesis. However, HRM's role is not clear: is it the solution to problems with the immediate employment issues of each unit within a network or a link in and within corporate alliances and network structures – a cultural facilitator? Is its future to provide coherence to the external boundaries of the firm and its flexible strategists? Or, should it also become flexible, networked and outsourced as HRM becomes the mechanism by which the network firm can be coordinated and the relationships across the network managed,

finding its most extreme expression in the fact that it may itself be subject to the logic of networking and new organizational forms and be subcontracted or even largely digitalized into systems that personnel are supposed to self-manage?

In the 1990s as work–life balance issues were added to equity issues and diversity management, HRM departments could become internal moral auditors and sanction, or warn, wayward departments who were not doing the 'right thing'. They could help departments navigate the ethical minefields of current management practice, legislation, political correctness and changing values. New issues offered plenty of opportunity for new training and learning – both individually and organizationally – opportunities that HRM might colonize so as to attach themselves to fashionable signifiers such as knowledge work, knowledge workers and the knowledge economy.

The knowledge that counts most in business is how to improve the bottom line. Increasingly, the challenge for HRM is to identify and correlate work practices with performance. For many HRM scholars this direction represents a possible way into the harder and more glamorous world of accounting and financial legitimacy, as a part of the professionalizing project. However, it is evident that the re-branding of HRM is still less than wholly convincing or successful.

What is the moral responsibility of managers in contemporary organizations? At one extreme, there are views that see responsibility as a relation primarily between managers and shareholders – the principal responsibility of the managers is to be a good steward of assets and to increase their return for those who own them. In recent years there has been a significant broadening of the discourse of responsibility as it applies to organizations; from these perspectives the shareholder value argument is a somewhat restricted view, as the development of broader stakeholder models suggests. Indeed, a new field of macro-organizational behavior, that of 'corporate social responsibility' (CSR) has developed to address the relations between organizations, their management and a range of stakeholders.

The widespread publicity given to a number of major corporate scandals in recent times has done much to place the issue of responsibility on the business school agenda. Of course, it is fairly clear that responsibility can be attributed in legal proceedings. Doing wrong is a clear instance of being less than morally responsible, even when it serves organizational self-interest. Reference to moral responsibility in business is largely concerned with the relation between self and other interests. Being responsible to the interests of others as one might be to the interests of ones self is, in Christian tradition, the basis of certain conceptions of morality, but, as Carl Rhodes and Alison Pullen argue, it has long been a central consideration of moral philosophy that can be traced back to Aristotle's *Nichomachean Ethics* (2004).

Rhodes and Pullen chart the notion of moral responsibility as it has evolved in modern business discourse from Adam Smith's day to its contemporary incarnation in Milton Friedman's (1970) famous dictum that 'the social responsibility of business is to increase profits'. As they note, Friedman's views were developed in opposition to the questioning of this narrow purpose by those who assumed that business might have social responsibilities, and that it was not an oxymoron to speak of 'corporate social responsibilities'. Indeed, as the authors chart, there are plenty of accounts that argue that if business looks after its corporate social responsibilities it will also be good for the bottom line, although other accounts note the importance of being socially responsible as a desirable end in itself rather than seeing it as a means to the ultimate ends of business being defined as being profitable. As such a desirable end, the idea of social responsibility can be attached to what are assumed to be various 'interests', such as 'community', 'ecology', and so on. As they note, in terms of a moralizing turn away from the pursuit of shareholder value, it is not uncommon for the ethical position taken in stakeholder theory and CSR to be self-righteous, simplistic and lacking in

deliberation. It is also, as they go on to argue, often based on an ethic of calculation, a 'calculus of advantage' that sees good strategy in being responsible.

What might be an alterative to a calculative ethics? Rhodes and Pullen find inspiration in the recent ethical theory developed by the sociologist, Zygmunt Bauman. Here the notion of responsibility can be located in terms of the relations between the business organization and the 'social' as a more or less generalized other. Following Bauman, consideration of the others to whom an organization might be responsible is achieved differently depending on the relative proximity with which those others are conceived. Some such as employees and local communities may be relatively close at hand; others such as suppliers or customers may be quite distant. Building on Lévinas' (1969) ethics, how the organization assumes responsibility will be evident in the way in which it deals with these others both close and far as both particular and unknowable. At best, the authors suggest, responsibility requires a relation that does not violate the particularity of the other by subsuming them under category headings but as treating them as authentic selves and others. The categories of stakeholder are an organization construct, serving organization self-interest, an attempt to manage any potentially authentic selves by denying their authenticity through categorization devices. As they say, 'to consider others as stakeholders can easily become a glib excuse for *not* dealing with others as real and particular people – an easy way out of the very question of responsibility'. It becomes a way of evading the moral mazes of everyday organizational life. Using Derridean terms they suggest that responsibility requires undecidability, which can never be pre-empted by organizational rules, rationalities and codes of ethics. It entails managers *being responsible beings* and that entails constant attention. The upshot is that managers need to be their own moral philosophers – a fairly daunting process, perhaps. The freedom of the manager to act and make decisions is, they suggest, the very condition of responsibility. It is a kind of *phronesis*, or practical wisdom (Flyvbjerg, 2006).

The issues of responsibility are, perhaps, no more evident that when considered in the context of what has come to be called 'sustainability'. As Suzanne Benn writes, discourses of sustainability developed as attempts to resolve increasingly evident tensions between the goals of economic growth, the desire for social equity and the limits to natural resources. Development is, broadly, defined as sustainable when it meets the needs of the present without compromising the ability of future generations to meet their own needs; it means in even simpler terms, taking nothing away from nature and adding nothing that impairs or blights that nature. Judged thus, the whole project of industrialization has been a grievously unsustainable trajectory that scholars and practitioners have only recently sought to arrest and redirect. The redirection has been promulgated in terms of three principles: intergenerational equity, intragenerational equity, and the precautionary principle. As Benn observes, however, beyond these broad brush strokes the discourse is essentially contested, with little agreement on its key tenets, texts, or topics. Nonetheless, she establishes a case for organizational decision makers to exercise their ethical responsibilities in terms of balancing relationships between humans and the rest of the biosphere, present and future generations, and the developing and developed worlds. In organizational behavior to the present, these relations have been conceptualized in terms of two dominant schemas within the overall discourse: the win-win and the moral imperative. Win-win discourses stress the good business case for being sustainable: minimizing waste, cutting costs, and being a good organizational citizen. The moral imperative case is based on various formulations of the manager as a *social* being: it is normative, drawing on business ethics principles to advocate sustainability as ethical practice morally transformational leaders should engage in. The tone is one of ecological evangelism, sure in the certainty of the correctness of its own beliefs, and often associated with various consultancy models and practices that can help organizational behavior 'go green'. Benn explores the growth of these discourses and their ramifications on organizational behavior.

More recently, in making the links between sustainable development and organizational behavior Benn notes that there will have to be a profound cognitive and cultural change in individual attitudes and beliefs if the agenda is to be developed in both theory and practice. One positive sign might be the emergence of the 'Bottom of the Pyramid' market – the 4 billion people living on less than $2 per day who organizations are increasingly being urged to target with affordable goods and services, who can be reached by engaging with civil society organizations and local governments to stimulate local innovations and entrepreneurship. Promising as this might seem, however, Benn argues that we need an organizational behavior discourse that draws on the field of environmental sociology, especially that strand within it known as reflexive ecological modernization. For ecological modernists, a form of hyper-industrialization, premised on technological innovation, needs to be developed under different conditions of leadership, notably a commitment to the precautionary principle.

Reflexive ecological modernization sees sustainability issues arising as unintended risks produced by the success of rationality, such as global warming, competition and conflict over increasingly scarce natural resources such as water, toxic environments, and weapons of terrorism. The reflexive component refers to the need constantly to question and interrogate existing modes of rationality, in order to implement increasingly precautionary and sustainable forms of development. Often the questioning will be led by non-conventional stakeholders, such as green activists, NGOs, and other civil society organizations that impose themselves as stakeholders on previously less reflective organizational behavior.

The key issue for organizational behavior is the development of its discourse as sufficiently critically self-aware, learning-oriented, and open to broadly based conversations, while giving regard to precaution, ensuring concern with the international dimensions of development, and giving consideration to the multiple and interdisciplinary possibilities for environmental and social solutions to negative impacts of development. Organizational behavior has nothing to lose but its blinkers as a handmaiden only of organizational orthodoxy according to these perspectives. It has to open itself to new stakeholders, issues and develop authentic concerns that are quite distinct from the traditional pursuits of leadership or OD. The study of the social production and use of statistics could facilitate our understanding of how managers, leaders, employees, make sense of risks facing them, their organization, society and the planet. Thus, rather than merely helping interpret existing tools for calculation or developing new tools for performance appraisal considered in terms of traditional role requirements, the new macro-organizational behavior should be changing the priorities and changing the tools.

Three priorities are essential. Corporate leaders have to accept the precautionary principle. Organizations need to become less centralized and more networked into grass-roots movements, understandings and politics. Business and industry need to work within the context of a more active civil society, in which government organizations support less resourced actors with knowledge and other tools and facilities in order to ensure a more inclusive political community. Fittingly, the chapter concludes with a discussion of a case in point: the Chinese city of Dongtan, an attempt to build a community based on ecologically reflexive modernization principles.

The previous three chapters clearly point to the centrality of how organizations express who they are and what they stand for to all of their internal and external stakeholders, which is the topic of the chapters by Majken Schultz and Mary Jo Hatch. There are, they suggest, many reasons why organizations are devoting increasing energy and resources to expressive organizational practices: competitive pressures to differentiate the business offering; stakeholder pressures from new actors in their environment, such as those that Benn has described, and changing norms about the meanings that should surround the cash and customer nexus. The expression of the organization is an important arena in which organization control is tested; the occasions for expression are often quite local and uncoupled from central management control; they are often contested, sometimes by highly resourceful and provocative organizations and other actors who 'target' specific corporate or other organizational expressions.

The field of organizational expression is challenging for the organization behavior specialist also. No one academic discipline 'owns' it: researching how the managing of organizational expression is done entails a multidisciplinary and multifunctional approach. It means looking at what organizations do not merely in the terms of any one specialism but in terms that capture the members' usage and sense of what they are doing. In this context, organization theory approaches such as institutional theory, can be useful: what are the forms of mimesis shaping organizational expression? But they are limiting – because the whole point of organizational expression is to situate the organization as distinct, different, apart from the crowd. Additionally, organizational expression should not just tell generalized others what the organization is, what it means; it should also be expressive of the identity that those significant others who are employees or customers are encouraged to develop.

Expressiveness depends on context as well as the uses made and meanings given to them by their audiences. These shift fast and subtly and study of the semiotics of symbolic meaning must be a core task in researching organizational expression. How members and users of organizations embed their understanding of culture, identity and difference is of the utmost significance. What are the significant rites, rituals and rhetoric that do this work? Thus, organization culture studies have a key role to play in research into organizational expression, as do studies of corporate identity, branding, and communication. A cross-disciplinary framework is required that builds on these approaches and incorporates other elements as necessary. For instance, the study of organizational communication, audiences and message reception will be important.

In practical terms this means that organizational expression will be an activity in which cross-functional boundaries must be spanned, local professional politics will flourish, and disciplinary identities will be blurred in practice. Management needs to pay attention to the macro-cultural context within which meaning are constituted, circulate, and change as well as the identity conflicts that are important to their key audiences. Doing this will often mean sacrificing a few sacred tenets held by some of the disciplines, such as marketing. Additionally, it will mean acknowledging that some of the most important shapers of organizational expression may not be at all amenable to managerial design and control – think of the impact of the McLibel campaign on McDonalds, for instance. It is all too easy for organizational expressions, dominated by consumerism, to be transformed by culture-jammers from once meaningful expressions originating in the organization's culture into empty speech cluttering the marketplace, subject to derision. Fiat's campaign for the Fiat 127 comes to mind: the catchline went something like: 'If this car was a woman, it would get its bottom pinched'. The graffiti artist who corrupted one poster with the riposte 'If this woman was a car, she'd run you down', gained a permanent place in advertising folklore, and spawned a huge industry of feminist culture-jamming. In the future managers will have to learn to manage organizational expressiveness with all its semiotic complexity, subtlety and political nuances. Stakeholders will often push and twist messages where they were not intended to go and managers need to be reflexive about these possibilities, and understand local cultures, styles and tastes, as well as the

nature of the local politics of gender, of class, of ethnicity, that might appropriate their expressions. (Think of US rappers and Cristal champagne or UK 'chavs' and Burberry.)

René ten Bos and Stefan Heusinkveld contribute the last chapter in this part of the book, on 'management fashion and organizational behaviour'. They open with a fascinating history of self-help manuals, spiritual tracts, and their increasingly bizarre 'new age' descendants, all oriented to fashioning employees and entrepreneurs that fit the changing times. One focus was on self-helping working men and another on their organizational adaptability. In the first, a focus on religion was evident; in the second set, organizational aspects as well as the emotional posture of the employee were engaged. Emotion was regarded with ambivalence, as potentially useful, if managed properly, and threatening if not. Both sets of discourses become interrelated into contemporary management fashion. As the authors observe, notions such as self-help, spirituality, emotion, harmony, and many more are still prevalent in the work of consultants, gurus, and others who have the wish to appeal to contemporary managerial taste.

Three distinct 'lines' may be identified in this contemporary advice industry shaping management fashions. First, those rationalist accounts that use a conception of science which is general, timeless, abstract, objective, and axiomatic. Second, the more politically engaged argument that popular management ideas should be condemned for their manipulative and inhumane tendencies. As the authors note, the 'humanistic-political approach' shares a desire to debunk the managerial 'hypes' and 'fads' with the rational approach but from a political rather than rationalist perspective. A third approach accepts that fashion in general is an unmistakable part of current developments in our society and that what is important is to study how fashion stylists, such as management gurus, express themselves. These ideas are then developed and worked out in the chapter.

For the future, they argue that overly normative approaches of management fashion will not dominate future research. Some key areas for further research are identified. These include the role of knowledge entrepreneurs, such as consultants and gurus; the necessity of studying the social-cultural context of fashion, especially, in a liquid modernity, in which the authority of science in legislating everyday truths seems to have declined from its rationalist heyday. Hence, it is not so much to the production of science that we should look for the recipe knowledge that circulates in the marketplace but more commercial circuits of production. Additionally, there should be continuing attention paid to the consumption of management fashions: *how* and *why* does *what* get to be widely consumed or not by *whom*? What are the dynamics of 'cool'? Moreover, what are the ethical implications of all this consumption?

## ORGANIZING ON A MACRO-SCALE

Organizational behavior might have begun in psychology with a primarily individual focus but it soon moved on to more collective phenomena, such as organization change, which David Wilson explores in his contribution to the volume. In this chapter Wilson traces the theoretical and empirical development of research into change as a discrete phenomenon of organized society. It shows how management theory colonized change theories and, at first, assumed that change could be planned and implemented via managerial agency. The chapter then develops a series of perspectives in which managerial agency is questioned and in which change and organization are viewed as inextricably interlinked processes.

Exploring the antecedents for change involves a wide range of disciplines including philosophy, psychology, economics and sociology as well as disciplines explicitly attached to researching organizing and organization. Within each of these disciplinary areas there will be rival accounts of change phenomena. Between disciplines there is a great deal of incommensurability – but this also characterizes within disciplinary discourses,

such as microeconomics, macroeconomics and international economics.

An adequate account of change has to include reference to the importance of context (primarily an assessment of where change takes place such as the type of organization or society – is it highly developed or less developed, for instance); content (meaning what the change is about, such as the adoption of a new technology – does it have system transforming implications or does it slot in to what is already extant) and process (describing the characteristics of the change journey from first idea to implementation – is the journey straightforward, highly problematic, involve many others or few, are there many recursive loops or few, and so on), argues Wilson. Temporality is also important: change can be slower or faster; evolutionary or revolutionary; its scope may be highly focused or diffuse, specific or general, long term or immediate. Despite the importance of these features, increasingly identified in the research literature, there are still many apparent tendencies to talk about change as if it were linear, rational, and easily manageable – especially in the organizational behavior literature.

Amongst macro-organizational behavior approaches to change, that known as Organizational Development (OD) is one of the best known. OD approaches involve senior managers creating a vision, developing commitment and motivation for its accomplishment, by capturing and developing political and behavioral support from various stakeholders within and outside the organization.

Wilson suggests we should consider whether change is envisaged as a planned or *emergent* process and the extent to which the course of change might be seen as *voluntarist* or *determined*. Planned change describes a sequence of steps or stages which prescribe what managers should do. Emergent perspectives view change as a process which is almost never planned, but is one which emerges from a host of organizational and individual activities. Four distinct perspectives can be mapped on to these broad-brush accounts: life-cycle theories; teleological theories; dialectic theories, and evolutionary theories.

For the future, the agenda of change research should focus on change across levels of analysis and emphasize the interplay of organization, group and individual levels. The organizations studied should be extended from large commercial enterprises to small and medium firms, public sector and not-for-profit organizations. New hybrid forms of networks are emerging that demand analysis likely to uncover quite different mechanisms at work compared with classical bureaucracy. Of course, as the previous analysis of management fashions established, there will be no shortage of nostrums, solutions and recipes available in the market for managing change and sometimes the analysis of change and these prescriptions for change will become entangled.

Change and its direction is seen as serious work in organizations, best done by those serious people who populate the top management teams – the élites, in other words. In his contribution titled 'We have always been oligarchs', David Courpasson considers the actual power of leaders. To understand how certain actors have the power to change things significantly we need to grasp how structural forces constrain élites and how, nonetheless, individuals can still shape phenomena in more or less determinate ways by mobilizing diverse actors. In considering the role of élites in the past debate has often veered between accounts of oligarchic bureaucracies; Courpasson wants to introduce a more 'hybrid' context that he terms *polyarchy*. The chapter addresses the sort of leaders that are being shaped that fit these polyarchies.

The existence of organization as more or less similar to an archetype of polyarchy or bureaucracy is a matter of organizational design, which Gerard Fairtlough and Rosemary Beckham address in their chapter on 'organizational design'. (Sadly, Gerard died whilst this volume was being finalized.) As in so much else of consequence in the field the origins of a concern with organizational design were established by Max Weber. Weber was concerned principally with the bureaucratic type; today the design of new organizations and the redesign of existing ones is a widespread practice within business, government and civil society. Whatever the design, these authors contend, the main reason why organization design can be contentious or emotional is its connection with power and status – usually organized in a hierarchical way – as in a bureaucracy.

There are, according to Fairtlough (2005), two fundamental alternatives to hierarchy. The first is heterarchy, which involves multiple sources of rule rather than the single rule of hierarchy. An organizational example is the relationship between the partners in a traditional law firm, where all partners are of roughly equal status, sharing decision making, risks and rewards. The second alternative is responsible autonomy, under which an individual or a group has autonomy to decide what to do, but is accountable for the outcome of the decision, as in privately owned businesses that operate autonomously, providing they satisfy their creditors, and basic scientific research, in which principal investigators are free to choose their line of enquiry, providing it leads to results judged valuable by peer review. The chapter elaborates the corollaries and consequences of these 'three ways of getting things done' and relates them to a broader set of theories from the field as well as providing examples drawn from practice.

Increasingly, organizational behavior is likely to take place in projects. Projects are a form of organizing in which individuals are temporarily but interdependently linked to achieve a specific outcome or set of outcomes. These outcomes can include the production of ideas or products, solutions to problems, provision of a service, or the construction of public or private infrastructure; they may be innovation projects, where the outcomes are very exploratory or they may be explicitly mission-based – such as putting a man on the moon.

Carlsen and Pitsis argue that projects, even ones that fail to come in on time and budget – which is the vast majority of mega-projects – can, nonetheless, be ideal arenas of positive personal and organizational change. They demonstrate this proposition through three carefully delineated case studies of the development of an IT application for collecting dependency allowance debt; the case of oil exploration in a peripheral license in the North Sea, and a major construction project for cleaning up Sydney's waterways. What they see unifying these three very different projects is that they are typified by the production of narrative capital that generates positive organizational change. Narrative capital is repeatedly drawn upon and used for future oriented purposive action.

A focus on projects and projection may be considered particularly valuable in studying processes of positive organizational change and their temporal-relational contexts. The authors note many examples of projects that affirm life in the sense that they continue to capture the imagination of people irrespective of generation or nationality. What is attractive in projects, they argue, even those that are more mundane than the major historical ones that they enumerate, is how projects constitute moving horizons of collective engagement and meaning that live on and inform organizational behavior long after the project has elapsed. To understand this meaningfulness they draw on phenomenological psychology, seeing it as an underutilized resource in the construction of positive organizational psychology (see Chapter 5). To this end, they draw out and develop the four key processes of expansive connecting, extending, instantiating and creating deviance that inform their view of projects for life.

Corporate governance provides a focus upon the organizational and political processes involved in resolving disputes and conflicts of interest between participants in corporate organizations. Corporate governance varies widely between societies but the main focus of its reform in recent years has been in the Anglo-Saxon countries, especially the UK and the US, which are the focus of the penultimate chapter by Rob Watson. It is in these societies that shareholder capitalism has flourished. In the US and UK, the institutional and legal framework has always supported the principle that, in the absence of financial distress, executive discretion ought to be exercised in accordance with the financial interests of the company's shareholders. The chapter, taking this corporate context for granted, discusses the major advantages of the corporate model and the unique governance problems associated with this organizational structure. The distinctive and novel feature of this organizational form is that it has a separate legal status completely independent from that of its owners (i.e., the shareholders that provide the firms' risk capital) and/or its senior executives (i.e., the employees responsible for corporate strategy and operational management). This legal fiction, the product of eighteenth and nineteenth century legislators in the UK and US, implies that the company, not its owner-managers, is the contracting party with respect to all business dealings and that, as a consequence, the owner-managers ought not to be held personally responsible should the company at some stage be unable to honor its financial obligations.

Of course, most corporations today are not owner-managed but exist under conditions of a separation of ownership and control. Corporate strategy and the control of resources reside in the hands of professional managers, so shareholders have to rely on the decision making discretion of senior executives. Senior executives, however, may have different interests from those of shareholders. Thus, a central issue for corporate governance, as Watson elaborates, is how these differing interests might be aligned. It is the effectiveness of the various legal, organizational and market-based incentives and constraints upon managerial discretion that constitute the primary concern of corporate governance. Not surprisingly, given the publicity that has attached to a number of spectacular corporate cases of collapse and malfeasance, the traditional solutions to governance problems have been found lacking. The chapter concludes with a brief review of alternative 'stakeholder' views regarding objectives of corporate decision making and the corporate governance systems found in other developed and developing economies that appear to embody in their systems of corporate law and practice similar stakeholder notions. This includes an analysis of how these alternatives differ from the Anglo-US model and an assessment of whether they appear to have any advantages that could usefully be incorporated into the current shareholder oriented systems of the UK and US.

In the final chapter Stewart Clegg and Chris Carter discuss globalization. They focus on its role in shaping the world of organizational behavior. The role of globalization is contested; some authorities are as fervently 'for' it as others are 'against' it. Globalization or tradition seems to be a stark choice that is faced in such contests. What is constituted as global innovation or as local tradition is, however, always categorically framed in simple rhetoric that clouds complex politics. Key actors and moments in these politics are identified – multinationals, management gurus, accounting firms, governments, political sloganeering, and the financialization of everyday life and the carnivalization of occasions of state, for instance.

## CONCLUSION

We have no doubt that much of organizational behavior in the future will engage with the macro-concerns and agenda sketched here; it will need to if it is to remain relevant to the changing conditions of contemporary existence. However, much will remain more tightly coupled to the psychology roots of the organizational behavior discourse. There are many good reasons of professional formation, tradition and disciplinary training and inclinations why this should be the case. Nonetheless, as we have sought to argue in this volume, there are even more compelling reasons why the field needs to drop its blinkers and address the rich vistas that a concern with macro-organizational behavior opens up.

## REFERENCES

Albert, S. and Whetton, D. (1985) 'Organizational identity', *Research in Organizational Behaviour*, 7: 263–295.

Aristotle (2004) *The Nichomachean Ethics*. Harmondsworth: Penguin.

Baldamus, W.I. (1961) *Efficiency and Effort: An Analysis of Industrial Administration*. London: Tavistock.

Clarke, A. (1993) *Diaries*. London: Weidenfeld & Nicolson.

Clegg, S.R. (1981) 'Organization and control', *Administrative Science Quarterly*, 26: 545–562.

Clegg, S.R., Hardy, C., Lawrence, T. and Nord, W.R. (2006) *The Sage Handbook of Organization Studies*. London: Sage.

Courpasson, D. (2006) *Soft Constraint: Liberal Organizations and Democracy*. Oslo/Copenhagen: Liber/CBS Press.

Cyert, R.M. and March, J.G. (1963) *A Behavioral Theory of the Firm*. Englewood Cliffs, NJ: Prentice Hall.

Fairtlough, G. (2005) *The Three Ways of Getting Things Done: Hierarchy, Heterarchy, and Responsible Autonomy in Organizations*. Axminster: Triarchy Press.

Flyvbjerg, B. (2006) 'Making organization research matter: Power, values and phronesis', in Clegg *et al.* (op. cit.). pp. 370–287.

Foucault, M. (1977) *Discipline and Punish: The Birth of the Prison*. Harmondsworth: Allen Lane.

Foucault, M. (1979) 'Governmentality', *Ideology and Consciousness*, 6: 5–21.

Friedman, M. (1970) 'The social responsibility of business is to increase its profits', *New York Times Magazine*, 30 September.

Gall, G. (1999) 'A review of strike activity in Western Europe at the end of the second millennium', *Employee Relations*, 21 (4): 357–377.

Garfinkel, H. (1967) *Studies in Ethnomethodology*. Englewood Cliffs, NJ: Prentice Hall.

Goffman, E. (1959) *Asylums*. Harmondsworth: Penguin.

Gramsci, A. (1971) *Excerpts from the Prison Notebooks*. London: Lawrence and Wishart.

Lévinas, E. (1969) *Totality and Infinity*, trans. Alphonso Lingis. Pittsburgh: Duquesne University Press.

Lukes, S. (1974) *Power: A Radical View*. London: Macmillan.

Lukes, S. (2005) *Power: A Radical View* (Second Edition). London: Palgrave-Macmillan.

Marx, K. (1976) *Capital*. Harmondsworth: Penguin.

Peters, T. (2003) *Re-imagine! Business Excellence in a Disruptive Age*. London: Dorling Kindersley.

Schutz, A. (1967) *The Phenomenology of the Social World*. Evanston, IL: Northwestern University Press.

Simmel, G. (1950) *The Sociology of Georg Simmel* (edited and translated by Kurt Woolf). New York: The Free Press.

Viber (2004) *Theories of Macro-organizational Behavior: A Handbook of Ideas and Explanations*. New York: M. E. Sharpe.

# PART ONE

# Framing the Field: Introducing Some Big Questions

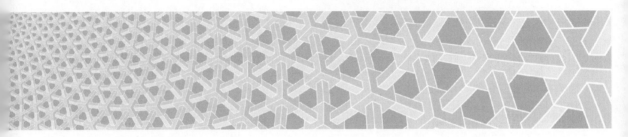

# 1

# What Do OB Tools and Practices Do?

André Spicer

## INTRODUCTION

Many people ask what theories of organizational behaviour actually do. Students are notorious for prodding their teachers about the use of sometimes seemingly baroque theories. Practitioners enjoy the sport of mocking researchers for their quaint irrelevance. Producers of theories of organizational behaviour are also prone to engaging in a little self-flagellation when they ask questions such as: 'Aren't these theories just a fancy version of common sense' (Gordon *et al.*, 1978), 'can't any relatively intelligent person pick these ideas up on the job' (Pfeffer and Fong, 2002, 2004), 'What is the point of an education in all these silly models which bear little relationship to what managers do' (Mintzberg, 2004), 'don't theories of OB stunt peoples moral and ethical development' (Leavitt, 1989), 'Why do theories ignore real world problems' (Hambrick, 1993), 'Why do we ignore the external validity of our theories' (Kilmann, 1979), 'How relevant are the theories which we develop to the real world?'

(Starkey and Madan, 2001; Starkey, Hauchlet and Tempest, 2004), and 'Are we using the right style to communicate our ideas' (Grey and Sinclair, 2006).

Some scholars have directly reacted to these concerns by arguing that the purpose of organizational behaviour should be the development of knowledge, not a desperate quest for relevance. For instance, during a speech at a large scholarly conference, Jim March (2000) commented that the purpose of management research 'is not in trying to identify factors affecting corporate performance, or in trying to develop managerial technology. It is in raising fundamental issues and advancing knowledge about fundamental processes affecting management'. For March and many others like him, the purpose of theory is to expand our understanding of the organizational world. It is not to provide relevant tools for managers to fiddle about with.

In this chapter, I will look at the conundrum that people who engage with management theory face. The question at the centre of this chapter is what do organizational behaviour theories do? In order to answer this question, I will begin by giving a brief sketch of what it is that we mean by the idea of theory. In the second part, I will consider why theories matter by looking at empirical research that has investigated the impact that management ideas have on organizations. I will use this research to make the case that theories of management have a profound and far-reaching affect on organizational life. In the third part of the chapter, I consider the way that management knowledge is used. I argue that theories of organizational behaviour can be used for four purposes: *predicting* how an organization may work, *understanding* why organizations operate as they do, *critiquing* the way that organizations currently work, and *creating* new ways of organizing. I conclude the chapter by arguing that a competent user of theories of OB should try to develop skills in each of these areas.

## WHAT IS THEORY?

Think of the typical tools and practices that managers use. These tools are not things like a hammer or an egg beater. Rather, they are neatly packaged theories. Some examples include batteries of personality tests that are used during recruitment, ideas about team formation that are pushed into practice during a project, or theories about organizational structure that are put into play during corporate change processes. So in order to know what an OB tool or practice can do, it is vital that we consider what theories do.

The first question we must clearly answer is this: What exactly do we mean by theory? The word 'theory' is derived from the Greek word, *theoria*. This means contemplation, speculation or taking a view of things. The modern usage of the word owes a great deal to the sciences. A scientific approach tends to define theories as 'a statement of relations among concepts within a set of boundary assumptions and constraints' (Bacharach, 1989: 496. For a similar example see Dubin, 1969 and Whetten, 1989). A few things jump

out if we unpick this terse definition. First, theory is about concepts. That is, a theory is made up of abstract representations of reality that are embodied in some kind of language or symbolism. For instance, the theories of power are typically made up of abstract concepts such as 'networks' and 'power' (for examples of network and power research see: Burt, 1992). These concepts are abstract because they include a whole range of empirical instances. For instance, the abstract concept of networks can be used to describe a relationship between friends, lovers, or colleagues.

The second characteristic of theory is that it is about the relationship between concepts. That is, a theory seeks to establish how two abstract representations fit together. For instance, a theory of power might suggest that powerful organizational members (the first abstract representation) have a diverse social network (the second abstract representation). Notice that these two abstract representations are linked by a causal relationship. This theory states that diverse social networks cause an individual to be powerful. According to some, rooting out these causal relationships is the bread and butter of theory. The job of the theorist is to suggest possible relationships between concepts which the more empirically inclined can go away and test.

The third characteristic of theory is that it seeks to explain why concepts fit together as they do. This involves developing an explanation of exactly why concept one might have an affect on concept two. For instance, theories of network power provide an explanation of why more network = more power. They do this by suggesting that social networks provide individuals with access to valuable information, resources, and opportunities to influence decision makers which in turn provide an individual with power. Such explanations require the theorist to argue out the links between the two concepts. This can be done by careful logical deduction where the theorist argues if A is the case, then B must be true. It can also be done by deducing links between concepts from previously undertaken empirical work.

For instance, studies of network power have pieced together empirical evidence from existing empirical studies of power and resources, information and opportunities. No matter which way theorists go about this task, they must substantiate a link between concepts.

The final aspect of theory is the identification of the broad context or constraints under which it works. To put this in a different way, a theory involves identifying the conditions under which two concepts relate. For instance, a theory about power and networks might identify the idea that bigger networks = greater power works in some cultural contexts rather than others. Often an enthusiastic theory builder will try to bracket off these potentially pesky problems by labelling them as 'contextual variables'. For instance, the theory about networks and power might identify cultural context as a contextual variable. By identifying when and where a concept might work and when and where it might not work, a theorist is able to make her model more bounded and potentially more convincing.

The sciences certainly provide us with a very clear and well defined answer to what a theory might be. However, this approach does not provide the only indication of what theory can be. A second, quite different approach to theory can be found in the humanities. This sense of what theory is was produced by the theoretical turn that occurred during the second part of the twentieth century. At a minimum, theory in this tradition involves an 'abstention from empiricist or positivist knowledges through insight into their sleeping structures' (Hunter, 2006: 87). That is, the theorist is not so concerned with simply describing the world of happenings and events as it appears to them. In fact, the theorist is profoundly suspicious of any sense data that comes their way. For them, our experiences and understandings of the social world are mediated by some kind of theory. In revealing how a theory mediates data, they dig out the 'sleeping structures' that arrange and order our experiences of the social world. This involves a kind of revelation whereby the theorist seeks to identify and discover the ancient ideas that infuse how we see the world. This act of rooting out the theories we use to see the world also involves changing ourselves. For Terry Eagleton, 'theory of this kind comes about when we are forced into a new self-consciousness about what we are doing' (2003: 27). Indeed, theory ultimately aims to help us cultivate a certain sense of 'openness to being' (Hunter, 2006) that might involve not only the ability to recognize ourselves as if for the first time, but also see the world anew. According to proponents in the humanities, theory is not a model which relates a set of concepts. Rather, theory is a way of approaching the world based on constant questioning and looking beyond the immediate data and common sense which come so easily to hand.

## DOES THEORY MATTER?

Now that I have established what theory is, let me ask a slightly more troubling question: does theory actually matter? People dealing with theories of organizational behaviour are often very sceptical. They regard theory as nothing more than something to keep credulous managers amused, consultants paid, and academics busy. However, this assumption does not seem to stack up against the evidence. Studies of the impact of management theories have noted the widespread and profound affect that management ideas have on organizations and our lives more generally. They include a profound affect on routines, cognitions, fashion, ideology, language, distribution of capital, and technology. Let us consider each of these points in turn.

One of the first areas of research that noticed the profound affect that management ideas had on organizational life was the field of routines. Researchers working in this field argue that organizations are not only groups of people who do things. They are also collectives who act together. Studies of organizational routines show how collective processes of trial and error gradually become the everyday practices of an organization

(Levitt and March, 1988; Feldman, 2003). These routines, which we take for granted, are often the result of hard-won collective lessons. For instance, the process of hiring a new candidate usually involves a well trodden routine. However, these routines are often the result of incremental and collective processes of learning in organizations. Collective trial-and-error processes are brought together as a theory proper through some kind of scientific endeavour. For instance, the practices of corporate culture during the 1980s were later rationalised and mapped out in formal theories of the organization (Barley, Meyer and Gash, 1989). What had been a rather fluid and fuzzy collection of practices developed into a theory. The greatest advantage is that these ideas could be transported and translated across different workplaces (Czarniawska and Sevon, 1996). Theories about how we do relatively mundane things such as hire people, fix a minor problem, or communicate with our boss are gradually embedded in our practices, but our routines are rarely the result of our own learning. If this was the case, our routines would be quite stunted. Rather, routines are often the result of the learning of others which have been packaged into theories. Consider the example of hiring again. When a newly minted HR manager is faced with the prospect of hiring new staff, they do not just rely on their own experience. Instead, they reach for some of the standard templates of how you hire. The result is that one template of hiring quickly becomes the common sense that managers cling to. This reminds us that theories of organizational behaviour matter because they can rapidly become embedded into our un-thought everyday actions.

Once researchers had begun to recognize how theories could have a profound affect on routines, they began to ask how this occurred. One result was that new theories changed how people in organizations thought about and understood the social world. This stream of research has repeatedly uncovered how shared theories focus the minds of people working in certain industries (Lant, 2002), which happens when a certain 'cognitive scheme' spreads throughout an industry. Such schemes typically shape how people think about and interpret that industry. For instance, the rise of new understanding of what the Catholic church should do during the 1960s led to fundamental changes in the structure of the organization, how priests relate to the laity, and how religious services should be conducted (Bartunek, 1984). Similarly, who companies understand to be their competitors are shaped by collective theories which circulate within an industry (Porac and Thomas, 1990). For instance, members of the Scottish textile industry thought about it using common cognitive schemes which were divided along the lines of Hosiery, Knitware and Lace (Porac, Thomas and Baden-Fuller, 1989). These divisions were based on shared cognitive schemes. The result was that companies operating in each sector of the market understood their competitors in a rather limited and circumscribed fashion. Shared cognitive schemes can shape what skilled groups understand as appropriate and reasonable at certain moments. For instance, in his re-reading of the Mann Gulch disaster, Karl Weick (1993) argues that a group of firefighters refused to drop their heavy tools and run from a dangerous wildfire because they understood their tools as being part of their professional identity as firefighters. The theories of fire-safety which were drummed into these unfortunate young men during their training and socialization cost them their lives. The lesson that we can draw from these studies is that theories can become inscribed into shared cognitive schemes within organizations, sometimes with life and death consequences.

Theories don't just shape our routines and our thinking. They can also create whole industries. Studies of management fashions have pointed out that there is a whole sector of the economy in many advanced capitalist countries that is devoted to the development and circulation of management ideas (Abrahamson, 1991; Abrahamson and Fairchild, 1999). Participants in this economy include the producers of fashionable new ideas such as academics, intellectuals, and management gurus. There is also a large group of people whose time is devoted to circulating management fashions such as management consultants, advisers, and the business press. Finally, there are many willing and eager consumers of management knowledge such as governments, employees and, of course, management themselves. Indeed the management knowledge sector plays an increasingly important role as part of the post-industrial economy. In fact, some of the more desirable jobs that the young and ambitious aspire to occupy are as circulators of management fashion. These positions are so coveted because not only do they pay well, but they also confer on the position holder a degree of status; their holders are the witch doctors of the post-modern metropolis, able to prescribe all sorts of common sense and hokum tricked out with fancy trappings.

Theories are not just people's bread and butter. They also provide an orientation and collective sets of ideas. Indeed, these ideas provide strict and appealing normative schemes for managers. They give a set answer to disturbing questions such as what is right and wrong, what we should strive for, and what we should do. In short theories of organizational behaviour can act as ideologies. Many commentators on contemporary societies have noted that some of the most widespread and surprising ideologies of our day are ones associated with management (Chiapellio and Boltanski, 2005). Just think of the fanatical commitment that we all seem to have towards leadership (Calás and Smircich, 1991). Whole nations have been driven into neurotic fits of self-scrutiny when they feel they 'lack leadership'. Many millions are spent on nurturing leadership. Today, even schools have downplayed teaching 'content' (such as history or chemistry) in favour of instruction in the illustrious process of leadership. As a theory gradually becomes an ideology, it typically provides a justification for particular relations of power within a society. The ideology of leadership, for instance, provides an alluring justification for why it is that we should sit back and follow the demands of a leader, no matter how harmful. This is because the ideology of leadership leads us to assume that leadership is good and thoroughly necessary.

Theories tell us what to value. They also provide us with a language we can use to talk about the world. Indeed management has become a widely accepted *lingua franca* of social life (Grey, 1999; Grant *et al.*, 2004). Theories of management have gradually become the way many people talk about the world. Talk about team work has become a way we discuss group relations. Entrepreneurship has become a widespread parlance for understanding nearly any setting from education to the organization of medical services (Jones and Spicer, forthcoming). We use ideas of management to talk about even the most mundane aspects of everyday life from sleep to home decor (Hancock and Tyler, forthcoming). The spread of management as a discourse is particularly important for a number of reasons. First, management talk provides us with a limited set of ways of describing the social world. This means that we begin to have a very complex and well crafted repertoire for acts that involve telling others what to do. More than this, discourses of management also begin to shape how we understand and interpret social life. For instance, the language of entrepreneurialism means that we understand the social world as one huge set of opportunities which only need to be seized by a wily operator. Indeed, studies of entrepreneurial discourse go as far as claiming that the language of entrepreneurship 'makes up' our sense of who we are as people (Du Gay, 1996). For instance, the rise of entrepreneurship discourse means that professionals drop their sense of identity in favour of a new more entrepreneurial outlook.

Theories of management are rarely picked up because they directly lead to greater productivity or more effective organizations. Rather, theories of management are often adopted by managers in their quest to gain legitimacy (Meyer and Rowan, 1977). That is, theories of management which are widespread and relatively well accepted become a way people seek to be seen as being a good player in an industry. The result is that companies often pick up and use management theories even when they have little or no direct practical benefit. However, what these management theories actually do is to confer a sense of status and legitimacy on the firm, which can have quite widespread and practical implications. For instance, putting into practice a theory such as total quality management, which is seen to have widespread importance in an industry, may mean that potential investors will look on the company more favourably. In turn, this might result in a better valuation by financial analysts, a better share price or a better chance for the company to survive in a competitive market. So the central lesson here is that theories of management can make a significant difference to the status and legitimacy of managers and organizations.

The final way that theory makes a difference in organizations is by becoming part of the technologies that are vital to the daily functioning of the organization. If we look carefully at many of the technologies that are frequently used in organizations, we find that they embody particular theories. Accounting systems embody theories of double-entry bookkeeping. Group-ware systems embody ideas of collaborative working. The new open-planned office environment embodies ideas of knowledge sharing. Recruitment systems embody ideas of human resource management. In each of these cases what were once complex and quite fluid ideas have been tied up and packaged into rather neat technologies (Latour, 2005). The result is that the user does not necessarily have to think in any depth about the ideas. Rather, the theory has become almost automated – it does it on its own. In many ways, theories of organizational behaviour have become part of the ubiquitous 'software' of organizational life.

## HOW CAN YOU USE THEORY?

OB theories are powerful tools and practices that profoundly influence organizational life. However, like any tools, it is not good enough

to know what they are and what they can do. We must also know exactly how these tools and practices can be used. One thing of which we can be certain is that theories about organizations are a special kind of tool. They are not blunt instruments which one can use as a paperweight. Rather, they are performative things. By this, I mean theories are a set of words which can be used to do things (Austin, 1969). Indeed, people do things with theories all the time. They use them to restructure, chastise, reflect, comment and convince (Cooren, 2000). Indeed, using a theory is a kind of practical act that has various affects in the world (Spicer *et al.*, 2007). If using a theory has affects, then we must ask what kinds of things we use theory to do. Jürgen Habermas (1987) provides a neat answer to this troubling question. He argues that we use theories to pursue particular interests. There are three distinct interests he identifies: explaining causal relations, understanding and interpreting, and critiquing the world. In what follows I shall expand on these three uses of theory. I will also suggest that theories of organization can have a fourth use: creating new modes of organizing.

Perhaps the most widespread way that theories can be used is to predict and control aspects of the social world. In order to do this, a theorist would set out to identify two or more concepts and posit a causal relationship between them. For instance, a theorist of power may suggest that the more scarce resources that an individual has at their disposal, the more powerful they will be (Pfeffer and Salancik, 1978). Having identified this relationship, the theorist would then seek to predict it. They might try to predict how much power an individual will have in an organization on the basis of the resources that they have at their disposal. Finally, a theorist might go a step further. On the basis of their theoretical knowledge, they may seek to control this relationship. For instance, a theorist might be concerned about the lack of power that immigrants have in the labour market. In order to rectify this, they might seek to provide immigrants with some scare resource (such as specialist skills) which would make them more powerful. Underlying this approach to theory is a deeper assumption about the nature of the social world. This assumption is that social life is made up of a complex web of causal relations. Moreover, these causal relations can be objectively known and understood through careful testing. Finally, by using a theory to predict social relations we usually end up conserving or, at the best, incrementally changing existing social relation because we are using evidence of how organizations are in order to build a theory. The result is that what we end up producing as truth what already exists, not what could possibly exist. Using theory to predict certainly has some strong advantages. Perhaps the major advantage is that it allows the theorist to identify clear causal patterns in organizations. As a rhetorical move, giving the audience a clear and uncomplicated message about causal relations can be very convincing indeed. It makes nice news stories and can appeal to the busy practitioner who does not have the time or effort for 'partially this, partially that' stories. However, such certainties come at a high cost. By making rigid rule like statements, much of the ambiguity and uncertainty that characterize social life is completely written out of the picture. The result is that we develop a one-dimensional and rather unsupple understanding of the social world. At times we can end up in a situation where our law-like generalizations act as mechanisms that reproduce existing patterns of domination and subjection. This means our theories can act as a brake on social change and enforce a single dominant version of how things should be.

A second way that we can use theory is to interpret the social world. This involves using theory as a perspective or point of understanding to sort out the buzzing confusions and complexities of the social world. Following this approach, the moment of doing theory is a moment of trying to generate meaningful understanding of the social world. Often this involves trying to recover the folk theories that people press into service in their everyday attempts to negotiate and make sense of the social world (Glaser and Strauss, 1968). For instance, some studies of power have sought to undercover the interpretive schemes that people working in organizations use to negotiate certain situations. One example is the practical negotiations which go on around how a contract should be interpreted on a building site (Clegg, 1975). This process of interpretation largely involved attempts to recover the ways people interpret the social world in order to create a degree of mutual understanding between actors. The idea is that we should try to communicate how other people interpret and understand the social world. Underpinning this approach to doing theory is the assumption that the social world is saturated in meaning. It also assumes the way that we can understand this social world is through an effort to recover the patterns of meaning and interpretation of actors. Thus, it is first and foremost an attempt to root out the practical knowledge of actors as they go through the social world. In doing so, we continue to have a rather conservative approach to the social world. This is because we seek to root out the interpretive schemes that are already existing within a society. We do not make the more difficult move of innovating, of actually trying to posit radically new ways of interpreting and understanding the social world. This approach to theorizing certainly has some distinctive and notable strengths. First, it allows us to develop situated, rich, and meaningful descriptions of social life (Latour, 2005). These descriptions of social life can often prove to be engaging and intuitively convincing. They are stories that speak to our experience of the social world as a space of ambiguities, meaningfulness and complexities. However, in providing a deep and detailed description of what happens in a particular setting, we end up with an endless list of specific knowledge. It is difficult to develop any generalized theory which can be usefully used to mediate between different contexts and even more difficult to turn theory building into a progressive enterprise where new theories build on existing ideas. The result is that theorists can continually engage in a process of reinventing the wheel. Using theory to interpret social reality can mean that it is very difficult to question existing patterns of social life. When interpreting, all a theorist can do is to affirm the existing stock of practical knowledge. Calling this knowledge into question is seen to be somewhat arrogant and belittling to the stock of practical knowledge of our research subjects.

The third way that theory can be used is as a tool for critique. This involves using our ideas to call into question existing social relations and ways of organizing. Theory becomes a kind of negative capability. This is the capability of 'being in uncertainties, mysteries, doubts, without any irritable reaching after fact and reason' (Keats, 1970: 43; see also: Bion, 1984). This ability to live with the unknown involves a willingness to unfold and unpick our deeply held assumptions and perspectives on organizations. Moreover, it involves a willingness to deliberately destabilize our existing understandings and dearly held theories about social life. Using theory to call into question established perspective works through a process of questioning. It sets out to reveal the assumptions and political commitments that underlie existing approaches to the social world. Once these underlying assumptions are identified, the theorist proceeds to dismantle each and every one of these assumptions. Studies of power in organizations often take this route. Instead of seeking to recover the interpretive schemes and practical knowledge of actors, they seek to call this practical reason into question. For instance, Burawoy's (1979) study of power in a factory showed how the practical knowledge of the employees that they used to help the time pass during the boring work day actually made them complicit in their own subordination. Seeing things way this allowed Burawoy to call into question the structures of power and domination that underpin the organizational life world of these workers. Using this approach to critique he sought to reveal the structures of domination and power that infest social life. Doing so involves an attempt to grasp the possibility and potentialities of creating radical social change. Underlying such efforts is the assumption that social reality is something that is structured around struggles and patterns of domination. The theorist seeks to know the world by throwing that world into question. Knowledge, according to critical theory, is first and foremost a process of asking questions in order to create some kind of radical or emancipatory social change. Such procedures of critique certainly allow the theorist to do some interesting things. It allows them to reveal relations of power and domination that often underlie existing theories. It also means that the theorists do not unconditionally accept existing bodies of ideas. Rather, they seek relentlessly to call these bodies of ideas into question. Doing so means that we are not fated to merely accept existing folk theories as the way things are and indeed should be. Rather, it allows them to call into question these folk theories in ways that may lead to human emancipation. Indeed, it was this very negative capability of questioning and critique that underpinned some of the great movements such as the Enlightenment, the Reformation, and the French Revolution (Withnow, 1989). While such negative capabilities certainly can produce large scale social change, they can also lead to more sinister outcomes. Perhaps one of the most questionable consequences of using theory as a tool for critique is that it leads theorists in a relentless cycle of destructive tearing down of any ideological edifice they are faced with. The result is two-fold – first, it makes it very difficult, if not impossible to identify what the theorist actually supports (Böhm, 2006). Second, it leads to a kind of resentful dependence on the very thing which we set out to critique (Brown, 1995). Thus critique has a kind of parasitic dependency on the existing bad guys at whom it takes pot-shots. Finally, critique can seduce the theorists into making rather grand claims in a way that disregards folk theories. The rich world of everyday ideas is replaced with a monolithic single commitment to critique which effectively wipes out the diversity of local knowledge that critique is supposed to celebrate. It also can sap energy from the many practical efforts to change organizational life to which critique is apparently so committed.

After Habermas, some other theorists have developed a further way that theory might be used in the world, not for prediction, understanding, or critique but innovation. The final way that theory can be used is in the creation of new ways of being and organizing, an approach to doing theory that involves creating new concepts that allow us to think about organizations in a different way. This process of concept creation proceeds through the encounter with thought and the world, an encounter which will certainly reveal things which are mysterious and cannot be adequately explained (Alvesson and Kärreman, 2007). In order to provide explanations, we are then pushed to create concepts (Deleuze and Guattari, 1996). This involves crafting new representations and ways of being which reveal unthought aspects of social life. It gives us a language through which we can begin to think what was previously unthinkable. For instance, some theorists of power have taken the risk of creating new ways of understanding and enacting relations of power within organizations. This process of concept creation can produce new ways of doing power within organizations. Thinking about organizational power relations as a kind of social movement allows us to imagine new ways of relating to one another in organizations (e.g., Davis *et al.*, 2005). By inventing new ways of thinking through power relations, we are able to open up the world by drawing out the potentialities that dwell all around us. The act of doing theory should be understood first and foremost as an act of theorizing. Approaching theory as a creative act assumes that the organizational world is one which is at least partially confronted through and in the theories which we have of it. These theories can certainly be investigated and understood, but they can also be reworked to draw out potentialities in the social world. Doing so helps to make incremental and sometimes potentially radical changes to the social world.

Instead of these changes being made through a negative destabilizing of existing social relations, they can be made through a generous contribution of new ways of existing and living. The process of doing theory involves contributing new ways of theorizing. Going through this process helps us to bring into being new ways of understanding and being within organizations. It expands our theoretical imaginations. It provides us with new ways of thinking and talking about the social world. It also gives a sense of what might be possible within organizations, but perhaps most importantly, if we approach the process of theorizing as one of concept creation, we are able to hold the process of theorizing consistently open to potentialities which we cannot yet imagine. While all this sounds promising, the act of theorizing as a process of creation comes with less lustrous baggage. Because of the commitment to consistent openness, it can lead to the undisciplined creation and multiplication of concepts. While this can create an attractive and exciting fair of ideas, it can also create a lack of any progressive research programme. In addition, it may nurture a commitment to the outlandish, novel and freakish rather than what is actually 'true'. It might even produce a disorientating and rather confusing landscape of ideas for the neophyte to negotiate. Along with the excitement might come a sense of confusion and disorientation.

## CONCLUSION

Theory matters. At least this is the argument I have tried to make here. I have argued that when we use OB tools and practices we are largely using theories. They may be naïve theories or complex theories, but they are theories all the same. These theories have a range of affects in organizations such as changing people's routines, influencing the technologies they use to get the job done, and changing the very job which is to be done. Furthermore, I have argued that theory can be used for a number of purposes including prediction, understanding, critique and creation. What remains is the question of exactly how a theorist of organizations can fit these different ways of doing theory together.

One way people think about how different theories are used is to think in terms of conflicting paradigms (e.g., Burrell and Morgan, 1979). Such an orientation involves recognizing that the different approaches to doing theory rely on mutually exclusive assumptions which cannot and should not be mixed. All one can do is be certain about exactly what kind of theorist one is and remain true to the cause. As an approach, it certainly has its charms. It clarifies the underlying theoretical positions we come from when we think about organizations. It also identifies why it is sometimes so difficult for different theorists to work together. However, it can lead to a rather unproductive situation where there is no possible or practical interaction between different theoretical approaches. The result is the carnage of paradigm warfare with little border traffic between different approaches.

A second way of thinking about how these different ways of doing theory fit is in terms of the political standards which are used to think through the doing of theory (e.g., Contu and Willmott, 2005; Böhm, 2006). Following this approach, each of the different ways of doing theory are said to be based on different political agendas. Any attempts to mix different theoretical positions would ultimately involve wavering between what should be considered to be incoherent political positions, meaning that one would dilute their political commitments and projects. The upshot is that one should remain committed to their position and attempt to build a movement around it. Doing so would see the position gain strength and steeling itself from attack from other conceptual movements. While this approach is certainly good advice for the theoretical field marshal, it can fall victim to an absolute elision of theory and politics. For sure, our theorizing always has political commitments, but it is never *only* politics. Theory can be and indeed should be far more than this. It can overflow the possibility of

petty wars of dominance in favour of an encounter with the rich strangeness of the world.

So if not paradigms or politics, what then? I would like to suggest that doing theory can involve a kind of practical stance. This is a stance where we realize that when we do theory, we are performing certain things. The question then is not first and foremost about our commitment to certain theoretical positions or political causes. Rather, the key question is about what the task at hand might be and how theoretical practice, of whatever kind, can be used to do it (Spicer *et al.*, 2007). Taking this approach involves asking exactly what I am hoping to do with this theory, who will benefit, and what might be the best way of going about doing it. This would probably necessarily involve a movement between different positions when investigating different questions. By asking somewhat more loose and experimental questions, the practice of theory may become one which is not dominated by hard and fast commitments. Rather it becomes a practice that is more supple and able to answer the pressing concerns at hand. This would make the task of doing theory something which does not involve dogmatic commitments. Rather it would become an act of testing and experimentation (Ronnell, 2006). Doing theory would be about remaining open to the world and the constant possibility that this world will overflow the ideas we already have at hand. Most importantly, it would cultivate the ability to listen for and experience the mystery that is how people behave in organizations.

## REFERENCES

Abrahamson, E. (1991) 'Managerial fads and fashions: The diffusion and rejection of innovations', *The Academy of Management Review*, 16 (3): 586–612.

Abrahamson, E., and Fairchild, G. (1999) 'Management fashion: Lifecycles, triggers, and collective learning processes', *Administrative Science Quarterly*, 44: 708–740.

Alvesson, M. and Kärreman, D. (2007) 'Constructing mystery: Empirical matters in theory development', *Academy of Management Review*, 32 (4).

Austin, J.L. (1969) *How to Do Things with Words*. London: Penguin.

Bacharach, S.B. (1989) 'Organization theories: Some criteria for evaluation', *Academy of Management Review*, 14 (4): 496–515.

Barley, S., Meyer, G.W. and Gash, D.C. (1988) 'Cultures of culture: Academics, practitioners and the pragmatics of normative control', *Administrative Science Quarterly*, 33: 24–60.

Bartunek, J.M. (1984) 'Changing interpretive schemes and organizational restructuring: The example of a religious order', *Administrative Science Quarterly*, 29: 355–372.

Bion, W. (1984) *Attention and Interpretation*. London: Karnac.

Böhm, S.G. (2006) *Repositioning Organization Theory*. London: Palgrave.

Brown, W. (1995) *States of Inquiry*. Princeton, NJ: Princeton University Press.

Burawoy, M. (1979) *Manufacturing Consent*. Chicago: University of Chicago Press.

Burrell, G. and Morgan, G. (1979) *Sociological Paradigms and Organizational Analysis*. London: Heinemann.

Burt, R. (1992) *Structural Holes: The Social Structure of Competition*. Cambridge: Harvard University Press.

Calás, M. and Smircich, L. (1991) 'Voicing seduction to silence leadership', *Organization Studies*, 12 (4): 567–602.

Chiapello, E. and Boltanski, L. (2005) *The New Spirit of Capitalism*. London: Verso.

Clegg, S.R. (1975) *Power, Rule and Domination*. London: Routledge Kegan Paul.

Contu, A. and Willmott, H. (2005) 'You spin me round: The realist turn in organization and management studies', *Journal of Management Studies*, 42 (8): 1645–1662.

Cooren, F. (2000) *The Organizing Property of Communication*. Amsterdam: John Benjamins.

Czarniawska, B. and Joerges, B. (1996) 'Travels of ideas', in B. Czarniawska and G. Sevon (eds) *Translating Organizational Change*. Berlin: de Gruyter, pp. 13–48.

Davis, G., McAdam, D., Scott, W. Richard and Zald, M.Z. (eds) (2005) *Social Movements and Organization Theory*. Cambridge: Cambridge University Press.

Deleuze, G. and Guattari, F. (1996) *What is Philosophy?* New York: Columbia University Press.

Dubin, R. (1969) *Theory Building*. New York: Free Press.

Du Gay, P. (1996) *Consumption and Identity at Work*. London: Sage.

Eagleton, T. (2003) *After Theory*. New York: Penguin.

Feldman, M. and Pentland, B. (2003) 'Reconceptualizing organizational routines as a source of flexibility and change', *Administrative Science Quarterly*, 48: 94–118.

Glaser, B.G. and Strauss, A.L. (1967) *The Discovery of Grounded Theory: Strategies for Qualitative Research*. New York: Adeline de Greuter.

Gordon, M.E., Kleiman, L.S. and Hanie, C.A. (1978) 'Industrial organizational psychology: Open thy ears o house of Israel', *American Psychologist*, 33 (10): 893–905.

Grant, D., Hardy, C., Oswick, C. and L. Putnam (eds) (2004) *The Sage Handbook of Organizational Discourse*. London: Sage.

Grey, C. (1999) 'We are all managers now, we always were: On the development and demise of management', *Journal of Management Studies*, 36 (5): 561–586.

Grey, C. and Sinclair, A. (2006) 'Writing differently', *Organization*, 13 (3): 443–453.

Habermas, J. (1987) *Knowledge and Human Interests*. Cambridge: Polity.

Hambrick, D. (1993). 'What if the Academy actually mattered?', *Academy of Management Review*, 19 (1): 11–16.

Hancock, P. and Tyler, M. (forthcoming) *The Management of Everyday Life*. London: Palgrave.

Hunter, I. (2006) 'The history of theory', *Critical Inquiry*, 33: 78–112.

Jones, C. and Spicer, A. (forthcoming) *Unmasking the Entrepreneur*. Cheltenham: Edward Elgar.

Keats, J. (1970) *The Letters of John Keats: A Selection*. R. Gittings (ed.). Oxford: Oxford University Press.

Kilmann, R.H. (1979) 'On integrating knowledge utilization with knowledge development: The philosophy behind the MAPS design technology', *Academy of Management Review*, 4: 417–426.

Lant, T. (2002) 'Organizational cognition and interpretation', in Joel Baum (ed.) *The Blackwell Companion to Organization*. Oxford: Blackwell, pp. 344–362.

Latour, B. (2005) *Reassembling the Social: An Introduction to Actor-network Theory*. Oxford: Oxford University Press.

Leavitt, H.J. (1989) 'Educating our MBAs: On teaching what we haven't taught', *California Management Review*, 31: 38–50.

Levitt, B. and March, J. (1988) 'Organizational learning', *Annual Review of Sociology*, 14: 319–340.

March, J. (2000) 'Citigroup's John Reed and Stanford's James March on management research and practice', *Academy of Management Executive*, 14: 52–64.

Meyer, J. and Rowan, B. (1977) 'Institutional organizations: Formal structures as myth and ceremony', *American Journal of Sociology*, 83: 340–362.

Mintzberg, H. (2004) *Developing Managers Not MBAs*. London: FT Prentice Hall.

Mitroff, I.I., Betz, F., Pondy, L.R. and Sagasti, F. (1974) 'On managing science in the systems age: Two schemas for the study of science as a whole systems phenomenon', *Interfaces*, 4 (3): 46–58.

Pfeffer, J. and Fong, C. (2002) 'The end of business schools? Less success than meets the eye', *Academy of Management Learning & Education*, 1: 78–95.

Pfeffer, J. and Fong, C. (2004) 'The business school "business": Some lessons from the US experience', *Journal of Management Studies*, 41 (8): 1501–1520.

Pfeffer, J. and Salancik, G.R. (1978) *The External Control of Organizations: A Resource Dependence Perspective*. New York: Harper and Row.

Porac, I., Thomas, H. and Baden-Fuller, C. (1989) 'Competitive groups as cognitive communities: The case of Scottish knitwear manufacturers', *Journal of Management Studies*, 26: 397–416.

Porac, J.F. and Thomas, H. (1990) 'Taxonomic mental models in competitor definition', *Academy of Management Review*, 15 (2): 224–240.

Ronnell, A. (2006) *The Test Drive*. Urbana, IL: University of Illinois Press.

Spicer, A., Alvesson, M. and Kärreman, D. (2007) *Critical Performativity: The Unfinished Business Critical Management Studies*. Paper presented at The Academy of Management Annual Conference, Philadelphia.

Starkey, K. and Madan, P. (2001) 'Bridging the relevance gap: Aligning stakeholders in the future of management research', *British Journal of Management*, 12: Special Issue, December, S3–26.

Starkey, K., Hauchlet, A. and Tempest, S. (2004) 'Rethinking the business school', *Journal of Management Studies*, 41 (8): 1521–1531.

Weick, K.E. (1993) 'The collapse of sensemaking in organization: The Mann Gulch disaster', *Administrative Science Quarterly*, 38 (4): 628–652.

Whetten, D.A. (1989) 'What constitutes a theoretical contribution?', *The Academy of Management Review*, 14 (4): 490–495.

Withnow, R. (1989) *Communities of Discourse: Ideology and Social Structure in the Reformation, the Enlightenment, and European Socialism*. Cambridge, MA: Harvard University Press.

# 2

# What Does Knowledge Work Do?

Tim Ray

Proclaiming that we live in a Knowledge Age has become fabulously fashionable. Competitive success in the Knowledge Economy relies on Knowledge Workers who *do* Knowledge Work. Using the abstract noun 'knowledge' as if it were an adjective has produced some terms that sound weighty and worthy, but do these innovative uses of knowledge achieve anything useful? Certainly, economists have long been aware that knowledge is important in economic development. Yet, as Edith Penrose famously pointed out, economists have, for the most part, found the whole subject of knowledge 'too slippery to handle with even a moderate degree of precision' (Penrose, 1995: 77). Organization behaviourists have been less cautious. In an attempt to avoid slipperiness and recklessness, this chapter argues that knowledge work does not *do* anything. *People* do things. The exploitation of knowledge relies on *knowers*: the people who *know* how to act and think in appropriate ways. And therein lies the managerial problem: if people – knowledge workers – are paid to 'act and think for themselves', how can they be relied upon to do the 'right' thing?

## INTRODUCTION

Daughter:  Daddy, how much do you know?
Father:    Me? Hmm – I have about a pound of knowledge.
D:         Don't be silly. Is it a pound sterling or a pound weight?
           I mean *really* how much do you know? (Gregory Bateson 2000: 21, original emphasis)

Getting the measure of knowledge work and what it *does* is not easy. According to Peter Drucker, the person responsible for coining the term 'knowledge worker' was Peter Drucker.[1] For Drucker (2001: 194), knowledge work requires each knowledge worker to act and think as if he or she were a Chief Executive Officer. Moreover, knowledge workers are specialists: 'knowledge workers, whether their knowledge is primitive or advanced, whether they possess a little of it or a great deal, will, by definition, be specialized' (Drucker, 2003: 308). Drucker (2001: 149–50) also noted that the largest and fastest growing group of knowledge workers do both knowledge work *and* manual work; he called them 'technologists'; and proposed that they include those who apply knowledge of the highest order (such as surgeons), along with people (such as lab technicians) who rely upon the autonomous use of more modest, but nevertheless specialized, knowledge. In short, knowledge workers see themselves as 'professionals' (Drucker, 2002: 239) who are expected to *get the right things done*, which Drucker (1988: 1) argued, is simply saying that they are expected to be 'effective'.

In the opening chapter of his book, *The Effective Executive* (first published in 1967), Drucker portrayed the problem of expecting knowledge workers to behave as trusted agents with elegant simplicity.

> A cartoon in The New Yorker magazine some time ago showed an office on the door of which was the legend: 'Chas. Smith, General Sales Manager, Ajax Soap Company'. The walls were bare except for a big sign saying 'Think'. The man in the office had his feet propped up on his desk and was blowing smoke rings at the ceiling. Outside two older men went by, the one saying to the other: 'But how can we be sure that Smith thinks soap?'
>
> One can indeed never be sure what the knowledge worker thinks – and yet thinking is his specific work, it is his 'doing'. (Drucker, 1988: 3)

Agent Smith's autonomy encapsulates the fundamental problem with managing knowledge work: how can organizations secure the intelligent cooperation of those who are paid to act and think for themselves? Smith might bubble with soapy thoughts, but dream of working somewhere else: is he being *effective* or *defective*?

On the one hand, managers might see effectiveness in terms of *efficiency*. If the division of labour is *perfected* and economies of scale *maximized*, waste could be *minimized*. And the combination of efficiency and significant market share can make it hard for new suppliers to gain a foothold.

Although the American sociologist, George Ritzer, has made it clear that he does not bear any particular animus towards the fast-food colossus, McDonald's (Ritzer, 2004a: xiii), his work on the 'McDonaldization of society' offers a compelling insight into processes by which contemporary bureaucracies exploit Max Weber's 'iron cage' of rationality (ibid.: 27–8) to gain an iron grip on global markets (Ritzer, 2004b). Command and control bureaucracies transmit authority from those at the top, who 'do the thinking', to those who 'do the doing'. As manufacturing migrates to China and other places where labour is cheap, McDonaldization has transposed production-line principles to many aspects of service-sector work. In a McDonaldized world, each employee's job is specified by rules that 'cage' creativity to ensure that any suitably qualified person could do the job: whoever 'does the job' *does the same thing*.

On the other hand, the capacity to innovate and compete effectively involves *flexibility*. Knowledge workers explore new possibilities that might stretch or break the 'rules of the game'. Their autonomy allows them to do *different things*, which can be crucial in the pursuit of differences that 'make a difference', but it does not make sense to expect someone to 'do the right thing' in the face of uncertainty, if you do not trust and respect their judgement: listening to knowledge workers and the capacity to empathize with 'the world as they see it' is often vital to securing their intelligent cooperation. Knowledge workers have to be treated as human beings, as opposed to 'human resources'. In a world where effective knowledge workers manage themselves, trust and respect are fundamental to a process in which knowledge work becomes embedded in a way of life. Technological advances make it possible to work from almost anywhere: e-mails can be checked from holiday hotels and 'doing knowledge work' does not necessarily mean being 'at work', but what is it that knowledge workers *do*?

Focusing on the abstract noun 'knowledge' does not offer obvious pointers. You cannot see, hear, smell, taste or feel an abstract noun, but some abstract nouns, such as 'knowledge', 'truth' and 'wisdom', can focus diffuse emotions. A good school might have them written above the gate. They are akin to flags that stir feelings in ways that defy deconstruction; it is possible to support the flag without saying what you are supporting (see Polanyi and Prosch, 1977: 72). Moreover, mindless enthusiasm for waving the knowledge flag can be infectious. In opening his book, *Knowledge Work and Knowledge-Intensive Firms*, Mats Alvesson (2004: 1) opines that knowledge 'is very difficult to define and delimit: like many other common terms, it covers everything and nothing'. Undaunted, Alvesson (2004: 1) summarizes his provisional approach to defining knowledge in terms of *judgement* 'backed up to a high degree by theoretical, intellectual knowledge', but this does not specify what 'theoretical, intellectual knowledge' *is*; although the full force of the problem floods forth at the end of the book, where Alvesson comes clean: 'Of course, "knowledge" has no essential meaning, and people use the term in an infinite number of ways' (Alvesson, 2004: 231). He cautions that, far from being a six-lane highway that gets people to where they want to go, knowledge could be seen as a 'dead end' (see Alvesson, 2004: 228–31); knowledge could be the road to *nowhere*. So, what is the nature of this wrong turning and is there a more promising path that might take us *somewhere*?

Although knowledge is an abstract noun, it is often used as if it were a concrete noun. For example, information that has been produced by the scientific method and approved by the international community of practising scientists is often referred to as knowledge, because – in the realist view of science – it corresponds to what 'really exists'. In the manner of a portrait painter, the scientist aims at producing concrete knowledge that is a 'true' likeness of the 'real thing', but scientists cannot see the real thing that they are trying to represent. All that they can do is use scientific experiments to compare different models of what the real thing might be like and reject those that do not fit with experimental findings. Progress relies on eliminating what is 'wrong' to distil what might be 'right'.

Science has emerged as a reliable way of knowing that can be refined and extended by successive generations of scientists – and its cumulative achievements further the idea that 'realism works'.

According to the respected British philosopher and media personality, A. C. Grayling, realism is familiar 'because we all, in our non-philosophical moments at least, believe it' (Grayling, 2007: 109). Notwithstanding the gratuitously extravagant nature of Grayling's claim to know what we all believe, ordinary language routinely uses knowledge as if it were a representation of something 'real' – thereby hijacking scientific realism as a vehicle for lending weight to whatever people happen to think. For Simon Blackburn, who is another respected British philosopher and media personality, this gives the green light to relativism. Today's relativists, he objects, feed on the desecrated corpse of reason: 'Astrology, prophecy, homeopathy, Feng Shui, conspiracy theories, flying saucers, voodoo, crystal balls, miracle-working, angel visits, alien abductions, management nostrums and a thousand other cults dominate people's minds' (Blackburn, 2005: xiv). And the cult of management nostrums based on 'knowledge' – which Alvesson cautions 'has no essential meaning' – seems to have befuddled normally serious journal editors and others who guard the gates of social science.

During the second half of the 1990s, Anglophone management science became bewitched by a curious departure from its realist roots, as oriental oracular mystique shaped the rise of new nostrums. According to Japanese academics, Ikujiro Nonaka and Hirotaka Takeuchi, what the Hungarian-born scientist Michael Polanyi (1891–1976) called tacit knowledge, which is in the heads of persons and entirely subjective, could be converted into universally comprehensible explicit knowledge objects that can be managed (see Tsoukas, 2003; Ray, 2008a). Unlike Polanyi, who was one of the world's leading physical chemists, tipped for a Nobel Prize (which is an honour that was subsequently bestowed on his son, John) and committed to the personal search for an absolute truth, Nonaka and Takeuchi advocated unconstrained relativism. Truthfulness is *not*, Nonaka and Takeuchi (1995: 58) suggested, an essential attribute of knowledge. Rather, as Nonaka and colleagues explained in later work, truth, like beauty, is 'in the eye of the beholder' (Nonaka, Toyama and Konno, 2000: 7): it can be whatever takes your fancy, although the baying of those who believe that tacit-explicit knowledge-conversion is the basis for Knowledge Management (KM) tends to ignore the casuistry. References to Polanyi abound in a KM literature that feasts on the desecrated corpse of his ideas.

When the daughter, in Gregory Bateson's metalogue asked her father 'Daddy, how much do you know?' she is asking him to tangle with the inexpressible parts of his mind. He *does not know* – in wholly lucid, wholly explicit terms – *what he knows*. Nonetheless, through shared experience, Bateson's father and daughter might develop the capacity to trust their respective judgements about what the other might know. Building on Ernst von Glasersfeld's (2002) radical constructivism, this chapter argues that the construction of human knowing cannot transcend the limits of human experience. However, in contrast to Nonaka's implicit nihilism (which rejects truth in favour of unconstrained personal opinion), radical constructivism proposes that personal knowing is *constrained* by the individual's developing sense of what is *viable*. We are the *subjects* of what we have learned in the course of our experience: *all knowing is subjective*. While interaction with other people nurtures the development of *intersubjectively viable* communication, the sense that each individual makes of words and numbers – explicit knowledge – is always personal. The Ajax Soap Company can never be sure that Agent Smith 'thinks soap' and it cannot be confident about the results of any attempt to coerce Agent Smith into confessing what he really thinks. Unwarranted pressure might prompt Agent Smith to respond with worthless words and gestures. Managing knowledge workers effectively relies on the capacity to establish and sustain their intelligent cooperation.

## ANTECEDENTS: FROM ACTIVE LEARNING TO FICTITIOUS COMMODITIES

It is so difficult to find the *beginning*. Or, better: it is difficult to begin at the beginning. And not try to go further back. (Ludwig Wittgenstein, *On Certainty*, 1972: Sec. 471, original emphasis)

Conceivably, there was a time when advanced primates – our ancestors – *knew* that they could scramble around on floating branches and *learned* how to use those branches to do useful things. S. C. Gilfillan's (1935: 18–19) book, *Inventing the Ship*, cited swimming and playing around a floating log as the first of nine possible stages in the evolution of the dugout canoe. Gradually, learning by doing – experience – that was shared by successive generations gave rise to the modern boat. Gilfillan did not suggest that this is the only way in which boats originated: the waterproofed basket boat of the Tigris Euphrates, or the coracle, or the bark canoe, or something else, might have come earlier, but they were not, he argued, in the main line of descent to the modern ship in the way that the dugout was. For Gilfillan, 'use promotes improvement' (Gilfillan, 1935: 276). Building a better boat – or a better version of anything – involves *learning* about what is viable in the pursuit of what is perceived to be more advantageous.

With the rise of capitalism, the concept of 'more advantageous' became aligned with 'more profitable'. In his magnum opus, *The Great Transformation: The Political and Economic Origins of Our Time*, Karl Polanyi (Michael Polanyi's elder brother) marshalled an astonishingly comprehensive array of evidence to press the point that capitalism transformed markets from reliable 'servant' to uncompromising 'master'. Before the great transformation, markets were never seen as more than 'accessories of economic life' but a market economy is controlled, regulated and directed by market prices (Polanyi, 2001: 71). Notwithstanding the capacity of markets to generate hitherto unimagined material wealth, Polanyi argued that they could have catastrophic consequences.

Since it was first published in 1944, Karl Polanyi's book has become a classic text. In his foreword to the 2001 edition, the distinguished economist and Nobel Laureate, Joseph Stiglitz, noted that Polanyi's account of the great transformation of European civilization is analogous to the transformation that confronts today's developing countries. Specifically, Stiglitz declared that policies advocated by the International Monetary Fund, World Bank and United Nations might have been much more effective if they had taken serious account of the lessons in Polanyi's book. However, any suggestion that Stiglitz is about to specify Karl Polanyi's message with laser-like precision is immediately dispelled: 'It is hard, and probably wrong even to attempt to summarize a book of such complexity and subtlety in a few lines' (Stiglitz in Polanyi, 2001: vii). Nevertheless, it is comparatively easy and probably right to quote a few lines from Polanyi that could be used to summarize what is wrong with the factors of production – land, labour and capital – deployed in neoclassical economic theory: they are 'fictitious'.

> Labor is only another name for a human activity which goes with life itself, which in its turn is not produced for sale but for entirely different reasons, nor can that activity be detached from the rest of life, be stored or mobilized; land is only another name for nature, which is not produced by man; actual money, finally, is merely a token of purchasing power which, as a rule, is not produced at all, but comes into being through the mechanism of banking or state finance. None of them is produced for sale. The commodity description of labor, land, and money is entirely fictitious. (Polanyi, 2001: 75–6)

Yet, those who see competitive markets as the key to an efficient allocation of scarce resources, and regard it as right that organization behaviours comply with the exigencies of effective markets, often overlook the fictitious nature of commodities. And that solecism is often compounded by a failure to specify the nature of competition. As Paul McNulty pointed out, the economic conception of competition is both fundamental to economics and divorced from the verb 'to compete' (McNulty, 1968: 640, 650).

Neoclassical economics perfected the idea that competition could be used to define the structure of a 'perfect' market. Hence, 'perfect competition' exists when a large number of buyers and sellers produce an identical product; all firms have equal access to the factors of production; there is no scope for collusion between buyers or sellers, and every participant in the market has instantaneous and perfect information about everyone else's prices. The interaction of supply and demand fixes a market price that cannot be changed by the action of any individual buyer or seller. No one can change anything. Everyone is powerless. The price is 'perfect'. Thus, those who believe in the perfection of competition might claim that they have perfected a 'physics of society' in which practitioners apply a single universally valid model of the world (see Solow, 1985: 330). Perfect competition is divorced from the verb 'to compete' in ways that echo the distinction between objective knowledge and transitive uses of the verb 'to know'.

Scientific detachment relies on transcending people and the practice of power to produce knowledge that is objective. Science is a non-rivalrous good: more for you does not mean less for me, but there is a widespread willingness to supplement science with the objectification of subjective personal knowledge. This second kind of knowledge is often presented as a rivalrous resource: the 'fourth factor of production'. By representing what a person knows as knowledge that has become coded as information, it is possible to treat personal knowledge as a scarce commodity that could be priced according to the laws of supply and demand: thereby adding a fourth fictitious commodity to Karl Polanyi's trilogy. However, such a sleight of hand is not without its complications: information has some peculiarly slippery qualities. If you sell information, you still have the thing that you sold.

Also, if you ask to inspect information for sale, the seller would no longer have anything to sell. Yet, whatever the difficulties of conceptualizing the economics of knowledge production, few would disagree with the proposition that learning how to do new things is essential to economic progress. Similarly, attempts to articulate the importance of innovation and organizational learning have become axiomatic to OB's axis of spin.

Innovation is impelled by a complex inter-action between the quest for new possibilities and the evolution of user needs. In one early conception of entrepreneurial capitalism, the inventive process was seen as *exogenous*: heroic entrepreneurs established new firms and thereby gave economic significance to imaginative thinking. However, sustaining the trajectory of competitive innovation placed a premium on *endogenous* creativity – for example, by using Research and Devel-opment (R&D) to 'invest in invention' – and that raised new issues for economists (Schumpeter, 1928: 384–5). In contrast to the single controlling mind associated with the heroic inventor-entrepreneur, knowledge work in complex organizations involves many minds. Different knowledge workers see their roles in different ways and information that flows easily in one part of the organization might not find sympathetic ears in other places. For example, the R&D department may not be able to create what the marketing department dream of selling. Understanding the circumstances of other people and the capacity to empathize with their problems offers an obvious route to improved flexibility, but the struggle to develop intersubjectively viable communication is often overshadowed by the deification of objectivity.

## CENTRAL APPROACHES: FROM SCIENTIFIC MANAGEMENT TO KNOWLEDGE MANAGEMENT

The principal object of management should be to secure the maximum prosperity for the employer, coupled with the maximum prosperity for each employee. (Frederick Winslow Taylor, 1998: 1)

The above sentence opened Frederick Winslow Taylor's monograph, *The Principles of Scientific Management* (first published in 1911). Taylor wanted to increase the efficiency of work and thereby produce a bigger economic pie that would benefit both employer and employee – although it is not hard to see why his attitudes to employees were controversial. Consider, for example, his comments about the requirements of a person who could be regarded as fit to handle pig iron.

Now one of the very first requirements for a man who is fit to handle pig iron as a regular occupation is that he shall be so stupid and so phlegmatic that he more nearly resembles in his mental make-up the ox than any other type. The man who is mentally alert and intelligent is for this very reason entirely unsuited to what would, for him, be the grinding monotony of work of this character. Therefore the workman who is best suited to handling pig iron is unable to understand the real science of doing this class of work. He is so stupid that the word 'percentage' has no meaning to him, and he must consequently be trained by a man more intelligent than himself into the habit of working in accordance with the laws of this science before he can be successful. (Taylor, 1998: 28)

For Drucker, Taylorism constituted an impor-tant step towards the knowledge economy: 'Taylor, for the first time in history, looked at work itself as deserving the attention of an educated man' (Drucker, 1992: 271), but Taylor's science owes little to objectivity. Rather it is presented as a tool that the 'intelligent' can use (according to their *subjective* sense of what is required) to command and control the 'stupid'.

In 1945, the Austrian-born British thinker and joint winner of the 1974 Nobel Prize for Economics, Friedrich Hayek, published a paper entitled 'The Use of Knowledge in Society'. At a time when central planning was being advocated as an alternative to the market-rational economy, Hayek was concerned with the control of knowledge that could never be given to a single mind. In the case of scientific knowledge, he claimed, it was possible that 'a body of suitably chosen experts may be in the best position to command all the best knowledge available' (Hayek, 1945: 521) – all one had to do was chose the experts – but what about the economic significance of non-scientific knowledge?

> Today it is almost heresy to suggest that scientific knowledge is not the sum of all knowledge. But a little reflection will show that there is beyond question a body of very important but unorganized knowledge which cannot possibly be called scientific in the sense of knowledge of general rules: the knowledge of the particular circumstances of time and place. (Hayek, 1945: 521)

The popular assumption that everyone had more or less perfect knowledge, Hayek dared to suggest, overlooked the possibility that different people might know different things. In Hayek's view, the 'marvel' of the market stemmed from the way in which price signals *transmit* information without the involvement of a single controlling mind. If the scarcity of a raw material causes the price to go up, for example, people use it more sparingly, without anyone telling them what to do. As Hayek explained: 'I have deliberately used the word "marvel" to shock the reader out of the complacency with which we often take the working of this mechanism for granted' (Hayek, 1945: 527). Clearly, differences in what different people know have profound implications for the way in which markets operate, but the marvel of the market *fails* in areas where knowledgeable people might triumph, not least of all in their ability to anticipate the value of things that have yet to be invented and their sensitivity to side effects, such as pollution, poverty and other 'externalities' that discontent those who are affected by other people's passion for market-rational principles (see Stiglitz, 2002).

After the World War II, it seemed to many in Britain and America that science had played a decisive role in their victory. Progress in science-related technologies, such as nuclear power, jet engines, radar, rockets, penicillin and plastics, promised to sustain a so-called 'linear model of innovation' in which science discovered, technology applied and everything else took care of itself.

Government investment in science would generate the knowledge that was necessary to compete. Or so it appeared, until Japan and other countries, which did not '*do* science', started to do rather well. How could this be when their government expenditure on basic research was relatively low when judged against British or American standards?

Amid concerns that the Japanese were 'borrowing' inventions from elsewhere and developing them into commercially viable products and production processes, Anglo-American concerns led to 'research into research' and efforts to understand the interaction between organizations and the sources of technological innovation. These included the landmark investigation, *Wealth from Knowledge* (Langrish et al., 1972: 39), which concluded that the transition from 'pure knowledge' – science – to wealth is less simple and less direct than was commonly supposed. On occasions, scientific progress can generate the basis for new avenues of technological development but subsequent progress relies on improvement innovations that are grounded in the knowledge of the particular circumstances of time and place. As a follow-up to *Wealth from Knowledge,* subsequent research indicated that cultivating the capacity to support 'post-innovation performance' typically relies on endogenous learning *within* the organization (Georghiou et al., 1986) – which could be seen as the Anglo-Saxon equivalent of Japanese-style 'knowledge-creation'.

Michael Gibbons and his colleagues (Gibbons et al., 1994; Nowotny et al., 2001) developed the 'knowledge as science' versus 'non-scientific but useful knowledge' divide using new terms. What Gibbons et al. called the 'Mode 1' production of science was only part of the picture; people, who were concerned with doing things in a specific context, also produced useful knowledge, which they dubbed Mode 2 knowledge production. Whereas Mode 1 knowledge production might be seen as a cooperative venture among scientists who trust each other to deploy the scientific method in their search for metaphysical truth, Mode 2 knowledge production is anchored in practical, context-specific here-and-now problems. While Mode 1 knowledge production is disciplinary, Mode 2 knowledge production is typically transdisciplinary and might rely on informal cooperation among practitioners and users from a variety of backgrounds. For example, the design of an artificial heart valve could bring together expertise from a range of backgrounds that include medicine, engineering, healthcare and views from patients. Such knowledge was presented as a commodity that could be exchanged in market-like institutions involving the crystallization of 'Mode 2 objects' and 'trading zones' (Nowotny *et al.*, 2001: 144). Suddenly, it seemed as if commodified personal knowledge could be treated as if it were a piece of cake that could be shared among those who needed to know, but how do you know if a cake baked by a stranger is safe to eat and how does 'the price of cake' avoid problems that bedevil trading in information?

Trying to be practical about knowledge, by detaching it from metaphysical truth and presenting information as a rivalrous commodity, tends to make the whole subject more slippery. For Blackburn (2005: xiv) losing faith in truth is redolent of G. K. Chesterton's remark about people who lose their faith in God: it is not so much that they will believe in *nothing* that is the problem, but that they will believe in *anything*. In addition, if Mode 2 knowledge production constituted tentative steps into a world where 'anything goes', Nonaka *et al.*'s proclamation that truth is 'in the eye of the beholder' signalled a stampede. In a paper first published by *Harvard Business Review* in 1991, Nonaka appeared to appeal to oracular mystique in his statement that 'To convert tacit knowledge into explicit knowledge means finding a way to express the inexpressible' (Nonaka, 2004: 36). Similar sentiments were developed in Nonaka and Takeuchi (1995: 11): 'The explanation of how Japanese companies create new knowledge boils down to the conversion of tacit knowledge to explicit knowledge'. Furthermore, explicit knowledge was portrayed as a transferable object, which contained a universally comprehensible meaning that could be conveyed through communication: 'For tacit knowledge to be communicated and shared within the organization, it has to be converted into words or numbers that anyone can understand' (Nonaka and Takeuchi, 1995: 9). As if by magic, the hitherto ineffable dimension of a person's subconscious would become common currency in a 'perfect language' that everyone understands and no one misunderstands.[2]

According to Nonaka and Takeuchi, Frederick W. Taylor 'failed to perceive the experiences and judgments of the workers as a source of new knowledge' (Nonaka and Takeuchi, 1995: 36). Their approach stressed that everyone within a Japanese organization is viewed as being on the same team: worthwhile ideas could come from anyone. Top-down management is blended with bottom-up management in a process of 'middle-up-down-management'. Everyone from every part of the organization contributes to a creative churning of different points of view. Whereas Taylor argued that a single controlling mind – an 'intelligent' person – should take responsibility for the 'stupid', Nonaka and Takeuchi were eager to stress that the pursuit of effective communication enabled everyone in the organization to participate in the creation of organizational knowledge. They painted a picture in which incandescent endogenous innovation appears to feed on the oxygen of mutual understanding among 'insiders', but what stops the metaphorical 'glass envelope' (that contains 'high-temperature' creativity among organizational insiders) from shattering? What prevents the middle-up-down creation of innovative thinking coming to the attention of 'outsiders'? To answer such questions, we have to avoid organizational behaviour's general assumptions about ubiquitous practices and pay particular attention to the specific context in which Nonaka and Takeuchi generated their peculiar ideas.

Arguably, the ability of Japanese organizations to take the long-term loyalty of their knowledge workers for granted stems from deeply embedded institutional expectations about the role of 'company as family' workplace organizations in Japanese society. The implicit, but mutually binding, contract between leading organizations and their knowledge workers is a long-term affair. Even in twenty-first century Japan, the stigma against job-hopping for permanent male employees persists (Ray, 2008b). and, whatever the outcome of contemporary debates about 'changing Japan', so-called lifetime employment was taken for granted in 1980s Japan, when Nonaka and Takeuchi (1995: 17) did most of the research for their book. Yet, Nonaka and Takeuchi seem to have overlooked the power implications that arise from limited labour mobility (Ray and Clegg, 2007). Close community relationships shape communication within Japanese organizations: it is relatively easy for insiders to imagine what might be in each other's minds and offer their intelligent cooperation to the articulation of novel thinking. The employee's future is linked to the organization's success. Cooperation among colleagues is natural and the ease of communication makes it easy for insiders to ostracize and retaliate against those who break their unspoken code: as the Japanese aphorism warns: 'the nail that sticks out is hammered down'. Self-policing discipline helps insiders to see things in an aligned way and underpins impressive flexibility. Many activities that would require managerial coordination in a British or American organization occur 'automatically' as colleagues, who know each other well, act and think in cooperative ways without being told to do anything.

Nonaka and Takeuchi's model, however, excluded the practice of power from the process of managing people within a Japanese organization. While they saw knowledge as something that is created by individuals (Nonaka and Takeuchi, 1995: 59, 239), they insisted that what an individual knew could be converted into explicit knowledge that *anyone* could understand. It appeared as if personal knowledge could be extracted from the person and the power relations, which shape an insider's actions and thoughts, could be ignored. In a way, this is hardly surprising: as Japanese insiders, Nonaka and Takeuchi were commenting on what happened, as a matter of course, inside Japanese organizations – there was no need to make the question of *why* such things happened anthropologically strange. Of course, translating their ideas to other contexts without paying attention to the local interaction of power and knowledge, which shapes acting and thinking inside Japanese organizations, would constitute cavalier anthropology. However, anthropological sensitivity hardly featured in the process by which KM infiltrated standard OB practice. When Nonaka and Takeuchi concluded their book with the claim that they had transformed the 'enigma' of knowledge-creating processes in Japanese organizations into something that is 'universal' (Nonaka and Takeuchi, 1995: 246), KM supporters seemed oblivious to the need for caution. Subjective knowledge could be converted into universally comprehensible knowledge, while any concern with truth or the practice of power could be ignored. It was as if the desecrated corpse of reason had been laid out for an all-you-can-eat feast.

The editors of a major handbook on organizational learning and knowledge management suggested that Nonaka and Takeuchi (1995) 'set the standard' for the emergent field of 'organizational knowledge' (Easterby-Smith and Lyles, 2003: 11). Meanwhile, Nonaka and Takeuchi have claimed that Drucker called their book a 'classic' (Takeuchi and Nonaka, 2004: ix). The editors of *Organization*'s January 2007 special issue on 'The Philosophical Foundations of Knowledge Management' suggested that Nonaka and Takeuchi's book is 'surely KM's most influential work' (Spender and Scherer, 2007: 5). Explicit knowledge came to be seen as a management 'solution' to the 'problem' of controlling tacit knowledge. Even though early signs suggested that KM offered an opportunity to 'learn from failure' (Storey and Barnett, 2000), interest in Nonaka and Takeuchi's 'New Taylorism' remained buoyant.

# CRITICAL ISSUES

> Why, sometimes I've believed as many as six impossible things before breakfast (The White Queen in *Through the Looking Glass*, Lewis Carroll, 1982: 173)

In Lewis Carroll's classic story, *Through the Looking Glass*, Alice objected to the White Queen's demand that she believe in the impossible, but the Queen had no patience with Alice's commitment to common sense: 'Try again' the Queen admonished, 'draw a long breath, and shut your eyes' (Carroll, 1982: 173). While Alice, aged seven and a half, remained defiant, many people with more experience of life appear more fickle.

The arresting influence of Nonaka and Takeuchi's argument about converting what Polanyi called tacit knowledge into explicit knowledge, which could be clicked across cyberspace, seems to have eclipsed interest in what Polanyi actually wrote. Short of a brain transplant, personal knowledge is in the heads of persons. It is *not* a transferable commodity and communication is *not* a form of conveyance. Yet, the KM faithful seem incapable of seeing through mysticism's beatific and seemingly imperishable smile. Many appear happy to accept Nonaka and Takeuchi's version of Polanyi's philosophy – as Haridimos Tsoukas has explained.

> Ever since Nonaka and Takeuchi (1995) have published their influential *The Knowledge-Creating Company*, it is nearly impossible to find a publication on organizational knowledge and knowledge management that does not make a reference to, or use the term 'tacit knowledge'. And quite rightly so: as common experience can verify, the knowledge people use in organizations is so practical and deeply familiar to them that when people are asked to describe how they do what they do, they often find it hard to express it in words [...]
>
> My argument will be that popular as the term 'tacit knowledge' may have become in management studies, it has, on the whole, been misunderstood. (Tsoukas, 2003: 412)

Tsoukas went on to develop his critique with regard to Nonaka and Takeuchi's flagrant contradiction of Polanyi's model of tacit knowledge. And there are good reasons to return to Polanyi's original treatment of the subject, as we will see in a moment. But there is also a critical issue associated with Polanyi's philosophy that Tsoukas overlooked: Polanyi's passionate faith in the possibility of discovering the truth.

Polanyi protected his model of personal knowledge from the charge of relativism by insisting that each person should be committed to the responsible search for the absolute truth about an independent reality. Everyone was expected to believe that they were searching for the same thing.

> I believe that in spite of the hazards involved, I am called upon to search for the truth and state my findings. (Polanyi, 1974: 299, original emphasis)

Polanyi argued that different people might have different beliefs about what constitutes the truth, but there is only one truth (Polanyi, 1974: 315). Writing elsewhere, he noted that 'If all men were exterminated this would not affect laws of inanimate nature' (Polanyi, 1969: 225). That is quite a leap of faith, which is even more shocking when translated from the state of nature to the state of human affairs and organizational behaviour. Without the White Queen's willingness to believe in impossible things, even the most committed practitioner might struggle with 'laws' of management that would not be affected if all of an organization's members, customers, suppliers and so on were exterminated. To say the least, it would be difficult to relate Polanyi's search for the truth to management science. Nevertheless, if we simply consider his concept of personal *knowing* (without regard to the metaphysics of *being*), there might be merit in using the tacit dimension as a conceptual tool.

As Polanyi pointed out in his famous observation, '*we can know more than we can tell*' (Polanyi, 1983: 4, original emphasis): we can recognize our friend's face in an instant from one in a thousand or one in a million, but we cannot say what we recognize.

We attend *from* subsidiary awareness (the subconscious interpretation of sense perceptions that contribute to gestalt integration) *to* conscious focal awareness (gestalt integration of subsidiary details). Recognition of our friend enters consciousness as if it were a ready-made entity; we know, in a flash – 'that person is our friend!'

We might speculate that our friend's eyes were an important part of our subsidiary awareness, but we cannot be focally aware of the gestalt whole *and* focally aware of its subsidiary details. The focal and subsidiary categories require each other but also mutually exclude one another. If we shift out attention to what might have been a subsidiary detail (such as our friend's eyes), the sense of seeing our friend's face as an integrated entity goes out of focus. We can only be focally aware of one thing at a time. What we know consciously is always enabled and constrained by what we know tacitly, but this tacit coefficient is, by definition, something that we know but cannot tell.

In Polanyi's model, we learn how to act and think *without being aware of what and how we learn*. Focal awareness of what we might have learned comes later (for example, when we suddenly became focally aware of mastering a new skill), but this takes the form of an edited highlight. It is distilled from an otherwise tacit learning process.

> *All knowledge fails into one of these two classes: it is either tacit or rooted in tacit knowledge.*
>
> The ideal of a strictly explicit knowledge is indeed self-contradictory; deprived of their tacit coefficients, all spoken words, all formulae, all maps and graphs, are strictly meaningless. An exact mathematical theory means nothing unless we recognize an inexact non-mathematical knowledge on which it bears and a person whose judgment upholds this bearing. (Polanyi, 1969: 195, original emphasis)

Nevertheless, separating explicit knowledge from its tacit coefficient (and thereby producing something that Polanyi saw as 'strictly meaningless') is at the heart of Nonaka and Takeuchi's influential argument. The White Queen might well have approved.

## NEW APPROACHES: WHOM CAN YOU TRUST?

The only given is the way of taking. (Roland Barthes, quoted by von Glasersfeld, 2002: epigraph)

In a paper entitled the 'Republic of Science', Polanyi argued that science constituted a self-organizing community in which mutual authority (exercised *between* scientists *not* over them) shaped the development of coherent theories: 'scientists, freely making their own choice of problems and pursuing them in the light of their own personal judgement, are in fact co-operating as members of a closely knit organization' (Polanyi, 1969: 49). However, Polanyi felt compelled to link this image of intersubjectively viable communication (the basis on which scientists trust and respect each other) to a search for, what he believed to be, an absolute truth. Yet, scientists cannot see beyond their experience. They lack a God's-eye-view of the 'real thing' and cannot see if their arrows of speculation have hit the truth.

In contrast, Nonaka *et al.*'s (2000) approach to the truth appears akin to shooting arrows at a barn door and then painting a target wherever the arrows land: every shot scores a bull's-eye – which is fine, *if* you are willing to accept that hitting the bull's-eye has lost its original meaning. Indeed, once you get into the realm of unconstrained relativism, anything is fine. Should you want to encourage a child to paint, it might be fine to put his or her painting on the refrigerator door and declare it a masterpiece, but what sense are we, Simon Blackburn (2005: 38) mused with incredulity, to make of an art establishment that exhibits dead pigs, blank canvasses, soiled underwear, buckets of offal and innards?

It seems as if we are caught between two absurdities: either we accept Polanyi's logic that it makes sense to shoot arrows at an invisible target – metaphysical truth – or we accept that truth is wherever an arrow lands. Yet, if we confine our investigation to the process of organizational behaviour as *intersubjectively viable knowing and learning*, without trying to engage with *being* and the nature of metaphysical truth, it is possible to preserve Polanyi's concept of personal tacit knowing and communities of interaction (as illustrated by mutual authority practiced in the Republic of Science) without tangling with his metaphysics. Focusing on intersubjectively viable knowing and learning, within and between different communities of interaction, might afford insights into where the marvel of the market fails. In the longer term, the art lover's willingness to pay inflated prices for dead pigs, the manager's trips to KM conferences, or the propensity of OB journals to publish yet more studies of the objective materialization of the subjective might be eclipsed by new and different fashions.

From a radical constructivist perspective, knowledge (no matter how 'knowledge' is defined) is in the heads of persons and the knowing subject has no alternative other than to construct what he or she knows using his or her experience (Glasersfeld, 2002: 1). Knowledge is *not* passively received, but actively constructed by the cognizing subject; it is *not* the 'discovery' of ontological reality, but the subject's cognitive capacity to organize his or her experiential world (Glasersfeld, 2002: 18). Contrary to claims that personal knowing is a recipe for nihilism or solipsism, we cannot construct the world in any way that we want: there are *constraints* (as we find whenever things as we see them are not as we want them to be). Nor is radical constructivism 'against science'. Quoting Humberto Maturana, von Glasersfeld (2002: 117) has offered a four-stage summary of 'the scientific method' that does not resort to metaphysical truth. In practice, what scientists do is: (1) specify the constraints under which a phenomenon is observed; (2) propose an explanation of interesting or surprising aspects of the phenomenon; (3) produce predictions; and (4) generate conditions that should lead to the observation of the predicted phenomenon. Viewed from a radical constructivist perspective, the process of building up scientific knowledge is *not* qualitatively different from learning in any other sphere of activity.

A radical constructivist approach to learning and knowing is commensurate with at least two aspects of Polanyi's philosophy: (1) we learn in the course of doing and (2) a person can never have a wholly explicit focal awareness of what he or she knows. Agent Smith cannot step out of his body, meet himself as an object, and be objective about what he knows. However, the intelligent cooperation of colleagues and others who are familiar with 'soapy thoughts' might establish a basis for an intersubjectively viable dialogue in which Agent Smith contributes to the construction of fresh thinking. Smith's bosses might become coaches or facilitators in communities of creative interaction; but unlike a Japanese organization, in which the long-term loyalty of knowledge workers can be taken for granted, negotiating Agent Smith's effective cooperation is subject to American expectations about the legitimacy of labour mobility and building a career by moving between organizations. Somehow, the Ajax Soap Company and Agent Smith have to nurture trust and respect that tends towards a 'loyalty beyond reason' (Roberts, 2004: 66) in which each could always count on the other. Of course, establishing the basis for loyalty beyond reason is no easy matter, as counsellors who deal in romantic relationships might testify. Although loyalty beyond reason might be entirely 'reasonable' when work involves a close-knit family business or takes place in a Japanese 'company as family' workplace organization, or some other context where the consequences of being rejected as 'unreasonable' are too painful to contemplate.

For those who believe in fictitious commodities and the marvel of the market, doing knowledge work effectively might involve a 'great transformation': one in which the welfare of those who matter is placed before ostensibly 'objective' indicators of efficiency. Nourishing the flexibility that is necessary to absorb uncertainty depends on trusting and respecting the knowledge workers on whom you rely. The rise of knowledge work heralds a world in which the committed knowledge worker does the acting and thinking – possibly late into the night – without the need for a Human Resources Manager to count the hours.

## CONCLUSION

I mean *really* how much do you know? (Gregory Bateson, 2000: 21, original emphasis)

Objectivist approaches, stretching from scientific management to knowledge management, have sought a 'sensible' answer to the Daughter's question in Bateson's metalogue. What do agents, ranging from pig iron workers to knowledge workers, *know*? How can the human-as-a-resource be managed? If everyone's knowledge were converted into a common currency, such as explicit knowledge, it would be possible to see what they *really* knew – just as Bateson's daughter demanded. For those who believe in KM, the objectification of knowledge provides the basis for shoehorning the personal capacity 'to know' into a command and control framework. Believing in impossible things is something that can appeal to people of any age.

In Lewis Carroll's story, the White Queen – shortly after issuing her edict to believe in the impossible – turned into a sheep. Quite what fate will befall tacit-explicit knowledge-conversion is unclear. Converting a queen into a sheep is shocking and the widespread willingness to convert a sentient person's capacity 'to know' into a *thing* – explicit knowledge – is also shocking. An uncritical sheep-like following of management fashion can give unwarranted succour to the enemies of common sense.

Rather than treat knowledge as an object among other objects, it might be more helpful to address the processes by which people learn how to 'do things' in concert with others. Personal relationships that foster trust and respect pave the way to loyalty beyond reason. While those who cherish objectivity might be apt to dismiss the subjective dimension of loyalty beyond reason, such an attitude leaves them vulnerable to the power that might be exercised by those who see things differently. An objective 'physics of society' would have nothing to say about subjectivity, intersubjective interaction and the power associated with knowing how to 'make a difference'; but ignoring, misinterpreting or misrepresenting others can reduce the stability of experiential reality by undermining the personal capacity to anticipate what might happen next. As the 9/11 attacks on America illustrated, what happened yesterday is not necessarily a reliable guide to tomorrow's possibilities. In an increasingly interconnected world, it is important to pay appropriate attention to the shifting 'force fields' of passion that drive thinking and acting within and between different nested and overlapping communities of interaction.

Knowledge work does not do itself. People do knowledge work. Knowledge work is what they do.

## ACKNOWLEDGEMENTS

I am grateful to the editors and Jacqueline Kenney for helpful comments on earlier versions of this chapter. Responsibility for what remains, of course, rests with me.

## NOTES

1 Drucker (2001: 194) claimed that he coined the term 'knowledge worker' in his book *The Age of Discontinuity* (Drucker, 1992), which was first published in 1969. (Although he might have chosen an earlier date; for example, his book, *The Effective Executive* [Drucker, 1988], first published in 1967, is replete with references to 'knowledge workers'.) Meanwhile, Drucker (1992: 263) acknowledged that Fritz Machlup coined the related term 'knowledge industries' in *Production and the Distribution of Knowledge in the United States* (Princeton University Press, 1962).

2 In common with 'perfect competition', 'perfect language' hardly fits with everyday experience: perfect speaking and perfect listening would imply that everyone already knew the meaning of every possible combination of every word and number. Saying something new is logically impossible: it would raise the possibility of being misunderstood and thereby render the language 'imperfect'. (See Grayling's [2007: 91–108] assessment of 'explicit speaker theory'.)

## REFERENCES

Alvesson, M. (2004) *Knowledge Work and Knowledge-Intensive Firms*. Oxford: Oxford University Press.

Bateson, G. (2000) *Steps to an Ecology of Mind*. Chicago: University of Chicago Press.

Blackburn, S. (2005) *Truth: A Guide for the Perplexed*. London: Allen Lane/Penguin.

Carroll, L. (1982) *The Complete Illustrated Works of Lewis Carroll*. London: Chancellor Press.

Drucker, P. (1988) *The Effective Executive*. Oxford: Elsevier Butterworth-Heinemann.

Drucker, P. (1992) *The Age of Discontinuity: Guidelines to Our Changing Society*. New Brunswick: Transaction.

Drucker, P. (1994) *Post-Capitalist Society*. New York: HarperBusiness.

Drucker, P. (2001) *Management Challenges for the 21st Century*. New York: HarperBusiness.

Drucker, P. (2002) *Managing in the Next Society*. New York: Truman Talley Books.

Drucker, P. (2003) *The Essential Drucker: The Best of Sixty Years of Peter Drucker's Essential Writings on Management*. New York: HarperBusiness.

Easterby-Smith, M. and Lyles, M. (eds) (2003) *The Blackwell Handbook of Organizational Learning and Knowledge Management*. Malden, MA: Blackwell.

Georghiou, L., Metcalfe, J.S., Gibbons, M., Ray, T. and Evans, J. (1986) *Post-Innovation Performance: Technological Development and Competition*. Basingstoke: Macmillan.

Gibbons, M., Limoges, C., Nowotny, H., Schwartsman, S., Scott, P. and Trow, M. (1994) *The New Production of Knowledge*. London: Sage.

Gilson, R. and Roe, M. (1999) 'Lifetime employment: Labor peace and the evolution of Japanese corporate governance', *Columbia Law Review*, 99 (2): 508–540.

Gibbons, M., Limoges, C., Nowotny, H., Schwartsman, S., Scott, P. and Trow, M. (1994) *The New Production of Knowledge*. London: Sage.

Gilfillan, S.C. (1935) *Inventing the Ship*. Chicago: Follett Publishing Company.

Gladwell, M. (2005) *Blink: The Power of Thinking without Thinking*. New York: Little, Brown.

Glasersfeld, E. von (2002) *Radical Constructivism: A Way of Knowing and Learning*. London: Routledge Falmer.

Grayling, A.C. (2007) *Truth, Meaning and Realism: Essays in the Philosophy of Mind*. London: Continuum.

Hayek, F.A. (1945) 'The use of knowledge in society', *The American Economic Review*, 35 (4): 519–530.

Langrish, J., Gibbons, M., Evans, W.G. and Jevons, F.R. (1972) *Wealth from Knowledge*. London: Macmillan.

McNulty, P. (1968) 'Economic theory and the meaning of competition', *Quarterly Journal of Economics*, 82 (4): 639–656.

Nonaka, I. (2004) 'The knowledge-creating company', in H. Takeuchi and I. Nonaka (eds) *Hitotsubashi on Knowledge Management*. Singapore: Wiley, pp. 29–46.

Nonaka, I. and Takeuchi, T. (1995) *The Knowledge-Creating Company: How Japanese Companies Create the Dynamics of Innovation*. Oxford: Oxford University Press.

Nonaka, I., Toyama, R. and Konno, N. (2000) 'SECI, ba and leadership: A unified model of dynamic knowledge creation', *Long Range Planning*, 33: 5–34.

Nowotny, H., Scott, P. and Gibbons, M. (2001) *Re-Thinking Science*. Cambridge: Polity.

Penrose, E. (1995) *Theory of the Growth of the Firm*. Oxford: Oxford University Press.

Polanyi, K. (2001) *The Great Transformation: The Political and Economic Origins of our Time*. Boston, MA: Beacon Press.

Polanyi, M. (1969) *Knowing and Being: Essays by Michael Polanyi*, M. Grene (ed.) Chicago, IL: University of Chicago Press.

Polanyi, M. (1974) *Personal Knowledge: Towards a Post-Critical Philosophy*. Chicago, IL: University of Chicago Press.

Polanyi, M. (1983) *The Tacit Dimension*. Gloucester, MA: Peter Smith.

Polanyi, M. and Prosch, H. (1977) *Meaning*. Chicago, IL: University of Chicago Press.

Ray, T. (2008a) 'Tacit knowledge', in S.R. Clegg, and J.R. Bailey (eds) *International Encyclopedia of Organization Studies*. Thousand Oaks, CA: Sage, pp. 1503–1507.

Ray, T. (2008b) 'Japanese management', in S.R. Clegg, and J.R. Bailey (eds) *International Encyclopedia of Organization Studies*. Thousand Oaks, CA: Sage, 731–735.

Ray, T. and Clegg, S. (2007) 'Can we make sense of knowledge management's tangible rainbow? A radical constructivist alternative', *Prometheus*, 25 (2): 161–185.

Ritzer, G. (2004a) *The McDonaldization of Society, Revised New Century Edition*. Thousand Oaks, CA: Pine Forge Press.

Ritzer, G. (2004b) *The Globalization of Nothing*. Thousand Oaks, CA: Pine Forge Press.

Roberts, K. (2004) *Lovemarks: The Future Beyond Brands*. New York: PowerHouse Books.

Schumpeter, J. (1928) 'The instability of capitalism', *The Economic Journal*, 38 (151): 361–386.

Solow, R. (1985) 'Economic history and economics', *American Economic Review*, 75 (2): 328–331.

Spender, J.C. and Scherer, A.G. (2007) The philosophical foundations of knowledge management: Editors introduction', *Organization*, 14 (1): 3–26.

Stiglitz, J. (2002) *Globalization and its Discontents.* Victoria: Allen Lane/Penguin.

Storey, J. and Barnett, E. (2000) 'Knowledge management initiatives: Learning from failure', *Journal of Knowledge Management*, 4 (2): 145–156.

Takeuchi, H. and Nonaka, I. (2004) *Hitotsubashi on Knowledge Management.* Singapore: Wiley.

Taylor, F.W. (1998) *The Principles of Scientific Management.* Mineola, NY: Dover Publications.

Tsoukas, H. (2003) 'Do we really understand tacit knowledge?', in M. Easterby-Smith and M. Lyles (eds) *The Blackwell Handbook of Organizational Learning and Knowledge Management.* Malden, MA: Blackwell, pp. 410–427.

Wittgenstein, Ludwig (1972) *On Certainty.* New York: Harper Torchbooks.

Wittgenstein, Ludwig (2001) *Philosophical Investigations.* Oxford: Blackwell.

# 3

# Organizing Freedom and Constraint Within the 'Neo-Liberal' Regime of Choice[1]

## Alan Scott and Richard Weiskopf

## INTRODUCTION

This growth of administration reflected the spirit of utilitarianism. Bentham's fabulous Panopticon, his most personal utopia, was a star-shaped building from the center of which prison wardens could keep the greatest number of jailbirds under the most effective supervision at the smallest cost to the public. Similarly, in the utilitarian state his favorite principle of 'inspectability' ensured that the Minister at the top should keep effective control over all local administration. The road to the free market was opened and kept open by an enormous increase in continuous, centrally organized and controlled interventionism.

Contemporary readers would be likely to attribute the above quotation to Michel Foucault, the reference to Bentham's Panopticon being the decisive clue. In fact, the author is the economic historian Karl Polanyi and it is from his major work of 1944, *The Great Transformation* (1957 [1944]: 55). Polanyi is describing the dialectic of freedom and constraint in modern market societies; a dialectic he seeks to capture via the metaphor of the 'double movement': 'the extension of the market organization in respect to genuine commodities was accompanied by its restriction in respect to fictitious ones [i.e., labour]' (ibid.: 76).

The moral, of course, is that the issue that we are discussing here – freedom and constraint under a 'neo-liberal' *regime of choice*[2] – may be novel in the form that it takes, but is a variation on a familiar theme: the promise of freedom vis-à-vis previous forms of personal subjection versus the reality of new material and bureaucratic (or 'post-bureaucratic') constraint. Karl Marx drew our attention to the matter time and time again, and so did Max Weber:

the labourer seeks money wages which free him from the dependence and good will of the landlord despite the economic decline that is a result. Just as money rent appeared to the medieval peasant as the most important sign of his personal freedom, so does money wage appear to today's worker. The rural worker forsakes positions that are often more favourable, always more secure, in a search for personal freedom. (Weber, 1894: 172)

The emphasis upon *personal* freedom is decisive in Weber's analysis, as it is in the very similar but more elaborate analysis offered by his contemporary, Georg Simmel, in the *Philosophie des Geldes* (1900, English translation 1990). For both Simmel and Weber, the social psychology behind workers' attitudes towards wage labour, and towards capitalism in general, was that the experience and collective memory of *personal* subjection under pre-capitalist conditions were so vivid and oppressive that the promise of freedom offered by the wage contract appeared to make the latter preferable and worth the risk. Flight from the land to the city was as much a search for personal freedom as it was for work. *Stadtluft macht frei* (city air makes us free). Since social action is at least as much backward-looking as it is goal-orientated and future-directed (cf. Hirschman, 1982), Weber and Simmel thought that in this social psychology lay in great part capitalism's attraction as well as – contra Marx – its source of relative stability, despite inherent class conflict. Furthermore, since one's personal fortune under capitalism can plausibly be attributed to impersonal factors, it has something of the quality of fate or luck, for which no individual agent, except perhaps oneself, may be held responsible.[3]

Marx, Weber, Simmel and Polanyi were discussing the emergence of the market society – of capitalism – as such. Whatever their differences, each rejected the notion – central to economic liberalism – of the market as a 'spontaneous order' and emphasized instead the regulatory and coercive measures necessary to establish it. They asserted too that the modern market subject was constituted within this historical process, rather than being its prime mover. And, finally, each sees the dialectic between freedom and constraint as key, though clearly it is here above all that fundamental differences emerge between, say, Marx and the liberal Simmel.

How much of all this is still relevant in discussing the more micro-level issue of the behaviour of subjects who are, firstly, already exposed to capitalist employment relations and, secondly, work *within* state and private enterprises? The transformation with which we are dealing here is not as 'great' as Polanyi's transformation from a pre-market to a market society, but how far must we adapt classical analysis of that wider shift in order to understand contemporary organizational change?

## THE PROMISE OF FREEDOM 'FREEDOM TALK'

It's over! It's over! Praise God … it's over. … The world in which 'we' – the best and the brightest, the college kids – depended on 'them', the Big Corps., to 'guide' (micromanage! Dictate! Control!) our careers. … But .. 'it' is finished. Kaput. Even if 'we' didn't want it to be (and there are literally millions who don't). It is O-V-E-R! New World (Economic) Order: We – white collar 'we' – are on our own. Our lives are more precarious. But they've been given back to us. The challenge: What are we going to make of them? (Peters, 2001: 12)

The parallels between capitalism's original promise to the serf – e.g., Weber's East Elbian farm labourers – and that of contemporary management's promise to the bureaucratic subject are not difficult to discern. A radical critique of bureaucracy and its constricting effects is the common denominator of the managerial discourse of enterprise for which Tom Peters and his various collaborators have all but become a synonym. The 'old management' or 'old rationality', it is argued, is no longer useful since it deadens the living element in business and economy. Bureaucracy in particular is held responsible for lack of flexibility and motivation. It is no longer portrayed, as it was by Weber, as the most *technically* efficient form of organization in and for capitalism, but as hindering and blocking economic development. Bureaucratic rules and norms, as well as analytical distinctions and divisions, are held responsible for the boredom and resentment which are sometimes associated with organizational contexts. They are accused of restricting the flexibility and creativity that is necessary for survival in the 'hyper competition' (d'Aveni, 1994) that characterizes the neo-liberal context.

In Tom Peters's *Liberation Management* (1992) these ideas are elaborated and radicalized. Management is no longer portrayed as an activity of rational structuring and directing. Rather the idea of (liberation) management is to act as a liberator that radically does away with anything that presents itself as an obstacle to creativity, engagement, entrepreneurial zeal and enthusiasm. According to Peters's own view, his best-selling *In Search of Excellence* (Peters and Waterman, 1982) was 'an out-and-out-attack on the excesses of the rational model' (Peters, 1992: xxxi). In the 1990s – the era of liberation management – the situation had changed yet again: 'curiosity, initiative, and the exercise of imagination are in' (ibid.: xxxii). The new form of management, which presents itself in the guise of a great liberator 'provides many people with a heavy dose of liberation, and God knows: it's disorganized' (ibid.: 701). In the chaos of disorganization, it is argued 'thrill' and 'symbioses' are necessary to create 'wow factories' (ibid.: 701).

Peters's radical critique of bureaucracy and his call for a 'passionate hatred of bureaucracy' displays some remarkable similarities to the arguments advanced by anarchist thinkers such as Michael Bakunin or Gustav Landauer[4] in order to free us from institutional constraints and bonds. In contrast, however, to the anarchists' outrage against repression and domination, it is lack of efficiency that is the object of Peters's opprobrium and provoked his battle cry. In this respect, Peters's radical critique is typical of the neo-liberal language of choice. The traditional 'values of bureaucracy' (du Gay, ed. 2005) – calculability, predictability, reliability, protection of the private sphere, equality of treatment – are thrown overboard and are recoded in the entrepreneurial revolution. They become vices to be hauled before the 'permanent economic tribunal' of the market (Foucault, 2004 [1979]: 342) since they are seen as blocking the dynamics of competition and the unfolding of productive potential.

Whereas Max Weber predicted that under conditions of capitalist rational organization charisma's path 'from a stormy emotional life that is indifferent to economic considerations [*wirtschaftsfremd*] to slow death by suffocation under the weight of material interests' (Weber, 1922: 661) is predetermined, the entrepreneurial revolution promises a paradoxical synthesis which realigns emotions, or even passions, with material interests. The 'new spirit of capitalism', as Boltanski and Chiapello call this discursive regime (see below), attempts to mobilize energies with the help of the spectacular staging of work, performance and productivity.

The traditional division between the work and the private sphere, between *Amt und Person* (office and person) is increasingly omitted; the boundaries increasingly blurred. Work is deterritorialized; every place (including the train in which this sentence is being written) becomes a potential workplace. In contrast to bureaucracy's constitutive distinction between organization and individual, the new discourse spreads out to form total inclusion. With respect to the limitations that are inherent to the model of bureaucracy, this points to the fundamental ambivalence of these organizational limitations. They are not only restrictions on individual freedom, but they are also a means of protecting individuals from *Willkür und Vereinnahmung* (from arbitrariness and monopolizing claims on the entire person). The delimitation in Peters's sense is paradoxical. It deterritorializes entrepreneurial action (via 'deregulation', and expansion of entrepreneurial principles to all spheres of life) and reterritorializes the unleashed forces by culturally re-codifying them and extending management's territorial reach into the realm of the irrational (see Thrift, 2000, and Krell and Weiskopf, 2006).

Entrepreneurial-managerial authors want to convince us 'what a wonderful force passion is' (Chang, 2002: 215), and that passion is 'the single, most important factor for realizing profit' (ibid.: 215). Passion in this view is no longer the opposite of the organizational world, rather it becomes a resource that 'can be controlled, cultivated, and directed to specific ends' (ibid.: 32).[5] It no longer belongs in 'the realm of the touchy-feely' (ibid.: 13). Rather it is a force that provides organizations with the necessary drive. It 'provides direction and focus', 'creates energy', 'fosters creativity', 'inspires action', 'attracts employees and customers', 'builds loyalty', 'unites the organization' and 'brings the organization to a higher plane'. In the end: 'passion heightens performance: Increased energy, focus, and creativity all contribute to one end: heightened performance. Passion drives improvements in both the quality and quantity of work performed' (ibid.: 14).

Of course, this is only half the story. The effectiveness of the entrepreneurial discourse relies not only on what is said but also in *what is not said*. The discourse of enterprise/ 'liberation management' conceals that these seemingly wonderful places – the 'passion-driven organizations' – do not only allow 'passion' but rather *demand* it, and thus create new pressures and unfreedoms. For those who cannot be convinced, the new freedom becomes a heavy burden: 'where associates cannot be convinced or inspired to be passionate about the organization or their work … there is usually little choice: they must leave' Chang tells us (2002: 198). The discourse of enterprise offers alternatives. For those who are not able or willing to be passionate in this sense, there is still the possibility – or the need – to become really 'autonomous', albeit in a very specific sense. Again, it is Tom Peters who has formulated the recipe: 'Fifty ways to transform yourself from an "employee" into a brand that shouts distinction, commitment and passion!' is the title of the little pamphlet that is offered as a signpost to 'the Liberating-New-World-Order-of-brand-new-Brand You' (Peters, 2001: 6).

## FREEDOM'S DUTIES: GOVERNMENTALITY AND THE CONDUCT OF CONDUCT

Twentieth century collective power was exercised through the Big State. Their welfare paternalistic,

handing down from on high. That won't do today. Just as mass production has departed from industry, so the monolithic provision of services has to depart from the public sector. People want an individual service for them. They want Government under them not over them. They want Government to empower them, not control them. And they want equality of both opportunity and responsibility. They want to know the same rules that apply to them, apply to all. Out goes the Big State. In comes the Enabling State. Out goes a culture of benefits and entitlements. In comes a partnership of rights and responsibilities. That's why we need reform. (Blair, Tony, 2002)

In one sense, however, the promise of freedom in contemporary managerial discourse is more radical than that of capitalism in its *Urform*. For Simmel, for example, it is enough that the worker is now theoretically free to *choose* his own master: 'by thus eliminating the pressure of irrevocable dependence upon a particular individual master, the worker is already on the way to personal freedom despite his objective bondage' (Simmel, 1990 [1900]: 300).[6] The modern post-bureaucratic subject, in contrast, is promised freedom from *any* master other than him or herself as entrepreneur – as a subject able to conduct his or her own conduct – under one condition: her or she must be able to act and think as a (self-)responsible entrepreneur; must become enterprising, that is to say, 'both an active self and a calculating self, a self that calculates about itself and that acts upon itself in order to better itself' (Rose, 1998: 154). We are free not to only to *choose* but also to *be* our own master in the one project that we can never leave: our own life as an entrepreneurial project.

In the contemporary regime of choice it seems that this freedom is less a right or a privilege than a *duty*. As Nikolas Rose has argued, 'there is an obligation to be free' (1990: 258). We are constituted as (self-)responsible, choosing subjects who 'competently' make use of our freedom and of our passions. We are responsible for our lives (for our success, for our health, for our family, etc.), for making a specific *use* of our freedom and for actively making choices for ourselves: 'we are obliged to fulfill our political role as active citizens, ardent consumers, enthusiastic employees, and loving parents as if we were seeking to realize our own desires' (ibid.: 258). In this context the role of the state is no longer to guarantee the freedom of the market (as in classical liberalism), rather the market and marketization is itself a governing principle that structures all spheres of life. Foucault's (1991) neologism of 'governmentality' (a combination of government and rationality, which, of course, also refers to a specific mentality of government) comprises the complex of notions, calculations and strategies through which diverse authorities attempt to act upon the lives and conduct of others (Rose, 1998: 152). *Enterprise* characterizes governmental rationality (neo-liberal governmentality) (Foucault, 2004). The vocabulary of enterprise here provides a language for articulating a political rationality and linking it to specific practices. As a language or discourse, enterprise 'not only designates a kind of organizational form, with individual units competing with one another on the market, but more generally provides an image of a mode of activity to be encouraged in a multitude of areas of life' (Rose, 1998: 154).

The language of enterprise serves to *problematize* organizational practices in a variety of different places. Public and private organizations, universities, hospitals, etc. are being increasingly re-imagined as 'enterprises', evaluated and recast in language of enterprise, re-modelled in the image of the firm (Marquand, 2004). If there are problems, they are attributed to the 'lack of enterprise', consequently our institutions/organizations have to become '(more) enterprising', that is restructured or re-formed along the principles of Enterprise. The same logic applies to individuals or 'human capital'. The worker here is no longer simply a passive 'factor of production', but rather a 'machine of competences' (Foucault, 2004) in which investment must be made. Even the unemployed or the 'job-seeker' has to become 'enterprising' in order to meet the challenge and to prove and improve his or her 'employability'. Unemployment benefits appear as part of the multiplicity of *investments* that the individual

has to make in order to optimize his or her performance.

We are not only 'obliged to be free' but we are also *obliged to be passionate* – and, as it seems increasingly – we are *obliged to be creative*. Creativity is no longer merely a human potential or capacity to be repressed in the name of order, clarity and efficient organization. Rather, creativity is a potential to be used and mobilized in the name of innovation, change and competitive advantage in the knowledge economy. Governing the 'autonomous subject' is not so much a matter of restricting and limiting individuals by defining rules and prescribing behaviour or certain choices (directly). Rather, government operates in a different way. Neo-liberals, such as Hayek and Friedman, have argued that the

> 'well-being of both political and social existence is to be ensured not by centralized planning and bureaucracy, but through the 'enterprising' activities and choices of autonomous entities – businesses, organizations, persons – each striving to maximize their own advantage by intervening and promoting new projects by means of individual and local calculations of strategies and tactics, costs and benefits' (Rose, 1998: 153).

Governing the autonomous subject works by providing technologies that allow the subject to reflect on possibilities and opportunities in terms of the discursive categories provided by government and diverse experts. The autonomy or the possibilities of choice are thus not so much restricted or limited from outside; rather, *certain* choices are encouraged and made more likely by defining the frame (laying down discursive categories) that makes choices plausible and attractive or not. Government now implies that individuals, private and public organizations, communities, universities, etc. are reconstituted and have to see themselves as 'partners' or 'agents' (of government as principle) that take a large part of the burden of responsibility, for resolving problems or, to put it in neo-liberal argot, 'meeting the challenge' to optimize one's life or project. The process of constituting 'partners' of government implies a double movement of 'responsibilization and autonomization'. Organizations and other agents that were once enmeshed in what are represented as the 'bureaucratic' lines of force of the welfare state are to be made more responsible for securing their own future survival and wellbeing. Yet, at one and the same time, they are to be steered politically from the centre, 'at a distance' through the intervention and deployment of a host of governmental techniques which can shape their action while at the same time attesting to their independence (du Gay, 2004: 40–1).

The specific concept of 'Enterprise' (with a capital E) that informs neo-liberal govern-mentality constitutes a mode of governing that is neither traditional Weberian bureaucracy nor a free market. As Paul du Gay (ibid.: 46) remarked, it is a 'governmentally constituted quasi-market' in which we make our 'free' choices:

> What we have here, then is neither traditional Weberian bureaucracy nor a free market but a governmentally constituted quasi-market. It is the *formation of opportunity structures and environmental parameters rather then routine daily decisions that is the object of organizational manipulation*. In the public services there is nothing at all subtle about this form of 'government at a distance.' For example, in all those many areas where the state is still paymaster, the price of units of resource is set centrally. By altering those nominal prices the state retains enormous power over those agencies to which it has also granted a degree of real autonomy. The newly free actors, whether organizations or individuals, find themselves responding to centrally determined decisions, but not as they once knew them. They may have no more influence over the formulation of policy, probably they have less, but they certainly have a lot more responsibility for the success or failure of 'outcomes'. (ibid.: 46–7, emphasis added)

Viewed from the perspective of the agent, the (entrepreneurial) regime of choice does more than merely create an obligation to think and act as an entrepreneur, to engage passionately in the project of realizing one's capacities and possibilities, to maximize one's own worth by optimizing one's own life as a 'project', to understand and enact one's life in terms of choice. It also transforms the ways in which individuals think and have to think about themselves: 'they must interpret their past and dream up their future as outcomes of choices made or choices still to make' (ibid.: 87). It also produces its own margins and marginalizations. Those who are excluded, who are not willing or able to 'competently' use their freedom of choice, are 'no longer embraced within a social politics of solidarity, are allocated to a range of new para-governmental agencies – charities, voluntary organizations supported by grants and foundations' (ibid.: 89). The traditional welfare state is supplemented by a host of advisers and agents who promise to 'empower' clients and enable them to 'meet the challenges' in a more efficient – entrepreneurial – way than did the institutions of the welfare state. Where the attempt 'to install the capacities for self-determination and self-mastery' (ibid.: 89) fails, the threat of exclusion is ever present.

Viewed from the perspective of the organization, the regime of choice creates, to adapt a phrase from urban studies, 'new organizational spaces'[7] in which the higher levels of the hierarchy are no longer responsible for the success or failure of each individual sub-level, but in which teams, set in competition with and against each other within the internal market, are freer to make their own strategic decisions, but also bear a correspondingly greater responsibility for their own fate. In the expectation of increasing efficiency by simultaneously lowing costs and raising the level of activity, the organization is no longer imagined as the Weberian cascading pyramid of command within a unified bureaucracy but as a network of nodal points, and a mix of audit and central price fixing has displaced the memo as the central steering mechanism.

## THE ANTI-BUREAUCRATIC MOMENT AND THE RENEWAL OF THE 'SPIRIT' OF CAPITALISM

How did we find ourselves in a position in which capitalism's original promise had to be renewed in this modified form? What conditions prompt attempts to revive the spirit of capitalism? One answer points to conjunctural factors such as increased competition and profit squeeze forcing managers to look for ways of raising productivity by emphasizing creativity and seeking to create 'fast' managerial subjects (see Thrift, 2000). A broader approach foresees such a 'crisis' emerging from the dynamic of capitalism itself. These styles of analysis are by no means incompatible, and they ascribe the aim of such organizational shifts to a common motive: the further increase of efficacy and rationality; the simultaneous lowering of costs and the raising of productivity. In the following discussion we use Weber's analysis in order to identify some of the longer-term factors, and Boltanski and Chiapello to illustrate a more conjunctural approach focusing on changes over the last quarter of a century.

Capitalism can be understood, in ideal-typical terms, as the child of Protestant individualism with its emphasis upon self-reliance and self-help, but also as contributing to a rationalization process in which effective power comes to be exercised on a day-to-day basis via routine administration (*Handhabung der Verwaltung*) (Weber, 1918a: 145). What Weber most feared in socialism was the restoration of essentially pre-capitalist conditions in which 'the master was not a simple employer, but rather a political autocrat' (1894: 161). Whereas capitalism divided political authority from relations of economic dependence, socialism reunites them, exposing workers to economic exploitation and political domination from a single source: the state as both ruler and employer (1918b). However, and this is the crucial point, the self same tendencies are inherent within capitalism itself (albeit in a milder form due to the at least formal differentiation – 'pillarization' – of state and market). This is so for two reasons: (i) the capitalist firm increasingly takes the form of a corporate bureaucracy (which includes the provision of stability of employment, relative security, and a fixed career structure); (ii) state welfare measures ascribe rights

on the basis of *occupation*, thus, as under socialism, fusing once more economic and political status. In this way a 'polity of estates' (*Ständestaat*) can re-emerge within capitalist society, but in a more rational, and thus still more oppressive, form. This scenario has occasionally been referred to as Weber's 'Egyptianization thesis', and his formulation of it is truly spine-chilling and worth quoting at length:

> A lifeless machine is *congealed spirit*. It is *only* this fact that gives the machine the power to force men to serve it and thus to rule and determine their daily working lives, as in fact happens in factories. The same *congealed spirit* is, however, also embodied in that *living machine* which is represented by bureaucratic organization with its specialization and trained, technical work, its delimitation of areas of responsibility, its regulations and its graduated hierarchy of relations of obedience. Combined with the dead machine, it is the process of manufacturing the housing of that future servitude to which, perhaps, men may have to submit powerlessly, just like the slaves in the ancient state of Egypt, *if they consider that the ultimate and only value by which the conduct of their affairs be decided is good administration and provision for their needs by officials (that is 'good' in the purely technical sense of rational administration)*. Bureaucracy achieves this, after all, incomparably better than any other structure of rule. This housing, so praised by our native littèrateurs, will be augmented by shackles chaining each individual to his firm (the beginnings of this are to be found in so-called 'welfare arrangements'), to his class (by an increasingly rigid structure of ownership) and perhaps at some time in the future to his occupation (by state provision of needs on a 'liturgical' principle, whereby associations structured along occupational lines carry a burden of state responsibilities). This housing would become more indestructible if, in the social area, as in those states in the past where enforced labour existed [*Fronstaaten*], an organization of the ruled based on their social and occupational status were to be attached (which in truth means subordinated) to the bureaucracy. An 'organic,' that is an Oriental-Egyptian social structure, would begin to emerge, but, in contrast to that ancient form, one which would be as strictly rational as a machine. (Weber, 1918a: 158–59)

The passage stands at the beginning of a long history of the critique both of bureaucracy and of the state as a source of welfare aimed at protecting the employee from his/her fate in the market, but the outline of this critique is already evident here; the 'road to serfdom' (Hayek) had already been marked out by Weber. Peters and Waterman, whom we discussed above, are merely the propaganda end of a much more sophisticated bureaucracy critique that finds its highest contemporary expression in public choice theory and in the theory of new public management. Rather than pursue those intellectual arguments further here,[8] we want to examine how the view, deduced from them, that the employee needs to be liberated yet again from his/her housing of present servitude translates into organizational practice; how a 'neo-liberal' regime of choice' has been (re-)constituted.

Probably the most comprehensive account of contemporary capitalism's recent attempt to avoid the fate that Weber foresaw for it, and certainly one that is gaining influence, is Luc Boltanski's and Ève Chiapello's 1999 text *Le nouvel esprit du capitalisme* (translated as *The New Spirit of Capitalism*, 2006a).[9] On their account, capitalism's 'new spirit' emerges as a response to, indeed partial absorption of, the capitalism critique of the 1960s, particularly as it had been articulated – and performed – by artists. This response is highly selective, retaining the emphasis on personal freedom, self-determination and authenticity, but ditching the social aspects of the 1960s' critique: its demands for equality, social justice and solidarity. While the economic justification of capitalism – as articulated in economic theory – remains stable over time, its social justification – which must demonstrate capitalism's 'excitement', 'security', and 'fairness' – is in periodic need of renewal. Taken together, the economic/theoretical and the social forms of legitimation constitute capitalism's 'justificatory regime' or 'order of worth' (*Cité*). The concept of *Cité* refers to the way in which philosophical notions of justice find their way into common sense and are echoed in everyday discourse and practice, thus acquiring 'validity' and providing legitimation for a variety of social (sub-) systems (see Boltanski and Thévenot, 1999). The new spirit of capitalism, which they see emerging since the 1980s, is characterized by the 'project-oriented *Cité*' (see below).

As for Weber's early Protestants, an intrinsically meaningless activity – work – which had previously been a means towards an end under the 'old economy', has become an end in itself, and thus has had to acquire meaning. However, whereas the famous conclusion to the *Protestant Ethic* suggests that this original meaning can fall away once this form of life – this 'coat' – has institutionalized itself into a 'steel-hard casing'[10] (2002 [1920]: 123), for Boltanski and Chiapello, institutionalization is not enough: work has to acquire a new meaning and a new significance once its previous legitimation has exhausted itself and been challenged. Habitualized patterns and/or external compulsion are insufficient. Work, where it has become our life, not only has to *have*, it also has to *give* meaning. Whereas for Weber rationalization processes take over where Protestant values leave off, for Boltanski and Chiapello, who reject the rationalization thesis, capitalism has to constantly renew itself, it has to periodically change its (moral) coat.

Although Boltanski and Chiapello are careful to note that their analysis of capitalism – developed on the basis of a broad and in-depth reading of managerial literature – may in some respects be specifically French, the picture they draw is familiar enough from other national contexts, perhaps unsurprisingly so given that a goodly proportion of that literature constitutes French translations of English-language (particularly North American) texts. Their argument concerning the emerging 'network polity' is not that networks, network organizations, project work, temporary contracts, and the rest are either qualitatively new or are replacing older forms, but rather that these already present aspects of capitalist production have recently (i.e., since the 1980s) taken on a central legitimizing function. In some fields they have at least supplemented, if not replaced, the 'industrial' justificatory regime with its emphasis on scale, stability, predictability, career, etc. The new 'project-orientated' *Cité* exists alongside other forms, just as it had long done as a peripheral part of the dual labour market at a time in which the industrial regime played this, largely unchallenged, central justificatory role, but now it has come to compete with the industrial regime.

Justificatory regimes are distinguished by a number of features: (i) the criteria of success and failure (or 'greatness' and 'smallness' as Boltanski and Chiapello put it) that are applied, and (ii) the kinds of test that individuals face in their work-related activities. For the new project subject, old-fashioned qualities of reliability (finishing the job), stability, and solidity give way to activity, process, and future orientation. Agents are led into an action trap in which they are propelled, or dragged, into an infinite, though poorly defined, future:

> In the project-oriented *Cité*, a 'great one' must be adaptable and flexible. He or she is polyvalent, able to move from one activity, or the use of one tool, to another. A 'great one' is also active and autonomous. He or she will take risks, make contact with new people, open up new possibilities, seek out useful sources of information, and, thus, avoid repetition. (Boltanski and Chiapello, 2006b: 169)

The emphasis upon risk taking, interpersonal skills and trust building, and networking abilities, plus the capacity to move between – and act effectively within – a variety of contexts or subsystems is the key. In return for success, the project subject must be willing to make an investment that may entail sacrifice: 'what is relevant is to always be pursuing some sort of activity, never to be without a project, without ideas …' (ibid.: 169); anything that could curtail one's availability must be abandoned. Project workers and their managers have to develop a set of complementary skills quite different from those of, say, the traditional bureaucratic subject. A spirit of public or organizational service is replaced by a 'just do it' culture in which due process is subordinated to outcome, and results trump correctness (cf. du Gay, 2000). The successful actor – unlike his or her bureaucratic predecessor – is no longer rewarded with a stable career, but with an increase in *employability*. If successful, they will have proven themselves, and on

that basis are in a better position to garner future contracts. Entrepreneurialism comes to replace loyalty as the personal quality that is recognized and rewarded within the new regime of choice.

Within the project-orientated polity, an agent's value is measured in terms of his/her degree of activity, their ability to adapt, and their flexibility and mobility. The inability to network, or to co-operate across a broader spectrum of social subsystems, is a sign of weakness. Projects are temporally limited; they are medium-term solutions within an increasingly insecure and unpredictable life course. Theories of social capital that verge on rational choice theory (e.g., Lin, 2001) view participation in collective life as motivated by the desire to access community resources out of essentially self-regarding considerations. Such an account chimes well with the activity of the project subject. In the process they are unable to pursue the kind of vocation (*Beruf*) – in the sense of a life-long commitment to a single project and its attendant values – of the professional and have more in common with the early Protestant entrepreneur than they do with the bureaucratic subject: self-monitoring, self-discipline, restlessness and anxiety (see Pasqualoni and Scott, 2006: 164–65 and Weiskopf and Loacker, 2006: 406–7). As with early Protestants, on Weber's account, hyper-activity and anxiety are the price of liberation from tradition.

### Example: The Creative Industries

To make this clearer, we shall briefly analyse one of the cutting-edge areas of capitalism in its neo-liberal guise: the creative industries. Creative Industries (CIs) are a heterogeneous and notoriously ill-defined field in which creativity counts as an essential factor for the provision of products or services (performances). Depending on political motivations and purposes, communication software, multimedia, Internet, games, fashion, design, visual/performing arts, museums, architecture, music and literature are all subsumed under this label. On the other hand, CI is a discourse, which emerged in the context of neo-liberal restructuring in the United Kingdom from the 1980s onwards. 'Cool Britannia', coined at the time of Tony Blair's New Labour ascension to government in 1997, emerged as a label that signified a new attractiveness, attributed to the 'creative' professions. Ever since, CIs have gained a growing significance in economic-political discussion. They are widely considered and discursively constructed as both a powerful motor of a modern economy and as a model for dynamism and innovation (see, for example, Caves, 2000; Florida, 2002; Jones and Thornton, 2005; Lash, Lury and Boden, 2006).

The CIs are examples of capitalism's ability to transform itself by integrating critique. What Boltanski and Chiapello call the 'artistic critique' (in contrast to the 'social critique'), which focused on the boredom and lack of creativity, the lack of possibilities of self-actualization and expression that character-ized the traditional regimes of production, just as much as the bureaucratic organization, has been turned into a central resource of production. Contemporary capitalism seeks its own renewal and dynamic in innovative and creative fields. The artist as the exem-plar of the 'creative worker' is no longer constructed as representing the strict and radical opposition to the economic system and rationality. Rather, the artist turns into a new role model (Menger, 2003). The artist is an exemplar of 'greatness' in Boltanski and Chiapello's sense; a new 'cultural *Held der Arbeit*' (lit. 'Work Hero,' honorary title in the GDR). To work creatively and intensively, flexibly and passionately, as an artist, is presented as an attractive and more exciting alternative to traditional office work. Work in the creative field promises to realign material and expressive rewards. It promises possibil-ities of creative self-expression and to give meaning to individual lives. 'Creative work' is hard work but it also provides lots of 'fun'. Risk taking, the avoidance of repetition and the ability to move from one project to the next are essential attributes of the entrepreneurial subject in the cultural field (see, for example, Storey, *et al.*, 2005). Characteristically, the ideology of the autonomous, creative and

ever-active, artist who constantly (re-)invents him- or herself serves as a legitimatory principle that supports the readiness and openness to change. 'Thinking differently', being different and 'making one's life a work of art'[11] which the artistic (and philosophical) avant-garde once saw as an attempt to break out of a regulated and conventionalized world, has become a norm itself: 'Be distinct ... or extinct!' (Peters, 2001, front cover).

With respect to the modes of organizing work, CIs belong to a 'precursor group' (Voß and Pongratz, 2004). A great many *workers* in the CIs are both *highly qualified and underemployed* (Menger, 1999). *Flexibility,* self-organization and self-management are imperatives which dominate work and life practices that are often precarious. The CI can be considered as exemplifying project- and network-based forms of organizing work. As Menger (2003) put it, the CIs are a 'field of experimentation of flexibility'. *Structurally* the employment relations in this field are characterized by high inter-/trans-organizational mobility, flexible work times and wages schemes, temporary contracts, high levels of self-responsibility, unclear boundaries and insecure incomes.

## THE STRUGGLE AGAINST THE OLD ORDER AND THE INSTALLATION OF THE NEW

With respect to the issue of the new constraints that accompany the alleged shift to a neo-liberal world of choice, we need to walk a narrow line. If our aim is an account that is adequate at the level of meaning, then we need to avoid mere ideology critique that treats these freedoms as illusory and the promise as entirely empty. As Simmel (1990 [1900]) showed, if we contextualize these choices, then, remembering that freedom is negative in the sense of freedom *from* a given and known source of subjugation, the alternative is indeed liberating, whatever its attendant risks and costs. Neither the choice, however constrained, of the rural labourer nor that of the contemporary worker opting for life in the project world are irrational when we examine the experiences that have given rise to them. At the same time, we need to acknowledge, first, that those actors will inevitably be confronted with, and caught within, what the Weberian scholar Wilhelm Hennis calls new 'orders and powers' (Hennis, 2000), second, that these orders and powers may indeed be more – or more rationally – constraining than those left behind. In other words, we are not dealing with illusion (or ideology in the Marxist sense), but with logic of disappointment (*Enttäuschung*, dis-illusion): in the search for the opposite to that of which we have personal and historical experience, we fly into the arms of regimes that bring with them a contrasting set of frustrations and dilemmas (see Hirschman, 1982). Since there is 'a conflict in each between the ways they free and enslave us', the latter may turn out to be even harsher, making the former appear in retrospect as a 'happy past' (Deleuze, 1995: 178).

However, what might be said about the new orders and powers of the supposedly post-bureaucratic, flat and teamwork- and project-based entrepreneurial organization? Are, for example, these new forms of work organization accompanied by some equivalent of the Benthamite principle of 'inspectability?' Is Karl Polanyi's 'double movement' hypothesis – greater freedom for goods; greater restriction on labour – valid for this renewal of the spirit of capitalism? There is now a vast body of work in recent critical management studies and elsewhere arguing that the current emphasis upon 'transparency' and 'measuring everything' is indeed the contemporary equivalent of the inspectability principle, and that audit is the technical instrument of its realization (Power, 1997 and Strathern, ed. 2000 are key references). Since this matter is covered elsewhere in this volume, we want to focus on the means and problems of realizing the neo-liberal organizational form. To do so, we shall continue to move back and forth between contemporary analysis of the renewal of the spirit of capitalism, and classical accounts of its original form.

We need to acknowledge, first, that in a 'neo-liberal' regime of choice' not all actors are at the cutting edge and in the exciting world of the CIs, but rather many work *within* large-scale (and in many ways 'traditional') organizations, which, however, in order to retain legitimacy, must accommodate themselves and make reference to the dominant discourse, thus creating greater homogeneity in organizations that seek to imitate the dominant model within their organization field; a process that neo-institutionalists characterize as 'institutional isomorphism' (see di Maggio and Powell, 1991). Second, we also have to recognize that the response of actors is often more complex than is frequently acknowledged, and is sometimes downright contrary and bloody-minded in its refusal to grasp the freedoms offered. It is important to avoid an overly functionalist language in which the subject is constituted – in one smooth movement – simply by being 'interpellated' as the new entrepreneurial self (Jones and Spicer, 2005).

We need, in other words, accounts of the ways in this regime fails, as well as accounts, whether panglossian or critical, of the way in which it succeeds. This entails acknowledging that the subject is a historical form rather than an essence, existing only in the embryonic form of its becoming; in 'forms which are far from being completed' (Foucault, 1989: 263). The constitution of the *form* (i.e., the entrepreneurial self) is always supplemented by the logic of *life*, which always partially escapes the forming imperatives. The infinity of manifestations of life escapes the cultural formation (e.g., of the neo-liberal subject of choice) and can never be fully captured (cf. Simmel, 2005 [1916], ch., 1). All efforts to establish performance criteria – supposedly capable of anticipating even that which cannot be anticipated – are supplemented by the dissipative logic of life; by intrinsically nomadic forces of life that are 'not just changeful, but intrinsically complex, heterogeneous, multiple and surprisingly novel at every turn' (Chia, 1999: 214). Technologies of organizing need to be 'applied,' that is they have to be 'folded back' to the immediate context of life. Application is not a linear transferring of imperatives, rather it is a *social process* in which these organizational imperatives are adapted, modified, and changed in the process of *application* (which more closely resembles bricolage rather than technical engineering).

In *Economy and Society*, Weber draws a useful ideal typical distinction that makes this struggle to constitute the new subject quite apparent, namely that between two types of *revolution*: the charismatic and the bureaucratic. Despite the fame of the triad: tradition-bureaucracy-charisma, this particular use of the schema has gone largely unnoticed in organizational studies, but it provides a novel approach to the issues with which we are concerned. Both bureaucratic and charismatic revolutions are ways of breaking the hold of tradition; of disrupting 'patterns', to use the more contemporary language of neo-institutionalism, but they work in different ways. The charismatic revolution seeks to change actors from within by altering their basic convictions.[12] In contrast, the bureaucratic revolution works from without by changing 'facts and routines' [*Dinge und Ordnungen*], and then, on that basis, people; the latter by altering the conditions to which they must adapt [*Anpassungsbedingungen*] and then perhaps by increasing their possibilities of adaptation [*Anpassungsmöglichkeiten*] to the outside world by setting rational ends and means' (Weber, 1922: 657). The charismatic revolution appeals to emotions, and its mode is that of quasi religious *conversion*. The bureaucratic revolution appeals to reason; to us as calculating rational actors (*Homo economicus*), and its mode is that of *rational persuasion*, including the use of incentives and sanctions, and *law*. The former works on our imagination, on desire, on passion, on fantasy; the latter on behaviour. The former demands inner conviction, faith; the latter conformity, obedience. It is thus not surprising that Weber concludes that:

> Charisma is *the* great revolutionary force in tradition-bound epochs. In contrast to the likewise revolutionizing force of '*ratio*' [reason] that works precisely from outside – either through change in the conditions and problems of life and thus indirectly [affecting] the orientation to these, or through intellectualization – charisma *can* be a

reformation from within which, born out of necessity or enthusiasm, means a change in the direction of core convictions [*Gesinnungen*] and actions under a completely new orientation of all attitudes towards all forms of life and to the 'world' in general. (ibid.: 142)

However, it is the bureaucratic rather than the charismatic revolution that, for Weber, characterizes the modern fight against tradition, because charisma *in its pure form* is at best indifferent, and at worst hostile, to rational and economic considerations. It seeks 'to shape facts and routines according to its own revolutionary intent' (ibid.: 658), and is thus anathema to the central principles of the 'new economy': goal-directedness and efficiency; in other words, rationalization. However, most of what we have described earlier – particularly the evangelical (a more accurate term than the self-ascription 'liberation') management of Peters and Waterman, looks remarkably like Weber's charismatic revolution in its appeal to passion and in its irrationalism. If a charismatic revolution is more effective, but less controllable, than a bureaucratic one, then a synthesis combining the power of the former with the controllability of the latter would be a more effective modernizing tool than either in its pure form. What Weber calls 'bureaucratic domination' the political anthropologist James Scott has more recently labelled 'cadastral rule', rule via cadastral maps such as organizational charts, bench marking reports, etc. Cadastral rule simplifies complex realities and exercises power by seeking to make the material conform to the schema. For Scott, cadastral rule is the typical mode in which power is exercising within 'high modernity'. As well as tracing its irrational consequences – from Corbusian utopian city planning through to still more terrible cases such as the forced collectivization of agriculture – James Scott also draws our attention to its relative weakness, namely the gap between the map and the territory:

> Redesigning the lines and boxes in an organizational chart is simpler than changing how that

organization in fact operates. Changing the rules and regulations is simpler than eliciting behavior that conforms to them (Scott, J.C., 1998: 255).

It is this relative weakness of the bureaucratic revolution and of cadastral rule that may help to explain a seeming paradox of the modern, flatter 'post-bureaucratic' organization: while the language is vaguely 'post-modern' in its anti-rationalism, and vaguely libertarian in its emphasis upon individual freedom, the technical means adopted for the realization of these aims are, on Weber's definition, strictly bureaucratic-rational, and, on James Scott's, high modernist. We are back here to Karl Polanyi's 'double movement', but in a modified form: not merely the freeing of goods and the restricting of labour, but the *simultaneous loosening and tightening* of control (see Le Galès and Scott, A. 2008). Part of this double movement is the, again seemingly paradoxical, simultaneous emphasis upon flatter organization and the growing centralization of power within contemporary organizations;[13] a process that delayering has reinforced.[14] This Janus-faced character of modern organizational change – this combination of ir- or at least non-rational rhetoric and highly rational technique – is reflected in contemporary managerial discourse.

## CONCLUSION

It would be tempting at this point to characterize the regime of choice as the new steel-hard casing. Weber's frightening Egyptionization thesis might even be trumped. It relied upon bureaucratic power alone, whereas here we seem to be dealing with an even more potent combination of charisma and refined bureaucratic technique, but we should resist this temptation. The regime of choice is, above all, a programme; an attempt to bring about the conditions that it asserts are already in place. First, it does not follow that the rhetoric will work on all of the target actors all of the time. As the Marxist historian Christopher Hill noted of the seventeenth-century enclosures

of the commons: 'propagandists were upset by the failure of the poor to understand that it was in their interests to quit the relative security of the village in order to work for others elsewhere' (Hill, 1996: 40). Once exposed to, or faced with the prospect of, the new work conditions, the language of neo-liberal choice may be as likely to induce boredom or cynicism as to muster enthusiasm and mobilize passion. This can be expected partly because the everyday experience of those who are called upon to act as entrepreneurs *for* rather than servants *of* an organization (Scott, A., 1996: 104) is so manifestly different from that of the (supposedly) free-floating creative workers upon whom they are exhorted to remodel themselves. The precariousness of work may become just as heavy a burden as the imperative to constantly reinvent oneself. Besides this, so much of the routine work still required simply does not demand creativity while, on the other hand, creative work (or the work of 'creatives' as they are known in the trade) is increasingly subjected to control and proletarianized (see Zukin, 1988 for an influential early account). Second, even the combination of emotional appeal and further rationalized means of control does not guarantee projected or planned outcomes, nor necessarily secure conformity. In perhaps what is the best contemporary analysis we have of the complexities of micro-level responses to organizational management and their macro implications for organizations, Christopher Hood's *The Art of the State*, it is argued that no 'polar' form of management is immune to 'reverse effects' – i.e., achieving 'the very opposite of the desired effect' (Hood, 1998: 210), and furthermore that the responses of actors at lower-levels of the organization can wring concessions from managers that can systematically subvert the latter's reform intentions ('placation'). Hood's analysis is a sobering reminder that it is not the job of the organizational analyst to mistake organizations for managerial prescriptions or talk *about* organizations, or to confuse 'managerial subjectivity' (Thompson and Findlay, 1999: 172) with organizational practice.

What summary conclusions might be drawn about the dialectic of constraint and freedom under the 'neo-liberal' regime of choice from the above discussion?

(1) The regime of choice is a discursive construct, or, less politely, a 'modernizing rhetoric' (Hood), or, less politely still, propaganda, but, in order to be effective, it must address and articulate agents' frustrations with the forms of (personal) subordination that they have experienced (Simmel) and offer them a contrasting alternative;

(2) The promise to free actors from *particular* forms of subordination (e.g., those associated with highly welfarist corporations) is in principle realizable;

(3) Not realizable, even in principle, however, is the explicit or implicit claim to release actors from *all* forms of control other than those they opt to exercise over themselves. This is to be viewed primarily as an attempt to shift responsibility – occasionally blame – from a collective agent (the 'organization') to the individual 'owner' of the problem (Foucault and Rose). We remain caught within 'orders and powers' of some sort or other (Hennis), and we continue to be ruled or governed in some way or other (Weber and Foucault); often more rationally, but perhaps less personally (Simmel), than before;

(4) Where accompanied by such exaggerated claims, the language of organizational and employee choice seeks to (i) cloak and supplement highly, and increasingly, rationalized forms of organizational control with a non-rational (or even irrational) charismatic appeal such that the actor is addressed as an emotional and not merely as a rational being; (ii) vie to become the dominant form of organizational legitimation to which all organizations have to appeal if they are not to appear out-dated and lose external legitimacy (di Maggio and Powell, 1991);

(5) A language of choice has perhaps as much to do with legitimation (Boltanski and Thévenot, 1999) as it does with actually changing the organization or behaviour within it, since, first, as authors such as James Scott and Christopher Hood have shown, managerial claims, however they are cast, often go unrealized; organizational re-engineering does not necessarily induce genuine change, and, secondly, in the 'post-bureaucratic' organization, bureaucracy is, in respect of control, more

itself than ever, having been stripped of its 'cumbersome' and 'inflexible' accompanying ethic of correct procedure (du Gay, 2000 and 2005).

Under these conditions, the language of choice may have become primarily a type of legitimation that has generally been neglected, namely self-legitimation: the ways in which powerful actors explain and legitimize their actions *to themselves and to each other* (see Barker, 2001). It may, in other words, become, above all, a form of talk among those with considerable power resources about themselves and about – and indeed to – those who are subordinate to them, casting the former in a positive, and the latter, on occasion, in a negative, light.

## NOTES

1 This chapter is informed by two research projects in which the authors are separately engaged: 'European governance: multi-level or post-democratic?' funded by the Austrian Ministry of Science (www. NODE-research.at) (Scott) and 'Re-creating organization: Organizing work and the work of organizing as ethico-aesthetic practice,' funded by the Austrian Science Fund (FWF grant no. FP 190260) (http://www. re-creating.org) (Weiskopf).

2 The term 'regime of choice' is taken from Nikolas Rose. See, for example, Rose, 1999: 87–89. We discuss his analysis below.

3 And thus not a question of justice or injustice for libertarians such as Robert Nozick, 1974.

4 Or indeed by Chairman Mao during the Cultural Revolution.

5 This supports Weber's view that 'rational discipline' must include the instrumentally rational channelling of irrational forces (the 'moral element'). Weber traces the techniques required to achieve this back to military discipline and the conduct of war. See Weber, 1922: 682.

6 For a detailed discussion of the implications of Simmel's analysis for organization studies, see Scott, A., 2008.

7 The phrase is 'new state spaces' (e.g., Brenner, 2004). The argument is the same, but at the level of the state: 'spatial post-Keynesianism' 'rescales' the state, which no longer seeks to govern a unified object – 'the nation' – but reconstitutes the subject of governance as 'the entrepreneurial city', 'the learning region', etc. Again, these are set up in competition (*Standortpolitik*; the politics of locational advantage) in the expectation of lifting general standards by

simultaneously lowering costs and raising the level of activity.

8 For a review of the main lines of argument and critique of new public management, see Palumbo, 2001.

9 The following discussion of the *New Spirit* is a slightly modified version of Pasqualoni and Scott, A. 2006. We would like to thank *Max Weber Studies* and Pier-Paolo Pasqualoni for allowing us to use this material. A briefer – article length – version of the new spirit of capitalism argument can be found in Boltanski and Chiapello, 2006b.

10 This is a more accurate translation of *strahlendes Gehäuse* or *stahlhartes Gehäuse* than is the more familiar 'iron cage'.

11 Foucault (1982: 237) famously concluded from his refusal of an essential or timeless subject: 'there is only one practical consequence: we have to create ourselves as a work of art'. Some decades earlier Max Weber had warned: 'Even with a personality of Goethe's standing, it would have been disastrous, as far as his art was concerned, if he had taken the liberty of trying to make his "life" into a work of art. And ever if one doubts this, one would have at least to be Goethe to allow oneself to try at all. At the very least, everyone would admit that even in the case of someone like him, who appears every thousand years, such a liberty has its price' (Weber 1919: 11). It is a matter for research and personal experience what price has to be paid in following the advice or imperative, and if the gains in freedom are worth it.

12 The term Weber uses is *Gesinnung*, which is broader and deeper than conviction. In English its equivalent would be a family of terms: conviction, mind-set, cast of mind, orientation, perception, general outlook (the stem is *Sinn*, sense). The term is thus, for example, less behaviouristic and external than Pierre Bourdieu's influential notion of 'habitus'.

13 At a more macro (political and economic) level, Andrew Gamble characterized Thatcherism as the combination of 'free economy and strong state' (Gamble, 1988). Although his main theoretical inspiration came from Gramsci, there are, again, clear echoes of Polanyi's great transformation thesis in this formulation.

14 Again, a more macro level, in this case that of politics, Colin Crouch (2004) has argued that the increasing 'disembedding' of élite actors – i.e. growing distance and lack of democratic control from below – encouraged the emergence of 'post-democratic practices,' styles of political governance that are increasingly monocratic and monological. Crouch, like a number of contemporary analysts, is thus aware of the interrelatedness of organizational and political governance. Chapter Ten of Sheldon Wolin's 1960 text *Politics and Vision* – 'The age of organization and the sublimation of politics' – remains the classic expression of this view.

# REFERENCES

Barker, R. (2001) *Legitimizing Identities: The Self-Presentation of Rulers and Subjects.* Cambridge: Cambridge University Press.

Blair, T. (2002) 'At our best and boldest', Speech to the Labour Party Conference in Blackpool. http://politics.guardian.co.uk/labour2002/story/0,12294,802604,00.html. Last accessed 28.08.2007.

Boltanski, L. and Chiapello, È. (1999) *Le Nouvel Esprit du Capitalisme.* Paris: Gallimard.

Boltanski, L. and Chiapello, È. (2006a) *The New Spirit of Capitalism.* Translated by Gregory Elliot. London: Verso.

Boltanski, L. and Chiapello, È. (2006b) 'The new spirit of capitalism', *International Journal of Politics, Culture and Society,* 18: 161–188.

Boltanski, L. and Thévenot, L. (1999) 'The sociology of critical capacity', *European Journal of Social Theory,* 2.3: 359–377.

Brenner, N. (2004) 'Urban governance and the production of new state spaces in western Europe, 1960–2000', *Review of International Political Economy,* 11 (3): 447–488

Caves, R.E. (2000) *Creative Industries. Contracts between Arts and Business.* Cambridge, MA: Harvard University Press.

Chang, R. (2002) *The Passion Plan at Work. Building a Passion-driven Organization.* San Francisco: Jossey-Bass.

Chia, R. (1999) 'A "Rhizomatic" model of organizational change and transformation: perspective from a metaphysics of change', *British Journal of Management,* 10: 209–227.

Crouch, C. (2004) *Post-Democracy.* Cambridge: Polity Press.

d'Aveni, R. (1994) *Hypercompetition. Managing the Dynamics of Strategic Management.* New York: Free Press.

Deleuze, G. (1995) *Negotions. 1972–1990.* New York: Columbia University Press.

di Maggio, P.J. and Powell, W.W. (1991) 'The "iron cage" revisited: Institutional isomorphasism and collective rationality', in W.W. Powell and P.J. di Maggio (eds) *The New Institutionalism in Organizational Analysis.* Chicago: Chicago University Press.

du Gay, P. (2000) *In Praise of Bureaucracy.* London: Sage.

du Gay, P. (2004) 'Against enterprise (but not against "enterprise", for that would make no sense)', *Organization,* 11 (1): 37–57.

du Gay, P. (ed.) (2005) *The Values of Bureaucracy.* Oxford: Oxford University Press.

Florida, R. (2002) *The Rise of the Creative Class: And How It's Transforming Work, Leisure, Community and Everyday Life*. New York: Basic Books.

Foucault, M. (1982) 'On the genealogy of ethics: An overview of work in progress', in H.L. Dreyfus and P. Rabinow (eds) *Michel Foucault: Beyond Structuralism and Hermeneutics*. Chicago: University of Chicago Press.

Foucault, M. (1989) *Foucault Live: Interviews, 1966–1984*. New York: Semiotext(e).

Foucault, M. (1991) 'Governmentality', in G. Burchell, C. Gordon and P. Miller (eds) *The Foucault Effect. Studies in Governmentality*. London: Harvester Wheatsheaf.

Foucault, M. (2004) *Naissance de la Biopolitique: Cours au Collège de France* (1978–1979). Paris, Seul.

Foucault, M. (2004) '[1979]: Vorlesung 10 (Sitzung vom 21. März 1979)', in M. Sennelart (ed.) *Michel Foucault. Geschichte der Gouvernementalität II. Die Geburt der Biopolitik. Vorlesungen am Collége de France 1978–1979*. Translated by Jürgen Schröder. Frankfurt am Main: Suhrkamp.

Gamble, A. (1988) *The Free Economy and the Strong State*. London: Macmillan.

Hennis, W. (2000) *Max Weber's Central Question* (2nd edn). Translated by Keith Tribe. London: Threshold Press.

Hill, C. (1996) *Liberty Against the Law: Some Seventeenth-Century Controversies*. London: Allen Lane The Penguin Press.

Hirschman, A. (1982) *Shifting Involvements*. Oxford: Blackwell.

Hood, C. (1998) *The Art of the State: Culture, Rhetoric, and Public Management*. Oxford: Oxford University Press.

Jones, C. and Spicer, A. (2005) 'The Sublime Object of Entrepreneurship', *Organization*, 12: 223–246.

Jones, C. and Thornton, P.H. (eds) (2005) *Transformation in Cultural Industries*. Amsterdam: Elsevier.

Krell, G. and Weiskopf, R. (2006) *Die Anordnung der Leidenschaften*. Vienna: Passagen.

Lash, S., Lury, C. and Boden, D. (2006) *Global Culture Industry: The Mediation of Things*. Cambridge: Polity Press.

Lassman, P. and Speirs, R. (eds) (1994) *Weber: Political Writings*. Cambridge: Cambridge University Press.

Le Galès, P. and Scott, A. (2008) 'Une révolution bureaucratique britannique?', *La Revue Française de Sociologie*, 49 (2): 317–346.

Lin, N. (2001) *Social Capital: A Theory of Social Structure and Action*. Cambridge: Cambridge University Press.

Marquand, D. (2004) *Decline of the Public*. Cambridge: Polity Press.

Menger, P.M. (1999) 'Artistic labor markets and careers', *Annual Review of Sociology*, 25: 541–574.

Menger, P.-M. (2003) *Portrait de l'Artiste en Travailleur. Métamorphoses du Capitalisme*. Paris: Seuil.

Nozick, R. (1974) *Anarchy, State and Utopia*. New York: Basic Books.

Palumbo, A. (2001) 'Administration, civil service and bureaucracy', in K. Nash and A. Scott (eds) *The Blackwell Companion to Political Sociology*. Oxford: Blackwell.

Pasqualoni, P.-P. and Scott, A. (2006) 'Capitalism and the spirit of critique: Activism and professional fate in a contemporary social movement/NGO', *Max Weber Studies*, 6 (1): 147–170.

Peters, T. (1992) *Liberation Management. Necessary Disorganization for the Nanosecond Nineties*. New York: Alfred A. Knopf.

Peters, T. (2001) *Reinventing Work. The Brand You. Or: Fifty Ways to Transform Yourself from an 'Employee' into a Brand that Shouts Distinction, Commitment, and Passion*. New York: Alfred A. Knopf.

Peters, T. and Waterman, R. (1982) *In Search of Excellence: Lessons from America's Best-run Companies*. New York: Harper & Row.

Polanyi, K. (1957) [1944] *The Great Transformation*. Boston: Beacon Press.

Power, M. (1997) *The Audit Society: Rituals of Verification*. Oxford: Oxford University Press.

Rose, N. (1990) *Governing the Soul. The Shaping of the Private Self*. London: Routledge.

Rose, N. (1998) *Inventing Ourselves. Psychology, Power, and Personhood*. Cambridge: Cambridge University Press.

Rose, N. (1999) *Powers of Freedom: Reframing Political Thought*. Cambridge: Cambridge University Press.

Scott, A. (1996) 'Bureaucratic revolutions and free market utopias', *Economy and Society*, 25 (1): 89–110.

Scott, A. (2008) 'Georg Simmel: The individual and the organization', in P.S. Adler (ed.) *Oxford Handbook of Sociological Theory and Organization Studies: Classical Foundation*. Oxford: Oxford University Press.

Scott, J.C. (1998) *Seeing Like a State: How Certain Schemes to Improve the Human Conditions Have Failed*. New Haven: Yale University Press.

Simmel, G. (1990) [1900] *Philosophy of Money* (2nd enlarged edn). Edited and translated by T.B. Bottomore and D. Frisby. London: Routledge.

Simmel, G. (2005) [1916] *Rembrandt: An Essay in the Philosophy of Art*. Edited and translated by A. Scott and H. Staubmann. New York: Routledge.

Storey, J., Salaman, G. and Platman, K. (2005) 'Living with enterprise in an enterprise economy: Freelance and contract workers in the media', *Human Relations*, 58: 1033–1054.

Strathern. M. (ed.) (2000) *Audit Cultures*. London: Routledge.

Thompson, P. and Findlay, P. (1999) 'Changing the people: Social engineering in the contemporary workplace', in L. Ray and A. Sayer (eds) *Culture and Economy After the Cultural Turn*. London: Sage.

Thrift, N. (2000) 'Performing cultures in the new economy', *Annals of the Association of American Geographers*, 90 (4): 674–692.

Voß, G. and Pongratz, H. (eds) (2004) *Arbeit und Subjektivität*. Berlin: Edition Sigma.

Weber, M. (1894) 'Developmental tendencies in the situation of East Elbian labourers', in K. Tribe (ed.) *Reading Weber*. London: Routledge, 1989.

Weber, M. (1918a) 'Parliament and government in Germany under a new political order', in P. Lassman and R. Speirs (eds) op. cit.

Weber, M. (1918b) 'Socialism', in P. Lassman and R. Speirs (eds) op. cit.

Weber, M. (1919) 'Science as a vocation', in P. Lassman and I. Velody (eds) *Max Weber's 'Science as a Vocation'*, London: Unwin Hyman (1989).

Weber, M. (1922) *Wirtschaft und Gesellschaft*, Studienausgabe [1972]. Tübingen: J.C.B. Mohr.

Weber, M. (2002) [1920] *The Protestant Ethic and the Spirit of Capitalism*. Translated by S. Kalberg. Oxford: Blackwell.

Weiskopf, R. and Loacker, B. (2006) '"A snake's coils are more intricate than a mole's burrow". Individualization and subjectification in post-disciplinary regimes of work', *Management Revue*, 17 (4): 395–419.

Wolin, S.S. (2004) [1960] *Politics and Vision*. Extended and Revised Edition. Princeton: Princeton University Press.

Zukin, S. (1988) *Loft Living: Culture and Capital in Urban Change*. London: Radius.

# 4

# Managerialism and its Discontents

Martin Parker

## INTRODUCTION

Slave rebellions, peasant revolts, and mass revolutions are not merely interruptions to history, but a continual counter-point to any and all concentrations of authority.[1] This chapter is concerned with a modern version of power, and a modern version of resistance. Managerialism, as I will define it here, is a relatively recent invention (Jacques, 1996), and it is important to begin by suggesting that it partly emerges as a rationalist and meritocratic response to feudal concentrations of inherited power. For many nineteenth century authors, the idea of expert organisers was a profoundly radical one. It was an idea that in some senses transcended the distinction between capital and labour, and promised to end some older struggles altogether. For Saint-Simon, for example, the dream of an organised technocracy was constitutive of social progress, of a new order that swept away old despotisms. Yet, even before Saint-Simon, other Frenchmen such as Vincent de Gournay had suggested that 'bureaumania' was in danger of giving petty clerks too much power, and stifling the proper exercise of enterprise. Even before its invention, managerialism was provoking discontent.

As management strengthened its grip during the twentieth century, so did the criticisms become more ubiquitous. Indeed, in most of popular culture (from the cartoon boss to the mad CEO) we find a portrayal of managers as stupid, selfish, evil, conspiracists and so on. These popular images often echo some more fully articulated complaints from elsewhere. From the right, often the attack has been that the managerialists and modernising technocrats failed to understand the cultural distinctions that were central to legitimating a divided society with low social mobility. They do not, in other words, know their station. From the point of view of those on the left, the technocrats operate on behalf of the powerful, hiding class interests in their rhetoric about impartiality and markets. They do not, in other words, tell the truth about who they are working for. Rather more bizarrely though, we can now also see managerialism as under attack by consultants and academics who claim that doing business within global e-capitalism means that management (being here a synonym for grey bureaucracy) is too slow and too hierarchical anyway. The new facilitator of networks demands that the manager gives up the key to their private toilet. Finally, in the most radical critique of all, there is a lengthy tradition of anti-authoritarian positions that could be broadly characterised as anarchist, workerist, feminist and environmentalist. All of these positions, in very different ways, add up to a trenchant attack on hierarchy and expertise, and demand the end of the manager.

In this chapter, I will explore these portrayals of management over the past 250 years or so. Whilst I certainly don't want to reduce centuries of dissent, resistance and activism to some simplistic categories, I intend to make two main points. First, that managerialism has been under continual attack throughout the modern period, and that contemporary forms of Critical Management Studies are hence often articulating some elderly themes. I find this disquieting, since many contemporary academic critiques of managerialism don't seem to be very aware of their historical location, and perhaps of possible connections they might make with other ideas. My second point is that many critiques of managerialism end up (inadvertently I suspect) being rather conservative about the possibilities for alternative forms of organisation. Not all of them though, since the more anti-authoritarian varieties appear to open the possibility that the 'manager' might be a temporary character on the historical stage, and this, I suggest, is a possibility that is well worth exploring.

## THE RELIGION OF NEWTON

Marie-Jean-Antoine-Nicholas de Caritat, Marquis de Condorcet was a supporter of the French revolution who proposed a highly influential theory of human progress in 10 stages, relying heavily on ideas about the usefulness of reason, invention and science. Written whilst in hiding, Condorcet's (1743–94) posthumously published *Sketch*

*for a Historical Picture of the Progress of the Human Spirit* suggested that the revolution had inaugurated the tenth age of humankind. This would be a golden age in which state education was central to ensuring absolute equality of opportunity and gradual eugenic and health improvements. He supported the emancipation of women, civil marriages, divorce and birth control and felt that the advanced application of social statistics would be able to guarantee effective pension and insurance systems. His New World would have no wars, and a universal language that would help communication and speed intellectual development. He died at the hands of his fellow revolutionary Robespierre, largely on account of his aristocratic background.

Claude-Henri de Rouvroy, Comte de Saint-Simon was also born into an ancient aristocratic family in Paris in 1760. Saint-Simon refused communion at the age of 13, was imprisoned and then escaped. He acted as an officer on the American side during the American Revolution, fought at the battle of Yorktown, and was again imprisoned. During the French revolution, despite renouncing his title, he was imprisoned for a while, and spent the rest of the time speculating in land in order to develop a fortune to support his various grand undertakings (which included what is now the Panama Canal). It was said that his valet had orders to wake him with the phrase, 'Remember, monsieur le Comte, that you have great things to do'. By his 40s, he had squandered his fortune, and began to write, though with little notice until a few years before his death in 1825.

What society needed, he thought, was a new stable social order in which the chiefs of industry would control society. These men of science, by virtue of their intelligence and training in philosophy, science and engineering, would be able to rule with the best interests of everyone in mind. Saint-Simon suggests a progressive development towards larger units of 'association' and away from 'subjection'. This 'spontaneous harmony' was a result of industrialism, and could even result in a European state with homogenous institutions (perhaps led by England). Though his writings are confused and contradictory, in *Du Système Industriel* (1821) and *Catéchisme des Industriels* (1824), he puts forward a meritocratic hierarchy in which science is used to produce things which are useful for all. New institutions, such as the chambers of 'Invention', 'Examination' and 'Execution' would organise public works and festivals. Politics would disappear, and become a branch of economics since efficiency and production would be all that mattered in the new order.

After his death, several of his disciples (particularly Barthelemy-Prosper Enfantin and Saint-Amand Bazard) established a short-lived journal (*Le Producteur*) and attempted some experiments in communal living, incorporating radical ideas about 'free love' and the equality of the sexes. However, it was Saint-Simon's collaboration with Auguste Comte on the journal *L'Organisateur* from 1819 that was crucial in developing his reputation more generally, since Comte's rather mystical faith in science and progress almost entirely echoed Saint-Simon and Condorcet's ideas. As Clegg and Dunkerley (1980) suggest, Saint-Simon is perhaps best seen as the grandfather of management,[2] and his faith in a technocratic élite finds clear echoes in later organised utopias (Parker *et al.*, 2007) as well as ideas about the importance of the welfare state, administration and bureaucracy. Saint-Simon was certainly a radical, and hostile to inherited privilege, but his radicalism was of a particular kind. Science, being a firm and certain kind of knowledge, a 'religion of Newton' or 'cult of Reason', essentially would play the key role in social engineering. Science, through its élite of experts, would 'shift the Earthly Paradise and transport it from the past into the future'.

## GOVERNMENT FROM DESKS

One element of early managerialism is precisely this radical commitment to re-organising the world more 'scientifically', but it is also difficult to disentangle it from an earlier word, 'bureaucracy'. *Bureaucratie*,

rule from the desk, was coined by Vincent de Gournay (1712–59) at least a century before Saint-Simon was born. De Gournay was one of the French 'physiocrats' or 'economists' who stressed a dynamic view of the circulation of wealth against centralised state protectionism. He was, in other words, keen on freeing up the hidden hand of the market, and allowing the merchants and the bourgeoisie freedom to make their money, and trickle down wealth to the poor. For de Gournay, *Bureaucratie* was a form of governance by officials which protected state interests, an 'illness', an impediment to the proper exercise of commercial freedoms. As the word moved across Europe, it took with it this connotation of interference, of meddling in things that are best left alone. In 1830s England, the term was often used in resistance to the centralisation of poor relief and public health measures. Thomas Carlyle, in 1850, referred to it as 'the continental nuisance' and John Stuart Mill, in 1860, as an inadequate alternative to democracy within which 'the work of government has been in the hands of governors by profession' (Mitchell, 1968).

The social theorist who partially rescued bureaucracy from this opprobrium is undoubtedly Max Weber, whose *Wirtschaft und Gesellschaft* (*Economy and Society*) was published in 1921. Weber saw the advance of bureaucratisation as inevitable but tied it to a larger sociological thesis about the development of forms of legitimacy. He argued that, in every sphere of social life, from music to war, charismatic and traditional forms of authority are increasingly routinised into legal-rational, or bureaucratic, authority, but Weber's ambivalence about the advance of bureaucracy is clear. On the one hand, he lists its advantages:

> The fully developed bureaucratic mechanism compares with other organisations exactly as does the machine with the non-mechanical modes of production.
> Precision, speed, unambiguity, knowledge of the files, continuity, discretion, unity, strict subordination, reduction of friction and of material and personal costs – these are raised to the optimum point ... (Weber, 1948: 214)

Yet he is also painfully aware of its consequences:

> Its specific nature, which is welcomed by capitalism, develops the more perfectly the more bureaucracy is 'dehumanised', the more completely it succeeds in eliminating from official business love, hatred and all purely personal, irrational, and emotional elements which escape calculation.
>     ... the professional bureaucrat is chained to his activity by his entire material and ideal existence. In the great majority of cases, he is only a single cog in an ever-moving mechanism which prescribes to him an essentially fixed route of march. (1948: 215–216, 228)

Weber's ambivalence echoes through the twentieth century. Harold Laski, in 1930, defines bureaucracy as 'a system of government the control of which is so completely in the hands of officials that their power jeopardises the liberties of ordinary citizens'. In 1950, Harold Lasswell and Abraham Kaplan refer to it as 'the form of rule in which the élite is composed of officials' (Nelson, 1985). Indeed, much of US sociology and psychology after World War II was concerned with various ways in which the authoritarian Fascist or Communist versions of bureaucracy could be better understood and avoided. Descriptions of authoritarian personality types, experiments on the willingness of subjects to obey people in white coats, groupthink and conformity, and accounts of the dysfunctions of bureaucracy abound. One of the most perceptive of these commentators suggested that most of us have used Eichmann's banal excuse that he 'was merely following orders' (Arendt, 1963/1994). In his celebrated book, *The Organization Man*, William Whyte describes the 'social ethic' (which 'could be called an organisation ethic, or a bureaucratic ethic') as a pervasive form of dull conformity (1961: 11). For Whyte this is a climate that 'inhibits individual initiative and imagination, and the courage to exercise it against group opinion' (op. cit: 365). Around the same time, Herbert Marcuse (who cites Whyte approvingly) characterised modern societies as one-dimensional in the sense that people at work, and in their leisure, were becoming mere instruments for the mechanical organisation of capitalism (1964), and situationists like Vaneigem and Debord launched an assault on a culture based on:

> time-which-is-money, submission to bosses, boredom, exhaustion ... The organisation of work and the organisation of leisure are the blades of the castrating shears whose job is to improve the race of fawning dogs. (Vaneigem, 1967/1992: 52, 55)

More lately, and more carefully, both MacIntyre (1981) and Bauman (1989) have complained that management and bureaucracy are narrowing human sensitivities. For different reasons, both these authors end up arguing that the calculating human is replacing the feeling human. They take aim at instrumental forms of utilitarianism which efface the possibility of asking more general questions about values and ethics because a boundary is constructed between personal convictions and organisational duty.

One of the most pervasive things about this diagnosis of government from desks is the idea that bureaucracy somehow restricts agency. In an echo of Rousseau, free people are constrained, whether they are the bureaucrats or their clients; the victims of Fascism or the victims of Stalinism; the executives or their customers. de Gourney might have felt that the constraint was primarily a commercial one, whilst Bauman felt it was a moral one, but the linking theme is that bureaucracy stops us from doing things. It places red tape around our freedom, and ties us to desks.

## FOUR FORMS OF DISCONTENT

The word 'bureaucracy' does not mean the same as the word 'management', but they are certainly very overlapping concepts. Management, in an etymological and common sense way, also has some connotation of being led by the nose (Jackson and Carter, 1998), and that sense of constraint certainly informs its critics. Yet there are some very different complaints about managerialism, both in terms of explaining what it is, and what we should do about. Hence, if we want to understand what it means to be 'against management' (Parker, 2002) we need to acknowledge its rather complex history. From de Gournay to the present day, there are a variety of positions, and a variety of forms of discontent. In other words, lots of people don't like management, but their reasons differ considerably. Within Critical Management Studies, many authors have worried a lot about what the word 'critical' means (Fournier and Grey, 2000). In order that the boundary between 'us' and 'them' is clear, it is necessary to distinguish between the sort of critique that is morally righteous and that which is self-interested posturing. The problem is that there are lots of people who claim to be critical of the current climate of managerialism – business ethicists, opportunistic management gurus, relativising postmodernists, consumer champions, doctrinaire Marxists, careful reformers and the sort of people who throw bricks through McDonalds' windows. These people do not themselves agree on the distribution of the righteous and the self-interested. Indeed, they actually agree about very little. Perhaps even calling this a rainbow coalition is stretching the coverage of rainbows a little too far.

For example, if we take many state leftist critiques of management, it is usually the case that the central target is not management as a specific way of thinking about authority relations and expertise, but rather as a representative for the interests of capitalists. In that sense, Marx, Lenin, Mao, Guevara and so on were rarely directly concerned with alternatives to technocratic governance. Either the assumption is made that the post-revolutionary leader will embody the 'real' interests of the governed, or that (at some unspecified point in the future) the institutions of the state and of capital will wither away to be replaced by a decentralised system of worker soviets. The former ends up with Lenin's enthusiasm for Taylorism, and the latter was actively resisted by those in power in Moscow and Beijing. Quite clearly, not all state communists are against management, even though they might have something to

say about ownership. So, if we disregard what I think are basically authoritarian critiques of authoritarianism, we are left with a variety of positions that actually engage with management and managerialism *per se*. I will divide this section into four parts, which broadly cover complaints rooted in nostalgia, modernisation, everyday cultural experience, and (most importantly, for my purposes) anti-authoritarianism.

## *Nostalgic critique*

Consider Protherough and Pick's (2002) *Managing Brittania*, an exploration of the culture of managerialism in Blair's Britain. The authors seem to detest much about the age that they live in, and they believe that 'management' is the problem. Theirs is the sort of conservatism that rails against 'bureaumania' in the name of personal freedoms. Management is a bad thing because it is an extension of the petty mentality of the *petit bourgeois* once they move into positions of responsibility and power. The state has mutated into a sprawling apparatus based around the idea that everything must be controlled. Government becomes a gigantic nosy neighbour, and no Englishman can now claim that his home is still his castle. Protherough and Pick seem to believe that the past was a lot better – when the local baker made wholesome bread and good administrators displayed wholesome traits of personal character, and then the world started to change for the worse. This, I think, is a form of anti-managerialism that has some ancient ancestors and some rather conservative implications.

Indeed, many cultural nostalgics, from John Ruskin and William Morris to Matthew Arnold and T.S.Eliot seem to have equated cultural decline with bureaucratisation and commerce. More lately, George Ritzer has replayed this attitude with a Weberian spin in his McDonaldization thesis (2000). It seems to me that Protherough and Pick's attempt to rescue culture from the 'robotic grasp of the bureaucrats' (2002: 205) exemplifies this long-standing theme. This is the nostalgic liberalism of 'intellectuals' who fear that commerce and mass administration are replacing warm human values. To be clear here, Protherough and Pick are not anarcho-libertarians in the sense that they wish to argue against any and all forms of intervention. They seem happy enough for the state to exist, and for organisations to do whatever it is that they do. What seems to annoy them most is that *certain* forms of culture and language are being degraded by the shrill demand for key performance indicators. They spend almost no time worrying about the call centre, but vent a great deal of spleen against those who have tried to claim that universities, art galleries, theatres, churches and culture itself should be subjected to the same kind of intrusive controls. This is an aesthetic judgement of the 'how dare they!' variety. It is the crassness and vulgarity of these jumped-up traffic wardens that seems to annoy them most, and the 'deadening' effects of managerial language that provide their most common illustrations.[3]

Protherough and Pick's is a kind of anti-modern critique, one engaged in the lengthy class-inflected debate between conservatives and reforming utilitarians. Though they are never explicit about what they *do* want to sponsor (being happier bashing everyone else) they seem to have a faith in the intrinsic qualities of a particular form of life, a romanticised version of occupation as vocation. They complain that 'the British worker is no longer a craftsman or professional, but has been forced into acting as a state controlled automaton' (op cit: 42). Working class struggle against capitalist deskilling in the workplace, and the self-interested market strategies of highly paid élites, are reduced to a lost idyll of happy industrial feudalism. What Protherough and Pick want is 'proper, old fashioned management' (205) which pits 'common sense' against the halogen brightness of nasty 'modern' management (193).

So management here stands for a series of connected elements of modern life – urbanisation, rationalisation, the division of labour, and social mobility. For many European writers, management often also means something rather brash, brutal and North American. It is important to note that conservative and radical nostalgic critiques can end up in rather similar places, with Ruskin and Morris's hostility to industrialism chiming with craft and guild ideas from a romanticised pre-capitalist economy. The accountant, the buzz word and the MBA become emblems of cultural decline and we wait for the return of the local, the authentic and the re-establishment of legitimate authority. Probably the most important element in this nostalgic critique is this last one. It is not a question of the refusal of hierarchy in itself, but rather the insistence that modern hierarchies are based on vulgar or incorrect criteria. This is not a denial of leadership, but an insistence that we are currently being led by the wrong people. Managers need to be put back in their place.

### Modernising critique

In precisely the place that we might expect to find a certain defensiveness about attacks on management, we also find that some modernising radicals are against it too (Koch and Godden, 1996). With the growth of state and corporate administrations throughout the twentieth century, some new de Gournay's wish to once again claim that there is not enough enterprise going on anymore. Consultants can describe themselves as 'revolutionaries', and claim to be hostile to the sclerotic effects of management as a new kind of 'bureaumania'. In much of the first world, the 1960s saw the beginnings of a long attempt to articulate administration as solid and inflexible compared to fast moving 'organic' organisations that would be able to survive in a hyper-global market (Grey, 1999). Futurologists could claim that an older world was sliding away, and that the new post-whatever times needed to be post-bureaucratic too. Consultants could sell ideas about culture (not structure), re-engineering (not incrementalism), and spirit (not loyalty). A decentralised network was talked into being, and dot coms replaced automobile companies as the exemplars of a new age (Gourvennec, 2005).

In its most contemporary form then, management has now become another word for dull grey administration, and been replaced by leadership or, even better, transformational leadership. The charismatic leader returns, slashing bravely through the thickets of departments and memoranda. Being against management means being for the customer, understanding the market, being able to change strategy rapidly and so on. In terms of organisational structure, big unwieldy dinosaurs are to be chopped up into smaller and more focused units. In terms of individual psychology, the winners are the innovators, the non-conformists, the intrapreneurs. Authors such as Thomas Frank (1998, 2000) and Heath and Potter (2005) have nicely demonstrated how easily this patina of radicalism can be grafted on to what Frank calls 'market populism'. In other words, it is the fault of management that public services don't work well, or that commercial organisations can't satisfy our every whim. We must ditch hierarchy and embrace heterarchy (Fairtlough, 2005), or whatever neologism is proposed as a critique of the present and a solution for the future.

Within the public sector, a pale ghost of this libertarianism embraces ideas about leadership and decentralisation too, and is similarly excoriating about bureaucracy. Yet, as Paul du Gay has noted (2000), the problem with too warm an embrace from this side is the contradictions that it so rapidly has to deal with. Libertarians, whether left or right, can dismiss the state and leave things up to the market. Modernising 'third way' policy makers might like to be quoted making similar pronouncements, but are necessarily always located within a department of Saint-Simon's technocratic apparatus. If they were not, their policy announcements would either not be heard, or only heard once, as they become their own gravediggers. In other words, unlike the free market libertarians, the third way modernisers can never be that consistent about their anti-managerialism.

## Cultural critique

The two forms of engagement above are both, more or less, 'political', in the sense that they clearly and deliberately engage in a criticism of the language, strategy and character of management. Yet we don't need to go to the bookshop or library to find these sorts of ideas. In the *Futurama* episode 'Mars University' from 1993, Farnsworth, a rather mad scientist, is having a conversation with Gunther, a monkey who has been wearing a hat that makes him very clever. At the end of the episode, he decides that the hat caused more trouble than it was worth.

Farnsworth: But what about your super-intelligence?
Gunther: When I had that, there was too much pressure to use it. All I want out of life is to be a monkey of moderate intelligence who wears a suit. That's why I've decided to transfer to business school.
Farnsworth: Noooooooooooooo!

Whether we are considering film, TV, comic books, advertising or the Internet this is a ubiquitous and semi-invisible form of critique (Parker, 2006). In workplaces, we find notice boards containing multiply photocopied witticisms about the nature of work; spam e-mails have attachments that pretend to be a PowerPoint from the boss; MBA students and their teachers read *Dilbert*; and small *Books of Management Bollocks* are for sale in gift shops (Ackroyd and Thompson, 1999; Westwood and Rhodes, 2007). Websites and blogs offer ways of getting back at your boss, often using extreme violence, and tales of cubicle slavery are documented in the imagined freedom of cyberspace. On the small screen, bosses and management are endlessly lampooned in situation comedies. Over-promoted, power-crazed dumbwits parade their insecurities in front of sarcastic employees, and, since the 1970s, contemporary films, whether realist or fantastic, have managers in the role that would traditionally have been played by the mafia mobster, or the cowboy in the black hat.

Blockbusters as varied as *Spiderman*, *Bridget Jones' Diary* and *Monsters Inc.* all have plots that revolve around managerial conspiracies. Sometimes this is explicitly thematised, as in films such as *You've Got Mail* or *Disclosure*, sometimes it is a feature of the back story that allows us to easily understand why the bad guy is bad, as in *Robocop* or *Mission Impossible 2*. Indeed, I would argue that almost the only place you can find a good manager in English-speaking culture nowadays is in the B-School penumbra of consultants, textbooks and training courses.

Yet, as with other forms of anti-managerialism, this is not new. In a strong stream of quasi-gothic imagery, the cultural critique of managerialism goes much further back than this (Parker, 2005). In Dickens, Zola, Gaskell and other industrial commentators of the mid-nineteenth century we find a series of complaints about the character of the manager, of the emergence of bureaumania and the soaring hierarchies of organisations. Even Gilbert and Sullivan, in their 1893 operetta *Utopia Unlimited*, gently parodied the brigh-eyed optimism of people who believed that joint stock companies would solve all their problems. The turn of the twentieth century and the rise of robber baron capitalism articulated discontent in much more powerful ways. The Czech dramatist Karel Capek introduced the word 'Robot' into English through his 1922 play *R.U.R* – 'Rossum's Universal Robots'. In the play the robots (from the Czech *robota* meaning drudgery, with connotations of serfdom) are produced as 'living machines' without souls. Of course, at that time – immediately after the 'Great' War – Taylor, Bedeaux, Gantt, Gilbreth and so on were suggesting that it really was possible to control employees in increasingly mechanical detail. Within the organisation, aliens with little English, like Frederick Taylor's 'dumb ox' Schmidt, had to be disciplined, shaped and moulded before they could become useful for the scientific manager.

Like the robotic workers in films like *Metropolis* (1926) and *A Nous La Liberté* (1932), Charlie Chaplin's defiant little tramp in *Modern Times* (1936), or Simone Weil's writings on factory time (see Grey, 1996) these humans become part of factory or office machines – black and white characters marching to the timings of the machine whilst their bosses smoked big cigars upstairs. Franz Kafka's books *The Trial* (1925) and *The Castle* (1926) capture a more general sense of these organisational nightmares. Within their labyrinths of mysterious conspiracies, helpless individuals endlessly attempt to understand the reasons for their circumstances, and bureaucrats defer to rulebooks and superiors that are nowhere to be found. These concerns with rationalisation and hierarchy are nicely echoed in Aldous Huxley's 1932 *Brave New World*. Set in the World State's Western European Zone, Huxley named his 'Fordship' the Controller Mustapha Mond, after Sir Alfred Mond, the first Chairman of Imperial Chemical Industries. The key problem for this dystopia, as in Yevgeny Zamayatin's explicitly Taylorist 'OneState' of *We* (1924) or Orwell's later *1984* (1948) is how the individual can resist the anti-human bureaucracy that wishes to practice what Huxley prophetically called 'Human Element Management'.

In the US context there had also been growing suspicion of increasing corporate power from the beginning of the century onwards. Ambrose Bierce, in his *Devil's Dictionary* of 1911, defined the corporation as 'An ingenious device for obtaining individual profit without individual responsibility'. The organisation of the US economy under the control of the so-called 'trusts' ensured that prices were set in smoke-filled rooms and profits guaranteed. Yet, after World War I, the Great Depression, the stockmarket crash, muckraking journalism, substantial attempts at union organisation by the IWW and the CIO together with violent resistance by industrialists, all turned this sense of unease into widespread social concern. The rise of the Progressive Party and the 'trustbusters' was in some sense a response to the widespread sense of corruption and collusion, and the perception that both big business and big politics were effectively in each other's pockets.

The brave promise of an America of social opportunity now sees the 'little guy' suffering under the new yoke of big organisation. Social commentary books such as Matthew Josephson's *The Robber Barons* (1934), Frederick Lewis Allen's *The Lords of Creation* (1935) and Thurman Arnold's *The Folklore of Capitalism* (1937) all took aim at the new decadent American aristocracy.

In short order the railroad presidents, the copper barons, the big dry-goods merchants and the steel masters became Senators, ruling in the highest councils of the national government, and sometimes scattered twenty-dollar gold pieces to the newsboys of Washington. But they also became in even greater number lay leaders of churches, trustees of universities, partners or owners of newspapers or press services and figures of fashionable, cultured society. (Josephson, in Beder, 2000: 53)

There was a widespread hostility in the US to the robber barons in their skyscrapers, the con-artists on Wall Street and their stooges in the government. Films like *Mr Smith Goes to Washington* (1939) and *It's a Wonderful Life* (1946) are centrally organised around a dichotomy between the little guy and the bad politician or financier. In the latter, George Bailey, the long suffering owner of Bailey Savings and Loan, prevents the town of Bedford Falls from falling into the clutches of the evil Mr Potter and his big bank. The narrative of community and common virtue versus big business was certainly the most common mythical subtext in the US, whilst in Europe these concerns seemed to focus more on bureaucratic rationalisation and the simultaneous rise of worker's associations and socialist politics. On both sides of the Atlantic, management was getting a bad press.

Whether Gradgrind in Dickens' *Hard Times*, or David Brent in *The Office*, cultural discontent about managerialism often has diffuse targets. Since there is no definitive 'reading' of any cultural text, it would be difficult to definitively decide whether the

'against' was management, rationalisation, capitalism or work itself. Nonetheless, the figure of the manager is central here. Whether demonic and conspiratorial, or ridiculous and self-obsessed, the point is that they are a culturally troubling figure. They appear to represent an occupational group with the potential for great evil and coercion, a power with a legitimacy that is highly suspicious, or even with the hint of illegitimacy concerning their social mobility. Whether cultural discontent is the same as dissent, or even resistance, is not the question here. If we add in the nostalgic or modernising complaints, we appear to have a variety of positions from which management is being attacked, and that is before we even start to think about the serious alternatives.

## Anti-authoritarian critique

Before the words management and bureaucracy had been coined, there were slaves and masters, ecclesiastical hierarchies, patriarchal and ethnic hierarchies, imperial states, feudal structures of land ownership, and the East India Company. There were also Amazons, Cathars, Diggers, Levellers and Dissenters (Parker *et al.*, 2007). My point is that dissent to managerialism is one small element of dissent aimed at all sorts of other sorts of authority relations. Once again, it is well worth re-emphasising that versions of managerial rationalisation were often enough seen as a radical improvement to the capricious power of kings. From Thomas More's original 1516 *Utopia* onwards, a consistent theme in Western utopianism has been the well-ordered city-state. In works such as Campanella's *City of the Sun* (1602), Etienne Cabet's *Voyage to Icaria* (1839) or Edward Bellamy's *Looking Backward* (1888), the managerial meritocracy is very clear, and they are all forms of order that anticipate Weber's description of bureaucracy.

Yet these autocratic utopias also have their counterpoint in a utopianism and politics that rejects hierarchy, and treats issues of organisation and order as potentially distributable across a community that is organised differently. William Morris's celebrated *News from Nowhere* (1890) is, in part, a reaction to Bellamy's *Looking Backward*. Where Bellamy was lauding a technologically sophisticated version of strong state socialism, Morris is describing an arcadia of small market towns in which production and ownership are communal. Morris wants work to be desired, to be a natural part of the human condition. People gather together in 'banded workshops' to enjoy the exercise of their craft, but there is no compulsion to work. Such compulsion would simply produce ugly objects, and debased people. *News from Nowhere* can easily be read as an anarchist eco-topia, set in a future that is producing a new kind of people, freed from relations of slavery and repression.

In that sense, the key set of thinkers who should be considered as early anti-managerialists are those generally associated with anarchism of various kinds (Marshall, 1993; Reedy, 2002; Ward, 2004). Anarchism is organisation theory in the truest sense, a contingency theory without boundaries. Rather than assuming, as many more conservative organisational theorists do, the existence of the division of labour, capitalism, hierarchy and so on, all these 'facts' become questions. No 'natural order' is assumed, and issues of governance, control, decision making, production and so on are all assumed to be matters that the autonomous individual can make intelligent choices about. Management, in anything other than the role of a temporary co-ordinating function, is simply superfluous since people can usually organise themselves. More damagingly, management also disempowers, appropriates and dominates. Unsurprisingly, given that anarchists are not keen on being told what to do, there is little agreement on any other guiding principles. Writers such as Godwin, Stirner, Proudhon, Baukunin, Kropotkin, and Tolstoy rarely suggest similar solutions to similar problems. Some stress forms of association at the local level; others assume that autonomy is a value that should not be compromised by any constraints. Many assume that certain rules are acceptable in order to maintain a minimal

social order, but there would be considerable debate about the nature and force of any coercion or shared legislation. Whatever the view, the privileges of managerialism would certainly be questioned in most forms of anarchist thought.

However, when we move towards the anarcho-syndicalist versions of anarchism, the importance of more elaborate organisational forms becomes apparent. Since the aim of syndicalists is primarily large scale political change, then the use of industrial action, particularly the general strike, is seen as a means of defending the interests of workers against management and of overthrowing the present order. However, in order to achieve this, labour organisations need to develop the self-governing structures that will form the basis of subsequent worker's control of production. It is here that more centralised forms of authority might become tolerated for tactical reasons, something that we also see in many cooperatively run organisations. Nonetheless, syndicalists pursue a long-term strategy that intends to result in forms of workplace democracy and worker self-management[5] (Vanek, 1975; Albert and Hahnel, 1991; Rocker, 2004). There is a considerable continuum of work and practice here, ranging from forms of minimal involvement and ownership that retain most managerial privileges (such as employee share ownership, and versions of empowerment), through to fully fledged co-operative forms of ownership and control. The latter are particularly vibrant today in Italian workerism, combined with a variety of forms of anti-corporate protest and attempts to unionise precarious workers (Wright, 2002). Most importantly for the argument in this chapter, these ideas are again not new, and can be dated back, at least, to the English labour economists, Robert Owen, the Rochdale Pioneers and so on (Davis and Parker, 2007).

That being said, another current of anti-managerial thought is rather more recent, and is associated with versions of radical and anarcho-feminism. Patriarchy is here argued to be the original form of oppressive authority from which all others develop. Feminists (and perhaps pro-feminist men) should thus struggle against all forms of hierarchy, and perhaps towards ways of being that are more collective and supportive. It could be argued that Emma Goldman (1869–1940) was the originator of this simultaneous attack on both liberal feminism and managerial capitalism (Marshall, 1993). However, as with anarchism and workerism, there are many inflections within feminist resistance to authority (Ferree and Martin, 1995). Feminists might take their principal problem to be men, leading to separatist forms of organisation. Or they might articulate the problem as patriarchal relations, or capitalist relations, or some combination of both. As we will see below, the intersections between feminism and forms of environmentalism are also particularly strong. However, whatever the accent, the general point would be that radical feminists would be suspicious about the naturalisation of authority, the division of labour, and any separation between public and private action, such as that embodied in a Weberian description of bureaucracy (Bologh, 1990). Managers tend to operate without hatred or passion, and in so doing, end up assuming both separation and dominance.

We find a similar diversity of anti-authoritarian positions within green or environmentalist thought. In this case, it is very often the human relationship to nature that is articulated as an original hierarchy, though ecofeminist positions would also argue that this is a peculiarly male way of relating to the natural world. So if positions of dominance and exploitation are problematic, then it is obvious enough that more collective and cooperative relations should be encouraged within our work and our communities. Of crucial importance here is the trend to localisation, to the grassroots (Fournier, 2002). As Schumacher said, small is beautiful, and the sorts of organisational relations sponsored by green activists and writers would tend to be based on ideas of the eco-village and the sustainable community. Coordination may require a limited division of labour, but the general principal would usually be that

hierarchy should be minimised, and forms of collective decision making would be the norm. Again, it needs to be noted that there is no 'one' enviromental position. Variants of collectivism and individualism, as well as diagnoses of the source of the problem, shade over into feminist, socialist and anarchist positions (Naess, 1989; Bookchin, 1997; Warren, 1997). Uniting these varieties of thought and practice would be metaphors of 'working with' and being 'close to', which would tend to refuse the physical or intellectual separations on which managerialism needs to rely.

Anti-authoritarian critiques of managerialism are clearly entangled with a variety of other complaints, but they all share a deep distrust of the notion of the expert organiser. The idea of the manager, as someone with more status and reward who is not involved in day-to-day organising, is entirely antithetical to most anarchist, workerist, feminist, and environmentalist thinkers. In addition, these ideas are inextricably entangled with actual practices. Whether we look at the long history of intentional communities, co-operatives, alternative economic practices or contemporary attempts to resist the hegemony of the capitalist work organisation, these are discontents that produce alternatives, and these are not temporary, minor or historical alternatives, but a continual stream of practical opposition that is as vibrant now as it has ever been.

## AGAINST MANAGEMENT?

If we take the picture as a whole then, it is clearly not the case that 'management' (broadly conceived) has only recently come under sustained criticism. Certain authors (including this one) have tended to focus on business ethics, critical management studies, and anti-corporate protest as if these were manifestations of a peculiarly modern (post 1970s) set of complaints or understandings. In this chapter, I have argued that the growth of managerialism has always been contested, and from a wide variety of theoretical and political locations.

At the risk of simplification, let me propose a way of classifying these discontents. What I called the nostalgic critique is generally aimed from 'above' management, both in terms of social class and claimed moral elevation. It is essentially a 'high cultural' discontent that suggests that management is a debasing force, an example of the way in which modernity corrupts a more authentic authority structure. Very often, the people doing the complaining might well feel that their position or profession is insufficiently respected, and that modernisation means increasing marginalisation. The modernising critique is different in that it appears to originate from 'alongside' management. It is a form of discontent that seeks to move management over in order that a new order can occupy its place. This is the voice of a putative 'new generation' of organisers, a group of young princes inviting their elderly relative to vacate the site of power. The complaint is simply that management could be done better, often by calling it something else.

By contrast, the cultural and anti-authoritarian critiques appear to be located 'below' management. In the case of the former, pretty much by default since the location of the reader of the cultural text is assumed to be someone who shares the assumption that all managers are, by definition, shits. Popular culture, in the broadest sense, speaks for the popular, for the people, and hence rarely provides a sympathetic account of the troubles of those with power. Those with power are assumed to be quite capable of doing that for themselves. The second critique from 'below' is rather more nuanced, in that it does attempt to speak for various interests that it claims have not been represented within contemporary market managerialism. Whether articulating the distinctive voices and possibilities of women, workers, nature, community, or the individual, the general point is that these are proposals (and often experiments) in organising that are quite self-consciously anti-managerial. They open the possibility that managerialism be seen as only one form of organising, and not a synonym for

organisation in general. However, this is not to say that they all share a common agenda, just that they are generally opposed to similar things. The nature of this opposition means that they all articulate management as a discipline, occupation or activity which constrains and disempowers. Hence words like collectivity, democracy, and autonomy are likely to be seen as part of the solution.

Yet we can't assume that 'above', 'alongside' and 'below' are themselves incommensurable or timeless positions. Perhaps it would be better to describe them as tendencies, since they can be combined in various ways. For example, William Morris appears to combine medieval nostalgia with a proto-communist sensibility and some highly prescient nods towards environmentalism. Radical cyber-libertarians often propose modernisation precisely in order that decision making can be distributed, and networks take the place of hierarchies. Cultural critique is not insulated from alternative organisation, but can be used to pursue explicitly political ends, as in the case of situationism and autonomism. Finally, anarchists can be nostalgics or modernisers too; it depends on their attitudes to technology, the urban, and the relations between human and 'nature'. In sum, we should not expect that anti-managerial positions will be simple, because managerialism is not simple. It gets inflected differently in different times and places, and hence invites different condemnations. Many are contradictory in their implications, only joined together by a vague common enemy, a sense that 'management' stops people from doing things that they might otherwise rather like to do.[6]

To conclude then. It is often enough assumed that we are better at organising things nowadays, and that the rise and rise of the manager reflects the need for professionally trained organisers to deal with more and more complex organisation. This chapter has shown that this is a very one-sided history, and that it opens into a future that is eminently contestable. Aside from reflecting the interests and dreams of a powerful occupational ideology, there are all sorts of ways of thinking against management, and there always have been. Critical Management Studies did not begin with Alvesson and Willmott (1992). At the same time that Saint-Simon was writing, across the channel William Blake was opposing the consequences of industrialism, the 'dark satanic mills', slavery and sexual inequality. An anarchist before the word had been coined, he rejected all forms of imposed authority and said (in his 1821 *Jerusalem*) 'I must Create a System or be enslav'd by another Mans.' Just as Saint-Simon was celebrating order, so was Blake viewing society as inevitably restricting the freedoms derived from intuition and spontaneity. He would have been against management too, had he known about it.

## NOTES

1 Thanks to Stewart Clegg for his help with this chapter.

2 Of course other starting points could have been chosen – the arsenale at Venice, the Jesuits, a slave plantation, the Springfield Armoury, West Point Military Academy or a railway company. History rarely has clear places where things begin.

3 For a sloppy left intellectual example of a similar argument, see Wheen, 2004.

4 A cartoon series by Matt Groening, developer of *The Simpsons*.

5 The inclusion of the word 'management' in this phrase tells us something about some of its assumptions about scale and hierarchy.

6 Pretty much the same thing could be said of Critical Management Studies too.

## REFERENCES

Ackroyd, S. and Thompson, P. (1999) *Organisational Misbehaviour*. London: Sage.

Albert, M. and Hahnel, R. (1991) *Looking Forward: Participatory Economics for the 21st Century*. Cambridge, MA: South End Press.

Alvesson, M. and Willmott, H. (eds) (1992) *Critical Management Studies*. London: Sage.

Arendt, H. (1963/1994) *Eichmann in Jerusalem: A Report on the Banality of Evil*. London: Penguin.

Bauman, Z. (1989) *Modernity and the Holocaust*. Oxford: Polity.

Beder, S. (2000) *Selling the Work Ethic: From Puritan Pulpit to Corporate PR*. London: Zed Books.

Bologh, R. (1990) *Love or Greatness: Max Weber and Masculine Thinking*. London: Unwin Hyman.

Bookchin, M. (1997) *The Murray Bookchin Reader*. New York: Continuum International Publishing.

Clegg, S. and Dunkerley, D. (1980) *Organization, Class and Control*. London: Routledge and Kegan Paul.

Davis, P. and Parker, M. (2007) 'Co-operatives, labour and the state: The English labour economists revisited', *Review of Radical Political Economy*, 39 (4): 523–542.

du Gay, P. (2000) *In Praise of Bureaucracy*. London: Sage.

Fairtlough, G. (2005) *The Three Ways of Getting Things Done: Hierarchy, Heterarchy and Responsible Autonomy in Organizations*. Axminster: Triarchy Press.

Ferree, M. and Martin, P. (1995) *Feminist Organizations*. Philadelphia: Temple University Press.

Fournier, V. (2002) 'Utopianism and the cultivation of possibilities: Grassroots movements of hope', in M. Parker (ed.) *Utopia and Organization*. Oxford: Blackwell.

Fournier, V. and Grey, C. (2000) 'At the critical moment: Conditions and prospects for critical management studies', *Human Relations*, 53 (1): 7–32.

Frank, T. (1998) *The Conquest of Cool: Business Culture, Counterculture, and the Rise of Hip Consumerism*. Chicago, IL: University of Chicago Press.

Frank, T. (2000) *One Market Under God*. London: Secker and Warburg.

Gourvennec, Y. (2005) *Of Networks and Men: Information Society, Networks and Postmodern Management*. http://visionarymarketing.com/articles/ofnetworksandmen0.html (accessed 5/2/07).

Grey, C. (1996) 'Towards a critique of managerialism: The contribution of Simone Weil', *Journal of Management Studies*, 33 (5): 591–611.

Grey, C. (1999) '"We are all managers now"; "We always were": On the development and demise of management', *Journal of Management Studies*, 36 (5): 561–585.

Heath, J. and Potter, A. (2005) *The Rebel Sell: How the Counter Culture Became Consumer Culture*. Mankato, MN: Capstone.

Jackson, N. and Carter, P. (1998) 'Labour as dressage', in A. McKinlay and K. Starkey (eds) *Foucault, Management and Organization Theory*. London: Sage, pp. 49–64.

Jacques, R. (1996) *Manufacturing the Employee: Management Knowledge from the 19th to the 21st Centuries*. London: Sage.

Koch, R. and Godden, I. (1996) *Managing Without Management: A Post-Management Manifesto for Business Simplicity*. London: Nicholas Brealey.

MacIntyre, A. (1981) *After Virtue*. London: Duckworth.

Marcuse, H. (1964) *One Dimensional Man*. London: Routledge and Kegan Paul.

Marshall, P. (1993) *Demanding the Impossible: A History of Anarchism*. London: Fontana.

Mitchell, G. (1968) *A Dictionary of Sociology*. London: Routledge & Kegan Paul.

Naess, A. (1989) *Ecology, Community and Lifestyle*. Cambridge: Cambridge University Press.

Nelson, M. (1985) 'Bureaucracy', in A. Kuper and J. Kuper (eds) *The Social Science Encyclopedia*. London: Routledge & Kegan Paul, pp. 79–81.

Parker, M. (2002) *Against Management*. Oxford: Polity.

Parker, M. (2005) 'Organisational Gothic', *Culture and Organization*, 11 (3): 153–166.

Parker, M. (2006) 'The counter culture of organisation: Towards a cultural studies of Representations of Work', *Consumption, Markets and Culture*, 9 (1): 1–15.

Parker, M., Fournier, V. and Reedy, P. (2007) *The Dictionary of Alternatives*. London: Zed.

Protherough, R. and Pick, J. (2002) *Managing Brittania. Culture and Management in Modern Britain*. Norfolk: Edgeways, Brynmill Press.

Reedy, P. (2002) 'Keep the black flag flying: Anarchy, utopia and the politics of nostalgia', in M. Parker (ed.) *Utopia and Organisation*. Oxford: Blackwell.

Ritzer, G. (2000) *The McDonaldization of Society*. London: Sage.

Rocker, R. (2004) *Anarcho-Syndicalism: Theory and Practice*. Oakland, CA: AK Press

Vaneigem, R. (1992) *The Revolution of Everyday Life*. London: Left Bank Books & Rebel Press.

Vanek, J. (ed.) (1975) *Self-Management: Economic Liberation of Man*. Harmondsworth: Penguin.

Ward, C. (2004) *Anarchism: A Very Short Introduction*. Oxford: Oxford University Press.

Warren, K. (ed.) (1997) *Ecofeminism*. Bloomingtom: Indiana University Press.

Weber, M. (1948) In H.H. Gerth and C. Wright Mills (eds) *For Max Weber*. London: Routledge and Kegan Paul.

Westwood, B. and Rhodes, C. (eds) (2007) *Humour, Organization and Work*. London: Routledge.

Wheen, F. (2004) *How Mumbo Jumbo Conquered the World*. London. Fourth Estate.

Whyte, W.H. (1961) *The Organisation Man*. Harmondsworth: Penguin.

Wright, S. (2002) *Storming Heaven: Class Composition and Struggle in Italian Autonomist Marxism*. London: Pluto Press.

# 5

# Positive Organizational Scholarship: What Does It Achieve?

Arran Caza and Kim S. Cameron

Positive Organizational Scholarship (POS) is a relatively new development in organization studies, having formally begun with a 2003 edited collection of the same name (Cameron, et al., 2003b). Since that time, it has attracted considerable attention (e.g., George, 2004; Caza and Roberts, 2006; Fineman, 2006; Caza, 2008). The theoretical basis and scope of POS have been addressed quite recently (Dutton and Glynn, 2007; Dutton and Sonenshein, 2007), so this chapter only summarizes these issues, in favor of concentrating on the research and practice of POS. After discussing the domain and precursors of POS, primary attention is given to what POS has accomplished to date. These accomplishments have two facets, as POS involves a research perspective and an approach to managing organizations. This chapter considers the accomplishments of POS in both areas.

## NATURE OF POSITIVE ORGANIZATIONAL SCHOLARSHIP

In the eponymous book that launched POS (Cameron et al., 2003b), the editors began by contrasting two extreme, hypothetical worlds: one of greed, manipulation, and distrust; the other of appreciation, collaboration, and meaningfulness. They then characterized POS as recognizing the importance of the first world, but intentionally emphasizing the second. 'POS is concerned with the study of especially positive outcomes, processes, and attributes of organizations and their members' (Cameron et al., 2003a: 4). POS promotes the study of enablers, motivations, and effects associated with positive phenomena, with the aim of revealing positive states and processes that would otherwise be missed or obscured by traditional, 'non-POS', perspectives.

The creation of the label POS was described as a deliberate one, with each element of the acronym intended to signify an important element of the perspective (Cameron et al., 2003a). The use of 'positive' declared 'an affirmative bias and orientation [toward] exceptional, virtuous, life-giving, and flourishing phenomena' (Cameron et al., 2003a: 5). The term 'organizational' was meant to stress the emphasis on organized contexts, as opposed to purely individual phenomena (see Dutton and Glynn, 2007). Finally, the 'scholarship' label was used to make theoretical explanation and empirical support an explicit requirement for inclusion. In sum, POS calls for scholarly research examining positive phenomena in organizations (Cameron et al., 2003a: 11).

While the intended meaning of 'organizational' and 'scholarship' seem relatively straightforward, questions have been raised about what constitutes 'positive' (e.g., George, 2004; Fineman, 2006). The issue is addressed in more detail later in this chapter, but the uncertainty about the precise nature of positiveness reflects the fact that no formal definition has been offered, either in the original book (Cameron et al., 2003b) or in subsequent statements about the nature of POS (Cameron and Caza, 2004; Roberts, 2006; Caza and Caza, 2008). Instead, general descriptors and evocative examples have been used to imply the meaning of positiveness. These include references to elevating processes, excellence, human strength, resilience, vitality, and meaningfulness (Cameron et al., 2003a; Cameron and Caza, 2004; Roberts, 2006). However, the exact nature of positiveness remains unclear.

In many ways, the POS emphasis on how to see, rather than exactly what to see, bears an affinity to the technique involved in seeing an auto-stereogram. Readers will recall the popular culture boom of 'magic eye' pictures in the 1990s. In these pictures, if individuals focused their vision in just the right way, a three-dimensional image would seem to emerge from a field of random dots. With these pictures, those who had already seen the image tended to tell others how to look at the

picture, rather than telling them to look for a specific object. Moreover, the act of properly seeing a given magic eye picture was initially difficult, but once one was able to see the image in the dots, it became hard to believe that anyone could fail to see it.

POS has been characterized in comparable terms. The POS perspective promises a different way of looking at familiar organizations to see that which has previously been missed, but which is clearly evident and important once one recognizes it. The notion of a different way of perceiving, and of subsequent revelation, is shared by all statements of the aims and nature of POS (Cameron et al., 2004, 2003a; Roberts, 2006). In this sense, POS is like many other conceptual labels in organization studies, serving as an umbrella term to unite a range of theories and investigations that share a common theme (Dutton and Glynn, 2007). 'POS draws from the full spectrum of organizational theories to understand, explain, and predict the occurrence, causes, and consequences of positivity' (Cameron et al., 2003a: 5).

## PRECURSORS OF POSITIVE ORGANIZATIONAL SCHOLARSHIP

Obviously, POS did not create the notion of positive behaviors, processes, and outcomes in organizational settings. Numerous research traditions addressed such phenomena before POS was established. The most relevant of these are discussed here, including positive psychology, community psychology, positive organizational behavior, prosocial organizational behavior, organization development, and corporate social performance.

### Positive psychology

Positive psychology is a movement initiated in 1999 by then-president of the American Psychological Association Martin Seligman (Seligman, 1999). He called for psychologists to study positive subjective experience, positive individual traits, and positive institutions. The stated intent of positive psychology was to counter the overwhelming research focus on pathology, and to develop 'a science that takes as its primary task the understanding of what makes life worth living' (Seligman and Csikszentmihalyi, 2000: 13). In the years following Seligman's call, positive psychology has had considerable popularity and success, generating extensive research and education (Snyder and Lopez, 2002; Peterson, 2006), including a positive companion to the established handbook of mental pathology (American Psychiatric Association, 1994; Peterson and Seligman, 2004) and several interventions for increasing happiness (Seligman *et al.*, 2005). POS is often described as the organizational equivalent of positive psychology (Cameron *et al.*, 2003a; Roberts, 2006; Dutton and Sonenshein, 2007), and positive psychology scholars were invited to offer advice in the initial POS book (Peterson and Seligman, 2003).

## Community psychology

Community psychology is a predecessor of positive psychology. Community psychologists have advanced principles and practices for fostering wellness, such as positive self-attitudes, wholesome growth, and personal integration (e.g., Jahoda, 1958). The emphasis in community psychology has been on preventing illness, rather than curing it, with the goal of enhancing wellness, instead of reducing sickness (see Durlak and Wells, 1997 for a review). In this way, community psychology shares the POS emphasis on desirable, positive phenomena, rather than negative ones.

## Positive organizational behavior

Building on the work of the Gallup organization and its emphasis on strengths in the workplace, Luthans (2002) called for organizational research on individuals' state-based strengths and capacities, under the label of positive organizational behavior. Self-identified researchers of positive organizational behavior describe themselves as distinct from POS on the grounds that POS is 'more macro-oriented' (Luthans *et al.*, 2005: 251) than their emphasis on

psychological capacities (Luthans and Avolio, 2003). Nonetheless, the inaugural POS book (Cameron *et al.*, 2003b) addressed both macro and micro topics and included a chapter from the leading scholars of positive organizational behavior (Luthans and Avolio, 2003). As such, this chapter makes no distinction between positive organizational behavior and POS.

## Prosocial organizational behavior

A variety of altruistic 'citizenship' behaviors have been studied in organizations (see Ilies *et al.*, 2007 and Podsakoff *et al.*, 2000 for reviews). This research tradition grew out of the early recognition that organizations depend upon individuals to do much more than is formally required of them (Katz, 1964), and led to the study of voluntary efforts to benefit coworkers and the organization. The focus of this research was thus consistent with, and supportive of, the eudemonic assumption of POS, given that citizenship behaviors were defined as benefiting others while providing no formal reward to the individual engaged in them (Smith *et al.*, 1983).

## Organization development

Organization development (OD) provides a series of techniques for changing and enhancing organizational functioning (Cummings and Worley, 2005) and is thus concerned with many of the same matters as POS. Of particular importance to POS is the OD approach known as Appreciative Inquiry, originated by Cooperrider and Srivastava (Cooperrider *et al.*, 2000). Appreciative Inquiry is a technique for guiding organizational change based on previous successes and peak performance. In Appreciative Inquiry, designing a future state based on the best of the past serves as a source of learning and power for future organizational growth (Cooperrider and Whitney, 2005). Formal research on the effects and contingencies of Appreciative Inquiry is limited as yet (see Burke, 2001), but the approach is widely employed among OD practitioners.

## Corporate social performance

Federal governments and international bodies have urged large organizations to assist in promoting social welfare (e.g., OECD, 2000), although opinions about doing so remain divided. While this debate about the social responsibilities of corporations predates the discipline of organization studies (e.g., Berle, 1932; Dodd, 1932), corporate social performance has become an active research literature among organization scientists. Margolis and Walsh (2003) identified 127 studies of the relationship between companies' social and financial performance. Similarly, stakeholder theories of organization examine the potential social benefits that large organizations can produce (Donaldson and Preston, 1995; Hoffman, 1996; Morris, 1997).

## ASSUMPTIONS INHERENT IN POSITIVE ORGANIZATIONAL SCHOLARSHIP

Before examining what POS has accomplished, an important point about initial assumptions should be addressed. POS is premised on the belief that 'the desire to improve the human condition is universal and the capacity to do so is latent in most systems' (Cameron *et al.*, 2003a: 10). Like the humanism movement in psychology (Maslow, 1968; Rogers, 1980), POS takes it as given that individuals and their institutions are inherently eudemonic, that they seek goodness for its intrinsic value (Dutton and Sonenshein, 2007). This can be contrasted with other initial assumptions, such as the Freudian view of humanity's conflicted nature (Freud, 1938) or Hobbes' (1651) belief in humanity's essential brutishness. Postmodern assumptions about the subjectivity of experience also disagree with the humanism of POS, since postmodern views tend to reject the existence of any universal aspect of human nature (e.g., Giddens, 1979; Scheurich, 1997). This issue of initial assumptions is important, because all argumentation depends on beginning from some fixed point of first principle. An assumption of one kind or another is inevitable, and what follows from it only makes sense in the context of that assumption. Since POS begins with the

assumption that individuals are inherently driven to seek that which is positive, most of its claims depend upon the truth of that assumption.

The logic for grounding POS in the eudemonic assumption was based on the heliotropic effect (Cooperrider, 2000). Heliotropism is defined as the tendency of living systems to seek that which is life-giving and to avoid that which is life-depleting. This effect is shown when organisms move away from darkness toward light or positive energy (e.g., a plant bending toward the sun). Evidence that living systems have an inherent inclination toward positive energy and disinclination toward negative energy has been observed in a variety of disciplines, including the social and biological sciences.

In the social sciences, numerous instances have been found where individuals show a preference for positiveness. For example, it has been found that people are more accurate in learning and remembering positive terms than neutral or negative terms (Matlin, 1970; Kunz, 1974), and that they are more accurate in recalling positive stimuli (Thompson, 1930; Akhtar, 1968; Rychlak, 1977). In free association tasks, people tend to respond with positive rather than negative words (Wilson and Becknell, 1961; Silverstein and Dienstbier, 1968), and positive items take precedence when people make lists (Matlin *et al.*, 1979). People more frequently recall positive life experiences than neutral or negative ones, and they mentally rehearse positive items more than negative items (Meltzer, 1930; Stang, 1975). People seek out positive stimuli and avoid negative stimuli (Luborsky *et al.*, 1963; Day, 1966). Moreover, when people see positive and neutral stimuli equally often, they report that the positive stimuli are more frequent (Matlin and Stang, 1975; Stang, 1975). Positive stimuli are judged to be larger in size than negative or neutral stimuli (Stayton and Wiener, 1961). Over time positive memories replace negative memories, and negative memories diminish (Holmes, 1970; Yarrow *et al.*, 1970).

A similar positive bias is found in language. Positive words have higher frequencies in most languages, including English, French, German, Spanish, Chinese, Urdu [India and Pakistan], Russian, Italian, Dutch, Belgian Flemish, Iranian Farsi, Mexican Spanish, Swedish, Turkish, and Serbo-Croatian. A preponderance of positive words is present in all types of literature, in formal and informal language, in written and spoken communication, and among both adults and children (Boucher and Osgood, 1969; Matlin and Stang, 1978). It has also be shown that positive words typically enter English usage more than 150 years before their negative opposites, so that people were 'better' before they were 'worse,' and 'clean' before they were 'dirty' (Mann, 1968; Zajonc, 1968; Boucher and Osgood, 1969; Matlin and Stang, 1978). Osgood and Richards concluded that: 'It would appear that from time immemorial humans have been differentially reinforced for strength (rather than weakness), for activity (rather than passivity), ... that humans have found believing more reinforcing than doubting, certainty more than uncertainty, plentitude more than scarcity, asserting more than denying – and congruity ... more than incongruity' (1973: 410).

There is equally diverse evidence of heliotropism in the biological sciences. The basis of evolution is heliotropic, that organisms persist to the extent that they acquire life-giving resources, processes, and attributes (Smith, 1993). Experiments with a range of life forms, from bacteria to mammals, find that living organisms possess an inclination toward heliotropism (e.g., Smith and Baker, 1960; D'Amato and Jagoda, 1962; Mrosovsky and Kingsmill, 1985). Photosynthesis – the molecular process of using the sun's energy to create oxygen and biological energy – also illustrates the relationship between positive energy, in the form of light, and life-giving processes (Blankenship, 2002).

For the purposes of this chapter, the heliotropic effect was accepted. The approach taken below is to allow the assumption that human beings are naturally inclined toward positiveness, so as to take stock of POS on its own terms. However, to the extent that one believes some other initial assumption

is more appropriate, he or she will view POS as inherently flawed because it begins from a 'mistaken' assumption. It is beyond the scope and concerns of this chapter to debate the relative merits of one initial assumption over another, but this issue has been discussed elsewhere (Fineman, 2006; Roberts, 2006).

## POSITIVE ORGANIZATIONAL SCHOLARSHIP: RESEARCH

As noted earlier, this chapter focuses on the empirical accomplishments of POS, so only research articles are reviewed here. Others have reviewed the theoretical basis of POS (Dutton and Glynn, 2007; Dutton and Sonenshein, 2007). Furthermore, this chapter reviews only articles that could be objectively classified as 'self-identified' POS research. In March 2007, a three-part search for POS articles was conducted, including: articles listed on the web page of the Center for Positive Organizational Scholarship (http://www.bus.umich.edu/Positive), an ISI Web of Knowledge search for works citing the three published statements of POS (Cameron et al., 2003b; Cameron and Caza, 2004; Roberts, 2006); and a search of both the PsycINFO and Proquest databases using variations of the term 'positive organization' in the years 2003 to 2007. The search identified 21 articles that reported research which was explicitly aligned with the POS perspective (see Table 5.1). These are discussed below, in six themes.

However, before proceeding, it should be noted that the list in Table 5.1 is potentially controversial. It includes work by researchers who are not otherwise affiliated with POS, and excludes work by researchers who are closely affiliated. A useful example of the later is a paper by Quinn (2005). This paper uses empirical evidence to advance a model of flow, which is a desirable, high performance work state (Csikszentmihalyi, 1996). The author, Ryan Quinn, is listed as a member of the POS community of scholars (http://www.bus.umich.edu/Positive), and one might

**Table 5.1    Summary of POS research articles**

| Article | Relevant findings |
| --- | --- |
| Andersson *et al.*, 2007 | Given hope, gratitude increases organizational concern for social issues |
| Avey *et al.*, 2006 | Psychological capital reduces absenteeism |
| Bono and Ilies, 2006 | Positive emotion is a source of charismatic leadership |
| Bright *et al.*, 2006 | Leadership responsibility increases organizational virtue; organizational virtue buffers against the negative effects of downsizing |
| Britt *et al.*, 2007 | Morale is distinct from depression; meaningful work fosters morale |
| Cameron *et al.*, 2004 | Organizational virtue improves organizational performance |
| Duchon and Plowman, 2005 | Unit spirituality leads to greater customer satisfaction |
| Dutton *et al.*, 2006 | Traditional organizational systems can be redirected to organize and support expressions of compassion |
| Ellis *et al.*, 2006 | Failure teaches more than success |
| Fry *et al.*, 2005 | Leader spirituality increases follower well-being, commitment, and productivity |
| Giacalone *et al.*, 2005 | Virtuous consumers are more concerned with the social performance of organizations |
| Gittell *et al.*, 2006 | Positive relations improve organizational performance |
| Kellet *et al.*, 2006 | Empathy is a source of leadership ability |
| Losada and Heaphy, 2004 | Positive communication creates interpersonal connection, leading to better group performance |
| Luthans and Jensen, 2005 | Psychological capital increases commitment to the organization |
| Luthans *et al.*, 2005 | Psychological capital improves individual performance |
| O'Donohoe and Turley, 2006 | Organizational compassion leads to more care for customers |
| Peterson and Luthans, 2003 | Leader hope increases profit, retention, and satisfaction |
| Pittinsky and Shih, 2004 | Career mobility does not reduce commitment to the organization |
| Verbeke *et al.*, 2004 | Pride can benefit individual performance |
| Wooten and Crane, 2004 | Valuing relationships improves unit performance |

reasonably assume that flow is a POS phenomenon, even though it predates POS. However, there is nothing in the article itself which explicitly classifies it as POS research. Unfortunately, while this particular instance seems straightforward, there are many more cases where the decision to include or exclude an article would be highly subjective.

The ideal search criteria would have been either a list of POS phenomena or a concrete definition of 'positiveness.' However, as noted above and discussed below, neither is currently available. As such, we chose conservative, objective search criteria that limited our review to those articles that explicitly connected their research to POS. Therefore, the list in Table 5.1 should not be construed as a judgment. It simply reflects the belief that it would be inappropriate, and likely misleading, to make a list from our own, inevitably biased, perceptions.

### Individual virtue and social concern

A survey study of white-collar workers examined the relationship linking hope, gratitude, and responsibility (Andersson et al., 2007).

Hope was defined as a motivational state of felt agency, as the belief that one could achieve a desirable effect. Gratitude was a moral affective state, in which the individual feels motivated toward prosocial behavior, to 'give back' in return for whatever caused the feeling of gratitude. In this study, the researchers found that gratitude led to greater feelings of responsibility for employees and social issues if high hope was present. That is, if individuals felt both grateful and hopeful, then they also felt greater responsibility for other members of the organization and for extra-organizational social matters.

Similar results were shown in two surveys that linked positive psychology character strengths to concern about corporate social performance (Giacalone *et al.*, 2005). In the first survey, consumers who scored high on trait-based gratitude and hope were also more concerned that organizations serve multiple purposes so as to benefit society, rather than simply maximizing profits. The second survey linked similar concerns about corporate social performance to the traits of spirituality (transcendent ideals and a desire for meaning in community) and generativity (concern for future generations). Together, these results suggest that individual virtue is an important factor in understanding how individuals judge organizations.

## Leadership

There have been several investigations of the role of POS phenomena in explaining leadership. Bono and Ilies (2006) described a series of studies showing that leaders who express more positive emotions engender the same emotions in followers, who then perceive that leader as more charismatic and effective. Similarly, another study found that Army leaders who expressed more vision and love satisfied their followers' needs for the same, fostering greater well-being, commitment, and productivity among followers (Fry et al., 2005). In the fast food industry, leader hope has been linked to follower satisfaction and retention (Peterson and Luthans, 2003). Similarly, a simulation study showed that group members' assessment of an individual's leadership ability was influenced by that individual's displayed level of empathy (Kellett et al., 2006). As a set, these studies indicate that POS phenomena can assist in predicting and explaining effective leadership.

## Organizational virtue

A number of studies have examined virtues as organizational phenomena, with virtue broadly defined as selfless action taken for the sake of others. For example, one study described how members of a business school were able to redirect existing organizational systems to support compassionate responses to individual tragedy (Dutton et al., 2006). Similarly, O'Donohoe and Turley's (2006) interview study of newspaper staff dealing with bereaved clients found the staff engaging in 'philanthropic emotion management,' in which they made personal sacrifices for the sake of grieving clients, even though these sacrifices were neither required nor rewarded by the organization.

There have also been several studies linking virtue to performance. One study within a healthcare network showed how units that

were supportive of their members' spirituality produced higher levels of customer satisfaction (Duchon and Plowman, 2005). Another study, among Dutch sales staff, found that pride was a source of self-worth, motivation, creativity, and altruism, and thus led to higher levels of adaptive selling, individual effort, self-efficacy, and citizenship behavior (Verbeke et al., 2004). Consistent with both of these studies, Cameron and colleagues' (2004) report of survey data used organizational forgiveness, trust, optimism, compassion, and integrity to predict measures of innovation, quality, turnover, customer retention, and profitability. In a related paper, Bright and colleagues (2006) found that leaders who took responsibility for the disruptive effects of downsizing received more forgiveness from followers, and this forgiveness reduced the performance losses usually created by downsizing.

One feature that all of these studies have in common is a consideration of the organizational nature of virtue. While it was obviously individuals experiencing or expressing virtuous behavior, these studies suggest that such expressions of virtue have the potential to become collective phenomena. Through emotional contagion, reciprocity, and institutionalization, organizational contexts can potentially engender virtuous behavior in individuals.

## Positive relationships and performance

Relationships are another important source of potential performance benefits investigated by POS. A study of the airline industry found that carriers with better internal relations showed greater resilience in the post-9/11 economy; airlines with better internal relations had lower costs, fewer layoffs, and quicker recovery to pre-9/11 stock prices (Gittell et al., 2006). Similarly, an ethnographic study of a midwifery practice showed how that practice's emphasis on social relationships and humanistic values benefited patient service and staff development (Wooten and Crane, 2004). And in a study of management teams, Losada and Heaphy (2004) described how the highest performing teams on unit profitability, customer satisfaction, and 360-degree evaluations were characterized by more positive communication and interpersonal connection among members.

Interestingly, the performance effects observed in all of these studies resulted from combining positive relationships with some other 'non-POS' factor. For example, Gittell and colleagues (2006) found that airlines recovered more quickly when they had positive relations and greater financial resources. Similarly, the successful management teams in Losada and Heaphy (2004) could be identified by their ratio of positive to negative communication. Interactive effects of this sort suggest the need to simultaneously consider both POS and 'non-POS' phenomena in studying organizational behavior.

### Psychological capital

This is a second-order construct comprised of resilience, optimism, self-efficacy, and hope (Luthans et al., 2007). Several studies have examined its effects in organizations. One study linked psychological capital to reduced absenteeism, and found it was a better predictor of involuntary absenteeism than job satisfaction or organizational commitment (Avey et al., 2006). In another study, nurses' psychological capital predicted their own intentions to stay in their job and their supervisors' ratings of their organizational commitment (Luthans and Jensen, 2005). A third study found that psychological capital predicted supervisory ratings of worker performance (Luthans et al., 2005). As such, the positive individual state of psychological capital has been linked to improved health, motivation, commitment, and performance, suggesting its potentially broad importance in understanding organizational behavior.

### Absence of negativity

The importance of a POS perspective depends on positive phenomena involving more than the absence of negative ones (Cameron and Caza, 2004; Dutton and Glynn, 2007). If one can achieve POS processes and outcomes simply by eliminating ineffective practices,

then there is little that is unique about positiveness. However, if there are important differences between reducing the negative and increasing the positive, then distinct study of positive phenomena is merited (Roberts, 2006).

Britt and colleagues' (2007) results suggest that there is indeed a difference between that which is positive and an absence of that which is negative. Their survey study of soldiers deployed in Kosovo tested the idea that morale, defined as a positive construct of individual motivation and enthusiasm to accomplish the organizational mission, was distinct from depression (Britt et al., 2007). The authors challenged the prevailing view that morale and depression were opposing anchors of a single dimension and used their survey results to show that the two were distinct constructs. While both were influenced by individuals' confidence in their leaders, meaningful work was only important to morale, whereas stress was only a predictor of depression. Since morale and depression had different antecedents, they were distinct phenomena, and this implies that positiveness is not simply an absence of negativity.

In a similar vein, Pittinsky and Shih (2004) presented indirect support for the value of a POS perspective. Their survey of Internet and software workers showed that, contrary to traditional expectations, job change did not reduce commitment to the organization during tenure. In an era of portfolio careers and high organizational mobility, most individuals can expect to work for multiple companies, and this would seem to reduce the potential for commitment to any particular organization, especially in contrast to an individual who has lifetime employment with one organization. However, Pittinsky and Shih (2004) showed that this is not necessarily true, and that commitment was possible even among highly mobile knowledge workers.

However, not all results were so clearly supportive. Ellis and colleagues' (2006) lab study suggested that a positive focus is not helpful for task learning. They used a computer-based business simulation to test the effect of different post-event review strategies.

Participants completed the simulation, and then took part in facilitated interventions to help them improve their performance. There were three interventions, one each focusing on successes, failures, or both success and failure. The results from a second round of the simulation showed that those who focused only on success did no better than a control group with no intervention, and that an analysis of failures tended to produce the greatest increase in subsequent performance. These results may raise some questions about success-focused interventions, and certainly serve to emphasize the need to address both positive and negative phenomena in organizations (e.g., Bagozzi, 2003).

### Summary

The studies described above include a wide range of methods and contexts, and they cross all levels of analysis. It is therefore clear that POS is not a focused analytic approach in the way that population ecology or network theory are defined approaches. However, there are notable regularities across these studies. One concerns the location of the POS phenomena. Eighteen of the papers used distinctively POS phenomena to explain traditional outcomes, while only six studied specifically POS outcomes. Therefore, although POS has been described as the study of positive enablers, processes, and outcomes, the research conducted thus far has been primarily concerned with using POS to explain familiar, 'non-POS,' outcomes such as profit and retention.

One can also conclude from these studies that there is value in a POS perspective. The evidence reviewed here suggests that positiveness is more than the absence of negativity, and so there is a need to study positiveness as such. At the same time, it seems clear that the ideal approach would be to study relevant positive and negative phenomena simultaneously. It has been shown that, under some conditions, positive phenomena can produce undesirable results (e.g., reduced learning from a focus on success, Ellis *et al.*, 2006 or overconfidence resulting from pride, Verbeke *et al.*, 2004). Likewise, the benefits

of positive behaviors may be contingent on the presence of other behaviors that are more traditionally studied in organization studies, such as morale's dependence on confidence in leadership (Britt *et al.*, 2007), or positive relationship benefits depending on adequate financial reserves (Gittell *et al.*, 2006).

## POSITIVE ORGANIZATIONAL SCHOLARSHIP: PRACTICE

Practicing and applying POS in organizations has taken a variety of forms, including the writing of case studies to document especially positive organizational performance, developing specific tools and techniques for generating positive effects among workers, and designing university courses and executive education programs centered on POS knowledge. Examples include Hess and Cameron's (2006) case studies of the positive practices used in a variety of organizations. In addition, specific tools and techniques aimed at enhancing positive outcomes for individuals or organizations have been developed, such as the Reflected Best-Self Instrument (Quinn *et al.*, 2003; Roberts *et al.*, 2007), the Reciprocity Ring (Baker, 2007), Appreciative Inquiry Summits (Cooperrider and Whitney, 2005), and supportive communication techniques (Dutton, 2003a; Cameron, 2007). These tools, and others, are being applied in a variety of organizational settings. Case studies of extraordinary leaders or organizations also have been produced for teaching purposes (e.g., Dutton *et al.*, 2002; Baker and Gunderson, 2005; Bek *et al.*, 2007). In addition, undergraduate and graduate courses based on POS have been designed and taught in several colleges and universities (syllabi for many of these courses are available from the Center for POS at http://www.bus.umich.edu/Positive).

Relative to this volume of applied work, there has been relatively little formal study of the effect of POS interventions. This is primarily due to the constraints of detecting effects from planned organizational interventions while controlling for possible confounds.

Moreover, organization-level interventions have been rarer than individual-level ones. However, some reports have been made, with results suggesting that positivity in practice is associated with higher levels of performance.

For example, Cameron and Lavine (2006) studied the exceptional performance of a company that cleaned up and closed a nuclear production facility 60 years ahead of schedule, $30 billion under budget, and to standards 13 times greater than federally required. This was arguably the most remarkable example of organizational success in recent memory. More than three million square feet of buildings had to be decontaminated and removed, over 100 tons of plutonium residues had to be neutralized and disposed of, and numerous protesters had to be converted into supporters and advocates. During the cleanup, union members were motivated to work themselves out of a job as quickly as possible, an approach contradictory to traditional union priorities, while maintaining levels of morale and safety that exceeded industry averages by a factor of two. Cameron and Lavine (2006) explained this remarkable performance as a product of 21 different positive organizational practices.

Another intervention study was reported in which two different organizations which had been suffering through periods of downsizing and deteriorating performance each implemented a new change agenda grounded in POS practices. In both of these organizations performance improvements were significant, and employees attributed the success to the implementation of POS principles (Cameron, 2003). Of course, causality could not be determined in either of these two organizations because data were collected after the turnaround had begun to occur.

In contrast to the limited study of organization-level practice, there has been more extensive study of positively oriented interventions at the individual level, largely as a result of positive psychology (e.g., Seligman *et al.*, 2005). However, because the emphasis here is on POS, only those individual interventions with a specifically organizational focus are considered. One example

is work by Grant and associates (2007) that found that the perceived meaningfulness of work could be enhanced by personal interaction. Workers who had direct contact with the beneficiaries of their work subsequently displayed more task persistence. These workers also had significantly greater productivity in routine tasks, producing more than one and a half times the output of those who did not have contact with beneficiaries.

Baker, Cross, and Wooten (2003) discovered that 'positive energizers' (individuals who uplift and boost others) had higher performance than 'negative energizers' (people who deplete the good feelings and enthusiasm of others). In fact, individuals who provided positive energy to many people were four times more likely to succeed than individuals who were at the center of information or influence networks. Moreover, the performance enhancement associated with positive energy was also conveyed to those interacting with the energizer. Baker, Cross, and Parker (2004) further reported that high performing organizations have three times as many positive energizers as average organizations. Because positive energy is not a personality trait, but rather a behavioral attribute, training in the enhancement of positive energy was reported to be part of an intervention agenda in some of these organizations.

The strengths-based research of the Gallup Organization has also led to a number of organizational training activities. Reports from this training suggest that identifying employee strengths and then providing the opportunity to use those strengths produces significant performance enhancements. For example, managers who spent more time with their strongest performers, as compared to spending it with their weakest performers, achieved double productivity in their units. Likewise, in organizations where workers were given a chance each day to do what they do best, productivity was one and a half times greater than in the typical organization (Clifton and Harter, 2003).

Taken together, these examples provide some support for the benefits of POS-related practices in real-world work settings. As yet, not enough is known to draw firm conclusions regarding the what, how, or when of such interventions, but there is suggestive evidence that practices based on POS can benefit individuals and organizations. Thus, in addition to the personal benefit, there may be organizational reasons to enhance virtues such as gratitude, foster positive energy, increase work meaningfulness, and build on individual strengths.

## CHALLENGES AND OPPORTUNITIES

The most fundamental challenge to POS is clearly whether (or when) its fundamental humanistic assumption is appropriate. As noted earlier, Fineman (2006) provides a cogent discussion on this topic, so it will not be duplicated here. However, even when one accepts the starting premise of POS, a number of important challenges and opportunities remain. These are discussed below.

### Clarifying 'positive'

As noted at the outset, POS has yet to offer a definitive statement about what constitutes positiveness in organizations. The language used often implies that there is some universal standard by which positiveness can be judged, but that standard has yet to be specified (e.g., Cameron *et al.*, 2003a; Cameron and Caza, 2004). Most likely there is no easy resolution to this matter, as shown by the challenges of definition faced in other fields. Biologists, engaged in the study of life, do not have a universally accepted definition of life, and most of their proposed definitions involve outcomes rather than independent criteria (e.g., it is alive if it metabolizes, reproduces, and adapts). Similarly, Justice Stewart's (Jacobellis v. Ohio 1964) famous remarks about not being able to define pornography, but knowing it when he saw it, suggest that recognizing a phenomenon and succinctly defining it are very different endeavors (also see Dutton, 2003b).

At present, consistent with the humanism at the heart of POS, it seems to be assumed that enabling the inherently eudemonic nature of individuals and their organizations will lead to positive behavior, create positive dynamics, and produce positive results. Unfortunately, the empirical evidence suggests more complex relationships. Positive emotions can produce negative behaviors (Verbeke *et al.*, 2004), negative emotions can produce positive behaviors (Bagozzi, 2003), and positive behaviors may produce negative results (Lee *et al.*, 2003; Ellis *et al.*, 2006). Given this, one has to wonder what ultimately counts as positive. If a cause or process is only labeled positive when it produces a positive result, then the definition threatens to become circular or meaningless. For example, if it is true that positive phenomena rarely arise from blissful or tranquil circumstances (Cameron and Caza, 2004), then discord and turmoil play a crucial role in generating positive phenomena. Given this, if a positive process is defined by its positive product, then discord and turmoil would be positive enablers.

There seem to be at least two possible responses to the challenge of defining positiveness. One would be adopting some prescriptive norm of positiveness. Some POS researchers seem inclined in this direction (e.g., Spreitzer and Sonenshein, 2003), and this is the solution used by positive psychology. Although there is some debate about specifics (e.g., Beutler and Malik, 2002), the *Diagnostic and Statistical Manual of Mental Disorders* (American Psychiatric Association, 1994) provides a broadly accepted description of normal psychology. As such, it is straightforward for psychologists to define negative as worse than normal and positive as better than normal. One option for POS is to develop a comparable standard to serve as the basis for judgments of positiveness. The other option would be more contingent, requiring specification of the factors and processes that condition the local meaning of positiveness (e.g., Bagozzi, 2003; Lee *et al.*, 2003). Whichever solution is adopted, clarity about positiveness seems crucial to the continued development and coherence of POS as a perspective.

## Positive–negative interactions

It has been noted that the most dramatic examples of positive outcomes are observed amidst poor conditions (Cameron and Caza, 2004). Moreover, it is intuitively obvious that some positive behaviors require negative conditions. There is no need for forgiveness without offense and resilience is meaningless without hardship. Consistent with this, statements of POS stress the intent to counter an undue emphasis on negative phenomena, but not to call for an end to such study (Cameron et al., 2003a; Dutton and Glynn, 2007; also see Luthans and Youssef, 2007). Nonetheless, the excitement generated by POS has the potential to lead to over-correction, and the failure to consider the role of non-positive phenomena (e.g., Bono and Ilies, 2006). Such over-correction should be avoided, as behavior in organizations is complex and reliably multi-causal (Mohr, 1982). The full insight of the POS perspective can likely only be realized in interaction with non-positive phenomena, as shown by the results reviewed earlier. Consider, for example, that pride can produce positive and negative outcomes simultaneously (Verbeke et al., 2004), and that group performance is explained by the ratio of positive to negative communication (Losada and Heaphy, 2004). As these examples show, organizational behavior may be best understood by addressing all relevant phenomena, whether positive or not.

## Integration

One of the early concerns raised about POS was construct proliferation (George, 2004). This concern is an instance of a more general issue facing POS, one which is both a challenge and an opportunity, and that is the integration of POS research. Even just within POS, there are exciting possibilities for integration. For example, the study described above by Ellis and colleagues (2006) found that focusing only on success produced little improvement in subsequent task performance. This seems to suggest that focusing on failures is the best way to learn from experience. However, one may interpret these results differently in light of the findings

in Losada and Heaphy (2004). This latter study found that management teams were most successful when their communication consisted of approximately 85% positive comments and 15% negative comments. As such, one wonders if the best post-event learning strategy might not require finding the optimal ratio in which to focus on success and failure. More generally, this example shows the potential benefit of tighter integration within POS research. The excitement of a new perspective may create a heady, open frontier feeling, but it seems that theory would advance more quickly with closer connection between studies.

Of course, the benefits of integration with the larger field of organization studies are of the same sort, only many times greater (see Dutton and Glynn, 2007). POS faces the need to carefully link its new constructs to relevant existing ones. The work on leadership offers an easy example, where the findings about emotion and mood (e.g., Peterson and Luthans, 2003; Kellett et al., 2006) seem quite consistent with pre-existing treatments of leadership (e.g., Pescosolido, 2002). Similarly, there would seem to be natural affinities between the POS work on how virtues influence expectations of corporate social performance (e.g., Giacalone et al., 2005; Andersson et al., 2007) and the existing work on how corporate reputation influences individuals (e.g., Fombrun and Shanley, 1990; Turban and Greening, 1997; Albinger and Freeman, 2000). Such integration will also be important for establishing the discriminant validity of POS constructs. While there is evidence that hope and self-efficacy are distinct, despite their apparent similarity (Magaletta and Oliver, 1999), many other POS constructs have yet to have their independence verified.

## Cultural specificity

POS has been promoted, and primarily studied, in developed Western cultural settings. However, given the POS assumption that all individuals share an inherent desire for that which is positive, comparative cross-cultural research seems essential.

For example, comparative anthropologists have shown that nearly all human societies have some form of incest taboo (Wolf and Durham, 2005), experimental psychologists have shown that the fear of snakes and spiders is a universal human trait (Ohman et al., 2001), and positive psychologists have found evidence of shared values in world religious traditions (Dahsgaard et al., 2005). Demonstrating similarly wide-ranging findings would greatly bolster POS claims about universal drives. Without such evidence, any particular researcher's description of a positive behavior or outcome is subject to criticisms of being culture-bound, or even hegemonic (e.g., Fineman, 2006). Moreover, exploring the dynamics of positive organizing in other cultures would serve to enhance the underlying theory as refinements would surely be required to correct the cultural idiosyncrasies unconsciously included in the initial theory.

Psychological capital provides an illustrative example of this potential (also see Schaufeli et al., 2006). When researchers tested the four-part construct of psychological capital in China, they found that only three of the four components were relevant. Resilience, optimism, and hope were measured as usual, but self-efficacy was dropped from the analysis (Luthans et al., 2005). Although the authors did not explain this omission, it presumably reflects the unique nature of American self-concepts. Kitayama and colleagues (1997) found that American self-esteem benefited from positive feedback, whereas the absence of negative feedback was more beneficial to Japanese self-esteem. If the same is true in China, then it is not surprising that the American notion of positive self-efficacy was uninformative when applied to Chinese workers. Moreover, since the three-part measure of psychological capital had the predicted relationship with performance, it suggests that self-efficacy may be ancillary to the core construct. Self-efficacy may be highly correlated with psychological capital in America, but not in other cultures. As this example shows, POS needs cross-cultural research, both to buttress its claims of universality and to refine its theory.

## Other boundary conditions

Cultural specificity is only one example of potential boundary conditions relevant to POS. The importance of boundary conditions is clearly recognized in most theoretical treatments of POS. However, relatively little research effort has been directed to such issues as yet, though some interesting possibilities have been identified. For example, Andersson and colleagues (2007) found that hope and gratitude predicted concern for employees and social problems, but not for economic, safety, or financial issues. Understanding why would surely enrich theories of hope and gratitude. An important direction for POS will thus be defining boundary conditions, and particularly why positive phenomena are so rare.

The issue of rarity is also important because it raises a potential paradox at the heart of the POS perspective. When thinking about positive phenomena, one may reasonably ask whether the positiveness derives from the activity or its rarity. In other words, is an exceptional behavior positive because it produces a desirable outcome, or because it produces a desirable outcome that is also rare? Most discussions have described POS as the study of positive deviance, as the study of that which is both positive and exceptional (Cameron et al., 2003a; Peterson and Seligman, 2003; Cameron and Caza, 2004; Dutton and Sonenshein, 2007). Given this, suppose that an intervention succeeded in making a positive behavior commonplace. Would that behavior stop being relevant to the concerns of POS? If anyone could do it, would it still be positive? Of course, this returns to the issue of defining positiveness, and thus underscores how fundamental that issue is for the advancement of POS (also see Weick, 2003).

## POS outcomes

As noted in the literature review, most research attention has been devoted to understanding how POS phenomena produce familiar outcomes such as profit and retention. This is presumably to be expected, as the new perspective seeks to establish its validity within the larger field. However, it may be that POS can make its most important contributions by offering alternatives to the familiar outcomes. Given growing public concern about the social role of large organizations (Mitchell, 2001; Margolis and Walsh, 2003), POS may be ideally positioned to contribute to this discussion by suggesting precisely what organizations should be concerned with, in addition to profit and retention (e.g., Dutton *et al.*, 2006).

In concluding this chapter, it is worth noting that the discussion thus far has omitted what may be the most important accomplishment of POS, both in practice and research: excitement. In its first four years, POS has generated books, articles, presentations, cases, workshops, undergraduate and graduate curricula, corporate programs, and dedicated research centers. Moreover, anecdotal evidence indicates that many of those involved in POS derive great motivation and satisfaction from it (e.g., Luthans, 2002; Bernstein, 2003; Dutton, 2003b). For these reasons, it seems wise to remain conscious of the tension between the specificity demands of theoretical precision and the openness that allows the widest range of inclusion and discovery.

## ACKNOWLEDGEMENT

We are grateful to Brianna Caza, Jane Dutton and Bob Quinn for assistance with early drafts of this chapter.

## REFERENCES

Akhtar, M. (1968) 'Affect and memory: An experimental note', *Pakistan Journal of Psychology*, 1: 25–27.

Albinger, H.S. and Freeman, S.J. (2000) 'Corporate social performance and attractiveness as an employer to different job seeking populations', *Journal of Business Ethics*, 28 (3): 243–253.

American Psychiatric Association (1994) *Diagnostic and Statistical Manual of Mental Disorders*, 4th edn. Washington, DC: American Psychiatric Association.

Andersson, L.M., Giacalone, R.A. and Jurkiewicz, C.L. (2007) 'On the relationship of hope and gratitude to corporate social responsibility', *Journal of Business Ethics*, 70: 401–409.

Avey, J.B., Patera, J.K. and West, B.J. (2006) 'The implications of positive psychological capital on employee absenteeism', *Journal of Leadership and Organizational Studies*, 13 (2): 42–60.

Bagozzi, R.P. (2003) 'Positive and negative emotions in organizations', in K.S. Cameron, J.E. Dutton and R.E. Quinn (eds) *Positive Organizational Scholarship: Foundations of a New Discipline*. San Francisco, CA: Berrett-Koehler Publishers Inc., pp. 176–193.

Baker, W. (2007) *The Reciprocity Ring*. University of Michigan: Center for Positive Organizational Scholarship.

Baker, W. and Gunderson, R. (2005) *Zingerman's Community of Businesses*. University of Michigan: Center for Positive Organizational Scholarship.

Baker, W., Cross, R. and Parker, A. (2004) 'What creates energy in organizations?', *Sloan Management Review*, 44: 51–56.

Baker, W., Cross, R. and Wooten, M. (2003) 'Positive organizational network analysis and energizing relationships', in K.S. Cameron, J.E. Dutton and R.E. Quinn (eds) *Positive Organizational Scholarship: Foundations of a New Discipline*. San Francisco, CA: Berrett-Koehler Publishers Inc., pp. 328–342.

Bek, J., Benedetto, K., Feldman, E., Goldenberg, S., Jaffe, A., Lavery, B., Martin, C., Waller, A., Dutton, J.E., Grant, A.M. and Russo, B. (2007) *A Foundation of Giving: How One Company Cares for Its Employees*. University of Michigan: Center for Positive Organizational Scholarship.

Berle, A.A.J. (1932) 'Corporate powers as powers in trust', *Harvard Law Review*, 45 (6): 1049–1074.

Bernstein, S.D. (2003) 'Positive organizational scholarship: Meet the movement: An interview with Kim Cameron, Jane Dutton, and Robert Quinn', *Journal of Management Inquiry*, 12 (3): 266–271.

Beutler, L.E. and Malik, M.L. (eds) (2002) *Rethinking the DSM: A Psychological Perspective*. Washington, DC: American Psychological Association.

Blankenship, R.E. (2002) *Molecular Mechanisms of Photosynthesis*. London: Blackwell.

Bono, J.E. and Ilies, R. (2006) 'Charisma, positive emotion and mood contagion', *Leadership Quarterly*, 17: 317–334.

Boucher, J. and Osgood, C.E. (1969) 'The Pollyanna hypothesis', *Journal of Verbal Learning and Verbal Behavior*, 8: 1–8.

Bright, D., Cameron, K.S. and Caza, A. (2006) 'The ethos of virtuousness in downsized organizations', *Journal of Business Ethics*, 64 (3): 249–269.

Britt, T.W., Dickinson, J.M., Moore, D., Castro, C.A. and Adler, A.B. (2007) 'Correlates and consequences of moral versus depression under stressful conditions', *Journal of Occupational Health Psychology*, 12 (1): 34–47.

Burke, R.M. (2001) *Appreciative Inquiry: A Literature Review*. Appreciative Inquiry Commons Working Paper.

Cameron, K.S. (2003) 'Organizational virtuousness and performance', in K.S. Cameron, J.E. Dutton, and R.E. Quinn (eds) *Positive Organizational Scholarship: Foundations of a New Discipline*. San Francisco, CA: Berrett-Koehler Publishers Inc., pp. 48–65.

Cameron, K.S. (2007) 'Building relationships by communicating supportively', in D.A. Whetten and K.S. Cameron (eds) *Developing Management Skills*. Upper Saddle River, NJ: Prentice Hall, pp. 229–272.

Cameron, K.S. and Caza, A. (2002) 'Organizational and leadership virtues and the role of forgiveness', *Journal of Leadership and Organizational Studies*, 9 (1): 33–48.

Cameron, K.S. and Caza, A. (2004) 'Contributions to the discipline of positive organizational scholarship', *American Behavioral Scientist*, 47 (6): 731–739.

Cameron, K.S. and Lavine, M. (2006) *Making the Impossible Possible*. San Francisco, CA: Berrett-Koehler.

Cameron, K.S., Bright, D. and Caza, A. (2004) 'Exploring the relationships between organizational virtuousness and performance', *American Behavioral Scientist*, 47 (6): 766–790.

Cameron, K.S., Dutton, J.E. and Quinn, R.E. (2003a) 'Foundations of positive organizational scholarship', in K.S. Cameron, J.E. Dutton and R.E. Quinn (eds) *Positive Organizational Scholarship: Foundations of a New Discipline*. San Francisco, CA: Berrett-Koehler Publishers Inc., pp. 3–13.

Cameron, K.S., Dutton, J.E. and Quinn, R.E. (eds) (2003b) *Positive Organizational Scholarship: Foundations of a New Discipline*. San Francisco, CA: Berrett-Koehler Publishers Inc.

Caza, B.B. and Caza, A. (2008) 'Positive organizational scholarship: A critical theory approach', *Journal of Management Inquiry*, 17 (1): 21–33.

Clifton, D.O. and Harter, J.K. (2003) 'Investing in strengths', in K.S. Cameron, J.E. Dutton and R.E. Quinn (eds) *Positive Organizational Scholarship: Foundations of a New Discipline*. San Francisco, CA: Berrett-Koehler Publishers Inc., pp. 111–121.

Cooperrider, D.L. (2000) 'Positive image, positive action: The affirmative bias of organizing', in D.L. Cooperrider, P.F. Sorenson, D. Whitney and T.F. Yeager (eds) *Appreciative Inquiry*. Champaign, IL: Stipes, pp. 29–53.

Cooperrider, D.L. and Whitney, D. (2005) *Appreciative Inquiry: A Positive Revolution in Change*. San Francisco, CA: Berrett-Koehler Publishers, Inc.

Cooperrider, D.L., Sorenson, P.F., Whitney, D. and Yeager, T.F. (eds) (2000) *Appreciative Inquiry*. Champaign, IL: Stipes.

Csikszentmihalyi, M. (1996) *Creativity: Flow and the Psychology of Discovery and Invention*. New York: Harper Collins.

Cummings, T.G. and Worley, C.G. (2005) *Organization Development and Change*, 8th edn. Mason, OH: Thomson South-Western.

D'Amato, M.R. and Jagoda, H. (1962) 'Effect of early exposure to photic stimulation on brightness discrimination and exploratory behavior', *Journal of Genetic Psychology*, 101 (2): 267–271.

Dahsgaard, K., Peterson, C. and Seligman, M.E.P. (2005) 'Shared virtue: The convergence of valued human strengths across culture and history', *Review of General Psychology*, 9 (3): 203–213.

Day, H. (1966) 'Looking time as a function of stimulus variables and individual differences', *Perceptual and Motor Skills*, 22: 423–428.

Dodd, E.M.J. (1932) 'For whom are corporate managers trustees?', *Harvard Law Review*, 45 (7): 1145–1163.

Donaldson, T. and Preston, L.E. (1995) 'The stakeholder theory of the corporation: Concepts, evidence, and implications', *Academy of Management Review*, 20 (1): 65–91.

Duchon, D. and Plowman, D.A. (2005) 'Nurturing the spirit at work: Impact on work unit performance', *Leadership Quarterly*, 16: 807–833.

Durlak, J.A. and Wells, A.M. (1997) 'Primary prevention programs for children and adolescents: A meta-analytic review', *American Journal of Community Psychology*, 25: 115–152.

Dutton, J.E. (2003a) *Energizing Your Workplace: Building and Sustaining High Quality Relationships at Work*. San Francisco: Jossey-Bass.

Dutton, J.E. (2003b) 'Breathing life into organizational studies', *Journal of Management Inquiry*, 12 (1): 5–19.

Dutton, J.E. and Glynn, M. (2007) 'Positive organizational scholarship', in C. Cooper and J. Barling (eds) *Handbook of Organizational Behavior*. Thousand Oaks, CA: Sage.

Dutton, J.E. and Sonenshein, S. (2007) 'Positive organizational scholarship', in S. Lopez, and A. Beauchamps (eds) *Encyclopedia of Positive Psychology*. Malden, MA: Blackwell Publishing.

Dutton, J.E., Quinn, R. and Pasick, R. (2002) *The Heart of Reuters*. University of Michigan: Center for Positive Organizational Scholarship.

Dutton, J.E., Worline, M.C., Frost, P.J. and Lilius, J. (2006) 'Explaining compassion organizing', *Administrative Science Quarterly*, 51 (1): 59–96.

Ellis, S., Mendel, R. and Nir, M. (2006) 'Learning from successful and failed experience: The moderating role of kind after-event review', *Journal of Applied Psychology*, 91 (3): 669–680.

Fineman, S. (2006) 'On being positive: Concerns and counterpoints', *Academy of Management Review*, 31 (2): 270–291.

Fombrun, C. and Shanley, M. (1990) 'What's in a name? Reputation building and corporate strategy', *Academy of Management Journal*, 33 (2): 233–258.

Freud, S. (1938) *The Basic Writing of Sigmund Freud*, translated by A. A. Brill. New York: Modern Library.

Fry, L.W., Vitucci, S. and Cedillo, M. (2005) 'Spiritual leadership and army transformation: Theory, measurement, and establishing a baseline', *Leadership Quarterly*, 16: 835–862.

George, J.M. (2004) 'Book review of 'positive organizational scholarship: Foundations of a new discipline', *Administrative Science Quarterly*, 49(2): 325–330.

Giacalone, R.A., Paul, K. and Jurkiewicz, C.L. (2005) 'A preliminary investigation into the role of positive psychology in consumer sensitivity to corporate social performance', *Journal of Business Ethics*, 58: 295–305.

Giddens, A. (1979) *Central Problems in Social Theory: Action, Structure, and Contradiction in Social Analysis*. Berkeley, CA: University of California Press.

Gittell, J.H., Cameron, K., Lim, S. and Rivas, V. (2006) 'Relationships, layoffs, and organizational resilience: Airline industry responses to September 11', *Journal of Applied Behavioral Science*, 42 (3): 300–329.

Grant, A.M., Campbell, E.M., Chen, G., Cottone, K., Lapedis, D. and Lee, K. (2007) 'Impact and the art of motivation maintenance: The effects of contact with beneficiaries on persistent behavior', *Organizational Behavior and Decision Processes*, 103 (1): 53–67.

Hess, E.D. and Cameron, K.S. (2006) *Leading with Values: Positivity, Virtue, and High Performance*. Cambridge: Cambridge University Press.

Hobbes, T. (1651) *Leviathan: The Matter, Forme, and Power of a Common-wealth Ecclesiasticall and Civill*. London: Andrew Crooke.

Hoffman, A.J. (1996) 'A strategic response to investor activism', *Sloan Management Review*, Winter: 51–64.

Holmes, D.S. (1970) 'Differential change in affective intensity and the forgetting of unpleasant personal experiences', *Journal of Personality and Social Psychology*, 15: 234–239.

Ilies, R., Nahrgang, J.D. and Morgeson, F.O. (2007) 'Leader-member exchange and citizenship behaviors: A meta-analysis', *Journal of Applied Psychology*, 92 (1): 269–277.

Jahoda, M. (1958) *Current Concepts of Positive Mental Health*. New York: Basic Books.

Katz, D. (1964) 'The motivational basis of organizational behavior', *Behavioral Science*, 9: 131–133.

Kellett, J.B., Humphrey, R.H. and Sleeth, R.G. (2006) 'Empathy and the emergence of task and relations leaders', *Leadership Quarterly*, 17: 146–162.

Kitayama, S., Markus, H.R., Matsumoto, H. and Norasakkunkit, V. (1997) 'Individual and collective processes in the construction of self: Self-enhancement in the United States and self-criticism in Japan', *Journal of Personality and Social Psychology*, 72: 1245–1267.

Kunz, D. (1974) 'Response faults on word association as a function of associative difficulty and of affective connotation of the words', *Journal of Consulting and Clinical Psychology*, 42: 231–235.

Lee, F., Caza, A., Edmondson, A.C. and Thomke, S. (2003) 'New knowledge creation in organizations', in K.S. Cameron, J.E. Dutton and R.E. Quinn (eds) *Positive Organizational Scholarship: Foundations of a New Discipline*. San Francisco, CA: Berrett-Koehler Publishers Inc., pp. 194–206.

Losada, M. and Heaphy, E.D. (2004) 'The role of positivity and connectivity in the performance of business teams', *American Behavioral Scientist*, 47 (6): 740–765.

Luborsky, L., Blinder, B. and Mackworth, N. (1963) 'Eye fixation and recall of pictures as a function of GSR responsivity', *Perceptual and Motor Skills*, 16: 469–483.

Luthans, F. (2002) 'The need for and meaning of positive organizational behavior', *Journal of Organizational Behavior*, 23: 695–706.

Luthans, F. and Avolio, B. (2003) 'Authentic leadership development', in K.S. Cameron, J.E. Dutton and R.E. Quinn (eds) *Positive Organizational Scholarship: Foundations of a New Discipline*. San Francisco, CA: Berrett-Koehler Publishers Inc., pp. 241–258.

Luthans, F. and Youssef, C.M. (2007) 'Emerging positive organizational behavior', *Journal of Management*, 33 (3): 321–349.

Luthans, F., Avey, J.B., Avolio, B.J., Norman, S.M. and Combs, G.M. (2006) 'Psychological capital development: Toward a micro-intervention', *Journal of Organizational Behavior*, 27: 387–393.

Luthans, F., Avolio, B.J., Walumbwa, F.O. and Li, W. (2005) 'The psychological capital of Chinese workers: Exploring the relationship with performance', *Management and Organization Review*, 1 (2): 249–271.

Luthans, F., Youssef, C.M. and Avolio, B.J. (2007) *Psychological Capital*. Oxford: Oxford University Press.

Luthans, K.W. and Jensen, S.M. (2005) 'The linkage between psychological capital and commitment to organizational mission: A study of nurses', *Journal of Nursing Administration*, 35 (6): 304–310.

Magaletta, P.R. and Oliver, J.M. (1999) 'The hope construct, will and ways: Their relations with self-efficacy, optimism, and well-being', *Journal of Clinical Psychology*, 55: 539–551.

Mann, J.W. (1968) 'Defining the unfavorable by denial', *Journal of Verbal Learning and Verbal Behavior*, 7: 760–766.

Margolis, J.D. and Walsh, J.P. (2003) 'Misery loves companies: Rethinking social initiatives by business', *Administrative Science Quarterly*, 48: 268–305.

Maslow, A. (1968) *Toward a Psychology of Being*. New York: Van Nostrand.

Matlin, M.W. (1970) 'Response competition as a mediating factor in frequency-affect relationship', *Journal of Personality and Social Psychology*, 16: 536–552.

Matlin, M.W. and Stang, D.J. (1975) 'Some determinants of word frequency estimates', *Perceptual and Motor Skills*, 40: 923–929.

Matlin, M.W. and Stang, D.J. (1978) *The Pollyanna Principle: Selectivity in Language, Memory, and Thought*. Cambridge, MA: Schenkman Publishing.

Matlin, M.W. Stang, D.J., Gawron, V.J., Freedman, A. and Derby, P.L. (1979) 'Evaluative meaning as a determinant of spew position', *Journal of General Psychology*, 100 (1): 3–11.

Meltzer, H. (1930) 'The present status of experimental studies on the relationship of feeling to memory', *Psychological Review*, 37: 124–139.

Mitchell, L.E. (2001) *Corporate Irresponsibility: America's Newest Export*. New Haven, CT: Yale University Press.

Mohr, L.B. (1982) *Explaining Organizational Behavior*. San Francisco, CA: Jossey-Bass.

Morris, S.A. (1997) 'Internal effects of stakeholder management devices', *Journal of Business Ethics*, 16 (4): 413–424.

Mrosovsky, N. and Kingsmill, S.F. (1985) 'How turtles find the sea', *Z. Tierpsychology*, 67: 237–256.

O'Donohoe, S. and Turley, D. (2006) 'Compassion at the counter: Service providers and bereaved consumers', *Human Relations*, 59 (10): 1429–1448.

OECD (2000) '*Is there a new economy?*' Technical report, Organisation for Economic Co-operation and Development, Paris, France.

Ohman, A., Flykt, A. and Esteves, F. (2001) 'Emotion drives attention: Detecting the snake in the grass', *Journal of Experimental Psychology: General*, 130 (3): 466–478.

Osgood, C.E. and Richards, M.M. (1973) 'From Yang to Yin to and or but', *Language*, 49 (2): 380–412.

Pescosolido, A.T. (2002) 'Emergent leaders as managers of group emotion', *Leadership Quarterly*, 13 (5): 583–599.

Peterson, C. (2006) *A Primer in Positive Psychology*. New York: Oxford University Press.

Peterson, C. and Seligman, M.E.P. (2003) 'Positive organizational studies: Lessons from positive psychology', in K.S. Cameron, J.E. Dutton, and R.E. Quinn (eds) *Positive Organizational Scholarship: Foundations of a New Discipline*. San Francisco, CA: Berrett-Koehler Publishers Inc., pp. 14–28.

Peterson, C. and Seligman, M.E.P. (2004) *Character Strengths and Virtues: A Handbook and Classification*. New York: Oxford University Press.

Peterson, S.J. and Luthans, F. (2003) 'The positive impact and development of hopeful leaders', *Leadership and Organization Development Journal*, 24 (1): 26–31.

Pittinsky, T.L. and Shih, M.J. (2004) 'Knowledge nomads: Organizational commitment and worker mobility in positive perspective', *American Behavioral Scientist*, 46 (6): 791–807.

Podsakoff, P.M., MacKenzie, S.B., Paine, J.B. and Bachrach, D.G. (2000) 'Organizational citizenship behaviors: A critical review of the theoretical and empirical literature and suggestions for future research', *Journal of Management*, 26 (3): 513–563.

Quinn, R.E., Dutton, J.E. and Spreitzer, G.M. (2003) *Reflected Best Self Exercise*. University of Michigan: Center for Positive Organizational Scholarship.

Quinn, R.W. (2005) 'Flow in knowledge work: High performance experience in the design of national security technology', *Administrative Science Quarterly*, 50 (4): 610–641.

Roberts, L.M. (2006) 'Response – Shifting the lens on organizational life: The added value of positive scholarship', *Academy of Management Review*, 31 (2): 292–305.

Roberts, L.M., Dutton, J.E. and Spreitzer, G.M. (2007) *Bringing My Reflected Best Self to Life*. University of Michigan: Center for Positive Organizational Scholarship.

Rogers, C.R. (1980) *A Way of Being*. Boston, MA: Houghton Mifflin.

Rychlak, J.F. (1977) *The Psychology of Rigorous Humanism*. New York: Wiley-Interscience.

Schaufeli, W.B., Bakker, A.B. and Salanova, M. (2006) 'The measurement of work engagement with a short questionnaire: A cross-national study', *Educational and Psychological Measurement*, 66 (4): 701–716.

Scheurich, J.J. (1997) *Research Method in the Postmodern*. Washington, DC: Falmer Press.

Seligman, M.E.P. (1999) 'The president's address', *American Psychologist*, 54: 559–562.

Seligman, M.E.P. and Csikszentmihalyi, M. (2000) 'Positive psychology: An introduction', *American Psychologist*, 55: 5–14.

Seligman, M.E.P., Steen, T.A., Park, N. and Peterson, C. (2005) 'Positive psychology progress: Empirical validation of interventions', *American Psychologist*, 60 (5): 410–421.

Silverstein, A. and Dienstbier, R.A. (1968) 'Rated pleasantness and association value of 101 English nouns', *Journal of Learning and Verbal Behavior*, 7: 81–86.

Smith, C.A., Organ, D.W. and Near, J.P. (1983) 'Organizational citizenship behavior: Its nature and antecedents', *Journal of Applied Psychology*, 68 (4): 653–663.

Smith, J.C. and Baker, H.D. (1960) 'Conditioning in the horseshoe crab', *Journal of Comparative and Physiological Psychology*, 53 (3): 279–281.

Smith, J.M. (1993) *The Theory of Evolution* (Canto edition). Cambridge: Cambridge University Press.

Snyder, C.R. and Lopez, S.J. (2002) *Handbook of Positive Psychology*. New York: Oxford University Press.

Spreitzer, G.M. and Sonenshein, S. (2003) 'Positive deviance and extraordinary organizing', in K.S. Cameron, J.E. Dutton and R.E. Quinn (eds) *Positive Organizational Scholarship: Foundations of a New Discipline*. San Francisco, CA: Berrett-Koehler Publishers Inc., pp. 207–224.

Stang, D.J. (1975) 'Student evaluations on twenty-eight social psychological tests', *Teaching of Psychology*, 2: 12–15.

Stayton, S.E. and Wiener, M. (1961) 'Value, magnitude, and accentuation', *Journal of Applied Psychology*, 62: 145–147.

Thompson, R.H. (1930) 'An experimental study of memory as influenced by feeling tone', *Journal of Experimental Psychology*, 13: 462–467.

Turban, D.B. and Greening, D.W. (1997) 'Corporate social performance and organizational attractiveness to prospective employees', *Academy of Management Journal*, 40 (3): 658–672.

Verbeke, W., Belschak, F. and Bagozzi, R.P. (2004) 'The adaptive consequences of pride in personal selling', *Academy of Marketing Science Journal*, 32 (4): 386–402.

Weick, K.E. (2003) 'Positive organizing and organizational tragedy', in K.S. Cameron, J.E. Dutton and R.E. Quinn (eds) *Positive Organizational Scholarship: Foundations of a New Discipline*. San Francisco, CA: Berrett-Koehler Publishers Inc., pp. 66–80.

Wilson, W.R. and Becknell, J.C. (1961) 'The relationship between the association value, pronouncability, and affectivity of nonsense syllables', *Journal of Psychology*, 52: 47–49.

Wolf, A.P. and Durham, W.H. (eds) (2005) *Inbreeding, Incest, and the Incest Taboo: The State of Knowledge at the Turn of the Century*. Stanford, CA: Stanford University Press.

Wooten, L.P. and Crane, P. (2004) 'Generating dynamic capabilities through a humanistic work ideology: The case of a certified-nurse midwife practice in a professional bureaucracy', *American Behavioral Scientist*, 47 (6): 848–866.

Yarrow, M.R., Campbell, J.D. and Burton, R.V. (1970) 'Recollections of childhood: A study of the retrospective method', *Monographs of the Society for Research in Child Development*, 35: Serial 5.

Zajonc, R.B. (1968) 'Attitudinal effects of mere exposure', *Journal of Personality and Social Psychology*, 9: 1–27.

# PART TWO

# Macro-Organizational Behaviour and Immanent Processes

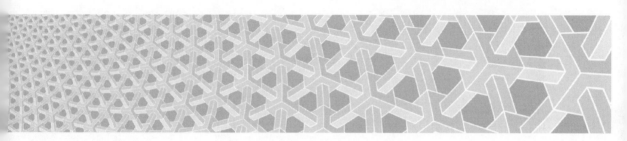

# 6

# Organizational Learning: The Dynamic Flow of Macro and Micro Forces

Elena P. Antonacopoulou

## INTRODUCTION

If learning is an integral part of living; if working life demands learning as a condition of survival; if learning is an essential human condition, why is it that we have such difficulty engaging with the phenomenon? The intimate relationship between learning and working life is one that does not easily lend itself to analysis partly because it is embedded in the dynamics of our human engagement with the challenges of living and working. Learning is both process and product, a cause, a consequence and context in which emerging life and work patterns co-evolve and, in turn, organize learning. No one single perspective in current learning theory is sufficient to capture fully the multiple connections and possibilities that learning creates and from which it emerges. Yet, if we seek to move the learning debate forward we must learn to work and live with the complexity of learning in ways that we

can usefully engage and employ to help us address many of the challenges that working life presents.

The need to capture the dynamics of learning in working life is a long-standing challenge in learning research. There has been a tendency to examine learning by using change as a measure for such dynamics. Therefore, much current thinking equates learning with change and presents them as interdependent, even synonymous (Alderfer and Brown, 1975; Friedlander, 1984; Handy, 1989). This perspective is dominant in views which position learning as important for surviving the challenge of change (Heywood, 1989; Clark, 1991; Cunningham, 1994), as well as, views which argue that for effective change to take place organizations and individuals must first learn (Fiol and Lyles, 1985; Argyris, 1993; Srivastva et al., 1995). Some commentators refer specifically to Ross Ashby's law of requisite variety (Lessem, 1993; Dixon, 1994). The law of requisite variety states that for an organism/system to survive, its rate of learning must be equal or greater ($L \geq C$) than the rate of change in its environment (Ross Ashby, 1958). Some commentators, however, also present a counter argument drawing on empirical findings at the group (Cook and Yanow, 1993) and individual levels (Antonacopoulou, 1998; 1999; 2004a). Their analysis suggests that the social, emotional and political forces at play in the process of learning do not always lead to change and transformation. Instead, learning aims to provide a degree of stability by reinforcing the status quo through a focus on what is known rather than a drive towards the unknown.

We need to move beyond conceptualisations of learning and changing as stable patterns of routines and practices. We need to embrace more fully the emergent, self-organizing practices that shape learning in relation to the multiplicity of forces constitutive of work and working life. In pursuing this challenge we need to first carefully reflect on the range of disciplines, which inform the learning debate and take stock of their fundamental epistemological and ontological assumptions about learning. Each of the dominant disciplines (psychology, sociology, philosophy and anthropology; see Easterby-Smith, 1997) that have so far informed the learning debate bring a different set of assumptions to their conceptualization of learning. If we are to come closer to capturing and representing the richness of the learning phenomenon we need to make a concerted effort to integrate these diverse perspectives and assumptions, as they reveal different aspects of learning. Only then can we begin to engage more fully with the complexity of learning as a phenomenon. Some of the principles of complexity theory which is considered as a trans-disciplinary science may be useful in our efforts to embrace learning more holistically. Ideas from complexity theory (Dooley *et al.*, 2003) and process theories of becoming (Clegg *et al.*, 2005) enable us to explore learning as a flow expanding the space of possibilities. Such a definition of learning employs a mode

of thinking consistent with 'trialectic logic' (Ichazo, 1976; Horn, 1983; Soja, 1997).

Ford and Ford (1994) understand trialectics as a logic strongly related to the science of complexity. The science of complexity might provide a new avenue for rethinking learning. Trialectics offers an alternative logic to formal and dialectic logic, one that focuses on the forces that create different possibilities. The ontological focus is not on the epiphenomena but the unfolding of the phenomena in time and space. Applying this logic to rethinking the nature of learning we can explore not only the synthesis of potentially opposing perspectives as suggested in dialectics or formal logics of change. Additionally, learning can also emerge as different connections and possibilities are explored. Learning therefore, emerges as a space/choros where these possibilities can be contained and it is also a process and product of a multiplicity of interconnections (Antonacopoulou, 2000a; 2002, 2008a).

In this chapter the nature of learning is examined by focusing on the complex interconnections between learning and working life. The analysis paves the way for a re-conceptualisation of learning in relation to work practices. The section which follows introduces a more dynamic way of engaging with learning complexity highlighting interconnectivity, diversity self-organization and politics as key, yet neglected, dimensions in learning debates. These dimensions will be analysed by drawing on the main principles of complexity theory and a new conceptualisation of learning as a flow will be presented. The notion of learning-in-practise will then be introduced as a new perspective drawing attention to the fluidity of learning as a mode of living and working. The chapter concludes with a review of the main implications for future learning research in complex social arrangements such as work organizations.

## LEARNING AS A FLOW

Although complexity science has its roots in the physical sciences, it is increasingly employed to understand social phenomena, including organizations (Ofori-Dankwa and Julian, 2001; Dooley *et al.*, 2003) and their social complexity (Antonacopoulou and Chiva, 2007) as well as specific management issues such as strategic management (Stacey, 1993), strategic change (Stacey, 1995; Brown and Eisenhardt, 1997), innovation management (Cheng and Van de Ven, 1996), and design management (Chiva, 2004). It is also penetrating into adult education debates (Fenwick, 2003) and more recently organizational learning debates (Antonacopoulou and Chiva, 2007).

It is beyond the scope of this discussion to provide a review of the main principles of complexity science (for such reviews see Tsoukas, 1998; Mitleton-Kelly, 2003; Antonacopoulou and Chiva, 2007). It is important to clarify however, that complexity science sets out to devise mechanisms to create and maintain complexity, and to produce tools for its description and analysis (Simon, 1996). Complexity science covers many fields of scientific research, including chaos theory, the study of fractals and the idea of complex adaptive systems (CAS). The ideas of CAS enable us to understand system behaviour in relation to simple actions that may create multiple effects as interacting 'agents' follow rules and influence their local and global environments (Sherman and Schultz, 1998). One of the most important characteristics of CAS systems is their capacity to learn (Gell-Mann, 1994; Stacey, 1995, 1996). Previous research also shows that CAS ideas are relevant in identifying the essential factors that facilitate organizational learning (Chiva, 2003).

Three key principles of complexity science will be employed here to illustrate dimensions of learning for which current debates do not fully account. These are: *interconnectivity, diversity* and *self-organization*. A fourth and equally neglected element in both complexity and learning debates is *politics*. The re-conceptualisation of learning as a complex social process demands that we also pay attention to the socio-political dimensions of complexity.

## INTERCONNECTIVITY

Appreciating the complexity of learning implies a need to understand the interconnections among parts of the process that constitute learning (Kauffman, 1995; Axelrod and Cohen, 1999). Interconnections reflect the fractal nature of learning and demonstrate that a number of elements combine to create what we understand learning to be. Learning is not only a cognitive process resulting from the neural connections as information is connected to create meaning. By the very process of developing meaning, learning is also a highly emotional process that influences how we react and respond to experiences we encounter. These responses generate different psychological states that, combined with related actions are, in turn, contained within structures and systems defined and negotiated by social actors. These social structures, by extension, provide meaning to social interactions and, at the same time, provide an understanding that defines one's identity in the context of one's role in different settings. Therefore, learning as a system is embedded within biological, psychological, social, cultural, and emotional systems, amongst other viable systems, all of which co-exist and co-evolve in relation to internal and external conditions within an ecosystem.

The institutionalisation of learning processes within any (social) system will be subject to ongoing institutional transformations caused by learning practices instituted by social structures. These social structures however, are also constantly negotiated as diverse social forces (agents and structures) interact in the heterogeneous nature of self-organization. Therefore, if learning is about connecting, interconnectivity implies the co-existence of heterogeneous forces (Gell-Mann, 1994).

## DIVERSITY

Heterogeneity and diversity are key dimensions of learning. Diversity is what feeds learning in the way conditions that underpin interactions and connections between systems create tensions. That multiple dimensions exist in tension is to reflect the multiplicity of possibilities each dimension can create by being attracted to different possibilities. Tensions dissolve into the space of possibility and become ex-tensions of current reality. These ex-tensions reflect the elasticity of processes such as learning, as multiple possibilities emerge in the way interconnections are explored. Interconnections are reflective of the in-tension to learn which brings at-tension to some specific possibilities, which are more relevant at different moments in time. Ultimately, this suggests that tensions are not only born out of conflict, power and political differences privileging one mode of reality over another. Instead, tensions are also attractions to different possibilities. It is the way learning space expands to embrace the new spaces learning creates. Therefore, learning is 'the edge of chaos' in the way the tensions between competing forces drives the possible connections that can be productively created as a result of their interaction. Engaged interaction, as opposed to instrumental transaction, challenges conditions of power and control in heterogeneous forces, a perspective that implies that the learning space embraces different perspectives and engages actants in a reflective and reflexive process of learning. In other words, inherent diversity need not lead to a synthesis of conflicting perspectives, as the dialectic logic would suggest. Instead, diversity needs to be maintained as it is a source of dynamism driving self-organization, which is a basic cause, consequence and context for learning, which we frequently refer to as 'understanding'.

## SELF-ORGANIZATION/EMERGENCE

That learning connects heterogeneous forces reflects the ultimate quality of learning; surprise. Learning is not a matter of chance. Learning is part of the stream of practices that constitute organization. Such practices are reflected in routines (Axelrod and Cohen, 1999; Bechky, 2003); models (Stacey, 1996); strategies (Gell-Mann, 1994); culture (Gell-Mann, 1994); or the dominant logic (Bettis and Prahalad, 1995). Regularities in practices enable a system to determine the nature of further experience and make sense of it (Stacey, 1996). Reconfigurations in practices are a consequence of a process of self-organization and co-evolution. Learning practice, therefore, can be re-conceptualized as a process and product of the ongoing mutations in relation to the governing practices and the way these co-evolve in time and space in response to endogenous and exogenous forces. Learning not only arises as a result of noticeable shifts (formal logic) in practices or re-integration of otherwise conflicting perspectives (dialectic logic). Learning also emerges from multiple possibilities previously not explored. Such possibilities may be interpreted as surprise or serendipity depending on whether they are considered relevant or attainable. No single experience determines learning practice, which is unpredictable and uncontrollable (Goodwin, 1994) due to its social nature (Elkjaer, 1999).

Learning therefore, emerges as a natural condition accompanying the creation of a new order that is characterized by self-organization as diverse elements within a system co-evolve and provide both negative and positive feedback to support single loop learning (negative feedback) and double loop learning (positive feedback) (Argyris and Schön, 1978; Stacey, 1996). Essentially, self-organization is the process of re-ordering different aspects of learning, such that new learning can emerge in a cyclical process of ongoing evolution. Learning is, therefore, not only a mode of connecting or an expanse of diverse elements and forces. Learning is also the foundation of learning's possibility as such. Learning provides the energy for connections to be made and highlights the gaps that exist while it also provides the scope for bridging these gaps. Moreover, learning shapes the emerging models that define the boundaries of action while it also opens up multiple modes of interaction. Modes of interaction are not only the emerging patterns of thinking and action, they are also the very social structures that are constantly evolving as social actors become sensitised to new possibilities for learning. These new possibilities are also central to self-organization and the inherent nature of social systems to renew themselves. This process of renewal and ongoing transformation is made possible because learning is endemic to living.

Moreover, learning is central to the systemic nature of social evolution because it highlights the complex (infusion) of connecting forces and the conditions that support their interaction. With such a perspective one not only captures the fluidity that is so central to social systems but also is challenged to explore learning as an integral part of what it means to be a viable system (see Beer, 1972). In other words, self-organization is an inherent mechanism for reaching internal consistency in relation to external forces, a critical point, because it reaffirms the political nature of learning.

## POLITICS AND POWER

The political nature of learning remains one of the biggest challenges in learning research. Researchers who focus on the political nature of learning (Coopey, 1995; Antonacopoulou, 2000b; 2001; 2006b; Lawrence *et al.*, 2005) highlight the inequalities of power and control, the tensions between individual and organizational priorities in learning or the different perspectives and motives underlying learning and knowledge. The politics of learning clearly illustrate that learning does not take place in a vacuum. Learning is a connection of possibilities stimulated by the signals received within the context in which learning takes place. These signals, however, are subject to multiple interpretations which define the actions one takes to make life and work more meaningful. A key dimension of the political nature of learning is revealed at this point, which has been so far neglected,

partly because we have paid insufficient attention to the power of learning. The power of learning is at the core of what makes knowing political. Learning entails responsibility and accountability. It is rather common that social actors tend to negate the responsibility that learning entails by proposing sad excuses about their inability to learn. These defensive routines, as Argyris (2004a) clearly demonstrates in his research, reflect a reluctant tendency to learn even when the need to learn is obvious. Antonacopoulou (1998) describes this state as 'mathophobia', which is reflective of the power of learning to steer a whole host of emotions. It is also the powerful connection between learning and what people do in the name of learning.

To learn therefore, is to make viable connections between a diverse set of emerging possibilities that affect action and interaction with others. To be accountable for one's actions is one of the defining characteristics of those who chose to lead a life of learning (Antonacopoulou and Bento, 2003; Antonacopoulou, 2004b). Responsible action reinforces that learning only gains meaning in the process of interacting with others. This point reasserts the social and political significance of learning, reminding us that learning is not a controllable entity. Rather, learning is better understood as a dynamic complex process, which is embedded in the ways social forces within systems define the conditions of their interaction. Therefore, to say learning is social and political is to appreciate the multiple ways in which learning is manifested in action. How and why people act in relation to their work is defined by their learning and, in turn, defines their understanding, which subsequently guides their actions. In short, political learning is reflective of the emerging tensions that occur as different learning opportunities in life are explored.

All these aspects illustrate the complexity of learning and reinforce the need to explore learning as a complex flow unfolding from the emerging tensions of work practices. It is also these dimensions of learning that we can usefully draw from as we develop further our understanding of the patterns, practices and routines that give life to learning-in-practice.

## LEARNING-IN-PRACTICE

The characteristics of learning as a flow renew the importance of the embeddedness and situatedness of learning, an observation consistent with a growing shift towards a practice-based view, one which has been marked in recent years in many different parts of social science (Schatzki *et al.*, 2001). In management, this has been reflected in an increasing concern with what people actually do as a necessary preamble to theorisation about organizations and organizing (Barley and Kunda, 2001; Nicolini *et al.*, 2003; Whittington, 2003).

The practice-based view has been particularly prominent in the organizational learning and strategy debates where the focus tends to be on the set of actions or activities (praxis of practitioners) and the mediating objects that constitute part of a practice (Gherardi, 1999; 2000; Johnson *et al.*, 2003). It also emphasises the importance of communities of practitioners as the space where the social dynamics of learning are negotiated, thus reinforcing principles of interconnectedness and interdependence between agency and structure, a point which is central both in structuration theory (Giddens, 1984) and in actor network theory (Law, 1999), and, of course, consistent with much thinking underpinning the pragmatist framework that Dewey (see Elkjaer, 2004) introduced to understand participation and experience as integral aspects in the learning process. Therefore, these perspectives encourage us to explore 'learning-as a-practice' engaging not only actions and activities in relation to learning, but also the role of language and other cultural and material artifacts, the nature of social interactions and not least the tacit, situated and almost instinctive responses of actors in the socially networked worlds in which they live. Conceptualizing learning as a practice (Nicolini *et al.*, 2003), reminds us that practices are influence by forces that are

both inside and outside of the organization (Gherardi and Nicolini, 2002; Bechky, 2003). The co-existence of multiple adjoining and interlocking practices forms the heart of their evolution. The normal, everyday execution of practice thus becomes the context of tensions amongst different practices and the groups that embody them. Learning in relation to practice is therefore, an emerging powerful force expanding the space of possibility by connecting actors, work systems and artefacts together. By focusing on this emerging, powerful and connective force we can also open the possibility of engaging with the fractality of practices.

Therefore, if we are to understand this self-organizing process evident in the way practitioners and their practices are interconnected, two issues need to be further developed. One issue is the definition of practice, which needs to become more 'elastic' and multifaceted. The existing literature, provides a number of different perspectives on practice as action (Bourdieu, 1980); practice as structure – language, symbols, tools (Turner, 1994); practice as activity system (Engeström, Miettinen and Punamäki, 1999); practice as social context (Lave and Wenger, 1991); practice as knowing (Nicolini *et al.*, 2003). The literature on organizational routines, as a special kind of practice, becomes relevant here, with their conceptions of routines as sources of efficiency, memory and social order (Nelson and Winter, 1982), flexibility (Pentland and Rueter, 1994; Adler, Goldoftas and Levine, 1997), connections (Feldman and Rafaeli, 2002), change (Feldman and Pentland, 2003) and the creation of resources (Feldman, 2004). A full description of the processes of emergence and self-organization needs consideration of many aspects of practice at the same time.

The second issue that needs theoretical development is the dynamics of the practice. Because of the multi-faceted nature of practice, the existing conceptualizations of institutionalization (Selznick, 1957; Berger and Luckmann, 1966) are potentially reductive, when talking about practice. Studies of institutionalization processes, in fact, tend to emphasize the end result, the institutionalized practice. We need to appreciate that there is no end result to this process, as the view of learning as a flow, introduced in the previous section, suggests there is only a continuous unfolding of what could be referred to as practising. This is an important point that, on the one hand, introduces a trivial distinction between practice and practise; however, on the other hand, it sensitizes us to an important qualitative difference between *a* practice and *its* practise. The Oxford dictionary defines practice as 'the actual doing of something' or 'a way of doing something that is common, habitual or expected' such as the work of a doctor working in general practice. Practise on the other hand, is defined as 'to do something repeatedly or regularly in order to improve one's skill' or 'to do something regularly as part of one's normal behaviour', e.g., to work as a doctor is to be in practise.

Therefore, whilst practice and practicing (Gherardi, 2004) focus on the institutionalization of activities and routines, practise and practising focus on the holistic and emergent nature of practice (Antonacopoulou, 2007). Practice can be conceptualized as a dynamic social process that emerges over time; such a view entails at its core practising attempts which seek to accommodate endogenous and exogenous forces, brought about by ecological, economic, social and political dynamics (Antonacopoulou, 2006b, 2008b). Connections between practices form the core of learning-in-practise as it describes how practices evolve and how learning unfolds through repeated enactments, which configure multiple arenas for negotiations of order, thus involving multiple interdependent stakeholders whose interactions are supported by the degree of learning collaborations they seek to explore (Antonacopoulou and Méric, 2005). By focusing on practise and its emergence, it is possible to map the social network that has an impact on the way practices are orchestrated, through practising attempts. By placing learning practise at the centre of the investigation, it is possible to account more fully for the diverse interests and political forces underpinning learning in time

and space. A practise-centred perspective, as a new dimension in future learning research, can help us potentially develop methodologies for studying the fluidity and interconnectivity of complex social processes, such as learning and working.

There is a critical need, therefore, to refocus attention in future learning research not only on the changes resulting from learning practices but also the practising attempts behind those practices and the changes they entail. Not only a different mode of thinking is entailed but also a different set of epistemological and ontological positions if one is to engage with such fluidity. Epistemologically this would encourage us to explore the practice of learning and working in different contexts, to pay attention to the dynamic relations between individual agency, social structures and systems embedded in social systems, and the complexity of tasks that shape the focus and orientation of learning and experiences of living in such organized arrangements. Ontologically, in extending process research (Pettigrew, 1989; Langley, 1999; Lewis and Grimes, 1999; Scandura and Williams, 2000), instead of studying processes as objects located in time and space, we can embrace the challenge of using the process itself as a foundation for studying the same process. This could be described as a cosmological approach to studying learning, one which would have the capacity to integrate macro and micro dimensions of learning (see Antonacopoulou, 2002).

In capturing the dynamic nature within which practices such as learning emerge, we need also to explore how a practice is practised i.e., rehearsed in performance, if we are to more fully account for how learning is the condition for learning in the same way as change is a condition for changing. The underlying ethos of practise (i.e., the values, beliefs and interpretations surrounding a practice) is just as critical as understanding the behaviours, activities and actions that constitute a practice. This view implies that learning one's practice is not sufficient; practising one's practice is more important (Antonacopoulou, 2004b).

One cannot really master one's practice unless one is prepared to practise it. In other words, by practising one's practice one refines, improves, changes elements of the practice, elements of one's praxis and, ultimately, elements of one's self (e.g., identity).

In the context of this analysis, practice is not only what one does, what actions one takes, but also how one learns to discover the intricate aspects and meanings of one's practice, with the socialisation aspects that are implicit in that. Learning-in-practise reflects the power of learning as part of working life as an extension of practising so that living is purposeful and working can be meaningful.

## CONCLUSIONS

This chapter has outlined the unfinished and ever evolving relationship between learning and working life. The re-conceptualisation of learning extends the view of learning-as-practice to embrace the co-existence of multiple adjoining and interlocking practices which form the heart of learning as part of a co-evolving process of living and working. Learning is, therefore, conceptualized as a flow where multiple and heterogeneous macro and micro forces attract each other and create interconnections that define the emerging purpose of learning, in different contexts, as self-organizing attempts exposing different political agendas. Therefore, learning is not only a practice. It is also a practise; a flow, a flexible ever-changing mode of connecting different practices in ways that enrich learning practice and working life.

The argument has several implications for future learning research. For one, the study of learning needs to advance by recognizing the value of viewing and researching the phenomenon as a connecting force between people, systems and other processes that define the social complexity it seeks to engage with and represent. Therefore, learning is not only the institutionalisation of practices but also a reflection of the self-organizing nature of learning routines, processes and practices.

These issues raise a number of methodological implications for future research in learning, particularly in relation to capturing the social complexity underpinning learning. As others (Argyris, 2004b; Easterby-Smith *et al.*, 2004) have recently pointed out in outlining future research directions in learning research, learning needs to describe the universe as completely as possible. For that it is critical that learning scholars reflect on their learning scholarship and constantly renew their learning practices as they practise, with their emerging ideas about learning. Unless learning scholars learn how to (un)learn, learning research will not progress. The chapter signals the enormity of the task ahead, if learning research is to be driven by its own efforts to support learning about learning.

## ACKNOWLEDGEMENTS

The author would like to acknowledge the support of the ESRC/EPSRC Advanced Institute of Management Research under grant number RES-331-25-0024 for this research. My thanks to Chris Argyris and Tara Fenwick for feedback on an earlier draft of this chapter.

## REFERENCES

Adler, P.S., Goldoftas, B. and Levine, D.I. (1997) 'Flexibility versus efficiency? A case study of model changeovers in the Toyota production system', *Organization Science*, 10 (1): 43–68.

Alderfer, C.P. and Brown L.D. (1975) *Learning from Changing: Organisational Diagnosis and Development.* Thousand Oaks, CA: Sage.

Antonacopoulou, E.P. (1998) 'Developing learning managers within learning organizations', in M. Easterby-Smith, L. Araujo and J. Burgoyne (eds) *Organizational Learning and the Learning Organization: Developments in Theory and Practice.* London: Sage, pp. 214–242.

Antonacopoulou, E.P. (1999) 'Individuals' responses to change: The relationship between learning and knowledge', *Creativity and Innovation Management*, 8 (2): 130–139.

Antonacopoulou, E.P. (2000a) 'Reconnecting education, training and development through learning: A holographic perspective', *Education and Training*, Special Issue on 'Vocational Education and Training in SMEs', 42 (4/5): 255–263.

Antonacopoulou, E.P. (2000b) 'Employee development through self-development in three retail banks', *Personnel Review*, Special Issue on 'New Employee Development: Successful Innovations or Token Gestures?', 29 (4): 491–508.

Antonacopoulou, E.P. (2001) 'The paradoxical nature of the relationship between training and learning', *Journal of Management Studies*, 38 (3): 327–350.

Antonacopoulou, E.P. (2002) Learning as Space: Implications for Organisational Learning. Manchester Business School Research Paper series, No. 443.

Antonacopoulou, E.P. (2004a) 'The dynamics of reflexive practice: The relationship between learning and changing', in M. Reynolds and R. Vince (eds) *Organizing Reflection*. London: Ashgate, pp. 47–64.

Antonacopoulou, E.P. (2004b) 'The virtues of practising scholarship: A tribute to Chris Argyris a "Timeless Learner"'. Special Issue: 'From Chris Argyris and Beyond in Organizational Learning Research', *Management Learning*, 35 (4): 381–395.

Antonacopoulou, E.P. (2006a) 'Working life learning: Learning-in-practise', in E.P. Antonacopoulou, P. Jarvis, V. Andersen, B. Elkjder and S. Haeyrup (eds) *Learning, Working and Living: Mapping the Terrain of Working Life Learning*. London: Palgrave, pp. 234–254.

Antonacopoulou, E.P. (2006b) 'The relationship between individual and organizational learning: New evidence from managerial learning practices', *Management Learning*, 37 (4): 455–473.

Antonacopoulou, E.P. (2008a) 'On the practise of practice: In-tensions and ex-tensions in the ongoing reconfiguration of practice', in D. Barry and H. Hansen (eds) *Handbook of New Approaches to Organization Studies*. London: Sage, pp. 112–131.

Antonacopoulou, E.P. (2008b) 'Strategizing as practising: Strategic learning as a source of connection', in L.A. Costanzo and R.B. McKay (eds) *Handbook of Research on Strategy and Foresight*. London: Sage.

Antonacopoulou, E.P. and Bento R. (2003) 'Methods of "Learning Leadership": Taught and Experiential', in J. Storey (ed.) *Current Issues in Leadership and Management Development*. Oxford: Blackwell, pp. 81–102.

Antonacopoulou, E.P. and Chiva, R. (2007) 'The social complexity of organizational learning dynamics of learning and organizing', Special Issue, *Management Learning*, 38 (3): 277–296.

Antonacopoulou, E.P. and Méric, J. (2005) 'From power to knowledge relationships: Stakeholder interactions as learning partnerships', in M. Bonnafous-Boucher and Y. Pesqueux (eds) *Stakeholders and Corporate Social Responsibility – European Perspectives*. London: Palgrave.

Argyris, C. (1982) *Reasoning, Learning and Action*. San Francisco: Jossey-Bass.

Argyris, C. (1993) *On Organisational Learning*. Cambridge, MA: Blackwell.

Argyris, C. (2004a) *Reasons and Rationalizations: The Limits to Organizational Knowledge*. Oxford: Oxford University Press.

Argyris, C. (2004b) 'Reflecting and beyond in research on organizational learning', Special Issue: 'From Chris Argyris and beyond in research on organizational learning', *Management Learning*, 35 (4): 507–509.

Argyris, C. and Schön, D.A. (1978) *Organisational Learning: A Theory in Action Perspective*. Cambridge, MA: Addison Wesley.

Axelrod, R. and Cohen, M.D. (1999) *Harnessing Complexity*. New York: The Free Press.

Barley, S.R. and Kunda, G. (2001) 'Bringing work back in', *Organization Science*, 12 (1): 76–95.

Bechky, B. (2003) 'Sharing meaning across occupational communities: The transformation of understanding on a production floor', *Organization Science*, 14 (3): 312–330.

Beer, S. (1972) *Brain of the Firm*. London: Penguin.

Berger, P.L. and Luckmann, T. (1966) *The Social Construction of Reality: A Treatise in the Sociology of Knowledge*. London: Penguin.

Bettis, R.A. and Prahalad, C.K. (1995) 'The dominant logic: Retrospective and extension', *Strategic Management Journal*, 16: 5–14.

Bourdieu, P. (1980) *The Logic of Practice*. Stanford, CA: Stanford University Press.

Brown, S.L. and Eisenhardt, K.M. (1997) 'The art of continuous change: Linking complexity theory and time-paced evolution in relentlessly shifting organizations', *Administrative Science Quarterly*, 42: 1–34.

Cheng, Y.T. and Van de Ven, A.H. (1996) 'Learning the innovation journey: Order out of chaos?', *Organization Science*, 7 (6): 593–614.

Chiva, R. (2003) 'The facilitating factors for organizational learning: Bringing ideas from complex adaptive systems', *Knowledge and Process Management*, 10 (2): 99–114.

Chiva, R. (2004) 'Repercussions of complex adaptive systems on product design management', *Technovation*, 24: 707–711.

Clark, N. (1991) *Managing Personal Learning and Change: A Trainer's Guide*. London: McGraw-Hill.

Clegg, S.R., Kornberger, M. and Rhodes, C. (2005) 'Learning/becoming/organizing', *Organization*, 12 (2): 147–167.

Cook, S.D.N. and Yanow, D. (1993) 'Culture and organisational learning', *Journal of Management Inquiry*, December, 2 (4): 373–390.

Coopey, J. (1995) 'The learning organisation: Power, politics and ideology', *Management Learning*, 26 (2): 193–213.

Cunningham, I. (1994) *The Wisdom of Strategic Learning: The Self-managed Learning Solution*. London: McGraw-Hill.

Dixon, N. (1994) *The Organisational Learning Cycle: How Can We Learn Collectively*. London: McGraw-Hill.

Dooley, K.J, Corman, S.R., McPhee, R.D. and Kuhn, T. (2003) 'Modeling high resolution broadband discourse in complex adaptive systems', *Nonlinear Dynamics, Psychology, and Life Sciences*, 7 (1): 61–85.

Easterby-Smith, M. (1997) 'Disciplines of organizational learning: Contributions and critiques', *Human Relations*, 50 (9): 1085–1113.

Easterby-Smith, M., Antonacopoulou, E.P., Lyles, M. and Simms, D. (2004) 'Constructing contributions to organizational learning: Argyris and the new generation', Special Issue: 'From Chris Argyris and beyond in organizational learning research', *Management Learning*, 35 (4): 371–380.

Elkjaer, B. (1999) 'In search of a social learning theory', in M. Easterby-Smith, J. Burgoyne and L. Araujo (eds) *Organizational Learning and the Learning Organization*. London: Sage Publications, pp. 75–91.

Elkjaer, B. (2004) 'Organizational learning: The third way', Special Issue: 'From Chris Argyris and beyond in organizational learning research', *Management Learning*, 35 (4): 419–434.

Engeström, Y., Miettinen, R. and Punamäki, R.-L. (1999) *Perspectives on Activity Theory*. Cambridge: Cambridge University Press.

Feldman, M.S. (2000) 'Organizational routines as a source of continuous change', *Organization Science*, 11 (6): 611–629.

Feldman, M.S. (2004) 'Resources in emerging structures and processes of change', *Organization Science*, 15 (3): 295–309.

Feldman, M.S. and Rafaeli, A. (2002) 'Organizational routines as sources of connection and understanding', *Journal of Management Studies*, 39 (3): 309–331.

Feldman, M.S. and Pentland, B.T. (2003) 'Reconceptualizing organizational routines as a source of flexibility and change', *Administrative Science Quarterly*, 48 (March): 94–118.

Fenwick, T. (2003) 'Reclaiming and re-embodying experiential learning through complexity science', *Studies in the Education of Adults*, 35 (2): 123–141.

Fiol, C.M. and Lyles, M.A. (1985) 'Organisational learning', *Academy of Management Review*, 10 (4): 803–813.

Ford, J. and Ford, L.W. (1994) 'Logics of identity, contradiction, and attraction in change', *Academy of Management Review*, 19 (4): 756–785.

Friedlander, F. (1984) 'Patterns of individual and organisational learning', in P. Shrivastava (ed.) *The Executive Mind*. San Francisco: Jossey-Bass.

Gell-Mann, M. (1994) *The Quark and the Jaguar. Adventures in the Simple and the Complex*. New York: WH Freeman.

Gherardi, S. (1999) 'Learning as problem-driven or learning in the face of mystery?', *Organization Studies*, 20 (1): 101–124.

Gherardi, S. (2000) 'Practice-based theorizing on learning and knowing in organizations', *Organization*, 7 (2): 211–223.

Gherardi, S. and Nicolini, D. (2002) 'Learning in a constellation of interconnected practices: Canon or dissonance?', *Journal of Management Studies*, 39 (4): 419–436.

Giddens, A. (1984) *The Constitution of Society*. Cambridge: Cambridge University Press.

Goodwin, B. (1994) *How the Leopard Changed its Spots: The Evolution of Complexity*. London: Weidenfeld and Nicolson.

Handy, C. (1989) *The Age of Unreason*. London: Arrow.

Heywood, J. (1989) *Learning Adaptability and Change: The Challenge for Education and Industry*. London: Paul Chapman.

Horn, R. (1983) *Trialectics: Towards a Practical Logic of Unity*. Lexington, MD: Information Sources.

Ichazo, O. (1976) *The Human Process for Enlightenment and Freedom*. New York: Arica Institute Press.

Johnson, G., Melin, L. and Whittington, R. (2003) 'Guest editors' introduction: Micro strategy and strategizing: Towards an activity-based view', *Journal of Management Studies*, 40 (1): 3–22.

Kauffman, S.A. (1995) *At Home in the Universe*. Oxford: Oxford University Press.

Langley, A. (1999) 'Strategies for theorizing from process data', *Academy of Management Review*, 24: 691–710.

Lave, J. and Wenger, E. (1991) *Situated Learning: Legitimate Peripheral Participation*. New York: Cambridge University Press.

Law, J. (1999) 'After ANT: complexity, naming and topology', in J. Law and J. Hassard (eds) *Actor Network Theory and After*. Oxford: Blackwell Publishers, pp. 1–14.

Lawrence, T.B., Mauws, M.K., Dyck, B. and Kleysen, R.F. (2005) 'The politics of organizational learning: Integrating power into the 4I framework', *Academy of Management Review*, 30 (1): 180–191.

Lessem, R. (1993) *Business as a Learning Community*. London: McGraw-Hill.

Lewis, M.W. and Grimes, A.J. (1999) 'Meta-triangulation: Building theory from multiple paradigms', *Academy of Management Review*, 24: 672–690.

Mitleton-Kelly, E. (2003) *Complex Systems and Evolutionary Perspectives on Organizations: The Application of Complexity Theory to Organizations*. London: Elsevier.

Nelson, R.R. and Winter, S.G. (1982) *An Evolutionary Theory of Economic Change*. Cambridge, MA: Belknap.

Nicolini, D., Gherardi, S. and Yanow, D. (2003) 'Introduction: Towards a practice-based view of knowing and learning in organizations', in D. Nicolini, S. Gherardi and D. Yanow (eds) *Knowing in Organizations: A Practice-Based Approach*. London: M. E. Sharpe, pp. 3–31.

Ofori-Dankwa, J. and Julian, S.D. (2001) 'Complexifying organizational theory: Illustrations using time research', *Academy of Management Review*, 26: 415–430.

Pentland, B.T. and Rueter, H.H. (1994) 'Organizational routines as grammars of action', *Administrative Science Quarterly*, 39 (3): 484–510.

Pettigrew, A.M. (1989) 'Longitudinal methods to study change: Theory and practice', in R. Mansfield (ed.) *Frontiers of Management Research and Practice*. London: Routledge.

Ross Ashby, W. (1958) 'Requisite variety and its implications for the control of complex systems', *Cybernetica*, 1 (2): 83–99.

Scandura, T.A. and Williams, E.A. (2000) 'Research methodology in management: Current practices, trends and implications for future research', *Academy of Management Journal*, 43: 1248–1264.

Schatzki, T.R., Knorr Cetina, K. and Von Savigny, E. (2001) *The Practice Turn in Contemporary Theory*. London: Routledge.

Selznick, P. (1957) *Leadership in Administration*. Berkeley: University of California Press.

Sherman, H. and Schultz, R. (1998) *Open Boundaries*. New York: Perseus Books.

Simon, H.A. (1996) *The Sciences of the Artificial*. Cambridge, MA: MIT.

Soja, E.W. (1997) *Thirdspace, Journeys to Los Angeles and Other Real-and–Imagined Places*. Oxford: Blackwell.

Srivastva, S., Bilimoria, D., Cooperrider, D.C. and Fry, R.E. (1995) 'Management and organisational learning for positive global change', *Management Learning*, 26 (1): 37–54.

Stacey, R.D. (1993) 'Strategy as order emerging from chaos', *Long Range Planning*, 26 (1): 10–17.

Stacey, R.D. (1995) 'The science of complexity: An alternative perspective for strategic change processes', *Strategic Management Journal*, 16: 477–495.

Stacey, R.D. (1996) *Complexity and Creativity in Organizations*. San Francisco: Berret-Koehler Publishers.

Tsoukas, H. (1998) 'Introduction: Chaos, complexity and organization theory', *Organization*, 5 (3): 291–313.

Turner, S. (1994) *The Social Theory of Practices: Tradition, Tacit Knowledge and Presuppositions*. Cambridge: Polity.

Whittington, R.E. (2003) 'The work of strategizing and organizing: For a practice perspective', *Strategic Organization*, 1 (1): 117–125.

Zollo, M. and Winter, S.G. (2002) 'Deliberate learning and the evolution of dynamic capabilities', *Organization Science*, 13 (3): 339–351.

# 7

# Shaping Organizational Commitment

Robert A. Roe, Omar Solinger and
Woody Van Olffen[1]

## INTRODUCTION

The chapter offers a critical discussion of the background, meaning and operational significance of the concept of organizational commitment in organizational research. It is asserted that the notion of organizational commitment has its roots in contract-based labor relations as are prevalent in North America, and that it has gained popularity as a conceptual counterweight to deteriorating labor relations that resulted from the wave of industrial restructuring that began in the 1980s. An analysis of the concept of organizational commitment as used in organization research confirms this interpretation. It makes clear that commitment expresses to a large degree a concern about unwanted employee turnover. A concise review of the literature shows that employee commitment matters. Since most studies have been cross-sectional, little is known about the way in which commitment emerges and how it develops over time. It is argued that a temporal perspective will help to gain a better understanding of what commitment actually is and how it affects the way in which people in organizations behave. After a discussion of the 'best' level of commitment, which shows the idea of 'the more the better' to be untenable, we discuss the question 'what can be done to shape commitment?' Referring once again to the labor relations context we conclude that managers' wish to shape commitment is subject to a paradox. The more commitment is under pressure because of threat of job loss or poor employment conditions, the less managers can do to prevent it from falling – let alone raise it. In as far as commitment can be shaped it is at the start of the employment relationship. Maintaining it seems to be a matter of keeping promises and striking a balance between organizational and employee interests.

In the recent literature on organizational behavior there is a great interest in understanding and influencing the commitment of employees towards their organizations. It gives the impression that control over employee commitment is key to successful management of organizational transitions in times of strategic change. In this chapter we will first explore why organizational commitment has become such an important issue, looking at fashions, structural economic changes and institutional contexts as explanatory factors. Next, we will discuss the nature of commitment as it has been established in organizational behavior research, and examine the meanings assigned to it in different institutional contexts. Finally, we will investigate the relevance of lower and higher degrees of commitment for the way in which members of organizations behave and perform, and discuss whether and to what degree managers can indeed shape the commitment of their employees.

## SINCE WHEN HAS ORGANIZATIONAL COMMITMENT BEEN AN ISSUE AND WHY?

Scientific interest in the relationship between the organization and its employees has a respectable history (Hrebiniak and Alutto, 1972; Steers, 1977; Mowday, Steers and Porter, 1979; Mowday, Porter and Steers, 1982; Reichers, 1985). Since the early days of the industrial revolution management theorists have given attention to such notions as worker obedience, satisfaction, enjoyment of work, and work motivation on the positive side, and to turnover, absenteeism, stress and work pressure on the negative side. Organizational commitment only became popular in the late 1980s at a time when interest in worker satisfaction was fading. Since then it has competed for primacy as a hot topic with more recent favorites such as trust, organizational citizenship behavior, and extra-role behavior. More negative worker-related concepts, such as counterproductive behavior and anti-organizational behavior have also appeared (see e.g., Giacalone and Greenberg, 1997). The angle from which organizational researchers have studied the organization-employee relationship has changed over time, and the focus has moved back and forth from positive to negative notions.

The pendulum movement seems to coincide with the interest of managers in shaping different facets of employee behavior under varying social and economic conditions. As Abrahamson has outlined in a series of papers on management fashions (Abrahamson, 1997; Abrahamson and Fairchild, 1999) the demand for and emergence of management concepts and techniques is influenced by long-wave macro-economic cycles of expansion and contraction, each lasting about 25 years, that alternately stress either capital efficiency or labor productivity. From this perspective, the interest in commitment may be explained from a long-run contraction phase, in which it competes with earlier and later normative rhetoric (e.g., worker participation, quality circles, empowerment and trust) and occasional rational rhetoric (e.g., BPR in the 90s).

From another perspective the interest in organizational commitment may be seen as a response to a unique, path-dependent process of economic restructuring. In this context it is worth noting that the growing interest coincides with the increasing influx of foreign capital into Western business organizations and the resulting wave of mergers, acquisitions, restructuring and downsizing that began in the early 1980s. Organizational commitment seems to have become an issue in times when shareholder interest took dominance over employee interests, creating a degree of estrangement of employees from their employing organizations. Another factor may be the increasing dependency of managers on employees' qualifications, due to advances in technology as well as increases in workers' education and emancipation. These improved qualifications reduced the effectiveness of traditional command and control management. This points at the management control aspect of fostering commitment. The growing reliance on teamwork and non-traditional working arrangements (e.g., distance workers) have decreased the observability of employee behavior and thus the effectiveness of traditional control mechanisms like behavior control (Ouchi and Maguire, 1975; Eisenhardt, 1985). As dynamic task contexts make outcome specifications uncertain as well, more indirect personnel or normative control mechanisms are needed and put in place. Developing commitment may be seen as alternative control strategy in which employees 'control themselves' (Herriot, 2001).

Whatever the exact cause, while commitment had already been studied in the 1960s and 1970s, it only became popular in the 1980s. Key publications from these early days included Walton (1985), who triggered the interest of managers in 'managing-by-commitment' instead of 'management-by-control,' and Mowday, Porter and Steers (1982) and Reichers (1985), who inspired researchers to investigate the nature of organizational commitment and its origins and effects.

Apart from variations over time, there appears to be varying interest in organizational commitment amongst different parts of the world. Although employees having variable degrees of commitment towards their organizations is probably a universal phenomenon, the interest in understanding and controlling it seems strongest in the Western industrialized world. Originally, the study of organizational commitment was an almost exclusive concern of North American researchers. Many US authors wrote about the phenomenon and designed empirical studies based on employee surveys. They typically adopted an instrumental point of view, uncritically assuming that commitment is something managers can create or change at will by way of persuasion, operant conditioning, identity-manipulation, normative pressure or exchange-based reciprocation. Underlying these tactics was the guiding conviction that managers can motivate employees who 'can be trusted to use their discretion to carry out job tasks in ways that are consistent with organizational goals' (Arthur, 1994: 672). As Collins and Smith (2006) summarize the literature '... a consensus exists that companies can manage the employer-employee relationship and motivate employees through HR practices with a commitment orientation ...' (op. cit.: 546). Herriot (2001) in a critical analysis of employment relationships gives the following account of managerial rhetoric: 'From a shared set of values and assumptions arises a shared commitment. . . . This commitment is towards the organization, and contains a strong affective component: the employee feels favorably towards the organization, identifies with its failures and successes, and is willing to go the extra mile on its behalf. The committed employee is constructive and productive, and furthermore, feels tied to the organization so that he or she wishes to stay. . . . The employees share the values and assumptions of the business, and so are in business for themselves. They have bought into, and taken part ownership of, the business. Therefore they can be expected to accept responsibility and accountability' (op. cit.: 180).

Inspired by the work of American scholars (e.g., Mowday, Porter and Steers, 1982; Allen and Meyer, 1990; Caldwell, Chatman and O'Reilly, 1990; Meyer and Allen, 1991) and their belief in the control of employee commitment, many researchers in Europe and other continents have launched similar investigations into commitment, although commitment never became an equally important research topic among European researchers. A possible explanation for this difference in emphasis may be found in the different types of labor relations of North America and Europe. While American labor relations are mainly short-term and contract-based, the prevailing European model is based on a long-term covenant that implies mutual obligations of employers and employees. Americans might feel a greater *need* to highlight organizational commitment as it is less likely to develop under labor relations governed by flexible, short-term contracts. In this context it is worth noting that commitment is a consistent element in American models of employee turnover (March and Simon, 1958; Angle and Perry, 1981; Price and Mueller, 1981; Steers and Mowday, 1981; Hom and Griffeth, 1995). Europeans may take organizational commitment for granted as an existing part of their 'covenant-type' (Kaplan and Kaplan, 1979) labor relations. This view is in line with the observation that there is a paradox in the descriptions of HRM by American and European authors (Van Diepen, Van Iterson and Roe, 2006). 'In North America, the practice of instrumental, contract-based employee relations is complemented with rhetoric of employee devotion and loyalty to the company. In Europe, on the contrary, protracted employee relations are so self-evident that no special emphasis on positive employee attitudes and behaviors is needed' (op. cit.: 81). A similar contrast is identified in Guest's analysis of the nature of HRM in the United States and Europe (Guest, 1990; Sturges *et al.*, 2005).

Instead of commitment, European research interest has been more in the *psychological contract* and its development over time (Herriot, Manning and Kidd, 1997; Anderson and Schalk, 1998; Sparrow, 1998; Kluytmans and Ott, 1999; Beaumont and Harris, 2002; De Witte and Näswall, 2003; Guest, 2004; Conway and Briner, 2005). The popularity of this topic suggests that in Europe relatively more attention is paid to how employees *perceive* taken-for-granted exchange relationships between the organization and themselves. Still, although the roots of the commitment concept may be American (Argyris, 1960; Rousseau, 1995), it is nowadays part of the conceptual 'OB toolkit' of managers and scholars in Europe as well as other parts of the industrialized world. The globalization of management and organization knowledge is, in fact, a virtual Americanization, because the influences rarely flow the other way.

## WHAT DOES ORGANIZATIONAL COMMITMENT MEAN?

For a number of reasons organizational commitment is not easy to define. While it is often assumed that commitment is an attitude of employees vis-à-vis the employing organization, authors have given definitions that comprise other elements as well. In their often quoted definition Mowday, Porter and Steers (1982) included identification and a desire to remain a member of the organization. They refer to commitment as 'the relative strength of an individual's identification with and involvement in a particular organization. Conceptually it can be characterized by three factors: (a) a strong belief in and acceptance of the organization's goals and values; (b) a willingness to exert considerable effort on behalf of the organization; and (c) a strong desire to maintain membership of the organization' (p. 27). Allen and Meyer (1990) defined organizational commitment as a 'psychological state that binds an individual to an organization (i.e., makes turnover less likely)' (op. cit.: 1). Their well-known model of commitment distinguishes three dimensions, referred to as affective, normative and continuance commitment (Allen and Meyer, 1990, 1996), and their research is characterized by a strong focus on turnover, or more precisely on preventing the individual employee from leaving the organization. In all this the focus is on the individual employee and the perspective is that of social psychology.

An etymological analysis by Solinger (2004) supports this view, suggesting that the core of commitment is a 'state of being bound' that can be recognized in the Latin word '*committo.*' As shown by the expression 'to commit oneself,' commitment is apparently self-imposed as distinct from being imposed by someone else. Interestingly, the Latin root of the word 'engagement' (i.e., gage), which is often used as synonym of commitment, literally means 'pledge.' A commitment typically comes into being when some sort of a pledge – or a binding vow – is made. Signing an employment contract is an unequivocal example of making a pledge, implying from that moment on a self-imposed responsibility and obligation towards an employer. This meaning is not exclusively English – it can also be found in other languages. For instance, in Mandarin Chinese commitment can be directly translated into '承诺,' which means to promise to do something according to certain agreements. (The meaning for the first character '承' means to carry on, to take over, or 'shoulder.' The second character is '诺,'

which means to promise, agree or permit.) The same meaning can be found in the Russian word (ОБЯЗАТЕЛЬСТВО), which bears notions of bond, plight, engagement, guaranty, responsibility, duty, recognizance, and trust. Thus, it seems that commitment is a widely known concept that designates the phenomenon of people being bound to a promise to be of service to someone else or some social entity.[2]

In the commitment literature the notion of '*affective attachment*' to the employing organization has been most popular when referring to the organizational commitment phenomenon, alluding to affective states like belongingness, togetherness and identification, but also to more cognitive states like the internalization of the goals, norms and values of an organization (e.g., Buchanan, 1974; Barling, Wade and Fullagar, 1990). Organizational commitment also has a motivational meaning, as the affective relationship can be the source of a *readiness to act* for the benefit of the organization. Such action readiness does not refer to a specific behavior, but to a broad range of behaviors that can be relevant to serve the interest of the organization at a particular moment (Solinger, Van Olffen and Roe, 2008). For example, a committed individual can choose to work overtime on a Friday night, and engage in fundraising activities over the weekend because his/her commitment implies a general readiness to perform behaviors that serve the organization's purposes. Therefore, we have referred to this behavioral aspect of commitment as a 'generalized behavioral pledge' (ibid.: 80).

Taking these facets together, it appears that the term commitment refers to a psychological phenomenon that reflects the conjugation of the classic attitudinal triplet of affect, cognition, and action readiness (Hollander, 1971; Ajzen and Fishbein, 1980; Eagly and Chaiken, 1993; Ajzen, 2000). Following a strictly attitudinal conceptualization, organizational commitment can be defined as an attitude of an employee vis-à-vis the organization reflected in a combination of affect (emotional attachment, identification),

cognition (identification and internalization of its goals, norms and values), and action readiness (a generalized behavioral pledge to serve and enhance the organization's interests) (Solinger, Van Olffen and Roe, 2008, op. cit: 80). Conceived in this way, organizational commitment appears to be a universal phenomenon. This does not mean, of course, that its prevalence, its importance, or the norms regarding the desired level and proper display of commitment are the same everywhere. In fact, studies of commitment in different countries (Meyer *et al.*, 2002; Gelfand, Erez and Aycan, 2007) have shown that commitment is embedded in diverging patterns of behavior which may be attributed to different cultures and institutional settings. Considering organizational commitment as an individual attitude raises the question how the individual defines and perceives the organization, perhaps the most problematic part of the notion of commitment. As a matter of fact, individuals may hold different views of what the organization *is* – some may think of the larger whole (the legal entity and everything it represents) whereas others may think of a plant, a division, a department, or alternatively, the management, the colleagues etc. Research on commitment foci suggests that this is a theoretically and practically meaningful issue (Reichers, 1985; Randall, 1988; Gregerson, 1993; Mueller and Lawler, 1999; Cohen, 2003). Indeed, people might have multiple organizational commitments and these do not have to be the same for all employees. It seems likely that organizational commitment to one's colleagues or one's department develops differently and is more resistant to change under adverse conditions, than commitment to the management or the organization as a whole. Some preliminary theoretical and empirical findings seem to support this supposition (Lawler, 1992; Gregerson, 1993; Mueller and Lawler, 1999).

Interestingly, research on organizational commitment has tended to give much more attention to measurement issues than to conceptual issues. Therefore, the discourse on what organizational commitment means has mainly been driven by empirical studies conducted with instruments that were created without much conceptual analysis (Bergman, 2006). A large part of the discourse has centered around the dimensions or components of commitment, as proposed by Meyer and Allen (1991). The discussion has overlooked one important point, i.e., that the three components (affective, continuance, and normative commitment) imply different attitude objects (Solinger, Van Olffen and Roe, 2008). While affective commitment pertains to the organization, as meant above, the other components refer to a *specific action* (i.e., leaving the organization). Although this emphasis may be understood from the interest of (especially North American) managers in curtailing turnover, it does not make much sense to consider this specific action as central to the concept and to discard other behavioral acts that are potentially relevant to the organization. It is even more questionable in the light of a recent meta-analysis reporting that organizational commitment only yields small to moderate effect sizes on employee turnover (Griffeth, Hom and Gaertner, 2000), in spite of the fact that turnover has been included in many organizational commitment measures. Other developments in turnover research show that people who leave are relatively satisfied with their jobs and that their reasons for leaving lies mostly in off-the-job factors (e.g., Cady, Boyd and Neubert, 2001). Therefore, the current focus on leaving the organization in commitment theory and research seems disproportionate and not consistent with recent empirical findings (Solinger, Van Olffen and Roe, 2008).

All this confirms the idea that the interest in organizational commitment is a disguised concern about unwanted employee turnover, largely stemming from American labor relations frameworks governed by short-term contracts. When looked upon from a wider perspective, the question is whether the prevailing conceptualization of organizational commitment in the North American literature, i.e., that of Meyer and Allen (1997), sufficiently captures the nature of commitment as it is experienced in other parts of the world. It seems that the more confined notion of affective commitment better grasps the essence of organizational commitment and therefore makes sense in a wider range of cultural contexts (Palich, Hom and Griffeth, 1995; Wasti, 2003), which may have been the reason that it has been preferred by many researchers.

## DOES ORGANIZATIONAL COMMITMENT MATTER?

Even though one can argue about the quality of instruments used for measuring organizational commitment, it is apparent from the many studies that commitment does matter. That is, employees with low and high organizational commitment differ markedly in other work-related attitudes and behaviors. Although it has occasionally been observed that high commitment can have negative consequences for the individual worker as well as for the organization and its clients (Whyte, 1956; Randall, 1987; Schwartz, 1987), it is widely assumed that positive effects prevail (Meyer *et al.*, 2002). Empirical research seems to confirm this assumption. If we confine ourselves to measures of 'affective commitment,' we can conclude that organizational commitment co-varies positively with various other measures, ranging from job involvement, job-, pay- and co-worker-satisfaction to job performance, citizenship behavior (OCB) and the absence of stress and turnover intentions. These robust associations were demonstrated across studies in meta-analyses (Mathieu and Zajac, 1990; Tett and Meyer, 1993; Allen and Meyer, 1996). Even non-work life satisfaction is related positively to affective commitment (Romzek, 1989). Of course, it should be noted that most of these studies are of a cross-sectional nature, and tell us little about the consequences that *changes* in commitment have for organizational behaviors, subjective well-being, and performance. Studies that have investigated the effects of profound organizational events, such as organizational restructuring, downsizing and outsourcing, show that a decline in organizational commitment is associated with a host of negative effects, both in attitudes and performance (Brockner *et al.*, 1997; Burke and Nelson, 1998; Luthans and Sommer, 1999; Isaksson and Johannson, 2003; Kalimo, Taris and Schaufeli, 2003; Bentein *et al.*, 2005).

Altogether, these studies indicate that commitment does matter. There are clear differences between employees who hold positive attitudes toward their organization and those who do not. The direction of the relationship between commitment and other attitudes and behaviors is not always the same. Although, many studies have provided evidence of robust linear relationships, suggesting that commitment is a 'good thing,' it would be premature to conclude that higher commitment will always lead to more positive outcomes. As Randall (1987) has argued, high commitment may lead to negative outcomes for the organization (e.g., ineffective utilization of human resources, lower flexibility and innovation, illegal or unethical acts on behalf of the organization) as well as for the individual (e.g., limited time for non-work, social and work-family conflicts, stress, reduced mobility). It is certainly conceivable that commitment relates to other variables in a curvilinear rather than linear way. In fact, such a relationship was found by Somers and Casal (1994) in a study on whistle-blowing. They found that the highest degree of whistle-blowing was present among employees with average commitment scores. Whether such relationships exist in other domains as well, remains to be investigated. In this context it is good to underline the necessity to go beyond cross-sectional research and to engage in more (quasi-) experimental research to investigate effects of increasing and decreasing commitment on other attitudes and behaviors (Stinglhamber and Vandenberghe, 2003).

In discussing the implications of commitment, we should keep in mind the institutional and cultural context. In a recent meta-analysis Meyer and colleagues (Meyer *et al.*, 2002) have observed differences in strengths of relationships findings from studies done in North America (mainly the US) and other

countries. Interestingly, the differences in correlations with other variables are greatest for normative and continuance commitment. In North American studies, correlations with organizational citizenship behaviors were typically weaker than in non-North American studies. For affective commitment the differences were less outspoken. Unfortunately the number of non-North American studies is small and it is not possible to isolate data from European studies.

Yet, it seems possible to interpret the findings from the institutional angle that was mentioned before. To the degree that differences are present, the correlations are lower in North America where labor relations are characterized by short-term employment contracts. Employee behaviors in such circumstances might not be governed by feelings of being bound by a pledge or by norms and obligations. In the case of affective commitment, where differences were found to be small, a hidden contextual effect may be present. That is, with correlations being roughly the same, the actual implications of commitment for organizational citizenship behavior or turnover may be different. The difference may reside in the social norms inherent in the labor system. In a 'contract-environment' characterized by short-term contracts, the norm is likely to be low commitment, a low degree of OCB and a strong tendency to look for a better job. In such an environment, more typical in North America and other Anglo-Saxon countries, a higher level of commitment may be associated with more display of OCB and a lower likelihood to leave – which is perceived as 'better' from a managerial point of view. In contrast, in an environment characterized by long-term covenant-based relationships, the norm is likely to be high commitment, a high degree of OCB and a weak tendency to look for a better job. In such an environment, more typical in continental Europe, a higher level of commitment will not have much consequence but a lower level of commitment will be associated with less display of OCB and a greater likelihood to leave – which is perceived as 'worse.'

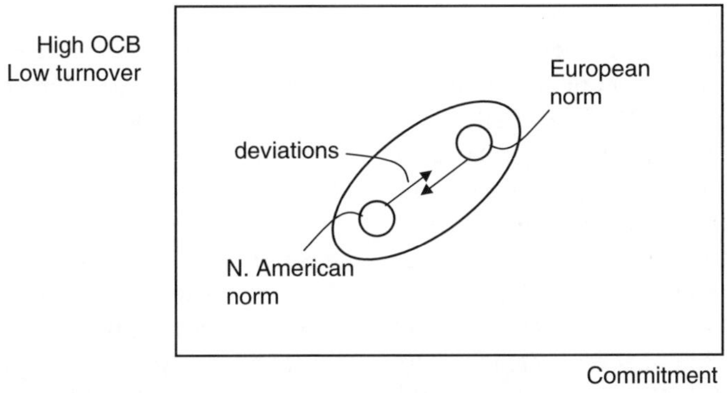

High OCB
Low turnover

European
norm

deviations

N. American
norm

Commitment

**Figure 7.1   Hypothetical model of cultural commitment norms.**

Figure 7.1 gives an illustration of the asymmetrical and opposing effects that may result from prevalent social norms. In the first case there is a positive (or 'additive') effect which becomes visible when there *is* commitment, while in the second case there is a negative (or 'subtractive') effect which is noticeable when commitment *is not* there. A difference as postulated here would imply that an intermediate level of commitment would be considered low in Europe and high in North America. Although data to make such comparisons are currently lacking, it would be worth investigating this issue.

## HOW DOES COMMITMENT DEVELOP OVER TIME?

In spite of a large body of empirical studies about organizational commitment little is as yet known about how it emerges, and how it develops over time. The available evidence suggests that organizational commitment is evoked in the early stages of employment, or even in the pre-contractual phase when the individual and the organization negotiate about the future labor contract (Damos and Koonce, 1997). Moreover, early experiences – during the first few months of employment – seem to be critical for the level of commitment that establishes itself.

Although this way of describing the emergence of commitment suggests that it is largely a matter of trading expectations between the individual and the (representative of the) organization, especially at an early stage of the relationship, it is important to realize that commitment can also been seen as part of a wider social phenomenon (Salancik and Pfeffer, 1978; Lawler, 1992), and establishing commitment may be part of socialization into an organizational community. Here social norms can come into play. In a covenant-based environment, where mutual obligations are more or less self-evident, the norm may make a newcomer feel obliged to accept a high degree of commitment. In a contract-based environment, on the other hand, the norm may be to start with a low level of commitment and to reciprocate whatever the organization is offering. In the first case a low degree of (initial) commitment would be inappropriate, whereas in the second case a high degree of commitment would be out of place.[3]

Individual, exchange-based experiences may differ, leading to differences between employees in how their commitment develops over time. Apart from the initial period, little is known about the development of commitment over longer periods of time. Intra-individual changes are rarely reported, if studied at all. Some scholars account for a relative stability in the commitment phenomenon (e.g., Mowday, Porter and Steers, 1982) while others view the concept as inherently dynamic (Beck and Wilson, 2001). There is some evidence that organizational commitment can remain stable, at least when the exchange relationship with the organization remains intact or key expectations are met (Sturges *et al.*, 2005). Theoretical arguments on post-decisional justification and the need for behavior-attitude consistency suggest that organizational commitment might strengthen over time (Salancik, 1977; O'Reilly and Caldwell, 1985; Brickman, Dunkel-Schetter and Abbey, 1987). There is considerable cross-sectional and correlational evidence that organizational commitment increases with age and years of service (Buchanan, 1974; O'Reilly and Caldwell, 1985; Morrow and McElroy, 1987; Mathieu and Zajac, 1990; Adelman *et al.*, 1993). However, results should be interpreted with caution because correlations seem to differ in various tenure time-frames and age cohorts (Beck and Wilson, 2001), which reminds us that cross-sectional studies do not provide information of within-person changes over time.

Most longitudinal studies of commitment have confined themselves to the first months of employment. Several of these studies have focused on causal relationships among antecedents and consequences of commitment and not on the temporal dynamics of the commitment phenomenon itself. Some studies show a somewhat counterintuitive trend: commitment seems to *start off high* on the first day of work and then gradually *declines over time* (Van Maanen, 1977; Vandenberg and Self, 1993; Damos and Koonce, 1997; Beck and Wilson, 2000). The decline is attributed to entry shock, unmet expectations, exposure to negative work experiences, and social norms in the particular work setting. It has been suggested that after a period of initial decline the exchange relationship between the employee and the organization determines the level of organizational commitment (Beck and Wilson, 2000), potentially leading to sharp increases or decreases depending on the exchange relationship (Stinglhamber and Vandenberghe, 2003; Sturges *et al.*, 2005). Research on organizational restructuring, downsizing and outsourcing that was mentioned before, shows declines of organizational commitment in a large part of the work force. Among 'survivors' of downsizing there is some evidence that after a steep drop, commitment may increase again (Brockner *et al.*, 1987;

Allen et al., 2001; Spreitzer and Mishra, 2002). However, there is reason for caution in interpreting these developmental patterns as they may also reflect shifts in the *meaning* of commitment over time (Vandenberg and Self, 1993).

If one adopts a broader temporal perspective it is obvious that the individual's organizational commitment is temporally bounded and confined to the phase of the career in which a work (employment) relationship with a particular organization is maintained. This is also implied in the definition of organizational commitment. Some longitudinal studies have found convincing evidence that turnover behavior is preceded by a decline in organizational commitment (Bentein *et al.*, 1989; Cohen and Freund, 2005; Kammeyer Mueller *et al.*, 2005). Thus, organizational commitment can be said to have a 'life cycle' that begins around the start of the relationship and terminates somewhere around the end of the relationship. The overall shape of the curve describing the development of commitment possibly follows an (imperfect) inverted U-shaped pattern. Although empirical research on this matter is still lacking, it seems plausible that the origin lies in a narrow time-band around the start (shortly before, at, or shortly after), while the end may fall in a much wider interval. Theoretically, one may expect that some people, especially those experiencing a violation of their psychological contract, will show a drop in commitment a substantial time before the end of their employment. Others (e.g., those retiring) may anticipate the end of the relationship and gradually loose commitment towards the end. Perhaps some people, who had a high commitment to their organization, may still be committed after the relationships ends (think of retiree and alumni networks). All this will, of course, depend on the quality and duration of the employment relationship.

Which patterns actually occur and which factors they depend on is something to be revealed by future research, but it is important to acknowledge that organizational commitment is not something 'that is simply there.'

As is also apparent from the interest of managers and researchers in finding how commitment can be influenced, we must assume that it is open to change. Commitment as a collective phenomenon may change over time as well. This is especially likely under conditions of incisive organizational change (restructuring, downsizing and outsourcing, mentioned earlier), that provoke sensemaking processes resulting in shifts in people's shared ideas and attitudes. Several sources (e.g., Brockner *et al.*, 1997; Kalimo, Taris and Schaufeli, 2003; Moore, Grunberg and Greenberg, 2004) have given evidence of declining morale in such circumstances, going hand-in-hand with an overall loss of trust, an increase in cynicism, and a drop in commitment. It is obvious that such changes can be a powerful source of resistance that managers have to cope with.

## HOW MUCH COMMITMENT?

Organizational commitment is among the many concepts in OB for which no precise, criterion-referenced measures exist. All measures in use are norm-referenced, that is, scores are compared to those of other people in the same or similar organizations. To our knowledge, there are not even standardized norm groups for comparison. Nevertheless, the question may be raised how much commitment is beneficial for the organization, at least from the manager's perspective. For researchers and managers who study commitment in order to limit turnover, the prevailing idea seems to be 'the higher the better.' However, older studies indicate that high commitment may have significant disadvantages (Whyte, 1956). There is also evidence suggesting that employees with high organizational commitment, especially those who had a long-term relationship with the employer, experience greater difficulty when they face a takeover or termination of the organization, or the necessity to leave the organization and move to another one (Ashforth, 2001). This is especially an issue in the case of outsourcing. Thus,

high commitment may be associated with considerable resistance to change (Randall, 1987), which is seen as negative from a managerial perspective. Again a cultural factor may come into the picture. We would expect these effects of high commitment to be more visible in covenant-based as compared to contract-based settings where long-term employment contracts prevail.

Is low commitment a bad thing? One can argue about the lowest acceptable level of organizational commitment. Although the prevailing idea is that low commitment is undesirable, this position may be qualified as well. Referring to the exchange relationship between the organization and the employee, it might be argued that a low level of commitment is the appropriate response to a low employment security offer. We refer to the discussion about changing psychological contracts (Herriot, 1992; Anderson, Herriot and Hodgkinson, 2001; Conway and Briner, 2005). Especially in environments where employers insist on a flexible work force that receives employability rather than secure employment, low organizational commitment can be a functional, i.e., adaptive response that psychologically protects the individual against arbitrary managerial action, but low commitment can have other advantages. It can stimulate individual creativity, innovation and originality, enhance the chance of turnover among those who don't feel well placed, and facilitate whistle-blowing which can prevent damage to the organization (Randall, 1987). Another aspect, linked to the notion of multiple commitment foci (Reichers, 1985), is that people who feel little commitment to the organization may still feel commitment to their fellow employees.

Although it is at odds with common management rhetoric, the desired level of employee commitment may well be variable over time. Managers may expect high commitment in times of expansion but low commitment in times of restructuring and downsizing. From an employee point of view such changing expectations are inconsistent and often a source of distrust and cynicism. Also, this form of managerial inconsistency may create *unintended effects* in an employee's commitment levels. If managers did not consistently create conditions under which commitment can flourish, a sudden emphasis on an employee's commitment – e.g., in times of expansion – may have contrary effects. To employees this sudden emphasis may seem opportunistic, hollow rhetoric or even manipulative, fostering forms of organizational cynicism rather than organizational commitment (Naus, 2007). A likely paradoxical consequence is that employee commitment declines rather than rises as intended. This resonates with the idea that leadership has to be perceived as *authentic* in order to have impact on followers (Gardner *et al.*, 2005).

## SHAPING COMMITMENT

Much of the extant literature gives the impression that managers can shape the organizational commitment of their employees at will. Many authors have given recommendations how to instill a greater level of commitment. Among them are developing a common vision (Senge, 1990), creating a strong normative environment (O'Reilly and Chatman, 1986; Finegan, 2000), and adopting a transformational leadership style (Podsakoff, MacKenzie and Bommer, 1996). During the past decade most interest has been devoted to what HRM can do to create a highly committed workforce. Therefore, we will consider this line of research in some detail.

Many authors have investigated whether so-called 'High-commitment HR-practices' lead to superior organizational performance. The term is loosely used to indicate practices such as selective staffing, developmental appraisal, competitive and equitable compensation, and comprehensive training and development activities (e.g., Whitener, 2001) Although many studies have indeed shown links between certain HR practices and firm *performance* (Huselid, 1995; MacDuffie, 1995; Niehaus and Swiercz, 1996; Collins

and Clark, 2003; Bou and Beltrán, 2005), it is questionable whether these practices do produce high *commitment*, and whether it is indeed high commitment which explains better performance at the firm level. Analyses have shown that HR-practices come in certain 'bundles' (e.g., related to recruitment or employee development) but the conceptual status of these bundles and the relationship to commitment are doubtful, and evidence regarding links to employee commitment is virtually non-existent. In fact, the correlations between so-called High commitment HR-practices and outcomes may well be explained by other mediating factors, such as stability of employment, teamwork, social climate, or level of trust in management (Gould-Williams and Davies, 2005; Collins and Smith, 2006). A 'labor process explanation,' assuming work intensification and a change in task controls, has also been tested (Ramsay, Scholarios and Harley, 2000) but could not be confirmed.

The relationships might alternatively be attributed to underlying labor relations and hence considered to be spurious. This possibility could explain why findings from comparative research, involving the US and European countries, are not very consistent (Black, 1999). Different types of labor relations – more contract-based in Anglo-Saxon countries, and more covenant-based in continental Europe, operating in combination with national cultures may lead to different bundles of HR-practices that differ in their relationships with outcomes. For instance, it seems that what is perceived as innovative High-commitment HR in the US corresponds to a fairly traditional pattern in Europe out of which various national variants have developed. Differences between industries, and between the public and private sector (Boyne, Jenkins and Pools, 1999) also play a role, making the picture more complex.

Next to the inability to rule out alternative explanations of company performance and the cultural relativity of 'what works,' the research on High-commitment HRM is plagued with conceptual and methodological problems (Delery, 1998; Truss, 2001). Among them is the distorting effect of high measurement error resulting from reliance on a single informer to gain information on corporate HR practices (Wright *et al.*, 2001). Another problem is the possibility of reversed causal order. A study by Wright *et al.* (2005) demonstrated that HR practices are related to earlier, as well as later, firm performance, and that the effect of HR-practices virtually disappears when earlier performance is partialled out. A lack of measurement equivalence makes it hard to interpret result from comparative research (e.g., Black, 1999).

Finally, there is a logical problem, namely that one cannot make causal inferences about changes in HRM from cross-sectional studies that establish associations between HRM practices and performance of different organizations. We are not contesting that certain HR-practices can have positive outcomes for the employees and the firm, but we consider that the assumption that they serve to control employee commitment is highly questionable.

Earlier, we have made a distinction between organizational commitment as an individual and a collective phenomenon. Commitment in the first sense is 'a state of being bound to the organization' that individual workers impose upon *themselves*. Commitment in the second sense is a shared attitude of members of a collective, based on a social norm of what is appropriate in the relationship with the organization. This norm is typically embedded in and supported by a broader *institutional context* of established labor relations, national laws and industrial norms of conduct. Thus, when asking the question what organizations – or rather the managers representing them – can do to shape the commitment of employees, we face the logical difficulty that commitment, in either sense, is something that cannot be influenced directly by another party. Only individual employees themselves can establish their degree of commitment, and they can only do so within the limits set by the collective. People other than the employees themselves – particularly

managers – cannot influence commitment directly; they may only create conditions under which employees are inclined to raise or maintain their degree of commitment and their common norm. Although one would expect that covenant-based labor relations generally offer a better climate for this route to shaping commitment, the questions of what the precise conditions are that can sustain it, and what can be achieved, are still unanswered.

Making a distinction based on segmentation of the employee's organizational commitment life-cycle, we propose three types of moments at which interventions aiming at individual commitment might be launched. The first is in an early stage, when the employment relation begins. Here, commitment might be influenced by raising the employees' expectations. This is a potentially risky option since too high expectations have a higher chance of not being met, with a subsequent decline of commitment as the likely outcome. Second, there is the stage – earlier or later in the life-cycle – when commitment comes under pressure because of unmet expectations or adverse events. At this stage, the question is what can be done to prevent the decline that is likely to occur. This is a matter of 'repairing' or of bolstering existing commitment in order to give it a resilient character. And third, towards the end of the employment period, there is a similar question, i.e., how to prevent or delay the decline of commitment that is natural to occur. Here, the issue is how to support and respectfully see out employees retiring or otherwise leaving the organization. Framing the issue of shaping commitment in these terms makes clear that it is not easy for managers to really *shape* commitment, unless promises made at an early stage are consistently kept and employees are safeguarded from threatening events and developments. This is in line with evidence that has shown experienced fairness to be a strong antecedent of commitment (e.g., Cohen Charash and Spector, 2001). Especially in contract-based environments creating high commitment may be a wish that is hard to fulfill, however much it is emphasized in common rhetoric. Also, efforts to raise commitment may produce other results than those aimed for, including employee cynicism, especially when rhetoric is incongruent with managerial practice.

An implicit assumption in the foregoing is that shaping commitment is essentially a matter of raising commitment, but this interpretation is not the only one possible. If one accepts the idea that commitment can be too high, shaping commitment can also be a matter of reducing it (Randall, 1987). How could managers possibly achieve such a reduction? Due to the bias towards high commitment there is little to learn about this topic from the research literature. In practice managers may lower employee expectations and withhold expected rewards, in order to curtail commitment (and resistance to change), but again this is very likely to evoke opposition from employees and mobilize forces that jeopardize management's objectives and seriously undermine labor relations. Apart from this, such practices can be regarded outright unethical and should be avoided on moral grounds.

It would not be very fruitful to frame the issue of shaping individual commitments merely in terms of short-term exchange relationships. As said, there is a collective dimension to commitment as well. Individuals will base their commitment on shared and institutionalized ideas and standards, and they will rely on others in interpreting the meaning managerial actions. Moreover, they will not only consider current moves by management but also recall past actions. Thus, as several studies have demonstrated, employees have a collective memory. Survivors of drastic organizational change continue to distrust their managers and to disbelieve what they are told. As a result managers 'may be forced to accommodate employees with reduced levels of commitment although they believe that high levels of commitment are desirable' (Randall, 1987: 468). An interesting finding is that after a major reorganization, the turnover rates were higher and persisted at higher levels for years, even among *new* employees (Krug, 2003). The subjects in this study

were not ordinary employees but executives! Another factor to consider is that managers are taken as example by employees. Managers who stay with an organization for a short period will therefore have to realize that the perceived contradiction between their own commitment and the commitment they expect from their employees may evoke serious cynicism among the latter (Naus, 2007).

The implication of all this is that shaping commitment is not just a matter of winning the hearts of employees by making new promises and introducing new incentives. Commitment can only be effectively influenced as part of a stable and trustworthy pattern of labor relations that allow people to voluntarily commit themselves.

## THE FUTURE OF COMMITMENT

An intriguing issue emerging from the foregoing is whether the phenomenon of high commitment among employees – as a reality and as something aimed for – is stable over time. If one takes a look at employment and labor relations from a historical perspective it is obvious that high commitment has not always been the rule. In the nineteenth century and the first half of the twentieth century the majority of workers were hired on contracts of limited duration, working conditions were often poor, and relations between workers and firm owners (or managers) were antagonistic rather than harmonious, also in Europe. We have only to recall the years of the Great Depression and World War II to remind us of circumstances that were unfavorable for the development of high- and long-term employee commitment. Although empirical data to test this assumption are lacking, it may well be that the development of committed employees is more typical for the post-war years when Western economies expanded, living and working conditions improved, unemployment was minimal, indeed virtually non-existent up until the later 1960s, and industrial democracy spread. It is worth noting, in this context, that Whyte's book, *The Organization Man*, which deals with the phenomenon of the highly committed employee, was published in 1956, in the middle of the post-war boom.

What does the future look like from this long-term perspective? Many authors in the field of organizational behavior have pointed at the great changes that have occurred and are currently taking place in the world of work. Although the rate of development may be different in North America, Europe and other parts of the world, the trend is in the same direction. Faced with relentless competition in inherently unstable global markets, firms adopt a variety of strategies with different emphases on innovation, flexibility and leanness. The implications for employees are often profound. For most, employment and income security is declining while work content and careers become increasingly unpredictable. In response to this – sometimes forced by 'hard lessons' of restructuring, downsizing and outsourcing – workers have learned to depend less on their employer and take more control of their own fate. Profiting from better education and greater awareness of the value of their knowledge, many – but not all of them – emancipate and actively manage their own career.

These changes have led to another type of psychological contract, focused more on short-term and mutually profitable exchange rather than long-term mutual obligations. In a somewhat pessimistic mode De Meuse and Tornow (1990) wrote: 'Nowadays, a new corporation-person bond is emerging, one that assumes each party is much less dependent on the other, one in which mutual loyalty is rapidly disappearing, and in which mutual trust may be at an all time low' (op. cit.: 203–204). As new generations appear on the labor market the attitude of employees and managers may change. 'New age employees' (Mir, Mir and Mosca, 2002) may look for positive aspects of the flexible employment relationship and develop another – more short-term and conditional – form of commitment than we have known before. In this situation it would be quite

inappropriate for employers to keep striving for high commitment by offering employees all sorts of promises that can only evoke wrong expectations and lead to frustration because they cannot be lived up to. Rather than trying to instill psychological contracts that are inherently untrustworthy and are consummated by the inability to deliver, managers might do better to adopt a more pragmatic attitude and try to openly make realistic short-time deals with workers they want to employ. The same applies to individual workers. For them it might be better to negotiate short-term but realistic employment conditions, than to aim for long-term outcomes that the employer will ultimately not be able or willing to deliver. There are some studies suggesting that this kind of negotiating is taking place with some degree of success (e.g., Parks, Kidder and Gallagher, 1998; Storey *et al.*, 2002; Guest, 2004).

Of course, such 'new deals' will imply some degree of commitment towards the organization, but as Baruch (1998) suggests, it will not be a type of 'high commitment' so often described in the literature, unlimited in scope and time, and serving as the basis for good performance and all sorts of organizational citizenship behaviors. It will be a commitment of a conditional type, focused on a narrowly defined range of task or role behaviors and limited in time, as defined by the deal. If both parties are satisfied and able to continue, a second deal may follow, and commitment may be continued accordingly. If the deal is ending both parties will loose their commitment, and look for new partners to whom they will become committed again. The implication for workers and employers in an environment characterized by such episodic employment relations is that they have to manage commitment dynamically. For both the challenge is 'binding and letting-go,' preferably with some degree of synchrony and mutual agreement.

The scenario depicted here is not the only possible one. If we look at the broader context, particularly in our Western societies that have seen a great deal of individualization during the past decades, it is well conceivable that new generations will want to restore some of the social relations that got lost. Some may want to do this mainly at the level of the family and the community, putting work in second place, whereas others may prefer to look for stronger social ties in the sphere of work, that is, in professional networks or in the organization. A combination, in the form of a balance between social life in the context of family and community, and that of work is also possible. Whatever form people will prefer, organizational commitment may get a new meaning because of the *social aspect* of belonging to an organization. These alternative ways of bonding and developing commitment – implying different foci – are clearly a topic that deserves future research attention.

Another development that we might see occurring in our post-Fordist society (Alonso and Lucio, 2006) is the differentiation of preferences regarding patterns of commitment. While some people may indeed opt for the bounded commitment that was described above, aiming for the successive fulfillment of jobs with different employers – perhaps also as self-employed – that suit their personal career plan. Such a differentiation between people, perhaps along generational lines, might result in a 'blended' work force in which people have different commitments. The picture reminds us of the 'shamrock model' of the organization proposed by Handy (1989) in the late 1980s. His description of the organization as offering three types of employment, stable employment to core workers, limited-term employment to important but non-essential workers, and contingent employment to workers doing temporary tasks, might match this idea of a workforce with mixed preferences regarding employment, career and lifestyle. To put it in present day terms, the organization would need core workers to preserve tacit and specialized organizational knowledge, and to look after the organization's key assets. In addition, it would need a continuous flow of labor entering and exiting on the tide of the market serving as a means to fulfill basic functions, while supporting innovation and knowledge exchange. All other work would be left to contingent workers hired for the time they are needed.

Handy's model was proposed in a time when globalization had only begun and a big wave of scale outsourcing and off-shoring was still to come. While his categorization still makes sense, the ongoing process of globalization intertwined with technological innovation and concentration of international capital, make it hard to foretell how the future development of Western organizations will be, what type of workforce they will need, and what type of labor markets will evolve. However, it is equally hard to predict which mix of preferences people will develop with regard to different types of commitment – different in scope and duration, and perhaps in foci. Whatever pattern will emerge, employee commitment will somehow continue to play a role but not in the way proposed by current management rhetoric. If there is anything to learn from the past, it is the necessity for another, more open and two-sided approach to employment relations (cf. Herriot, 2001), in which managers and workers alike face the new reality and adjust their expectations regarding commitment accordingly. We expect that this will help to understand and acknowledge how commitment is shaping itself.

## NOTES

1 The authors gratefully acknowledge the helpful comments of Ad van Iterson and Stewart Clegg on an earlier version of this text.

2 This does not necessarily imply that commitment to organizations is a universal phenomenon. It should be noted that a commitment assumes the possibility of making a choice. In certain economies people may not have the choice to commit themselves and rather be forced to submit themselves. In such cases one would not expect to find evidence of *organizational* commitment.

3 Of course, social norms can also differ for various categories of people, depending on their occupation (e.g., salesmen, production workers, middle managers) or level of education (e.g., unskilled laborers, academics). This underlines the relevance of studying commitment from a sociological angle in addition to the prevailing psychological approach.

# REFERENCES

Abrahamson, E. (1997) 'The emergence and prevalence of employee management rhetorics: The effects of long waves, labor unions, and turnover, 1875 to 1992', *Academy of Management Journal*, 40 (3): 491–533.

Abrahamson, E. and Fairchild, G. (1999) 'Management fashion: Lifecycles, triggers, and collective learning processes', *Administrative Science Quarterly*, 44: 708–740.

Ackerman, P.L. (1989) 'Within-task intercorrelations of skilled performance: Implications for predicting individual differences? A comment on Henry and Hulin, 1987', *Journal of Applied Psychology*, 74 (2): 360–364.

Adelman, L., Cohen, M.S., Bresnick, T.A. and Chinnis, J.O. (1993) 'Real-time expert system interfaces, cognitive processes, and task performance: An empirical assessment', *Human Factors*, 35: 243–261.

Ajzen, I. (2000) 'Nature and operation of attitudes', *Annual Review of Psychology*, 52: 27–58.

Ajzen, I. and Fishbein, M. (1980) *Understanding Attitudes and Predicting Social Behavior*. Upper Saddle River, NJ: Prentice Hall.

Allen, N.J. and Meyer, J.P. (1990) 'The measurement and antecedents of affective, continuance and normative commitment to the organization', *Journal of Occupational Psychology*, 63: 1–18.

Allen, N.J. and Meyer, J.P. (1996) 'Affective, continuance and normative commitment to the organization: An examination of construct validity', *Journal of Vocational Behavior*, 49: 252–276.

Allen, T.D., Freeman, D.M., Russell, J.E.A., Reizenstein, R.C. and Rentz, J.O. (2001) 'Survivor reactions to organizational downsizing: Does time ease the pain?', *Journal of Occupational and Organizational Psychology*, 74 (2): 145–164.

Alonso, L.E. and Lucio, M.M. (eds) (2006) *Employment Relations in a Changing Society: Assessing the Post-Fordist Paradigm*. Basingstoke: Palgrave Macmillan.

Anderson, N. and Schalk, R. (1998) 'The psychological contract in retrospect and prospect', *Journal of Organizational Behavior*, 19: 637–647.

Anderson, N., Herriot, P. and Hodgkinson, G.P. (2001) 'The practitioner-researcher divide in industrial, work and organizational (IWO) psychology: Where we are now, and where we do we go from here?', *Journal of Occupational and Organizational Psychology*, 74 (4): 391–411.

Angle, H.L. and Perry, J.L. (1981) 'An empirical assessment of organizational commitment and organizational effectiveness', *Administrative Science Quarterly*, 26: 1–14.

Argyris, C. (1960) *Understanding Organizational Behavior*. Homewood, IL: Dorsey Press.

Arthur, J.B. (1994) 'Effects of human resource systems on manufacturing performance and turnover', *Academy of Management Journal*, 37 (3): 670–687.

Ashforth, B.E. (2001) *Role Transitions in Organizational Life: An Identity-based Perspective*. Mahwah, NJ: Lawrence Erlbaum Associates.

Barling, J., Wade, B. and Fullagar, C. (1990) 'Predicting employee commitment to company and union: Divergent models', *Journal of Occupational Psychology*, 63: 49–61.

Baruch, Y. (1998) 'The rise and fall of organizational commitment', *Human Systems Management*, 17 (2): 135.

Beaumont, P.B. and Harris, R.I.D. (2002) 'Examining white-collar downsizing as a cause of change in the psychological contract: Some UK evidence', *Employee Relations*, 24 (4): 378–388.

Beck, K. and Wilson, C. (2000) 'Development of affective organizational commitment: A cross-sequential examination of change with tenure', *Journal of Vocational Behavior*, 56 (1): 114–136.

Beck, K. and Wilson, C. (2001) 'Have we studied, should we study, and can we study the development of commitment? Methodological issues and the developmental study of work-related commitment', *Human Resource Management Review*, 11: 257–278.

Bentein, K., Vandenberghe, C., Vandenberg, R. and Stinglhamber, F. (2005) 'The role of change in the relationship between commitment and turnover: A latent growth modeling approach', *Journal of Applied Psychology*, 90 (3): 468–482.

Bergman, M.E. (2006) 'The relationship between affective and normative commitment: Review and research agenda', *Journal of Organizational Behavior*, 27: 645–663.

Black, B. (1999) 'National culture and high commitment management', *Employee Relations*, 21 (4/5): 389–404.

Bou, J.C. and Beltrán, I. (2005) 'Total quality management, high-commitment human resource strategy and firm performance: An empirical study', *Total Quality Management & Business Excellence*, 16 (1): 71–86.

Boyne, G., Jenkins, G. and Pools, M. (1999) 'Human resource management in the public and private sectors: An empirical comparison', *Public Administration*, 77 (2): 407–420.

Brickman, P., Dunkel-Schetter, C. and Abbey, A. (1987) 'The development of commitment', in C.B. Wortman and R.M. Sorrentino (eds) *Commitment, Conflict and Caring*. Englewood Cliffs, NJ: Prentice-Hall, pp. 145–221.

Brockner, J., Grover, S., Reed, T., Dewitt, R. and O'Malley, M. (1987) 'Survivors' reactions to layoffs: We get by with a little help for our friends', *Administrative Science Quarterly*, 32 (4): 526.

Brockner, J., Hurley, R., Dewitt, R.L., Wiesenfeld, B., Grover, S., Stephan, J. *et al.* (1997) 'The effects on layoff survivors of their fellow survivors' reactions', *Journal of Applied Social Psychology*, 27 (10): 835–863.

Buchanan, B. (1974) 'Building organizational commitment: The socialization of managers in work organizations', *Administrative Science Quarterly*, 19 (4): 533–547.

Burke, R.J. and Nelson, D. (1998) 'Mergers and acquisitions, downsizing and privatization: A North American perspective', in M.K. Gowing, J.D. Kraft and J. Campbell Quick (eds) *The New Organizational Reality: Downsizing, Restructuring and Revitalization.* Washington, DC: American Psychological Association, pp. 21–54.

Cady, S.H., Boyd, D.G. and Neubert, M.J. (2001) 'Multilevel performance probability: A meta-analytic integration of expectancy and self-efficacy', *Psychological Reports*, 88 (3, Pt2): 1077–1090.

Caldwell, D.F., Chatman, J.A. and O'Reilly, C.A. (1990) 'Building organizational commitment: A multifirm study', *Journal of Occupational Psychology*, 63 (3): 245–261.

Cohen, A. (2003) 'Multiple commitments in the workplace: An integrative approach', *Series in Applied Psychology.* Mahwah, NJ: Lawrence Erlbaum.

Cohen, A. and Freund, A. (2005) 'A longitudinal analysis of the relationship between multiple commitments and withdrawal cognitions', *Scandinavian Journal of Management*, 21: 329–351.

Cohen Charash, Y. and Spector, P.E. (2001) 'The role of justice in organizations: A meta-analysis', *Organizational Behavior and Human Decision Processes*, 86 (2): 278–321.

Collins, C.J. and Clark, K.D. (2003) 'Strategic human resource practices, top management team social networks, and firm performance: The role of human resource practices in creating organizational competitive advantage', *Academy of Management Journal*, 46 (6): 740–751.

Collins, C.J. and Smith, K.G. (2006) 'Knowledge exchange and combination: The role of human resource practices in the performance of high-technology firms', *Academy of Management Journal*, 49 (3): 544–560.

Conway, N. and Briner, R.B. (2005) *Understanding Psychological Contracts at Work: A Critical Evaluation of Theory and Research.* Oxford: Oxford University Press.

Damos, D.L. and Koonce, J.M. (1997) 'Methodological and analytical concerns on the pilot selection research of Park and Lee (1992)', *Human Factors*, 39 (1): 9–13.

Delery, J.E. (1998) 'Issues of fit in strategic human resource management: Implications for research', *Human Resource Management Review*, 8 (3): 289.

De Meuse, K.P. and Tornow, W.W. (1990) 'The tie that binds – Has become very, very frayed!', *Human Resource Planning*, 13 (3): 203–213.

De Witte, H. and Näswall, K. (2003) '"Objective" vs "subjective" job insecurity: Consequences of temporary work for job satisfaction and organizational commitment in four European countries', *Economic & Industrial Democracy*, 24 (2): 149.

Eagly, A.H. and Chaiken, S. (1993) *The Psychology of Attitudes.* Orlando, FL: Harcourt.

Eisenhardt, K.M. (1985) 'Control: Organizational and economic approaches', *Management Science*, 31 (2): 134–149.

Finegan, J.E. (2000) 'The impact of person and organizational values on organizational commitment', *Journal of Occupational and Organizational Psychology*, 73 (2): 149–169.

Gardner, W.L., Avolio, B.J., Luthans, F., May, D.R. and Walumbwa, F. (2005) '"Can you see the real me?" A self-based model of authentic leader and follower development', *Leadership Quarterly*, 16 (3): 343–372.

Gelfand, M.J., Erez, M.J. and Aycan, Z. (2007) 'Cross-cultural organizational behavior', *Annual Review of Psychology*, 58: 479–514.

Giacalone, R.A. and Greenberg, R.A. (1997) *Antisocial Behavior in Organizations.* Thousand Oaks, CA: Sage.

Gould-Williams, J. and Davies, F. (2005) 'Using social exchange theory to predict the effects of HRM practice on employee outcomes', *Public Management Review*, 7 (1): 1–24.

Gregerson, H.B. (1993) 'Multiple commitments at work and extra-role behavior during three stages of organizational tenure', *Journal of Business Research*, 26: 31–47.

Griffeth, R.W., Hom, P.W. and Gaertner, S. (2000) 'A meta-analysis of antecedents and correlates of employee turnover: Update, moderator tests, and research implications for the next millennium', *Journal of Management*, 26 (3): 463–488.

Guest, D. (1990) 'Human resource management and the American dream', *Journal of Management Studies*, 27 (4): 377–397.

Guest, D. (2004) 'Flexible employment contracts, the psychological contract and employee outcomes: An analysis and review of the evidence', *International Journal of Management Reviews*, 5/6 (1): 1–19.

Handy, C. (1989) *The Age of Unreason.* London: Business Books.

Herriot, P. (1992) *The Career Management Challenge: Balancing Individual and Organizational Needs.* London: Sage Publications, Inc.

Herriot, P. (2001) *The Employment Relationship.* Hove: Routledge.

Herriot, P., Manning, W.E.O. and Kidd, J.M. (1997) 'The content of the psychological contract', *British Journal of Management*, 8 (2): 151.

Hollander, E.P. (1971) *Principles and Methods of Social Psychology.* New York: Oxford University Press.

Hom, P.W. and Griffeth, R.W. (1995) *Employee Turnover.* Cincinatti, OH: South/Western.

Hrebiniak, L.G. and Alutto, J.A. (1972) 'Personal role-related factors: In the development of organizational commitment', *Administrative Science Quarterly*, 17: 555–573.

Huselid, M.A. (1995) 'The impact of human resource management practices on turnover, productivity, and corporate', *Academy of Management Journal*, 38 (3): 635.

Isaksson, K. and Johannson, G. (2003) 'Managing older employees after downsizing', *Scandinavian Journal of Management*, 19 (1): 1–15.

Kalimo, R., Taris, T.W. and Schaufeli, W.B. (2003) 'The effects of past and anticipated future downsizing on survivor well-being: An equity perspective', *Journal of Occupational Health Psychology*, 8 (2): 91–109.

Kammeyer Mueller, J.D., Wanberg, C.R., Glomb, T.M. and Ahlburg, D. (2005) 'The role of temporal shifts in turnover processes: It's about time', *Journal of Applied Psychology*, 90 (4): 644–658.

Kaplan, R.N. and Kaplan, M. (1979) 'Covenant versus contract as two models of relationship orientation: On recording possibility and necessity', *Journal of Psychology and Judaism*, 4 (2): 100–116.

Kluytmans, F. and Ott, M. (1999) 'Management of employability in The Netherlands', *European Journal of Work & Organizational Psychology*, 8 (2): 261–272.

Krug, J.A. (2003) 'Why do they keep leaving?', *Harvard Business Review*, 81 (2): 14–15.

Lawler, E.J. (1992) 'Affective attachments to nested groups: A choice-process theory', *American Sociological Review*, 57 (3): 327–336.

Luthans, B.C. and Sommer, S.M. (1999) 'The impact of downsizing on workplace attitudes: Differing reactions of managers and staff in a health care organization', *Group & Organization Management*, 24 (1): 46–70.

MacDuffie, J.P. (1995) 'Human resources bundles and manufacturing performance: Organizational logic and flexible production systems in the world auto industry', *Industrial & Labor Relations Review*, 48 (2): 197–221.

March, J.G. and Simon, H.A. (1958) *Organizations.* New York: Wiley.

Mathieu, J.E. and Zajac, D.M. (1990) 'A review and meta-analysis of the antecedents, correlates and consequences of organizational commitment', *Psychological Bulletin*, 108: 171–194.

Meyer, J.P. and Allen, N.J. (1991) 'A three-component conceptualization of organizational commitment', *Human Resource Management Review*, 1: 61–89.

Meyer, J.P. and Allen, N.J. (1997) *Commitment in the Workplace: Theory, Research and Application.* Thousand Oaks, CA: Sage.

Meyer, J.P., Stanley, D.J., Herscovitch, L. and Topolnytsky, L. (2002) 'Affective, continuance, and normative commitment to the organization: A meta-analysis of antecedents, correlates, and consequences', *Journal of Vocational Behavior*, 61: 20–52.

Mir, A., Mir, R. and Mosca, J.B. (2002) 'The new age employee: An exploration of changing employee-organization relations', *Public Personnel Management*, 31 (2): 187.

Moore, S., Grunberg, L. and Greenberg, E. (2004) 'Repeated downsizing contact: The effects of similar and dissimilar layoff experiences on work and well-being outcomes', *Journal of Occupational Health Psychology*, 9 (3): 247–257.

Morrow, P.C. and McElroy, J.C. (1987) 'Work commitment and job satisfaction over three career stages', *Journal of Vocational Behavior*, 30: 330–346.

Mowday, R.T., Steers, R.M. and Porter, L.W. (1979) 'The measurement of organizational commitment', *Journal of Vocational Behavior*, 14: 224–247.

Mowday, R.T., Porter, L.W. and Steers, R.M. (1982) *Employee-organization Linkages: The Psychology of Commitment, Absenteeism and Turnover.* New York: Academic Press.

Mueller, C.W. and Lawler, E.J. (1999) 'Commitment to nested organizational units: Some basic principles and preliminary findings', *Social Psychology Quarterly*, 62: 325–346.

Naus, F. (2007) *Organizational cynicism: On the nature, antecedents, and consequences of employee cynicism toward the employing organization.* Maastricht: Maastricht University (PhD Thesis).

Niehaus, R. and Swiercz, P.M. (1996) 'Do HR systems affect the bottom line? We have the answer', *Human Resource Planning*, 19 (4): 61–63.

O'Reilly, C.A. and Caldwell, D.F. (1985) 'The impact of normative social influence and cohesiveness on task perceptions and attitudes: A social information processing approach', *Journal of Occupational Psychology*, 58: 193–206.

O'Reilly, C.A. and Chatman, J. (1986) 'Organizational commitment and psychological attachment: The effects of compliance, identification, and internalization on prosocial behavior', *Journal of Applied Psychology*, 71 (3): 492–499.

Ouchi, W.G. and Maguire, M.A. (1975) 'Organizational control: Two functions', *Administrative Science Quarterly*, 20 (4): 559–569.

Palich, L.E., Hom, P.W. and Griffeth, R.W. (1995) 'Managing in the international context: Testing cultural generality of sources of commitment to multinational enterprises', *Journal of Management*, 21 (4): 671–690.

Parks, J.M., Kidder, D.L. and Gallagher, D.G. (1998) 'Fitting square pegs into round holes: Mapping the domain of contingent work arrangements onto the psychological contract', *Journal of Organizational Behavior*, 19 (7): 697–730.

Podsakoff, P.M., MacKenzie, S.B. and Bommer, W.H. (1996) 'Transformational leader behaviors and substitutes for leadership as determinants of employee satisfaction, commitment, trust, and organizational citizenship behaviors', *Journal of Management*, 22: 259–298.

Price, J.L. and Mueller, C.W. (1981) *Professional Turnover*. Bridgeport, CT: Luce.

Ramsay, H., Scholarios, D. and Harley, B. (2000) 'Employees and high-performance work systems: Testing inside the black box', *British Journal of Industrial Relations*, 38 (4): 501–531.

Randall, D.M. (1987) 'Commitment and the organization: The organization man revisited', *Academy of Management Review*, 12 (3): 460–471.

Randall, D.M. (1988) 'Multiple roles and organizational commitment', *Journal of Organizational Behavior*, 9: 309–317.

Reichers, A.E. (1985) 'A review and reconceptualization of organizational commitment', *Academy of Management Review*, 10: 465–476.

Romzek, B.S. (1989) 'Personal consequences of employee commitment', *Academy of Management Journal*, 32 (3): 649–661.

Rousseau, D.M. (1995) *Psychological Contracts in Organizations. Understanding Written and Unwritten Agreements*. Thousand Oaks, CA: Sage.

Salancik, G.R. (1977) 'Commitment and the control of organizational behavior and belief', in B. Staw and G. Salancik (eds) *New Directions in Organizational Behavior*. Chicago: St. Clair Press, pp. 51–59.

Salancik, G.R. and Pfeffer, J. (1978) 'A social information processing approach to job attitudes and task design', *Administrative Science Quarterly*, 23: 224–253.

Schwartz, H.S. (1987) 'Anti-social actions of committed organizational participants: An existential psychoanalytic perspective', *Organization Studies*, 8 (4): 327–340.

Senge, P. (1990) *The Fifth Discipline: The Art and Practice of the Learning Organization*. New York: Doubleday.

Solinger, O.N. (2004) *The Effect of Linguistics, Motivation and Temporality on Organizational Commitment Conceptualization. A New Conceptual Model*. Maastricht, The Netherlands: Maastricht University. Faculty of Economics and Business Administration. Department of Organization and Strategy.

Solinger, O.N., Van Olffen, W. and Roe, R.A. (2008) 'Beyond the three-component model of organizational commitment', *Journal of Applied Psychology*, 91 (1): 70–83.

Somers, M.J. and Casal, J.C. (1994) 'Organizational commitment and whistle-blowing: A test of the reformer and the organization man hypothesis', *Group & Organization Management*, 19 (3): 270–284.

Sparrow, P.R. (1998) 'Reappraising psychological contracting', *International Studies of Management & Organization*, 28 (1): 30–63.

Spreitzer, G.M. and Mishra, A.K. (2002) 'To stay or to go: Voluntary survivor turnover following an organizational downsizing', *Journal of Organizational Behavior*, 23 (6): 707–729.

Steers, R.M. (1977) 'Antecedents and outcomes of organizational commitment', *Administrative Science Quarterly*, 22: 46–56.

Steers, R.M. and Mowday, R.T. (1981) 'Employee turnover and postdecision accommodation processes', in L.L. Cummings and B.M. Staw (eds) *Research in Organizational Behavior* (Vol. 3). Greenwich, CT: JAI Press, pp. 235–281.

Stinglhamber, F. and Vandenberghe, C. (2003) 'Organizations and supervisors as sources of support and targets of commitment: A longitudinal study', *Journal of Organizational Behavior*, 24: 251–270.

Storey, J., Quintas, P., Taylor, P. and Fowle, W. (2002) 'Flexible employment contracts and their implications for product and process innovation', *International Journal of Human Resource Management*, 13 (1): 1–18.

Sturges, J., Conway, N., Guest, D. and Liefooghe, A. (2005) 'Managing the career deal: The psychological contract as a framework for understanding career management, organizational commitment and work behavior', *Journal of Organizational Behavior*, 26: 821–838.

Tett, R.P. and Meyer, J.P. (1993) 'Job satisfaction, organizational commitment, turnover intention, and turnover: Path analyses based on meta-analytic findings', *Personnel Psychology*, 46: 259–293.

Truss, C. (2001) 'Complexities and controversies in linking HRM with organizational outcomes', *Journal of Management Studies*, 38 (8): 1121–1149.

Van Diepen, B., Van Iterson, A. and Roe, R.A. (2006) 'Human resources management in Europe and North America: Similarities and differences', in C. Cooper and R. Burke (eds) *The Human Resources Revolution: Research and Practice*. New York: Elsevier.

Van Maanen, J. (1977) 'Police socialization: A longitudinal examination of job attitudes in an urban police department', *Administrative Science Quarterly*, 20: 207–228.

Vandenberg, R.J. and Self, R.M. (1993) 'Assessing newcomers' changing commitments to the organization during the first 6 months of work', *Journal of Applied Psychology*, 78 (4): 557–568.

Walton, R.E. (1985) 'From control to commitment in the workplace', *Harvard Business Review*, 63 (2): 77–84.

Wasti, S.A. (2003) 'Organizational commitment, turnover intentions and the influence of cultural values', *Journal of Occupational and Organizational Psychology*, 76: 303–321.

Whitener, E.M. (2001) 'Do "high commitment" human resource practices affect employee commitment? A cross-level analysis using hierarchical linear modeling', *Journal of Management*, 27 (5): 515–535.

Whyte, W.N. (1956) *The Organization Man*. New York: Simon and Schuster.

Wright, P.M., Gardner, T.M., Moynihan, L.M., Park, H.J., Gerhart, B. and Delery, J.E. (2001) 'Measurement error in research on human resources and firm performance: Additional data and suggestions for future research', *Personnel Psychology*, 54 (4): 875–901.

Wright, P.M., Gardner, T.M., Moynihan, L.M. and Allen, M.R. (2005) 'The relationship between HR practices and firm performance: Examining causal order', *Personnel Psychology*, 58 (2): 409–446.

# 8

# Power in Organizational Behaviour

Raymond Daniel Gordon

The purpose of this chapter is to provide a critical review of what writers in the field of organization behaviour have had to say about power. The critique is framed within a comparative model where the approach to power adopted by these writers is compared to that adopted by key writers from broader fields related to organization studies. The comparative model shows that the literature on power in organizations has largely developed along two separate paths, one path having an idealist orientation and the other having a pragmatist orientation.[1] It is acknowledged that not all contributions to the literature are covered in the review; the charter for the chapter restricts the review to key contributions. Furthermore, there are incidents where a crossover between the paths could be argued, that is, some works categorized as being part of the idealist path promote a practical orientation towards the management of power in organizations. However, these works are categorized as idealist here because they are underpinned by a distinctly normative position: they promote an idea about how power 'ought' to be in organizations.

The chapter will begin by reviewing the literature that constitutes an idealist path. Marx and Weber are acknowledged as the foundering fathers of this literature; their work however will not be reviewed in detail – numerous other writers have already done this (see Clegg and Dunkerley, 1980 for example).

The community power debates that took place during the 1950s and 1960s made a significant contribution to this body of literature; when reviewing the literature chronologically, it is from these debates that what has become known as the 1st, 2nd and 3rd dimensions or faces of power appear to emerged. As shall be seen, organizational behaviour literature largely ascribes to the 1st dimensional view of power.

The chapter then reviews the literature that constitutes a pragmatist path. The organizational behaviour literature has largely neglected and in some case condemned this literature (Clegg *et al.*, 2006). Machiavelli and

Nietzsche are acknowledged as the founders of this literature, while the main contributor in regard to contemporary work on power in organizations is Foucault. Machiavelli and Nietzsche's writings will not be reviewed in detail; the objective here is to show how particular accounts of power in organizations emerge from their work.

While it is acknowledged that there are many writers who have employed Foucauldian analytics, the chapter focuses on the work of four contemporary post-Foucauldian theorists (Clegg, 1989; Haugaard, 1997; Flyvbjerg, 1998; Courpasson, 2000) who are recognized as leading writers in the field. The work of these theorists has contemporary significance and offers alternative theoretical and methodological insights into the nature of power in organizations.

Finally, the chapter explicates the differences between the idealist and pragmatist paths of literature and argues with reference to the context in which organizations find themselves today, that the field of organization studies and especially the field of organizational behaviour would benefit from a greater acceptance of research endeavours conducive with the conceptual and empirical frameworks presented in the pragmatist path of literature.

## IDEAS ABOUT HOW POWER 'OUGHT' TO BE

Weber and Marx are recognized as the founders (Hardy and Clegg, 1996) of this path of literature. Both, like writers[2] before them, adopt a common agency model in regard to power (Ball, 1978). A common agency model views power as being held by entities – for instance a person, group or department is viewed as having more or less power. Both also focus on the way in which power is derived from owning and controlling the means of production and how this power is reinforced by organizational structures and rules of governance. The differences in their approach to power, however, provides a 'fork in the road' in regard to the development of this path of literature. The 1st dimensional view of power reflects Weber's work while the 2nd and 3rd dimensional view of power is rooted in the work of Marx.

## The 1st dimensional view of power

During the 1950s and 1960s political theorists such as, Dahl (1957, 1961) and Polsby (1963) were focusing their research on how the way decisions were made in a community illustrated the nature of power relations in this community. Two opposing theories of what constituted 'good' government emerged – *élitism* and *pluralism*. In short: if the same groups or individuals were found to make most of the decisions in the key decision-making arenas, the community was said to be *élitist*; if decisions were made in different arenas by different groups the community was said to be *pluralist*.

Dahl (1957, 1958, 1961, 1968), an advocate of pluralist government, is recognized as the main contributor to the Community Power Debate literature. In a series of publications, he mapped out a behavioural science oriented response to what he described as the much less rigorous work of the 'élitist' theorists – Hunter and Mills. Dahl regarded the work of the élitist theorists as being methodologically slack. Subsequently, for Dahl the concern was with the construction of a methodological approach that could capture and provide a formal model of power. To acquire precision, Dahl employed the principles of mechanics and focused on cause and effect relationships between forms in motion: the power of 'A' could be measured through the reaction of 'B' (Clegg, 1989). That is, when 'A' makes 'B' do something that 'B' would not have otherwise done, 'A' has exercised power over 'B'. This definition resonates with the work of Weber, who defined power as the chance of a person or number of persons to realize their own will in a communal action, even against the resistance of others (Weber, 1948).

In addition to this somewhat mechanistic definition of power, underpinning the community power debates and subsequently the 1st dimensional view of power is the grounding of power to decision-making scenarios. That is, central to a first dimensional view of power is the assumption that all individuals are aware of the 'state of play' in regard to power and politics in their social environments and how this state of play impacts them; for the behaviourists, non-participation in decision making simply indicated that individuals were satisfied with the state of play. Such a view also necessarily grounds power to conflict situations; that is, individuals will participate in decision making when the decision scenario impinges on their interest. Furthermore, this approach to power necessarily assumes that power resides with people, that is, power does not exist unless people exercise it and, some people have more or less power than others (Bachrach and Baratz, 1963; Lukes, 1974; Clegg 1989; Hardy and Clegg, 1996; Hardy and Leiba-O'Sullivan, 1998).

When one considers the organizational behaviour literature more specifically the relative neglect of power becomes apparent. Organization behaviour texts make reference to Weber's work on rational legal power and authority and the early work of researchers such as Thompson (1956), Bennis (1959), Crozier (1964), French and Raven (1968) and more recently Pfeffer (1981) and Mintzberg (1983). Geoffrey Pfeffer is perhaps the most renowned writer in the field and in 1992 advocated a seven-point plan for getting things done through the use of power and influence: decide your goals; diagnose patterns of dependence and interdependence; including which individuals are influential; establish their views of your goals; identify their power bases in comparison to yours; determine effective strategies and choose a course of action. While each of these earlier studies made a major contribution to our understanding of power in organizations, little has been done since. Generally speaking, in the field of organization behaviour power is only implicitly addressed by studies that have an alternative research focus. If one picks up any organizational behaviour text book today and turns to the pages discussing

power, invariably much of the space is devoted to discussions on hierarchical and authoritarian forms of power along with French and Raven's bases of power model or some version there of. In short, in general the organizational behaviour literature remains entrenched in 1st dimensional view of power.

By way of critique, as Hardy and Clegg (1996) pointed out, when it comes to the legitimacy of power, contributors to the 1st dimensional view appear to have a preoccupation with rational legal authority and have consequently:

> rarely felt it necessary to explain why it is that power should be hierarchical. In other words, in this stream of research, the power embedded in hierarchy has been viewed as 'normal' and 'inevitable' following from the formal design of the organization. As such, it has largely been excluded from analyses, which have, instead, focused on 'illegitimate' power, i.e. power exercised outside formal hierarchical structures and the channels that they sanction (Hardy and Clegg, 1996: 624).

Contributors to the 1st dimensional view separated power and authority: authority, because it is associated with the organization's formal structure, rules and regulations, was considered unquestionably legitimate and consequently viewed as something different to power, which is attributed to political action on behalf of those actors who are not formally sanctioned with authority. According to this approach, those who are not sanctioned with authority in an organization have a duty to obey those who are; when one has a duty to obey, one 'should' not engage in conflict. This observation adds weight to why these early works necessarily associated power with conflict situations in which individuals engaged in political activities to realize their own vested interests at the expense of the organization's interest as a whole. For instance, in one of his earlier work's is Pfeffer (1981: 7) argues:

> It is clear that political activity is activity, which is undertaken to overcome some resistance or opposition. Without opposition or contest within the organization, there is neither the need nor the expectation that one would observe political activity.

Here, Pfeffer implies that in an organization context those sanctioned with authority, namely managers, only engage in politics to overcome resistance on behalf of workers, which results in an inefficient and ineffective use of an organization's resources; power and politics would not even occur if workers did not resist management (see Gandz and Murray, 1980; Enz, 1988 for similar views). Mintzberg (1983: 172) adds:

> Politics refers to individual or group behaviour that is informal, ostensibly parochial, typically divisive, and above all, in the technical sense, illegitimate – sanctioned neither by formal authority, accepted ideology, nor certified expertise (Mintzberg, 1983: 172).

Arguments like these from such prominent writers are indicative of an overriding focus on how to defeat power and conflict (Hardy and Clegg, 1996). Such a focus however, is premised on the assumption that those sanctioned with authority are capable of achieving rationally in the purest sense: 'the possibility that managers might seek to serve their own vested interests [in a given context] is largely ignored' (Hardy and Clegg, 1996: 629).

This body of literature considers formal structure as a legitimate equilibrium starting point from which a version of how power 'ought' to be in an organization is promulgated: it is only rational that power 'ought' to be in the hands of those formally sanctioned with authority. This starting point misrepresents the complex nature of power and consequently, especially in the organizational behaviour literature, other topics such as leadership, culture and decision making are largely treated as being politically neutral, inevitable and hence, unproblematic (Hardy and Clegg, 1996; see also Deetz, 1985; Clegg, 1989; Knights and Willmott, 1992).

## The 2nd dimensional view of power

Bachrach and Baratz (1962), questioned the 1st dimensional view of power by arguing that access to decision making scenarios was not available to all members of a social system and consequently, non-participation in decision making does not necessarily reflect satisfaction with the 'state of play' by non-participants. Bachrach and Baratz, and later others (Lukes, 1974; Clegg, 1975; Saunders, 1979), asserted that just because conflict was not observable did not mean that it did not exist; perhaps the interests and grievances of people remained unspoken and thus, never voiced in the decision-making scenario (Saunders, 1979; Gaventa, 1980). Schattschneider (1960) argued that rather than non-participation signalling agreement with decision outcomes, such inaction may be due to the suppression of information that, if not suppressed might compel non-participants to act. In short, the suppression of information may limit non-participants knowledge and compound their ignorance of variables that could significantly influence the decision process.

Building on this insight Bachrach and Baratz (1962; 1963) developed what has now become known as the 2nd dimension of power. They argued that a variety of previously unconsidered options were available to more powerful members of organizations who could use these options to prevent less powerful members from participating in decision situations. For instance, Parry and Morris (1974) argued, that managerial decision making took on an élitist character. They demonstrated empirically how, due to the endless committees, enquiries, or co-optations that constituted life at the top of organizations, managers rarely took the time to 'hear' the viewpoints or demands of their subordinates.

Non-decision-making can also operate through Friedrichs's (1937) 'rule of anticipated reaction' where a person anticipates a powerful other's likely opposition and consequently does not raise an issue. In short, 'Potential protagonists remain mute, from the expectation that they would invoke strenuous opposition' (Clegg, 1989: 79). Resonating with the 'rule of anticipated reaction' is Schattschneider's (1960) 'Mobilization of Bias', which refers to an unobtrusive system of order that privileges certain groups and individuals. Saunders (1979: 30–31) explains in more detail that a mobilization of bias,

> refers to those situations where dominant interests may exert such a degree of control over the way in which a political system operates, and over the values, beliefs and opinions of less powerful groups within it, they can effectively determine not only whether certain demands come to be expressed and needed, but also whether such demands will ever cross people's minds ... Crucial issues thus never emerge for public debate, and to study the course of contentious issues (as Dahl did in New Haven) is merely to study what happens to the political crumbs strewn carelessly about by an elite with its hands clasped firmly around the cake.

This suppression of crucial issues is an example of what Bachrach and Baratz (1962: 950) refer to as a non-decision-making process, where 'latent' power conflicts a never subject to public debate; decision scenarios are confined to 'the dominant values and the political myths, rituals, and institutions which tend to favour the vested interests of one or more groups'. Bachrach and Baratz's 2nd dimension of power is concerned with how some people are prevented from participating in decision making and thus marginalized. In this sense, they argue that power 'ought' to be democratic.

### The 3rd dimensional view of power

Lukes (1974) argued that Bachrach and Baratz did not go far enough, they still focused much upon issues about how 'decisions' were made, albeit 'non-decisions' (Ranson et al., 1980: 8). Central to his view of power was doubt in regard to the necessity for conflict between parties for non-decision-making power to be evident. He built on the work of Bachrach and Baratz to develop what is now known as the 3rd dimension of power by theorizing that power could be used to prevent conflict from occurring through the management of meaning. That is, by shaping people's

> perceptions, cognitions and preferences in such as way that they accept their role in the existing order

of things, either because they can see or imagine no alternative to it, or because they view it as natural and unchangeable, or because they value it as divinely ordained and beneficial (Lukes, 1974: 24).

Here, Lukes argues that power cannot be confined to observable conflict, to the outcomes of decisions, or to the suppression of information; it must also consider the question of political quiescence (Hardy and Clegg, 1996). In this sense, Lukes is concerned with how, through the natural-order-of-things, people might be 'duped, hoodwinked, coerced, cajoled or manipulated into political inactivity' (Saunders, 1979: 22). For Lukes, this use of power helped élite groups and individuals to sustain their dominance and reduce the likelihood of subordinates exercising the discretionary power they possessed. Along these lines, 'power is most effective when it is unnecessary' (Ranson et al., 1980: 8).

Accordingly, Lukes was concerned to interpret those mechanisms which perpetuated the status quo. His approach was characterized by a Marxian heritage (Clegg, 1989) because of his use of Gramsci's concept of 'ideological hegemony', which is a concept used to describe situations where 'a structure of power relations is fully legitimized by an integrated system of cultural and normative assumptions' (Hyman and Fryer, 1975: 199). The right to power of élite individuals or groups (to make decisions) becomes reified over time through the routine normalcy of their exercise of such power. In short, the perceived superiority and right to power for social élites, such as owners, leaders and managers becomes part of the natural-order-of-things. Lukes (1974), sees power operating when people have no awareness of, let alone the desire to realize, how the actions of others impact their interests: they are unaware of their 'real interests'.[3] While Lukes' 3rd dimensional view of power clearly moves beyond Bachrach and Baratz's 2nd dimensional view, he is similarly concerned with the emancipation of those marginalized by the hegemonic system in which they exist and therefore is also promulgating that power 'ought' to be democratic.

## THE PRAGMATIST STREAM: ACCOUNTS OF HOW POWER 'ACTUALLY' IS

Contributors to the 'pragmatists stream' are not concerned with telling people how power 'ought' to be in organizations, rather they are concerned with studying 'how' power comes to be exercised in the way that it is. The founding voices of the stream are Machiavelli and Nietzsche, while the main contributor from which much of the contemporary work on power in organizations has developed, is Foucault. As shall be seen, the work of both Machiavelli and Nietzsche is central to what Foucault has to say about power.

The achievement of order for Machiavelli does not come from a commitment to an ideal form of governance through a rational and benevolent leader; rather it is secured by a strategically minded prince (Machiavelli, 1958) who is adept at acting politically. The Prince's,

> focus is on strategies, deals, negotiation, fraud and conflict in which myths (ideals) concerning moral action become game players' resources (tools or weapons) rather than a topic which frames what the game should be (Clegg, 1989: 30).

Rather than an idealist framework, Machiavelli conceived power in terms of pure expediency, as distinctly empirical, with workings not independent of but dependent on context (Bauman, 1982). Machiavelli (1958: 91) maintains, 'a man who neglects what is actually done for what should be done learns the way of self-destruction'. In a similar, but later vein, Nietzsche (1968) argues that ideals are myths and lies, claiming that rather than a will to ideals, morals and values, people have a will to power. Nietzsche further argues in regard to the virtues of rationality, 'rationality at any cost ... in opposition to instincts has itself been no more than a form of sickness' (1968: 34). What he means is that

it is impossible to achieve rationality and that we often mislead ourselves in its pursuit.

For contributors to the idealist path of literature, such views are likely to be considered vulgar and divisive. However, rather than marginalizing what Machiavelli and Nietzsche have to say about power, this chapter considers their statements to be valuable in the sense that they act as beacons that remind us that people cannot divorce themselves from contextual pressures and that having faith in the way things 'ought' to be risks blindness to the more complex workings of power. In this sense, the work of Machiavelli [4] and Nietzsche can be seen not so much as a challenge but as a check in regard to how we pursue our ideals, including the modern ideals of 'rationality' and 'democracy' (Flyvbjerg, 1998; 2001).

Following Machiavelli and Nietzsche, Foucault was interested in the micro-dynamics of power and focused on the relationship between power and knowledge in social systems. Foucault's work is not easily understood and, for management and organizational behaviour writers, appears quite revolutionary. Many authors have embraced his ideas, but in translation the diversity of interpretation has resulted in a voluminous secondary literature that is fragmented and often contradictory. Here, both Foucault's work and interpretations of it, principally Clegg's (1989), Haugaard's (1997) and Flyvbjerg's (1998) will be addressed. Other writers who provide excellent interpretations of Foucault's work are Bauman (1982), Rabinow, (1984), Smart (1985) and Gane (1986).

Foucault argues that knowledge is socially constructed and reflects the outcomes of historical struggles for power; thus conceptions of 'truth' and 'reality' are not, in the scientific sense, 'out there' waiting to be discovered. Rather, they are historically constituted in our knowledge and subsequently reflect how histories, experience and learning. In this sense they are distinctly empirical, grounded in context and culturally specific. One can appreciate what Foucault means by recognizing that the systematic organization of knowledge reflected upon by cultures, such as in indigenous cultures similar those of different clans of Australian aboriginals, is based on myths, stories and legends – the Dreamtime. The knowledge of such indigenous cultures will differ from that of members from another culture who reflect upon knowledge constituted by religious doctrines, and differ again from those who reflect upon knowledge based on the principles of science. Each culture has its own set of historical antecedents and thus constitution of knowledge; if people from different cultures are reflecting on different bodies of knowledge when they make sense of the world, it is highly likely that the sense they make will also differ.

Reflecting on the writings of Foucault, Haugaard (1997: 43) observes that if knowledge is culturally specific, 'there is no "true" or "correct" interpretation based upon the discovery of the truth'. Idealists may critique Haugaard's observation by asking, 'How can it be true that there is no truth'. Such critique however, which is distinctly modern in the sense that it seeks absolutism, misses the point of Haugaard's observation. Foucault would alter Haugaard's observation slightly so that it read, 'hence, there is no *single* "true" or "correct" interpretation based upon the discovery of truth'. In other words, Foucault acknowledges that people do have a perception of truth, but their perception of this truth comes from reflection upon their cultural antecedents or historically constituted knowledge: different cultures have different histories, different antecedents, different versions of knowledge, and therefore, viewpoints about 'truth'. In this sense, there are *multiple* 'true' and 'correct' interpretations of truth.

Foucault goes further by showing how the historically constituted knowledge of reality that members of a cultural setting have acts as a meaning system – a meaning system is a historical *a priori* system of order that makes it possible for individuals to make sense of their world (Foucault, 1970). In a way that is not dissimilar to the work of Weber (1968). Foucault shows that in each cultural setting there are hidden rules or codes of order members of the setting need to follow in order to be seen by others as making sense: these codes of order unobtrusively constitute power structures, discipline behaviour and through this the construction of meaning and knowledge in the setting.

For Foucault, learning and the dynamic of knowledge, which he refers to as 'truth production', are situated in a theory of power. He argues, 'truth is linked in a circular relation with systems of power which produce and sustain it, and to the effects of power that induce and extend it' (Foucault, 1980: 133). Thus, it is the exercise of power, constrained by a social system's codes of order, which enables, drives and shapes the production of new 'truths' and subsequently extends knowledge within this system.

It follows from this that knowledge and power are inseparable and that the production of 'truth' in any social system, reflects the outcome of a struggle for power. Haugaard (1997: 68) interprets the notion of this struggle as suggesting that there will be a disqualification of some representations of knowledge (as idiocy), and a fight for others, all in the name of 'truth'. Foucault (1977) adds that when the struggle for power gives rise to a representation being seen as 'truth' and therefore established as valid knowledge, there has been a positive outcome of power. This is what Foucault means by power in a positive form. He does not see this as positive in the sense that it is something people should welcome. Rather he sees it as merely being positive because it introduces change into a system by virtue of creating new realities, truths and knowledge (Haugaard, 1997). It is positive in the sense of making something happen: it induces change.

In contrast to much of what is promulgated within the idealist path of literature, Foucault's work suggests that power can no longer be seen as a convenient, manipulatable and deterministic resource. It is more than just something that 'A' does to 'B' to make 'B' do something that 'B' wouldn't otherwise do. One cannot simply argue that power can be explained as 'A' making 'B' do something against 'B's' interests, as is in the case of Lukes' 3rd dimensional view. Foucault's work, while indirectly sympathetic to the critical approach adopted by Lukes (1974), has no space for the concepts of 'real interests'. By way of explanation, for Foucault (1990) the discursive nature by which meaning systems are constituted renders the notion of ideology problematic and any conception of false consciousness implausible; ideology and false consciousness are deemed untenable because they are ultimately grounded in an essentialist conception of society and social agency (Clegg, 1989). The former conceptualizes society as an 'intelligible totality', similar to the classical Marxist base/superstructure model, where the ideological totality is assumed to be 'the' underlying principle of intelligibility through which social order is constituted in society; in short, 'the' version of how things 'ought' to be. The problem with conceptualizing an intelligible totality or a version of how things 'ought' to be is that it is culturally specific. Bearing in mind that there is no culture on earth that doesn't believe that its truth is not true (Haugaard, 1997), one must ask the question, which versions of how things 'ought' to be is correct?

Foucault's work inextricably links power and knowledge, it shows that, 'It is not possible for power to be exercised without knowledge, it is impossible for knowledge not to engender power' (Foucault, 1980: 52). This power/knowledge nexus, places people within a web of power relations from which there is no escape; not just the privileged, but everyone has access to power (Hardy and Clegg, 1996). Thus, what is ordinarily taken to be knowledge and from knowledge as versions of how things 'ought' to be, has been constituted by the struggle for power.

The plurality of 'truth' is the reason why Foucault distrusts ideology (Haugaard, 1997). He maintains that commitment to ideology bounds one to mythical ideas of how things 'ought' to be, rather than how they actually are. Foucault's use of the term 'distrusts' rather than 'dispels', indicates that he is neither a nihilist nor relativist. Not trusting

one's ideology does not leave one valueless or norm-less. What Foucault means by not trusting ideology is that while he does have ideals and values, he does not see them as representing essential or fixed truths; rather, he acknowledges that through learning from the experience of social life his ideals and values have not only been historically constituted by the struggle for power but are open to change by the same means. He argues against allowing ones attitude to social phenomena and events to be based on an idiosyncratic morality or personal preference. In doing so, he places an emphasis on the socially and historically conditioned context and not a rational and universal grounding perceived and promoted by some philosophical idealist – grounding (not unlike that promoted by Marx and Lukes), which to this day is yet to be achieved (Flyvbjerg, 2001).

Furthermore, Foucault's genealogical analysis shows all interpretations are open for relative testing but not all interpretations are equal, which would be a case for relativism. Rather, in social systems, the acceptance of an interpretation must be built upon a claim of validity, part of which is acquiring legitimacy over alternative interpretations. Thus, while interpretations may well be influenced by *a priori* knowledge, the process by which one interpretation gains legitimacy over others indicates that the representation of interpretations is subject to the influence of contextual variables. This process of acquiring legitimacy illustrates that the means by which an interpretation acquires validity is not simply ideologically grounded (i.e., based on some preconceived idea of how things 'ought' to be) but that it also has a discursive dimension that is distinctly political: a dimension that is strategic, empirical and thus, context dependent.

Several contemporary writers in the broader field of organization studies contribute to the pragmatist path of literature. Stewart Clegg (1975; 1989; 1990) is perhaps the most renowned contributor. Rather than viewing power as something exercised when illegitimate use of system resources prevailed – as do those who contribute to the idealist path of literature, Clegg shows that it is an inherent characteristic of every aspect of organizational life, from the discourses that organizations produced, the subject of his earlier work (Clegg, 1975), to the structuring of organizations as sedimented selection rules in his slightly later work (Clegg, 1975; Clegg and Dunkerley 1980), through to the two major statements of his position in *Frameworks of Power* (Clegg, 1989) and *Power and Organizations* (Clegg et al., 2006). The former of these later two works introduced his conception of power as essentially a circulatory, relational property, using the model of circuits of power, while the latter incorporated insights from both the work on sedimentation and a radical re-reading of the history of organization studies as a story of power drilling into body, soul and mind.

Other contributors include Townley (1993) who explores the relevance of Foucault's power/knowledge nexus to the management of human resources; Hardy, who along with Clegg offers a critique of how the management literature has addressed power; Flyvbjerg (1998) who empirically illustrates how managers and political figures in a Danish council strategically legitimize their preferred course of action and ultimately rationalize their own versions of rationality – giving rationality a plurality – to convince themselves and others that their actions are legitimate; Courpasson (2000) who empirically illustrates how the introduction of new organizational structures, aimed at empowering lower level workers, are underpinned by unobtrusive forms of power (he terms these forms of power 'soft bureaucracy') continue to centralize power into the hands of managers and surreptitiously control the behaviour of lower level workers; and Gordon (2007), who, similar to both Flyvbjerg and Courpasson, empirically illustrates how certain officers in a police organization attempting to implement democratic control mechanisms remain subject to a despotic organizational social system and subsequently, because a narrow constitution of knowledge prevents

them from doing otherwise, continue to rationalize unethical and corrupt behaviour as not only 'rational', but 'right' and 'just'– termed by the officers as 'noble-cause-corruption'.

## CONCLUSION

The 1st, 2nd and 3rd dimensional views of power are recognized as being fundamentally underpinned by an attempt to promulgate a certain idealist view of how power 'ought' to be in social settings; this literature is subsequently termed the 'idealist path' of the power in organizations literature – the mainstream organizational behaviour literature adopts 1st dimensional view of power and is primarily based on the resource dependency model of power.

The alternative path of the power literature moves from the work of Machiavelli and Nietzsche, through to Foucault and on to contemporary writers such Clegg, Haugaard and Flyvbjerg. The chapter illustrates how this literature does not concern itself with how power 'ought' to be in organizations but how it actually is; accordingly this path of literature is termed the 'pragmatist stream'.

Much of that which is promulgated in the idealist stream is informative in regard to the workings of power in social settings, but, because of its normative grounding, fails to capture the broader complexities of power in organizations. Nietzsche's and Foucault's work challenges the validity of any ideal; for them, ideals represent a grand narrative or 'truth' about how things 'ought' to be, which leaves members of society with the problem of deciding which is the grandest 'ought' of them all. Contributors to the pragmatist path of literature turn the notion of ideals as versions of 'truth' on its head by illustrating how 'truth', rather than being outside of human influence waiting to be discovered, is a result of power. That is, 'truth' is socially constructed and is thus culturally significant and context dependent: ideals such as 'truth', 'rationality' and 'democracy' therefore are not singular but instead they have a plurality. For Foucault and his followers, 'power does not involve taking sides, identifying who has more or less of it, as much as seeking to describe its strategic role – how it is used to translate people into characters or articulate an organizational morality play' (Hardy and Clegg, 1996: 631). Rather than idealistic, the pragmatist path of literature is strategic.

When compared to the 'pragmatist stream' the 'idealist stream' of literature, while offering valuable insights and hence a contribution to the understanding of power in organizations does not provide an in-depth account of power. This is because the contributors to the 'idealist stream' adopt equilibrium starting points that ground the study power to episodic and causal situations; in short, they employ research frameworks that amputate important contextual variables that are significant in regard to the workings of power, more specifically, how and why power comes to be exercised in particular ways. The pragmatist path of literature, by focusing on the actual workings of power, attempt to employ broader research frameworks that are not limited by some preconceived idea of how power 'ought' to be and subsequently provide a more in-depth account of the balance and workings of power in organizations.

The pragmatist path of research into power argues that organizations are complex arenas of negotiation, contestation and struggle, rendering them 'subject to multivalent powers rather than monadic sites of total control … It is in these struggles that power and resistance are played out in dramatic scenes that those approaches influenced by Foucault seem best able to appreciate because they are not predisposed to know in advance who the victorious and vanquished *dramatis personae* "should" be' (Hardy and Clegg, 1996: 633). For this reason, management and especially organization behaviour theorists might benefit from theoretical and research frameworks consistent with the pragmatist path of literature, at the very least the field needs to move beyond the 1st Dimensional view of power.

## NOTES

1 It is acknowledged that the literature outside of that which is recognized as mainstream may not fit this categorization.

2 For instance, the seventeenth-century English political theorist Thomas Hobbes' (1839) ideas, despite being presented centuries beforehand, are evident in the modern era's approach to power in organizations. He promotes a legislative approach to power (Bauman, 1987; Clegg, 1989), meaning that he was concerned with legislating 'what' power is. Indeed, he provides one of the first accounts of a governance model that rationalized the use of power to achieve an ordered society and 'relatively autonomous, self managing discourse' (Bauman, 1987: 2).

3 It is Lukes' concept of real interest that renders his 3rd dimension of power problematic. Following Benton's (1981) paradox of emancipation, to assume that one knows the real interest of others better than they do themselves adopts a normative view and a position of moral and intellectual superiority, which, in a pluralist world is arrogant and in a cultural sense ethnocentric.

4 I acknowledge that Machiavelli is given some attention in the management literature (Gable and Topol, 1991), but not in the same vein as it is here. His work is addressed normatively and is often referred to in distinctly negative terms.

## REFERENCES

Bachrach, P. and Baratz, M.S. (1962) 'Two faces of power', *American Political Review*, 56: 947–952.

Bachrach, P. and Baratz, M.S. (1963) 'Decisions and non-decisions: An analytical framework', *American Political Review*, 57: 641–651.

Bachrach, P. and Baratz, M.S. (1970) *Power and Poverty: Theory and Practice*. Oxford: Oxford University Press.

Ball, T. (1978) 'Two concepts of coercion', *Theory and Society*, 5 (1): 97–112.

Bauman, Z. (1982) *Memories of Class: The Pre-History and After-Life of Class*. London: Routledge and Kegan Paul.

Bauman, Z. (1987) *Legislators and Interpreters*. Cambridge: Polity Press.

Bennis, W.G. (1959) 'Leadership theory and administrative behavior: The problems of authority', *Administrative Science Quarterly*, 4: 259–301.

Benton, T. (1981) '"Objective" interests in the sociology of power', *Sociology*, 15 (2): 61–184.

Clegg, S.R. (1975) *Power, Rule and Domination*. London: Routledge and Kegan Paul.

Clegg, S.R. (1989) *Frameworks of Power*. London: Sage.

Clegg, S.R. (1990) *Modern Organizations: Organizations in the Post Modern World*. London: Sage.

Clegg, S.R. and Dunkerley, D. (1980) *Organisation, Class and Control*. London: Routledge and Kegan Paul.

Clegg, S.R., Courpasson, D. and Phillips, N. (2006) *Power and Organizations*. Thousand Oaks, CA: Sage.

Courpasson, D. (2000) 'Managerial strategies of domination: Power in soft bureaucracies', *Organization Studies*, 21 (1): 141–162.

Crozier, M. (1964) *The Bureaucratic Phenomenon*. London: Tavistock.

Dahl, R.A. (1957) 'The concept of power', *Behavioural Science*, 2: 201–205.

Dahl, R.A. (1958) 'Critique of the ruling elite', *American Political Science Review*, 52: 463–469.

Dahl, R.A. (1961) *Who Governs? Democracy and Power in an American City*. New Haven: Yale University Press.

Dahl, R.A. (1968) 'Power', in *International Encyclopaedia of the Social Sciences*. New York: Macmillan, pp. 405–415.

Deetz, S. (1985) 'Critical-cultural research: New sensibilities and old realities', *Journal of Management*, 11 (2): 121–136.

Dubin, R. (1957) 'Power and union-management relations', *Administrative Science Quarterly*, 2: 60–81.

Enz, C.A. (1988) 'The role of value congruity in interorganizational power', *Administrative Science Quarterly*, 33: 284–304.

Flyvbjerg, B. (1998) *Rationality and Power: Democracy in Practice*. London: University of Chicago Press.

Flyvbjerg, B. (2001) *Making Social Science Matter: Why Social Inquiry Fails and How It Can Succeed Again*. Cambridge: Cambridge University Press.

Foucault, M. (1970) *The Order of Things*. London: Routledge.

Foucault, M. (1977) *Discipline and Punish*. London: Allen Lane.

Foucault, M. (1980) In C. Gordon (ed.) *Power/Knowledge: Selected Interviews and Other Writings 1972–1977*. Brighton: Harvester Press.

Foucault, M. (1990) *The Care of the Self: The History of Sexuality, Volume 3: The Care of the Self*. Harmondsworth: Penguin.

French, J. and Raven, B. (1968). 'The bases of social power', in D. Cartwright (ed.) *Studies in Social Power*. Ann Arbor, MI: Institute for Social Research.

Friedrich, C.J. (1937) *Constitutional Government and Democracy*. New York: Gipp.

Gable, M. and Topol, M.T. (1991) 'Machiavellian managers: Do they perform better?', *Journal of Business and Psychology*, 5 (3): 355–365.

Gandz, J. and Murray, V.V. (1980) 'The experience of workplace politics', *Academy of Management Journal*, 23 (2): 237–251.

Gane, M. (1986) 'Review: The form of Foucault', *Economy and Society*, 15 (1): 110–122.

Gaventa, J.P. (1980) *Power and Powerlessness: Quiescence and Rebellion in an Appalachian Valley*. Urbana: University of Illinois Press.

Gordon, R.D. (2007) *Power, Knowledge and Domination*. Libre: Copenhagen Business School Press.

Hardy, C. and Clegg, S.R. (1996) 'Some dare call it power', in S.R. Clegg, C. Hardy and W.R. Nord (eds) *Handbook of Organization Studies*. London: Sage, pp. 622–641.

Hardy, C. and Leiba-O'Sullivan, S. (1998) 'The power behind empowerment: Implications for research and practice', *Human Relations*, 51 (4): 451–483.

Haugaard, M. (1997) *The Constitution of Power*. Manchester: Manchester University Press.

Hickson, D.J., Hinings, C.R., Lee, C.A., Schneck, R.E. and Pennings, J.M. (1971) 'A strategic contingencies theory of intra-organizational power', *Administrative Science Quarterly*, 16: 216–29.

Hobbes, T. (1839) *The English Works of Thomas Hobbes*, Vols 1 and 2 (ed. by Sir William Molesworth). London: J. Bohn.

Hyman, R. and Fryer, B. (1975) 'Trade unions: Sociology and political economy', in J.B. McKinlay (ed.) *Processing People: Cases on Organizational Behaviour*. London: Holt, Rinehart & Winston.

Knights, D. and Willmott, H. (1992) 'Conceptualizing leadership processes: A study of senior managers in a financial services company', *Journal of Management Studies*, 29: 761–782.

Laclau, E. and Mouffe, C. (1985) *Hegemony and Socialist Strategy*. London: Verso.

Lukes, S. (1974) *Power a Radical View*. London: Macmillan.

Machiavelli, N. (1958) *The Prince*. London: Everyman.

Mechanic, D. (1962) 'Sources of power of lower participants in complex organizations', *Administrative Science Quarterly*, 7: 349–364.

Mintzberg, H. (1983) *Power In and Around Organizations*. Englewood Cliffs, NJ: Prentice Hall.

Neitzsche, F. (1968) *The Will to Power*. New York: Vintage Books.

Parry, G. and Morris, P. (1974) 'When is a decision not a decision?', in Icrewe (ed.) *British Political Sociology Yearbook*, Vol. 1: *Elites in Western Democracy*. London: Croom Helm, pp. 317–337.

Pettigrew, A.M. (1973) *The Politics of Organizational Decision-Making*. London: Tavistock Publications.

Pfeffer, J. (1981) *Power in Organizations*. Marshfield, MA: Pitman.

Pfeffer, J. (1992) *Managing with Power: Politics and Influence in Organizations*. Cambridge, MA: Harvard Business School Press.

Pfeffer, J. and Salancik, G. (1974) 'Organizational decision making as a political process', *Administrative Science Quarterly*, 19: 135–151.

Polsby, N. (1963) *Community Power and Political Theory*. New Haven: Yale University Press.

Rabinow, P. (1984) *The Foucault Reader*. London: Penguin.

Ranson, S., Hining, R. and Greenwood, R. (1980) 'The structuring of organizational structure', *Administrative Science Quarterly*, 25 (1): 1–14.

Saunders, P. (1979) *Urban Politics: A Sociological Interpretation*. Harmondsworth: Penguin.

Schattschneider, E.E. (1960) *The Semi-Sovereign People: A Realist's View of Democracy in America*. New York: Holt, Rinehart & Winston.

Smart, B. (1985) *Michel Foucault*. London: Tavistock.

Thompson, J.D. (1956) 'Authority and power in identical organisations', *American Journal of Sociology*, 62: 290–301.

Townley, B. (1993) 'Foucault, power/knowledge, and its relevance for human resource management', *Academy of Management Review*, 18: 518–545.

Weber, M. (1947) *The Theory of Social and Economic Organization* (trans. Talcott Parsons and A.M. Henderson). New York: Free Press.

Weber, M. (1948) *From Max Weber: Essays in Social Theory*. London: Routledge and Kegan Paul.

Weber, M. (1968) *Economy and Society: An Outline of Interpretive Sociology* (edited and with an introduction by G. Roth and C. Wittich). New York: Bedminster Press.

# 9

# On the (be)Coming and Going of Organizational Change: Prospect and Retrospect in Sensemaking

Ian Colville

Recently there has been growing demand for organizational research that is *both* theoretically rigorous *and* relevant to practice; moreover, 'practice' as the subject of organizational theory has made something of a comeback as is evident in conferences themed around, for example, 'A Return to Practice: Organization as it Happens' (*Organization Studies Summer Workshop*, 2006) and is also reflected in the burgeoning literature on strategy-as-practice (Johnson, Melin and Whittington, 2003; Jarzabkowski, 2004; Whittington, 2006). The return to practice is echoed throughout the social sciences and is not confined to the field of organizations and their behaviour and study (e.g., Schatzki, Knorr-Cetina and Von Savigny, 2001).

Despite this renewed interest, the challenge of achieving the both/and quality of *both* theoretical rigour *and* practical relevance is difficult. Some have taken to calling it the 'double–hurdle' (Pettigrew, 1997) and many fall at one or the other, leaving a metaphorical trailing leg: the tendency is to gain one, theoretical rigour or practical relevance, at the expense of the other. What this means is that management academics who prize theoretical rigour bemoan the fact that they don't matter outside their own closed circle (Hambrick, 1994, 2005) and that nobody seems to use their knowledge. Practitioners, meanwhile, and this includes sophisticated users such as governments or savvy captains of industry, ask why academics churn out so much complex 'claptrap'. Not surprisingly, those looking for practical relevance (and they include the very government departments funding academic management research) turn to management consultants who quite happily dispense prescriptions with more confidence than general practitioners, with even less science, and charge considerably more. Academics for their part dismiss the consultants' work as so much simple 'claptrap'.

The chapter argues that sensemaking, when understood as *both* a resource *and* a topic (Colville, Waterman and Weick, 1999a; Weick, 2005), furnishes an understanding of this double hurdle and also offers the possibility of jumping it. Sensemaking when viewed as a resource allows us to understand why those on either side of the theory/practice or rigour/relevance divide see each other as speaking so much claptrap or nonsense. Viewing sensemaking as a topic shifts attention to a more academic consideration, and as the particular topical focus here is organizational change, it is also intended to speak to issues of practical relevance. This will be illustrated through a case about the efforts of a CEO of a private London bank to create change by attempting to shape new meanings amongst the bank personnel as to who/what the bank was becom*ing*, where it was head*ing* and what chang*ing* this involved. Finally we look back at what happened and use these attempts at sense giving (Gioia and Chittipeddi, 1991) on the part of the leader. We do so by regarding these attempts as a means of shaping change, from which we develop a model for making sense of the prospective (be)coming of change (Tsoukas and Chia, 2002) with its retrospective going back on what has elapsed in order to make meaning.

The chapter is structured in three sections which are then followed by a conclusion. Section 1 provides an introduction to sensemaking that is composed in the style of sensemaking. It argues that when viewed as a resource, sensemaking can speak to both theory and practice. It then considers the more specific theoretical argument of change, showing how sensemaking when viewed as a topic, can advance our understanding of the (be)comings and goings of change.

Section 2 tells the story of attempts to change a former merchant bank in the City of London into a private bank and how that resulted in the bank being sold. Section 3 then interprets this story in contrast to the theorizing previously outlined in Section 1.

The final section, the Conclusion, then reflects on what this suggests for the future, both in terms of sensemaking and the contribution it can make to the very idea of jumping the double hurdle. Ironically, we conclude that we need to take 'claptrap' more seriously and that understanding the 'double dialectic' may be a precursor to the 'double hurdle'.

## SECTION 1: AN INTRODUCTION TO SENSEMAKING

There is more to sensemaking than Karl Weick, but it doesn't make a lot of sense without him (Colville, 1996). The sensemaking perspective (Weick, 1995, 2001) and its progenitor in the organizing model (Weick 1969, 1979) are, perhaps more than any other perspective in organization studies, closely associated with a single living person, reflected in a recent Special Issue of *Organization Studies* in his honour (Sutcliffe, Brown and Putnam, 2006). The trouble with this is that no man can be a perspective entirely to himself and it is difficult to talk of a legacy unless others can follow and enrich the seam of work.

Weick's work was the point on which Pfeffer (1995) and Van Maanen (1995) failed to agree, in quite an acrimonious but riveting manner, in what became known as the 'paradigm wars'. Van Maanen (1995) argued that the job of organizational theorists was to persuade readers that what we [organization theorists] have to say is correct, important and well worth heeding (1995:134). If the purpose of theory, as suggested by Van Maanen, is to communicate understandings to readers – the more the better – then as T.S. Eliot (1969) has it in *Sweeney Agonistes*, 'I got to do it with words', and as a consequence the author's style is part and parcel of theory. Van Maanen argued his position by using Weick as the example of style as theory *par excellence* in organization studies. It is appropriate that we quote a poet, Eliot, because Czarniawska (2003) picking up on the debate between Pfeffer and Van Maanen, describes Weick's style as poetic, but you can't replicate or imitate a poet – it is their voice and use of words that makes them unique as poets. It is that quality that allows you to recognize Seamus Heaney, for example, but if it is that unique and inimitable, then it isn't social science according to Pfeffer (1995) – even if it is Weick – and there is no legacy beyond and after the author.

The purpose is not to rekindle the paradigm wars but rather to make two points integral to the positioning of our argument. First, that while acknowledging the great debt this paper and sensemaking owes to Weick, in the future there has to be very much more than Weick to sensemaking or it will end with him. The editors of the *OS* Special Issue say as much in their introduction (Sutcliffe, Brown and Putnam, 2006) and note that others can be influenced and inspired. It happens in poetry. Paul Muldoon, a much celebrated poet and currently chair of creative writing at Princeton, pays testimony to how Heaney awakened his interest and desire for poetry (interview with Wroe, 2007). Indeed, Heaney even taught him at university – but Muldoon has since gone on to find his own voice: a different voice but one that follows on from Heaney and extends the tradition. As Sutcliffe, Brown and Putnam (2006) note, the invitation is not to imitate – you can't because the Weickian style is unique – but to enrich the sensemaking perspective by coming, literally and metaphorically *after* Weick.

The second point that Van Maanen notes is that a key element of the Weickian style is presence. Presence keeps the reader's attention pointed towards features of the text they deem the most important.

> Presence is magnified by such practices as repetition, amplification, enumeration, figuration, provision of concrete details and so forth. It is something of a substitute for a formalist strategy of proof and analysis. Support for an idea or position by the use of presence means repeating it time and time again, each time with a twist, a little differently so that various shades of meaning can be discerned. Redundancy is the key. Contrasted to the spare plain speaking, sequential, one-thing-at-a-time simplicity of a good deal of writing in organization theory, presence is indeed an unusual textural feature. Van Maanen 1995:138

If you felt we had reached the stage in this section where what was required was a plain speaking, one-thing-at-a-time definition of sensemaking, this is a way of explaining why that isn't quite so easy. It is not that Weick doesn't provide any definitions of sensemaking. He provides numerous ones dotted all over his writings – and we will get to some of them shortly – but as Van Maanen so astutely points out, they are all repetitions, saying the same thing only with a subtle twist bespoke to the purpose in hand.

Presence brings to the foreground issues that are germane to our current purpose. It highlights the fact that any writer first has to get the attention of the reader before s/he can convince them of the merits of what s/he is saying. Regardless of how good or relevant what it is you are saying is, if you can't get the attention of those you seek to influence, then you are lost. In a world in which there is so much competition for peoples' attention and where attention spans are becoming shorter, people have to find what you are saying of interest to them and engaging their interest is how you grab their attention. People find theories interesting, according to Davis (1971), where they constitute an attack on their taken for granted assumptions. They find uninteresting those propositions that affirm their assumptive grounds (that's obvious), that do not speak to their assumptive grounds (that's irrelevant), or that deny their assumptive grounds (that's absurd). Davis, as reported by Weick (1979:51) goes on to point out a dilemma that exists when anyone seeks to assert something interesting to *both* laymen *and* experts which he labels the 'double dialectic':

> On the one hand, the proposition will interest experts only if it denies the ground assumption of their discipline. On the other hand, the proposition will interest only laymen if it denies a ground assumption of their common sense world. But since the ground assumption of experts is already a denial of a ground assumption of laymen, any proposition that interests experts (because it denies their ground

assumption) will not interest laymen (because it affirms their ground assumption), and vice versa. What will be interesting to one will be obvious to the other. (Davis (1971: 331)

Davis was not writing with the discipline of management in mind but if we cast the Academy of Management as the experts and the managers as lay people drawing largely on their commonsense world of practice, then we can begin to see why academics and managers may have difficulty finding what the other asserts as interesting and may even be thought to be so much claptrap (obvious, absurd or irrelevant). Where the sensemaking and organizing perspective stands a better chance than many in organization studies of resolving the dilemma of the double dialectic is because it takes as its point of departure the everyday world of practice.

The organizing model was defined as 'a consensually validated grammar for reducing equivocality by means of sensible interlocked behaviours' (Weick 1979: 3) The statement is not as opaque as it reads. All it says is that there is a deal of uncertainty (equivocality, more correctly) as to what is going on and it can be difficult to figure out what a person should do next. When you are in uncertainty, you generally turn to someone else to see if you can jointly make sense of what is happening and what action you both can take (interlocked behaviour cycles). Consensual validation is described as 'common sense of a high order' or simply agreement as to what is real and what is illusory (Weick, 1979: 3). It would be a mistake to suggest that sensemaking is commonsensical but it would not be mistaken to suggest that sensemaking is concerned with how people engage in common-sensemaking although that process is itself not commonsensical. Geertz (1983) for one, has argued that it forms a cultural system and it needs to be studied as such.

The intellectual roots that inform sensemaking show a concern with everyday reality as it embraces a wider social scientific literature that includes: social psychology (e.g., Festinger, 1954); micro sociology

(e.g., Goffman, 1974); ethnomethodology (e.g., Garfinkel, 1967); cultural anthropology (e.g., Geertz, 1983), with symbolic interactionism being described as the unofficial 'house' theory (Weick 1995: 43). Czarniawska (2006) makes a similar observation in writing of the golden braid that links Weick with Gofffman (1974) and Allport (1957). Philosophically, there are strong resonances with European phenomenology and North American pragmatism. It turns out Weick is not a perspective entire to himself but he has a style that is. These are not common sense philosophies but they each take seriously and try to account for the commonsense world of everyday life. Theorists and the people who inhabit the particular aspect of the social world under investigation all try to answer the perennial question, 'what is going on here?' (Goffman, 1974), which is what is understood as sensemaking in the organizational behaviour literature (Weick, 1979, 1995; Colville, 1994).

The social researcher and those being researched have different motives and methods for answering this question, but they begin from the same place. To that extent, those doing everyday sensemaking are in a position to get the attention of non-experts (in academic management) and tell them something interesting about their worlds which transcends the double dialectic. Such an ability makes the work potentially relevant to academic and practitioner: sensemaking in minimal form is about finding out what the story is here (Weick, Sutcliffe and Obstfeld, 2005), and telling stories is one of the best ways of getting anyone's attention, as Peters and Waterman (1982) proved many years ago when they made sense of the times for many practitioners and theorists alike, by using sensemaking as a resource (Colville, Waterman and Weick 1999a).

## ORGANIZATIONAL CHANGE AS SENSEMAKING

The story of organizational change in the academic literature has been largely one of change rather than chang*ing*. For Tsoukas and Chia (2002) in a major reworking of the concept of change, this had lead to a situation where traditional approaches to change were dominated by assumptions privileging stability, routine and order, giving rise to stability being seen as the norm and change, the exception. Change is the filling in of the Lewinian sandwich of unfreeze/change/refreeze. If, on the other hand, you understand the essence of life and organizations to be their continually changing character then, Tsoukas and Chia argue, change rather than stability is the norm. This reversal of ontological priorities from stability to change sensitizes us to how pervasive change already is and allows us to see that change is potentially there, if only we choose to look for it (2002: 568). Change, from such a view, never starts, because it never stops (Weick and Quinn, 1999). Organizations are always in a dynamic ongoing process which is conveyed by the term organizational *becoming*.

Pettigrew, as we have seen, also makes the observation that human conduct is perpetually in a process of becoming, hence the overriding aim of the process analyst is to 'catch reality in flight' (1997: 33). The *ing* factor, whether it is in strategizing, changing, organizing, leading or simply the do*ing* of manag*ing* (Mangham and Pye, 1991) does signal an attempt to recognize a more dynamic and ongoing view. It is also one arguably attributed to early calls in the organizing and sensemaking model to stamp out nouns and to use verbs and adverbs (Weick, 1979). However, while broadly sympathetic to the process view, as understood by Toukas and Chia (2002), there is a tension in organizing and sensemaking between the process-oriented becoming and the more deliberated retrospective assessment of what has happened.

This tension is encapsulated in Kierkegaard's observation that life is lived forward but understood backwards (cited by Dru, 1938). This suggests a prospective forward-living of life that has a quality of becoming, with the retrospective understanding of what happened, which has

the quality of time passed, or going. If living forward is about leading and process, then understanding backwards is about learning through punctuating that process with pauses in order to look backward to make sense retrospectively. Put differently, pauses provide moments in time, interrupting momentum through time, that allow you to take stock of what has just happened in order to answer the question, 'what is the story here?'

## SECTION 2: BANKING ON CHANGE: A SHORT STORY

### *A beginning*

The story begins with how an insightful and well informed Chief Executive, Stephen Reading,[1] who had seen an uncertain and troubled future, sought to bring about change so that he and the bank he led would survive. The story, not a short story, was observed closely as it unfolded over a four-year period as part of a PhD (Carter, 2001). The case data were gathered by participant observation, coupled with interviews at regular intervals throughout the period. Taped interviews were transcribed and copious field notes were taken throughout the duration of the fieldwork. Analysis was conducted systematically through coding to identify patterns in the storyline (Miles and Huberman, 1994; Golden-Biddle and Locke, 1997). What follows is a stripped down version of the case account, presented (with permission) to help illuminate the concepts being explored in this chapter.

The story begins with a relatively small, independent City of London bank, here called Parvin May which in May 2002 was considering an opportunity to attempt to transform itself from a traditional merchant bank to a private one. Merchant banks arrange the funding of corporate clients, often for the purposes of raising funds and/or with a potential flotation on the stock exchange in mind. Private banks tend to focus on private individuals or 'high net worth' clients, with large sums of money.

Stephen Reading took the view that although the bank had a full listing on the London Stock Exchange, it really did not have the funds to compete on the corporate scene domestically, let alone internationally: in order to survive the bank was going to have to become a different type of bank and it would do that by ceasing merchant bank activities and increasing its private bank role. At this stage, Stephen was joint Chief Executive and John, the co-CEO, resisted this change: John saw a future in commercial banking. Both co-CEOs made presentations of their respective visions of the future to the board of directors. Stephen's vision was endorsed by the board and in particular, by the Chairman, Henry Sims, who had a substantial shareholding in the bank.

John immediately left. For Stephen, this was not a risky move: he was a relatively young man (mid-30s) who had identified what he saw as a potential problem in the bank's liquidity. He acted when he felt that there was a very real chance that he may have been associated with the failure of the bank which could jeopardize his future career prospects. Divesting the bank of commercial activities was, for him, a form of risk reduction rather than risk taking. At the time of writing this chapter, the escalating perils of liquidity problems in banking in the UK are only too clear in the case of Northern Rock – but that is another story. Stephen saw challenging his fellow joint chief executive not as a high risk strategy of political brinkmanship but as a means of reducing personal risk.

If I had stayed and said nothing, we would have failed. If they had chosen John's option, then I could have left before the bank was seen to fail. I didn't want to be associated with failure so either I stayed and changed things or I went before it failed. Either way was better for me than doing nothing.

### A middle

The middle of the story sees Stephen trying to bring about change. He is reluctant to share his central concern about the bank with the general organization populous for fear of either alienating his senior mangers or

shocking the rest of the organization into a state of inaction or worse, chaos. The bank is, by tradition, risk averse and conservative. A change or die approach allied to a burning platform could also have the effect of sending a signal to those inside and given the City grapevine and appetite for rumours to those outside, that all was not well with the bank. Confidence in the bank could be reduced and a loss of confidence might be self-fulfillingly fatal.

He thus chose to bring about a transformational change: the bank would make the transition from being a merchant bank to becoming a private bank, through incremental change on an ongoing basis. He wanted the bank to realize for itself why it needed to shed its old identity of merchant banking and take on a new one, becoming a private bank, through evolution. In doing this, he also wanted to encourage the bank to become less risk averse and to take on the set of skills that went with being a private bank. The vulnerability of the bank Stephen saw as stemming from its low return on capital (7%). If merchant banking was based on valuing relationships, then private banking was focused on profit. The fear that Stephen had, and it was not one that he shared openly in case it caused panic, was that if the bank was taken over while underperforming, all staff including himself would be vulnerable: the assets would be stripped and the staff dismissed.

Stephen used strategy weekends to get change going. At these, he engaged in 'clue dropping exercises', in the hopes that the penny would drop and staff would realize for themselves that more risk and initiative would have to take place. Later, we will call these attempts in sensegiving, but Stephen found the inability of senior staff to pick up on his clues and cues most frustrating: if he was waiting for the penny to drop, it was only happening *very* slowly.

One unanticipated outcome of this change from collective risk responsibility, typical of the old merchant bank, to a more individual approach to risk, associated with private banking, was that a group of senior mangers felt that their individual shouldering of this new risk was worthy of reward and they asked to be promoted to the board. Seven were made directors although at the same time, the board changed to meeting only every three months instead of monthly and meetings were, apparently, shorter.

> I knew something was amiss when we didn't get sandwiches – the old smaller board always got tea and sandwiches. We don't get sandwiches, we aren't there long enough to eat them! It's a joke, we are on the board without catering.

Promoted members were assuaged by large salary increases which would cover the cost of most sandwiches.

At this time some three years in, Stephen's strategy was beginning to bear fruit and as such:

> Now is not the time to lose any of these people. We are on our way but it is fragile and so in order to keep people where they are we have to be competitive.

### An end

The end is surprising, or at least, it came as a surprise to Stephen. As the strategy of change started to take hold, Stephen and Henry, the chairman (with a substantial personal shareholding) began to realize that not only was the bank surviving but, as a niche private bank, it was beginning to attract the attention of bigger players.

> Henry retires relatively soon and none of his family wants to get involved with the bank. What we are doing, and this is the plan, is putting the bank in a position to be taken over. We (Henry and Stephen) have been positioning the bank so that the right buyer goes for the whole team – that is why we have to keep them together. The way I see it is the directorate will be given shares and told to carry on and grow the bank more. Then they sell again, only this time we get real money out of it as well as the shareholders.

Would any of the team at the strategy weekend be briefed on this? Stephen thought not.

> No, it is not something I can discuss but I rather hope that if I make the right sounds, they might conclude this outcome themselves.

Stephen had predicted the future correctly in terms of a takeover, but he had not foreseen where it would place him.

Shortly before his retirement as Chairman, Henry issued the following notice to shareholders on the takeover of the bank by a larger bank, Hamworths.

> The Board of Directors of Hamworth's (UK) and the Board of Parvin May are pleased to announce the terms of a recommended cash offer.

> - The Offer of £9.50 per share represents a premium of 43.9% to the closing price;
> - Hamworth's (UK) has received irrevocable undertakings to accept the Offer in respect of 73.7% of Parvin May's existing share capital.

The note concluded:

> Following the strategic review which was initiated five months ago, the Board of Directors of Parvin May believes that the offer represents the most attractive means of realising value for Parvin May shareholders.

The bank had been sold.

Stephen Reading was not retained in the new company. Within two years, the only director who was still employed by the newly acquired bank was the IT director. With hindsight, Stephen's initial concern that if the bank was underperforming when it was taken over, then the whole team would go, starting with him, was prescient. It was just that he didn't believe the bank was underperforming when the momentum stopped, and the moment of truth arrived.

## SECTION 3: REVIEWING THE STORY

It is now time to review some assertions which were made at the outset in order to make a renewed sense of them in the light of what has been written in the chapter. That is what sensemaking is – the ongoing development of plausible images that rationalize what people are doing (Weick, 2005: 397). Whether these are people going about their everyday lives, trying to manage and make do, or social scientists theorizing about how these people are organizing and leading, the argument was that they were engaged essentially in the same project. This was why I believe that sensemaking stands a better chance of being seen as interesting and hopefully relevant to the world of practice. Practice and sensemaking speak the same language even if, when sensemaking is viewed as a topic rather than a resource, the approaches use different words.

Sensemaking when viewed as a topic and applied to the question of organizational change furnished a reading that was closer in conception to the process view of Tsoukas and Chia that saw change, or more appropriately changing as being constitutive of reality. From such a position, which requires a micro-perspective to see the ongoing adaptation and adjustment (Orlikowski, 1996), change becomes the reweaving of actors' webs of belief and habits of action to accommodate new experiences obtained through interactions (Tsoukas and Chia, 2002: 567).

However, the promise of a processual view is overblown and partial from a sensemaking perspective if it ignores the essential stabilities that make the process – e.g., journeying, becoming – possible in the first place. It draws attention away from the stepping aside to retrospect, from bracketing, repetition, recurrence, routine, self-imposed constraints, habits etc. In turn, this blinds us to those essential stabilities without which we cannot detect flow (Colville, Waterman and Weick, 1999b). At heart, what is being argued is that while change rather than stability is the norm (and this underpins the process view of change), if people continually live within ongoing streams, they aim to create some sort of stability because if they don't, they can't answer the question, 'what is going on here?' some stable substrate: and without that answer (i.e. change) erodes identity such that they can't answer the subsidiary question, 'who is going on here?'

When Tsoukas and Chia (2002) speak of the becoming of change and Pettigrew (1997) the becoming of social reality, all is process, all is flux, but there is no sensemaking because

there are no events being carved out of this stream to reflect on when all is process. Sensemaking is about turning circumstances into situations (Taylor and Van Every, 1999). It is about how something becomes an event for organizational members, what that event means, and how that influences future action (Weick, Sutcliffe and Obstfeld, 2005: 410). Without the delimiting of an organizational event, there is nothing for sensemaking to work on.

The problem that Stephen had was that giving cues as to what was required to begin with, and then waiting for the penny to drop, just did not create any sense of situations and events for most organization's members. They didn't know what to think: when scrutinizing an event, a sensible event is one that resembles something that has happened before (Weick, 1995: 170). Put more pointedly, history, memory, structure is the natural and first attitude taken in sensemaking and process is the unnatural or second attitude. If the first question is 'what is going on here?' then the second question must be 'is it still possible to go on the way we have?'. So it is the becoming and going that have to be considered when seeking to understand change (and order).

To lose sight of stabilities is to lose sight of change, which would be particularly disappointing, given that we have had to switch ontologies, according to Tsoukas and Chia, in order to see changing at all, but if this switching means that we close our eyes to stabilities, then we are left with a process view which approximates the situation proposed by Whorf who argued that, in a universe in which everything is blue, the concept of blueness cannot be developed for lack of contrasting colours (quoted by Watzlawick, Weakland and Fisch, 1974: 2). What this comes down to saying was best said by John Dewey, building on William James and quoted by Weick (2006: 1731) in an essay in the *Special Issue* in his honour:

In every waking moment, the complete balance of the organism [system] and its environment is constantly interfered with and is constantly restored. Hence 'the stream of consciousness' in general, and in particular, the phase of it celebrated by William James as alteration of flights and perchings: life is interruptions and recoveries. (Dewey 1922/2002: 178–179)

This provides Weick with another definition, with order, interruptions and recovery being described as 'sensemaking in a nutshell' (Weick, 1995: 37)

Our purpose here is better served by James's idea of life as an alteration of flights and perchings. Processual understandings are about flow, flights and becomings but they are brought into being and given shape through essential stabilities, perchings and goings.

Schutz (1967) explains why the attribution of meaning is always about goings and the past:

When, by my act of reflection, I turn my attention to my living experience, I am no longer taking up my position within the stream of pure duration, I am no longer simply living with that flow. The experiences are apprehended, distinguished, brought into relief, marked out from one another; the experiences which were constituted as phases within the flow of duration now become objects of attention as constituted experiences.... *For the Act of Attention* – and this is of major importance for the study of meaning – presupposes an elapsed, passed away experience – in short, one that is already in the past. (Schutz, 1967: 51)

Sensemaking lies in the reflective glance because meaning-making is usually attending to a flow that has already elapsed or thought of as if it were elapsed in some future perfect (Weick, 1995). Against this, Seamus Heaney says that it is in the realm of the glimpsed potential that the future takes shape (Heaney, 2002). Here, between the glimpses of the future and the glances to the past, we are caught between the living life forward and understanding it backwards: we are caught between foresight, process and change, and hindsight, structure and order.

Yet we know also that the flights of process require the perchings of stabilities and vice versa. Stephen Reading, as leader, as we have seen, is trying to create a new future for the bank. He is trying, against a culture of past memories and sensemaking, to

introduce a change of direction of behaviours and, ultimately, of identity. As such, he is very much on the front foot of leading organizational life forward but he is acutely aware that the weight of history will condition the type of change that is possible and the sense that will be made of it. He is trying to shape change and shape the meaning that will historically be attached to that change.

It was almost as if Stephen had read Gioia, Corley and Fabbri (2002: 632)

[the] point to emphasize about organizational change and the malleability of history is the indelible link between history and identity.
   … one way to conceptualize revisionist history, then, is as a bridge between organizational identity and organizational change. Successful change requires a union of the valued past with the hoped-for future. Subtly revising the past to better align with the desired future facilitates the change process.... (Gioia, Corley and Fabbric, 2002: 632)

It may be the case that we are the way we were, as James Joyce has it, but Gioia *et al* (2002) remind us that history is always open to reinterpretation when viewed from the present and with the future in mind:

Leadership vision for change might usefully be construed as an ability to foresee a desired state of affairs and then anticipate the likelihood of being able to influence (now) the future perception of the present and the past should such a state be achieved.... Equally important is the wisdom to select a vision that is ambiguous enough and robust enough to support many possible interpretations and many plausible stories. Consequently, leaders need to create the future context for maintaining a credible story line in describing the organization's history as it is being written. That story line must, of course, be able to reasonably and retrospectively account for actions taken in the present. In this fashion, it is possible to conceive of using history to manage the future proactively. (Gioia, Corley and Fabbric, 2002: 631)

Gioia *et al.* (2002) cite the case of a large university whose strategy was to get graduates to provide funds that would enhance the standing of the university in the future. People 'bought into the idea' that in the future they will have gone to a better university than they actually went to, at least in terms of the all-powerful US Business School rankings. However, the future is unknowable and even when it looks as if things are going to plan there are always unintended consequences that become eventful along the way.

Stephen Reading set out three objectives for his change initiative:

- Change the bank from a merchant to private bank
- Increase profitability
- Get individuals to take more responsibility and initiative consistent with a private bank.

All of this was undertaken with the aim of making sure the bank survived. A funny thing happened on the way to the future, however, and with the relative success of the change initiative, Stephen and Henry realized the bank was now an attractive takeover target, leading to the establishment of a new strategy which was to sell the bank, but it was a strategy that emerged after the event. If strategy was good luck rationalized with hindsight (de Bono, 1984: 143), then this is an excellent case in point.

There is a gap between living forward with flawed foresight and understanding backward with equally flawed but mischievously seductive hindsight (Weick, 1999: 134), but the gap is bigger on the living forward trajectory. The reason that the gap is greater going forward is because the possibilities of what might happen are more various than the probabilities of what did. Stephen easily alighted on the strategy-with-hindsight and yet, making his foresight come about was much more uncertain. To turn the glimpses into reality involved him in the rather difficult task of providing prospective meanings of who and what the bank was becoming.

These prospective meanings by leaders in change processes have been described as sensegiving (Gioia and Chittipeddi, 1991). The problem is, however, that the meaning of an action to a large extent lies in response (Mangham and Pye, 1991, drawing on Peckham, 1979) and that response is conditioned by equivocality on the part of the sensegiver, the sense receiver and the context and culture against which this all takes place.

The whole process is fraught with complexity or, as Stephen said before a strategy weekend:

I have got to focus them (the directors and assistant directors) on profit, but I have to do it in a way that makes them feel it is their idea. If I just say it's about making more profit, they will say I have carved up the weekend. If I say what is on my mind, it will scare them. But these people do not see it.

If we do not turn this around, somebody else is going to come in and do it better. And what happens to the staff? They get sacked and who wants a bunch of failures? It might work out for them but as a CEO, there is nowhere for me to go and I am not going to sit back and let it happen.

Stephen was partly successful in shaping prospective meaning but he never managed to get profit and individual risk-taking fully accepted as a way of working. The traditional way of working was through committee and collective responsibility. In promoting individual risk-taking and a more entrepreneurial approach to drive profits up, Stephen was working against the grain of history and culture. If some of the communication did get through about individual action and responsibility being rewarded, it unexpectedly resulted in another unintended consequence of individuals asking for a pay rise.

At the time of the above quote, Stephen would not have been receptive to such a request. However, events had moved on and the strategy of selling the bank had now emerged as the overriding objective. It made good sense for Stephen to accede to their demand at that point in time.

Note that Stephen's sensemaking changes over time, but you have to be close up and tracking it over time to catch the meaning. This is organizing as it happens (Boden, 1990), the constant reweaving of actors, webs of beliefs and habits of action to accommodate new experiences obtained through interaction (Tsoukas and Chia, 2002).

Gioia (2006) retreats from his view on sensegiving, to see it as part of the idea of retrospective sensemaking, holding that 'sensemaking is the predominant way of going about our most essential human task – and one of the biggest academic projects of our time – understanding how people make sense of experience' (Gioia, 2006: 1719).

The position outlined here would ask Gioia to think again. We have been at pains to suggest that you cannot understand process without structure, prospect without retrospect and becomings without goings. Having established that caveat or connection, we still have to pay attention to the flights as well as the perchings, to the living forward and the understanding backward.

Sensemaking as topic – incorporating sensegiving and sensetaking – still allows us to do that in looking with both eyes at change. Sensemaking as resource says that our theories of practice err on the side of understanding backwards but that most practitioners are concerned with living life forward. Weick, as usual, puts it best:

> Better theorising lies in 'keeping up with what perhaps is going on' through the use of tactics that weaken hindsight, highlight interruptions, articulate the nature of ready-to-hand alertness, fold action and cognition together, and focus on projects as the unit of analysis. Weick (2006: 1732).

We have attempted to 'keep up with what was going on' in the bank. We have attempted to furnish an answer to the question as to 'what's the story here?'

It turns out it is an everyday story of change: an everyday story that accepts the becoming of change, as long as it is tempered with its goings; that recognizes flights and perchings, prospective and retrospective meanings. It also suggests that if we explore the gap on the living forward side more wholeheartedly, our theories might just interest thinking practitioners and academics.

## SECTION 4: CONCLUSION

Most people ignore organization theory because most organization theory ignores people. If we really do want to be taken seriously as theorists then we have to take people seriously. One consequence would be that the double dialectic would become an essential first step to jumping the double hurdle. If being rigorous results in not being interesting then we will be marginalized and seen as irrelevant, absurd or obvious by those who claim to practice management and who claim to know how if not know why.

The argument being advanced here is that sensemaking and organizing is in a good (but by no means unique) position of being able to engage interest, by virtue of a perspective which says that sensemaking is about understanding social conduct. Whether that conduct is undertaken by people qua practitioners in organizational settings or people qua academics theorizing about what this behaviour means, makes little difference as they are both engaged in sensemaking: 'what is going on here?' and 'what do we do next?'.

In this way, sensemaking can act *both* as a resource *and* a topic. In both guises, sensemaking holds that in order to get things done it is more important to capture attention than intention. Intention is neither a necessary nor sufficient condition for action (Weick, 2001: 52). The best way to get attention is to interest people in what you have to say. Theory that hovers close to the descriptions of everyday life from which it proceeds (Geertz, 1983) and which puts a twist on what it is people assume they know has a chance of doing that. If the topic in hand is also of immediate relevance to managers, then the chances of solving the dilemma of the double dialectic are also increased.

The risk, identified at the outset, is that you fall foul of the double dialectic and academics and practitioners hear each other talking so much claptrap and nonsense.

However, if you look up the *Concise Oxford English Dictionary* definition, you may get a surprise. There is another, in fact the original, definition of 'claptrap' which is a device or trap for attracting clapping or applause. It is a device known to those rock bands who, on their last number, encourage the audience to raise their hands above their heads and to clap along in time with the music. At the end of the song, they stop and if the trap has been sprung properly, the audience go on clapping.

If as Van Maanen (1995) tells us (and we deliberately use the rhetorical tactic he identified of 'nuanced repetition'), the *raison d'être* of organization theory [read: organization studies and/or organization behaviour] is to communicate understanding and to persuade as many people as possible that we have something important to say and it is worth heeding, then we need to take 'claptrap' seriously.

Consultants, gurus (and good writers) seem to have developed the knack of getting peoples' attention through claptrap and more to the point, influence action. Perhaps we can learn to speak claptrap. Claptrap defined is literally what it says it is, namely a trap for clapping. Sensemaking defined is literally what it says it is, namely making something sensible (Weick, 1995: 16). Speaking claptrap is part and parcel of making sense. If speaking claptrap is also a way of speaking differently then it is also very much part and parcel of the (be)coming and going of change.

> What the Romantics expressed as the claim that imagination, rather than reason, is the central human faculty was the realization that a talent for speaking differently, rather than arguing well, is the chief instrument of cultural change. (Rorty (1989) quoted in Weick *et al.*, 2005: 1724)

Now, that is interesting.

## ACKNOWLEDGEMENT

The author would like to express his gratitude to Dr Mike Carter for permission to use case material generated during PhD research supervised by the author.

## NOTE

1 All names of managers and the bank in this case have been disguised.

## REFERENCES

Allport, G. (1957) 'The structuring of events: Outline of a general theory with applications to psychology', *Psychological Review*, 61: 281–303.

Boden, D. (1990) 'The world as it happens: Ethnomethodology and conversation analysis', in G. Ritzer (ed.) *Frontiers of Social Theory: A New Synthesis*. New York: Columbia University Press.

Carter, M. (2001) *The Sensemaking of Adaptive Change: A Perspective*. Unpublished PhD thesis, University of Bath.

Colville, I.D. (1994) 'Searching for Karl Weick and reviewing the future', *Organization*, 1 (1): 218–224.

Colville, I.D. (1996) 'Making sense of sensemaking', *Management Learning*, 27 (3): 151–153.

Colville, I., Waterman, R. and Weick, K. (1999a) 'Organizing and the search for excellence: making sense of the times in theory and practice', *Organization*, 6 (1): 129–148.

Colville, I., Waterman, R. and Weick, K. (1999b) 'Making sense of change: Essential stabilities in breathless journeys'. Symposium presentation to the Annual Meeting of the Academy of Management, Chicago.

Czarniawska, B. (2003) 'The styles and the stylists of organization theory', in H. Tsoukas and C. Knudson (eds) *The Oxford Handbook of Organization Theory*. Oxford: Oxford University Press.

Czarniawska, B. (2006) 'A golden braid: Allport, Goffman and Weick', *Organization Studies*, 27 (11): 1661–1674.

Davis, M. (1971) 'That's interesting: Towards a phenomenology of sociology and a sociology of phenomenology', *Philosophy of Social Science*, 1: 309–344.

de Bono, E. (1984) *Tactics: The Art and Science of Success*. Boston: Little Brown.

Dru, A. (1938) *The Journals of Kierkegaard*. Oxford: Oxford University Press.

Eliot, T.S. (1969) *The Complete Poems and Plays*. London: Faber & Faber.

Festinger, L. (1954) 'A theory of social comparison', *Human Relations*, 7: 117–140.

Garfinkel, H. (1967) *Studies in Ethnomethodology*. Englewood Cliffs, NJ: Prentice-Hall.

Geertz, C. (1983) *Local Knowledge: Further Essays in Interpretive Anthropology*. London: Basic Books.

Gioia, D. (2006) 'On Weick: An appreciation', *Organization Studies*, 27 (11): 1709–1722.

Gioia, D. and Chittipeddi, K. (1991) 'Sensemaking and sensegiving in strategic change', *Strategic Management Journal*, 12: 433–448.

Gioia, D., Corley, K. and Fabbri, T. (2002) 'Revising the past (while thinking in the future perfect tense)',

*Journal of Organizational Change Management*, 5 (6): 622–634.

Goffman, E. (1974) *Frame Analysis*. London: Penguin.

Golden-Biddle, K. and Locke, K. (1997) *Composing Qualitative Research*. London: Sage.

Hambrick, D. (1994) 1993 'Presidential address: What if the academy actually mattered?', *Academy of Management Review*, 19 (1): 632–636.

Hambrick, D. (2005) 'Venturing outside the monastery', *Academy of Management Journal*, 48 (6): 961–963.

Heaney, S. (2002) *Finders Keepers: Selected Prose 1971–2001*. London: Faber & Faber.

Jarzabkowski, P. (2004) 'Strategy as practice: Recursiveness, adaptation, and practices-in-use', *Organization Studies*, 25 (4): 529–560.

Johnson, G., Melin, L. and Whittington, R. (2003) 'Micro strategy and strategizing: Towards an activity-based view', *Journal of Management Studies*, 40 (1): 3–22.

Mangham, I.L. and Pye, A.J. (1991) *The Doing of Managing*. Oxford: Blackwell.

Miles, M.B. and Huberman, A.M. (1994) *Qualitative Data Analysis*. London: Sage.

*Organization Studies* Second Summer Workshop (2006) Re-turn to practice: Understanding organization as it happens. Mykonos, Greece, 15–16 June.

Orlikowski, W. (1996) 'Improvising organizational transformation over time: A situated change perspective', *Information Systems Research*, 7 (1): 63–92.

Peckham, M. (1979) *Explanation and Power: The Control of Human Behaviour*. New York: Seabury Press.

Peters, T.H. and Waterman, R.H. (1982) *In Search of Excellence*. New York: Harper & Row.

Pettigrew, A.M. (1997) 'The double hurdles for management research', in T. Clarke (ed.) *Advancement in Organizational Behaviour: Essays in Honour of D.S. Pugh*. London: Dartmouth Press, pp. 277–296.

Pfeffer, J. (1995) "Mortality, reproducibility, and the persistence of styles of theory", *Organization Science*, 6 (6): 681–686.

Rorty, R. (1989) *Contingency, Irony and Solidarity*. Cambridge: Cambridge University Press.

Schatzki, T., Knorr-Cetina, K. and von Savigny, E. (2001) *The Practice Turn in Contemporary Theory*. New York: Routledge.

Schutz, A. (1967) *The Phenomenology of the Social World*. Chicago, IL: Northwestern University Press.

Sutcliffe, K., Brown, A. and Putnam, L. (2006) 'Guest editorial to special issue on "Making sense in honor of Karl Weick"', *Organization Studies*, 27 (11): 1573–1578.

Taylor, J.R. and Van Every, E.J. (1999) *The Emergent Organization: Communication as its Site and Surface*. Mahwah, NJ: Lawrence Erlbaum.

Tsoukas, H. and Chia, R. (2002) 'On organizational becoming: Rethinking organizational change', *Organization Science*, 13 (5): 567–582.

Van Maanen, J. (1995) 'Fear and loathing in organization studies', *Organization Science*, 6 (6): 687–692.

Watzlawick, P., Weakland, J.H. and Fisch, R. (1974) *Change: Principles of Problem Formation and Problem Resolution*. San Francisco: Jossey-Bass.

Weick, K.E. (1969) *The Social Psychology of Organizing*. Reading, MA: Addison-Wesley.

Weick, K.E. (1979) *The Social Psychology of Organizing*. Reading, MA: Addison-Wesley.

Weick, K.E. (1995) *Sensemaking in Organizations*. London: Sage.

Weick, K.E. (2001) *Making Sense of the Organization*. Oxford: Blackwell.

Weick, K.E. (2005) 'The experience of theorizing: Sensemaking as topic and resource', in K.G. Smith and M.A. Hitt (eds) *Great Minds in Management*. New York: Oxford University Press.

Weick, K.E. (2006) 'Faith, evidence and action', *Organization Studies*, 27 (11): 1723–1736.

Weick, K.E. and Quinn, R. (1999) 'Organizational change and development', *Annual Review of Psychology*, 50: 361–386.

Weick, K.E., Sutcliffe, K. and Obstfeld, D. (2005) 'Organizing and the process of sensemaking', *Organization Science*, 16 (4): 409–421.

Whittington, R. (2006) 'Completing the practice turn in strategy', *Organization Studies*, 27 (5): 613–634.

Wroe, N. (2007) 'Invisible threads', Paul Muldoon interviewed by Nicholas Wroe, *Guardian*, 24th March.

# 10

# Organizational Identity

Andrew D. Brown

## INTRODUCTION AND OUTLINE OF THE CHAPTER

'Organizational identity' is currently a major domain of inquiry for scholars in organization studies, and a significant preoccupation for managers. From a practitioner perspective, as Cheney (1991: 201) has observed, the management of multiple identities and identifications is *the* key issue for modern organizations. This is, in part, because of increased pressures on managers to differentiate their organization from competitors while retaining the support of key stakeholders. Complementarily, contemporary research agendas have evolved from the broad interest in identity issues which spans the social sciences and humanities, and an earlier focus on the cultures of organizations (Brown, 2001). One more immediate spur that has prompted identity studies among sociologically informed organizational researchers has been the rise to prominence of a postmodern analysis of our world as increasingly fragmented, discontinuous and crisis-ridden – one in which identity issues are both highlighted

and problematized (Giddens, 1991). In such analyses, as modernity 'displaces, disturbs, deconstructs and redeploys' so the construction of an identity as a self, including an organizational 'self', is revealed as 'a struggle at best won only provisionally' (Frosh, 1991: 191, 187).

Another impetus for the growth of the literature on identity has been the claim that the concept has potential as a means of cohering and fostering linkages between different levels of analysis, heterogeneous organizational processes, and disparate communities of scholars. Polzer (2000: 628), for example, has suggested that 'Identity concepts are powerful in part because they cut across individual, group and organizational levels of analysis' while Ashforth and Mael (1996: 4) have argued that there 'are few conceptual bridges for linking macro- and micro-level structures and processes' and 'that the concept of identity provides one such bridge'. While most attention has undoubtedly been devoted to individual and societal levels of analysis organization, theorists have increasingly turned their gaze to identity, arguing that it is 'because identity is problematic – and yet so critical … that the dynamics of identity need to be better understood' (Albert, Ashforth and Dutton, 2000: 14). As a result, since the mid 1980s, there have been many attempts to define the concept. While Stimpert, Gustafson and Sarason (1998: 87) have defined identity as '*the theory that members of an organization have about who they are*' it is most often regarded as an internalized cognitive structure that defines what an organization stands for, and what it wants to become (Brown, 2007). These definitions are evidently quite different from each other, and incorporate the ideological preferences of the authors for particular identity-focused research agendas. Definitional disputes are strongly suggestive of the fractured and factitious nature of the organizational identity literature – features which earlier characterized and, some scholars thought, marred the development of the related literature on organizational culture. Such pluralism, though, has its supporters (cf. Glynn, Barr and Dacin, 2000).[1]

The chapter is structured into four major sections. First, I provide an account of the origins of the 'organization identity' concept with particular reference to Albert and Whetten (1985) and intellectual antecedents of their theorizing, especially the work of psychologists such as Freud and the sociologists Cooley, Mead and Goffman. Second, I give an account of some of the central approaches and main theories pertaining to organizational identity which I label 'functionalist', 'interpretive', 'psychodynamic' and 'postmodern'. Third, I examine a number of critical issues in organizational identity research: (i) conceptions of organizational identity as a construct, a question and a metaphor; (ii) identity multiplicity; (iii) continuity and change; (iv) linkages between the notions 'identity', 'reputation' and 'image', and (v) identification. In the final section I consider some new directions for the future, namely issues centred on the definition of organizational identity, the management of identity and the need for the establishment of a critical perspective on organizational identity issues.

## ORIGINS AND ANTECEDENTS

### *Origins*

Most accounts of the origins of contemporary views on 'organizational identity' begin with Albert and Whetten's (1985) seminal paper. Spurred by a recognition that enduring disagreements or confusions in organizations tend often to prompt identity questions such as 'Who are we?' and 'What do we want to become?' their espoused aim was to devise a 'scientifically tractable' concept that would render visible multiple empirical questions and hypotheses which would together form a distinctive research agenda. An adequate statement of an organization's identity should, they suggested, satisfy three criteria: (i) it should point to features that are understood to be the 'essence' of an organization (the criterion of claimed central character); (ii) it should reference features that 'distinguish' the organization from others (the criterion of claimed distinctiveness); and (iii) it should include features that exhibit a degree of 'sameness' or 'continuity' over time (the criterion of claimed temporal continuity). As a scientific concept, they argued, the criteria of central character, distinctiveness and temporal continuity were each necessary and as a set sufficient for defining identity.

While this formulation has been widely appropriated and deployed by scholars, Albert and Whetten themselves recognized a number of complications. Some of the most important of these have helped to structure ongoing debates in the field. For example, they noted that leaders may make many alternative statements regarding their organization's identity, and that these may be compatible, complementary, unrelated, or perhaps contradictory. In addition, they considered the formulation of a statement of an organization's identity to be a political-strategic act (by leaders) that was often (perhaps in part deliberately) imprecise and ambiguous. Moreover, rather than being characterized by a single identity, most organizations, according to Albert and Whetten, are in fact 'hybrids' combining two or more identities which may either be shared across an organization as a whole (holographic hybrids) or associated with specific sub-units of an organization (ideographic hybrids). To complicate matters still further, they theorized that identity is not a purely internal matter as, in defining who they (collectively) are, leaders create or invoke classification schemes in order to locate their and other organizations, and develop statements of identity in interaction with a range of external stakeholders.

While Albert and Whetten's work has been the point of origin for most research on organizational identity in organization studies, we should note that they, and others, have drawn on a wide variety of identity literatures in the Arts, Humanities and the Social Sciences.

## Antecedents

Although relatively new to organization studies, the concept of 'identity' has a lengthy history of development in fields as diverse as philosophy, literary theory, psychology and sociology. This diverse and heterogeneous body of work has served as a valuable resource from which theorists have drawn in their efforts to establish, theorize and research issues of organizational identity. Contemporary interest has its origins largely in social psychology and sociology. Studies of (or linked to) identity issues have long dominated research in psychology. Of the many psychologists who have been influential in developing notions of individual identity that have then been drawn on by organizational theorists, the most pervasive has been Freud. Freud's (1914) theory of narcissism, conception of self-esteem, and elaboration of the ego-defences has had particular impact. More recently, the social identity theory developed by Tajfel and Turner (1986), which suggests that individuals identify with a group using social comparison processes driven by a desire to enhance self-esteem, has been used to explain how organizational identities are developed, maintained and reproduced. A huge number of other theorists and researchers ranging from developmental psychologists such as Erikson (1965) to narrative psychologists such as Sarbin (1986) and Polkinghorne (1988) have also been influential in the evolution of the organizational identity literature.

Hatch and Schultz (2004) have highlighted the importance of sociologists such as Cooley, Mead and Goffman who, they claim, laid some of the foundations for later theorizing. Cooley (1902/1964) was influential in promoting understandings of individuals as inseparable from the society in which they participated: man '... is all social in the large sense, is all a part of the common human life ... everything human about him has a history in the social past' (Cooley, 1902/1964: 47–8). Mead (1934) defined two aspects of the self, the 'I' and the 'me', which constitute different phases of a social process in which the 'I', being historically prior, gives rise to the 'me'. Goffman (1959) suggested that identity is a performance which is managed by individuals in order to leave an impression on audiences that is, generally, favourable. Each of these themes, the social nature of individual selves, the distinction between an 'I' who creates and a 'me' that is authored, and the idea that identities are performed for external audiences, have all been explored and made use of by scholars of organizational identity. However, as with the field of psychology, a very large number of other thinkers from Durkheim to Foucault are also frequently referenced in works on organizational identity.

While the organizational identity literature has drawn broadly on the resources associated with, *inter alia*, interpretive sociology and social psychology, as it is used in organization studies the concept is, perhaps, most directly related to that of 'organizational culture'. Interest in the culture of organizations dates from the late 1970s (e.g., Pettigrew, 1979), was a major preoccupation throughout the 1980s, and remains the focus of considerable research attention (Brown, 1998). In their original paper, Albert and Whetten (1985) recognized that 'culture' and 'identity' were cognate terms, and were concerned to distinguish between organizations' cultures and identities both empirically and theoretically. Their efforts were, however, not wholly successful, and subsequent authors have confused matters further by implicating the two terms in definitions of each other. Dutton and Dukerich (1991: 546), for example, have argued that '... an organization's identity is closely tied to its culture because identity provides a set of skills and a way of using and evaluating those skills that produce characteristic ways of doing things'. Other theorists have responded by seeking to distinguish clearly between them. For example, Hatch and Schultz (2002) have argued that identity is the product of an ongoing 'conversation' between an organization's culture and the images of it held by key stakeholders, culture being relatively more contextual, tacit and emergent while identity is more textual, explicit and instrumental. Despite such efforts, there is as yet no clear consensus regarding how the two concepts are related, a fact which is strongly suggestive of the deeply embedded links between the two literatures.

## CENTRAL APPROACHES AND MAIN THEORIES

Part of what I seek to accomplish in this chapter is to highlight the huge diversity in approaches to the study of organizational identity, a feature of the literature not lost on other commentators, and which has led Porter (2001: 1) to argue that 'Not least among the interesting questions being posed about organizational identity concerns the process of its theorizing'. In this section I outline four perspectives on identity issues which I label 'functionalist', 'interpretive', 'psychodynamic' and 'postmodern'. It should at the outset be noted that these are arbitrary labels, and that this classification scheme disguises as much as it reveals. This is in part because there are relatively few published texts that do not incorporate elements from two or more of these perspectives. Albert and Whetten's (1985) original formulation of the organizational identity concept, for example, combines arguments that may be understood as incorporating both functionalist and interpretive assumptions. This said, separating these perspectives into 'ideal types' is instructive as it permits a clearer analysis of their key claims (and weaknesses).

### Functionalist perspectives

The functionalist perspective suggests that the identities of organizations are constituted by objective, often tangible, features such as corporate logos, brand management programmes, and strategic reports. As Soenen and Moingeon (2002) have made clear, these views on organizational identity which focus on physical manifestations that are, to varying degrees, controllable, is particularly dominant in fields such as marketing and brand management (e.g., Olins, 1989; van Riel & Balmer, 1997). Typical of this research stream is Brun's (2002) account of identity change constituted by a new logo and visual identity system at France Telecom. Recognizing the considerable scope for confusion, organization researchers (i.e., non-marketeers) such as Rindova and Schultz (1998) have sought to distinguish the targeted visual presentation of an organization's identity which they term 'corporate identity' from 'organizational identity'. Their concern has been to differentiate what they understand to be different levels of the same broad concept so that organization theorists do not 'miss some of the critical mechanisms through which identity is created, managed, interpreted, and changed' (Rindova and Schultz, 1998: 49). The phrase 'corporate identity' has become a focus of research inquiry for those interested in analysing identity issues using positivistic methods (e.g., Balmer and Gray, 1999; Alessandri, 2001; Balmer, 2001; Cornelissen and Elving, 2003; Alessandri and Alessandri, 2004).

Functionalist approaches are, however, also prevalent, perhaps dominant, in the organization studies literature, where they tend often to be associated with attempts to categorize organizational identities, and with efforts to define formal identity constructs with explanatory and predictive powers.

For example, Whetten (2006) has sought to develop a conception of organizational identity that has 'construct validity', which refers to supposedly objective 'referents' that are actually central, distinctive and enduring features of an organization, and which 'lends itself to model building, hypothesis testing, and empirical measurement' (p. 229). While recognizing other aspects of organizational identity, Fombrun (2002: xvi) argues that 'Identity is more or less *functional* – it helps organize the sense-making experiences of individuals'. These versions of organizational identity treat it as an inherent characteristic, property or essence that belongs to, and is located within, the entity to which it is ascribed (Porter, 2001). The identity literature developed specifically for managers rather than academics has also most usually adopted functionalist assumptions, and, incidentally, implicated the concept as a key source of strategic competitive advantage (cf. Stimpert *et al.*, 1998). While hugely popular, research on organizational identity from a functionalist perspective has been criticized as naïvely simplistic, reliant on an 'over-socialized' view of organizational participants, preoccupied with the ideas and practical concerns of senior managers, and unable to deal adequately with the cognitive and emotional dimensions of the identity concept (Porter, 2001; Brown, 2006).

## Interpretive perspectives

From an interpretive perspective, organizational identity is a social construction that results from the efforts of organizational members to understand their collective selves. Organizational identities reside within groups of individuals, and refer to those characteristics that members feel are, following Albert and Whetten (1985), central, distinctive and enduring. Such identities tend to be characterized as flexible, emergent, group-level constructs that reflect and incorporate individually internalized beliefs, assumptions and perceptions and which exist to the degree that members are aware of them. These identities are most usually said to

become shared through generalized processes of socialization, though some versions also privilege senior leaders and/or external stakeholders. For example, Scott and Lane (2000: 45) characterize organizational identity construction as a 'dynamic, reciprocal and iterative' set of processes which involve 'managers' and stakeholders' reflection on the meaning of organizational events, policies and actions ...' Pratt (2003) identifies two interpretive theories of collective identity: an 'aggregate' perspective, in which collective identity resides within the mind of each individual member (i.e., is a summation of individual views); and a 'gestalt' perspective, which postulates that collective identities reside in the relationships/relational ties that cognitively bind people together.

Many empirical studies of organizational identity have adopted an interpretive perspective (e.g., Golden-Biddle and Rao, 1997). One stream of research has centred on the putatively multiple identities of organizations. In analysing the identity of a psychiatric hospital Harrison (2000) found that members continually re-imagined the institution, and that few of them 'felt the need for any unified understanding of the institution or were convinced that it could ever be achieved or that it was even desirable' (p. 453). Glynn's (2000) study of the Atlanta Symphony Orchestra revealed that different groups had fundamentally opposed conceptions of the organization, with musicians championing normative artistry and administrators emphasizing the importance of utilitarian economics. Other studies have discovered how conceptions of identity, including future desired identities, are instrumental in inhibiting, guiding and facilitating processes of change (e.g., Dutton and Dukerich, 1991; Gioia and Thomas, 1996). Gioia and Thomas (1996), for instance, argue that 'A plausible, attractive, even idealistic future image would seem to help organization members envision and prepare for the dynamic environment implied by strategic change' (p. 398). Perhaps most attention has been focused on the linkages between organizational identity and individual members' identification with an organization and the implications of this for other aspects of processes of organizing such as patterns of social interaction, loyalty and commitment (e.g., Dutton, Dukerich and Harquail, 1994).

## Psychodyanmic perspectives

With its origins in the work of Freud, psychodynamic/psychoanalytic perspectives have a lengthy history in organizational studies (Jacques, 1955; Bion, 1968). Some of this early work, notably that of Schwartz (1987), which treated organizations as if they had collective self-conceptions, has been extremely influential. More recent work has made explicit reference to the notion of 'organizational identity'. One of the most thorough treatments of the subject has been offered by Diamond (1993), who defines organizational identity as '... the totality of repetitive patterns of individual behaviour and interpersonal relationships that, when taken together, comprise the unacknowledged meaning of organizational life'. For Diamond, organizational identity is a (not necessarily conscious) 'defensive solution' to psychological threats to members. These threats emanate from the contradictory motives and conflicting aims of organizational participants themselves, threats that are mitigated through the imposition of notionally 'rational' administrative processes which structure and define organizational life. Organizational identity thus not only defines 'who we are as a group', but does so in ways that satisfy individuals needs for security and self-esteem. According to Porter (2001: 21) the most significant contribution from psychodynamic approaches is that they draw attention to important unconscious processes in organizations which other perspectives ignore, appreciation of which can be used to supplement realist and rationalist perspectives in order to broaden and deepen our understanding of identity issues.

A wide-ranging conceptual analysis of the psychodynamics of organizational identities has been outlined by Brown (1997) and Brown and Starkey (2000). Predicated on

Freud's (1914) theory of narcissism, which leads to an understanding of organizations as means for regulating collective self-esteem, Brown (1997) showed how ego-defence mechanisms function at individual, group and organizational levels in order to ameliorate anxieties. Some of the principal ego-defences include the *denial* of what we find unacceptable about ourselves, the *rationalization* (attempt to justify) our consciously intolerable views or behaviours, and our tendency to attribute negative consequences to external causes and positive outcomes to ourselves (termed *attributional egotism*). This theorization has been complemented by Brown and Starkey (2000), who argue that the regressive tendencies associated with extreme forms of ego-defences may be mitigated through the pursuit of judicious management practices. That is, organizations need not be trapped by fantasies of omnipotence, idealization or denial etc., but are able to learn, develop and to adapt by engaging in three sets of interrelated processes: (i) critical self-reflexivity (genuine exploration of key tenets of collective identity); (ii) the promotion of a sophisticated dialogue regarding future possible organizational identities; and (iii) engagement in a quest for an attitude of 'wisdom' which focuses on the development of a willingness to explore ego-threatening matters.

## Postmodern perspectives

As Dunn (1998: 2) has pointed out, '... *the concept of the postmodern itself was an attempt to articulate a growing sense of the problematization of identity as a generalized condition of life in postwar society*'. In general, the label 'postmodern' refers to a disparate group of loosely related approaches that focus on organizational identities as discursive (linguistic) and/or imagistic constructions. For example, Coupland and Brown (2004) have argued that the identities of organizations are authored in 'conversations' between notional 'insiders' and 'outsiders' and that processes of identity construction are best regarded as ongoing arguments that, while never finally 'won', may be temporarily quietened by recourse to 'witcraft'. Brown and Humphreys (2006) have theorized organizations as texts, constituted in discourse, and organizational identities as unstable social constructions constituted through acts of languaging. From more extreme postmodern positions, however, the concept of 'organizational identity' fractures into a plethora of disparate images: 'Identity no longer holds a distinct and persistent core of its own but becomes a reflection of the images of the present moment' (Gioia, Schultz and Corley, 2000: 72). Organizational identity is revealed as a necessary illusion (Rosenau, 1992), a myth invented by leaders to exercise power, and a 'comforting falsification' for organizational members anxious in regard to their personal fate in times of accelerating crisis and change (Baudrillard, 1988; Gioia, Schultz and Corley, 2000: 73).

Perhaps the most fruitful language-based way forward for theorizing organizational identity is that rooted in what Fisher (1985) has referred to as the narrative 'metaparadigm'. A number of authors have sought to carve out a distinctively 'narrative' approach to organizational identity (Czarniawska-Joerges, 1994; Humphreys and Brown, 2002a; Kahane and Reitter, 2002; Chreim, 2005; Brown, 2006). In her attempt to 'depsychologize' the concept of organizational identity, and to free it from sociological determinism, Czarniawska-Joerges (1994: 198) has suggested that we regard '... identity construction as a continuous process of narration where both the narrator and the audience formulate, edit, applaud, and refuse various elements of the ever-produced narrative'. This insight has been used by Brown (2006) to argue that organizations' identities are constituted by the identity-relevant narratives that their participants' author about them. In this formulation, identity-relevant narratives are stories about organizations that actors author in their efforts to understand the collective entities with which they identify. Organizational identity, from this perspective, is a linguistic construct which 'resides' in the collective identity stories that people

tell to each other and outsiders in their conversations, write into corporate histories, and encode on websites. It is an approach that focuses attention on organizations as locales of power, and the reflexive, voiced, plurivocal, temporally continuous and quasi-fictional nature of identities (cf. Brown, Humphreys and Gurney, 2005).

## CRITICAL ISSUES FOR THE PRESENT

There is a huge range of currently unresolved (and quite possibly unresolvable) issues in organizational identity theory and research. Fundamental disagreements remain regarding how the concept should be defined, the most appropriate methodological approaches for its study, and what aspects of organizing notions of organizational identity are equipped to explain and analyse. In this section I will consider five of the most significant debates in this field: (i) Is organizational identity a construct, a question or a metaphor? (ii) Are organizations most appropriately characterized as having one or multiple identities? (iii) Are organizational identities enduring or mutable? (iv) How does the concept of organizational identity relate to cognate notions such as 'reputation' and 'image'? (v) What does an interest in organizational identity teach us about processes of identification?

### Construct, question or metaphor

In seeking to analyse the phrase 'organizational identity' theorists have suggested that it may be regarded as a construct, the answer to a question, or a metaphor (e.g., Albert, 1998). The idea that organizational identity is best regarded as a construct is most closely associated with functionalist approaches. Haslam, Postmes and Ellmers (2003: 359), for example, have argued that organizational identity 'can be defined and measured as a distinct psychological construct that plays a specific role in organizational behaviour'. The issue of 'construct validity' is also key for the work of Whetten (2006) who is primarily concerned to formulate a concept of organizational identity that can be distinguished analytically from related notions such as culture and image, and which can be used operationally to study '… bona fide organizational identity claims and associated identity-referencing discourse' (p. 219). Other authors, particularly those working from interpretive and postmodern perspectives, have criticized conceptions of organizational identity as a 'construct' as unnecessarily homogenizing and restrictive. Gioia, Schultz and Corley (2000: 76), for instance, have asserted that '… we believe it is necessary to encourage the study of identity as something other than an enduring, reified concept'.

Several theorists have suggested that organizational identity is most appropriately considered to be the answer, or set of answers, that members' give in response to questions such as 'who are we?' and 'who do we want to become?' Marziliano (1998: 5) argues that 'Summarizing identity answers the question "What do we believe we are?"' Fiol, Hatch and Golden-Biddle (1998: 57) contend that '… identity answers the question "who are we?" in relation to larger contexts of meaning'. Brown and Humphreys' (2006: 232) study of identity focuses on 'identity questions such as "what is important about this organization?" and "what is the future for us?"' These formulations, of course, beg the issue of what form answers to identity-prompting questions might take. A diverse set of responses have been suggested, from fairly standard verbal *claims* made by members, to more imaginative notions of identity as series of *conversations* between insiders and/or between insiders and outsiders. While much research that treats organizational identity as relating to one or more questions assumes that such questions do in fact have answers, this may not always be the case. As Albert (1998: 11), contends, 'sometimes … the unanswerability of a question (perhaps akin to undecidability in logic) is its defining feature'.

Metaphors mediate analogies (structural correspondences) between putatively disparate concepts. They are heuristic devices

from which may be derived new insights about a phenomenon (such as organized activity), or indeed specific propositions or new hypotheses (Morgan, 1980, 1983). Although work on metaphor has a lengthy history in organization studies, relatively few theorists have sought systematically to analyse 'identity' as a metaphor for understanding organizations. One exception is Cornelissen (2002: 159) who has attempted to evaluate 'whether we can [justifiably] project the idea of an "identity" upon organizations to describe and explain their dynamics'. His core argument, derived by Mackenzie (1978), is that it is not logically possible to equate a collective with an individual-level concept because to do so is to reify organizations and to ignore issues of individual agency. Cornelissen's conclusion is that, because there is little if any degree of structural similarity between 'individuals' and their identities on the one hand and 'organizations', and their notional identities on the other, there is no reasonable ground for using the 'metaphysical' phrase 'organizational identity'. Cornelissen's arguments have been firmly rebutted by Gioia, Schultz and Corley (2002), who point out that self-reference, reification and levels of analysis difficulties can all be overcome through careful definition/specification of the organizational identity concept. These intriguing debates, however, seem set to continue for the foreseeable future.

## Identity multiplicity

While some researchers have chosen to analyse organizations as if they possessed just one identity, most theorists recognize that organizations are generally characterized by identity multiplicity (Ashforth and Mael, 1989; Elsbach, 1998; Foreman and Whetten, 2002). In so doing, the organizational literature takes its lead from the individual-level identity literature which suggests that people have multiple personal identities (Gecas, 1982; Deaux, 1991), role identities (McCall and Simmons, 1978; Burke, 1980) and social identities (Allen *et al.*, 1983;

Hogg, 1996). Perhaps unsurprisingly, what is implied by phrases such as 'identity multiplicity' is itself contested by theorists working from the many diverse perspectives on organizational identity. That said, Pratt and Foreman's (2000: 20) formulation is, perhaps, a reasonable starting point: '*Organizations have multiple organizational identities when different conceptualizations exist regarding what is central, distinctive, and enduring about the organization*'. One curiosity to note is that most of the research that has been undertaken has tended to suggest that organizations have relatively few – generally no more than two or at the most three 'primary' identities.

Multiple identities have been researched in an array of organizations, including higher education institutions (Albert and Whetten, 1985; Humphreys and Brown, 2002a,b), non-profit organizations (Golden-Biddle and Rao, 1997), telecommunications firms (Sarason, 1995), agricultural cooperatives (Foreman and Whetten, 1997), nuclear power plants (Osborn and Ashforth, 1990), high technology manufacturing firms (Reger *et al.*, 1994), an orchestra (Glynn, 2000) a travel agency (Brown, Humphreys and Gurney, 2005), and a psychiatric hospital (Harrison, 2000). Private hospitals in particular have been singled out as being especially prone to 'possessing' multiple competing identities as they seek to combine a high concern with patient care with a high concern for investor returns (Starr, 1982; Stevens, 1989; Pratt and Foreman, 2000; Foreman and Whetten 2002). Despite this wealth of research, however, many issues are yet to be clarified. For example, it is unclear exactly how multiple identities are able to co-exist, under what conditions multiple identities tend to be discussed or are rendered invisible, what makes the same people attribute multiple identities to an organization, and in what circumstances different people attribute different identities to an organization.

In seeking to make sense of 'identity multiplicity' various typologies have been deployed. For example, in addition to Albert and Whetten's (1985) original distinction between 'holographic' and 'ideographic' identities, researchers have often made use of Etzioni's terminology to categorize identities into 'utilitarian', 'economic' and 'normative'. Some authors have sought to identify different kinds of identity common to all or most organizations. Soenen and Moingeon (2002), for example, have argued that there are four types of organizational identity (actual, communicated, ideal and desired) and five 'facets' of collective identities: *professed* identity (what a group or an organization professes about itself); *projected* identity (the elements an organization uses, in more or less controlled ways, to present itself to specific audiences); *experienced* identity (what members experience, more or less consciously, with regard to their organization); *manifested* (or 'historical') identity (a specific set of more or less tightly coupled elements that have characterized the organization over a period of time); and *attributed* identity (the attributes that are ascribed to an organization by its various audiences). While Soenen and Moingeon's framework has not achieved widespread popularity, it has occasionally been used to structure empirical studies (e.g., Albert and Adams, 2002).

One ongoing stream of research is concerned with the notional costs and benefits to organizations of their multiple identities (Pratt and Foreman, 2000). It has been suggested that, on the 'plus' side, multiple identities may be advantageous because sufficient requisite variety is required in order to meet (or at least be seen to meet) the diverse expectations of large numbers of internal and external stakeholders (Nkomo and Cox, 1996). An organization that is able to blend successfully multiple identities may also gain a significant competitive advantage by attracting a broad range of people to work for it who can enhance its capacity for creativity, adaptive flexibility and learning (Ashforth and Mael, 1989; Fiol, 1994). Moreover, not having a sufficient repertoire of available identities may be problematic because it might result in insufficient response strategies to cope with complex social environments (Thoits, 1986).

The potential 'costs' of harbouring multiple identities, especially if those identities are in conflict, are often said to be no less significant. In such circumstances, identity multiplicity may lead to inaction, vacillation or inconsistent behaviour with the result that resources are squandered (Golden-Biddle and Rao, 1997), and strategic decision-making impaired (Fiol and Huff, 1992). Further research, it has been suggested, is required in order to assess whether there is an optimum level of identity multiplicity/consensus, and the forms that this may take, which ensures legitimacy while minimizing conflict (Brown, 2007).

## Identity continuity and change

Of the three key tenets of Albert and Whetten's (1985) original definition of organizational identity, their suggestion that identities are relatively enduring has received the most critical attention. Building on individual-level conceptions of identity which suggest that identities are resistant to change, foster stability of sensemaking and provide a psychological anchor that promotes good mental health, Albert and Whetten (1985: 277) stated: '... organizations tend to become committed to what they have been and seldom substitute new characteristics for old ones'. The idea that identities tend to endure for extended time periods is still cherished by some scholars, and is pragmatic in that it simplifies the task of longitudinal identity research. One reason why identities are held to be resistant to change is that they are generally the products of unique and complicated historical processes that result in sets of institutional practices that participants are cognitively and affectively attached to. Cheney and Christensen (2001: 258), for instance, have theorized identities as 'stable yet responsive entities', while the difficulties associated with efforts of senior managers to deliberately alter organizational identities have been well documented (e.g., Humphreys and Brown, 2002a; Brown and Humphreys, 2003).

However, the assumption that identities exhibit stability has been challenged by other theorists, who prefer to regard organizations' identities as changeable, malleable, or incrementally adaptive. Gioia, Schultz and Corley (2000), for example, argue that the apparent durability of identity is an illusion perpetuated by the stability of the labels that are used by members to express their beliefs about their organization. That is, identity labels are enduring, but the meanings that members associate with those labels are mutable, so organizational identities are, in fact, at least potentially, precarious, feature both flux and stability, and are best regarded as adaptively unstable. While there are still only a few empirical studies of identity change, Chreim's (2005) analysis of a Canadian bank suggests that organizational identities are neither simply enduring nor constantly changing but, rather, unstable and 'subject to continual reconstitution' (p. 588). Even psychodynamic analyses of organizational identities, which emphasize their conservative tendencies, nevertheless also recognize the potential for organizations to mitigate the regressive influence of ego-defences and to learn and develop (Brown and Starkey, 2000). At a time when many business environments are changing rapidly the idea that identities are inherently unstable, and that change occurs to maintain continuity, has proven persuasive, and most commentators now regard organizational identities as dynamic rather than enduring.

## Identity, reputation and image

There is a consensus that organizational identities, however these are conceived, are not merely products of internal processes. Rather, they are formed through interactions between organizational members and external constituencies such as the media, competitors, regulatory institutions, shareholders, and customers (e.g., Dutton and Dukerich, 1991; Elsbach, 1994; Coupland and Brown, 2004). This is in line with the institutional perspective on organizations which suggests that organizational activities are constrained by mimetic, coercive and normative forces which curtail an organization's ability to manipulate identity at will (Powell and DiMaggio, 1991). Recognizing that organizations vary in the degree to which they acquiesce, resist, or proactively manipulate external influences and demands, Scott and Lane (2000) have sought to analyse the factors that make external stakeholders more/less important in identity issues. They suggest that the greater the *network density* in which an organization subsists, the more *central* it is in its stakeholder network, and the more power managers believe stakeholders to have, the more influential external constituencies will in fact be in determining an organization's identity (p. 55).

An understanding that identity involves interactions and interrelationships between insiders and outsiders, and also insiders' perceptions of outsiders' impressions (Gioia *et al.*, 2000: 70), has resulted in an explosion of identity-related concepts and models to explain these processes. Unfortunately, terminology has not been consistently applied by theorists and researchers. This said, terms such as 'reputation', 'construed external image' and 'desired future image' have gained some traction and are widely used. 'Reputation' is generally understood to refer to outsiders' relatively stable, long-term, broadly held understandings of an organization's identity (Fombrun, 1996; Rindova and Fombrun, 1998). More sophisticated versions, however, acknowledge that the homogenization of outsider views implied by this definition is unrealistic, that different external stakeholders may often have diverse perceptions, and that an organization may reasonably be said to have multiple 'reputations' just as it may be said to have multiple identities (Dukerich and Carter, 1998). 'Construed external image' refers to organization members' perceptions of how outsiders perceive their organization (Dutton and Dukerich, 1991; Dutton *et al.*, 1994). Yet again, though, given that many organizations are typified by multiple internal constituencies sensitive to the views of different external stakeholder groups, it may

be more appropriate to recognize that a single organization can have many construed external images (Brown, 2007).

Scholars working from functionalist and interpretive perspectives have sought to distinguish between the actual identity (or actually held perceptions of the identity) of an organization and a variety of other kinds of putative identities. Gioia and Thomas (1996) have termed 'desired future image' the identity senior managers would like internal and external members to attribute to the organization in the future. The phrase 'projected image' has been deployed by Alvesson (1990) to mean the identity created by an organization's leaders for consumption by others. Berg (1985) and Grunig (1993) have described the 'transient impressions' (a phrase coined by Gioia, *et al.* (2000) to refer to the short-term and highly changeable interpretations people make of organizations. The importance of these, and other conceptualizations, is not to be underestimated. These kinds of organizational images, it is frequently argued, may destabilize members' conceptions of identity, leading to profound bouts of reflexivity, and (possibly) new formulations of collective identity (e.g., Elsbach and Kramer, 1996). The oil company Shell's experiences of identity change as a result of environmentalists' challenges to its actions is an often quoted example of how construed external image can lead to self-questioning and transformation (Gioia, *et al.*, 2000; Coupland and Brown, 2004).

## *Identity and identification*

One reason why so much attention has been focused on the concept of 'organizational identity' is that it has been interpreted as a vehicle for understanding and explaining how individuals relate to organizations via the notion of 'identification' (Foreman and Whetten, 2002). Rooted in the social psychological literature on social identity and self categorization theory, identification is generally said to occur '*when an individual's beliefs about his or her organization become self-referential or self-defining*' (Pratt, 1998: 172).

In broad terms, identification may be understood as 'a response to social influence brought about by an individual's desire to be like the influencer' (Aronson, 1992: 34). Identification is an active process with multiple components or dimensions. It implies a cognitive aspect (in the sense of awareness of membership), an evaluative component (in that it is related to some value connotations), an emotional dimension (i.e., it engages us not merely through logic or rational argument), and it is bound up with sensemaking (of ourselves and our relationships with others). It may be conceived as a process of affinity and one of emulation, and is prompted by basic psychological needs for safety, self-enhancement, and meaningful existence. Drawing on social identity theory Pratt (1998) has argued that identification with an organization is more likely when certain categorization and self-enhancement antecedents are in place. Distinctive organizations with high prestige and attractive images, salient out-groups, and minimal intra-organizational competition, he suggests, tend to have higher levels of member identification (Dutton *et al.*, 1994).

Based on social identity literature authors such as Elsbach (1999) have sought to refine general notions of 'identification' into a larger number of more specific descriptions of the kinds of relationships individuals may have with their organizations. Elsbach identifies four such categories: identification, dis-identification, schizo-identification, and neutral identification. Identification implies a self-perception of an active and positive connection between the self and the organization. Dis-identification describes a self-perception of an active and negative connection between the self and the organization. Schizo-identification describes individuals who simultaneously identify and dis-identify with (different aspects) an organization. Finally, neutral identification refers to an individual's self-perception of impartiality with respect to an organization's identity, in which there is an explicit absence of either identification or dis-identification. This classification scheme offers more analytical

potential than the notion of 'identification' alone, and has been co-opted by those working from a narrative perspective (Humphreys and Brown, 2002a). The deployment of this framework using narrative theory rids 'identification' of its social psychological underpinnings, and leads to the analysis of the identification (and dis-/schizo- and neutral identification) stories that people tell in their efforts to account for their relationships with organizations. This is instructive because it is emblematic of how ideas, models and schema developed to explain identity processes from one perspective may be appropriated and redeployed by scholars with different epistemological and ontological premises and diverse methodological preferences.

## CONCLUSION: NEW DIRECTIONS FOR THE FUTURE

There is no shortage of new directions and challenges for the burgeoning literature on organizational identity to deal with. Cornelissen's (2002: 264) challenging position that 'organizational identity' should '… be replaced by an alternative concept of metaphor' must act as a constant spur for researchers to adapt and develop their identity theorizing. Similarly, conceptions of 'organizational identity' which assume that organizations are distinct entities with clear boundaries need to be re-examined. Virtual organizations, those that form elements of closely bound co-operatives and other trading blocks, and organizations engaged in ever more intimate forms of partnership sourcing, all provide challenges to scholars interested specifically in organizational identity. Moreover, there is a growing recognition that the notional frontiers of even conventional organizations are not merely permeable but symbolically enacted, which raises questions regarding attempts to locate their putatively unique identities (Cheney and Christensen, 2001). Whetten's (2002) argument that prevailing conceptions of organizational identity are neither 'identity enough' nor 'organizational enough', requires serious attention, even if his preferred solution of defining identity 'as the categorical self-descriptors used by social actors to satisfy their identity requirements' (Whetten and Mackey, 2002: 396) seems unappealing. Two issues in particular seem set to dominate debates in the immediate future, namely those centred on definitional problems and those relating to the management of organizational identities.

While there is a '… lack of consensus regarding the meaning and definition of the terms organization identity and identification' (Albert, Ashforth and Dutton, 2000: 15), this is not necessarily problematic. Multiple perspectives – functionalist, interpretive, psychodynamic, postmodern etc. – on organizations almost inevitably mean that such terms will be contested. It also means that rather than a homogenized, univocal discourse on identity issues which cherishes just one research agenda, there is scope for a pluralistic, multifaceted set of interlinked identity-centred conversations. Unfortunately, there is little evidence that authors are becoming sufficiently broadminded to see beyond their own narrow paradigmatic assumptions. van Riel (1995: 72) has complained that 'One must, unfortunately, accept that at a conceptual level, there is no … generally accepted definition of corporate identity'. Whetten (2006: 220) has expressed concern that '… the concept of organizational identity is suffering an identity crisis', and Pratt (2003: 162) worries that '… identity – as an explanatory concept – is often overused and under specified'. Rather than seek to restrict the scope for debate, scholars interested in organizational identity may be better advised to recognize, appreciate and accept that there are many ways in which the concept may be defined and deployed and that none of these is inherently more worthwhile than any other.

Narrow debates regarding the extent to which senior managers are able to author the kinds of organizational identities they choose, might benefit from an understanding that identities are suffused with power. Scholars working from functionalist and interpretive perspectives have often written blithely of organizations creating and maintaining desired identities, albeit generally within some set of internal and environmental constraints (e.g., Cheney, 1991; Elsbach and Kramer, 1996; Pratt and Foreman, 2000). Cheney (1991: 174), for instance, advises that '*If leaders, or controlling members of an organization wish to alter the organization's identity in significant ways, they must ground their call for change in the interests of at least some considerable parts of the organization*'. By focusing on those who are hierarchically privileged, such views downplay the significance of other actors, both internal and external, and fail to appreciate adequately the highly politicized nature of organizations. While centripetal forces mobilized by dominant groups may produce some shared meanings and understanding, leaders are unlikely ever to be able to exercise total control. The hegemonic impositions of élites may temporarily mobilize and reproduce the active consent of dominated groups, but as Humphreys and Brown (2002a,b) have shown, organizations tend to be characterized by multiple identities. In short, organizational identities are power effects, and it is to be hoped that a thorough-going critical perspective on organizational identity will be developed in the near future.

## NOTE

1 Coherence may be sacrificed, but a diverse literature provides a more nuanced view of the world in which cohesion, integration and unification are problematized, and an emphasis on variety precludes a bland homogenization.

## REFERENCES

Albert, A. (1998) 'The definition and metadefinition of identity', in D.A. Whetten and P.C. Godfrey (eds) *Identity in Organizations, Building Theory through Conversations.* Thousand Oaks, CA: Sage, pp. 1–13.

Albert, S. and Whetten, D.A. (1985) 'Organizational identity', in L.L. Cummings and B.M. Staw (eds) *Research in Organizational Behavior*, 7. Greenwich, CT: JAI Press, pp. 263–295

Albert, S. and Adams, E. (2002) 'The hybrid identity of law firms', in B. Moingeon, and G. Soenen (eds) *Corporate and Organizational Identities*. London: Routledge, pp. 35–50.

Albert, S., Ashforth, B.E. and Dutton, J.E. (2000) 'Introduction to special topic forum. Organizational identity and identification: Charting new waters and building new bridges', *Academy of Management Review*, 25: 13–17.

Alessandri, S.W. (2001) 'Modeling corporate identity: A concept explanation and theoretical explanation', *Corporate Reputation Review*, 4: 173–182.

Alessandri, S.W. and Alessandri, T. (2004) 'Promoting and protecting corporate identity: The importance of organizational and industry context', *Corporate Reputation Review*, 7: 252–268.

Allen, V.L., Wilder, D.A. and Atkinson, M.L. (1983) 'Multiple group membership and social identity', in T. Sarbin, and K.E. Scheibe (eds) *Studies in Social Identity*. New York: Praeger, pp. 92–115.

Alvesson, M. (1990) 'Organization: From substance to image?', *Organization Studies*, 11: 373–394.

Aronson, E. (1992) *The Social Animal*, 6th edn. New York: W.H. Freeman.

Ashforth, B.E. and Mael, F. (1989) 'Social identity theory and the organization', *Academy of Management Review*, 14: 20–39.

Ashforth, B.E. and Mael, F.A. (1996) 'Organizational identity and strategy as a context for the individual', *Advances in Strategic Management*, 13: 19–64.

Balmer, J.M.T. (2001) 'Corporate identity, corporate branding, and corporate marketing: Seeing through the fog', *European Journal of Marketing*, 35: 248–291.

Balmer, J.M.T. and Gray, E.R. (1999) 'Corporate identity and corporate communications: Creating a competitive advantage', *Corporate Communications*, 4: 171–176.

Baudrillard, J. (1988) 'Simulacra and simulations', in M. Poster (ed.) *Jean Baudrillard: Selected Writings*. Stanford, CA: Stanford University Press, pp. 166–184.

Berg, P.O. (1985) 'Organization change as a symbolic transformation process', in P. Frost *et al.* (eds) *Reframing Organizational Culture*. Beverly Hills, CA: Sage, pp. 281–300.

Bion, W.R. (1968) *Experiences in Groups*. London: Tavistock.

Brown, A.D. (1997) 'Narcissism, identity and legitimacy', *Academy of Management Review*, 22: 643–686.

Brown, A.D. (1998) *Organizational Culture*, 2nd edn. London: FT Pitman.

Brown, A.D. (2001) 'Organization studies and identity: Towards a research agenda', *Human Relations*, 54 (1): 113–121.

Brown, A.D. (2006) 'A narrative approach to collective identities', *Journal of Management Studies*, 43 (4): 731–753.

Brown, A.D. (2007) 'Organizational identity', in S. Clegg and J.R. Bailey (eds) *International Encyclopedia of Organization Studies*. Los Angeles, CA: Sage, pp. 1077–1081.

Brown, A.D. and Humphreys, M. (2003) 'Epic and tragic tales: Making sense of change', *Journal of Applied Behavioral Science*, 39 (2): 121–144.

Brown, A.D. and Humphreys, M. (2006) 'Organizational identity and place: A discursive exploration of hegemony and resistance', *Journal of Management Studies*, 43: 231–257.

Brown, A.D. and Starkey, K. (2000) '"Organizational identity and learning": A psychodynamic perspective', *Academy of Management Review*, 25: 102–120.

Brown, A.D., Humphreys, M. and Gurney, P.M. (2005) 'Narrative, identity and change: A case study of Laskarina Holidays', *Journal of Organizational Change Management*, 18 (4): 312–326.

Brun, M. (2002) 'Creating a new identity for France Telecom, beyond a visual exercise', in B. Moingeon and G. Soenen (eds) *Corporate and Organizational Identities*. London: Routledge, pp. 133–155.

Burke, P.J. (1980) 'The self: Measurement requirements from an interactionist perspective', *Social Psychology Quarterly*, 43: 18–29.

Cheney, G. (1991) *Rhetoric in an Organizational Society, Managing Multiple Identities*. Columbia, SC: University of South Carolina Press.

Cheney, G. and Christensen, L.T. (2001) 'Organizational identity, linkages between internal and external communication', in F.M. Jablin & L.L. Putnam (eds) *New Handbook of Organizational Communication*, Thousand Oaks, CA: Sage, pp. 231–269.

Chreim, S. (2005) 'The continuity-change duality in narrative texts of organizational identity', *Journal of Management Studies*, 42 (3): 567–593.

Cooley, C.H. (1902) *Human Nature and the Social Order*. New York: Charles Scribner's Sons.

Cornelissen, J.P. (2002) 'On the "organizational identity" metaphor', *British Journal of Management*, 13: 259–268.

Cornelissen, J.P. and Elving, W.J.L. (2003) 'Managing corporate identity: An integrative framework of dimensions and determinants', *Corporate Communications*, 2: 114–120.

Coupland, C. and Brown, A.D. (2004) 'Constructing organizational identities on the Web: A case study of Royal Dutch Shell', *Journal of Management Studies*, 41 (8): 1323–1347.

Czarniawska-Joerges, B. (1994) 'Narratives of individual and organizational identities', in S. Deetz (ed.)

*Communication Yearbook.* Newbury Park, CA: Sage, pp. 193–221.

Deaux, K. (1991) 'Social identities: Thoughts on structure and change', in R.C. Curtis (ed.) *The Relational Self: Theoretical Convergences in Psychoanalysis and Social Psychology.* New York: Guilford, pp. 77–93.

Diamond, M.A. (1993) *The Unconscious Life of Organizations, Interpreting Organizational Identity.* Westport, CT: Quorum Books.

Dukerich, J.M. and Carter, S.M. (1998) *Mismatched images: Organizational responses to conflicts between identity, shared external image, and reputation.* Paper presented at EGOS 14th Colloquium, Maastricht, The Netherlands.

Dunn, R.G. (1998) *Identity Crises, a Social Critique of Postmodernity.* Minneapolis: University of Minnesota Press.

Dutton, J.E. and Dukerich, J.M. (1991) 'Keeping an eye on the mirror: Image and identity in organizational adaptation', *Academy of Management Journal,* 34: 517–554.

Dutton, J.E., Dukerich, J.M. and Harquail, C.V. (1994) 'Organizational images and member identification', *Administrative Science Quarterly,* 39: 239–263.

Elsbach, K.D. (1994) 'Managing organizational legitimacy in the California cattle industry: The construction and effectiveness of verbal accounts', *Administrative Science Quarterly,* 39: 57–88.

Elsbach, K.D. (1998) 'The process of social identification: With what do we identify?', in D.A. Whetten and P.C. Godfrey (eds) *Identity in Organizations: Building Theory through Conversations.* Thousand Oaks, CA: Sage, pp. 232–237.

Elsbach, K.D. (1999) 'An expanded model of organizational identification', *Research in Organizational Behavior,* 21: 163–200.

Elsbach, K.D. and Kramer, R.M. (1996) 'Members' responses to organizational identity threats. Encountering and countering the *Business Week* rankings', *Administrative Science Quarterly,* 41: 442–476.

Erikson, E.H. (1965) *Childhood and Society.* Harmondsworth: Penguin.

Fiol, C.M. (1994) 'Consensus, diversity, and learning in organizations', *Organization Science,* 5: 21–50.

Fiol, C.M. and Huff, A. (1992) 'Maps for managers: Where are we? Where do we go from here?', *Journal of Management Studies,* 29: 267–285.

Fiol, C.M., Hatch, M.J. and Golden-Biddle, K. (1998) 'Organizational culture and identity: What's the difference anyway', in D.A. Whetten and P.C. Godfrey (eds) *Identity in Organizations, Building Theory through Conversations.* Thousand Oaks, CA: Sage, pp. 56–62.

Fisher, W.R. (1985) 'The narrative paradigm: An elaboration', *Communication Monographs,* 52: 347–367.

Fombrun, C.J. (1996) *Reputation: Realizing Value from the Corporate Image.* Boston: Harvard Business School Press.

Fombrun, C.J. (2002) 'Foreword', in B. Moingeon, and G. Soenen (eds) *Corporate and Organizational Identities.* London: Routledge, pp. xv–xvii.

Foreman, P. and Whetten, D.A. (1997) An identity theory perspective on multiple expectations in organizations. Working Paper. University of Illinois at Urbana-Champaign.

Foreman, P. and Whetten, D.A. (2002) 'Members' identification with multiple-identity organizations', *Organization Science,* 13: 618–635.

Freud, S. (1914) 'On narcissism: An introduction', Reprinted in J. Rickman (ed.) (1937) *A General Selection from the Works of Sigmund Freud. Psychoanalytical Epitomes, No. 1.* London: Hogarth Press, pp. 118–141.

Frosh, S. (1991) *Identity Crisis, Modernity, Psychoanalysis and the Self.* Basingstoke: Macmillan.

Gecas, V. (1982) 'The self concept', *Annual Review of Psychology,* 8: 1–33.

Giddens, A. (1991) *Modernity and Self-identity. Self and Society in the Late Modern Age.* Cambridge: Polity Press.

Gioia, D.A. (1998) 'From individual to organizational identity', in D.A. Whetten and P.C. Godfrey (eds) *Identity in Organizations, Building Theory through Conversations.* Thousand Oaks, CA: Sage, pp. 17–31.

Gioia, D.A. and Thomas, J.B. (1996) 'Identity, image, and issue interpretation: Sensemaking during strategic change in academia', *Administrative Science Quarterly,* 41: 370–403.

Gioia, D., Schultz, M. and Corley, K.G. (2000) 'Organizational identity, image, and adaptive instability', *Academy of Management Review,* 25: 63–81.

Gioia, D.A., Schultz, M. and Corley, K.G. (2002) 'On celebrating the organizational identity metaphor: A rejoinder to Cornelissen', *British Journal of Management,* 13: 269–275.

Glynn, M.A. (2000) 'When cymbals become symbols: Conflict over organizational identity within a symphony orchestra', *Organization Science,* 11: 285–298.

Glynn, M.A., Barr, P.S. and Dacin, M.T. (2000) 'Pluralism and the problem of variety', *Academy of Management Review,* 25 (4): 726–734.

Goffman, E. (1959) *The Presentation of Self in Everyday Life.* Garden City, NY: Doubleday.

Golden-Biddle, K. and Rao, H. (1997) 'Breaches in the boardroom. Organizational identity and conflict of commitment in a non-profit organization', *Organization Science*, 8: 593–611.

Grunig, J.E. (1993) 'Image and substance: From symbolic to behavioural relationships', *Public Relations Review*, 19 (2): 121–139.

Harrison, J.D. (2000) 'Multiple imaginings of institutional identity', *Journal of Applied Behavioral Science*, 36 (4): 425–455.

Haslam, S.A., Postmes, T. and Ellmers, N. (2003) 'More than a metaphor: Organizational identity makes organizational life possible', *British Journal of Management*, 14: 357–369.

Hatch, M.J. and Schultz, M. (2002) 'The dynamics of organizational identity', *Human Relations*, 55: 989–1018.

Hatch, M.J. and M. Schultz (2004) *Organizational Identity, a Reader*. Oxford: Oxford University Press.

Hogg, M. (1996) 'Social identity, self-categorization, and the small group', in J. Davis and E. Witte (eds) *Understanding Group Behaviour, Volume 2: Small Group Processes and Interpersonal Relations*. Hillsdale, NJ: Lawrence Earlbaum Associates, pp. 227–254.

Humphreys, M. and Brown, A.D. (2002a) 'Narratives of organizational identity and identification: A case study of hegemony and resistance', *Organization Studies*, 23 (3): 421–447.

Humphreys, M. and Brown, A.D. (2002b) 'Dress and identity: A Turkish case study', *Journal of Management Studies*, 39 (7): 927–952.

Jacques, E. (1955) 'Social systems as a defence against persecutory and depressive anxiety', in M. Klein, P. Heimann and R. Money Kyrle (eds) *New Directions in Psychoanalysis*. London: Tavistock, pp. 478–498.

Kahane, B. and Reitter, R. (2002) 'Narrative identity, navigating between "reality" and "fiction"', in B. Moingeon and G. Soenen (eds) *Corporate and Organizational Identities*. London: Routledge, pp. 115–129.

Mackenzie, W.J.M. (1978) *Political Identity*. Harmondsworth: Penguin.

Marziliano, N. (1998) 'Managing the corporate image and identity: A borderline between fiction and reality', *International Studies of Management and Organization*, 28 (3): 3–11.

McCall, G.J. and Simmons, J.L. (1978) *Identities and Interactions: An Examination of Associations in Everyday Life* (revised edn). New York: Free Press.

Mead, G.H. (1934) *Mind, Self, and Society*, C. W. Morris, (ed.). Chicago: University of Chicago Press.

Morgan, G. (1980) 'Paradigms, metaphors and puzzle solving in organization theory', *Administrative Science Quarterly*, 25: 605–622.

Morgan, G. (1983) 'Paradigms, metaphors and puzzle solving in organization theory', *Administrative Science Quarterly*, 28: 601–607.

Morgan, G. (1986) *Images of Organization*. Beverly Hills, CA: Sage.

Nkomo, S.M. and Cox, T. (1996) 'Diverse identities in organizations', in S.R. Clegg, C. Hardy and W.R. Nord (eds), *Handbook of Organization Studies*, Thousand Oaks, CA: Sage, pp. 338–356.

Olins, W. (1989) *Corporate Identity: Making Business Strategy Visible through Design*. Boston: Harvard Business School Press.

Osborn, R.N. and Ashforth, B.E. (1990) 'Investigating the challenge to senior leadership in complex, high-risk technologies', *Leadership Quarterly*, 1: 147–163.

Pettigrew, A.M. (1979) 'On studying organizational cultures', *Administrative Science Quarterly*, 24: 570–581.

Polkinghorne, D.E. (1988) *Narrative Knowing and the Human Sciences*. New York: State University of New York.

Polzer, J.T. (2000) 'Identity in organizations: Building theory through conversations', in D.A. Whetten and P.C. Godfrey (eds) Thousand Oaks, CA: Sage. (1998). Book review, *Administrative Science Quarterly*, 625–628.

Porter, T.B. (2001) *Theorizing organizational identity*. Paper presented at the AoM, Washington.

Powell, W.W. and DiMaggio, P.J. (1991) *The New Institutionalism in Organizational Analysis*. Chicago: Chicago University Press.

Pratt, M.G. (1998) 'To be or not to be? Central questions in organizational identification', in D.A. Whetten and P.C. Godfrey (eds) *Identity in Organizations, Building Theory through Conversations*. Thousand Oaks, CA: Sage, pp. 171–207.

Pratt, M.G. (2003) 'Disentangling collective identities', *Research on Managing Groups and Team, V: Identity Issues in Groups*, 161–188.

Pratt, M.G. and Foreman, P.O. (2000) 'Classifying managerial responses to multiple organizational identities', *Academy of Management Review*, 25 (1): 18–42.

Reger, R.K., Gustafson, L.T., DeMarie, S.M. and Mullane, J.V. (1994) 'Reframing the organization: Why implementing total quality is easier said than done', *Academy of Management Review*, 19: 565–584.

Rindova, V.P. and Fombrun, C.J. (1998) 'The eye of the beholder: The role of corporate reputation in defining organizational identity', in D.A. Whetten and P.C. Godfrey (eds) *Identity in Organizations, Building Theory through Conversations*. Thousand Oaks, CA: Sage, pp. 62–66.

Rindova, V.P. and Schultz, M. (1998) 'Identity within and identity without: Lessons from corporate and organizational identity', in D.A. Whetten and P.C. Godfrey (eds) *Identity in Organizations, Building Theory through Conversations*. Thousand Oaks, CA: Sage, pp. 46–51.

Rosenau, P.M. (1992) *Post-modernism and the Social Sciences: Insights, Inroads and Intrusions*. Princeton: Princeton University Press.

Sarason, Y. (1995) *Self-identity and the Baby Bells: Applying Structuration Theory to Strategic Management*. Doctoral dissertation, University of Colorado at Boulder.

Sarbin, T. (ed.) (1986) *Narrative Psychology: The Storied Nature of Human Conduct*. New York: Praeger.

Schwartz, H.S. (1987) 'On the psychodynamics of organizational disaster: The case of the Space Shuttle Challenger', *Columbia Journal of World Business*, 22: 59–67.

Scott, S. and Lane, V.R. (2000) 'A stakeholder approach to organizational identity', *Academy of Management Review*, 25: 43–62.

Soenen, G. and Moingeon, B. (2002) 'The five facets of collective identities, integrating corporate and organizational identity', in B. Moingeon, and G. Soenen (eds) *Corporate and Organizational Identities*. London: Routledge, pp. 13–34.

Starr, P. (1982) *The Social Transformation of American Medicine*. New York: Basic Books.

Stevens, R. (1989) *In Sickness and in Wealth: American Hospitals in the Twentieth Century*. New York: Basic Books.

Stimpert, J.L.L., Gustafson, L.T. and Sarason, Y. (1998) 'Organizational identity within the strategic management conversation', in D.A. Whetten and P.C. Godfrey (eds) *Identity in Organizations, Building Theory through Conversations*. Thousand Oaks, CA: Sage, pp. 83–98.

Tajfel, H. and Turner, J.C. (1986) 'The social identity theory of intergroup behaviour', in S. Worchel and W.G. Austin (eds) *Psychology of Intergroup Relations*, 2. Chicago: Nelson-Hall, pp. 7–24.

Thoits, P. (1986) 'Multiple identities: Examining gender and marital status differences in distress', *American Sociological Review*, 51: 259–272.

van Riel, C.B. and Balmer, J.M.T. (1997) 'Corporate identity: The concept, its measurement, and management', *European Journal of Marketing*, 31: 341–355.

Whetten, D.A. (2002) Making explicit our assumptions about the 'O' in organizational studies/theories. Meeting of the British Academy of Management, September 2002.

Whetten, D.A. (2006) 'Albert and Whetten revisited, strengthening the concept of organizational identity', *Journal of Management Inquiry*, 15 (3): 119–234.

Whetten, D.A. and Mackey, A. (2002) 'A social actor conception of organizational identity and its implications for the study of organizational reputation', *Business & Society*, 41 (1): 393–414.

# 11

# Organizational Conflict

### Stephen Ackroyd

## THE APPROACH TO ORGANIZATIONAL CONFLICT

Pre-modern societies are marked by more violence and other indicators of open conflict (assault, murder, mayhem, riots, insurrections and local wars) than modern ones. After reviewing much historical and anthropological evidence on aggression, violence and conflict, the evolutionary psychologist Steven Pinker concludes: 'The homicide rates in the most vicious American urban jungles today are twenty times lower than in many foraging societies. Modern Britons are twenty times less likely to be murdered than their medieval ancestors' (Pinker, 1997: 518). Such generalization is supported, though usually inexplicitly and indirectly, by a good deal of other evidence and argument from researchers, including many working in the organizational studies field. Indeed, as we shall see, there is much reason to think that the development of organizations has contributed to a transformation of conflict. Very simply put, what happens with the development of numerous organizations is a significant increase in the number and variety of the relationships in which people are enmeshed

(a greatly increased network density), making clear lines of cleavage and allegiance more difficult to sustain. Modern social life rests, not on a complete absence of conflict, but on a complicated gradation of indifferences, aversions and antipathies.

Societies that are largely constituted by organizations, or organizational societies (Presthus, 1979; Ahrne, 1990; see also Urry, 2000) feature only limited kinds of collective conflict. However, this conclusion does not mean that organizations themselves, or the kind of society largely constituted by organizations, have eliminated overt conflict. On the contrary, the opposite would be the appropriate conclusion: by channelling conflict, organizations are amongst the most significant remaining sites for its expression. Still less should we conclude that, by channelling conflict, organizations have somehow removed conflictive capacities from individuals and societies. As we shall suggest, conflict is a fundamental fact of organizations themselves and of organizational society. In the late modern period, conflict may have come to be subtly and effectively contained by extensive surveillance (Townley, 1998; Lyon, 2001) and soft constraint (Courpasson,

2005), but it has not gone away. Indeed, understanding the patterning of organizational conflict is important for at least two reasons: (a) it allows us to explain several key organizational processes as they exist today, and (b) it also allows a realistic assessment of the question of whether there may be significant changes in patterns of conflict in the future. The question of whether there could be atavistic reversion to overt and violent collective conflict is a concern that haunted a good deal of social science thinking of the nineteenth and twentieth centuries and is one which continues to have relevance today.

In the body of this chapter, there are three sections of roughly equal length. In the first two, we consider substantive work concerning organizational conflict. We find it convenient to divide the material on conflict into that which deals with conflict *in* organizations (intra-organizational conflict), and that *between* organizations (inter-organizational conflict). In the first of these substantive sections, there is a great variety of work that is relevant (Collinson and Ackroyd, 2005). Some schools of thought persist with the myth that most of what people do in organizations conforms to the purposes and goals of an organization, or management expectations regarding these. In this account, by contrast, research that suggests systematic tensions between the outlook and actions of different groups within organization will be given most attention. Second, work concerning conflict as it occurs or exists between organizations will be considered. Again, there is a great variety of work that could be considered in this section, and again, though the range of views is indicated, most space is devoted to the consideration of work produced by a subset of authors. Here attention is focused on the ways in which different kinds and forms of organization are pitted against each other.

In a third and final section of this chapter, how to make sense of the substantive findings that have been reviewed is considered. In this section, there is clearly a need to connect what is known about conflict within and conflict between organizations. Also, the work reviewed in earlier sections reveals that there are some very deep processes involved which are working themselves out over long periods of time. Hence there is a need to review our understanding within a historical as well as a theoretical framework. For this it is necessary to go back to a consideration of classical organizational and social theory. Hence, in this section, the work of Marx, Weber, Simmel, Schumpeter, Polanyi and Foucault is considered as it bears on the issues at hand.

## 1. CONFLICT WITHIN ORGANIZATIONS

Organizations are widely acknowledged to be the site of a good deal of conflict and contestation. Abundant evidence for conflict of various kinds – from absenteeism to zenophobia – has been turned up in the course of social science research over the last 100 years. Research has noted wide variation in the kind as well the intensity of conflict in organizations. It can vary from dissent (expressed failure to agree about ideas) to out-and-out violence and destructiveness (such as sabotage, riot, arson) as suggested by Figure 11.1. The existence of some sort of rudimentary political system in the workplace that is located in the interstices of the formal organization, through which conflict is represented and expressed, has been observed in so many organizations it may well be universal (Burns and Stalker, 1961; Zald and Berger, 1978; Buchanan and Badham, 1999; Noon and Blyton, 2002).

Scholars working in the organizational behaviour field (OB) frequently regard conflict in organizations as endemic, though they sometimes have a quite limited conception of it. In OB as it is constituted today, conflicting behaviour is perhaps most frequently labelled 'organizational *mis*behaviour' (Vardi and Weiner, 1996; Ackroyd and Thompson, 1999). However, a variety of other labels, such as 'workplace deviance' (Robinson and Bennett, 1995; 1997), 'anti-social behaviour' (Giacone and

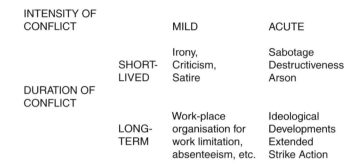

| INTENSITY OF CONFLICT | | MILD | ACUTE |
|---|---|---|---|
| | SHORT-LIVED | Irony, Criticism, Satire | Sabotage Destructiveness Arson |
| DURATION OF CONFLICT | LONG-TERM | Work-place organisation for work limitation, absenteeism, etc. | Ideological Developments Extended Strike Action |

**Figure 11.1    A range of behaviour indicative of intra-organizational conflict.**

Greenburg, 1997), 'dysfunctional behaviour' (Griffin, *et al.*, 1998) are also used. Clearly, some of this writing implies that employees recognize differences between their interests and those of their employers, but that they are mistaken or their perspective on this is somehow wrong, i.e., 'deviant', 'anti-social' or 'dysfunctional'. Some of this work explicitly denies that conflict arises from differences of interests that are rationally pursued by groups of employees. However, by no means all this work on organizational conflict implies that conflicts of outlook or interest are aberrant. The best and most reliable research assumes the opposite.

Recognition that there are conflicting interests between individuals and groups in organizations is difficult to avoid by anyone familiar with them. The first management theorists were under no illusion here. As is well-known, Frederick Taylor (1911), noticed conflict over the intensity of work, and made it basic to his policies. He noticed both a basic tendency to economy of effort on the part of employees (which he called 'natural soldiering') and the informal organization of such tendencies amongst workpeople (identified as 'systematic soldiering'). However, Taylor and his successors, management consultants and work analysts such as Gantt, the Gilbreths and Bedaux, somewhat naïvely assumed that there was an underlying correspondence of the interests between the ordinary employee and the managers. They thought that if the productivity of labour could be increased

by work study and kindred techniques, and some of this increase in value shared with the worker, cooperative activity would ensue, but this was naïve. For one thing, none of the early analysts had any intention of sharing the results of improved efficiency between the parties equally or fairly. They also assumed – quite wrongly – that the redesign of employees' work and the resulting deskilling and loss of control that employees experience, would be of no importance to them. Nor were those who adopted their ideas much interested in questions about a more equitable distribution of efficiency gains; they wanted the efficiency bonus and no additional costs. In retrospect, there was a failure to understand the relationship between manager and worker very adequately.

Conflict in organizations has been attributed to various causes. At a commonsense level it is often seen as the product of different personalities and individual incompatibility, simple bad management and so on. Considered more collectively, analysts have argued that distinctive forms of conflict are likely to arise wherever organizations exhibit particular configurations. Here we might cite the celebrated work of Zald and Berger (1978) in which they analyse the appearance of such things as organizational *coup d'état* or organizational insurgency movements. More recent writers are also very well aware of the politics of the workplace taking particular forms in appropriate circumstances

(Buchanan and Badham, 1999). At the deepest analytical level, however, the root of conflict has been seen as arising from capitalist economic organization. Paul Edwards argues that most conflicts in the workplace are traceable to what he calls the 'structured antagonisms inherent in private capitalism' (Edwards, 1986: 5). His account is supported by a good deal of other work (Freidman, 1977; Burawoy, 1975; Thompson, 1984), and is accepted here. Nevertheless, Edwards' abstract conception is difficult to use in research; neither does it provide the basic explanation of every kind of observed conflict. Hence, in practice, ideas about particular conflicts of interest (Swedburg, 2003) are used instead. Empirically, what we see are conflicts between individuals and groups. What they are ostensibly in conflict about varies a good deal. However, to take a historically very important instance, conflict between employers and employees is recurrent over such things as the duration of periods of work and or the intensity of working effort, as well as the use of the materials and equipment used in work performance (Ackroyd and Thompson, 1999). This example is compatible with the proposition that the conflict arises from the structured antagonisms of private capitalism.

The deep-seated and systemic nature of much intra-organizational conflict was gradually discovered in the second half of the twentieth century. This emerged with the development of more adequate research; the new work was both conceptually more rigorous than hitherto as well as being more sharply focused. One significant development was the application of anthropological study techniques, which required close and persistent observation of actual behaviour, to industrial settings. In the USA, from the early 1950s onwards, anthropological studies were undertaken of work behaviour in manufacturing industry (Dalton 1948; Roy 1952, 1953, 1954). In Britain the development of this sort of approach took longer (Lupton, 1963; Cunnison, 1964; Sykes, 1966). Both the Americans and the British discovered, through close observation, employees acting on what

they perceived to be divergent interests between themselves and their employers. They did this by various means but mainly by adjusting the amount of effort they expended. Where this was not possible, a variety of ways of adjusting what was called the 'effort bargain' or, more broadly the 'wage-work exchange', were in evidence. This finding was generalised in different ways by many researchers. In a penetrating series of case studies, researchers at Columbia University showed how interconnected activities in organizations are. In perhaps the most insightful of these, Gouldner (1954) showed that disturbance of the customary patterns of exchange of work for rewards could cause industrial action as well as new forms of work limitation. By the 1970s, there was emerging agreement that understanding behaviour at work usually involved some bargaining over rewards.

This key insight was applied in various areas of research. A second generation of industrial anthropologists revealed just how extensive the development of informal workplace organization in pursuit of benefits can be (Ditton, 1977; Mars, 1982). By the 1980s a general theory of the exchange of work for wages (especially as it applied to work in manufacturing production) was developed by industrial sociologists and others. Through meticulous studies of absenteeism and turnover in particular, researchers came to the conclusion that working effort was an area of active contest in many work organizations, and this conflict had numerous manifestations (Baldamus, 1961). Industrial relations analysts interested in the formal organization of the behaviour of groups in the workplace extended the range of anthropological and sociological insights to envisage the pervasiveness of conflict. Landmark research by Paul Edwards tied together the wide range of conflicting behaviour found in industrial settings from types which required only informal organization (such as absenteeism and utilitarian sabotage) to that which required some degree of formal union organization to be effective (such as working to rule) to that which obviously required much more extensive formal union coordination (such as strike action) (Edwards and Scullion, 1982; Edwards, 1986). Concepts derived from Marx as elaborated in the work of many researchers (Braverman, 1974; Friedman, 1977 and Burawoy, 1979 among them) and known as labour process theory (LPT) can be seen in many ways as the culmination of the intellectual developments outlined in which conflict is seen as a basic feature of workplace behaviour.

Analysis of the relationships between groups other than shop floor workers and managers were also given impetus by LPT. Some of the most interesting work in this respect is that which focuses on the processes by which occupational groups contest for ascendancy within management. Using the notion of the professional mobility project (Larson, 1977), Armstrong (1984, 1985, 1986) considered the ways in which professional groups within organizations change their situation. Armstrong not only identified the key conflicts between groups of 'professionals in management' but also considers particular professions – engineering, accountancy and personnel management – in terms of their attempts to broaden their jurisdiction, and in some cases to aspire to take over the general management of organizations. Other research has shown that even in industries where, of necessity, such professional occupations were strongly represented, such as engineering, senior engineers were often not a dominant voice on company boards. A study of the vehicle industry in Britain, for example, showed that, between the two World Wars and after, car companies reduced and marginalised the engineering professionals on company boards. Even where companies were set up by engineers in the first place, such as the Austin car company, directors of British car companies often were not able to ensure that product development concerns were given the highest priority when major strategic decisions were made (Ackroyd and Lawrenson, 1995). A profit-conscious and generalist management controlling industry, as is the case in Britain and the USA, has

been relatively unreceptive to the qualities of management by technically specialized professionals.

Another area of conflict and contestation in organizations that has been widely noted concerns the groups that control companies (Zald, 1969). Which groups are represented on boards can be decisive in deciding not only the strategy that a company adopts, but the uses to which assets are put and the distribution of rewards between groups. Much of what a board does is inherently political and the boardroom a likely site for conflict as different groups contest for ascendancy. In public limited companies, there are three parties to governance, each of which has overlapping membership. First, there are owners of the company – the shareholders – which can be a very large and diverse group. Size and diversity is a weakness when it comes to controlling a large company, and where this occurs this group has had declining influence. However, shareholders that hold many shares can expect not only to have their opinions heard, but also to have representation on the board of directors. Some will be individual holders of large blocs of shares (and some of these are becoming increasingly active in their demands). On the other hand, the largest shareholders may be institutions (such as pension funds or insurance companies). Second, there is the senior management of a company: some of whom will also be directors. Third, there are non-executive directors. These are mainly people supposedly selected because of their experience and knowledge, but we need not expect people from different walks of life to be represented – academics perhaps, or even trade union officials. Typically, non-executive directors are either serving executives of other companies or formerly were, and so this group usually has sympathy with the views and priorities of executives.

Board level politics is not to be understood simply in terms of the particular issues and debates occurring at a given time. Clearly, the legal forms and other rules which govern the form that the constitution of companies must take will also influence the patterns of politics (Charkham, 1994). It is also true that there are complex patterns of alliances that typically arise in the governance of companies to be observed, and these will influence outcomes typically agreed by boards (Scott 1984; 1986, 1997). In addition, there are long-term trends, describing the terms in which the parties to company governance contest with each other. For example, researchers have documented increases in the ascendancy of executives over shareholders over a long period. If we follow the ideas of economists about governance, and assume that a company exists for the sole benefit of the owners, we have to conclude that shareholders have often been weakly represented on boards and that the managers have too much power. The increasing independence of managers, as opposed to owners, is an issue first researched in the 1940s and often since then (Burnham, 1941; Berle and Means, 1947; Berle, 1955; Scott, 1984; Fligstein 1990).

Responses to this situation have been varied; but mostly there is acceptance of the point of view of the economists and accountants, that owners of the stock should have greater access to the distribution of the benefits flowing from the equity in the company. In order to deal with what is seen as the 'agency problem' in governance, top executives have in recent years been awarded large rises in their rewards mainly through share allocations and share 'options' – shares that they may buy at their discretion often at a fixed price. The rationale is to align the interests of executives more closely with those of shareholders. However, it seems very clear that these measures are not securing what they are supposed to, and the trend for executives to acquire even more independence continues. It can be argued that such things as the policy of managers to take their companies private, to take them over in management buyouts, or agree to their company being taken over by private equity interests, are all indications of managers' asserting their independence from owners and owners' interests.

From this discussion it should be clear that organizations are not fixed entities and the relationships between the groups that comprise them are being continuously negotiated, and that conflict (admittedly often on a modest scale) is the continuous accompaniment of this. Organizations reproduce themselves in roughly the same form much of the time, and change in the relative standing of groups is achieved in very small, incremental steps. That change occurs becomes clear only if we consider roles and relationships over long periods of time. Then we can perceive the effects of the negotiations between parties. Viewed in this way, organizations are what emerge from the relationships between the groups comprising them: conflict is integral to them. Indeed, it is possible to think in terms of a conflict theory of organization, in which any organization is seen as a coalition of different groups – each of which has some particular interest in the organization and access to some power relations. The organizational configuration considered as a whole comprises the relationships between all groups.

## 2. CONFLICT BETWEEN ORGANIZATIONS

So far it has been suggested that conflict within organizations arises from contestation between different social and economic groups. The conflict between groups, as it works itself out, causes organizational change. A similar conception of the effectiveness of agency (this time at the level of the organization) can be used when looking at such things as changes in populations of organizations (the totality of the organizations of a particular type) and or organizational fields (the sets of different organizations that constitute a given part of the economy or other institutional matrix). As particular bundles of social groups having distinctive orientations towards the world, the social projects that organizations have differ. As a result they can be seen as necessarily colliding with other organizations as they attempt to reach particular goals and to maximize what they understand to be their advantages.

To take an extreme example to exemplify the point: some organizations (for example, political parties or religious sects) may be seen as embodying the social aspirations of a particular group (Zald and Ash, 1966), and are a means by which the groups that created them seek to change the world. In a similar way, commercial organizations may be seen as principally driven by the socio-economic ends and aspirations of some group, though these may only be the money-making goals of the entrepreneurs that establish and own them. Even an orthodox new business does not necessarily or automatically achieve acceptance but has to struggle to find a place in the world.

Some indication of the range of possibilities, in terms of the types of collisions between organizations that can occur, is given in Figure 11.2. As is suggested, inter-organizational conflicts vary from mild and ephemeral to long-term and very acute.

By assuming that organizations will accommodate themselves to existing markets, much orthodox economics and organizational theory is ill-equipped to recognise the differences in outlook and objectives of organizations and the conflicts to which this routinely gives rise. There are some obvious examples of organizations, such as the Mafia or the IRA, that are oppositional to state and or other aspects of institutional life. Although such differences of outlook are clearly less extreme, organizations do have different reasons for their existence which differ from those of others and this may lead to collisions between them. As Etzioni argued some time ago, organizations of different types will involve very different patterns of motivation and modes of attachment by the groups that comprise them (Etzioni, 1961). Etzioni of course distinguished between coercive, utilitarian and normative organizations, but beyond this, there are finer differences within organizations of particular types, which do have an impact on the policy and strategy of firms. Organizations are often dissimilar in terms of the aspirations that drive their owners and leaders, the policies they conceive, and the objectives they seek. Market competition is itself only one type of institutionalised contestation, of course, in which conventions and laws supposedly regulate conduct, but seeing the market as a set of conditions, with which business must conform, is not something automatically accepted by business leaders. Although they are often ideologically disposed to approve of markets they will also seek to limit their effects or even avoid them. If they can be, market conditions will be altered. For an entrepreneur, what is seen is not a market, so much as business opportunities, in which the only rule is to raise profitability by any means possible (Anderson *et al.*, 1992). In favourable circumstances, there is the possibility of driving rival firms into bankruptcy, leaving the survivor as a monopoly. There is, of course, also a large literature that shows that business executives, having large resources at their disposal and much to gain by using them, are predisposed to break social rules concerning business practice, and often the law as well, in order to realize their

| INTENSITY OF CONFLICT |  | MILD | ACUTE |
|---|---|---|---|
|  | SHORT-LIVED | Achieving the acceptance of an new organisation | Resistance to take-over and industrial reconstruction |
| DURATION |  |  |  |
|  | LONG-TERM | Achieving the legitimacy of a new type of | Stand-off between class-based organisations |

**Figure 11.2   A range of examples of inter-organizational conflict.**

goals (Punch, 1996; Sayles and Smith, 2006).

In order to survive, organizations have to be much more active than either economic theory or orthodox organizational ideas, such as contingency theory, suggests. One of the reasons that contingency theory was finally found wanting and discarded, was because of its lack of political realism: it assumed an absence of political motivation on the part of groups, and indeed that any conflict arising in organizations was seen as both abnormal and necessarily dysfunctional (Mintzberg, 1989). There was also an inability or unwillingness to recognize that the activities of an organization's members were motivated by particular conceptions of their own interests, as well as in those of their organization. For this reason, organizations do not passively adapt to their circumstances, but actively pursue particular strategies and policies. New organizations, especially, have to make space for themselves and this usually requires an active stance towards other organizations that make up their field. More often than not there is a need to reallocate resources to new activities and displace other organizations. In organizational theory, the successors to contingency researchers fare better in recognising both the differences between organizations, and the need to account for the resulting politics between them.

Institutionalist writers recognize, at least, that institutional fields are actively coercive, as they assert that organizational fields exert pressures towards conformity. Clearly, organizations do have to obtain what they need to continue in business from the particular types of institutions, and pay the price if they are too dependent (Pfeffer and Salancik, 1978). In the institutional account, then, organizations largely conform to expectations other organizations have of them. The traffic is mostly one way: organizations adopt the patterns of organization typical in their particular field because doing so confers legitimacy. The social and economic aspirations people have must accommodate themselves to the expectations of the people serving them; this is especially true if they are dependent on the other institutions for access to key resources. The insitutionalist position offers an explanation of why the usual response to challenges to organizations is conformity.

In many ways, the perspective of population ecology (PE), the other major successor to contingency theory, more readily accommodates the view that organizations are vehicles for the aspirations of particular agents. PE is focused on the patterns of growth in specific organizational populations (i.e., sets of organizations of similar type), the innovation of a new type of organization follows a specific trajectory. All the examples of innovation of new types of organizations studied by PE analysts – from museums to new kinds of restaurants – generally show a similar trajectory. This is marked by very slow development in numbers in the early years, followed by rapid development once a certain density of the population is achieved, followed by stabilisation in the longer term. Both the slow initial development and eventual stabilisation of the population of a distinctive kind of organization implies that the organization has to establish itself. It only gradually gathers recruits and, in the early days, acceptance of the type of organization is limited. In the case of the rise of a new type of commercial organization, PE implies that the new type has to establish a market for the services it has to offer, and so to create a demand which, as time goes on, becomes so great that it is satisfied only by a large number of organizations of the type. Clearly, in this sort of case the creation of a new type of organization, may be seen as a kind of social movement in which the organization not only does something new, but also is the vehicle for the aspirations of a particular group – of museum curators, restaurateurs or whatever. In the language of PE, these processes are written about as new types of organizations invading an ecological niche which has finite resources. Considering the question of how this 'invasion' is achieved, the notion that new organizations have to struggle to achieve acceptance seems justified.

So far we have looked at examples of inter-organizational conflict which, even if we have a more accurate and realistic appraisal of them than is commonly envisaged, involve relatively minor conflicts. On the other hand, there clearly are examples where conflict between organizations is both widespread and acute. Such a case occurs when whole industries are reorganized, or, to use a fashionable, if euphemistic word, 'rationalized'. These periods of general economic transformation were what the institutional economist, Joseph Schumpeter, referred to as involving 'creative destruction' (1943) because, during them, large numbers of organizations are deliberately destroyed as well as created. For those whose businesses are forcibly downsized, split up, sold off or otherwise rationalized, this might sound too positive a description of what occurs. Indeed, what Schumpeter himself does not call attention to is the fact that these periods of transformation will be led by particular groups who have found new ways of making large gains. Such groups, fairly obviously, often meet widespread opposition, and acute conflict can arise. For example, the extensive period of transformation of US industry in the 1980s was brought about by several insurgent groups (mostly using new organizations which they controlled and through which they worked). First, there were the principals in new specialist finance houses who had invented new means of financing companies – from which they earned high fees (Johnston, 1987). The activities of these people and their organizations were contested by conventional bankers and business analysts and by regulatory officials. Second, there were corporate raiders with their conglomerates, interested in taking over and asset stripping rival companies (see for example, Fallon, 1991: 397–429). These were resisted as far as they were able by the companies that were their targets. Finally there are business executives who had to deal with the takeover bids of their companies, who fought back as best they could, with the help of their own professional lawyers and financiers. It is only a surprise that the big losers from these corporate transformations (which were largely about who would reap the benefits from exercises in corporate downsizing) – the hundreds of thousands of employees who lost their jobs (Lazonick and O'Sullivan, 2000; Lazonick, 2005) – did not cause much, if any, general political disturbance.

It is also important to recognize that there is – or has been – inter-organizational conflict that is both serious and which endured for long periods. The major example here is the conflict between the capitalist organizations which came to dominate the economy by the late nineteenth century and the institutions and practices developed by the working classes in response to them. In Britain and other parts of Europe, as the economy came to be dominated by large industry and modern management developed, oppositional politics itself underwent a transformation to more organized forms. Before the emergence of the modern economy, the pattern of conflict found in premodern and early modern societies would involve rioting, insurrection and rebellion, accompanied by widespread destructiveness and loss of life. In England until well into the nineteenth century rioting was common. The Riot Act of 1714, made the shooting of rioters by soldiers perfectly legal and this occurred periodically. The Act was replaced by the Public Order Act in 1986, which in some ways greatly extended police powers. However, with the development of large-scale industry and the emergence of trade unions (which were, increasingly, formally organized), insurrection and riot gradually gave way to striking as the predominant form of conflict. Writing about the evidence of conflict in Britain over the previous two centuries, Cronin (1979) argues that striking became slowly, but definitely, differentiated from general forms of political action such as rioting during the nineteenth century. According to Cronin, by the end of the third quarter of the nineteenth century, the strike gradually emerged as a new and distinctive from of collective conflict. Cronin argues:

> It is clear, then, that strikes became differentiated from earlier forms of collective action only slowly, and even in the nineteenth century

the separation has been at certain moments precarious... Nevertheless, there is some consensus that the strike became the 'natural' response to distress in England some time between 1850 and 1900. ... the break appears sharpest before and after 1870 .... However, the dynamism of protest did not diminish once the transition from the old to the new forms was accomplished (Cronin, 1979: 46).

For Cronin there is also a clear implication that, once the 'modernisation' of protest had been accomplished, there was small chance of turning back. By contrast, other researchers looking at similar evidence argue for continuing diversity in the forms of conflict, and argue that modern forms of conflict feature more diverse forms of social action (rallies and protest demonstrations) in addition to strikes. In the view of Charles and Louise Tilly, European populations have for long had available and used what they call 'repertoires of collective action' (Tilly and Tilly, 1981: 20) of which the capacity for strike action is but one. We shall return to the question of how general protest may best be interpreted in the final section of this article. However, it cannot be regarded as a matter of little importance to note that, since this historical and comparative work on the transformation of conflict noted here was completed in the 1970s and early 1980s, strike action (and indeed in some countries trade unionism itself) has collapsed.

## 3. ORGANIZATIONAL CONFLICT – ITS PAST AND ITS FUTURE

Though not the first to identify conflict as a significant factor in social life, Karl Marx was the first modern thinker to see conflict as both systemic within social formations and as the major cause of change. Although there are many aspects of his work that are questionable, it does contain a penetrating analysis of the rise of capitalism and the way in which conflict is integral to its development. In a certain sense, much of what later theorists of development were to do was a correcting and amending of Marx, and, in particular, a

reconsidering of the actual consequences of the rise of capitalism.

For Marx, of course, the socio-economic system found in any epoch is driven by the conflict between classes. Classes are defined as being differently placed with regard to ownership or control of the means of production. Within capitalism, the capitalist class owns the main means of production, which is capital. Capital, of course, can be moved between the liquid form of cash funds, to a material form when it is invested in buildings, plant and machinery and used in production. By contrast with this, the working classes own only their labour and, in order to live, have to sell it in return for wages. Marx's basic insight was that although all production of goods and services is done by labour (in what he called the labour process), ownership of the means of production allowed the capitalist to appropriate the full value of the goods produced (through what he called the valorisation process), whilst paying only a small proportion of its value out in wages. For this reason, there is a conflict over the work-wage exchange at the heart of capitalist organizations. This proposition, as we have seen, finds empirical support in a good deal of the research work reported in the first sections of this chapter. The conflicts in the workplace arising from this basic conflict have been discussed by numerous analysts, especially those concentrating on work in capitalist enterprises as they existed historically. Undoubtedly too, Marxian ideas are valuable in understanding why conflict can be extremely widespread, as in the recurrent waves of strikes, and diverse, as in the various forms of employee misbehaviour.

However, what we see in the longer term is not what Marx proposed would occur as a result of the development of capitalism. Clearly a build up of conflict leading to a final cataclysmic resolution between the organized capital and organized workers did not happen. For Marx, the basic conflict is between classes and, arguably, he did not analyse sufficiently the effects of the organizations in which these relationships are embodied. For Marx, conflict which originates in the economic sphere (in factories and workshops) can only intensify. Economic institutions generate tensions, but Marx assumed that these tensions cannot be resolved to any degree in the place they are generated. For him, intensifying conflict will eventually spill out from the economy into the political arena in increasing expressions of collective conflict. These will lead, eventually, to the revolutionary transformation of economy and society through political action. So it is for Marx that politics holds out the prospect of the resolution of conflict through the external reorganization of the economic sphere. Clearly there are some problems with this thesis. One is that this argument underestimates the capacity for economic organizations, and indeed reformed capitalist institutions more generally, to redirect, dissipate and diffuse conflict. Another, and much more fundamental objection, is the assumption that conflicts must be resolved at some point. As Georg Simmel suggested, after Marx's death, far from being unnecessary, conflict is constitutive of organizational and social systems and indeed a major source of whatever stability and dynamism such systems have (Simmel, 1902). Simmel points out that the caste type of society, which is very stable, is built on the exclusive, mutual repulsion of the castes. By extension, it is because the antagonisms within capitalism are actually less complete and less balanced, that contestation is active and ongoing, leading to a dynamic pattern of social organization. The consequences of conflict progressively unfold.

Viewed in this way, it is important to recognize that the rise of capitalism not only involves the change of economic systems but also that its rise is always accomplished by a particular social group, and the organizations that group created. These organizations redirect and channel conflicts in particular ways. In Britain, the site of the first industrial revolution, the advent of industrial capitalism was also a highly successful organizational development project of an industrial petit bourgeoisie. It is a little remarked point, but a highly important one, that the industrial

revolution in Britain was achieved by this group without any appropriate legal forms and supports (incorporation, limited liability), to say nothing of modern systems of management and organization, which had not yet been invented, but which were subsequently thought basic requirements for industrial capitalism. Apart from features of the English system of common law, which already allowed extensive freedom in the ownership and use of private property and which were soon extended to allow the emergence of free markets for labour (Polanyi, 1944), the development of industrial capitalism was first achieved without any very significant institutional support. The industrial workshop, the prototype of the modern factory, is the single most obvious organizational achievement of this group, and, though it is unremarkable by comparison with what came later, it is the source of the wealth of a whole new class. What this group did was rise to wealth and political influence against the values of the dominant culture, and without access to the land, stores of capital and other resources of the existing social élite. Viewed in this way, what the rising petit bourgeois class did by creating the first profitable industrial type of organization was no small achievement.

In a broader perspective, however, the dramatic reconstruction of the traditional economy – the destruction of the subsistence economy based on agriculture, the rise of industrial capitalism and the creation of labour markets – had the effect of creating new instability and unleashing ramifying conflict. Karl Polanyi, for example, has argued that the creation of a national market for labour in Britain had very extended social and political consequences. While it is true that conflict did not simply accumulate as Marx thought it would, it did not simply go away either and the consequences of this and their extent have been a matter of considerable debate. Conflict was redirected by modern capitalism and its associated system of organizations, but how far this was necessary and effective is not clear. As well as constituting the cause of conflict, industrial capitalism produced recognition that social projects and social problems can have organizational solutions. Thus, the development of the economy is accompanied by the development of the state, including nascent systems of pension and welfare provision, as well as oppositional parties and unions. In the longer term, we can see these new institutions redirecting the conflicts still embedded at the core of the capitalist economy. The development of the welfare state, in particular, had the indirect long-term effect of reducing industrial conflict (Hibbs, 1978; Ackroyd, 1997). Thus, Marx and Marxists have been said to have mistaken the outcroppings of extreme conflict (still to be observed in capitalism well into the twentieth century), as indications of impending final cataclysm, when they were not. In fact, viewed in the long term, widespread and violent industrial unrest was becoming increasingly rare, and conflict was gradually being re-routed through finer and more extensive institutional channels. Analytically, commentators on change can be classified into those who think that the channelling of conflict in the modern economy will be rapid and effective, and those who think that the instabilities arising will continue to be, potentially at any rate, deeply destabilizing.

A classic source supporting a conflict reduction thesis, in which organization will have a central role, is the work of Roberto Michels, a friend and colleague of Max Weber. Indeed, some have linked the ideas of Michels – who is famous for formulating what he called the 'iron law of oligarchy' – with Weber's ideas about the rationalization and bureaucratisation of the Western world. Both writers argue that the historical trend is for formal organization to take any radicalism out of potentially insurrectionary movements, such as revolutionary parties or militant trade unions. After an extended study of German political parties before World War I, Michels argued that socialist political parties, which, for ideological reasons formulated strict rules regarding democratic procedures and decision making in the early years of their existence, precisely to preserve the radicalism of their grass roots, would

nonetheless be traduced into conservatism by the inherent characteristics of modern bureaucracy (Michels, 1949). Bureaucracies are hierarchies controlled by élites, and Michels therefore suggested in a dictum for which he subsequently became famous: 'Who says organization says oligarchy'. Michels thought, among other things, that de-radicalisation will occur as radical policies had to be translated into actions by organizations governed by bureaucratic rules. The oligarchic monopolisation of control in bureaucratic structures would, Michels thought, dictate the failure of insurrectionary socialism. Before any left party had taken control of any country in the world, Michels wrote confidently: 'socialists may triumph, but not socialism'. However, there is a clear sense in which Michels and Weber foreclosed the debate about the effects of modern organization on insurrection and widespread conflict. Despite the fact that left political parties and trade unions inevitably became bureaucratised, as Michels said they would, this alone did not spell the end of their democratic tendencies, or the end of the conflicts to which they contributed.

Far from eliminating conflict, the formalisation of working class organization and the development of bureaucracy did not remove conflict. What happened was that trade union organization did not siphon off or institutionalise the radicalism of ordinary employees. The informal organization in workplaces, allowing for day-to-day resistance to management control, continued alongside the formal organization of trade unions. The two types of organization existed in a symbiotic and at times very uneasy relationship in some countries. In some industries in the UK, the majority of strike action was 'unofficial'; that is, mounted by workers but neither recognized by officials in the union organization nor sanctioned by the union bureaucracy. For long periods, strike action continued to be dependent on the informal organization of the employees in the workplace; not always, or even often, did it gain backing from the official union organization. Hence, although centralisation and bureaucratisation did become features of the trade unions, the informal oppositional organization of employees also persisted, and there was a mutual dependency between them. So it was that industrial protest and conflict was not eliminated very completely or quickly, as Michels and others predicted. Clearly, oppositional movements gain their vitality from the grievances formed in the collective experience of people, and for this reason conflict is constantly renewed.

Another thinker who contributed to the debate about the trajectory of capitalism, and who arguably overestimated the contribution of organization to the reduction of conflict, was Joseph Schumpeter, whose ideas we have already mentioned. Recognizing that the initial engine of capitalist development was the inventiveness of the bourgeoisie, Schumpeter nonetheless thought that the heavy infrastructure of organizations that emerged as capitalism developed, would contribute to the routinisation of entrepreneurial functions (1943). Schumpeter was actually one of the few economists to take seriously the capacity of capitalism to renew itself, and to find a place for the periods of convulsive change which periodically engulf any capitalist economy. In such times, when renewal gains ascendancy, productive resources are reconfigured to be used in new ways; *inter alia*, old types of organization and patterns of organization are discarded in favour of new ones. Be that as it may, Schumpeter did not see such processes of creative destruction as likely to occur indefinitely. He argued that, as they developed, large scale organizations would dispense with the need for entrepreneurship, through the routinisation of innovation. In the place of the entrepreneur large organizations would utilize research and development departments, corporate planning functions and the like. Schumpeter went so far as to suggest that the highly developed economy which was dominated by large and bureaucratised firms, interacting with equally large and bureaucratic institutions of the state, were in some ways indistinguishable from socialism. He even envisaged that a transition from highly developed capitalism

to socialism would be possible. However, in retrospect, Schumpeter clearly overestimated the effects of bureaucratisation, and indeed, the fundamental differences between capitalism and socialism. Indeed, the renewal of capitalism is the predominant tendency, and the shifting alliances which cause this, continue to produce organizational conflict and social instability. At present, the site of significant conflict has shifted, from tensions between the bottom and the top people in organizations, to disagreements between élite groups over their share of the spoils.

The verdict of many, perhaps most, contemporary writers and researchers into conflict in and around organizations, is that it has been finally domesticated and contained. Contemporary researchers and writers, particularly those taking a post-structuralist view, caution against the tendency to impute active resistance to people in organizations. The idea that any insurrectionary intent should be attributed to them is ruled out. Indeed, it seems to be true, that, although some behaviour in organizations can be seen as resistance to managerial control, it does not have subversive motives nor is it likely to be aimed at achieving transformatory effects. Drawing particularly on Foucault's ideas about discipline (1977), post-structuralist writers argue that contemporary managerial control is often exercised through new forms of workplace surveillance (computers, CCTV, appraisal, performance targets). Highlighting the ways that disciplinary processes often impact on employees' sense of themselves, post-structuralists also consider the analytical importance of the subjectivities that typically reflect and reinforce the exercise of power and resistance (Casey, 1995). Accordingly, many contemporary analysts seek to demonstrate the disciplinary effectiveness of managerial surveillance regimes (Sewell and Wilkinson, 1992; Willmott, 1993). Where conflict is manifested, it can have the unintended effect of reinforcing managerial control because opposition is then more visible. For example, Burrell argues that the effects of resistance frequently feed back into and strengthen control: 'discipline can grow stronger knowing where its next efforts must be directed' (1988: 228). In the understanding of many contemporary researchers, workplace conflict is likely to be small-scale, discontinuous and ineffective.

Arguably, however, some of this post-structuralist work is inconsistent with Foucault's own ideas and particularly with his (1977) assertion that power and resistance are reciprocally constituted. For Foucault power invariably produces resistance, especially in the form of local acts of defiance. The disciplinary effects envisaged by some writers are not inevitable and by no means all forms of resistance end in defeat for subordinates. In certain cases managerial attempts to render misbehaviour the target of further discipline may actually reinvigorate worker resistance. Collinson's (2000) study of resistance strategies found that persistence was more effective (but less common) than distancing. Shop floor workers distanced themselves from management and the organization, but paradoxically their counter-culture had the effect of reinforcing managerial prerogative and power. By contrast, employees who sought to render those in power more visible and accountable, through the persistent demand for more information and the questioning of decisions, were relatively more effective in achieving change. These two forms of resistance tended to reflect and reinforce quite distinct employee subjectivities, both of which contained important paradoxes, ambiguities and ironies.

In general, by questioning assumptions about subjectivity and identity, post-structuralists seek to produce new ways of thinking about power and resistance in the workplace. They argue that social scientists need to rethink the ways that they typically conceptualise particular practices as resistance (Jermier et al., 1994). Many post-structuralist writers also argue that resistance is not only a means by which employees may express their discontent about workplace processes, but it could also enable subordinates to construct an alternative, more positive sense of self to that provided, prescribed or circumscribed by the organization. Recent post-structuralist studies highlight the multiplicity, ambiguity and potentially contradictory outcomes of these resistant selves (Collinson, 2003). Since identities are never fully achieved, they must also be constantly reconstructed (Knights, 1990). Challenging conventional notions of identity as a fixed and objective essence, post-structuralists contend that oppositional selves are open, negotiable, shifting and ambiguous (Kondo, 1990). Hence post-structuralists view actors as decentred selves whose multiple identities and practices are frequently characterized by insecurities, contradictions and creative tensions. Given these ambiguities and subjective complexities, post-structuralists suggest that any examination of resistance needs to explore its interrelated conditions (that give rise to misbehaviour), processes (meanings, motives and diverse practices) and consequences (impact on selves and organizations). Such arguments are perfectly consistent with the idea that the long-term tendency is for the destabilizing effects of capitalism to be rerouted. There is not much disagreement between analysts over many of the features of contemporary conflict. However, what disagreement there is appears to be most acute over the question of whether conflict has been effectively dissipated, and whether it retains any capacity for structural change.

Throughout this chapter, there has been a recurrent theme in the writing that has been reviewed. This concerns the constitutive nature of conflict. It seems very clear in a great deal of work in this field, that conflict is not something that can be dispensed with, an aberration that can somehow be avoided or be done without. Conflict is endemic; and, as has been argued, it is constitutive of organizations. It certainly cannot be regulated out of existence, as management theorists and apologists assume. Indeed, the unusual situation is one in which there are no manifestations of conflict to be found in and around organizations. Conflict is the visible symptom of the existence power in organizations and its machinations. In this recognition resides the reason for durability and ubiquity of conflict. Indeed, we can go further and say that, to the extent that any recognition of conflict is missing from much management writing, such writing is likely to continue to inhabit a science fictional realm in which imagined actors do imagined things in imaginary organizations, and in which social reality remains, for the most part, chimerical.

# REFERENCES

Ackroyd, S. (1996) 'Organisation contra organisations: Professions and organisational change in the United Kingdom', *Organisation Studies*, 17 (4): 599–621.

Ackroyd, S. (1997) 'Don't care was made to care', in R. Hugman, M. Peelo and R. Soothill (eds) *Concepts of Care: Developments in Health and Social Welfare*. London: Arnold.

Ackroyd, S. and Lawrenson, D. (1995) 'Manufacturing decline and the managerial division of labour in Britain: The case of vehicles', in I. Glover and M. Hughes (eds) *The Professional-managerial Class*. Aldershot: Avebury.

Ackroyd, S. and Thompson, P. (1999) *Organisational Misbehaviour*. London: Sage.

Ahrne, G. (1990) *Agency and Organisation: Towards an Organisational Theory of Society*. London: Sage.

Anderson, R., Hughes, J.A. and Sharrock, W. (1989) *Working for Profit*. London: Croom Helm.

Armstrong, P. (1984) 'Competition between organisational professionals and the evolution of managerial control', in G. Thompson (ed.) *Work, Employment and Unemployment*. Milton Keynes: Open University Press, pp. 97–120.

Armstrong, P. (1985) 'Changing control strategies: The role of competition between accounting and other organisational professions', *Accounting, Organisations and Society*, 9 (2): 129–148.

Armstrong, P. (1986) 'Management control strategies and inter-professional competition, the case of accountancy and personnel management', in D. Knights *et al.* (eds) *Managing the Labour Process*. Aldershot: Gower, pp. 25–46.

Baldamus, W. (1961) *Efficiency and Effort*. London: Tavistock.

Berle, A.A. (1955) *The Twentieth Century Capitalist Revolution*. London: Macmillan.

Berle, A.A. and Means, G.C. (1947) *The Modern Corporation and Private Property*. New York: Macmillan.

Braverman, H. (1974) *Labour and Monopoly Capital: The Degradation of Work in the Twentieth Century*. New York: Monthly Review Press.

Buchanan, D. and Badham, R. (1999) *Power, Politics and Organizational Change: Winning the Turf Game*. London: Sage.

Burawoy, M. (1979) *Manufacturing Consent: Changes in the Labor Process under Monopoly Capitalism*. Chicago: Chicago University Press.

Burnham, J. (1941) *The Managerial Revolution*. Harmondsworth: Penguin.

Burns, T. and Stalker, G.M. (1961) *The Management of Innovation*. London: Tavistock.

Burrell, G. (1988) 'Modernism, postmodernism and organisational analysis: The contribution of Micheal Foucault', *Organisation Studies*, 9 (22): 221–235.

Casey, C. (1995) *Work, Self and Society: After Industrialism*. London: Routledge.

Charkham J. (1994) *Keeping Good Company: A Study of Corporate Governance in Five Countries*. Oxford: Oxford University Press.

Clegg, S. (1989) *Frameworks of Power*. London: Sage.

Clegg, S. and Dunkerley, D. (1980) *Organisations, Class and Control*. London: Routledge.

Collins, O., Dalton, M. and Roy, D. (1946) 'Restriction of output and social cleavage in industry', *Applied Anthropology*, 5 (Summer): 1–14.

Collinson, D.L. (1992) *Managing the Shopfloor: Subjectivity, Masculinity and Workplace Culture*. Berlin: William de Gruyter.

Collinson, D.L. and Ackroyd, S. (2005) 'Resistance, misbehavior and dissent', in S. Ackroyd *et al.* (eds) *The Oxford Handbook of Work and Organisation*. Oxford: Oxford University Press.

Courpasson, D. (2005) *Soft Constraint: Liberal Organisations and Domination*. Copenhagen: Liber and Copenhagen Business School Press.

Cronin, J.E. (1979) *Industrial Conflict in Modern Britain*. London: Croom Helm.

Cunnison, S. (1964) *Wages and Work Allocation*. London: Tavistock Publications.

Dalton, H. (1948) 'The industrial rate buster', *Applied Anthropology*, 7.

Ditton, J. (1977) 'Perks, pilferage and the fiddle: The historical structure of invisible wages', *Theory and Society*, 4 (1).

Edwards, P.K. (1986) *Conflict at Work*. Oxford: Blackwell.

Edwards, P.K. and Scullion, H. (1982) *The Social Organization of Industrial Conflict*. Oxford: Blackwell.

Fallon, I. (1991) *Billionaire: The Life and Times of James Goldsmith*. London: Hutchinson.

Fligstein, N. (1990) *The Transformation of Corporate Control*. Boston, MA: Harvard University Press.

Foucault, M. (1977) *Discipline and Punish*. London: Allen and Unwin.

Friedman, A. (1977) *Industry and Labour: Class Struggle at Work and Monopoly Capitalism*. London: Macmillan.

Giacalone, R.A. and Greenberg, J. (1997) *Antisocial Behaviour in Organisations*. Thousand Oaks, CA: Sage.

Gouldner, A. (1955) *Wildcat Strike: A Study of an Unofficial Strike*. London: Routlege

Griffin, R.W., O'Leary-Kelly, A. and Collins, J. (1998) 'Dysfunctional work behaviours in organisations', in C.L. Cooper and D.M. Rousseau (eds) *Trends in Organisational Behaviour*. Chichester: John Wiley.

Hibbs, D. (1978) 'On the political economy of long-run trends in strike activity', *British Journal of Political Science*, 8(1): 135–175.

Jermier, J.M., Knights, D. and Nord, W.R. (1994) *Resistance and Power in Organisations*. London: Routledge.

Johnston, M. (1986) *Takeover: The New Wall Street Warriors*. New York: Viking Penguin.

Knights, D. (1990) 'Subjectivity, power and the labour process', in D. Knights, and H. Willmott (eds) *Labour Process Theory*. London: Macmillan.

Kondo, D.K. (1990) *Crafting Selves: Power, Gender and Discourses of Identity in a Japanese Workplace*. Chicago: University of Chicago Press.

Larson, M. (1977) *The Rise of Professionalism: A Sociological Analysis*. Berkeley: University of California Press.

Lazonick, W. (2005) 'Corporate restructuring', in S. Ackroyd *et al.* (eds) *The Oxford Handbook of Work and Organisation*. Oxford: Oxford University Press.

Lazonick, W. and O'Sullivan (2000) 'Maximising shareholder value: A new ideology for corporate governance', *Economy and Society*, 29 (1): 13–35.

Littler, C. (1982) *The Development of the Labour Process in Capitalist Societies*. London: Heinemann.

Lupton, T. (1963) *On the Shop Floor*. Oxford: Pergamon.

Lyon, (2001) *Theorising Surveillance: The Panopticon and Beyond*. Portland, OR: Willan Publishing.

Mars, G. (1982) *Cheats At Work*. London: Counterpoint.

Michels, R. (1949) *Political Parties*. Glencoe, IL: Free Press.

Mintzberg, H. (1989) 'Politics and the political organisation', Chapter 13 of *Mintzberg on Management*. New York: Free Press.

Noon, M. and Blyton, P. (1997) *The Realities of Work*. London: Macmillan Business.

Pfeffer, J. and Salancik, G.R. (1978) *The External Control of Organisations*. New York: Harper Row.

Pinker, S. (1997) *How The Mind Works*. London: Allen Lane.

Polanyi, K. (1944) *The Great Transformation*. Boston, MA: The Beacon Press.

Powell, W.W. and DiMaggio, P. (eds) (1991) *The New Institutionalism in Organizational Analysis*. Chicago: University of Chicago Press.

Presthus, R. (1979) *The Organizational Society*. London: Macmillan.

Punch, M. (1996) *Dirty Business: Exploring Corporate Misconduct*. London: Sage.

Robinson, S.L. and Bennett, R.J. (1995) 'A typology of deviant workplace behaviours: A multidimensional scaling study,' *Academy of Management Journal*, 38 (2): 555–572.

Robinson, S.L. and Bennett, R.J. (1997) 'Workplace deviance: Its definition, its manifestations, and its causes', in R.J. Lewicki, R.J. Bies and B.H. Sheppard (eds) *Research on Negotiation in Organisations*. Greenwich, CT: Jai Press.

Roy, D. (1952) 'Quota restriction and goldbricking in a machine shop', *American Journal of Sociology*, 57 (5): 427–442.

Roy, D. (1953) 'Work satisfaction and social reward in quota achievement: An analysis of piecework incentives', *American Sociological Review*, 18 (5): 507–514.

Roy, D. (1954) 'Efficiency and the "fix": Informal heterosexual relations between supervisors and workgroups', in C.D. Bryant (ed.) *Deviant Behaviour*. Chicago: Rand McNally.

Sayles, L. and Smith, C.J. (2006) *The Rise of the Rogue Executive: How Good Companies Go Bad*. Saddle River, NJ: Pearson Education.

Schumpeter, J. (1943) *Capitalism, Socialism and Democracy*. London: Unwin University Books.

Scott, J. (1986) *Capitalist Property and Financial Power*. Hassocks: Wheatsheaf.

Scott, J. and Griff, M. (1984) *Directors of British Industry: The British Corporate Network*. Cambridge: Polity Press.

Scott, W.R. (1995) *Institutions and Organisations*. London: Sage.

Scott, W.R. and Meyer, J.W. and associates. (1994) *Institutional Environments and Organizations, Structural Complexity and Individualism*. London: Sage.

Sewell, G. and Wilkinson, B. (1992) 'Someone to watch over me: Surveillance, discipline and the just in time labour process', *Sociology*, 26 (2): 271–289.

Swedburg, R. (2003) *Principles of Economic Sociology*. Princeton, NJ: Princeton University Press.

Sykes, A.J.M. (1966) 'Joking relationships in an industrial setting', *American Anthropologist*, 68 (1): 188–193.

Taylor, F.W. (1911) *The Principles of Scientific Management*. New York: Harper and Row.

Thompson, P. (1989) *The Nature of Work*. London: Macmillan.

Thompson, P. and Ackroyd, S. (1995) 'All quiet on the workplace front? A critique of recent trends in British industrial sociology', *Sociology*, 29 (4): 615–633.

Tilly, A. and Tilly, C. (1981) *Class Conflict and Collective Action*. London: Sage Publications.

Townley, B. (1993) 'Foucault: Power/knowledge and its relevance to HRM', *Academy of Management Review*, 18: 518–545.

Urry, J. (2000) *Sociology Beyond Societies*. London: Sage.

Vardi, Y. and Wiener, Y. (1996) 'Misbehaviour in organisations: A motivational framework', *Organisation Science*, 7 (2): 151–165.

Weber, M. (1968) *Economy and Society*. London: Bedminster Press.

Willmott, H. (1993) 'Strength is ignorance, slavery is freedom: Managing culture in modern organisations', *Journal of Management Studies*, 30 (4): 515–552.

Zald, M.N. (1969) 'The power and functions of boards of directors', *American Journal of Sociology*, 75 (1): 97–111.

Zald, M.N. and Ash, R. (1966) 'Social movement organisations: Growth, decay and change', *Social Forces*, 44 (3): 327–341.

Zald, M.N. and Berger, M. (1978) 'Social movements in organisations: Coup d'état, insurgency and mass movements', *American Journal of Sociology*, 83 (4): 823–861.

# 12

# Organizational Careers

Kerr Inkson and Yehuda Baruch

## INTRODUCTION

For many individuals, their relationship with their employing organization is not a small or momentary thing – it is a critical element in their lives. If an individual's career is a journey – as it is most frequently conceptualized in metaphorical terms (Inkson, 2004, 2007) – then organizations are the most obvious and immediate parts of the context through which the individual travels. The paths along which people travel their careers are often determined by organizational structures, cultures, roles and pathways. And the journey is long – it may endure over 40 years and involve a long sequence of organizational roles. Through the institution of the career, the relationships between organizations and individuals constantly evolve and develop, often to mutual advantage. Organizational systems of career planning and managing, when professionally executed, generate and strengthen the bond between an organization and its employees. Thus, the understanding of careers and the understanding of organizations offer much to each other.

The study of organizational careers has its roots in early sociology (Moore, Gunz and Hall, 2006). Durkheim's principle of the division of labor and his conceptualization of occupational groups showed how individual lives and identities were shaped by the nature of their work, while Weber's modern bureaucracy depended on the development of career systems within organizations, such that individuals could be trained to acquire the qualifications enabling them to occupy higher and higher offices. This kind of thinking was a forerunner to the type of 'organizational career' theory and practice that first emerged in the business schools in the 1970s (Hall, 1976; Schein, 1978), and has been most recently epitomized in the resource-based view of the firm (Barney, 1991; Boxall and Purcell, 2003), which sees organizations as seeking to utilize the knowledge progressively accumulated in individuals' careers for the service of organizational objectives.

In this chapter we present the reader with the concepts and principles of organizational career planning and management, which we also critique in the light of contemporary developments. We aim to outline contemporary theories and developments, alongside the basic issues. We take a balanced approach to integrate traditional concepts with up to date, innovative inspirations as reflected in current scholarly work.

## ORGANIZATIONAL CAREER MANAGEMENT

People have always had careers, though in the far past most people's careers were simple and were determined by the careers of their parents, from whom they frequently inherited their ascribed status. Up to recent times, some 80–90% of careers were in agriculture. Early twentieth century studies of careers looked at them in a wider context: Hughes (1937) defined career as 'the moving perspective in which persons orient themselves with reference to the social order, and of the typical sequences and concatenation of office', thus indicating the delicate balance in careers, between organizational and individual forces. Careers can be viewed as the property of individuals, but for employed people, organizations can play a major role in planning and managing their careers.

To answer the question of who is in charge of one's career is rarely straightforward. Traditionally, prior to the existence of modern organizations, careers, insofar as they existed, were largely embedded in terms of guild organization. A career saw one progress from apprentice to journeyman, and maybe even become a Master. More recently, with the development of modern rather than guild organizations many of these organizations have become the major owners of careers, in particular large bureaucracies such as the Roman Army or the Church. Only later, as labor markets and the nature of work changed to give more power to people, did the responsibility for careers and their management begin to be perceived as something that belonged to individuals. The pendulum is still moving. While, as we will see later, it has swung to the view that individuals are basically in charge of their own careers, there are some who still claim that the focus of career development remains with the organization (Gutteridge, Leibowitz and Shore, 1993). We argue that both individuals and organizations are major

stakeholders in the management of careers, and the input of both is essential.

Irrespective of the focus on, and locus of, career, organizational structures, cultures and processes are essential inputs for career systems. For individuals, career is a major constituency of life that evolves around work and the workplace. Employers influence careers in many ways. According to Sonnenfeld (1989: 202) 'a career does not exist in a social vacuum but is in many ways directed by the employer's staffing priorities'. Organizations therefore seek to develop, control and utilize the careers of employees for commercial advantage. Because it is easier to predict and control the events that are inside the organization than those that are outside it, they have an interest in developing an internal labor market based on internal promotion and training, and a 'career system' to process employees' careers towards meeting organizational goals. Where there is a thoroughgoing internal labor market, careers tend to become organizational as well as (or instead of) occupational.

In the post- World War II era, the development of powerful internal labor markets and organizational careers, particularly for staff in technical, professional and managerial roles, became part of a powerful recipe for organizational success. The boom conditions and corporate philosophies existing in many countries for nearly 40 years following the end of World War II enabled many successful companies to meet exactly those conditions. Three very successful management books of the early 1980s promoted a vision of strong organizational careers within stable companies dedicated to excellent performance. In *Theory Z*, Ouchi (1981) idealized large Japanese *zaibitsu* such as Mitsubishi and Nissan, which achieved extraordinary employee loyalty and quality by recruiting only at the bottom of the organization chart, filling all other positions through their internal labor markets, promoting and transferring staff according to a highly predictable seniority system, and guaranteeing 'lifetime employment'. Although the authors of *In Search of*

*Excellence* (Peters and Waterman, 1982) pre-ferred performance to seniority as a basis for advancement, US-based organizations described in their book had long periods of successful growth and the HR policies described seemed similar, especially for managers. And in *Corporate Cultures*, Deal and Kennedy (1982) outlined means of adding sentimental constraints on mobility to those embodied in the structures of tangible rewards, and stressed the importance of building long-term workforces totally dedicated to their companies. Into the 1980s, organizational careers were a strongly recom-mended part of the recipe for organizational performance. And, in the more turbulent conditions of the twenty-first century, many organizations still see the advantages of retaining a committed core of organizational careerists (Pfeffer, 1998). Increasingly, to do so they develop organizational career management strategies.

## ORGANIZATIONAL CAREER MANAGEMENT AND STRATEGY

Organizational career management is the comprehensive system that organizations apply to manage their employees' careers. The *Career Active System Triad* (the CAST), introduced by Baruch (2004a), is a multi-level conceptual framework developed to help understand the human side of career management (Table 12.1).

The CAST is set at three levels of analysis: Values, Approaches, and Behaviors. The level of values – the principles, morals, and culture – is the basis from which the other levels emerge. The second level is of transforming and translating the values into the third level, that of action, behavior, and practice.

**Table 12.1   The career active system triad – levels presentation**

| Level | Individual | Organization |
|-------|-----------|--------------|
| **Values** | Aspirations | Philosophy (strategy) |
| **Approaches** | Attitudes | Policies |
| **Behaviors** | Actions | Practices |

The key managerial question is how to develop a match (following the person-organization fit concept), and which mecha-nisms to apply (following the organizational support concept). Herriot and Pemberton (1996) showed how both individual and organizational needs work together to achieve positive outcomes. The values convey the aspiration (for individuals) and strategy (for organizations) into the attitudes (for indi-viduals) and policies (for organizations) to direct them, so that in the final observed outcome, people will act and apply these at the practical level of behavior or operation, and organizations will utilize managerial prac-tices. What is proposed is an active system, always in a perpetual motion, responding to both external (environment, labor markets), and internal (both the organization and the people) dynamics.

Organizations develop career strategies. Sonnenfeld and Peiperl's (1988) model con-siders career management as a strategic response and therefore requires that career management fit with strategic organizational management. These authors posited that, rather than there being one best model for organizational careers, the particular type of career system to be applied should be appropriate to the firm's business strategy, in line with the typology of the four strategic types proposed by Miles and Snow (1978): *prospectors, defenders, analyzers, and reac-tors*. Thus, a 'baseball team' (prospector) will be open to external talent, will employ talent spotters, and will encourage compe-tition between members for top positions. A 'club' (defender) looks after its members, but may favor egalitarianism and seniority over merit as a criterion for development. An 'academy' (analyzer) will staff itself by means of the development of its own highly committed members. A 'fortress' (reactor) is more interested in the organization's survival than in what happens to its members, and its commitment to them will be low. These strategies are contingent on two contextual dimensions: supply flow, which ranges from completely internal supply to largely external supply of managerial labor; and assignment flow, which indicates the degree to which assignment and promotion decisions are based on individual performance as against overall contribution to the group or organization.

## ORGANIZATIONAL CAREER MANAGEMENT PRACTICES

Organizations vary in context and strategic orientation, and consequently in their strategies, policies and practices. Through these practices an underlying philosophy of organizational career management may be expressed in 'hands-on' practice designed to facilitate employees' career development to mutual benefit. But what are these career practices? Gutteridge and Otte (1983) and Tsui and Gomez-Mejia (1988) suggested lists of activities, programs, and methods with which the organization can handle HRM processes. Among these practices, we find those that have a close relationship with organizational career planning and its management: Organizational Career Management (OCM) involves activities relevant to the career development of its employees. Indirect activities may include selection, training, employee development, appraisal and compensation practices, while the provision of formal career paths, career planning and development exercises, mentoring and career counseling within the organization represent more direct approaches.

The importance and prominence of OCM has long been recognized by the scholarly community (Van Maanen and Schein, 1977; Walker and Gutteridge, 1979; Hall, 1986; Gutteridge *et al.*, 1993). Baruch (1999) reviewed the set of OCM practices available for organizations to apply. Later Baruch and Peiperl (2000) studied the actual application of OCM in organizations, indicating variations of sophistication and involvement. The list of practices is presented in Table 12.2 in descending order of frequency of their application in the UK.

Further, Baruch and Peiperl (2000) developed a two dimensional model to help companies building OCM systems (Figure 12.1)

**Table 12.2   Organizational career management practices, in decreasing order of frequency (Baruch and Peiperl, 2000)**

| Career practices |
| --- |
| Job postings |
| Formal education as part of career development |
| Performance appraisal as a basis for career planning |
| Career counselling by manager |
| Lateral moves to create cross-functional experience |
| Career counselling by HR |
| Retirement preparation programmes |
| Succession planning |
| Formal mentoring |
| Common career paths |
| Dual ladder |
| Books/pamphlets on career issues |
| Written personal career planning |
| Assessment centre |
| Peer appraisal |
| Career workshops |
| Upward appraisal |

## KEY TO FIGURE 12.1

### MD: Multi-directional

Peer appraisal

Upward appraisal

Common career paths

### FI: Formal

Written personal career planning

Dual career ladder

Career books and/or pamphlets

### AM: Active management

Assessment centres

Formal mentoring

Career workshops

### AP: Active planning

Performance appraisal as a basis for career planning

Career counselling

(1) by the direct supervisor

(2) by the HR department

Succession planning

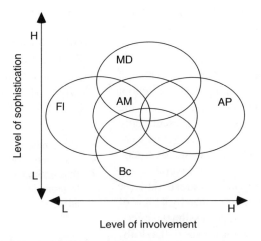

**Figure 12.1    Two dimensional model of career management practices.**

### Bc: Basic

Job posting

Formal education

Pre-retirement programmes

Lateral moves

What can managers learn from the model? HR managers charged with managing careers in organizations are typically faced with a plethora of choices concerning which elements to incorporate. They should develop career systems as sets of practices which naturally fit together, and are appropriate to the organization's stage of development, form, and/or industry. For example, companies seeking to provide the basic elements of a career system should consider first the elements of the *basic* cluster. Companies looking to sustain stable internal labor markets and offer longer-term careers may find the elements of the *formal* cluster appropriate. Organizations trying to maximize knowledge about individuals' potential, both for the individual and the organization, should consider using the somewhat resource-intensive practices of the *active management* cluster. At the other end of the spectrum, HR managers concerned with being cutting edge should consider the use of *multi-directional* practices, but should be aware that these are more common, possibly because they are more possible, in larger organizations with low unionization and high openness. Attempting to introduce such practices in small, unionized, or 'closed-culture' organizations might be difficult.

Furthermore, Baruch and Peiperl's (2000) emergent model suggests that when deciding on OCM practices generally, organizations would be wise to consider the level of involvement necessary from HR and line managers in order to make such practices work. Introducing highly demanding practices such as those in the *active planning* cluster may be inappropriate in situations where managers are not likely to be able to sustain the necessary effort to make them work, and may do more harm than good if they are seen by employees to be introduced only to be left unsupported.

## ALTERNATIVE PERSPECTIVES ON CAREER

In laying the foundations for organizational career theory and practice, Weber and his business-school successors also recognized the tension between organizational bureaucracy and individuals' needs for autonomy and growth, which at times may lead them to exercise their career behavior in directions which run counter to the orderly conduct of organizational business.

A critique of organizational careers and the interest taken in them by business school academics and managers might start with the point that such an approach represents only one of a number of perspectives that academics have used to better understand careers. Kanter (1989), for example, hypothesized three 'ideal types' of career: bureaucratic (or organizational) careers informed by a logic of advancement and status; professional careers, based on a logic of developing specialist skills, and entrepreneurial careers, characterized by a logic of adding value to one's enterprise. As Kanter noted, both professional and entrepreneurial careers can contribute to organizations, and most specific careers will probably be hybrids rather than pure ideal types, but her contribution calls attention to the need for wider conceptualizations of career/organization relationships and the influence on careers of forces at both a more macro-level and a more micro-level than the organization.

Careers have been theorized and studied, for example, by sociologists and psychologists. As might be expected, many sociologists regard individual careers as being determined largely by *social structure* in the form of such forces as broader institutional forms, social class, education, race, and gender (Johnson and Mortimer, 2002). In the career development movement of educationalists, psychologists and career counselors, the view predominates that careers are the result of successive personal choices based on rational decision making allied to maturing personal development, and that their key decisions concern choices of occupation rather than organization (Brown and Associates, 2002). Neither group would give much credence to the notion that employing organizations can, and should, influence their members' careers: in that respect, the business schools'

concept of organizational career management can look like self-seeking wishful thinking. A rapprochement between the three traditions within an integrated 'career studies' is long overdue (Inkson, 2007).

Starting from these wider perspectives of career studies, one review of career theories identifies four critical issues (Peiperl and Arthur, 2000). It labels these:

- Structure versus action;
- Stasis versus adaptation;
- Universalism versus particularism;
- Institutional knowledge versus individual knowledge.

*Structure versus action* asks the question
> Are careers the product of established societal, industry, occupational and organizational structures, or the product of individual action?

As indicated above, sociologists tend to believe that there are aspects of social structure that make this structure the major determinant of careers, while managers believe that organizational structures are critical. The view that it is individual action rather than structures that largely determines career, was initiated in the first-ever book about career choice, Frank Parsons' (1909) *Choosing a Vocation*. Parsons advocated that people should make good choices of occupation by striving to understand their own abilities and inclinations and the opportunities and difficulties of different lines of work, and should apply 'true reasoning' to relate these two groups of facts and find a suitable match. In its essentials, this is still the philosophy of much careers guidance today (e.g., Holland, 1997).

*Stasis versus adaptation* asks the question
> Are careers something relatively stable that you can rely on, or do they change as time goes by?

Are careers stable? For example, do people stay in the same jobs, occupations, and organizations for long periods? Do they retain their career goals over a lifetime? Some psychologists and career theorists argue that features of individual people, such as their basic level of ability, personality, values, and interests tend to remain similar over a lifetime (e.g., Schein's 'career anchors', 1993). Similarly, organizations, jobs and occupations have, and need, continuity. Job details may change, but society will always need, for example, doctors, teachers, salespeople and cleaners. Organizations need 'cores' of committed organizational members. A contrasting view is that in a society that changes with ever-increasing speed, the occupations and organizations in which people build their careers also change, so that change in careers and in the behavior needed to pursue careers, becomes inevitable (Collin and Watts, 1996), and that the key factors needed for career success are mobility and adaptability.

*Universalism versus particularism* asks the question

Are there universal laws which apply to all careers, or is every career unique?

This question poses the possibility of a research-based 'science of careers' enabling us to determine formal laws of career behavior. Examples of universalism are those theories asserting the principle of 'congruence' – stating essentially that careers with a good fit between individual and occupational characteristics will be more satisfying and successful (Dawis and Lofquist, 1984; Holland, 1997). Another is the 'age-stage' theory of career development, which asserts that all careers tend to pass through a fixed series of developmental stages (Levinson et al., 1978; Savickas, 2002, 2005). The universalist position seeks to bring order and predictability to the field of careers. On the other hand, as in other branches of social science, the findings of career studies about these presumed universals are at best inexact. For example, those who try to classify careers find that many careers obstinately resist classification as being one type or another, while those who seek to describe typical stages in a career find so many exceptions that the rule is essentially disproved (Arnold, 1997). Advocates of 'postmodernism' emphasize the influence on careers of idiosyncratic behavior and even chaos theory in ordinary day-to-day settings (Bright and Pryor, 2005).

*Institutional knowledge versus individual knowledge* asks the question

Where does the knowledge reside on which careers are based – in the individual or in the institutions related to his or her career?

Careers depend on knowledge, which is represented by such things as qualifications, background understanding, skills, practical experience, and know-how (Bird, 1996); but where does such knowledge reside? And who does it belong to? One view is that career-relevant knowledge is inherent in institutions such as professional associations and employing organizations. For example, an organizational member's knowledge of its products and processes may be regarded by the organization as its own intellectual property, which is entrusted to the stewardship of the member but is not to be shared externally (Sodergren, 2002). Such a view of career knowledge treats it as a set of formal principles held collectively, which the career actor is privileged to share, and implies that formal institutions have considerable 'knowledge power' over the person's career. The contrasting 'individual' view considers knowledge as personal, as residing in the minds of career actors rather than in the institutions, and as constituting a resource of the individual which can be used for the individual's own purposes (Bird, 1996). Individual knowledge accumulated in different career settings can be used to contribute to those settings, or can be carried across occupational and organizational boundaries in a form of cross-fertilization (Inkson and Arthur, 2001). Thus, a counterpart of the 'intelligent enterprise' (Quinn, 1992) is the "intelligent career" (Arthur, Claman and DeFillippi, 1995).

What we assert here is that the notion of organizational careers is viable to the extent that careers are:

- Determined by structure rather than action
- Stable rather than adaptive
- Seen to proceed according to predetermined laws rather than idiosyncratic behavior and change
- Based on institutional rather than individual knowledge.

Unfortunately, over the past 25 years, events in the developed world have conspired to move these underlying conditions of careers very much toward the end of the spectrum least supportive to organizational careers.

## THE DECLINE OF ORGANIZATIONAL CAREERS

In the more recent literature, organizational careers have increasingly been thought of as part of the past traditional, hierarchical and highly structured employment system, which is contrasted with a current business environment that is highly dynamic, even turbulent. Contemporary society and organizations, in particular, experience an accelerating pace of change. Organizations form the framework for most careers to occur and develop. Therefore, as organizations change, careers change too.

What advocates of organizational careers and stable staffing systems did not anticipate was the major questioning, in the 1980s and beyond, of the wisdom of the industrial state/large stable corporation view of economic development. Important external issues were technological advances (e.g., Kanter, 2001; Friedman, 2005) geo-political changes, in particular globalization (Bartlett and Ghoshal, 1989), the ever-changing processes of restructuring, often accompanied by redundancies, that have shattered traditional bureaucracies (Heckscher, 1995), and major shifts in the nature of the psychological employment contract (Rousseau and Wade-Benzoni, 1995; Conway and Briner, 2005).

With competition increasingly fiercely international, innovation rather than volume was becoming the key to sustained success, and innovation did not thrive best in the stuffy bureaucracies and closed cultures that fostered organizational careers. A fashion for organizations to focus on their 'core competencies' and 'flexible specialization', to offload or close businesses that they were not best equipped for or that were not clearly profitable, and to outsource supply,

led to the fragmentation and destabilization of both companies and company careers. Globalization relocated whole industries to different parts of the world; changing information technology required new skills and new, flexible people; new emphases on multi-skilling and teamwork weakened traditional job boundaries, and the feminization of the workforce introduced employees who needed new, more flexible patterns of work. The flames of organizational fragmentation were fanned by the free-market policies of politicians such as Ronald Reagan in the USA and Margaret Thatcher in Britain, and spread beyond Anglo-Saxon culture.

What followed seemed to many careerists to be a horrifying orgy of closures, takeovers, downsizings, flattenings and restructurings. Layoffs, transfers, demotions and career blockages multiplied (Inkson, 1995). By the middle 1990s a whole generation of organizational managers and professionals felt displaced, demoralized and betrayed by the organizations to which they had so recently felt loyal (Brockner, 1988; Goffee and Scase, 1992; Heckscher, 1995). Even in Japan, the 'lifetime employment' dream evaporated in the country's persisting recession (Hirakubo, 1999). The new career landscape and the blurring of boundaries in many facets of life have significant implications for careers, as they become multidirectional (Baruch, 2004b). However, this may be difficult for some people to cope with as new career patterns emerge to replace old ones (Arthur, Inkson and Pringle, 1999). Baruch (2006) offers a balanced view of the shared responsibility for careers and the need to have a realistic view of the dynamism of the system versus its stability.

In this maelstrom of change, can organizationally structured careers survive? One view is that in this unstable environment organizations should redouble their efforts to secure long-term individual commitment and energy, for example in 'high-commitment HRM' (Pfeffer, 1998). Others, most notably Hall (1996, 2002) and the entire career development movement of educators and career counselors (e.g., Brown, 2002) suggest that the individual is nowadays at the helm. The 'New Careers' (Arthur, Inkson and Pringle, 1999) may be a phenomenon requiring new approaches by organizations.

## NEW MODELS OF CAREER

Career scholars in the business schools have in recent years become increasingly interested in external labor markets, in careers *between* rather than *within* organizations, and in individuals as *agents* of their own career destinies. As a barometer of these changes, consider the research of Boston University academic Tim Hall. In the 1960s, Hall documented the importance of organizational socialization of young managers for their individual performance in the same organizations seven years later (Berlew and Hall, 1966). In 1976 he published *Careers in Organizations,* perhaps the first-ever comprehensive book on careers from an organizational perspective. However, that book contained a tiny addendum on 'the protean career', in which the individual rather than the organization was in charge of the career, where the individuals' values were those of autonomy and growth rather than power and advancement, mobility was high, and career success was measured by satisfaction rather than status and salary. Hall's 1996 book was called *The Career is Dead – Long Live the Career* (Hall and Associates, 1996), meaning that the traditional career was dead but the protean career was very much alive and thriving, and in 2002 he published *Careers in and out of Organizations.* Note, however, that these books do not suggest that organizations have no influence on the individual's career, merely that the balance has shifted in favor of the individual.

In recent years Hall (1996, 2002; Hall and Moss, 1998; Briscoe, Hall, and DeMuth, 2006) has further developed his conceptualization of the protean career. Its basis is that 'individuals are intent on using their own values (rather than organizational values for example) to guide their career ("values-driven") and take an independent role in managing their own vocational behavior ("self-directed")' (Briscoe, Hall and DeMuth, 2006: 30). These twin tendencies are supported by the learned career 'meta-competencies' of adaptability (valuable in the rapidly-changing environment), and awareness of identity (providing assurance that change remains consonant with the individual's core values). Thus is developed, to use Peters and Waterman's (1982) terms, a 'loose-tight' theory of careers in which tightness comes not from organizational goals or values but from the individual's own, while looseness arises from the concept of adaptability. In Hall's theory, the age-stage cycles of career development are replaced by 'mini-cycles' of learning in specific jobs and projects.

Equally influential as an alternative to the organizational career stereotype has been Michael Arthur's (1994; Arthur and Rousseau, 1996) concept of the 'boundaryless career'. Ashkenas *et al.* (1995) noted the phenomenon of the 'boundaryless organization': one major consequence of boundaryless organizations is the emergence of boundaryless careers – 'the opposite of organizational careers' (Arthur and Rousseau, 1996: 5), i.e., the career is *inter*-organizational. However, like the protean career, the boundaryless career has both objective and subjective aspects. Whereas the protean career is defined by the internal psychology of the careerist but is also likely to be mobile, the boundaryless career is defined by purposeful mobile behavior, but this is clearly predicated on a boundaryless *attitude* by the person concerned. Thus boundarylessness is represented in both behavior and in attitudes: mobility may be psychological as well as (or instead of) physical (Sullivan and Arthur, 2006).

Boundaryless careerists have career goals, expertise and networks that go beyond their current employer, and can therefore build their careers across a range of settings. Boundaryless careers have become more common (Ackah and Heaton, 2004) and are apparently functional in providing individuals with career success and 'marketability' both inside and outside the organization (Eby, Butts and Lockwood, 2003). And, in the international careers arena, the focus has moved steadily from approaches emphasizing the corporate management of expatriate assignments (Selmer, 1995) to the notion of global managers pursuing itinerant international careers (Suutari, 2003), thereby creating a new type of cosmopolitan international manager, the 'international itinerant' who self-manages his or her career, who is loyal to profession rather than organization, and who works for different organizations that are independent of each other (Banai and Harry, 2004). In a further variant, Peiperl and Baruch (1997) noted the trend of disillusioned corporate staff to develop their careers in small firms, entrepreneurial ventures and consultant roles, and coined the term 'post-corporate careers' to explain the phenomenon.

Accounts of the boundaryless career provide images of talented men and women, liberated from the crushing constraints of organizational life, moving freely and autonomously between exciting opportunities to develop ever more interesting and prosperous careers. On the other hand, even if organizational boundaries are permeated, 'boundaryless careers are embedded within social networks, institutional arrangements and communities' that may 'constrain careers in other ways' (Tams and Arthur, 2006; see also Inkson, 2006). A growing critique of boundaryless careers is developing around the notion that many individuals exposed to open labor markets – for example unskilled workers, women, ethnic minorities, and middle-aged managers with single-company career tracks, whose value in the open market is deemed low – may lack organizational and institutional protection and thus require and deserve the protection of employer patronage, which will be to the long-term benefit of organizations as well as individuals (Hirsch and Shanley, 1996; Pringle and Mallon, 2003).

For example, in a recent study, Currie, Tempest and Starkey (2006) noted that increased boundarylessness in the television industry had created skills shortages as mobile contractors went untrained and grouped together in specialist supplying organizations as a form of self-protection.

The same authors documented how, in a large retail bureaucracy, the exposure of managerial employees to the notion of boundarylessness following massive layoffs in middle management had caused the survivors to develop such a strong adherence to the notion of professional occupation – replacing the organizational boundary with a new one – as to be counter-productive to intra-organizational teamwork, mobility and competitiveness. Yamashita and Uenoyama (2006) found a similar phenomenon among Japanese hotel workers – increased crossing of between-organization boundaries was accompanied by greater reluctance to cross within-organization boundaries.

## ORGANIZATIONAL RESOURCES VERSUS INDIVIDUAL INVESTMENT

Inkson (2004, 2007) has recently drawn attention to the existence of various archetypal career metaphors, characterizing the images of career that different groups hold. The predominant metaphor in the consideration of many managers is implicit in the term 'human resource management'. The image of employees as integrated components in a broad mass of 'human resources', to be drawn on for the achievement of organizational goals, is now commonplace in business and managerial circles. Because employee expertise is not inherent in people, but accumulates over time as a result of career-related experiences, it is arguably the career rather than the individual that is the resource (Bird, 1996). In this view, careers are factories for expertise, which is built up by the individual almost inadvertently as he or she pursues increasingly responsible jobs while advancing in status along an organization-designed experience pathway.

In the resource-based view of the firm (Barney, 1991; Boxall and Purcell, 2003) the career is thus considered to be at the disposal of the organization, which may seek to utilize it as a stable component of its core; or as a repository of organization history, culture, expertise and skilled management. The practices and discourse of strategic human resource planning, performance evaluation, employee development, and succession planning ensure that the career resource is properly analyzed and improved, and that maximum value is extracted, thereby normalizing the employer's assumption of control. Organizational careers are of particular value, because they maximize opportunities to develop human assets to company advantage (Baruch, 1999; Baruch and Peiperl, 2000). The ceding of career development to the employer typically offers employees work security, advancement, personal development opportunities and significant material rewards. However, the resource metaphor also raises the issue of who the resources belong to and, in democratic societies, individual workers are free agents, able to walk away from their organization, possibly with some contractual constraints on their utilization of its intellectual property, and take an alternative job with another employer, perhaps even a competitor.

In the external labor market, actually or potentially each individual is a knowledge capitalist, a trader and investor of accumulated learning (Inkson and Arthur, 2001). As people continue in their careers, they invest in their organizations and the organizations invest in their careers, but capital accumulation is far from guaranteed: a dead-end job may reduce an individual's capital, make it obsolete and seriously deplete his or her employer's potential resource. If indeed the employee's career is a resource available to the organization in pursuit of company goals, then, from the perspective of the individual capitalist, the organization is likewise a resource available to him or her in pursuit of career goals. The processes of strategic human resource management outlined in the earlier part of this chapter, and the organizational inputs such as employee development opportunities, performance evaluation, and career guidance, can be utilized just as strategically by an individual – quite possibly a very mobile individual – as part of his or her individual career development.

## ORGANIZATIONAL MANAGEMENT AND THE NEW CAREERS

How can, and should, organizations respond to the new environment? Is it possible any longer to maintain that careers can be managed?

In the traditional paradigm of managing organizational careers, corporate strategy and structure were, at the individual level, embodied in the compartmentalization of the organization's intended work into a set of job descriptions, followed by the question, 'How do we acquire or develop a resource that can discharge these duties and thereby bring our predetermined objectives to fruition?' Individuals, if they had contrary career goals, were encouraged to modify them accordingly. Today's and tomorrow's paradigm, at least in part, must recognize the validity of employee aspirations, the likelihood that they may be best met in a succession of different organizations rather than in a single organization, and the labor market power that the employee possesses. The question must be, 'What are this person's aspirations, expertise and networks? How can these be utilized, at least temporarily, within our current plans and structures? And, is it worth considering whether we should change or add to our plans and structures to enable us to benefit from the person's career competencies?' Thus, the essence of the solution is to move from the management of careers as *resources* to the management of career-relevant *relationships*. As each employee is different, so it is likely too that a diversity of different relationships will exist with each employee (or contractor) according to their and the organization's needs: what Rousseau (2005) calls 'idiosyncratic deals' or I-deals. Employers must cede to employees the right to a personal careers perspective that may include other work partners.

Organizations can still benefit from the common orientation of mid-career professionals and managers to develop a stable, perhaps family-oriented, lifestyle, but they also need to become skilled and flexible at securing short-term commitment and teamwork from mobile professionals, contractors and contingent workers who seek to benefit from the excellence of their project work before moving on. New forms of project and occupational community may be utilized to replace the broad corporate communities and cultures emphasized in the management literature. Instead of merely worrying about the loss of institutional knowledge by departing staff (Currie *et al.*, 2006), managers should consider how to capture and institutionalize the expertise of newcomers so that it can be utilized after they have left. Also, organizations need to learn to be able to talk with employees openly about the latter's possibly boundaryless careers, and not to simply tag such individuals as 'disloyal'. Open discussion about such matters may paradoxically lead to greater long-term loyalty (Parker and Inkson, 1999).

a context of opportunity structures and mentorship that will enable employees to plan and control their own futures within the organizational context.

On the other hand, it is clear that many careers, particularly those of managers and professionals, have always diverged from the organizational form and that, apart from inter-organizational professional forms, new contextual conditions elicit many new career forms, including entrepreneurial, portfolio, protean, improvisational and boundaryless. The challenge for tomorrow's organizations is to find alternative forms of psychological contract that adequately reflect the range of employees' career objectives and strategies. We stress the need for a balanced view between the 'rigid, bureaucratic and structured' organization and the apparent fully dynamic, fluid boundaryless career.

## CONCLUSION

The impression portrayed in some contemporary literature is that organizations once had rigid hierarchical structures, and operated within stable environments. This enabled predictable, secure, and linear career structures. Now the system is dynamic and fluid, and as a result careers are unpredictable, vulnerable, and multidirectional. These depictions of the past and of the present are extreme scenarios. The true depiction is that much has shifted from the traditional and conventional mode, but many organizations still perform within a relatively stable environment and keep much of the traditional career system intact. Individuals take more control of their own career, but much in the career context remains for organizations to manage (Baruch, 2006).

The concept of the organizational career serves to remind organizations that the commitment of their employees may last a lifetime and is a precious resource, particularly if that lifetime encapsulates a career's-worth of relevant learning. Rather than managing employees' careers, organizations that think strategically have the opportunity to provide

## REFERENCES

Ackah, C. and Heaton, N. (2004) 'The reality of the "new careers" for men and women', *Journal of European Industrial Training*, 2 (4): 141–158.

Arnold, J. (1997) *Managing Careers into the Twenty-first Century*. London: Paul Chapman.

Arthur, M.B. (1994) 'The boundaryless career: A new perspective for organizational inquiry', *Journal of Organizational Behavior*, 15: 296–305.

Arthur, M.B., Claman, P.H. and DeFillippi, R.J. (1995) 'Intelligent enterprise, intelligent careers', *Academy of Management Executive*, 9 (4): 7–22.

Arthur, M.B. and Rousseau, D.M. (eds) (1996) *The Boundaryless Career: A New Employment Principle for a New Organizational Era*. New York: Oxford University Press.

Arthur, M., Inkson, K. and Pringle, J. (1999) *The New Careers: Individual Action and Economic Change*. London: Sage Publications.

Ashkenas, R., Ulrich, D., Jick, T. and Kerr, S. (1995) *The Boundaryless Organization: Breaking the Chains of Organizational Structure*. San Francisco, CA: Jossey-Bass.

Banai, M. and Harry, W. (2004) 'Boundaryless global careers', *International Studies of Management and Organization*, 34 (3): 96–120.

Barney, J. (1991) 'Firm resources and sustained competitive advantage', *Journal of Management*, 17 (1): 99–120.

Bartlett, C.A. and Ghoshal, S. (1989) *Managing Across Borders: The Transnational Solution*. Boston, MA: Harvard Business School Press.

Baruch, Y. (1999) 'Integrated career systems for the 2000s', *International Journal of Manpower*, 20 (7): 432–457.

Baruch, Y. (2004a) *Managing Careers: Theory and Practice*. Harlow: FT-Prentice Hall/Pearson.

Baruch, Y. (2004b) 'Transforming careers from linear to multidirectional career paths: Organizational and individual perspectives', *Career Development International*, 9 (1): 57–73.

Baruch, Y. (2006) 'Career development in organizations and beyond: Balancing traditional and contemporary viewpoints', *Human Resource Management Review*, 16 (2): 125–138.

Baruch, Y. and Peiperl, M.A. (2000) 'Career management practices: An empirical survey and theoretical implications', *Human Resource Management*, 39 (4): 347–366.

Berlew, D.E. and Hall, D.T. (1966) 'The socialization of managers: Effects of expectations on performance', *Administrative Science Quarterly*, 11: 207–233.

Bird, A. (1996) 'Careers as repositories of knowledge: Considerations for boundaryless careers', in M.B. Arthur and D.M. Rousseau (eds) *The Boundaryless Career: A New Employment Principle for a New Organizational Era*. New York: Oxford University Press, pp. 150–168.

Boxall, P. and Purcell, J. (2003) *Strategy and Human Resource Management*. New York: Palgrave Macmillan.

Bright, J.E.H. and Pryor, R.G.L. (2005) 'The chaos theory of careers: A user's guide', *Career Development Quarterly*, 53 (4): 291–305.

Briscoe, J.P., Hall, D.T. and DuMuth, R.L.F. (2006) 'Protean and boundaryless careers: An empirical exploration', *Journal of Vocational Behavior*, 69: 30–47.

Brockner, J. (1988) 'The effects of work layoffs on survivors: Research, theory and practice', in L.L. Cummings and B.M. Staw (eds) *Research in Organizational Behavior*. Greenwich, CT: JAI Press, pp. 213–255.

Brown, D. (ed.) (2002) *Career Choice and Development* (4th edn). San Francisco, CA: Jossey-Bass.

Collin, A. and Watts, A.G. (1996) 'The death and transfiguration of career – and of career guidance?', *British Journal of Guidance and Counseling*, 24: 385–398.

Conway, N. and Briner, R.B. (2005) *Understanding Psychological Contracts at Work*. Oxford: Oxford University Press.

Currie, G., Tempest, S. and Starkey, K. (2006) 'New careers for old? Organizational and individual responses to changing boundaries', *International Journal of Human Resource Management*, 17 (4): 755–774.

Dawis, R.V. and Lofquist, L.H. (1984) *A Psychological Theory of Work Adjustment*. Minneapolis: University of Minneapolis Press.

Deal, T.E. and Kennedy, A. (1982) *Corporate Cultures*. Reading, MA: Addison Wesley.

Eby, L.T., Butts, M. and Lockwood, A. (2003) 'Predictors of success in the era of the boundaryless career', *Journal of Organizational Behavior*, 24 (6): 689–708.

Friedman, T. (2005) *The World is Flat: A Brief History of the 21st Century*. New York: Farrar, Strauss, Giroux.

Goffee, R. and Scase, R. (1992) 'Organizational change and the corporate career: The restructuring of managers' job aspirations', *Human Relations*, 45: 363–365.

Gutteridge, T.G. and Otte, F.L. (1983) 'Organizational career development: What's going on out there?', *Training and Development Journal*, 37 (2): 22–26.

Gutteridge, T.G., Leibowitz, Z.B. and Shore, J.E. (1993) *Organizational Career Development*. San Francisco, CA: Jossey-Bass Pub.

Hall, D.T. (1976) *Careers in Organizations*. Pacific Pallisades, CA: Goodyear.

Hall, D.T. (1986) *Career Development in Organizations*. San Francisco: Jossey-Bass.

Hall, D.T. (2002) *Careers In and Out of Organizations*. Thousand Oaks, CA: Sage.

Hall, D.T. and Associates (1996) *The Career is Dead – Long Live the Career: A Relational Approach to Careers*. San Francisco, CA: Jossey-Bass.

Hall, D.T. and Moss, J.E. (1998) 'The new protean career contract: Helping organizations and individuals adapt', *Organizational Dynamics*, 26 (3): 22–37.

Heckscher, C. (1995) *White Collar Blues: Management Loyalties in an Age of Corporate Restructuring*. New York: Basic Books.

Herriot, P. and Pemberton, C. (1996) 'Contracting careers', *Human Relations*, 49 (6): 757–790.

Hirakubo, N. (1999) 'The end of lifetime employment', *Business Horizons*, 42, November–December, 41–46.

Hirsch, P.M. and Shanley, M. (1996) 'The rhetoric of "boundaryless" – or, how the newly empowered managerial class bought into its own marginalization', in M.B. Arthur and D.M. Rousseau (eds) *The Boundaryless Career: A New Employment Principle for a New Organizational Era*. New York: Oxford University Press, pp. 218–233.

Holland, J.E. (1997) *Making Vocational Choices: a Theory of Vocational Personalities and Work Environments* (2nd edn). Odessa, FL: Psychological Assessment Resources.

Hughes, E.C. (1937) 'Institutional office and the person', *American Journal of Sociology*, 43: 404–443.

Inkson, K. (1995) 'The effects of changing economic conditions on managerial job change and careers', *British Journal of Management*, 6: 183–194.

Inkson, K. (2004) 'Images of career: Nine key metaphors', *Journal of Vocational Behavior*, 65 (1): 96–111.

Inkson, K. (2006) 'Protean and boundaryless careers as metaphors', *Journal of Vocational Behavior*, 69 (1): 48–63.

Inkson, K. (2007) *Understanding Careers: The Metaphors of Working Lives*. Thousand Oaks, CA: Sage Publications.

Inkson, K. and Arthur, M.B. (2001) 'How to be a successful career capitalist', *Organizational Dynamics*, 31 (3): 48–61.

Johnson, M. and Mortimer, J. (2002) 'Career choice and development from a sociological perspective', in D. Brown (ed.) *Career Choice and Development*, (4th edn). San Francisco, CA: Jossey-Bass, pp. 37–81.

Kanter, R.M. (1989) 'Careers and the wealth of nations: A macro-perspective on the structure and implications of career forms', in M.B. Arthur, D.T. Hall and B.S. Lawrence (eds) *Handbook of Career Theory*. Cambridge: Cambridge University Press, pp. 506–521.

Kanter, R.M. (2001) *Evolve! Succeeding in the Digital Culture of Tomorrow*. Boston, MA: Harvard Business School Press.

Levinson, D.J., Darrow, C.N., Klein, E.B., Levinson, M.H. and McKee, B. (1978) *The Seasons of a Man's Life*. New York: Knopf.

Miles, R.E. and Snow, C.C. (1978) *Organizational Strategy, Structure, and Process*. New York: McGraw-Hill Book Co.

Moore, C., Gunz, H.P. and Hall, D.M. (2006) 'History of career studies', in J.H. Greenhaus and J.A. Callanan (eds) *Encyclopaedia of Career Development*. Thousand Oaks, CA: Sage.

Ouchi, W.G. (1981) *Theory Z*. Reading, MA: Addison Wesley.

Parker, P. and Inkson, K. (1999) 'New forms of career: The challenge to human resource management', *Asia-Pacific Journal of Human Resources*, 37 (1): 67–76.

Parsons, F. (1909) *Choosing a Vocation*. Boston, MA: Houghton Mifflin.

Peiperl, M.A. and Arthur, M.B. (2000) 'Topics for conversation: Career themes old and new', in M.A. Peiperl, M.B. Arthur, R. Goffee and T. Morris (eds) *Career Frontiers: New Conceptions of Working Lives*. New York: Oxford University Press, pp. 1–19.

Peiperl, M.A. and Baruch, Y. (1997) 'Back to square zero: The post-corporate career', *Organizational Dynamics*, 25 (4): 7–22.

Peters, T. and Waterman, R.H. (1982) *In Search of Excellence: Lessons from America's Best-run Companies*. New York: Harper & Row.

Pfeffer, J. (1998) *The Human Equation: Building Profits by Putting People First*. Boston, MA: Harvard Business School Press.

Pringle, J.K. and Mallon, M. (2003) 'Challenges to the boundaryless career odyssey', *International Journal of Human Resource Management*, 14 (5): 839–853.

Quinn, J.B. (1992) *Intelligent Enterprise: A Knowledge and Service Based Paradigm for Industry*. New York: Free Press.

Rousseau, D.M. (2005) *I-deals: Idiosyncratic Deals Employees Bargain for Themselves*. Armonk, NY: M. E. Sharpe.

Rousseau, D.M. and Wade-Benzoni, K.A. (1995) 'Changing individual-organization attachments: A two-way street', in A. Howard (ed.) *The Changing Nature of Work*. San Francisco, CA: Jossey-Bass, pp. 290–321.

Savickas, M.L. (2002) 'Career construction: A developmental theory of vocational behavior', in D. Brown (ed.) *Career Choice and Development* (4th edn). San Francisco, CA: Jossey-Bass, pp. 149–205.

Savickas, M.L. (2005) 'The theory and practice of career construction', in R.W. Lent and S.D. Brown (eds) *Career Development and Counseling: Putting Theory and Research to Work*. New York: Wiley.

Schein, E.H. (1978) *Career Dynamics: Matching Individual and Organizational Needs*. Reading, MA: Addison-Wesley.

Schein, E.H. (1993) *Career Anchors: Discovering Your Real Values*. London: Pfeffer.

Selmer, J. (ed.) (1995) *Expatriate Management: New Ideas for International Business*. Westport, CT: Quorum Press.

Sodergren, B. (2002), 'Paths to creativity for knowledge-intensive workers', in M.A. Peiperl, M.B. Arthur and N. Anand (eds) *Career Creativity: Explorations in the Remaking of Work*. Oxford: Oxford University Press, pp. 35–57.

Sonnenfeld, J.A. (1989) 'Career system profiles and strategic staffing', in M.B. Arthur, D.T. Hall and B.S. Lawrence (eds) *Handbook of Career Theory*. Cambridge: Cambridge University Press, pp. 202–224.

Sonnenfeld, J.A. and Peiperl, M.A. (1988) 'Staffing policy as a strategic response: A typology of career systems', *Academy of Management Review*, 13 (4): 568–600.

Sullivan, S.E. and Arthur, M.B. (2006) 'The evolution of the boundaryless career concept: Examining physical and psychological mobility', *Journal of Vocational Behavior*, 69: 19–29.

Suutari, V. (2003) 'Global managers: Career orientation, career tracks, life-style implications, and career commitment', *Journal of Managerial Psychology*, 18 (3): 185–207.

Tams, S. and Arthur, M.B. (2006) 'Boundaryless career', in J. Greenhaus and G. Callanan (eds) *Encyclopaedia of Career Development* (Vol. 1). Thousand Oaks, CA: Sage, pp. 44–49.

Tsui, A.S. and Gomez-Mejia, L.R. (1988) 'Evaluating human resource effectiveness', in L. Dyer (ed.) *Human Resource Management: Evolving Roles and Responsibilities, Series 1*. Washington, DC: ASPA/BNA, pp. 187–227.

Van Maanen, J. and Schein, E.H. (1977) 'Career development', in J.R. Hackman and J.L. Suttle (eds) *Improving Life at Work: Behavioral Science Approaches to Organizational Change*. Santa Monica, CA: Goodyear, pp. 30–95.

Walker, J.W. and Gutteridge, J.G. (1979) *Career Planning Practices: An AMA Survey Report*. New York: AMACOM.

Yamashita, M. and Uenoyamna, T. (2006) 'Boundaryless career and adaptive HR practices in Japan's hotel industry', *Career Development International*, 11 (3): 230–242.

# 13

# Top Management Teams and Team Working

Sarah MacCurtain and Michael A. West

## INTRODUCTION

As organizations wrestle with the need to constantly change and innovate in order to meet the challenges of the twenty-first century, the need for effective leadership at the top has never been greater. Since the publication of Hambrick and Mason's influential upper echelons theory in the 1980s, the top management team (TMT) has emerged as an important area of organizational research. Research relating to TMT structure, conflict and team performance indicates that the quality of the TMT as a whole, rather than the CEO in isolation, may be a better predictor of an organization's fate (Hambrick and Mason, 1984; Hambrick, 1994; Finkelstein and Hambrick, 1996). Although there are writers who either question the importance of the TMT (e.g., Starbuck, 1985; West and Schwenck, 1996) or at times dispute the appropriateness of working as a team at the top (Katzenbach, 1997), many practitioners and scholars argue that TMT dynamics and

the effective functioning of the team can enhance creative problem solving within the team and enable executives to draw on their diverse experiences and knowledge to make high quality decisions (Nadler, 1996; Edmondson et al., 2002). However, there is considerable evidence – both anecdotal and empirical – to suggest that TMTs do not always reach their full potential. It is therefore imperative to identify the factors that enhance or impede effective top team working and performance. This chapter will explore top management teams and team working in organizations and consists of four major sections and a conclusion. The first section reviews the research on top management team composition and diversity. The second section considers criticisms of this literature and the growth of attention to group processes. The third section considers the top management team and the organizational context. The final section examines critical issues for the present and new directions for the future.

# DEFINING THE TOP MANAGEMENT TEAM

There appears to be some debate in the literature about what constitutes a top management team (Carpenter *et al.*, 2004). Cyert and March's (1963) 'dominant coalition' is described as the group of powerful people that spans the boundary between the organization and the external environment and make decisions that have a significant impact on the organization. They suggest that top team membership can be identified by reference to senior hierarchical level (e.g., title or position) because, if they are at a strategic level, their actions will have such an impact on organizational outcomes. Alternatively, some studies follow Pettigrew's (1992: 178) assertion that titles/positions may not be the best way to determine top management team membership but rather to identify which players are involved in strategic decisions and why. Therefore many researchers rely on a CEO survey or interview to identify the top team (Bantel and Jackson, 1989; West and Schwenck, 1996; Knight *et al.*, 1999; Papadakis and Barwise, 2002; Collins and Clark, 2003). Finkelstein and Hambrick (1990) identify the top management team as members of the board while Boeker (1997) considers that the top team comprises all officers reporting to the CEO.

While researchers use a variety of methods to arrive at a measure of the top management team, it is evident from all the definitions of the TMT that such teams play a crucial role in determining organizational outcomes, for several reasons. They formulate and implement strategic decisions that have organization-wide impact; their actions carry considerable symbolic weight, and their influence on organizational culture and environmental sensemaking is pervasive (Finkelstein and Hambrick, 1996).

Given the importance of the TMT, effective intra-team working is paramount yet can be challenging. Such teams are often composed of independent and ambitious individuals, who are heads of functions as well as members of the top team, which can often impede

'true' team working. Functional goals and the overall team goals might sometimes conflict and there may be perceived differences in professional allegiances. There is also the added complication of the succession tournament where team members may be competing amongst themselves for the position of CEO.

Hambrick (1994) has exposed the fallacy so often implicit in the top team metaphor, stating that 'many top management teams have little teamness about them' and are often simply no more than a collection of people working individually. While it is debatable whether the team metaphor is suitable at all for describing the group of individuals who occupy the upper echelons of the organization (and one we will not engage in here), the importance of effective team working within such groups is generally recognized. Critchely and Casey (1984) argue that team working is the optimum organizational solution when there is high uncertainty, when the problem is complex, when the stakes are high and when there is maximum choice. Such conditions face the top 'team' and its members regularly.

# CENTRAL APPROACHES AND MAIN THEORIES: THE TOP MANAGEMENT TEAM COMPOSITION AND DIVERSITY

In terms of the individuals who comprise the team; who comprises the top team and do they make a difference? Hambrick and Mason's (1984) seminal upper-echelons (UE) theory hinges on the principle that they do and argues that the make-up of the top team, in terms of the age, education level, and tenure, can have a significant impact on organizational outcomes considered as proxies, 'albeit muddy and imprecise' (Hambrick, 2005: 11), for the underlying social psychological processes of the group that are difficult to measure. Hambrick (2005) argues that UE theory is essentially an information-processing theory, and helps to explain how the executive's orientation (measured using visible and measurable variables such as tenure, function and age) affects the selection, perception and interpretation of information and ultimately organizational outcomes such as innovation and company performance.

In addition to the main effect of demographic characteristics, demographic dispersion has been widely studied as a determinant of team behaviour and organizational outcomes (Peterson et al., 2003). A large proportion of the upper-echelons studies focus on the diversity (or lack thereof) of the top management team. Jackson (1996) and West et al. (1998) argue that diversity is most valuable when teams face a complex and creative task, which would suggest that TMTs are likely to benefit more from diversity than lower level teams. However, the research on top management teams and the effects of diversity on team/organizational outcomes is mixed and sometimes contradictory. Jackson (1996) suggests that task oriented measures of diversity (e.g., function, experience) are more likely to have positive effects than relations oriented diversity (e.g., age or gender). While this makes sense intuitively the research does not always support this assertion. For example, Smith et al. (1994) found diversity in experience to be negatively associated with performance whereas diversity in education was found to be positively associated with performance.

There is some empirical evidence supporting the upper echelons theory that the composition and diversity of the top team can influence organizational outcomes. Certain diversity measures provide more consistent results than others. For example, there is general agreement in the literature that the higher the level of education attained, the more receptive to creative solutions and innovation the person will be (Kimberly and Evanisko, 1981; Hambrick and Mason, 1984; Bantel and Jackson, 1989; Thomas, Litschert and Ramaswamy, 1991; Bantel, 1993). West et al. (1999) found educational level of the top management team to be the strongest predictor of profitability and, to a lesser extent, productivity of 160 UK manufacturing companies studied over 10 years. The vast majority of the research on educational diversity elicits similar results (Chaganti and Sambharya, 1987; Bantel,

1993; Smith et al., 1994; Hambrick et al., 1996).

While educational conformance on high achievement may be a positive, the majority of research on age diversity suggests negative results. It can result in dysfunctional conflict, lack of consensus and ineffective communication as age diversity can deter the development of a shared language between individuals that results from similar background and experiences (Pfeffer, 1983; Zenger and Lawrence, 1989). West et al.'s (1999) research found that the more teams differed in age, the worse the profitability of their company. In explaining this finding, they speculate that difference in age is associated with difference in worldviews. The less a team share a similar worldview or mental model of the task, the harder it is to communicate, collaborate and co-ordinate their strategies as a team. Very few studies reported a positive association between age diversity and organizational performance (with the exception of Sambharya, 1989; Kilduff et al., 2000).

While the majority of research on functional diversity and organisational outcomes suggests a positive relationship between the two (Carpenter, 2002), there are still inconsistencies. For example, Dearborn and Simon (1958) and Daellenbach, McCarthy and Schoenecker (1999) found that functional background played an important role in determining how executives approached problem solving and R and D intensity. Bantel (1993) found that functional diversity within teams leads to clearer corporate strategies and Hambrick, Cho and Chen (1996) have also found functional diversity to have positive effects for the firm, leading to market share and profit growth. Bantel and Jackson's (1989) study of the banking sector found a positive association between functional diversity and administrative innovations in the banking sector (interestingly, they found no association between functional diversity and technical innovations). Korn, Milliken and Lant (1992) found a positive relationship between TMT functional diversity and performance (as measured by increases in returns on assets) in the furniture industry but not in the software industry. Milliken and Martins (1996) argue that this finding suggests 'functional diversity in management teams may add value in terms of dealing with environmental complexity but that it may not facilitate coping with environmental volatility' (p. 411). Knight et al.'s (1999) study investigating how demographic diversity and group processes influence strategic consensus within TMTs found functional diversity hindered strategic consensus. Daellenbach et al. (1999) found functional diversity did not emerge as a predictor of innovation. In fact they found functional diversity often led to information overload.

Similarly, there are inconsistent findings when exploring the relationship between TMT tenure and team and organizational outcomes. Diversity in team tenure was found to decrease levels of cohesion and trust and lead to lower levels of group specific knowledge (Lawrence, 1997). O'Reilly and colleagues (1989) found tenure diversity was negatively related to group-level social integration as well as to individual integration and Wagner, Pfeffer and O'Reilly (1984) found a negative relationship between organizational tenure and turnover.

By contrast, there are also arguments suggesting tenure diversity may lead to positive cognitive outcomes. O'Reilly and Flatt (1989) and Katz (1982) argue that diversity in tenure leads to increased creativity and innovation. Diversity in tenure can benefit the team by adding fresh perspectives and objectivity as well as lessening the likelihood of 'groupthink', a phenomenon that occurs when groups become overly cohesive and can result in defective decision making. Boeker's (1997) research found positive associations between TMT tenure diversity and strategic change. Hambrick et al. (1996) found tenure diversity positively associated with increased market share and profit growth. Knight et al.'s (1999) study of US and Irish TMTs found that, contrary to their expectation, tenure diversity was positively related to strategic consensus.

Another possible explanation is that the relationship between tenure heterogeneity and outcomes is curvilinear. This suggestion supports Hambrick and D'Aveni's (1992) findings. In their study of team deterioration as part of a downward spiral of large corporate bankruptcies, they found that the teams of bankrupt firms were 'extreme in their amounts of tenure heterogeneity – some very homogeneous and some very heterogeneous – possibly revealing some instances of recent wholesale team replacement (homogeneous), some very long-standing teams (homogeneous), and some teams that were schismatic combinations of very long tenured and very short tenured members (heterogeneous)' (p. 1460).

Overall, the research in this area suggests that diversity tenure may have negative consequences for affective outcomes (e.g., reducing social integration and increasing turnover). The effects of tenure diversity on cognitive outcomes are mixed, but the majority of the literature suggests that tenure diversity increases the chance of the TMT engaging in debate, breaking with past practices and being more open to change (Wiersema and Bantel, 1992). This dichotomy is borne out in the research on other diversity measures. In reviewing the literature on team diversity, Milliken and Martins (1996) comment that much of the research on heterogeneity focuses on relationships between diversity and cognitive advantages to the group (more information, more debate etc.) while paying little attention to more affective outcomes. While the majority of the evidence suggests diversity may be positively related to cognitive outcomes, it is also argued that diversity can lead to 'process losses' (Milliken and Martins, 1996: 410). For example it has been suggested that functional heterogeneity can lead to conflict regarding group identity (Finkelstein and Hambrick, 1996) – do members see themselves as heads of their own functions (which may have goals that conflict with other functions) or members of the top team? Functional diversity may lead to increased politicking and hidden agendas hindering the implementation of innovative initiatives.

## CRITICISM OF UPPER ECHELONS THEORY

Faced with these inconsistencies, researchers have proposed theoretical and empirical refinements to enhance the explanatory and predictive powers of the upper echelons theory. Finkelstein and Hambrick (1990) extended their theory by including the concept of managerial discretion. Discretion is a 'means of accounting for differing levels of constraint facing different top-management groups' (Finkelstein and Hambrick, 1990: 485). Where the top team have low discretionary power, the role of the TMT is limited. Where discretion is high, top managers will have a significant impact on organizational outcomes and the upper echelons theory will have strong explanatory power. They argue that TMT discretion can be affected by environmental characteristics – industries described as highly uncertain allow executives greater discretion. Another possibility is that the very nature of membership of the top team itself can mean there is a tacit homogeneity in other areas more important than demographic variables. The measurement of demographic variables may mask similarity in world viewpoints and beliefs. There may be certain behaviours, values and experiences that facilitate membership of the top team such as loyalty, commitment, dedication and success. Team members may differ in terms of age and function but may be very similar in terms of how they view success and the types of business values to which they adhere. Therefore, teams that may seem diverse in terms of experience, function etc. (what Harrison et al., 2002, describe as surface level diversity) may be similar in terms of values, goals and beliefs and how they do business (deep level diversity, Harrison et al., 2002). Organizational culture and climate play a part in shaping the values adhered to within the organization – the organizational culture may support a certain 'type' of top manager regardless of age, function etc. and therefore culture and climate may be important additions in the UE literature.

Another enhancement to upper echelons literature would be the design of studies that allowed convincing conclusions about causal direction (Hambrick, 2005) and to take into account the fact that the impact of diversity may vary over time. One of the main criticisms of diversity research is the prominence of cross sectional studies. The few longitudinal studies conducted suggest that the effects of diversity do vary with time. For example, Watson, Kumar and Michaelson (1993) have found that homogeneous teams may perform better in the initial stages of group formation, but these effects dissipated over time and diverse teams later outperformed the homogeneous groups. Pitcher and Smith (2001) posit several possible explanations for the weak and inconsistent results associated with upper echelons theory. Perhaps, they suggest, the literature is plagued by weak and inconsistent findings because the hypothesized relationships are in fact non-significant; our theories are incorrect and the composition of the TMT is irrelevant. Or, they propose, the independent and/or dependent variable have been 'inadequately operationalized'; our theories are correct, but our measurement weak. Or alternatively, there are intervening variables obscuring or moderating the relationships hypothesized.

It is possible that it is not so much who comprises the TMT but what they do and how they do it that matters. The latter explanation has received much attention in the top team literature. Smith et al. (1994) agree that demographic variables alone are insufficient in predicting organizational outcomes as they found that TMT demography was indirectly related to performance through group process. They also measured the effects of process directly and found it to be a stronger predictor than TMT composition. Hambrick (2005) himself states that he is disappointed with the examination of the psychological and social processes that stand between executive characteristics and executive behaviour. Therefore, studying TMT diversity and organizational outcomes in isolation will never yield a conclusive understanding of the role of the TMT, let alone predict cause and effect relationships. However, studying TMT diversity in conjunction with other team and organizational variables can give rise to a more robust understanding of the TMT as a totality. While the literature on team diversity and its effect on organizational outcomes is often contradictory, there is consensus that certain group processes might play a crucial role in determining whether the outcome is a positive or negative one (Fredrickson, 1986; Dess, 1987; Smith *et al.*, 1994). However, there has not been consistency regarding what that role is and it is imperative to incorporate TMT processes into demographic models of team functioning.

## TMT GROUP PROCESSES

Team effectiveness is not only a function of team composition and team members' talents and abilities but also the processes teams engage in to accomplish their goals (Marks *et al.*, 2001). This realization has led to team processes playing a central role in the TMT literature in the last two decades. Marks *et al.* (2001: 357) provide a comprehensive definition of team process and describe it as 'members interdependent actions that convert inputs to outcomes through cognitive, verbal and behavioural activities directed towards organizational task work to achieve collective goals'. They differentiate process or team work from task work and argue that task work is *what* the team does and team work is *how* the team does it. The central tenet of the group process literature is that certain group processes provide greater effectiveness and efficiency. It is therefore important to take into consideration the psychological and task processes of the team. Research investigating the importance of group processes in understanding the consequences of TMT diversity and organizational outcomes has explored the roles played by conflict (Jehn, 1995; Amason, 1996; Knight *et al.*, 1999; Simons and Peterson, 2000), agreement seeking (Knight *et al.*, 1999), debate (Simons,

Pelled and Smith, 1999) and communication (Smith *et al.*, 1994).

Keck (1991) and Hambrick and D'Aveni (1992) have also attributed links between team diversity and organizational outcomes to unmeasured social and psychological processes. Their reasoning is that diversity influences team processes and these processes in turn influence organizational outcomes. Edmondson *et al.* (2002) reiterate the importance of considering team processes and extend the debate by introducing the concept of situation specific symmetries or asymmetries. They argue that team processes and outcomes may vary across the different situations faced by senior teams. Certain group processes may be appropriate in one situation but not in another. This view of the team as a dynamic entity (albeit with relatively stable characteristics such as composition) can help explain the variation in certain TMTs effectiveness over time. They argue that the match between the team's stable characteristics and the situation at hand (what they refer to as 'team-situation relationship') will vary depending on the context and identify two core dimensions of this 'team-situation relationship': 1. the distribution of relevant information/knowledge within the team ('situation specific information) and 2. the interests/goals of the TMTs ('situation specific interests').

Under certain conditions there may be an information asymmetry (TMT members have distinct and unshared information about the situation) and/or interest asymmetry (TMT members have divergent interests and hidden agendas) – in other situations the same team may achieve symmetry in one or both of these dimensions. For example, a TMT may achieve interest symmetry when facing a hostile takeover bid, yet experience interest asymmetry when agreeing budget allocation between departments (Edmondson *et al.*, 2002). Therefore, the type of situation facing the TMT can determine what team processes are appropriate. For example, they suggest the leader take a more directive role when there are interest asymmetries in order to avoid lobbying, politicking and conflict.

The consideration of the situation and the team-situation relationship provides a richer understanding of the team process literature. This chapter discusses a number of group processes identified in the literature as playing an important role in determining TMT effectiveness – TMT conflict, reflexivity and consensus.

## Conflict

Any discussion of top management teams would be incomplete if it did not address conflict and its consequences for the team. There is a wealth of literature discussing the importance of conflict, what type of conflict should be promoted and when. While conflict occurs at every level of the organization, the TMT is particularly vulnerable to conflictual situations. As mentioned previously, TMTs are often comprised of ambitious, individualistic people who are, in many instances, heads of their own functions (often with competing goals) and typically face stressful situations of high ambiguity and complexity. The presence of a succession tournament for the position of CEO further increases the potential for conflict within these teams.

Amason (1996) and Jehn's (1995) studies demonstrate how the impact of diversity can vary depending on the type of conflict experienced within the group. Diverse teams that engage in cognitive (or task) conflict are more likely to achieve positive outcomes than diverse teams experiencing high levels of affective (or relationship oriented) conflict. The presence of task conflict can prove invaluable in TMTs when making strategic decisions as such conflict promotes debate, critique and heightens the cognitive capabilities of the team. However, commitment to the implementation of such decisions is also important. Because of the nature of such decisions (i.e., they display ambiguity, complexity, multiple alternatives, time pressures) they are often difficult to discuss and implement. Herein resides the dilemma facing the top management team: task conflict is necessary in order to discuss problems in an open and critical manner; however, it is vital that such conflict does not trigger affective conflict that may potentially destroy the team's commitment to implementing the decision. The challenge of fostering functional conflict while avoiding dysfunctional conflict is one that faces all TMTs – and the two are generally positively correlated in teams. This is exacerbated by the possibility that affective conflict can sometimes pose as task conflict and vice versa. In research carried out by MacCurtain (2005) on TMTs in software companies, there was recognition that what sometimes seemed similar to task conflict in theory (e.g., questioning of ideas etc.) was intended (or perceived as intended) as affective conflict (e.g., to question one's credibility, damage reputation etc.). It was also suggested that on rare occasions when very high levels of trust existed, what appeared to be affective conflict may be simply an indication of high trust/closeness. For example, one particularly close knit, high-trust team reported that they frequently expressed frustration with each other and voices were sometimes raised but that it cleared the air and was quickly resolved because they trusted each other. While the dichotomy, suggesting that task conflict is functional, while affective conflict is dysfunctional may be sometimes overly simplistic, the overwhelming evidence suggests that, in general, task conflict at moderate levels is beneficial and affective conflict harmful to team functioning. The interaction between conflict and other team processes may help teams experience only functional conflict. For example, both conflict and consensus are needed in order to formulate high quality decisions and to ensure that such decisions get implemented.

Is the synthesis of conflict and consensus a contradiction in terms? The research would suggest not and indeed, many writers on TMTs and group processes suggest that the fusion of conflict and more consensus-seeking behaviour can be achieved and can enhance TMT performance. In their study of 76 TMTs in high technology firms, Knight et al.'s (1999) findings suggest diverse teams with low levels of interpersonal conflict and high levels of agreement-seeking achieve higher levels of strategic consensus.

They suggest that the encouragement of certain processes (cooperation, agreement seeking) might mitigate any potential negative effects of diversity.

## Consensus/agreement seeking

As discussed above, consensus is an important component of effective TMT functioning and may be complementary rather than opposed to other group processes such as conflict. If high quality strategic decisions are to be implemented in a timely fashion, there needs to be a certain amount of debate, but also consensus around that decision. As with many team processes, however, the relationship between consensus and effective outcomes is not straightforward. Consensus is a multi-dimensional concept involving both shared understanding and shared commitment. It also has a curvilinear relationship with certain team and organizational outcomes (Jarzabkowski and Searle, 2003) – if there is too much consensus, the group may become prone to 'group think' where harmony and adherence to the group's norms become more important than team effectiveness. As mentioned earlier, the level of consensus that is desirable can also depend on whether or not there is asymmetry of interest within the team. High asymmetry might require a less consensual, more directing approach whereas high levels of consensus work well when a team has symmetric interests (Edmondson et al., 2002). Consensus entails both a shared understanding of the problem and a shared commitment (Edmondson's 'interest symmetry') to solving the problem.

## TMT reflexivity

While there are relatively few empirical studies investigating the effects of reflexivity on organizational outcomes, the empirical work that has been done suggests this process plays a role in determining outcomes such as TMT innovative behaviour and innovation (De Dreu, 2002; Tjosvold et al., 2004), affective well being and team effectiveness (Carter and West, 1998), team performance (Schippers et al., 2003; Tjosvold et al., 2003) and also fosters gains in team processes

(Gevers et al., 2001). Swift and West (1998: 4) define reflexivity as the 'uniquely human ability to reflect upon processes, events, sensations, past experience and the physical being'. This definition can be applied to the team level where team reflexivity is 'the extent to which team members overtly reflect upon the group's objectives, strategies, and processes and adapt them to current or anticipated endogenous or environmental circumstances' (West, 1996: 559). Therefore, it is not enough to simply look back but also take into consideration the implications for the future. The 'looking forward' component of reflexivity is echoed by Swift and West (1998) who describe reflexivity as an iterative process comprising of three components: reflection – 'looking back', planning – 'looking forward' and action. Reflexivity is a concept that is growing in significance in organizational theory, but it has been found to be quite rare in practice (West, 2000; Mulder, Swaak and Kessels, 2004). In ever-changing, fast-paced dynamic environments the focus tends to be on moving forward and the process of reflection is often considered to be a luxury rather than a necessity, as illustrated by the following quote from a TMT member of a software company.

> We do not review and by not doing that we have bad experiences with failure – everyone has a different assessment of what went wrong when something fails. If you don't review, there is no collective memory – everyone has his or her own version. With time each version becomes fact. You end up having four different factual versions about what went right and what went wrong. We implement – but do not typically get together to question or review as we cannot afford the time.

However, this process can be invaluable for certain types of teams and West (1996) distinguished between simple decision-making groups and complex decision-making (CDM) groups when discussing the association between reflexivity and effectiveness. While reflexivity may not be necessary in routine decision-making groups working in certain and predictable environments, West (1996) proposes it is an important process for CDM groups making complex decisions under uncertain and unpredictable conditions (e.g., TMTs), if these teams are to achieve their goals. Changing circumstances often require a team to continually discuss what they are doing, how they are doing it, and why they are doing it. CEOs and TMT members need to encourage this activity within teams, focusing on both dimensions of reflexivity – reflection and adaptation. In order to do so, certain behaviours should become routine. These include questioning, planning, exploratory learning, analysis, making use of knowledge explicitly, planning and reviewing past events with self-awareness. CEOs and other TMT members can encourage these behaviours by questioning how particular actions or decisions should be viewed by the team, reviewing past decisions, successes and failures, developing plans for achieving goals and explicitly discussing assumptions within the team (Swift and West, 1998).

## TMT AND LEADERSHIP

While the CEO is rarely distinguished from the TMT as a whole (Peterson *et al.*, 2003) it is important to acknowledge the power differentials within the top management team. The probable imbalance of power within TMTs was recognized by Hambrick (1994) who noted that … 'everyday observations and a wealth of related literature indicates that the top group leader has a disproportionate, sometimes nearly dominating influence on the group's various characteristics and outputs' (p. 180). While CEOs are generally the most influential member of the group, there are circumstances when other TMT members may hold the balance of power due to their expertise, ownership position or external connections. Depending on the decision to be made or the action to be taken, power may fluctuate within the team at different times. Different sources of uncertainty require different individuals/departments to cope, hence power is never static. However, the majority of the literature would suggest that it is the CEO who is predominantly the most influential member of the top team and

there is considerable evidence that the CEO can influence organizational outcomes. For example, Miller, Kets de Vries and Toulouse's (1982) study on CEO locus of control and innovation found that CEOs with an internal locus of control (a personality factor that captures whether the individual believes they are in control of their own destiny) led companies that were more innovative and dynamic than CEOs with an external locus of control (individuals who believe their fate is outside of their control). Yet there are relatively few studies investigating the effect of the CEO on the functioning of the TMT.

Peterson *et al.*'s (2003) study on the impact of CEO personality on TMT dynamics is a notable exception and provides some interesting insights. Their study is significant in that they extend previous leadership personality studies by exploring the specific processes through which the CEO influences the TMT. Few other studies link specific leader personality traits with particular group processes (a possible reason for this may be the reluctance of CEOs to take part in personality research). Their findings suggest that a CEO's personality is significantly associated with how the TMT interacts. For example, they found that CEO conscientiousness was significantly related to team level concern for legality of their decisions, and CEO emotional stability was significantly related to team cohesion and intellectual flexibility. CEO agreeableness was significantly associated with team cohesion, decentralization of power and, interestingly, concern for legality (this may be, they suggest, due to the covariation that is usually observed between agreeableness and conscientiousness). They found that TMTs characterized by intellectual flexibility and cohesiveness all experienced significant income growth, suggesting that CEO personality can indirectly affect organizational outcomes through TMT dynamics. An area of significant interest with the leadership literature is that of emotional intelligence (EI) and Goleman (1995) argues that EI is a prerequisite of successful leadership. Leaders who are emotionally in tune with themselves and others are more likely to be transformational leaders (Barling, Slater and Kelloway, 2000) who create environments of trust and psychological safety. While there is little consensus about the exact nature of EI, there is some agreement in the literature that it comprises of five elements 1. understanding one's emotions, 2. managing one's emotions, 3. emotional self control, 4. empathy and 5. managing relations (Salovey and Mayer, 1990; Goleman, 1995). We will discuss the importance of emotion and the TMT in more detail later in the chapter.

## TMT AND ORGANIZATIONAL CLIMATE

The majority of the culture/climate literature focuses on the organizational leader as the prime influencer of organizational culture and climate (Schein, 1997); however, this focus is broadening to include the senior team as a whole (Seeger and Ulmer, 2003). Litwin and Stringer (1968: 1) define organizational climate as a 'set of measurable properties of the work environment perceived directly or indirectly by people who live and work in this environment and assumed to influence their motivation and behaviour'. Climate can be observed in the policies and procedures of the organization and is thought to be a 'direct behavioural manifestation of organizational culture, which is a deeper and less consciously held set of cognitions and affective attachments' (Janz and Prasarnphanich, 2003: 353). Albrecht and Travaglione (2003) position trust in senior management as a central factor in the way that employees experience aspects of organizational climate. There is considerable empirical evidence suggesting that the top management team influences organizational climate. How TMT managers interact with each other may have important consequences for the wider organization. For example, if the TMT members trust each other, they are more likely to engage in learning behaviour within the team (Edmondson, 1999) and facilitate the transfer of information across the organization. This behaviour will diffuse downwards throughout each of the different functions and may encourage others to do

the same (Zand, 1972). This supposition was supported by findings from a TMT study carried out by Flood *et al.* (2002), MacCurtain, West, Flood and Dawson (2005) and MacCurtain (2005). They found that affective tone and levels of trust within the top team influenced how employees outside the top team perceived the organizational climate. The higher the levels of trust between top team members, the more employees perceived the climate as one supportive of innovation, risk taking and experimentation. Therefore, TMT affective tone is important, not just in terms of the team itself but also in terms of the wider organization climate. As role models and as the symbolic representation of the organization, TMT members can influence the organizational climate through their own behaviours and priorities. For example, top team support for innovation is an important dimension of a climate for innovation (Anderson and West, 1998; Ragazzoni *et al.*, 2002). If employees perceive management as supporting and rewarding innovative behaviour, there will be higher levels of openness and risk taking (O'Reilly *et al.*, 1987), both of which are essential elements of a climate for innovation. Management can therefore influence organizational outcomes through the provision of a shared reality that prioritizes the organization's goals and moves away from a defensive culture.

## CRITICAL ISSUES FOR THE PRESENT

### Teams and global issues/ cross cultural management

Carpenter *et al.*'s (2004) comprehensive review and extension of the upper echelons literature highlights the growing research on global strategy and in doing so draws attention to TMT characteristics previously unexplored in the TMT literature. International diversification is a complex strategic decision for TMT members who are faced with the complexity and uncertainties in international markets. Tihanyi *et al.* (2000) suggest that TMT characteristics can have an impact on a firm's global strategy and their findings indicate that TMTs with lower average age, higher average tenure, higher average education, higher average international experience, and higher tenure heterogeneity are associated with firm's being more internationally diversified. The importance of having TMT members with international experience in a global era emerged in several other studies (Carpenter and Fredrickson, 2001; Carpenter *et al.*, 2003). Organizations with internationally experienced TMT members exhibited a greater propensity to enter into international partnerships and obtained foreign sales faster than companies with executives lacking such experience (Reuber and Fischer, 1997). The relationship may occur for several reasons (Tihanyi *et al.*, 2000). First, managers with international experience are more aware of opportunities in overseas markets. In addition, international experience helps them to understand diverse markets and reduce the anxiety and complexity associated with operating under conditions of greater uncertainty (Sambharya, 1996). Finally, Tihanyi *et al.* (2000) argue, while on international assignments, managers may network and make contacts that will be useful in future international ventures. Other studies found that TMT size was associated with the firm's global strategic posture (GSP); for example, Saunders and Carpenter (1998) found that larger TMTs were associated with having developed a GSP. One area that is missing from this stream of research is the national diversity of the top management team itself (Heijltjes, Olie and Glunk, 2003). To what extent are multinational companies run by multinational top management teams and does it matter? Heijltjes *et al.* (2003) suggest that very few companies are close to being what Hu (1992) describes as 'stateless'. Despite globalization and the economic integration of many states, the majority of multinational companies have a nationally homogeneous top management team. However, they do note a steady increase in the number of foreign members of company boards. The internationalization of top management teams, its antecedents and consequences, would make a valuable addition to the upper echelons research.

# NEW DIRECTIONS FOR THE FUTURE

## *TMT and emotionality*

The area of emotionality is one that has been neglected in the TMT literature. Much of the work on TMTs presents them as logical, rational problem solvers who leave their emotions behind once entering the organization. However, with the growth of interest in the area of emotions at work (cf. Fineman, 2001) and the realization of the importance of emotional intelligence in achieving individual, team and organizational goals, this area is beginning to receive the attention it deserves. In doing so, the literature focuses on three main areas: psychodynamic theory, affective tone of the team and emotional intelligence (the latter is explored under the section on leadership).

## *Psychodynamic approach to TMTs*

The role of the unconscious is seldom recognized in the TMT literature and when it is discussed, it is usually viewed as a peripheral and negative influence on decision-making, and one that must be removed (Stacy, 2007). However, it is important to recognize the role played by unconscious processes within top management teams engaged in the seemingly rational activities of managing and decision making. Under conditions of uncertainty, change and ambiguity, people can become uncomfortable and anxious. When this anxiety goes unchecked and escalates, individuals can engage in unconscious or irrational behaviour. Bion (1961) argues that when mature and competent managers get together as a team, each can bring with them the unconscious defence mechanisms of dependence (i.e., over reliance on another, abandonment of individuality), idealization (i.e., the idolization of the leader), denial (i.e., rejection of any threatening or uncomfortable information), splitting (i.e., two separate and contradictory views of reality may exist) and projection (i.e., projecting anxieties or hopes on to the leader). In situations that are particularly stressful, increased anxiety may trigger these defence mechanisms. Under such conditions, it is possible that mission statements, strategic plans and visions are being used as defence mechanisms (Stacey, 2007). Team members may cling to the old way of doing things or a dominant mindset, despite evidence to the contrary, because it is a way of lessening anxiety – they become psychological safety blankets. Stacey (2007: 113) suggests that 'a group of people can make rational decisions and learn only when they are able to contain the anxiety of organizational life, as opposed to avoiding it through covert politics, on the one hand, or becoming overwhelmed by it in the form of unconscious processes, on the other'.

The importance of dealing with defence mechanisms and unconscious processes appropriately is not just important for the team itself but also for the organization as a whole. Just as the leader can influence the affective tone of the group through emotional contagion, so too can the TMT affect the organization as a whole. TMT's fears and anxieties are often mirrored in the emotional tone and behaviour of the organization (Kets de Vries and Miller, 1984, 1991; Fineman, 2001). Paranoid, neurotic and narcissistic leaders can create suspicion, pessimism and anxiety in the top team; so too can the team create such emotional climates in the wider organization. This is particularly the case in smaller organizations where the top managers are not distant spectres but part of their everyday life (Miller and Toulouse, 1986). Undoubtedly, most emotionally intelligent leaders embody the positive aspects of leadership but there is growing interest in the 'darker' side of leadership, which explores how charismatic and emotionally astute but morally bankrupt leaders can use their skills to exploit and manipulate rather than empower. In a study carried out by Flood, MacCurtain and West (2001) many top managers cited managing egos as one of the biggest challenges of TMT membership. Many of the TMT members

interviewed reported encountering the darker side of charismatic leaders who one described as 'adept at spotting vulnerability and playing on that'. Such leaders can charm those above them and bully those below them. This would suggest that CEO personality, ethics and the emotional disposition of the CEO and the TMT need to be considered further. However, Fineman cautions against making cause and effect relations in such analyses and suggests that executives' anxiety may be a response to a work group's inability to cope.

The psychodynamic approach can help bridge the frequent disconnection between theory and practice. In taking a psychodynamic perspective, we can explore 'real life' successes and failures through a different lens. Hodkinson and Wright (2002: 949) draw on psychodynamic theory to explain the failure of a process intervention in a publishing company by suggesting that 'the participants adopted a series of defensive avoidance strategies amplified by a series of psychodynamic processes initiated by the Chief Executive Officer (CEO) ... that these defensive avoidance strategies served as a means of coping with the unacceptably high levels of stress, which arose as a result of having to confront a variety of alternatives, each with potentially threatening consequences for the long term well-being of the organization'. Their study provides unique insights into why the application of potentially powerful intervention tools may fail (in this case the use of scenario planning). The use of such a tool involved much reflection and dialogue in order to uncover taken for granted assumptions. What surfaced was a divergent view of the organization and its strategy and the TMT members' roles within the organization. Hodgkinson and Wright contend that such divergence of viewpoints proved immensely threatening to the team and the CEO in particular, invoking dysfunctional stress levels and subsequent scepticism and withdrawal from the process. In essence, 'the psychological reality of a cognitively disparate team faced with a highly uncertain future proved too stressful to bear for the CEO and other key participants engaged in the consultation process, giving rise to a variety of dysfunctional coping strategies, which undermined our best efforts to assist them in their deliberations' (p. 960). Such defence mechanisms can include withdrawal from the process, cynicism and ridicule, intimidation and control that surface under conditions of stress, uncertainty and change. While potentially uncomfortable group processes can trigger these defence mechanisms (e.g., deep reflection if the group is not ready as seen in Hodgkinson and Wright's study), the affective tone of the group can change the dominance of one emotional state over the other – insecurity to security, isolation to belonging and vice versa. It is with this in mind that we now turn to TMT affective tone.

### Affective tone

In order to contain the anxiety of organizational life, Stacey stresses the importance of managing the boundary conditions around the team, which include the nature and use of power, time pressures on the group and the trust levels and affective tone within the team. He highlights the importance of affective tone in overcoming negative unconscious processes within the team and to 'test reality rather than indulge in fantasy' (p. 117). Group affective tone consists of 'consistent or homogenous affective reactions within a group' (George, 1990: 108). It is the combined moods of the individual members of the group and if the moods of the individual group members are consistent, then group affective tone can be treated as a group property (George, 1990).

West *et al.* (1998) suggest that group affective tone is an important, if somewhat controversial, approach to understanding teams and suggest that positive affective tone can influence team behaviour and effectiveness. While little research focuses on the nature and consequences of affective tone (e.g., trust) within the top management team, what evidence there is suggests that trust within TMTs can positively impact on TMT dynamics. George (1996) suggests that cognitive flexibility will be enhanced in teams experiencing positive affective tone.

Where there are high levels of trust, there is more likely to be honest group discussion and reflection. Edmondson (1996) found that psychological safety within teams increased the potential for reviewing mistakes and reflecting upon them. West (1996; 2000) cautioned that certain processes such as reflecting back and discussing difficult issues can be discouraging for the team as it is likely that there will be a gap between the real and desired circumstances. When such discrepancies are revealed during reflexive practices the consequences can be 'aversive' leading to anxiety and uncertainty. Trust may play an important role in assuaging these worries. It can also be argued that the more team members trust in each other's competence and goodwill, the more likely it is they will admit to mistakes, question why projects failed and find innovative ways of rectifying those mistakes (Edmondson, 1999; Edmondson *et al.*, 2001). Simons and Peterson's (2000) noteworthy study of intragroup trust and conflict within 70 top management teams found intragroup trust moderated the relationship between task conflict and relationship conflict. Farrell *et al.*'s (2005) study found trust levels within the TMT moderated the relationship between transformational leadership and the ability to combine and exchange information. The affective tone of the top management team is therefore clearly important, yet remains an area neglected in TMT research.

## TOP MANAGEMENT TEAMS AND ETHICAL BEHAVIOUR

Concerns regarding corporate ethics and the organization's relationship with the environment have grown in recent years, particularly following scandals such as Enron and BP. The word Enron is now associated with corruption on a grand scale, however there was a time when the same company was heralded as an example of an economically and ethically sound organization. Enron's fall from grace highlights the importance of deeply embedding ethical values into the culture rather than simply relying on the cultural artefacts of ethical codes and ethical officers (Sims and Brinkmann, 2003). In order to move from the idea of ethics as abstract ideals towards one where ethics are rooted in everyday practices and actions, organization leaders must demonstrate behavioural integrity in which there is congruence between espoused and enacted values. Sims and Brinkman (2003) suggest that Schein's (1985) five primary mechanisms (i.e., attention focusing, reaction to crisis, role modelling, rewards allocation and criteria for hiring and firing) that are used to create and maintain certain cultures can help organizational leaders 'embed' ethical behaviour and prevent the use of ethics for mere façade and legitimation purposes. The growing concern with ethical behaviour emerges against a backdrop of declining trust in senior management (Albrecht and Travaglione, 2003). Leadership writers such as Terry (1993) and Simons (1999) note an increasing divergence between what managers say and what they do, rendering them untrustworthy and diminishing their credibility.

While a manager's ethical (or unethical) behaviour may be rooted in their personal stories, ambitions and personalities, there are societal, industry and organizational factors that may encourage or impede ethical behaviour. Zahra, Priem and Rasheed (2005) identify some of the organizational levels antecedents of top management fraud as being culture (i.e., norms of behaviour, 'toxic' cultures rewarding aggressive behaviour), board composition ('insider' vs 'outside' membership, separation of ownership and control) and senior leadership (leaders who espouse, enact and reward ethical values). The symbolic weight given to the senior management team's actions can promote similar actions by others in the organization. This is particularly the case when the leader is charismatic as this quality can lead to greater identification with the leader, as well as trust and obedience by employees (Ashforth and Anand, 2003), suggesting that sometimes a culture of 'organizational heroes' can be dangerous. Therefore, a charismatic but morally bankrupt leader can create an organizational culture where corporate illegal and unethical actions go unchecked and may even be celebrated. Corporate crime is an area that stirs the passions of many as the often devastating effects can be far reaching. The top management team play a pivotal role in developing a culture that emphasizes ethical behaviour in hiring, socializing, evaluating and rewarding employees (Zahra *et al.*, 2005).

## CONCLUSION

This chapter focuses on the members of the top management team – who they are, what they do and how they influence organizational outcomes. The top team is unique in many ways – their actions carry symbolic meaning both within the organization and externally, they make decisions critical to the survival of the organization, they provide vision and act as role models to other organizational members. It is therefore imperative that this team at the top is an effective one. However, this can be difficult to achieve given the variety of pressures that may mitigate team working at the top (i.e., leadership style, reward system, diverse and ambitious members, succession tournaments). While it is impossible to provide simple prescriptions for effective and ethical team working at the top, it is a challenge that must be faced by all senior managers. The need for moral as well as strategic leadership is even greater today as trust in senior management is at an all time low. The management of top management teams is in many ways the management of paradox. Such paradoxes include the creation of debate and conflict while simultaneously creating social integration; balancing long-term and short-term perspectives; creating top teams with members who are diverse but have shared meanings and 'fit'; balancing cooperation and competition; being both shapers of and shaped by the organizational context and the creation of a supportive yet challenging climate. The effective management of these polarities is the challenge facing every top team (Flood *et al.*, 2001). The overall vision of the team for the organization and clarity about their shared common purpose are the fundamental elements for their success.

# REFERENCES

Albrecht, S. and Travaglione, A. (2003) 'Trust in public sector senior management', *International Journal of Human Resource Management*, 14 (1): 76–93.

Amason, A.C. (1996) 'Distinguishing between the effects of functional and dysfunctional conflict on strategic decision-making: Resolving a paradox for top management teams', *Academy of Management Journal*, 39 (1): 123–149.

Anderson, N.R. and West, M.A. (1998) 'Measuring climate for work group innovation, development and validation of the team climate inventory', *Journal of Organisational Behaviour*, 19 (3): 235–259.

Ashforth, B.E. and Anand, V. (2003) 'The normalisation of corruption in organisations', *Research in Organizational Behaviour*, 25: 1–52.

Bantel, K.A. (1993) 'Top team, environment and performance effects on strategic planning formality', *Group and Organisational Management*, 18 (4): 436–458.

Bantel, K.A. and Jackson, S.E. (1989) 'Top management and innovations in banking: Does the composition of the top team make a difference?', *Strategic Management Journal*, 10 (Special Issue): 107–124.

Barling, Slater and Kelloway (2000) 'Transformational leadership and emotional intelligence: An exploratory study', *Leadership and Organization Development Journal*, 21: 157–161.

Bion, W. (1961) *Experiences in Groups and Other Papers*. London: Tavistock.

Boeker, W. (1997) 'Strategic change: The influence of managerial characteristics and organizational growth', *Academy of Management Journal*, 40 (1): 152–171.

Carpenter, M.A. (2002) 'The implications of strategy and social context for the relationship between top management team heterogeneity and firm performance', *Strategic Management Journal*, 23: 275–284.

Carpenter, M.A. and Fredrickson, J.W. (2001) 'Top management teams, global strategic posture and the moderating role of uncertainty', *Academy of Management Journal*, 44 (3): 533–546.

Carpenter, M.A., Pollock, T.G. and Leary, M. (2003) 'Testing a model of reasoned risk-taking: Governance, the experience of principals and agents, and global strategy in high-technology IPO firms', *Strategic Management Journal*, 24 (9): 803–820.

Carpenter, M.A., Geletkanycz, M.A. and Sanders, W.G. (2004) 'Upper echelons research revisited: Antecedents, elements and consequences of top management team composition', *Journal of Management*, 30 (6): 749–778.

Carter, S.S. and West, M.A. (1998) 'Reflexivity, effectiveness and mental health in BBC production teams', *Small Group Research*, 29 (5): 583–601.

Collins, C.J. and Clark, K.D (2003) 'Strategic human resource practice, top management team social networks, and firm performance: The role of human resource practices in creative organizational competitive advantage', *Academy Management Journal*, 46: 720–731.

Critchely, B. and Casey, D. (1984) 'Second thoughts on team building', *Journal of Management Education and Development*, 15 (2): 163–75.

Daellenbach, U.S., McCarthy, A.M. and Schoenecker, T.S. (1999) 'Commitment to innovation: The impact of top management team characteristics', *R & D Management*, 29 (3): 199–209.

Dearborn, D. and Simon, H. (1958) 'Selective perception: A note on the departmental identifications of executives', *Sociometry*, 21 (2): 140–145.

De Dreu, C.K. (2002) 'Team innovation and team effectiveness: The importance of minority dissent and reflexivity', *European Journal of Work and Organisational Psychology*, 11 (3): 285–298.

Dess, G.G. (1987) 'Consensus on strategy formulation and organisational performance: Competitors in a fragmented industry', *Strategic Management Journal*, 8: 259–277.

Edmondson, A.C. (1996) 'Learning from mistakes is easier said than done: Group and organisational influences on the detection and correction of human error', *Journal of Applied Behavioural Sciences*, 32 (1): 5–28.

Edmondson, A.C. (1999) 'Psychological safety and learning behaviour in work teams', *Administrative Science Quarterly*, 44: 350–384.

Edmondson, A.C., Bohmer, R.M. and Pisano, G.P. (2001) 'Disrupted routines: Team learning and new technology implementation in hospitals', *Administrative Science Quarterly*, 46: 685–716.

Edmondson, A.C., Roberto, M. and Watkins, M. (2002) 'A dynamic model of top management team effects: Managing unstructured task teams', *Leadership Quarterly*, 14: 297–325.

Farrell, J., Flood, P., MacCurtain, S., Hannigan, A., Dawson, J. and West, M. (2005) 'CEO leadership, top management team trust and the combination and exchange of information', *Irish Journal of Management*, 26 (1): 22–40.

Fineman, S. (2001) 'Emotions and organizational control', in R. Payne and C. Cooper (eds) *Emotions at Work: Theory, Research and Applications for Management*. Chichester: Wiley, pp. 219–241.

Finkelstein, S. and Hambrick, D. (1990) 'Top management team tenure and organisational outcomes: The moderating role of managerial discretion', *Administrative Science Quarterly*, 35: 484–503.

Finklestein, S. and Hambrick, D. (1996) *Strategic Leadership – Top Executives and their Effects on Organizations*. New York: West Publishing Company.

Flood, P., MacCurtain, S. and West, M. (2001) *Effective Top Management Teams*. Dublin: Blackhall Press.

Flood, P., Heffernan, M., Farrell, J., MacCurtain, S., O'Hara, T., O'Regan, P., Carroll, C., Dromgoole, T. and Mangan, J. (2002) *Managing Knowledge Based Organisations – Top Management Teams and Innovation in the Indigenous Software Industry*. Dublin: Blackhall Press.

Fredrickson, J.W. (1986) 'The strategic decision making process and organisational outcomes: The moderating role of managerial discretion', *Academy of Management Review*, 11: 280–287.

George, J.M. (1990) 'Personality, affect and behavior in groups', *Journal of Applied Psychology*, 75: 107–116.

Gevers, J.M.P., van Eerde, W. and Rutte, C.G. (2001) 'Time pressure, potency and progress in project groups', *European Journal of Work and Organizational Psychology*, 10 (2): 205–221.

Goleman, D. (1995) '*Emotional Intelligence*'. New York: Bantam Books.

Hambrick, D. (1994) 'Top management groups: A conceptual integration and reconsideration of the label "Team"', *Research in Organisational Behaviour*, 16: 171–213.

Hambrick, D. (2005) 'Upper echelons theory: Origins, twists and turns and lessons learned', in K.G. Smith and M. Hitt (eds) *Great Minds in Management*. Oxford: Oxford University Press.

Hambrick, D.C. and D'Aveni, R.A. (1992) 'Top team deterioration as part of the downward spiral of large corporate bankruptcies', *Management Science*, 38: 1445–1463.

Hambrick, D. and Mason, P.A. (1984) 'Upper echelons: The organisation as a reflection of it's top managers', *Academy of Management Review*, 9 (2): 195–206.

Hambrick, D., Cho, T.S. and Chen, M.J. (1996) 'The influence of top management team heterogeneity on firms' competitive moves', *Administrative Science Quarterly*, 41 (4): 659–684.

Harrison, D.A., Price, K., Gavin, J. and Florey, A. (2002) 'Time, teams and task performance: Changing effects of surface- and deep-level diversity on group functioning', *Academy of Management Journal*, 45: 1029–1045.

Heijltjes, M., Olie, R. and Glunk, U. (2003) 'Internationalization of top management teams', *European Management Journal*, 21 (1): 89–97.

Hodgkinson, G.P. and Wright, G. (2002) 'Confronting strategic inertia in a top management team: Learning from failure', *Organization Studies*, 23: 949–977.

Hu, Y.S. (1992) 'Global or stateless corporations are national firms with international operations', *California Management Review*, 34 (2): 107–126.

Jackson, S.E. (1996) 'The consequences of diversity in multidisciplinary work teams', in M.A. West (ed.) *Handbook of Work Group Psychology*. London: John Wiley and Sons, pp. 53–75.

Janz, B.D. and Prasarnphanich, P. (2003) 'Understanding the antecedents of effective knowledge management: The importance of a knowledge centred culture', *Decision Sciences*, 34: 351–383.

Jarzabkowski, P. and Searle, R. (2003) *Top management team strategic capacity: Diversity, collectivity and trust*. Aston Business School Research Paper.

Jehn, K.A. (1995) 'A multimethod examination of the benefits and detriments of intragroup conflict', *Administrative Science Quarterly*, 40: 256–283.

Katzenbach, J.R. (1997) 'The myth of the top management team', *Harvard Business Review*, 75 (6): 83–91.

Keck, S.L. (1991) *Top team executive structure: Does it matter anyway?* Paper presented at the Academy of Management Meeting, Miami.

Kets de Vries, M.F.R. and Miller, D. (1984) *The Neurotic Organisation* (2nd edn). San Francisco, CA: Jossey-Bass.

Kilduff, M., Angelmar, R. and Mehra, A. (2000) 'Top management team diversity and performance: Examining the role of cognitions', *Organizational Science*, 11: 21–34.

Kimberley, J. and Evanisko, M.J. (1981) 'Organisational innovation: The influence of individual, organisational and contextual factors on hospital adoption of technological and administrative innovations', *Academy of Management Journal*, 24: 689–713.

Knight, D., Pearce, C.L., Smith, K.G., Olian, J.D., Sims, H.P., Smith, K.A. and Flood, P. (1999) 'Top management team diversity, group process and strategic consensus', *Strategic Management Journal*, 20: 445–465.

Korn, H.J., Milliken, F.J. and Lant, T.K. (1992) *Top Management Team Change and Organisation Performance: the Influence of Succession, Composition and Context*. Paper presented at Annual Meeting of the Academy of Management, Las Vegas, NV.

Lawrence, B.S. (1997) 'The black box of organizational demography', *Organization Science: A Journal of the Institute of Management Sciences*, 8: 1–22.

Litwin, G.H. and Stringer, R.A. (1968) *Motivation and Organisational Climate*. Boston, MA: Harvard University Press.

MacCurtain, S. (2005) *An Exploration of the Determinants of Innovation: The Top Management Team, Organisational Climate and Organisational Learning*. PhD dissertation, Aston University, Birmingham, UK.

MacCurtain, S., West, M., Flood, P. and Dawson, J. (2005) *Top Team Trust, Innovative Climate and Organisational Learning*. Paper presented at *V International HRM Conference*, Seville, Spain, May 19–21.

Marks, M.A., Mathieu, J.E. and Zaccaro, S.J. (2001) 'A temporally based framework and taxonomy of team processes', *Academy of Management Review*, 26 (3): 356–376.

Miller, D. and Toulouse, J.M. (1986) 'Chief executive personality and corporate strategy in small firms', *Management Science*, 32: 1389–1409.

Miller, D., Kets de Vries, M.F.R. and Toulouse, J.M. (1982) 'Top executive locus of control and its relationship to strategy-making, structure and environment', *Academy of Management Journal*, 25: 237–253.

Milliken, F.J. and Martins, L.L. (1996) 'Searching for common threads: Understanding the multiple effects of diversity in organisational groups', *Academy of Management Review*, 21: 402–433.

Mulder, I., Swaak, J. and Kessels, J. (2004) 'In search of reflective behaviour and shared understanding in ad hoc expert teams', *CyberPsychology and Behaviour*, 7 (2): 141–145.

Nadler, D.A. (1996) 'Managing the team at the top', *Strategy and Business*, 2: 42–51.

O'Reilly, C.A., Chatman, J. and Anderson (1987) 'Message flow and decision making', in F.M. Jablin, L.L. Putman, K.H. Roberts and L.W. Porter (eds) *Handbook of Organisational Communication: An Interdisciplinary Perspective*. Newbury Park, CA: Sage.

O'Reilly C.A. and Flatt, S.F. (1989) *Executive Team Demography, Organisational Innovation and Team Performance*. Paper presented at the Academy of Management Conference, Washington, D.C.

O'Reilly, C.A., Caldwell, D.F. and Barnett, W.P. (1989) 'Work group demography, social integration and turnover', *Administrative Science Quarterly*, 34: 21–37.

Papadakis, V.M. and Barwise, P. (2002) 'How much do CEOs and top managers matter in strategic decision making?', *British Journal of Management*, 13: 83–95.

Peterson, R.S., Smith, D.B, Martorana, P.V. and Owens, P.D. (2003) 'The impact of chief executive officer personality on top management team dynamics: One mechanism by which leadership affects organizational performance', *Journal of Applied Psychology*, 88 (5): 795–809.

Pettigrew, A.M. (1992) 'On studying managerial elites', *Strategic Management Journal*, 13: 163–182.

Pfeffer, J. (1983) 'Organisational demography', in L.L. Cummings and B.M. Staw (eds) *Research in Organisational Behaviour*. Greenwich, CT: JAI Press, pp. 299–357.

Pitcher, P. and Smith, A.D. (2001) 'Top management team heterogeneity: Personality, power and proxies', *Organization Science*, 12 (1): 1–18.

Ragazzoni, P., Baiardi, P., Zotti, A., Anderson, N. and West, M. (2002) 'Italian validation of the team climate inventory: A measure of team climate for innovation', *Journal of Managerial Psychology*, 17 (4): 325–336.

Reuber, A.R. and Fischer, E. (1997) 'The influence of the management team's international experience on the internationalisation behaviours of SMEs', *Journal of International Business Studies*, 28: 807–825.

Salovey, P.and Mayer, J.D. (1990) 'Emotional Intelligence', *Imagination, Cognition and Personality*, 9: 185–211.

Sambharya, R.B. (1989) *Managerial Characteristics and MNC Performance*. Academy of Management Proceedings, pp. 111–116.

Sambharya, R.B. (1989) 'Foreign experience of top management teams and international diversification strategies of U.S. multinational companies', *Strategic Management Journal*, 17: 739–746.

Saunders, W.G. and Carpenter, M.A. (1998) 'Internationalization and firm governance', *Academy of Management Journal*, 41 (2): 158–178.

Seeger, M.W. and Ulmer, R.R. (2003) 'Explaining Enron', *Management Communication Quarterly*, 17 (1): 58–85.

Schein, E.H. (1997) *Organisational Culture and Leadership* (2nd edn). San Francisco, CA: Jossey-Bass.

Schippers, M.C., Den Hartog, D.N., Koopman, P.L. and Wienk, J.A. (2003) 'Diversity and team outcomes: Moderating effects of outcome interdependence and group longevity and the mediating effect of reflexivity', *Journal of Organisational Behaviour*, 24: 779–803.

Sims, R.R. and Brinkmann, J. (2003) 'Enron ethics', *Journal of Business Ethics*, 45: 243–256.

Simons, T. (1995) *Top Management Team Consensus, Heterogenenity and Debate as Contingent Predictors of Company Performance: The Complimentarity of Group Structure and Process*. Academy of Management Best Papers Proceedings, 62–66.

Simons, T. (1999) 'Behavioural integrity as a critical ingredient for transformational leadership', *Journal of Organizational Change Management*, 12 (2): 89–104.

Simons, T.L., Pelled, L.H. and Smith, K.A. (1999) 'Making use of difference: Diversity, debate and decision comprehensiveness in top management teams', *Academy of Management Journal*, 42 (6): 662–673.

Simons, T.L. and Peterson, R.S. (2000) 'Task conflict and relationship conflict in top management teams: The pivotal role of intra-group trust', *Journal of Applied Psychology*, 8: 102–111.

Smith, K.G., Olian, J., Sims, H.P., Scully, J., Smith, K.A. and O'Bannon, D. (1994) 'Top management team demography and process: The role of social integration and communication', *Administrative Science Quarterly*, 39 (3): 412–438.

Stacey, R.D. (2007) *Strategic Management and Organizational Dynamics: The Challenge of Complexity*. London: Prentice Hall.

Starbuck, W.H. (1985) 'Acting first and thinking later: Theory versus reality in strategic change', in J.M. Pennings (ed.) *Organisational Strategy and Change*. San Francisco, CA: Jossey-Bass, pp. 336–372.

Swift, T.A. and West, M.A. (1998) *Reflexivity and Group Processes: Research and Practice*. ESRC Centre for Organisation and Innovation, Institute of Work Psychology, University of Sheffield.

Terry, R.W. (1993) *Authentic Leadership: Courage in Action*. San Francisco, CA: Jossey-Bass.

Thomas, A., Litschert, R.J. and Ramaswamy, K. (1991) 'The performance impact of strategy-manager coalignment: An empirical investigation', *Strategic Management Journal*, 12: 509–522.

Tihanyi, L., Ellstrand, A.E., Daily, C.M. and Dalton, D.R. (2000) 'Composition of the top management team and firm international diversification', *Journal of Management*, 26 (6): 1157–1177.

Tjosvold, D., Hui, C. and Yu, Z. (2003) 'Conflict management and task reflexivity for team in-role and extra-role performance in China', *International Journal of Conflict Management*, 14: 141–164.

Tjosvold, D., Tang, M. and West, M. (2004) 'Reflexivity for team innovation in China', *Group and Organization Management*, 29 (5): 540–559.

Wagner, W.G., Pfeffer, J. and O'Reilly, C.A. (1984) 'Organisational demography and turnover in top management groups', *Administrative Science Quarterly*, 29: 74–92.

Watson, W.E., Kumar, K. and Michaelsen, L.K. (1993) 'Cultural diversity's impact on interaction process and performance: Comparing homogeneous and diverse task groups', *Academy of Management Journal*, 36: 590–602.

West, M.A. (1996) 'Reflexivity and work group effectiveness: A conceptual integration', in M.A. West (ed.) *Handbook of Work Group Psychology*. London: Wiley, pp. 555–579.

West, M.A. (2000) 'Reflexivity, revolution and innovation in work teams', in M.M. Beyerlein, D.A. Johnson and S.T. Beyerlein (eds) *Advances in the Interdisciplinary Study of Work Teams: Product Development Team*. Stamford, CT: JAI Press, pp. 1–29.

West, M.A., Borrill, C.S. and Unsworth, K.L. (1998) 'Team effectiveness in organisations', in C.L. Cooper and I.T. Robertson (eds) *International Review of Industrial and Organisational Psychology*. London: John Wiley and Sons.

West, M.A., Patterson, M.G. and Dawson, J. (1999) 'A path to profit?: Teamwork at the top', *Centre Piece: The Magazine of Economic Performance*, 4 (3): 7–11.

West, C.T. and Schwenk, C.R. (1996) 'Top management Team strategic consensus, demographic homogeneity and firm performance', *Strategic Management Journal*, 17 (7): 571–577.

Wiersema, M.F. and Bantel, K.A. (1992) 'Top management team demography and corporate change', *Academy of Management Journal*, 35: 91–121.

Zahra, S.A., Priem, R.L. and Rasheed, A.A. (2005) 'The antecedents and consequences of top management fraud', *Journal of Management*, 31 (6): 803–828.

Zand, D.E. (1972) 'Trust and managerial problem solving', *Administrative Science Quarterly*, 17: 229–240.

Zenger, T. and Lawrence, B. (1989) 'Organisational demography: The differential effects of age and tenure distributions on technical communication', *Academy of Management Journal*, 32: 353–376.

# 14

# Succession Management: Building Talent Across Organizational Generations

Jay A. Conger

## THE DYNAMICS OF THE TALENT MARKETPLACE

Few firms are prepared for what has come to be called the 'War for Talent' (Michaels *et al.*, 2001). With impending retirements of the baby boomer generation over this decade, most large companies will have to scramble to meet not only gaps in talent but gaps in the backgrounds of that talent. In the global economy of this century, firms will be competing for talent in most corners of the world. Managers themselves will need greater technological literacy, a sophisticated understanding of global marketplaces, fluency in multiple cultures, entrepreneurial skills, extensive networks of varied relationships, change management skills, and the ability to provide leadership in increasingly delay-ered and disaggregated organizations. Many companies do not have well honed inter-nal initiatives to develop such capabilities. Instead succession management is often a haphazard and opportunistic set of uncoordi-nated events. The price to be paid is a serious shortage of genuine managerial talent across the full range of workplace generations.

Acerbating this looming talent shortage is the greater mobility that successful managers and executives possess today. Over the last two decades, search firms have risen in size and power as the movers and brokers of talent. The research arms of the leading search firms compile vast directories of management talent and track the latest changes in the organiza-tional charts to see who might be available for opportunities. Each year they move thousands of managers across firms in every industry. In addition, career opportunities around the world are now easily identified on company and public internet sites. Job posting sites such as Monsterboard.com have significantly enhanced the visibility of opportunities and in turn mobility. As a result, many small and medium-sized companies can now target the same kinds of talent that has been historically reserved for large firms. These smaller firms can attract talent with greater opportunities for increased responsibility, impact, and wealth.

Feeding into these facilitators of mobility is a change in attitudes among the younger generations of managers. Witnesses of the massive downsizing initiatives of large corporations in the late 1980s and 1990s, younger generations have little commitment to the traditional notions of corporate loyalty. Their belief is that loyalty is no longer rewarded. Instead it is assumed that only by moving among different firms can one gain greater rewards and responsibility. In other words, opportunities for upward mobility are seriously limited by remaining in a single firm over one's career. This belief aided by search firms and the internet has accelerated company-hopping. For example, the average high performer may change companies a couple of times during a career. Some estimates suggest that today's average executives will have worked in five organizations over their careers.

## THE REINVENTION OF SUCCESSION MANAGEMENT

In response to these challenges, old succession management systems are being reinvented. A contemporary concern with both guarding one's talent and developing its capabilities to the fullest has led to the rediscovery and redesign of the old talent management systems. Much more than 'de-sexing' the old time 'manning charts', the new succession management brings a revival of certain old concepts with critical differences. Before we explain these differences, it is helpful to describe the old succession approaches to understand what they attempted to accomplish. From there, we can trace their evolution to today.

For decades, succession management's primary purpose was to identify replacements for *senior executives* who would eventually depart the organization for any number of reasons (Fulmer and Conger, 2004). There was little or no attention devoted to the

younger and more junior generations of talent. In many companies, succession also ended up a largely mechanical process. What we might call an 'annual event' – 'time to fill out those succession planning forms'. The possibility that it might be deployed for genuine development or for retention of talented individuals remained largely untapped. The assumption was that top managers were in place for the duration until some accident or health problem might remove them. It was even rare to think about the top person being lured away by another company. As a result, most companies focused their efforts on an essential, but unheralded succession management 'list'. The corporate succession list was to ensure that some thought had been given to identifying an adequate and appropriate pool of replacements should any of the senior-most managers leave the playing field. The primary focus was therefore on replacement rather than on development. For example, in 1967, the stated purpose of General Electric's Corporate Executive Manpower Staff list was, '… timely availability of *thoroughly experienced*, competent, and proven general managers for the Company's top positions'. Success was measured by the maintenance of a list of individuals ready to move up the corporate ladder.

Beyond their lack of an emphasis on development, these older models of succession management had other shortcomings. One was their singular focus on the executive level. The earlier systems were also quite formal. People had to create detailed and quite rigid replacement lists or *slates*. The process was bureaucratic and long term. As a participant, an individual would be moved methodically after a certain number of years from one step to the next. If someone proved to be a fast learner and a high performer, they still had to stay within the lock step of the career path. Ownership was relatively isolated within the senior levels of the operating units or at the 'corporate' headquarters. There was complete secrecy in the sense that only the most senior people knew where individuals were ranked on the list. So knowledge about when and how succession moves would be accomplished was limited to the executive levels of an organization.

Beginning in the late 1980s, many corporations became deeply interested in leadership development. The initial wave of development activities, however, focused primarily on training and education. Managers were sent off to business school programs or trainers were coming into companies to teach leadership skills. As the popularity of these programs grew, there was a concern that leadership development had positioned itself around a set of 'one time educational events'. Meanwhile research at the Center for Creative Leadership in Greensboro, North Carolina was demonstrating that jobs and bosses were often the best arenas to develop leadership (McCall, 1988). As a result, concern grew that educational interventions were insufficient to support genuine leadership development. Attention was directed towards succession planning with the possibility that such systems could be reinvented to support leadership development. The aim was to redeploy succession management towards a longer-term perspective where jobs and bosses became essential ingredients in developing leadership talent. The aim was also to move beyond the executive suite. Instead succession management would be deployed as a mechanism for *identifying* and *cultivating leadership talent* across the different organizational generations.

As a result, contemporary succession management no longer focuses solely on the *replacement* of executive talent but rather has broadened its emphasis towards the *development* of talent across generations. The new approaches take a much more systemic perspective towards the organization's talent strategy while proactively engaging company managers at many levels. A greater emphasis is on potential rather than simply on recent performance. For example, attention is given to how a certain assignment might develop an individual. Replacement lists are much more fluid and function as talent pools. Thanks to technology, the normal succession planning system is as simple as an Excel spreadsheet.

And, where the old systems were characterized by complete confidentiality and secrecy, today's succession systems actually encourage significant involvement by individuals who are participants and candidates. There is more developmentally oriented feedback and, in a few companies, actual transparency about where individuals stand on the succession rankings. As a byproduct of these changes, the more effective succession management approaches can program a continuous stream of challenges and job assignments for talented managers. They can also monitor the progress of a candidate and, when indicated, propose time in a new role that will keep that candidate challenged and growing. Organizations can also take a more disciplined view of where each promising individual is in his or her career. For example, are they getting sufficient developmental opportunities and the right bosses? What would be the ideal next job assignment? What experiences are needed to round out their skill set and to prepare them for new leadership roles? In a moment, we will examine the processes and practices they deploy to achieve these outcomes, but first it is important to understand the overarching aims of contemporary systems.

## THE GOALS OF SUCCESSION MANAGEMENT

The goal of a highly effective succession management system is two-fold. The first is to serve the needs of the organization by helping to provide a *continuous* and *deep supply* of talent. Many companies that grew rapidly in the 1990s discovered that they had also grown enormous gaps of internal talent. Today other gaps are associated with the impending retirement of aging baby boomer executives and the mobility of younger generations. Another set of gaps are being produced by fundamental shifts in the environment which demand new competences and capabilities. The ideal succession system therefore helps the corporation to plan for emerging needs at all management levels. The system can help fill in talent gaps and retain talent.

It can and should clarify the performance standards of the organization. Managers who get into the succession pool receive clear messages about what types of performance and behaviors will be rewarded. An effective system forces the organization to be very clear about the standards and competencies that will be used for measuring and rewarding managerial talent.

The second goal of an effective succession management is to serve the employees. Individual high performers always have external opportunities to go elsewhere. An effective succession management system can help to keep them challenged and motivated to prevent their migration to those external opportunities. In other words, *retention* and *development* are critical goals. High performers who find themselves stuck in jobs which they perceive as inadequate are prime targets for headhunters. An effective succession system helps talent to develop their potential by timely moves to opportunities that will match their needs and complement their current skill set. The best systems provide challenging opportunities and developmental feedback on performance and potential. An effective system should enable highly talented people to move on a faster, or at least, more appropriate track. It should also help them to avoid derailment in their careers.

## THE PRINCIPLES GUIDING 'BEST PRACTICE' SUCCESSION MANAGEMENT APPROACHES

If we examine the principles shaping the design features of 'best practice' succession management approaches, we find there are several critical ones (Fulmer and Conger, 2004). First, they are designed to be simple and easy to use by executives and line managers. All participants – not just those running the systems – have easy access. Data is secure but open to those who need it. They are non-bureaucratic processes. There is a unified approach to succession management to ensure consistency between different business units and geographic areas and maintain

objectivity of succession management. The overall approach is *developmentally* oriented rather than simply replacement oriented. The processes behind the system are more concerned with the continuing growth and development of the employee rather than in his or her ultimate job title.

The most effective systems always actively involve the very top officers of the organization. The CEO and his or her executive team are committed sponsors – proactively participating in determinations of talent and the next steps for the maximum development of their talented employees. Best practice succession systems are also effective at spotting gaps in talent and identifying 'lynchpin' positions. Lynchpin positions are those jobs which are critical to the success of the organization. These positions and the individuals who can fill them merit and receive regular and extensive attention.

Succession management still does the job of monitoring the succession process, enabling the company to make certain that the right people are moving into the right jobs at the right time and that gaps are being spotted early. Contemporary succession systems therefore incorporate frequent checkpoints throughout the year. These checkpoints monitor who is where and where they should be going next. A checkpoint function is built into the system to spot a problem before it becomes a problem.

Finally, well-run succession management operations are continually reinvented. Best-practice companies refine and adjust their systems as they receive feedback from line executives, experience shifts in the company's strategy, monitor developments in technology, and learn from other leading organizations. For example, the computer manufacturer Dell reduced the degree of computerization for succession management data in response to feedback from the field. To avoid the ever-present danger of becoming bureaucratized and mechanical, best practice systems therefore actively incorporate dialogues and debates about talent and about the succession process. There are continuous 'conversations' about what is needed for the future of each candidate, about who should be where, and when. There are continuous conversations on the part of the guardians and designers about the planning process and how its utilization can be improved.

## THE PRACTICES AND PROCESSES BEHIND 'BEST PRACTICE' SUCCESSION MANAGEMENT APPROACHES

Beyond the critical design principles, there are seven sets of practices and processes that form the actual mechanics of a 'best practice' succession management system (Fulmer and Conger, 2004). They include: 1) alignment of the succession strategy to the organization's overarching strategy, 2) senior level sponsorship and HR 'process' ownership, 3) identification and effective deployment of key linchpin positions, 4) rigorous talent identification processes, 5) strong developmental linkages that accompany talent identification, 6) multiple stakeholders assessments with developmental feedback, and 7) rigorous tracking and feedback metrics. Within each of these, there are a set of 'best practices' that distinguish the more effective succession approaches. We discuss each and their corresponding best practices below.

### 1) Strong alignment between the organization's strategy and its talent strategy

Succession management occupies a key position as an interface between the human resource function and the strategic direction of an organization. The company's strategy, its *marketplace* strategy and its *talent* strategy should be intertwined. Succession management then becomes a vital resource in anticipating the future needs of the organization in terms of finding, assessing, developing, and monitoring the human capital required by the organization's strategy. Several key questions must therefore be asked when making succession decisions for the organization. What are the strategic objectives of the company in terms of marketplaces and geography? What are the implications of that

strategy for talent development? In turn, what will be the talent strategies of the firm? And how do these translate into our succession systems?

For this 'translation' to work, there has to be a close partnership between the senior executive ranks and the human resource function. They are partners in understanding what the business strategy is and in preparing company talent to meet the demands of that strategy. For example, what types of skills and capabilities will be needed as we enter new markets or geographies or grow and reinvent our existing businesses? What types of developmental assignments will be needed most in the future as the firm unfolds its strategy ahead? Succession planning systems must be tightly linked to strategic objectives of the firm to be effective and to be credible. Thought has to be given to being responsive to emerging threats and opportunities and the implications of that for a talent strategy.

### 2) Senior level sponsorship and HR 'process' ownership

The sponsors and 'owners' of any succession system are critical to its usefulness and acceptance. Sponsorship must be at the very top, both at the top of the corporation and the top of functions and operating units. For example, at Dow Chemical, the process was designed with the active involvement of the CEO, the vice president of human resources, and the workforce planning strategic center. At other best practice companies such as General Electric or Pepsico, the CEO is the key sponsor for succession management, and a senior management committee of vice presidents steward the process at the corporate level. Sponsorship can take various forms but it always involves a serious time commitment on the part of the CEO and their executive team. For example, at the Sonoco Corporation, the top eight executives including the CEO, the vice president of HR, and the top group vice presidents meet annually for a week to discuss succession management. This is typical of companies whose senior teams are committed sponsors of succession management.

Without this level of critical support by the very top, succession management can end up a more mechanical process. Sensing that succession is simply a tangential activity, line executives can vary widely in their commitments to the development of subordinates. Operating groups and functions can hide and hoard their talent. Limited attention will be given to developmental assignments.

Ideally, the board of directors is also involved. They must be familiar with the system and its effectiveness. It is important that they be knowledgeable about succession candidates at the executive level. The ownership of the system, however, is usually shared among the business heads. Corporate Human Resources is the 'owner' of the processes and tools as well as serving as the system's guardian for the CEO. At the same time, line management owns the deliverables and is held accountable for the outcomes of the succession process. HR is held accountable for the system design and its effectiveness as a design and as a process. Periodic reviews by the senior executives and divisional heads ensure that the system continues to reflect the needs of the corporation.

### 3) Effective identification and deployment of lynchpin jobs

Best practice systems inventory their key positions across the organization from the executive level down to the director level. These are the positions considered critical to the success of the organization. They involve important skills, are often difficult to fill, and involve coordination with other parts of the organization. They could include regional management, key functional assignments, general management in a small business unit, or key staff assignments.

The more effective systems focus intensively on specific lynchpin positions – a select set of jobs that are essential to the long-term health of the organization. As William Rothwell (2001) points out, lynchpin positions are 'strategically vital leverage points ... which when they are left vacant ... the organization will not be able to meet or exceed customer expectations, confront

competition successfully, or follow through on efforts of crucial long-term significance' (p. 172). They are typically difficult to fill, rarely are individual contributor positions, and usually reside both in established areas of the business and those that will be critical to future success. In a professional services firm, for example, the partners managing critical industry sectors such as healthcare would be in lynchpin positions, as would partners managing emerging sectors such as biotech. In a retail organization, linchpin positions might range from regional managers to store managers of flagship operations. These positions require broad business perspective and experience. By monitoring the pipeline for these jobs, companies can focus development programs on ensuring an adequate supply of appropriate talent.

### 4) Rigorous talent identification processes

The fourth dimension is selection or identification of talent and the establishment of talent pools. The more effective systems base their assessments directly on the leadership and organizational competency models that are developed for each level. There is no universal competency model for the entire organization but rather there are multiple models, which vary by function and level. Furthermore, best-practice companies tend to use fewer competencies, feeling that simplicity and focus are stronger advantages than comprehensive efforts. Ideally, these models also contain 'derailing attributes' which provide a set of red flags to participants or reminders of the types of behaviors to avoid. In addition to competencies, there are tiered assessments of the readiness of an individual to be moved into a next position. These are staggered by 'readiness today', 'readiness in the near future', and 'readiness a year or two down the road'. People who might be ready to move into linchpin positions are identified. For the very top positions, there are position-specific determinations, but for the levels below, there are talent pools to ensure flexibility when it comes to needs.

After using the tools within the succession management process to identify future leaders, the next challenge is to organize high-potential talent. Talent pools increase the visibility of talent among the business units and provide a starting place for making decisions about talent movement. The size and scope of talent pools differ among organizations. For example, Dell uses two distinct pools, Eli Lilly uses four corporate pools, and Sonoco Products uses eight different pools. Within Dell's two pools, one is focused on talent at the corporate level while the other exists to classify talent at the business unit or functional levels. Employees designated as global corporate talent are profiled and reviewed by the Office of the Chief Executive and consist of individuals (fewer than 100) with the capability to run significant portions of a function or business and can leverage skills or experience on a global basis. Further, Dell tracks the movement and development of the global corporate talent pool on a quarterly basis and reports the results to the Office of the Chief Executive. Similarly, Dell's business units also have functional high-potential programs that identify talent deeper within their organizational structures. Unlike the global corporate talent pool, the functional high potentials are generally not reviewed during the Office of the Chief Executive presentations.

At Eli Lilly, the first two talent pools are the general manager and product team leader pools. They are composed of individuals who have cross-functional talent and can lead multiple disciplines. The third pool is for individuals who need an international assignment added to their experience base. The last pool moves individuals from function to function and develops behaviors. Individuals nominated for this pool must have at least director potential and must be supported by his or her home function.

### 5) Strong developmental linkages

The fifth dimension of an effective system is its developmental linkages. In other words, the system successfully identifies how positions are tied to an individual manager's development along with the superiors of those positions. It is critical that jobs identified for succession have specific opportunities related

to development. If a position is for a director level job for marketing in Shanghai, then what are the developmental opportunities that might lead up to that job? Stretch assignments also highlighted in terms of specific jobs. An effective succession system identifies shortages or gaps in the types of developmental experiences and jobs and is constantly working to increase the number of these. Finally, best-practice companies typically employ a wide range of developmental activities to engage leaders and extend their capabilities. While they believe that job assignments are the most significant developmental activity, many offer mentoring, coaching, and action learning along with educational programs to complement learning on the job.

### 6) Multiple stakeholder assessments with developmental feedback

The individuals who evaluate 'high potentials' and decide who gets promoted into what positions are major stakeholders in any succession management system. Multiple levels of assessors need to be involved. It is not simply an individual's superior who participates in the review, but also the superior's superior, and peers who possess a cross-functional perspective of a candidate's capabilities. Increasingly subordinates and external or internal customers are also involved in the assessment process.

Reviews include developmental dialogues with talent regarding their career interests and goals and the constraints they see. Individuals being assessed also receive information about suggested activities for further growth. These are complemented by individual developmental and career planning so that each participant is engaged to do reflective work. All of this is supplemented with feedback, such as 360-degree feedback, and coaching on the candidate's overall effectiveness in a particular job and his or her overall readiness to move to the next assignment.

The reviews and talent assessments of individual managers are rolled up the organization to assess the number of high potentials, how many of these are well placed, how many are ready for developmental assignments in the near term, and where are critical talent gaps and vulnerabilities. These reviews eventually reach up to the executive level so that the senior team has a good sense of the talent below them. For example, at the Bank of America, CEO Ken Lewis meets every summer with his top 24 executives to review the organizational health of the business. In two- to three-hour sessions with each executive, he probes the financial, operational, and people issues that will drive growth over the next 24 months, with the majority of time spent discussing the organizational structure, key players, and critical roles necessary to achieving the company's growth targets. These meetings are personal in nature, with no presentation decks or thick books outlining HR procedures, but they are rigorous. Business leaders come to the sessions with a concise document (three pages or less, to ensure simplicity) describing the unit's strengths and weaknesses in its talent pipeline. During these conversations, they make specific commitments regarding current or potential leaders – specifically identifying the next assignment, special projects, promotions, and the like. Lewis follows up with the executives in his quarterly business reviews, to ensure that they've fulfilled their commitments. In one of these talent review sessions last year, for example, one executive made a pitch to grow his business unit at a double-digit clip. This would require some shifts among top talent and a significant investment in building the sales and distribution workforce. Lewis agreed, and a year later in the talent review meeting, he requested specific progress reports relating to the change, checking that people had been put into the right roles and that the sales management ranks had been filled out.

### 7) Rigorous tracking and feedback metrics

Effective tracking in a succession system monitors progress and turnover. It records and analyzes exits of individuals who are talented and gaps at certain key levels and jobs, particularly lynchpin jobs. Two types of data are traditionally collected: *quantitative* data in terms of statistics of turnover and

placement rates, and *qualitative* data which analyzes why people are leaving, common problems that participants face in terms of their development and career progress, and dilemmas in using the succession system. Ideally, the tracking system also highlights the gap between planned assignments and actual assignments. This assessment enables top management to see whether or not the system is actually working according to the principles that guide it.

The use of technology for tracking in succession management varies widely within the best-practice organizations. Yet, Web-based systems seem to offer great potential for worldwide access and large-scale integration of data. The tracking process must be easy, accessible, and in an understandable format. For instance, Dell has moved from more extensive, global software applications to a much simpler MS Excel workbook to organize data.

In terms of metrics, there are generally two types: *individual* metrics, which rate the candidate on performance versus perceived potential, and metrics for the *overall system*, which highlight the number of openings that are successfully filled internally by the succession system. The latter highlights the number of individuals who are selected on the list of high potentials and who ultimately obtained jobs related to a targeted development assignment. There are also important metrics on diversity and cross-functional assignments that show how the organization is fulfilling key goals involving under represented segments of the workforce and general management development through multiple functional assignments.

Finally, there should be tracking systems and metrics that allow sponsors and owners to determine whether or not the succession system is working effectively to develop an adequate supply of leadership talent. For example, firms such as Dow and Eli Lilly measure the portion of key jobs that are filled by insider versus outsider candidates. Both firms believe that going outside the organization on a regular basis for key talent indicates that succession management is not working properly. Conversely, if all openings are filled by internal candidates, an organization might worry about not getting enough new perspectives into the ranks.

## CONCLUSION

At the foundation of the shift toward a more strategic approach to succession management is a belief that leadership talent directly affects the performance of the organization. This belief sets up a mandate for the organization – to get, promote, and keep leadership talent, which requires focusing with a 'talent mindset' on the part of the organization's most senior leaders. They must feel comfortable talking about their A-level talent as well as their low performers. Top performers must be rewarded with opportunities and stretch assignments while immediate action must be taken to address low performing talent. In contrast, many organizations have a tolerance for lower performers, but these individuals have important ramifications for succession management beyond the traditional measures of performance such as productivity. Sub-par talent can block key developmental positions. They may hamper the overall succession management process as their failure to develop subordinates properly can drive away high potential people. Top performing talent desire top performing superiors and great challenges at a fast pace. In closing our discussion, one of the most important underlying lessons is that good succession management is possible only in an organizational culture that encourages candor and a developmental mindset at the executive level. It also depends upon a deep comfort with differentiating individual performance and in turn a corporate culture where the truth is more highly valued than politeness or tolerance for average or poor performance.

## REFERENCES

Fulmer, R.M. and Conger, J.A. (2004) *Growing Your Company's Leaders: How Great Organizations Use Succession Management to Sustain Competitive Advantage.* New York: AMACON.

McCall, M. (1988) *Lessons of Experience: How Successful Executives Develop on the Job.* New York: Free Press.

Michaels, E., Handfield-Jones, H. and Axelrod, B. (2001) *The War for Talent.* Boston: Harvard Business School Press.

Rothwell, W.J. (2001) *Effective Succession Planning.* New York: AMACON.

# 15

# Rethinking Leadership and Followership

David Collinson

## INTRODUCTION

There is a growing challenge to the hegemony of US-centric leadership studies (Collinson and Grint, 2005). From a macro perspective, it is increasingly evident that leadership and followership dynamics take quite different forms in different societies (Bjerke, 1999) and that US cultural values cannot be transposed in any simple way to leadership theory, development and practice in other contexts. The multiple identities, values and cultures of followers (and leaders) in various diverse regions, societies and continents are likely to have a significant impact on the possibilities and limits of leadership practices. For example, whilst Western and North American societies typically subscribe to meritocratic principles based on individual achievement, Asian and Eastern societies adhere to more collectivist and ascriptive values that privilege, for example, kinship and age. Regions continue to be critical, but often neglected, units of analysis for cross-border, 'macro' leadership strategies. Ghemawat (2005) highlights the importance

of geographic, cultural, administrative and economic proximity for effective global leadership.

In his cross-cultural anthropological analysis of leadership development programmes in the US, Europe and China, Jones (2006) points to the disproportionate influence of US programmes in the global economy. He argues that US leader development focuses on individuals' self-knowledge, reflexivity and self-improvement. Jones suggests that this individualistic 'science of self' is informed by the cultural history of the US with its mythical heroes from the hunter-trapper to the Indian fighter, through the John Wayne cowboy figure, to the charismatic business entrepreneur.

Yet even in the US context, there is growing discontent about mainstream leadership thinking, particularly with regard to analysing relations between leaders and followers. Mintzberg (2006) has recently criticized the obsession with heroic leaders and its underlying 'syndrome of individuality' that, he believes, is undermining organizations and communities. For Mintzberg, the increasing tendency to try to separate leadership from management, results in the problem of 'macro managing' where senior managers remain highly detached, pronouncing from 'on high' their strategic intentions and abstract performance standards, whilst leaving others to implement their visions. Mintzberg argues in favour of 'communityship', of rethinking organizations as communities of cooperation and of encouraging distributed leadership where leadership roles are more fluid and shared by various people according to their capabilities.

Central to leaders' relations with followers is the issue of power. Gordon (2002) observes that, alongside the tendency to marginalize followers, questions of power have been largely overlooked in leadership studies. He argues that assumptions about a leaders' right to power and dominance are embedded at a deep structural level in most, if not all, organizations. This chapter highlights the value of rethinking leadership and followership in terms of their underlying power relations. Drawing on critical, post-structuralist and feminist insights, it examines the (neglected) importance of power for understanding leadership processes and outlines the need for more integrated analyses of leadership and followership. The chapter also seeks to examine these leadership power dynamics through dialectical perspectives that focus on the simultaneous interdependencies and asymmetries between leaders and followers as well as their ambiguous and potentially contradictory conditions, processes and consequences.

## MAINSTREAM PERSPECTIVES

A burgeoning literature now exists on the theory and practice of leadership. Much of this US-dominated, psychologically informed literature has produced useful insights about individual leaders' behaviours and competencies. However, in their concern to produce law-like, universal generalizations about what might constitute effective leadership, studies have tended to elevate and privilege leaders

to the neglect of both their relations with 'followers' and of wider economic, social, political, cultural and technological contexts.

It is often stated that the essence of leadership is followership, that without followers leaders do not exist and that leadership only exists in the interaction between leaders and followers. Yet, the full implications of these frequently articulated dictums have rarely been incorporated into leadership studies. Over the past 50 years, leadership researchers have developed numerous theories, most of which concentrate on leaders themselves and the qualities and behaviours deemed necessary to be an 'effective' leader. Informed mainly by functionalist assumptions,[1] the key concern of mainstream researchers has been what makes an effective leader? Yet, persuasive answers have proved elusive, findings have been inconclusive.

Situational leadership holds that 'effective leaders' should communicate by deploying a mix of directive and supportive behaviours compatible with followers' 'developmental levels' (e.g., Hersey and Blanchard, 1996). Path-goal theory suggests that leaders must choose leadership styles best suited to followers' experience, needs, and skills (e.g., House, 1971). Leader-member exchange theory observes that leaders tend to be open and trusting with 'in-group' followers, but distant with 'out-group' members (e.g., Graen and Uhl-Bien, 1995). Recent interest in 'emotional intelligence' suggests that effective leaders need to develop greater awareness of the emotional dynamics of leadership processes (e.g., Goleman, 2002).

Informed by the idea that leadership is primarily a group process, social identity theorists argue that leadership is contingent upon the degree to which leaders are perceived as 'prototypical' of the group's identity (e.g., van Knippenberg and Hogg, 2003). They predict that followers will endorse leaders who quintessentially embody the values of the group (Hogg, 2001). Identity construction is also central to Gardner and Avolio's (1998) focus on leaders' influence tactics through impression management (framing, scripting, staging and performing). Suggesting that leaders' own life histories can be a significant source of influence over followers, Shamir *et al.* (2005) illustrate how leaders can strategically construct their biographies to convey predefined messages.

Writers on transformational studies argue that charismatic leaders can inspire followers to greater commitment by satisfying their needs, values, and motivations (e.g., Burns, 1978). They also suggest that effective leaders should transform followers' identity (Lord and Brown, 2003). Arguing that people are motivated by concerns to express themselves and enhance self-esteem, these writers contend that charismatic leaders can validate followers' identities by, for example, acting as role models and encouraging followers' psychological identification and value internalization (Shamir *et al.*, 1993). From this perspective, leadership is defined as an influence process through which the leader changes the way followers envision themselves (e.g., by shifting the salience of different elements of subordinates' identities or by creating new aspects of their self-concept).

The foregoing approaches prioritize leaders, whilst addressing followers only in relation to their susceptibility to certain leader behaviours or styles.[2] In their search to render leadership a predictable practice and leadership studies a prescriptive endeavour, mainstream approaches tend to portray followers as 'an empty vessel waiting to be led, or even transformed, by the leader' (Goffee and Jones, 2001: 148) and tend to neglect important issues of power that lie at the heart of leadership dynamics.

## ROMANTICISM, DUALISM AND DIALECTICS

Meindl *et al.* (1985) were early critics of this tendency to 'romanticize leaders', either by crediting leaders for high organizational performance or by holding them personally responsible for workplace failures. Arguing that we have developed overly heroic and exaggerated views of what leaders are able to

achieve, they suggested that leaders' contribution to a collective enterprise is inevitably somewhat constrained and closely tied to external factors outside a leaders' control, such as those affecting whole industries. In his later work, Meindl developed a 'follower-centric perspective' (1995: 329) in which he recommended that researchers should no longer be concerned *at all* with leaders. Rather, he asserted that we should concentrate exclusively on followers' (romanticized) attributions of (charismatic) leaders and their views of themselves as followers, primarily for what they reveal about their own thought systems.

The critique of leadership romanticism has been particularly influential in developing a growing interest in followership (e.g., Shamir *et al.*, 2007). An increasing number of writers argue that 'exemplary', 'courageous' and 'star' followers are a precondition for high performing organizations (e.g., Chaleff, 2003; Kelley, 2004). These writers see 'effective followership' as particularly important in the contemporary context of greater team working, 'empowered' knowledge workers and distributed leadership (Raelin, 2003). Yet, rather than replace a 'leader-centric' approach with a 'follower-centric' analysis, as Meindl advocates, this chapter argues for a more dialectical understanding of the complex interactions between leaders and followers.

A number of critical leadership writers question the 'dualism' or false dichotomy underpinning the mainstream 'heroic' approach that conflates leadership with leaders and marginalizes followers (Gronn, 2002). Gordon (2002) argues that traditional studies take on a dualistic orientation in which leaders are privileged and given voice while followers are subordinated and rendered silent. He argues that the historical constitution of this differential in power between leaders and followers has resulted in mainstream theorists viewing leaders' apparent superiority as 'natural' and unproblematic. Furthermore, he suggests that emerging forms of dispersed leadership require new ways of conceiving leadership power relations. Fairhurst (2001) highlights the 'primary dualism' in leadership research as that between the individual and the collective, arguing that studies typically concentrate either on leaders, in ways that overlook the dynamics of the collective, or on the latter, thereby neglecting the former's basis for action. By contrast, she advocates dialectical approaches to leadership exploring the dynamic tension and interplay between seemingly oppositional binaries.

Debates about dualism(s) and dialectics have a longer history in social theory (e.g., the work of Hegel, Marx, Adorno and Derrida) and (to a lesser extent) in organization studies (Mumby and Stohl, 1991; Knights, 1997; Reed, 1997).[3] Giddens' structuration theory (1984, 1987) seeks to overcome the individual/society dualism by rethinking the 'dialectics of power relations'. He argues that human beings are knowledgeable social agents who, acting within historically specific (unacknowledged) conditions and (unintended) consequences, always retain a capacity to 'make a difference'. Rejecting more deterministic accounts in social theory, Giddens' 'dialectic of control' holds that, no matter how asymmetrical, power relations are always two-way, contingent and to some degree interdependent.

With regard to leadership an important implication of the dialectic of control is that leader-led relations are likely to be characterized by interdependencies and power asymmetries. Since power relations are always two-way, leaders will remain dependent to some extent on the led, while followers retain a degree of autonomy and discretion. If we rethink followers as knowledgeable agents, we can begin to see them as proactive, self-aware and knowing subjects who have at their disposal a repertoire of possible agencies within the workplace. Accordingly, power relations between leaders and followers are likely to be interdependent as well as asymmetrical and contested.

Seeking to develop a dialectical approach to understanding leadership power relations, the following sections now consider the inter-related dialectics of control/resistance, consent/dissent and men/women, highlighting

these as important, persistent and mutually reproducing features of leadership-followership dynamics.

## CONTROL/RESISTANCE

Mainstream leader- or follower-centred approaches share a tendency to underestimate questions of control and resistance (Ray et al., 2004). Assuming that the interests of leaders and followers automatically coalesce, orthodox studies view power and control as unproblematic forms of organizational authority whilst treating resistance as abnormal or irrational. Mainstream studies typically define leadership in terms of 'influence' (positive) and distinguish this from power (negative). In so doing, they fail to appreciate that the former may be one aspect of the latter. By contrast, a small number of more critical leadership studies recognize the importance of power.[4]

Informed by various perspectives (from labour process theory to radical psychology and post-structuralism), critical leadership writers recognize that leaders' power can take multiple economic, political, ideological and psychological forms (Grint, 2005). They show how control is not so much a 'dependent variable' as a deeply embedded and inescapable feature of leadership structures, cultures and practices. Indeed, leaders in organizations can exercise power and control in many ways, for example, by constructing corporate visions, shaping structures and cultures, intensifying and monitoring work, providing rewards, applying sanctions, and by making key strategic HR decisions and through hiring and firing. They can also exercise power by 'managing meaning' and defining situations in ways that suit their purposes (Smircich and Morgan, 1982).

Power is also an important concept within critical, post-structuralist organization studies (Hardy and Clegg, 1999). Influenced by Foucault's (1977, 1979) ideas, post-structuralists examine the ways that 'power/knowledge' regimes are inscribed on subjectivities. Foucault explored the 'disciplinary power' of surveillance that produces detailed information about individuals, rendering them visible, calculable and self-disciplining selves. He argued that by shaping identity formation, power is enabling and productive as well as subordinating. Foucault also highlighted the dialectic between power and resistance, asserting that 'resistance is never in a position of exteriority to power' (1979: 95). Even in the most totalitarian of power regimes, cleavages and contradictions arise that provide opportunities for resistance, especially in the form of localized acts of defiance. As Foucault argued, 'where there is power, there is resistance' (1979: 95).

Accordingly, post-structuralists assert that power/resistance are mutually implicated, co-constructed and interdependent processes that have multiple, ambiguous and contradictory meanings and consequences (Mumby, 2005). Viewing control and resistance as discursive and dialectical practices, they argue that the meanings of such practices are to some extent open-ended, precarious, shifting and contingent. From this perspective, power is seen as both disciplinary and enabling while practices of control and resistance are viewed as mutually reinforcing and simultaneously linked, often in contradictory ways (Collinson, 1992, 1994).

There is a considerable literature in organization studies indicating that forms of control (particularly coercive practices) can produce follower resistance. These studies suggest that followers are frequently more knowledgeable and oppositional than has typically been acknowledged in the leadership literature (either by leader-centric or follower-centric studies). Researchers have often drawn on Hirschman's (1970) ideas to argue that resistance enables subordinates to 'voice' dissent (e.g., Graham, 1986). Hirschman argued that in conditions of organizational decline individuals are likely either to resign (exit) or try to change (voice) products or processes they find objectionable. He suggested that voice is less likely where exit is possible and more likely where loyalty is present and when exit opportunities are limited.[5]

Critical researchers in organization studies reveal that oppositional practices can take numerous forms (Ackroyd and Thompson, 1999), including strikes, 'working to rule', output restriction, 'working the system', 'whistleblowing' and sabotage (Edwards et al., 1995). In exceptional cases, subordinates may even (seek to) depose leaders (Mole, 2004). Even in the military, there is a long history of outright rebellion, mutiny and spontaneous acts of 'follower' dissent (Prince, 1998). Through oppositional practices followers express discontent, exercise a degree of control over work processes and/or construct alternative, more positive identities to those prescribed by the organization (Jermier et al., 1994).

Clearly, not all follower dissent is aimed specifically at leaders. Moreover, followers do not invariably seek to resist those in leadership positions. In many everyday workplace settings, employees are concerned less with opposition and more with performing well and meeting expectations about their job performance. Indeed, research suggests that followers value leaders who exercise control and take responsibility and do so in clear, fair and transparent ways (Kouzes and Posner, 2004; Collinson and Collinson, 2005).[6] Employee resistance is more likely to emerge when they believe that leaders are exercising control in unfair, dictatorial, coercive, nepotistic, narcissistic and/or self-interested ways. Lipmen-Blumen (2005) argues that such 'toxic leaders' display dysfunctional personal characteristics such as lack of integrity, insatiable ambition, enormous egos, arrogance, reckless disregard for the effects of their actions on others and cowardice (e.g., the recent case of Enron).

Critical studies indicate that followers are much more likely to resist when they feel that their views have not been considered, when they perceive leaders to be 'out of touch' and when they detect discrepancies between leaders' policies and practices. Where followers perceive such inconsistencies, they can become increasingly cynical about leaders. Fleming's (2005) research in an Australian call centre found that, in the face of a corporate culture which treated workers like children, cynicism enabled employees to construct a new, opposing identity. Employees in a US Subaru Isuzu plant detected inconsistencies between the company's team working ideal and work intensification. Consequently they refused to participate in corporate rituals, sent highly critical anonymous letters to the company and used humour to make light of the company's team-working and continuous improvement philosophies (Graham, 1995).

In my own research over the past 25 years in various UK organizations, follower resistance has routinely emerged and has often been aimed specifically at leaders (Collinson, 2005a). While subordinates have complained about leaders being 'distant', their views of leaders have often been quite different to those which leaders hold of themselves. Employees have expressed considerable frustration that their voice is ignored, that they have suggestions on how to improve workplace processes, but that those in senior positions will not listen to their proposals. In such cases, followers can start to believe that it is impossible to achieve positive change and consequently may psychologically withdraw from the organization.

Research in a UK truck manufacturer demonstrated that a corporate culture campaign introduced by the new US senior management team to establish trust with the workforce had precisely the opposite effect (Collinson, 2006). Shopfloor workers dismissed senior management's definition of the company as a team. Fuelled by their perceptions of leaders' distance, managers' apparent disregard for workers' views, and their own sense of job insecurity, employees resisted by 'distancing' themselves, restricting output and effort, and by treating work purely as a means of economic compensation. The company's leaders remained unaware of how their strategies produced contrary effects on the shopfloor. This study showed how control and resistance can be embedded within a complex, mutually-reinforcing and dialectical vicious circle.

Post-structuralist studies suggest that follower dissent may be even more diverse than previously recognized and may be aimed at multiple audiences, such as the media (Real and Putnam, 2005) and customers (Leidner, 1993). Those working outside organizations can also express dissent. The campaign against Shell's plans to dispose of the obsolete Brent Spar platform by sinking it into the Atlantic Ocean illustrates how (external) resistance can change leaders' practices. After a Europe-wide boycott of their petrol stations, Shell eventually dismantled the platform on land in Norway. Klein (2000) has explored global protests against the leadership of the World Bank, the IMF and the World Trade Organization as well as more specific campaigns against companies like Nike, Reebock, McDonalds and Pepsi. The oppositional 'voices' of these 'external followers' may be less constrained than those of employees who are inevitably more 'disciplined' by employment contracts.

## DISSENT/CONSENT

Where subordinates are particularly concerned to avoid sanctions, they may resist in disguised and partial ways that blur the boundaries between dissent and consent. While (employed) followers might be highly critical of leaders' practices, they may decide to censor their views and camouflage their actions through a kind of resistance that 'covers its own tracks' (Scott, 1985). One of the reasons why opposition may be limited is because those who resist anticipate the disciplinary sanctions their actions may provoke and shape their actions accordingly. As Heifetz and Laurie (1997: 129) observe in their study of leadership, 'whistle-blowers, creative deviants and other such original voices routinely get smashed and silenced in organizational life'.

Subtle and routine subversions such as absenteeism (Edwards and Scullion, 1982), 'foot dragging' (Scott, 1990), 'disengagement' (Prasad and Prasad, 1998) and even irony and satire (Collinson, 2002) can be disguised and ambiguous, making them difficult for leaders to detect. Employees may even undermine leaders' change initiatives simply by doing nothing. Such inertia can result in leaders making all sorts of errors (Grint, 2005). Indeed in certain cases, even worker accommodation with managerial objectives can enable them to reassert control and conceal their resistance within the appearance of consent.

My own research suggests that disguised dissent is particularly likely to occur where surveillance has become increasingly pervasive, for example, where hierarchical control is being reconfigured through performance targets. As a consequence of their increased awareness of being monitored, followers may engage in ambiguous oppositional practices that embody elements of both dissent and consent. In particular, they may conceal and massage knowledge and information. Under the gaze of authority, individuals are increasingly aware of themselves as visible objects and, as a consequence, they can become increasingly skilled choreographers of self and information, learning to disguise their response to 'the gaze'.[7]

Research on North Sea oil installations found that, despite extensive leadership commitment to safety, many offshore workers were either not reporting accidents and 'near misses' or else they sought to downplay the seriousness of particular incidents (Collinson, 1999). While company leaders talked proudly about the organization's 'learning culture', offshore workers complained about a 'blame culture' on the platforms. Believing that disclosure of accident-related information would have a detrimental impact on their appraisal and consequently pay and employment security, offshore workers felt compelled to conceal or downplay information about accidents, injuries and near misses. Precisely because such practices constituted a firing offence, these workers also disguised their under-reporting. When a report based on these findings was presented to the company's senior managers, they expressed considerable surprise and their reaction illustrates how corporate leaders can become detached from followers and divorced from the realities of production.[8]

While the mainstream leadership literature tends to assume that it is primarily leaders who use impression management, a post-structuralist approach highlights the importance of followers' disguised dissent. Such dramaturgical practices can take primarily conformist (e.g., telling leaders what they want to hear) or more oppositional forms (e.g., knowledge and output restriction). They may also embody elements of both conformity and resistance. Accordingly, workplace power asymmetries can generate subtle forms of disguised dissent. Rather than being polarized extremes, dissent and consent may be inextricably linked within the same practices. This focus on the power/resistance dialectic does not imply that followers will invariably engage in resistance (in a kind of mechanical or predetermined way), or that their opposition is necessarily effective. Control may produce compliance and even conformity, while resistance can also have unintended and contradictory consequences.

From a feminist post-structuralist perspective, Kondo (1990) criticizes the tendency artificially to separate conformity or resistance into 'crisply distinct categories'. Arguing that there is no such thing as an entirely 'authentic' or 'pristine space of resistance' or of a 'true resister' (1990: 224), she contends that people 'consent, cope, and resist at different levels of consciousness at a single point in time' (1990: 224). Kondo's observations problematize the meaning of the term 'resistance' and warn us about the dangers of romanticizing followers' practices as well as those of leaders. While earlier radical writers might have been inclined to 'celebrate' workplace resistance, Kondo cautions against this tendency automatically to impute a subversive or emancipatory motive or outcome to resistance. Her analysis also highlights the importance of gender for understanding the control/resistance and consent/dissent dialectics of leadership.

## MEN/WOMEN

Feminist post-structuralist researchers argue that gender is a very important and frequently neglected feature of leadership dynamics. Observing that men tend to remain dominant in leadership positions, they reveal how masculinity continues to inform the models, styles, language, cultures, identities and practices of leadership (Collinson and Hearn, 1996). Since people are inherently gendered beings, the dialectic between men and women, masculinity and femininity is an inescapable feature of leadership dynamics. Bowring (2004) emphasizes that the binary opposition between leaders and followers is reinforced by a gender dualism in which men are viewed as the universal, neutral subject and women as 'the other'. She argues that we need to move towards greater fluidity in leadership research by recognizing that people have multiple, inter-related and shifting identities.

Post-structuralist gender studies illustrate how certain gendered, ethnic and class-based voices are routinely privileged in the workplace, whilst others are marginalized (Ashcraft and Mumby, 2004). Research on gender highlights the embedded-ness of masculine assumptions in organizational power relations, identities and practices. There is increasing recognition that the workplace is an important site for the reproduction of men's masculine power and status. Research suggests that masculinity can be embedded in formal organizational practices (e.g., recruitment and promotion) through to more informal, cultural dynamics (e.g., the social construction of skill). Central to men's valorization of 'work' is also a close identification with machinery and technology. Masculine dynamics at work can also be reproduced through men's sexuality and the sexual harassment of women. Writers illustrate how managerial control is often sustained through the gendered segregation of jobs. While romanticized notions of the heroic, 'tough' leader are saturated with masculinity, women continue to be largely excluded from senior positions (Sinclair, 1998). Male leaders' preoccupation with gender control can even be prioritized above (and be in conflict with) their commercial concerns (Collinson et al., 1990).

Post-structuralist feminist research demonstrates that resistance practices can also take gendered forms (e.g., Trethewey, 1997). Various studies reveal, for example, how male-dominated shop floor counter-cultures are frequently characterized by highly masculine breadwinner identities, aggressive and profane forms of humour, ridicule and sarcasm and the elevation of 'practical', manual work as a confirmation of working-class manhood and opposition to management (Willis, 1977).[9] Research also addresses the contradictions of subordinate resistance. Cockburn (1983) illustrates how male-dominated shop-floor counter-cultures can elevate men and masculinity whilst subordinating women and femininity. Willis (1977) describes how working-class 'lads' creatively constructed a counter-culture that celebrated masculinity and the so-called freedom and independence of manual work. Yet, this counter-culture facilitated the lads' smooth transition into precisely the kind of shop-floor work that then subordinated them, possibly for the rest of their working lives. This focus on the consequences of employee resistance avoids an overly romanticized interpretation that merely 'celebrates' rather than critically examines follower opposition (Collinson, 1992).

A small number of recent feminist post-structuralist studies focus specifically on leadership issues. They suggest that it is not merely followers but also those (broadly) defined as occupying leadership positions who may engage in resistance in seeking to promote change. Sinclair (2007) focuses on the 'subversive leadership' of two Australian leaders, a woman Chief Commissioner of Police and an aboriginal school principal who achieved radical change in moribund systems. Meyerson (2001) shows how senior managers can attempt to effect (gender) change whilst working within the organization. 'Tempered radicals' are frequently women in senior positions who are committed to their organization but also to a cause that is fundamentally at odds with the dominant workplace culture.

Seeking to maintain a delicate balance between pursuing change, whilst also avoiding marginalization, tempered radicals have to cope with various tensions and contradictions between potentially opposing 'personal' and 'professional' identities.

Ashcraft's (2005) research reveals how airline captains engaged in subversive practices but in this case their intentions were to undermine a change programme and to preserve their power and identity. Viewing the corporate enactment of a 'crew empowerment system' as a threat to their masculine authority and identity, pilots utilized numerous strategies to resist their loss of control, whilst also giving the appearance of supporting this change programme. These predominantly white professional men resisted the erosion of their authority by apparently consenting whilst actually resisting.

These studies reveal how resistance can symbolically invert the values and meanings of society and organization, but in ways that sometimes cut across emancipatory agendas, (unintentionally) reinforcing the status quo. A post-structuralist approach suggests that apparently oppositional practices may actually reinforce the very (dualistic) conditions that stimulated resistance in the first place. In turn, this raises important questions for critical leadership studies about the meaning of resistance, about who resists, how, why and when they do so, what strategies inform their practices, and what outcomes ensue.

Post-structuralist feminist studies also raise important questions about how to theorize the inter-relations between multiple leadership dialectics. There remains a significant challenge to show how these multiple dialectics relate to one another and intersect. Such challenges become even more acute when we start to take account of other important aspects of power, identity and diversity like race and ethnicity and recognize these as key aspects of leadership dialectics. Such differences and inequalities can take multiple forms (e.g., gender, ethnicity, age, disability, faith, sexual orientation, class, national origin, etc.) and different aspects of identity may be assessed by those in leadership positions in ways that reproduce disadvantage. In addition to the theoretical challenges they pose, these arguments highlight the need to develop new forms of more inclusive and integrated leadership practices that value diversity and difference.

To be sure, the three dialectics discussed here of power/resistance, consent/dissent and men/women should neither be reified and separated nor seen as exhaustive of the diverse dialectics in which leadership is situated. Rather, we need to rethink leadership and followership dynamics in ways that can incorporate these and other dialectics, to explore how they may be mutually reinforcing and/or might cut across and be in tension with one another. Suffice it to say here, that post-structuralist feminism draws our attention to the multiplicity of leadership dialectics and the need to find new ways to theorize these ambiguous and potentially contradictory inter-relations.

## CONCLUSION

This chapter has sought to rethink leadership and followership in terms of their power relations. Drawing on post-structuralist analysis, it has argued that dialectical perspectives, in particular, can facilitate new ways of thinking about the complex, shifting dynamics of leadership. This dialectical approach recognizes that leaders exercise considerable control and that their power can also have contradictory outcomes which leaders either do not always understand or of which they are unaware. Control and resistance are therefore viewed as mutually reinforcing, ambiguous and potentially contradictory processes.

While followers can express opposition in numerous ways, they often seek to protect themselves from sanctions. Leadership studies tend to assume that it is primarily leaders who use impression management. Yet, far from being passive 'followers' whose identities are shaped by charismatic leaders, employees at various hierarchical levels may manipulate information and identities to disguise their dissent. Equally, while control can stimulate resistance, it may also discipline, shape and restrict the very opposition it has provoked. Disguised dissent incorporates self-protective practices that may conceal opposition within ambiguous practices that blur boundaries between resistance and consent. These arguments, in turn, raise a number of under-explored issues about what it may mean to be a 'leader' and a 'follower' in contemporary organizations.

First, a dialectical approach questions the prevailing view that leader-led relations are inherently consensual. The legacy of orthodox studies is a rather uncontested notion of leadership. Yet, in leader-follower relations there is always the potential for conflict and dissent. Leaders cannot predict or assume followers' motivations, obedience or loyalty. Given the asymmetrical nature of workplace power, it is hardly surprising that followers often do conform or comply, but from a leadership point of view we need to know a lot more about the conditions and consequences of such practices. For example, when leaders surround themselves with sycophants and stifle dialogue, new ideas may well be blocked (Bratton *et al.*, 2004).

Second, post-structuralist feminist analyses highlight the gendered nature of these ambiguous and contradictory leader/follower, power/resistance, and consent/dissent dialectics. They demonstrate that leadership dynamics are inescapably situated within, and reproduced through multiple dialectics. Complex questions about how we theorize the interrelations between multiple dialectics are raised by such dialectics. It is quite possible for researchers in challenging one dualism to reproduce others. Just as resistance may paradoxically reproduce the very conditions that give rise to opposition, critical leadership studies may question certain dualisms, but in ways that reproduce other dichotomies. For example, while some critical researchers challenge the leader/follower dualism, they simultaneously neglect important relations between power and resistance and/or gender and/or identity and so on. Accordingly, addressing the diversity of these dialectics as well as finding ways to theorize their

interrelations remains a pressing challenge for leadership studies.

Third, there is a need to develop more nuanced accounts of the diverse economic, social, political and cultural contexts that typically reflect and reinforce leadership dynamics. For example, technological advances in communications and transportation increase the potential for cross-cultural interactions in all types of organizations. Globalization may facilitate trade and global capital flows, more integrated financial markets and reduce transportation costs (Bratton *et al.*, 2005). In the search for lower production and distribution costs, transnational corporations can transfer parts of their processes to other parts of the globe. These shifting local, regional, national and global contexts require more detailed analysis by leadership scholars.

Finally, a dialectical approach also raises questions about leaders' and followers' identities. The notions of 'the leader' and 'the follower' are deeply embedded identities, especially in Western societies (Sinclair, 2007). Yet, there is a growing concern that such traditional dualisms are no longer sustainable. Leadership power relations and identities are increasingly blurred and contradictory (Gordon, 2002). For example, whilst distributed leadership principles encourage followers to act as 'informal leaders', leaders in many contemporary organizations are subject to intensified pressures of accountability that render them 'calculable followers'. Accordingly, there is a need for more research to examine these multiple, shifting, and often simultaneous identities of 'leaders' and 'followers'. Exploring how these ambiguous subjectivities are negotiated in practice within contemporary power relations should further enhance our understanding of leadership dialectics.

## NOTES

1 Functionalism has been heavily criticized in social theory for interpreting conflict purely in terms of its contribution to social order and for aligning with the interests of the powerful. By also discounting

agents' reasons for their actions, functionalism, in Giddens' terms, tends to derogate the subject. Within leadership studies this deterministic tendency is particularly evident in the recurrent neglect of followers.

2 Situational leadership views followers through the static and objectified categories of 'enthusiastic beginners', 'disillusioned learners', 'reluctant contributors' and 'peak performers'. Path-goal theory treats leadership as 'a one way event – the leader affects the subordinate' (Northouse, 2004: 113). Leader-member exchange theory says little about the ways followers may influence the leader-member relationship or about the group and organizational dimensions of these relationships (Howell and Shamir, 2005). Transformational studies typically draw on highly gendered, heroic images of the 'great man', viewing leaders as dynamic agents of change and followers as passive and compliant.

3 Apparently opposing binaries can occur in many forms, including: rationality/emotion, material/symbolic, public/private, home/work, theory/practice, micro/macro and local/global. On the one hand, identifying structures, distinctions and boundaries is clearly important for making sense of the world, helping to create meaning and clarity (Surman, 2002: 221). Language itself typically embodies dualistic understandings based on subject-object separations (e.g., 'leader' and 'follower'). Yet, on the other hand, problems can arise when distinctions are reified as seemingly concrete, independent and ontological 'representations of reality', whilst interrelations and asymmetries are denied or underestimated.

4 However, some of these studies produce rather deterministic accounts that neglect follower resistance. Viewing leadership as a process of power-based reality construction, Smircich and Morgan (1982) conclude that leaders create situations in which followers are 'crippled' by powerlessness and are complicit in 'surrendering' their autonomy. Calas and Smircich (1991) contend that leaders are inevitably successful in 'seducing' followers. Gemmill and Oakley (1992) argue that 'leadership' induces 'massive learned helplessness' resulting in people becoming 'cheerful robots'.

5 Tending to neglect the asymmetrical power dynamics that can both stimulate and constrain follower dissent, Hirschman underestimates the costs and overestimates the possibilities for followers of both exit and voice. While he treats consumer and employee behaviour as synonymous, it is usually much easier for individuals to refuse to buy a product than it is to resign one's job. Assuming that managers will listen to employee voice and change their practices, Hirschman ignores the possibility of sanctions for those who risk dissent. Indeed where exit is possible, follower dissent may be more likely (rather than less, as Hirschman contends).

6 Some critical writers argue that, in their search for security, followers prefer the (perceived) safety of conformity to charismatic leaders, to whom they often attribute exceptional qualities through processes such as transference (Maccoby, 2007), fantasy (Gabriel, 1997), idealization (Shamir, 1999), seduction (Calas and Smircich, 1991) and reification (Gemmill and Oakley, 1992). While Milgram's (1963) experiments highlighted peoples' widespread willingness to obey authority, Fromm (1977) pointed to 'the fear of freedom' where individuals try to shelter in the perceived security of being told what to do and what to think, believing that this is a less threatening alternative to the responsibility of making decisions for themselves.

7 This dramaturgical notion of self applies Goffman's (1959) ideas of impression management to surveillance processes. Goffman argued that interaction is like an information game in which individuals strategically disclose, exaggerate, or deliberately downplay information.

8 The degree of leader 'distance' and 'proximity' is also a growing area of leadership research. Early writers argued that psychological leader distance was a precondition for sustaining charisma (Katz and Kahn, 1978). More recent research indicates that distance between leaders and led can take many different forms (e.g., Antonakis and Atwater, 2002). Distance may, for example, be social, hierarchical, physical and/or might be defined by interaction frequency. On the one hand, retaining a distance can be necessary for leaders to maintain a strategic overview, make 'hard' decisions and communicate 'difficult' information. On the other hand, however, leaders can become so detached from the led that their 'motivational' messages are no longer effective (Collinson, 2005b). Distance and proximity issues are particularly significant in the context of debates about global, regional and local leadership strategies.

9 Research on female-dominated shop-floors and offices suggests that women workers often engage in similarly aggressive, joking and sexualized cultures of resistance.

## REFERENCES

Ackroyd, S. and Thompson, P. (1999) *Organizational Misbehaviour*. London: Sage.

Antonakis, J. and Atwater, L. (2002) 'Leader distance: A review and a proposed theory', *Leadership Quarterly*, 13 (6): 673–704.

Ashcraft, K.L. (2005) 'Resistance through consent?', *Management Communication Quarterly*, 19 (1): 67–90.

Ashcraft, K.L. and Mumby, D.K. (2004) *Reworking Gender: a Feminist Communicology of Organization*. London: Sage.

Bjerke, B. (1999) *Business Leadership and Culture.* Cheltenham: Edward Elgar.

Bowring, M.A. (2004) 'Resistance is not futile: Liberating captain Janeway from the masculine-feminine dualism of leadership', *Gender, Work and Organization*, 11: 4381–405.

Bratton, J., Grint, K. and Nelson, D. (2005) *Organizational Leadership.* Mason, OH: South Western/ Thomson.

Burns, J.M. (1978) *Leadership.* New York: Harper Row.

Calas, M. and Smircich, L. (1991) 'Voicing seduction to silence leadership', *Organization Studies*, 12: 567–602.

Chaleff, I. (1995) *The Courageous Follower.* San Francisco, CA: Berrett-Koehler.

Chaleff, I. (2003) *The Courageous Follower*, 2nd edn. San Francisco, CA: Berrett-Koehler.

Cockburn, C. (1983) *Brothers.* London: Pluto.

Collinson, D. (1992) *Managing the Shopfloor: Subjectivity, Masculinity and Workplace Culture.* Berlin: Walter de Gruyter.

Collinson, D. (1994) 'Strategies of resistance: Power, knowledge and subjectivity in the workplace', in J. Jermier, D. Knights and W. Nord (eds) *Resistance and Power in Organizations.* London: Routledge, pp. 25–68. Republished in K. Grint (ed.) (2000) *Work and Society: A Reader.* Cambridge: Polity Press, pp. 163–198.

Collinson, D. (1999) 'Surviving the rigs: Safety and surveillance on north sea oil installations', *Organization Studies*, 20 (4): 579–600.

Collinson, D. (2002) 'Managing humour', *Journal of Management Studies*, 39 (2): 269–288.

Collinson, D.L. (2005a) 'Dialectics of leadership', *Human Relations*, 58 (11): 1419–1442.

Collinson, D. (2005b) 'Questions of distance', *Leadership*, 1 (2): 235–250.

Collinson, D.L. (2006) 'Rethinking followership: A post-structuralist analysis of follower identities', *The Leadership Quarterly*, 17 (2): 179–189.

Collinson, D. and Collinson, M. (2005) Blended Leadership. Centre For Excellence in Leadership Working Paper Series, Lancaster University.

Collinson, D. and Grint, K. (2005) 'Editorial introduction', *Leadership*, 1 (1): 5–9.

Collinson, D. and Hearn, J. (eds) (1996) *Men as Managers, Managers as Men: Critical Perspectives on Men, Masculinities and Managements.* London: Sage.

Collinson, D., Knights, D. and Collinson, M. (1990) *Managing to Discriminate.* London: Routledge.

Edwards, P.K.E. and Scullion, H. (1982) *The Social Organization of Industrial Conflict.* Oxford: Basil Blackwell.

Edwards, P.K., Collinson, D.L. and Della Rocca, G. (1995) 'Workplace resistance in Western Europe', *European Journal of Industrial Relations*, 1 (3): 283–316.

Fairhust, G.T. (2001) 'Dualisms in leadership research', in F.M. Jablin and L.L. Putnam (eds) *The New Handbook of Organizational Communication.* Thousand Oaks, CA: Sage, pp. 379–439.

Fleming, P. (2005) 'Metaphors of resistance', *Management Communication Quarterly*, 19 (1): 45–66.

Foucault, M. (1977) *Discipline and Punish.* London: Allen and Unwin.

Foucault, M. (1979) *The History of Sexuality.* London: Allen and Unwin.

Fromm, E. (1977) *The Fear of Freedom.* London: Routledge Kegan Paul.

Gabriel, Y. (1997) 'Meeting God: When organizational members come face to face with the supreme leader', *Human Relations*, 50 (4): 315–342.

Gardner, W.L. and Avolio, B.J. (1998) 'The charismatic relationship: A dramaturgical perspective', *Academy of Management Review*, 23: 32–58.

Gemmill, G. and Oakley, J. (1992) 'Leadership: An alienating social myth', *Human Relations*, 45 (2): 113–129.

Ghemawat, P. (2005) 'Regional strategies for global leadership', *Harvard Business Review*, December: 98–108.

Giddens, A. (1984) *The Constitution of Society.* Cambridge: Polity.

Giddens, A. (1987) *Social Theory and Modern Sociology.* Cambridge: Polity.

Goffee, R. and Jones, G. (2001) 'Followership: It's personal too', *Harvard Business Review*, 79 (11): 148.

Goffman, E. (1959) *The Presentation of Self in Everyday Life.* Harmondsworth: Penguin.

Goleman, D. (2002) *The New Leaders: Transforming the Art of Leadership into the Science of Results.* London: Time Warner.

Gordon, D. (2002) 'Conceptualising leadership with respect to its historical-contextual antecedents to power', *Leadership Quarterly*, 13 (2): 151–167.

Graen, G. and Uhl-Bien, M. (1995) 'Relationship-based approach to leadership: Development of leader-member exchange theory of leadership over 25 years', *Leadership Quarterly*, 6 (2): 219–247.

Graham, J.W. (1986) 'Principled organizational dissent', *Research in Organizational Behaviour*, 8: 1–52.

Graham, L. (1995) *On the Line at Subaru-Isuzu.* Ithaca: ILR Press.

Grint, K. (2005) *Leadership: Limits and Possibilities.* New York: Palgrave Macmillan.

Gronn, P. (2002) 'Distributed leadership as a unit of analysis', *Leadership Quarterly*, 13 (4): 423–452.

Hardy, C. and Clegg, S.R. (1999) 'Some dare call it power', in S.R. Clegg and C. Hardy (eds) *Studying Organization: Theory and Method.* London: Sage, pp. 368–387.

Heifetz R.A. and Laurie, D.L. (1977) 'The work of leadership', *Harvard Business Review*, Jan–Feb: 124–134.

Hersey, P. and Blanchard, K. (1996) *Management of Organizational Behaviour.* Englewood Cliffs, NJ: Prentice Hall.

Hirschman, A.D. (1996) *Exit, Voice and Loyalty.* Cambridge, MA: Harvard University Press.

Hogg, M. (2001) 'A social identity theory of leadership', *Personality and Social Psychology Review*, 5 (3): 184–200.

House, R. (1971) 'A path-goal theory of leadership: Lessons, legacy and a reformulated theory', *Leadership Quarterly*, 7 (3): 323–352.

Howell, J. and Shamir, B. (2005) 'The role of followers in the charismatic leadership process: Relationships and their consequences', *Academy of Management Review*, 30 (1): 96–112.

Jermier, J.M., Knights, D. and Nord, W.R. (eds) (1994) *Resistance and Power in Organisations.* London: Routledge.

Jones, A.M. (2006) 'Developing what? An anthropological look at the leadership development process across cultures', *Leadership*, 2 (4): 481–498.

Katz, D. and Kahn, R.L. (1978) *The Social Psychology of Organizations.* New York: Wiley.

Kelley, R.E. (2004) 'Followership', in *Berkshire Encyclopedia of World History.* Great Barrington: Sage Reference/Berkshire, pp. 504–513.

Klein, N. (2000) *No Logo.* London: Flamingo.

Knights, D. (1997) 'Organization theory in the age of deconstruction: Dualism, gender and postmodernism revisited', *Organization Studies*, 18 (1): 1–20.

Kondo, D.K. (1990) *Crafting Selves: Power, Gender and Discourses of Identity in a Japanese Workplace.* Chicago: University of Chicago Press.

Kouzes, J.M. and Posner, B.Z. (2004) 'Follower-oriented leadership', in *Berkshire Encyclopedia of World History.* Great Barrington: Sage Reference/Berkshire, pp. 494–499.

Leidner, R. (1993) *Fast Food, Fast Talk: Service Work and the Routinisation of Everyday Life.* Berkeley: University of California Press.

Lipmen-Blumen, J. (2005) *The Allure of Toxic Leaders.* Oxford: Oxford University Press.

Lord, R.G. and Brown, D.J. (2003) *Leadership Processes and Follower Self-identity.* Mahwah, NJ: Lawrence Erlbaum.

Maccoby, M. (2007) *Leaders We Need.* Boston, MA: Harvard Business School Press.

Meindl, J. (1995) 'The romance of leadership as a follower-centric theory: A social constructionist approach', *Leadership Quarterly*, 6 (3): 329–341.

Meindl, J., Ehrlich, S.B. and Dukerich, J.M. (1985) 'The romance of leadership', *Administrative Science Quarterly*, 30 (1): 78–102.

Meyerson, D.E. (2001) *Tempered Radicals.* Boston, MA: Harvard Business School.

Milgram, S. (1963) 'Behavioral study of obedience', *Journal of Abnormal and Social Psychology*, 69 (2): 137–143.

Mintzberg, H. (2006) 'The leadership debate with Henry Mintzberg: Community-ship is the answer', *The Financial Times*, October 23, 2006.

Mitchell, V. (1990) 'Everyday metaphors of power', *Theory and Society*, 19 (5): 545–578.

Mole, G. (2004) 'Can leadership be taught?', in J. Storey (ed.) *Leadership in Organizations.* London: Routledge, pp. 125–137.

Mumby, D. (2005) 'Theorizing resistance in organization studies', *Management Communication Quarterly*, 19 (1): 19–44.

Mumby, D. and Stohl, C. (1991) 'Power and discourse in organizational studies: Absence and the dialectic of control', *Discourse and Society*, 2 (3): 313–332.

Northouse, P.G. (2004) *Leadership Theory and Practice* (3rd edn). London: Sage.

Prasad, A. and Prasad, P. (1998) 'Everyday struggles at the workplace: The nature and implications of routine resistance in contemporary organizations', in P.A. Bamberger and W.J. Sonnenstuhl (eds) *Research in the Sociology of Organizations.* Stamford, CT: JAI, 15: pp. 225–257.

Prince, L. (1998) 'The neglected rules: On leadership and dissent', in A. Coulson (ed.) *Trust and Contracts: Relationships in Local Government Health and Public Services.* Bristol: The Polity Press, pp. 95–126.

Raelin, J. (2003) *Creating Leaderful Organisations.* San Francisco, CA: Berrett-Koehler.

Ray, T., Clegg, S. and Gordon, R. (2004) 'A new look at dispersed leadership: Power, knowledge and context', in J. Storey (ed.) *Leadership in Organizations.* London: Routledge, pp. 319–336.

Real, K. and Putnam, L. (2005) 'Ironies in the discursive struggle of pilots defending the profession', *Management Communication Quarterly*, 19 (1): 91–119.

Reed, M. (1997) 'In praise of duality', *Organization Studies*, 18 (1): 21–42.

Scott, J. (1985) *Weapons of the Weak: Everyday Forms of Peasant Resistance.* New Haven: Yale University Press.

Scott, J.C. (1990) *Domination and the Arts of Resistance.* New Haven: Yale University Press.

Shamir, B. (1999) 'Taming charisma for better understanding and greater usefulness: A response to Beyer', *The Leadership Quarterly*, 10 (4): 555–562.

Shamir, B., Dayan-Horesh, D. and Adler, D. (2005) 'Leading by biography: Towards a life-story approach to the study of leadership', *Leadership*, 1 (1): 13–29.

Shamir, B., House, R.J. and Arthur, M.B. (1993) 'The motivational effects of charismatic leadership: A self-based concept theory', *Organization Science*, 4 (4): 577–594.

Shamir, B., Pillai, R., Bligh, M. and Uhl-Bien, M. (2007) *Follower-Centred Perspectives on Leadership*. Greenwich, CT: Information Age.

Sinclair, A. (1998) *Doing Leadership Differently*. Melbourne: Melbourne University Press.

Sinclair, A. (2007) *Leadership for the Disillusioned*. London: Allen and Unwin.

Smircich, L. and Morgan, G. (1982) 'Leadership: The management of meaning', *The Journal of Applied Behavioural Science*, 18 (3): 257–273.

Surman, E. (2002) 'Dialectics of dualism: The symbolic importance of the home/work divide', *Ephemera*, 2 (3): 209–223.

Trethewey, A. (1997) 'Resistance, identity and empowerment: A postmodern feminist analysis of clients in a human service organization', *Communication Monographs*, 64: 281–301.

van Knippenberg, D. and Hogg, M. (eds) (2003) *Leadership and Power: Identity Processes in Groups and Organizations*. London: Sage.

Willis, P. (1977) *Learning to Labour*. Aldershot: Saxon House.

# PART THREE

# Macro-Organizational Behaviour and Key Practices

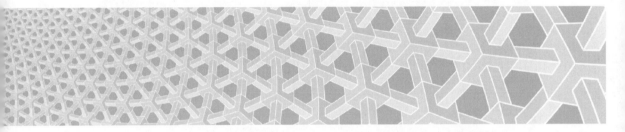

# 16

# The Labour Process, Surveillance, and the Person in the Sight of the Organization

Graham Sewell

## INTRODUCTION

The 'Labour Process' is a familiar term in industrial sociology and its related disciplines but mention it to specialists in organizational behaviour and you could well draw a blank. This is because orthodox labour process theory [LPT] consciously eschews the methodological individualism we associate with 'micro' approaches to organizational behaviour in favour of a methodological holism that attributes causal powers to social forces associated with aggregate social objects such as classes. This early reference to class is important for labour process theory in that it is signalling its alignment with a venerable intellectual tradition that has developed, on and off, since Karl Marx coined – or, at least popularized – the term, 'labour process', in *Capital*, his magnum opus of 1867. In an era where Marxist critique is no longer fashionable the main challenge for this chapter is to revisit the basic tenets of LPT under economic, organizational and technological conditions that bear little resemblance to those found in Victorian Britain. In this chapter I shall attempt to convince the reader that, by shifting its primary empirical focus from the disciplinary effect of bureaucratic control to a nuanced appreciation of the disciplinary effects of surveillance-based control systems, we can extend the usefulness of LPT well into the twenty-first century. In the process, I shall build an important bridge between our understanding of individual behaviour in the workplace and the operation of broader social forces we associate with late modernity. In this way it is hoped that the labour process can serve as a common focus for the 'micro' and the 'macro' traditions in organizational behaviour.

## LABOUR PROCESS THEORY: ORIGINS AND ANTECENDENTS

### A Fair Day's Work for a Fair Day's Pay? Time, Waged Labour, and the Origins of a Labour Theory of Value

Central to LPT is the understanding that modern work organizations are constituted through the operation of an employment relationship between a legal entity – whether it be known as the 'firm', the 'enterprise', the 'organization', or the 'employer' – and individual 'employees'. The employment relationship is normally governed by an explicit written contract that places certain expectations on employers and employees in terms of their conduct towards each other. In particular, the contract governs the employer's expectation of an employee's performance in his work role and, in return, the employee receives assurances about his terms, conditions and wages. This is so taken for granted by specialist scholars and lay people alike that we rarely reflect on the fact that it is a very recent development in human history. Of course, it is a truism to say that civilizations of the past must have had effective forms of organization to realize their great achievements – how could the pyramids of Geza have been built without coordinated human effort on the most massive scale? It is generally accepted by historians, however, that these achievements were founded on the extensive use of slavery and other forms of forced labour that reflected these civilizations' deep-seated customs and practices, as well as their economic reliance on imperial conquest. For example, the Athenians thought physical labour to be degrading and unbefitting of the free citizen; a convenient belief, of course, for an economic and political system based on slave holding (Westermann, 1955).

The ancient Greeks' well documented reliance on a complex and hierarchical system of forced labour – a combination of chattel slaves, debtor slaves, indentured labour, and serfdom (Westermann, 1955) – is not unusual among ancient civilizations and suggests the absence of the concept of waged labour (although Aristotle did develop a primitive labour theory of value). Setting out the circumstances under which slavery and, later, feudalism declined is crucial to my argument because the existence of waged labour is a *sine qua non* for Marx's conception of the labour process. There is much debate among historians about when and why waged labour emerged as an economic institution but there is some consensus that two momentous events propelled medieval Europe towards a proto-capitalist system where nominally free employees worked for employers in exchange for financial remuneration. The first is the Black Death in the middle of the fourteenth century. The massive decline in population (albeit uneven) caused a labour shortage that greatly disrupted the feudal system in Europe and also created the conditions where a minority of serfs became freemen and land-holders in their own right (in England there are many documented cases of serfs simply taking ownership of the fields they worked as their masters and fellow serfs died around them – Kelly, 2005). Although this labour scarcity forced land-owners to seek new ways of maintaining the productivity of their land it was not in itself a sufficient condition for the emergence of nominally free labour engaging in work effort in return for wages (for example, Saudi Arabia did not formally abolish slavery until 1962). Free labour required some notion of equivalence between effort (as measured by an input such as time spent labouring or an output such as productivity) and reward that allowed wages to be set. Again, although the exact details are historically controversial, there is a consensus that the Reformation played an important role in promulgating this notion throughout Protestant Europe. Max Weber (1894) famously observed that the Reformation was crucial in establishing an inner-worldly asceticism that provided the impetus for capitalism but equally important to Protestantism is the belief that one's salvation comes through a personal relationship with God, rather than simply through submitting oneself to the authority of the Church. An important corollary of this is that living a virtuous life becomes one's own responsibility. Even Protestant sects such as Calvinists who believed in predestination held that, because there was no way of telling who was a member of the elect and who was not, everyone should strive to live a life of virtue and hard work. Thus, financial success that was the result of one's own efforts came be to be seen as an outward symbol of virtuousness as well as a product of Weber's inner-worldly asceticism. This belief in the moral probity of worldly riches became a central element of the value theory of labour contained in John Locke's *Second Treatise on Government* (1690). Although primarily concerned with demonstrating that private property (in particular, cultivated land) was compatible with Protestant godliness, Locke noted that not only had God commanded man to labour since the Fall but '... the labour of his body and the work of his hands are properly his' (§26). From this observation he went on to argue that it was through labour that man transformed nature and thus imparted value to all things that did not occur naturally. He gave the simple example of picking up acorns that had fallen from an oak tree standing on common land – they were part of nature's bounty available to all but the act of labouring to pick them up imparted value on them and transformed them into a commodity. Because this labour was the possession of the labourer, acorns valorized in this way also legitimately became the property of the labourer. According to Locke, it was '... labour that puts the difference of value on all things' (§40), adding that when labour provided sustenance beyond subsistence levels then, 'by the common consent of men', this surplus value could be recognized and stored in the form of money. Importantly, not only did Locke's value theory legitimate the accumulation of private wealth but, at a time when for many centuries wages had been based on custom and tradition, it introduced in the public consciousness a consideration of the link between reward and effort at work (Thompson, 1963).

An important practical implication of this growing appreciation of the link between effort, reward, and the creation of value through labour can be seen in the development of penal institutions. This is doubly important from the perspective of this chapter because the emergence of the origin of the concept of the person in sight of the organization is also closely associated with the development of prisons where the behaviour of convicts became the focus of intense scrutiny by their captors (Melossi and Pavarini, 1981). For example, the sixteenth century Dutch *Rasphuis* – a form of hard labour where teams of convicts were put to work making sawdust using large two-handed saws – is a crucial historical moment in this nexus of the economic valorization of work effort and the control of human conduct in organizations. Of course, not only were the Dutch arch Protestants who fought a long and bloody war of independence against the Catholic Spanish around this period but they were also pioneers of early modern commerce. Thus, the principle of the *Rasphuis* sat well with Dutch religious and economic sensibilities.

Although the concept of a penal tariff that equates the severity of a crime with an amount of time needed for an offender to pay off their 'debt' to society is taken for granted today, this was a significant break from a European tradition where criminals were rarely incarcerated once they were convicted – as recently as the early nineteenth century an overwhelming majority of British convicts were either executed or transported to the colonies (Emsley, 1987). In this way, penal institutions can be seen as proto-modern organizations (Ignatieff, 1978) where familiar notions such as hierarchy, control, and subordination, which later became central to Marx's conception of the labour process, first took shape (Sewell, 2001). Nevertheless, it is fair to say that, however unruly they were, the majority of the population were unlikely to have direct experience of institutions of punishment and confinement such as prisons, bridewells, asylums, workhouses and lazarettos. Thus, it became crucial for the spread of modern organizations that the population be educated in the rhythms and cycles of industrial life (Mumford, 1934; Thompson, 1967). For example, Parisians in pre-revolutionary France enjoyed over 200 days a year where at least some of the local tradesmen, masters, and their apprentices were celebrating holidays (Treasure, 1985). In rural areas in Britain the story was similar with farm labourers being more accustomed to the longer rhythms of the changing seasons and what would be considered today as rather obscure religious holidays such as Rogation Days or Michaelmas instead of uniform 'factory time' (Thompson, 1967).

With the two necessary conditions of the capitalist labour process – a value-theory of labour based on nominally free employment governed by contract, combined with a uniform conception factory time – in place by the nineteenth century the time was ripe for critique of managerial control and employee subordination associated with industrial work. Of course, the huge economic, political and social upheaval of the Industrial Revolution made such a critique all the more pressing.

## Marx's critique of the capitalist labour process

Marx was not the first to offer a systematic critique of the early stages of modern capitalism. For example, a rich vein of proto-communistic thinking can be identified in post-revolutionary France where commentators such as the Comte de Saint-Simon (1760–1825) pointed out that the great mass of workers were free in name only when their only alternative was destitution. Charles Fourier (1772–1837) took these sentiments on board and incorporated them into his proposals for a form of cooperative and decentralized production where the full fruits of the participants' labour were distributed on the basis of need rather than ability. It was Fourier's insight – that workers received but a fraction of the value that their efforts created under capitalist production –

which was taken up with such penetrating force by Karl Marx (1818–1883). Reading Marx and Locke in parallel on labour as the source of value reveals that they had much in common, although their purposes were diametrically opposed. Unlike Locke and his successors (for example, Smith and Ricardo), who wanted to legitimate private property, Marx intended that his critique would demonstrate once and for all that capitalism was fundamentally exploitative and, in the process, would hasten the demise of a system based on the accumulation of private wealth. His explicit discussion of the labour process takes up only 10 of the 1000 plus pages of the first volume of *Capital* but the principles set out therein are central to his subsequent disquisition on the 'laws' of capitalist accumulation.

Marx begins his discussion of the labour process by drawing the important distinction between labour power (i.e., an individual's potential to labour) and labour power in use (i.e., the actual labour the individual ends up performing). In purchasing an individual's labour power, the capitalist sets it to work to produce a use value (i.e., a specified article that satisfies another's want). This difference is the source of what has become known by labour process theorists as the 'indeterminacy of labour' – whoever purchases labour power from another is unlikely ever to receive its full productive benefit; the challenge is to make an individual's labour effort approach their labour power. Effective organization of this consumption of labour power to produce use values is thus set out early on as the central problem of any labour process, regardless of the social conditions under which it takes place. There then follows a detailed discussion of the way in which nature is transformed by labour to produce value that is, in its central argument, almost indistinguishable from Locke's, save for one important respect. Although Marx's starting point is, like Locke, 'nature' in its most basic form he also recognizes that few material inputs into the industrial system have not been previously transformed by human labour, including things that we now call infrastructure. One of

Marx's quaint aphorisms, however, signals his main departure from Locke when he notes that, just as the taste of porridge doesn't tell you who grew the oats, so a product tells you little of the social conditions of capitalism under which it was made. First, the labourer works under the direction of the capitalist and, as a result, the actions of the labourer are subordinated to those of the capitalist. Second, the product of this labour remains the property of the capitalist and not the labourer. Moreover, the labourer, as the seller of labour power, receives its exchange value (as set by the labour market) while the capitalist, as buyer of labour power, receives its use value (as set by the product market). If it takes half a working day for the labourer to produce enough to pay for the exchange value of his labour for a whole day, then anything that accrues to the labourer's work for the rest of the day belongs to the capitalist. This constitutes a highly abbreviated description of Marx's theory of the production of surplus value; a theory which has been contested by labour economists ever since it was first put forward. Today the simplicity of Marx's nineteenth century examples of industrial labour – mainly cotton spinning – seem so far removed from current economic, political, and technological complexities that it seems difficult to accept the theory today. Yet, according to orthodox labour process theorists, so long as we can still observe the separation of mental and manual labour then Marx's fundamental observations apropos the subordination of labour to capital through management's monopoly of the conception of work are still as valid today as they were in 1867. If, however, in some circumstances managers no longer explicitly seek to monopolize the conception of work then it places severe strain on LPT, at least as it is commonly constituted. I will argue that LPT can still be tractable when it comes to understanding key problems associated with Marxist critique such as subordination and work intensification but it requires us to move from an exclusive focus on the separation of conception and execution and look to instances where management control

operates in circumstances where employees exercise a formally acknowledged degree of discretion, not only over *what* work is done but also *how* it is done. I will show that we can extend LPT to consider these conditions of nominal employee autonomy by thinking, perhaps counter-intuitively, of ceding discretion to employees as an alternative means of closing the gap between labour power and actual performed labour. As such, workers' conduct still needs to be controlled so that discretion is directed towards problems deemed to be in line with the explicit goals of the organization, such as continuous improvement. If, moreover, we think of this control as the continuous surveillance of employees who are exercising discretion, rather than the specification of work tasks by managers followed by intermittent checking to see if those tasks have been adequately performed (an essentially bureaucratic notion of control), then this raises the important matter of how we can theorize the disciplinary effects of this form of scrutiny. This opens up LPT to a consideration of recent social theory that places surveillance, vision, and the person-in-sight at the heart of its conceptualization of social order and cohesion.

## OCCULARCENTRISM, THE GAZE AND THE PERSON-IN-SIGHT

In his book, *Downcast Eyes*, Martin Jay traces the declining status of vision in French philosophy. Of course, sight was central to the Scientific Revolution and the subsequent project of Enlightenment, both literally and figuratively. Copernicus, Kepler, Gallileo and Brahe had demonstrated that visual observation was central to scientific advancement; from the Renaissance onward, optical instruments were hailed as the technological wonders of their age as the ability to see the very small or the very large opened up new horizons. Makers of optical instruments, moreover, were held in the highest regard and occupied important positions in the scientific community – for example, Spinoza earned his living as a lens grinder and, in the UK, Robert Hooke was major figure in the newly formed Royal Society. The emerging modern science of optics, as pioneered by Descartes and Newton, was itself seen as the very model of Reason and, in France, thinkers whose influence is still felt today – people such as Laplace, Fourier, and Fresnel – all made important contributions to the development of the discipline. At the same time, *Philosophes* such as Rousseau, inspired by this dynamism in the natural sciences, echoed classical philosophers such as Plato in their desire to '... lift the veil of appearance and reveal an essential truth beneath' (Jay, 1994: 91). According to Rousseau it was no longer the eye of God alone that was able to see what lay behind man's scheming and artifice; like the astronomer seeing into the heavens or the biologist peering into the smallest cell, man could now turn objective scrutiny toward the conduct of himself and others, dreaming of a new social order of '... beneficial mutual surveillance without reprobation or repression' (Jay, 1994: 92). Indeed, Rousseau and his confreres believed that the Enlightenment truly heralded a world where the darkest recesses of nature and humanity alike were to be illuminated by Reason.

Jay contends that this Enlightenment occularcentrism was essentially benign and optimistic but was gradually inverted in the twentieth century by French thinkers, to be replaced by a largely pessimistic stance where a malignant 'Gaze' is indeed implicated in reprobation and repression. This abrogation of Enlightenment principles is commonly conveyed by invoking Jeremy Bentham's Panopticon; the design for a prison where organization and sight meet in a utilitarian vision of perfected social control. Given that so much has been written about the Panopticon – a ring of cells overlooked by a central observation tower – in organizational literature in recent years, only the briefest description of its proposed operating principle is warranted here. Importantly, overseers in the tower could not be seen by the inhabitants

of the individual cells, leaving inmates with the impression that they could at any moment be under surveillance. This is the source of panoptic discipline: the effect of surveillance would appear to be continuous even if inmates were not necessarily under constant scrutiny.

In organizational literature the discussion of panoptic discipline has largely drawn on Michel Foucault's use of the Panopticon in his book, *Discipline and Punish*. While this work is obviously of the utmost importance to the matter at hand in this chapter it is, however, still worthwhile dwelling on other critics who have turned to Bentham's model as an idealized form of organization. It is also important to note that the disciplinary effect of perfect surveillance was familiar well before Bentham, although the all-seeing eye was usually associated with God rather than man. Most vividly, Hieronymus Bosch's painting, *The Seven Deadly Sins*, shows each of the sins in tableaux arrayed around the iris of an eye. The message would have been powerful and unambiguous when it was painted in 1470: God sees all and your sins shall find you out.[1]

Comparing Bosch's painting and Bentham's drawings one is struck by their almost identical composition: replace the tableaux of the sins with cells and the iris with the observation tower and you have the floor plan of the Panopticon (see Figures 16.1. and 16.2).[2] Himmelfarb (1968) contends that this is no coincidence for Bentham was inspired by religious imagery and she points to his annotation of one sketch with an excerpt from Psalm 139 as evidence.[3] Nevertheless, as an atheist Bentham was intent on replacing God's all-seeing eye with a rational machine. Yet even with these apparently high ideals, Himmelfarb depicts Bentham as a man driven, not by the high-minded idealism of a social reformer, but by personal greed. According to Himmelfarb, Bentham got the idea for the Panopticon from a workshop run by his brother in Russia and the reason he lobbied Parliament for over forty years to set up a pilot scheme was because it was always his intention to run the institution profitably for

**Figure 16.1    Hieronymus Bosch, *The Seven Deadly Sins*. Used with the permission of the Museo Prado, Madrid.**

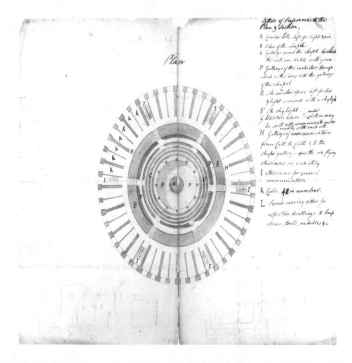

**Figure 16.2    Original plan of the Panopticon with Jeremy Bentham's own annotations. Used with the permission of the Bentham Papers, University College London Library Services, Special Collections.**

himself, not only as a private prison, but as 'manufactory' utilizing convict labour.

Miller (1975) is less worried about Bentham's pursuit of mammon and more interested in using the Panopticon as a way of conveying the difference between *l'oiel* [the eye] and *le regard* [the gaze] in Jacques Lacan's psychoanalytic theory. Thus, images captured through the eye belong to the solipsistic world of the individual-as-subject, but images captured through the gaze of a disembodied system of scrutiny marks out the identity of the individual-as-object differentiated from the mob. In this way Lacan's analysis of *voir* [to see] is linked to *savior* [to know] and *pouvoir* [to be able] (Jay, 1994). This is close to what Jay describes as Foucault's (1979) phenomenological account of surveillance as part of the lived spatial experience of the body in the world, but Foucault goes further than Lacan in adding an 'epistemic' account where the gaze is implicated in systems of classification. This is consistent with the continuing spatial obsession of the modern institutionalization of power – a place for everything and everything in its place that finds its apotheosis in Bentham's Panopticon. It goes beyond this, however, to incorporate a Nietzschean genealogy that rejects the anthropocentric fallacy of the ahistorical and unified subject in favour of the contingency of a historical and fragmented subject constituted through '… the acuity of a glance that distinguishes, separates, and disperses' (Foucault, 1977: 153). For the person in the sight in the organization, this epistemic gaze has important ramifications because, at any one moment, they are subjected to numerous forms of classification that render them – in their eyes and in the eyes of others – 'good' or 'bad', 'complaint' or 'recalcitrant', 'effective' or 'ineffective', etc. (or any combination of such qualities – Sewell, 1998). What's more, qualities once thought to be 'good' – say, obedience, steadiness, and a lack of imagination – can become 'bad' as organizations increasingly expect 'flexibility', 'innovation', or 'initiative' from their employees. In this way, workplace

surveillance reflects the control compulsion associated with 'Governmentality' – a higher order discourse about the forms of rationalization and control that are deemed necessary for the effective functioning of the modern state (Foucault, 2003; cf. Beniger, 1986). According to Marks (2000), Governmentality orders techniques of disciplinary power through the imperative of incorporating people into a greater 'societal body'. Historically, this involved a shift away from dealing with troublesome citizens on a case-by-case basis and towards preventing deviancy through a generalized process of 'policing' and 'normalization'. Thus,

> … a constant supervision of individuals by someone who exercised power over them – a schoolteacher, foreman, physician, psychiatrist, prison warder – and who, so long as he exercised power, had the possibility of both supervising and constituting knowledge concerning those he supervised. A knowledge that now was no longer about determining whether something had occurred; rather, it was about whether an individual was behaving as he should, in accordance with the rule or not, and whether he was progressing or not. This new knowledge was no longer organized around the questions: 'Was this done? Who did it?' It was no longer organized in terms of presence and absence, of existence and non-existence; it was organized around the norm, in terms of what was normal or not, correct or not, in terms of what one must do or not do (Foucault, 2000a: 59).

In effect, disciplinary techniques are localized responses to the challenge of Governmentality which, in organizations, confront the question: How do we get potentially unruly individuals from diverse backgrounds and with varying abilities to become 'useful' members of the organization (where the meaning of 'useful' is constantly changing)? In this way the consideration of the person in sight in an organization involves much more than identifying the technological systems approximating to the Panopticon that identify when and where employees diverge from norms of behaviour; it also requires us to consider how the purpose of surveillance and its consequences are constituted. This is, of course, also bound up with questions about how behavioural norms become established; a matter that is consistent with the position taken by Foucault in *Discipline and Punish*, which he later clarified as follows,

> Identifying a single automatic mechanism that allows power to operate is *absolutely not* the thesis of the book [*Discipline and Punish*]. Rather, it is the idea that, in the eighteenth century, such a form of power became desirable and possible. It is the theoretical and practical implications of the enduring will to create these kinds of mechanism that constitutes the object of my analysis. (Foucault, 1980: 37. Trans. Dreyfus and Rabinow, 1982 – my emphasis)[4]

Thus, under the particular expression of the obsession with obedience we now associate with the ideas of Frederick Winslow Taylor, control of the labour process was only concerned with ensuring that employees had performed their task in the manner specified by managers, whether it is enforced by direct overseeing, is fixed in the technology of production (i.e., via a moving assembly line), or is embedded in bureaucratic rules (Edwards, 1979). Under each of these conditions it is possible to deal with the indeterminacy of labour by maintaining the separation of conception and execution. This is consistent with orthodox labour process theory (Braverman, 1974), leading to a situation where managers determine behavioural norms on the basis of a putatively scientific analysis. The problems arises, however, that these managerially defined norms effectively become performance maxima: as an employee, why bother trying to improve upon what your manager had told you to do when this could be construed as a form of disobedience (even if you could do the job better than the way your manager had already specified)? This poses a dilemma for the manager who is trying to be true to the rhetoric of inclusion, empowerment and increased discretion recently popularized through organizational techniques like teamwork or continuous improvement, techniques that attempt to tap into the workforce's knowledge of the work

process (Sewell, 2005): If you do dissolve the separation of conception and execution and allow employees even the slightest degree of discretion over how they execute their work tasks then how can managers ensure that that discretion is used to the benefit of the organization (Sewell, 1998)? To do so requires a form of surveillance that not only identifies when workers have failed to live up to expectations but also identifies when they have exceeded them. In other words, surveillance must be able to identify when employees are exercising their intimate knowledge, expressed as personal mastery over the work process, so that that knowledge is made available to other employees in the organization (Sewell, 2005). This is an interesting extension of the control compulsion because it seems to offer, in Weber's (1962) term, a means of 'incorporating' employees into the value system of the organization in a manner that is not simply reactive and punitive (although those that are deemed to have fallen short of expectations can still be punished) but also appears to encourage employees to use their initiative in the pursuit of continuous improvement (Sewell and Barker, 2006). In the phraseology of LPT, surveillance ensures that a worker's executed labour approaches their labour power more effectively than under the strict separation of conception and execution associated with both Taylorism and bureaucratic rules of conduct. Of course, the concept of normative incorporation is well-established in organization and management studies (e.g., Ouchi, 1980), especially through discussions of 'strong corporate cultures' (e.g., Ray, 1986), although it is easy to exaggerate its effectiveness (Thompson and Ackroyd, 1995). Thus, surveillance provides a 'fail-safe' mechanism that ensures the gradual improvement of work processes should familiar techniques of normative incorporation fail to live up to their billing, a proposition that allows us to extend LPT into a new arena where, nominally at least, workers have greater discretion over how work is done. It also allows us simultaneously to consider the development of techniques of surveillance in the workplace as a form of control that extends the scope of Lacan's 'gaze' by marking out the prodigious from the mob. This trend is driven by the compulsive desire to rationalize conduct in the workplace that Foucault speaks of through his figurative use of the Panopticon.

## MARX, WEBER, NIETZSCHE, AND FOUCAULT: LABOUR PROCESS THEORY AND EMPLOYEE AUTONOMY

We can now return to a considerable challenge to the durability of LPT, for acknowledging even the slightest recombination of conception and execution would appear to undermine the fundamental Marxist notion of the division of labour into mental (i.e., managerial) and manual work. In short, by ceding discretion to workers, the basic source of alienation is removed. Previous attempts at recombination have been dismissed as a sham by Marxist critics (e.g., Friedman, 1977; Wright, 1985) but it is increasingly difficult to describe recent developments such as teamwork as a mere slight of hand when it comes to increased autonomy (Sewell, 1998). What a revitalized approach to LPT must do is to demonstrate how autonomy can lead to greater intensification of work and the creation of increased levels of surplus value. The key to this demonstration lies in grasping that attempts to normalize employee performance occur not just around the lowest common denominator (i.e., the least able), or even some notionally 'average' performer, but around the most able. For example, Barker (1993, 1999) has shown how teams that exercise a degree of autonomy over the conception and execution of work tasks indulge in group behaviour that places pressure on poorer performers to emulate their higher performing team mates (cf. Bauman, 2002). Importantly, individual performance data generated by surveillance systems can be used by team members to increase peer pressure on poorer performers to improve – that is, to make them useful to the team and, hence, the organization

(Sewell and Wilkinson, 1992; Sewell, 1998). We still need, however, to provide some kind of conception of how this usefulness is judged, not least because the orthodox Marxist account of control through the separation of conception and execution of work is no longer so compelling. So the question arises: How can LPT retain its critical edge and provide an account of control that is consistent with recent changes in organizational practice? My proposal is to revisit Max Weber's (1962) concise definitions of power, domination and discipline: the exercise of power relates to the opportunity existing within a social relationship which permits one to carry out one's own will even against resistance and regardless of the basis upon which this opportunity rests; domination is coextensive with the exercise of power in that it relates to the opportunity to have a command of a given specified content obeyed by a given group of persons in an organization; and, discipline relates to the opportunity to obtain prompt and automatic obedience in a predictable form from a given group of persons because of their practiced orientation towards a command. The Marxist's criticism of these definitions of power, domination and discipline (e.g., Wright, 1985) is that they take no account of the specific exploitative nature of the social relations of capitalist production; they could apply to any form of organization, regardless of whether capitalists were trying to exploit employees or masters were trying to exploit slaves. This is indeed an important point of difference between Marx and Weber for Marx contended that, under the social relations of communistic production, the absence of exploitation would lead to the withering of domination and subordination. In contrast, Weber took from Nietzsche (as did Foucault) the view that, regardless of whether an organization was capitalistic or communistic, domination and subordination would always be present wherever life was organized along bureaucratic lines (Gouldner, 1955; Coser, 1971; Turner, 1991). The fatalistic aspect of Weber's account of the inexorable rise of bureaucracy was famously taken up by Gouldner (1955) who described it as the 'metaphysical pathos of modernity'. Edwards' (1979) reaffirmed this position by identifying bureaucracy as an advanced and unobtrusive form of organizational control that had developed in response to the shortcomings of more overt and direct forms. Such fatalism has, however, been tempered by the rise of an anti-bureaucratic sentiment (see Heckscher and Donnellon, 1994: passim.), propelling things such as teamwork and empowerment to the fore in the management and business literature over recent decades. Developing in parallel with this anti-bureaucratic movement has been a growing awareness that surveillance has often acted as an adjunct to (if not a replacement for) bureaucracy as a means of controlling human conduct (e.g., Packard, 1964; Rule, 1973; Marx, 1988; Gandy, 1993; Lyon, 1994) and there have been several attempts at extending our understanding of workplace control with this consideration in mind (e.g., Burawoy, 1983; Attewell & Rule, 1984; Attewell, 1987; Prechel, 1994). What unites many of these treatments – even the earliest ones – is a focus on computers and increasingly sophisticated electronic systems as the means of workplace control but, as Bentham showed us, surveillance can potentially exert a strong disciplinary effect through very simple physical arrangements. The obvious constraint on isolating a worker in the manner demanded by Bentham's Panopticon, however, is that it is not conducive to the social and physical arrangements of today's workplaces. This has been the key insight of authors who have heralded the rise of an 'Electronic Panopticon' (e.g., Zuboff, 1988; Webster and Robins, 1989; Sewell and Wilkinson, 1992) – the advent of new technologies mean that surveillance is no longer dependent on a direct sight line between observer and observed which relaxes many constraints on the physical and social organization of work. As a result there has been a proliferation of research on the control of occupations previously thought to be impervious to rationalization and standardization, such as medical professionals (e.g., Kohli and Kettinger, 2004; Doolin, 2004).

It is, of course, possible to take the comparison between the Panopticon and electronic surveillance to the extreme, leading some researchers to overstate their claims about the totalising effect of workplace control (e.g., Fernie and Metcalf, 1999). It is a criticism that has been levelled by Foucauldian scholars (Knights and McCabe, 1999) and anti-Foucauldian scholars (e.g., Thompson and Ackroyd, 1995; Thompson, 2003) alike. Despite their obvious theoretical differences, these camps are united through their sceptical attitude toward the ability of surveillance to resolve the problem of the indeterminacy of labour and, in the process, deliver on its promise of creating a docile and compliant workforce. Indeed, the real question that emerges here is not so much why it is that surveillance works so well at maintaining organizational discipline but why we put so much effort into perfecting surveillance when we know from empirical studies of workplace resistance, misbehaviour and recalcitrance that it works so badly? Sewell and Barker (2005, 2006) have responded to this revised question of workplace surveillance by shifting the debate away from whether it can ever approach Bentham's panoptic ideal and toward a consideration of the Panopticon as a figurative expression of the desire to subsume all organizational conduct under a totalizing system of control. Whether it is pursued through the physical sequestration of an individual in time and space, through bureaucratic means, or through electronic surveillance, we nevertheless still ought to consider how we make sense of the purpose and consequences of control as it is deployed in the pursuit of Weber's versions of power, domination, and discipline. Drawing on the work of Gouldner (1955), Sewell and Barker (2006) draw attention to the way in which bureaucracy and, more recently, surveillance have been the focus of competing discourses that exert an epistemological force on the way in which we conduct research on organizational control. Importantly, these discourses can be in broad agreement on how control is achieved but differ markedly when it comes to identifying whose interests it serves.

# RETHINKING LABOUR PROCESS THEORY: SURVEILLANCE, KNOWLEDGE AND THE PERSON IN THE SIGHT OF THE ORGANIZATION

## Coercive versus protective surveillance

One of Alvin Gouldner's most interesting and sustained projects was, as he described it, to undertake a 'Marxist critique of Marxism'. By this he meant that we must see Marxism as an historical and social product with its own internal contradictions (Gouldner, 1973) and his discussion of bureaucracy as the 'metaphysical pathos of modernity' (Gouldner, 1955) was an early example of this kind of critique. For example, a command economy such as the Soviet Union was bound to be a highly bureaucratized society but, with its self-serving elites, it also appeared to be a perfect example of Michels' (1915) 'Iron Law of Oligarchy'. The apparent contradiction in a Communist society – that a political class instated to serve the masses ends up serving itself – no longer rings true, however, when we reconsider Weber's injunction that all relations in organizations are relations of power. It was this observation that led Gouldner (1955) to historicise bureaucracy by identifying two ways of understanding its purpose and consequences. These were aligned with Liberal and Radical ideological and intellectual traditions in the United States respectively. The former considered bureaucracy to be a legitimate means of exercising power by a few to serve the interests of the many while the latter considered bureaucracy to be an exploitative means of exercising power by the few to serve the interests of the even fewer (i.e., capitalists). Gouldner's identification of these Liberal and Radical traditions served as the inspiration for Sewell and Barker's (2006) reconsideration of the Panopticon as what White (1973) called an 'inaugural gesture' that provides researchers with a memorable way of reconsidering Gouldner's metaphysical pathos of modernity (Rose and Miller, 1992). Foucault (2000b) clarified this primarily figurative role of

the Panopticon by showing how we use it to convey the almost compulsive desire to know all there is to know about people and rely on this knowledge to regulate their behaviour (Hacking, 1983; Marks, 2000). The operational logic of the Panopticon suggests that the need to direct an employee's activities exclusively and continuously toward achieving an organization's goals is satisfied through the proximate and immediate disciplinary effect of surveillance rather than through a reliance on abstract and formal rules enforced through bureaucratic means (Jay, 1994). The particular depiction of the few watching the many sits well with current preoccupations with the almost limitless ability of information technology to provide constant surveillance of citizens or employees (Poster, 1990; Lyon, 1994; Bogard, 1996; Alge et al., 2004); technology that was, of course, unavailable in Weber's day. In this way, the Panopticon is a vivid metaphor of Weberian domination in an organizational setting that is more in tune with the experience of people who are increasingly conscious of the intrusion of surveillance into many aspects of their working lives. That is, the Panopticon captures both the ideal of universal and continuous surveillance in a compelling manner and creates the expectation that such 'total' surveillance is a possibility, spurring us on to pursue the ideal though various technological means (Heidegger, 1977), even if the practical results are often disappointing. Not that this quest always gives rise to a regressively constraining social dynamic for surveillance can conceivably protect us by preventing lapses into irrationality and chaos by contributing to the maintenance of order, but the pursuit of this degree of social control nevertheless necessarily involves the exercise of power, regardless of the political character of the regime that pressed it into service (Foucault, 2000c). This is why it is so important to address the normative question: When considering surveillance in organizations, in whose name are power, domination, and control exercised? We may know *how* surveillance works (or, at least, is supposed to work) but we also need to establish *why* it is enacted in the first place. This is why Sewell and Barker (2006) addressed the question of how Radical and Liberal discourses exert an epistemological influence on researchers who pursue characteristic research programmes in organizational surveillance.

## Labour process theory as a discourse of coercive organizational surveillance

Sewell and Barker (2006) contend that LPT displays a 'family resemblance' (Wittgenstein, 1958) to a Radical discourse of organizational control because it presents surveillance as a means of ensuring that the effort expended by employees gets as close as possible to their notional maximum capacity to work. In this way, the person-in-sight is problematized as an individual who is duty bound to act in a certain way. Thus, managers need to coerce employees into doing something they would otherwise not do – that is, to work as hard as they can all the time, even though such hard work may not obviously be in their own interests. The few watching the many is justified because it enables a small number of managers to exercise control over a larger and potentially unruly mass of employees through the monitoring of individual behaviour (Rushing, 1966). The prospect of constant surveillance is attractive to managers because it minimizes the opportunities for employees to avoid working as hard as they really can, even in circumstances that transcend the organizational arrangement traditionally associated with the separation of conception and execution. Consequently, a discourse of coercion focuses on two main roles: (1) the activities of managers who wish to guarantee the constant visibility of employees in order to maximize their effort; and (2) the activities of employees who wish to avoid this scrutiny in order to minimize their subordination to managers. Thus, managers become agents of oppression and, in this respect, the discourse of coercion concentrates on how surveillance allows

the more powerful to dominate the less powerful.

From this position on the purpose of organizational surveillance, empirical studies within this research programme tends to focus on identifying its localized disciplinary effects. In particular, researchers direct their attention towards how specific systems of surveillance track employees' positions in time and space and how managers use the data generated by these systems to expose those employees who are working 'hard' (and who are, therefore, setting an example to others) and those who are not 'pulling their weight' (and who should, therefore, be subjected to retraining or dismissal – Sewell, 1998). On the basis of such comparative performance monitoring, individuals may come to be seen (by themselves and by others) as 'lazy' or 'industrious', 'compliant' or 'recalcitrant', 'normal' or 'deviant', and so forth. Importantly, managers' efforts aimed at perfecting control through surveillance *and* employees' efforts at avoiding that control are seen as equally rational organizational behaviours (Fleming and Sewell, 2002). These efforts become an escalating 'battle of wits' in which mangers devise ever more sophisticated surveillance and employees use their ingenuity to circumvent it.

Setting out this coherent position on the coercive purpose of organizational surveillance and its consequences draws attention to the family resemblances that help us to place research (e.g., Garson, 1988; Sewell and Wilkinson, 1992; McKinlay and Taylor, 1996; Sewell, 1998; Marx, 1999; Bain and Taylor, 2000; Ball and Wilson, 2000; Thompson, 2003) in the Radical tradition. Generally speaking, by being critical of the way in which surveillance primarily serves the interests of an organizational minority (be it a 'managerial élite' or, ultimately, the 'capitalist class' itself), the discourse of coercion has informed research that is aligned with the critical thrust of LPT: documenting the extension of surveillance into new areas of organizational life; closing down the spaces in which workers could previously escape the gaze of managers, and exerting its disciplinary effect in circumstances where physical oversight or bureaucratic control are deemed to be impossible or undesirable. This move signals the prospect of work intensification and the erosion of employees' autonomy as they submit to the will of managers. An important implication of this Radical critique is that, if left uncorrected, the expansion and perfection of surveillance will ultimately lead to the complete subjugation of all employees who come to recognize the futility of dissent and end up supine and self-disciplining; a characteristically dystopian vision that this perspective on surveillance shares with other critical representations of complete organizational domination (e.g., Goffman, 1961). Nevertheless, this line of research also suggests avenues of resistance that are perhaps better suited to countering surveillance than blatant sabotage, industrial action, or other directly confrontational practices of traditional radicalism (Fleming and Sewell, 2002). For example, a subtle understanding of the practical limitations of surveillance can reveal the 'blind spots' in a network of control; areas where employees can escape the gaze of managers, thus providing them with space to manoeuvre (Knights and McCabe, 1999).

In contrast to this Radical research programme, Sewell and Barker (2006) go on to identify a Liberal research programme where the person-in-sight is problematized as an individual who has the potential to indulge in self-interested behaviour should he be left to his own devices. Thus, organizational surveillance (usually in the guise of individual performance monitoring) is deemed to be legitimate so long as: (1) it prevents antisocial individuals from taking advantage of the organization *and* their colleagues; (2) its operation is invested in the hands of impartial managers – Williamson, 1975); and (3) all members of the organization recognize both the reasonableness of surveillance as a course of action *and* trust in the impartiality of those responsible for its operation. In this way surveillance is seen to be benign and protects the interests of the majority of organizational members against the actions of a potentially disruptive or self-interested

minority of employees (Rushing, 1966). It is not necessary to go into the epistemological effect of this discourse here in any detail except to make three important observations. First, under this logic, anyone who objects to being placed under surveillance runs the risk of being labelled 'irrational' or a 'trouble-maker' (Fleming and Sewell, 2002). Second, research in this programme tends to focus its critical attention on issues such as the effective and equitable operation of surveillance in the name of 'procedural fairness' and involves considerations such as ensuring data accuracy at the point of collection, maintaining data integrity and security over time, and respecting the prevailing standards of privacy (e.g., Eddy *et al.*, 1999; Ambrose and Adler, 2000; Alge, 2001; Frayer, 2002; Moorman and Wells, 2003; Stanton and Weiss, 2003), rather than mounting a challenge to the basic legitimacy of the surveillance per se. Third, Sewell and Barker (2006) point out that these first and second points are rhetorically and conceptually compelling to the point that Radically inspired research often relies on them to legitimate its critique of surveillance. Thus, surveillance may be deemed to be acceptable in some circumstance (say, when matters such as health and safety are at stake – Findlay and McKinlay, 2003) or where it can be used to turn the scrutiny back on managers through some form of 'sousveillance' or 'undersight' (Mann *et al.*, 2003). For example, Mason *et al.* (2002) showed that work groups were able to make surveillance a 'disclosure' mechanism that confirmed they had performed to expected standards; something that gave them an advantage in negotiating new production levels and rewards. Similarly, McKinlay and Taylor (1996), Ezzamel *et al.* (2001), and Button *et al.* (2003) reported that, in some circumstances, employees were able to use data related to their own performance to highlight the hypocrisy of managers who had high expectations of others but exempted themselves from the same obligations. In some respects this strategy is hardly surprising: if you become aware of the disciplinary effects of the 'calculability' of your own position (Clegg, 1989; Covaleski *et al.*, 1998) then you are also likely to be aware that others – including those who are nominally your superiors – are themselves subject to similar forms of discipline. Thus, while being at odds with implacable opposition and repudiation, this strategy does allow for negotiations to take place around specific practices of surveillance that can then make recourse to legal injunctions (Mishra and Crampton, 1998; Frayer, 2002; Findlay and McKinlay, 2003) or cultural expectations such as privacy and mutual obligation (Stone and Stone, 1990).

## CONCLUDING REMARKS: LABOUR PROCESS THEORY AND THE INDETERMINACY OF KNOWLEDGE

To argue that research on surveillance has come under the epistemological influence of a Radical discourse is to historicize LPT in the way advocated by Gouldner (1973) with respect to the Marxian corpus. It is also an attempt to accommodate the kinds of technological developments we associate with a futuristic vision of the twenty-first century in a manner that retains the critical edge of a theory developed in the nineteenth century. But the more comprehensive and far-reaching surveillance becomes so the more spectacular are its failures. We can make a direct comparison with wider society here. We are living in an era where numerous states have abandoned hard-fought and long-held civil liberties in the name of security yet, when security systems fail (as they invariably do), the response is to impose even more restrictions on liberty. There are echoes of this in a paradox identified by Sewell and Barker (2006): Surveillance is a failure so let's do more of it! The irony is that we often rely on the rhetoric of Liberalism in order to sustain a Radical critique of surveillance in that some forms of managerially imposed scrutiny are tolerable and even desirable if they appear to protect the majority of organizational members from

a disruptive or criminal minority. One is struck by the similarity to Lenin's justification of workplace control undertaken by Communist apparatchiks in the Soviet Union – so long as it's done in the name of the masses then domination is just fine.

With these observations in mind, two things are left for us to consider. The first is to revisit the problem of the indeterminacy of labour. By insisting on the strict separation of conception and execution, Taylor's discussion of Scientific Management still serves, according to Braverman (1974), as the locus classicus when it comes to employees' subordination to management. By denying the worker any room to exercise their discretion, Taylor tried to create the circumstances where managers monopolized legitimate knowledge about the best way to organize work. Indeed, Taylor was only half-joking when he wished for workers who were 'trained gorillas' (Sewell, 2005). Under these conditions, the indeterminacy of labour was simply a question of physical effort – at any moment we are left to ponder whether employees are really working as hard as they can. Under conditions where managers do not try to enforce a monopoly over the conception of work – that is, where employees are expected to use their discretion to make improvements to work processes and products – the indeterminacy of labour now includes a cognitive element. In other words, the problem is expanded to include a consideration of whether employees are working their bodies *and* their minds as hard as they can? In this way, the labour process can be characterized as a problem of the 'indeterminacy of knowledge' where surveillance is implicated in a process of expropriating cognitive faculties including imagination, ingenuity, problem-solving skills and other forms of embodied knowledge (Sewell, 2005).

My second and final concluding thought is also a corollary of refocusing LPT on the problem of the indeterminacy of knowledge. It is also the area where the macro and micro traditions in organizational behaviour can enter into a beneficial dialogue. Clearly, individual cognitive faculties like imagination and problem-solving skills are the bailiwick of micro-organizational behaviour but, when these faculties are put to work in an organization they become the focus of a debate about what constitutes legitimate knowledge in the workplace. For example, an employee who directs his skills and expertise toward the continuous improvement of the production process is likely to be hailed by managers as a model corporate citizen (although some of his colleagues might think of him as a 'rate-buster' or 'company suck'). If, however, the employee used those very same skills and expertise to indulge in creating personal utility or even sabotage then managers would condemn him as disruptive and an undesirable influence on others (although some of his colleagues might consider him a hero). The important point to note here is that what constitutes legitimate knowledge (and, consequently, what constitutes *il*legitimate knowledge) is bound up with an understanding of the wider interests of different parties in the organization. Whether one's membership of these parties is determined by one's relationship to a particular class (in the Marxist sense), matters of identity (such as gender, age, ethnicity, culture, etc.) or professional affiliation is a matter of one's theoretical and ideological stance. A similar point was made by Rao and Pasmore (1989). In a surprisingly neglected article they argue that organization studies presents itself alternatively as: 1) a positivistic search for instrumental knowledge; 2) a critique of power and ideology for the purposes of emancipation; 3) a hermeneutic exercise aimed at initiating a discussion on the moral future of organizational society; and 4) a competition between specialist scholars intent on defining the most persuasive discourse. By thinking about the labour process as a research programme under the influence of a Radical discourse of surveillance we can bring together Rao and Pasmore's viewpoints in the following manner. Clearly, LPT presents itself as critique of power and ideology where knowledge is expropriated through surveillance and used against the very people who once possessed it to intensify their

work. As Sewell and Barker (2006) have demonstrated, however, this can be counter-posed with a Liberal discourse of efficiency and mutual obligation where knowledge is revealed through surveillance to serve the interests of all, making the organization more effective while organizational life becomes more congenial for everyone by reducing the chances of antisocial behaviour. Presenting them as competing discourses in this way highlights the primary moral question faced by the student of workplace control: Is surveillance coercive or is it protective? This is not, however, a simple Manichean moral dilemma although, prima facie, we might reasonably expect these discourses to be mutually exclusive; talking about surveillance in one way would seem to preclude the other. Indeed, the status of organizational surveillance is, much as bureaucracy before it, always likely to be theoretically and empirically ambiguous. An interesting outcome of this ambiguity is that it actually gives the supporters of rival discourses space to coexist. Thus, they are more likely to stand in an antinomian relationship to one another (Sperber and Wilson, 1986; Barley and Kunda, 1992; Trethewey, 1999), operating in parallel without obvious contradiction for most of the time – that is, although we may find surveillance intrusive and restrictive, we can still acknowledge (however grudgingly) that there may be occasions when it is able to protect us from the antisocial behaviour of others (and vice versa, of course). The net result is that we rarely have to confront the potential tension between coercion and protection and Rao and Pasmore's (1989) competition between specialist scholars intent on defining the most persuasive discourse – the 'language game', as they call it – may never eventuate. There may be times, however, when this competition will be felt most intensely; times when the contradictory character of these logically opposed views may become more obvious (Trethewey, 1999). Faced with this antagonism we are usually expected to decide whether surveillance is primarily coercive and should be resisted or primarily protective and should be supported. Yet it is at this very moment of paradox that the epistemological function of Liberal and Radical becomes blurred and we have difficulty 'knowing' organizational surveillance conclusively; moments at which we may be torn between seeing surveillance as being either protective or coercive. This is the great irony of workplace surveillance; one which we must bear in mind whether we are dyed-in-the-wool labour process theorists or management consultants designing a state-of-the-art employee monitoring system.

## NOTES

1 This picture hung on the wall of the pious King Philip II of Spain's personal bedchamber in the Escorial Palace as a reminder of God's omnipresence.

2 Bentham may have been aware of Bosch's painting but, in any case, similar paintings were common in English churches.

3 Psalm 139 – 'Thou art about my path, and about my bed: and spiest out all my ways'.

4 L'automaticité du pouvoir, le caractère mécanique des dispositifs où il prend corps n'est absolument pas la thèse du livre [Surveiller et Punir]. Mais c'est l'idée au XVIIIe siècle qu'un tel pouvoir serait possible et souhaitable, c'est la recherche théorique et pratique de tels mécanismes, c'est la volonté, sans cesse manifestée alors, d'organiser de pareils dispositifs, qui constitue l'objet de l'analyse.

## REFERENCES

Alge, B.J. (2001) 'Effects of computer surveillance on perceptions of privacy and procedural justice', *Journal of Applied Psychology*, 86: 797–804.

Alge, B.J., Ballinger, G.A. and Green, S. (2004) 'Remote control: Predictors of electronic monitoring and intensity', *Personnel Psychology*, 57: 377–410.

Ambrose, M.L. and Adler, G.S. (2000) 'Designing, implementing, and utilizing computerized performance monitoring: Enhancing organizational justice', *Research in Personnel and Human Resource Management*, 18: 187–219.

Attewell, P. (1987) 'Big Brother and the sweatshop: Computer surveillance in the automated office', *Sociological Theory*, 5: 87–100.

Attewell, P. and Rule, J. (1984) 'Computing and organizations: What we know and what we don't know', *Communications of the ACM*, 27:1184–1192.

Bain, P. and Taylor, P. (2000) 'Entrapped by the "Electronic Panopticon"? Worker resistance in a call centre', *New Technology, Work, and Employment*, 15: 2–18.

Ball, K. and Wilson, D. (2000) 'Power, control, and computer based performance monitoring: Subjectivity, repertoires, and resistance', *Organization Studies*, 21: 539–566.

Barker, J.R. (1993) 'Tightening the iron cage: Concertive control and self managing teams', *Administrative Science Quarterly*, 38: 408–437.

Barker, J.R. (1999) *The Discipline of Teamwork*. Newbury Park, CA: Sage.

Barley, S.R. and Kunda, G. (1992) 'Design and devotion: Surges of rational and normative ideologies of control in managerial discourse', *Administrative Science Quarterly*, 37: 363–399.

Bauman, Z. (2002) *Society under Siege*. Cambridge: Polity.

Beniger, J.R. (1986) *The Control Revolution: Technological and Economic Origins of the Information Society*. Cambridge, MA: Harvard University Press.

Bogard, W. (1996) *The Simulation of Surveillance: Hypercontrol in Telematic Societies*. Cambridge: Cambridge University Press.

Braverman, H. (1974) *Labor and Monopoly Capital: The Degradation of Work in the Twentieth Century*. New York: Monthly Review Press.

Burawoy, M. (1983) *Manufacturing Consent: Changes in the Labor Process under Monopoly Capitalism*. Chicago: University of Chicago Press.

Button, G., Mason, D. and Sharrock, W. (2003) 'Disempowerment and resistance in the print industry? Reactions to surveillance-capable technology', *New Technology, Work & Employment*, 18: 50–61.

Clegg, S.R. (1989) *Frameworks of Power*. London: Sage.

Coser, L. (1971) *Masters of Sociological Thought: Ideas in Historical and Social Context*. New York: Harcourt Brace Jovanovich.

Covaleski, M.A., Dirsmith, M.W., Heian, J.B. and Samuel, S. (1998) 'The calculated and the avowed: Techniques of discipline and struggles over identify in Big Six public accounting firms', *Administrative Science Quarterly*, 42: 293–327.

Doolin, B. (2004) 'Power and resistance in the implementation of a medical management information system', *Information Systems Journal*, 14: 343–362.

Dreyfus, H.L. and Rabinow, P. (1982) *Michel Foucault: Beyond Structuralism and Hermeneutics*. Hemel Hempstead: The Harvester Press.

Eddy, R.E., Stone, D.L. and Stone-Romero, E.F. (1999) 'The effects of information management policies on reactions to human resource information systems: An integration of privacy and procedural justice perspectives', *Personnel Psychology*, 52: 335–346.

Edwards, R. (1979) *Contested Terrain: The Transformation of the Workplace in the Twentieth Century.* New York: Basic Books.

Emsley, C. (1987) *Crime and Society in England, 1750–1900.* London: Longman.

Ezzamel, M., Willmott, H. and Worthington, F. (2001) 'Power, control and resistance in "the factory that time forgot"', *Journal of Management Studies*, 38: 1053–1079.

Fernie, S. and Metcalf, D. (1999) '(Not) hanging on the telephone: Payment systems in the new sweatshops', *Advances in Industrial and Labor Relations*, 9: 23–68.

Findlay, P. and McKinlay, A. (2003) 'Surveillance, electronic communications technologies and regulation', *Industrial Relations Journal*, 34: 305–318.

Fleming, P. and Sewell, G. (2002) 'Looking for the good soldier, Švejk: Alternative modalities of resistance in the contemporary workplace', *Sociology*, 36: 857–873.

Foucault, M. (1977) 'Nietzsche, genealogy, history', in D.F. Bouchard (ed.) *Language, Counter-memory, Practice: Selected Essays and Interviews.* Ithaca: Cornell University Press.

Foucault, M. (1979) *Discipline and Punish: The Birth of the Prison.* Harmondsworth: Penguin.

Foucault, M. (1980) *L'Impossible Prison: Recherches sur le Système Pénitentiaire au XIXe Siècle.* Paris: Seuil.

Foucault, M. (2000a) 'Truth and juridical forms', in J.D. Faubion (ed.) *Michel Foucault: The Essential Works, vol. 3.* New York: The New Press.

Foucault, M. (2000b) 'Governmentality', in J.D. Faubion (ed.) *Michel Foucault: The Essential Works, vol. 3.* New York: The New Press.

Foucault, M. (2000c) 'Questions of method', in J.D. Faubion (ed.) *Michel Foucault: The Essential Works, vol. 3.* New York: The New Press.

Foucault, M. (2003) 'Lecture: 17 March 1976', in M. Bertani and A. Fontana (eds) *Society Must Be Defended.* London: Allen and Lane, pp. 239–264.

Frayer, C.E. (2002) 'Employee privacy and Internet monitoring: Balancing workers' rights and dignity with legitimate management interests', *Business Lawyer*, 57: 857–876.

Friedman, A.L. (1977) *Industry and Labour: Class Struggle of Work and Monopoly Capitalism.* London: Macmillan.

Gandy, O. Jnr (1993). *The Panoptic Sort: A Political Economy of Personal Information.* Boulder, CO: Westview Press.

Garson, B. (1988) *The Electronic Sweatshop: How Computers are Transforming the Office of the Future into the Factory of the Past.* New York: Simon & Schuster.

Goffman, E. (1961) *Asylums: Essays on the Social Situation of Mental Patients and other Inmates.* Chicago: Aldine Press.

Gouldner, A. (1955) 'Metaphysical pathos and the theory of bureaucracy', *American Political Science Review*, 49: 496–507.

Gouldner, A. (1973) *For Sociology: Renewal and Critique in Sociology Today.* London: Allen Lane.

Hacking, I. (1983) 'Biopower and the avalanche of numbers', *Humanities in Society*, 5: 279–295.

Heckscher, C. and Donnellon, A. (1994) *The Post-bureaucratic Organization: New Perspectives on Organizational Change.* Thousand Oaks, CA: Sage Publications.

Heidegger, M. (1977) *The Question Concerning Technology, and other Essays.* New York: Garland.

Himmelfarb, G. (1968) *Victorian Minds.* London: Weidenfeld & Nicolson.

Ignatieff, M. (1978) *A Just Measure of Pain: The Penitentiary in the Industrial Revolution, 1750–1850.* London: Macmillan.

Jay, M. (1994) *Downcast Eyes: The Denigration of Vision in Twentieth-century French Thought.* Berkeley: University of California Press.

Kelly, J. (2005) *The Great Mortality: An Intimate History of the Black Death.* London: Harper Perrenial.

Knights, D. and McCabe, D. (1999) 'Are there no limits to authority? TQM and organizational power', *Organization Studies*, 20: 197–225.

Kohli, R. and Kettinger, W.J. (2004) 'Informating the clan: Controlling physicians' costs and outcomes', *MIS Quarterly*, 28: 363–395.

Locke, John (1960) [1690]. 'An essay concerning the true original extent and end of civil government', in J. Locke (ed.) *Two Treatises of Government.* Cambridge: Cambridge University Press.

Lyon, D. (1994) *The Electronic Eye: The Rise of Surveillance Society.* Cambridge: Polity Press.

Mann, S., Nolan, J. and Wellman, B. (2003) 'Sousveillance: Inventing and using wearable computing devices for data collection in surveillance environments', *Surveillance and Society*, 1: 331–335.

Marks, J. (2000) 'Foucault, Franks, Gauls. Il faut défendre la société: The 1976 lectures at the Colège de France', *Theory, Culture and Society*, 17: 127–147.

Marx, G.T. (1988) *Undercover: Police Surveillance in America.* Berkeley: University of California Press.

Marx, G.T. (1999) 'Measuring everything that moves: The new surveillance at work', *Research in the Sociology of Work*, 8: 165–189.

Marx, K. (1976) [1867]. *Capital: A Critique of Political Economy.* Harmondsworth: Penguin.

Mason, D., Button, G., Lanshear, G. and Coates, S. (2002) 'Getting real about surveillance and privacy at work', in S. Woolgar (ed.) *Virtual Society? Technology, Cyberbole, Reality*. Oxford: Oxford University Press.

McKinlay, A. and Taylor, P. (1996) 'Power, surveillance and resistance: Inside the factory of the future', in P. Ackers, C. Smith and P. Smith (eds) *The New Workplace and Trade Unionism*. London: Routledge, pp. 279–300.

Melossi, D. and Pavarini, M. (1981) *The Prison and the Factory: Origins of the Penitentiary System*. London: Macmillan.

Michels, R. (1968) [1915]. *Political Parties: A Sociological Study of the Oligarchical Tendencies of Modern Democracy*. New York: Free Press.

Miller, J.-A. (1987) [1975]. 'Jeremy Bentham's Panoptic Device', *October*, 41: 3–29.

Mishra, J.M. and Crampton, S.M. (1998) 'Employee monitoring: Privacy in the workplace?', *SAM Advanced Management Journal*, 63 (3): 4–15.

Moorman, R.H. and Wells, D.H. (2003) 'Can electronic performance monitoring be fair? Exploring relationships among monitoring characteristics, perceived fairness, and job performance', *Journal of Leadership & Organizational Studies*, 10 (2): 2–16.

Mumford, L.Q. (1934) *Technics and Civilization*. New York: Harcourt Brace.

Ouchi, W. (1979) 'The relationship between organizational structure and organizational control', *Administrative Science Quarterly*, 22: 95–113.

Ouchi, W.G. (1980) 'Markets, bureaucracies, and clans', *Administrative Science Quarterly*, 25: 129–141.

Packard, V. (1964) *The Naked Society*. London: Longman.

Poster, M. (1990) *The Mode of Information: Poststructuralism and Social Context*. Cambridge: Polity Press.

Prechel, H. (1994) 'Economic crisis and the centralization of control over the managerial process: Corporate restructuring and neo-Fordist decision-making', *American Sociological Review*, 59: 723–745.

Rao, M.V.H. and Pasmore, W.A. (1989) 'Knowledge and interests in organization studies: A conflict of interpretations', *Organization Studies*, 10: 225–239.

Ray, C. (1986) 'Corporate culture: The last frontier of control?', *Journal of Management Studies*, 23: 287–297.

Rose, N. and Miller, P. (1992) 'Political power beyond the state: The problematics of government', *British Journal of Sociology*, 43: 173–207.

Rule, J.B. (1973) *Private Lives and Public Surveillance*. London: Allen Lane.

Rushing, W.A. (1966) 'Organizational rules and surveillance: Propositions in competitive organizational analysis', *Administrative Science Quarterly*, 10: 423–443.

Sewell, G. (1998) 'The discipline of teams: The control of team-based industrial work through electronic and peer surveillance', *Administrative Science Quarterly*, 43: 397–429.

Sewell, G. (2001) 'The prison-house of language and the penitential discourse of organizational power', in R. Westwood and S. Linstead (eds) *Language and Organization*. London: Sage.

Sewell, G. (2005) 'Nice work? Rethinking managerial control in an era of knowledge work', *Organization*, 12: 685–704.

Sewell, G. and Barker, J.R. (2005) 'Max Weber and the irony of bureaucracy', in M. Korczynski, R. Hodson and P. Edwards (eds) *Social Theory at Work*. Oxford: Oxford University Press, pp. 56–87.

Sewell, G. and Barker, J.R. (2006) 'Coercion versus care: Using irony to make sense of organizational surveillance', *Academy of Management Review*, 31: 934–961.

Sewell, G. and Wilkinson, B. (1992) 'Someone to watch over me: Surveillance, discipline and the Just-in-Time labour process', *Sociology*, 26: 271–289.

Sperber, D. and Wilson, D. (1986) *Relevance: Communication and Cognition*. Oxford: Blackwell.

Stanton, J.M. and Weiss, E.M. (2003) 'Organisational databases of personnel information: Contrasting the concerns of human resource managers and employees', *Behaviour & Information Technology*, 22: 291–304.

Stone, E.F. and Stone, D.L. (1990) 'Privacy in organizations: Theoretical issues, research findings, and protection mechanisms', *Research in Personnel and Human Resources Management*, 8: 349–411.

Thompson, E.P. (1963) *The Making of the English Working Class*. London: Gollancz.

Thompson, E.P. (1967) 'Time, work-discipline, and industrial capitalism', *Past and Present*, 38: 56–97.

Thompson, P. (2003) 'Fantasy Island: A labour process critique of the "Age of Surveillance"', *Surveillance & Society*, 1: 138–151 (www.surveillance-and-society.org)

Thompson, P. and Ackroyd, S. (1995) '"All quiet on the workplace front": A critique of recent trends in British industrial sociology', *Sociology*, 29: 615–633.

Treasure, G. (1985) *The Making of Modern Europe, 1648–1780*. New York: Methuen.

Trethewey, A. (1999) 'Isn't it ironic: Using irony to explore the contradictions of organizational life', *Western Journal of Communication*, 63: 140–167.

Turner, B.S. (1991) 'Preface', in H.H. Gerth and C. Wright Mills (eds) *From Max Weber: Essays in Sociology*. London: Routledge.

Weber, M. (1962) *Basic Concepts in Sociology*. London: Peter Owen.

Weber, M. (1976) [1894]. *The Protestant Ethic and the Spirit of Capitalism*. London: Allen & Unwin.

Webster, F. and Robins, K. (1989) 'Plan and control', *Theory and Society*, 18: 323–351.

Westerman, W.L. (1955) *The Slave Systems of Greek and Roman Antiquity*. Philadelphia: American Philosophical Society.

White, H.V. (1973) 'Foucault decoded: Notes from underground', *History and Theory*, 12: 23–54.

Williamson, O.E. (1975) *Markets and Hierarchies, Analysis and Antitrust Implications: A Study in the Economics of Internal Organization*. New York: Free Press.

Wittgenstein, L. (1958) *Philosophical Investigations*. Oxford: Blackwell.

Wright, E.O. (1985) *Classes*. London: Verso.

Zuboff, S. (1988) *In the Age of the Smart Machine*. New York: Basic Books.

# 17

# Implementing Employment Equity in Gendered Organizations for Gendered Lives

Judith K. Pringle, Alison M. Konrad and Anne-Marie Greene

Within organization studies there has been a focus on the modernist project (Casey, 2002) together with a curious lack of attention to broader factors. The contextual embeddedness of organizations has been largely ignored. 'New structuralism' calls for inquiry into how society shapes organizations (Lounsbury and Ventresca, 2003) and for 'richer conceptualizations of social structure and process ... at the intersection of the sociology of culture, stratification and politics and institutional analysis' (Lounsbery and Ventresca, 2003: 464). Organization studies, particularly outside of Europe, have been strongly influenced by social and industrial psychology, resulting in focus on a micro level of analysis. It is a situation that

has been exacerbated by research being conducted from separate disciplinary silos, such as psychology and sociology, which once provided its framework (Lawrence, 2004). For more effective organizational analysis and change we need to take a more multi-level approach (Yammarino and Dansereau, 2004). In an effort to advance this project, we discuss the implementation of employment equity from three levels of analysis – micro, macro and meso (House, Rousseau and Thomas-Hunt, 1995; Mathieu and Taylor, 2007). In this chapter, micro and macro factors are considered in terms of their influence on the organization – the meso level – an approach that parallels a macro-organizational behaviour frame.

## GENDERED LIVES AND GENDERED ORGANIZATIONS: MICRO ANALYSIS

Gender equality in the workplace remains a distant goal. Workplaces continue to show inequality in wages, gender segregation of jobs and unequal access to high quality employment (Benschop, 2006). Although most members of contemporary industrial societies endorse women's equal participation in the public sphere (Bolzendahl and Myers, 2004), reactions to equality initiatives are mixed (Harrison *et al.*, 2006). It appears that people are more willing to verbalize support for gender equality than to support operational and material change.

The division of unpaid household labour continues to be unequal, with women doing more of the work and more of the repetitive, monotonous types of work (Coltraine, 2000; Eurostat, 2004). People express more willingness to work under a female manager (Moore, 2002), but female leaders are rated more negatively than their male counterparts, especially by men and in masculine domains (Eagly, Makhijani and Klonsky, 1992; Brett, Atwater and Waldman, 2005). Furthermore, the capitalist enterprise continues, more and more boldly and explicitly, to exploit women's bodies and sexuality for profit (Kilbourne, 2005; King, 2006). Yet despite extensive evidence to the contrary, substantial numbers of people argue that gender equality has been achieved and that the status of women is no longer a concern for public policy ('An Agency Well Pruned', 2006).

In this chapter, we will explore the problem of creating employment equity within organizations and societies that remain strongly gendered (Benschop, 2006). In this first section we begin by describing the status of women in contemporary industrialized societies, focusing on the aspects of gendered lives that most directly impinge upon efforts to achieve equality for women in the workplace. Then, we describe the state of contemporary work organizations, which have been in flux in response to the heightened competition resulting from the globalization of the business environment. Finally, we suggest that organizational responses to this environment are *unlikely* to lead to greater equality for women in the workplace.

### Status of women in business

In many countries, researchers have conducted careful surveys to measure the representation of women in senior business positions. Scrutiny of women in powerful positions is a desired outcome of a liberal feminist agenda, a dominant rationale for change within the women and management literature. Catalyst, a non-profit research and consulting organization based in North America, conducts a census of *Fortune* 500 (US) and *FP* 500 (Canada) firms every year, counting women directors in odd years and women executives in even years. Findings from the most recent Catalyst censuses show that in 2004, 7.9% of *Fortune* 500 and 7.1% of *FP* 500 executives were women, and in 2005, 14.7% of *Fortune* 500 and 12.0% of *FP* 500 directors were women (Catalyst, 2006a, 2006b).

Cranfield's School of Management (Singh and Vinnicombe, 2005) conducts an annual census of *FTSE* 100 (UK) boards, and the most recent findings indicate that 10.5% of directorships were held by women in 2005, up from 5.8% in 2000. Similarly the biannual New Zealand (NZ) census of women in management and the professions (McGregor and Fountaine, 2006) found that only 7% of board directors are women, even though there are high profile public positions held by women, e.g., the posts of Prime Minister, Chief Justice and the past Governor-General.

The European Professional Women's Network surveys the boards of the largest 300 European companies in even years. Their findings indicate that European companies vary greatly in the level of female representation on boards. The highest levels of female representation on the boards of large companies are found in Scandinavian countries, with women occupying 28.8% of these directorships in Norway, 22.8% in Sweden, 20% in Finland, and 17.9% in Denmark. The lowest levels of female representation are found in southern Europe. There are no women directors of large Portuguese companies and women hold only 1.9% of directorships in Italy, 4.1% in Spain, and 4.4% in Greece. Other European countries show the following low levels of representation of women on large corporate boards: 5.8% in Belgium, 6.5% in The Netherlands, 7.2% in Germany, 7.6% in France, 8.1% in Ireland, and 9.5% in Austria (Berry, 2006).

Extrapolating from the representation of women in line and staff positions in the top few layers of management in *Fortune* 1000 (US) firms, Helfat, Harris and Wolfson (2006) predicted that by 2010, at most, 6.4% of CEOs of these large US firms would be women. Their most optimistic scenario predicted that 12.8% of CEOs in these firms would be women by 2016. These numbers are far below parity, yet they still appear optimistic when one considers that in 2006, only 20 of the *Fortune* 1000 were led by female CEOs. Outside of Scandinavia, the growth of women's representation in European companies has also been described as slow (European Professional Women's Network, 2006).

The reasons for the lack of representation of women in top business positions are the subject of much debate. Evidence suggests that the division of labour in the family, gender stereotyping/categorization, and the objectification of women, all influence women's organizational experiences and can be detrimental to aspirations of employment equity.

## Division of labour in the family

Around the world, women take responsibility for two-thirds or more of caretaking and household labour (Bianchi *et al.*, 2000; Davis and Greenstein, 2004; Fuwa, 2004; Geist, 2005; Halleröd, 2005; Lee and Waite, 2005; Li, 2005). Family formation affects women's career development, and the impact differs in different societies. For instance, in Taiwan, almost a third of women leave the paid labour force upon marriage, and an additional 10% leave when they have children. By comparison, in mainland China, marriage and children have little impact on women's labour force participation (Yi and Chien, 2002). In the United States (US), marriage is no longer associated with women's labour force participation, but the arrival of children reduces women's participation in paid work (Cohen and Bianchi, 1999).

Family structures are also changing (Lobel, Googins and Bankert, 1999). One important shift has been the dramatic increase in the percentage of babies born to single mothers. Single mothers face the challenge of combining work and family effectively to both care for their children and provide income for the family. In addition, welfare reform efforts are moving poor women with children into the workforce, which is challenging employers to find ways of employing and retaining former welfare clients, many of whom must juggle paid work with considerable family obligations (Kossek *et al.*, 1997; Deckop *et al.*, 2006). Elder care responsibilities also result in increased work-family conflict, especially for women (Singleton, 2000).

In sum, many women in contemporary industrialized societies combine full-time employment with demanding family responsibilities. In response to overload, some women drop out of the labour force or engage in entrepreneurship (Arai, 2000), and employers are finding that they need to provide work-life flexibility benefits to retain female workers. Research supports the effectiveness of organizational work-life flexibility programmes for improving productivity (Konrad and Mangel, 2000), enhancing employee attitudes towards the organization (Kossek and Nichol, 1992; Grover and Crooker, 1995; Baltes *et al.*, 1999; Holtzman and Glass, 1999; Igbaria and Guimaraes, 1999), and increasing employee retention (Lyness *et al.*, 1999).

There is also some evidence that work-life flexibility benefits are associated with positive outcomes for women's careers (Dreher, 2003). However, work-life flexibility programmes are not sufficient for improving the status of women in business, unless they are fully integrated into organizational systems and processes, such that utilizing them is viewed as legitimate and routine. Unfortunately, in many organizations, utilizing work–life flexibility benefits is viewed as a career limiting move (Catalyst, 2005). Research has shown that people are unlikely to use work–life flexibility benefits unless they perceive the organization to have a supportive work-family culture (Thompson, Beauvais and Lyness, 1999). Furthermore, élite jobs are becoming more and more 'extreme' (Hewlitt and Luce, 2006), requiring 80-hour work-weeks, relentless travel, and unpredictable schedules. Although the women who have succeeded in these environments may say that it is 'worth it' (Hymowitz, 2006), these conditions preclude most women from reaching top business positions, and most holders of these élite top-paying jobs are men (Hewlitt and Luce, 2006).

## Gender stereotyping and categorization

Gender stereotyping is another factor that influences the behaviour and treatment of women in organizations. Gender stereotypes are beliefs about the attributes of women and men (Diekman *et al.*, 2005). Cross-national research has shown consistency in the contents of gender stereotypes such that men are expected to show more dominance, aggressiveness, achievement, autonomy, exhibitionism, and endurance while women are expected to show more affiliation, nurturance, succorance, deference and abasement (Williams and Best, 1990). Gender stereotypes are promulgated in various ways, including through the media and educational materials (Signorielli and Bacue, 1999; Döring and Pöschl, 2006). For instance, children's books still show substantially more male than female characters, depict female characters as nurturing and indoors, and assign female characters to traditionally feminine roles, such as homemaker (Hamilton *et al.*, 2006). The amount of gender stereotyping in children's books also has not declined between the 1980s and 1990s (Hamilton *et al.*, 2006).

Gender stereotypes are pervasive and activated automatically (Irmen, 2006). Recent research has shown that gender stereotyping continues such that university undergraduates use different standards to evaluate women and men (Prentice and Carranza, 2002). Specifically, students consider characteristics such as warmth, friendliness, interest in children and sensitivity to the needs of others to be more desirable in 'women' than in 'people' and more desirable in 'people' than in 'men'. Students consider characteristics such as decisiveness, ambition, risk-taking, and assertiveness to be more desirable in 'men' than in 'people' and more desirable in 'people' than in 'women'. Women are particularly penalized by students for being rebellious, stubborn, controlling, cynical, promiscuous, or arrogant, all of which characteristics are more acceptable in 'men' than in 'people' and more acceptable in 'people' than in 'women'. Hence, Prentice and Carranza (2002) argue that gender stereotypes are prescriptive as well as descriptive, and affect how people are judged by others.

Given the contents of gender stereotypes, it is not surprising that leadership is viewed cross-culturally as more consistent with masculinity than with femininity (Schein, 2001; Powell, Butterfield and Parent, 2002; Sümer, 2006). Recent research has shown that women and men view the roles of chief executive officer (CEO), vice president (VP) or mid-level manager in industry to be equally desirable but that women are less likely than men to see these roles as possible for themselves (Killeen, López-Zafra and Eagly, 2006). Indeed, if people view assertiveness, decisiveness, and risk-taking as less desirable in women than in men, then evaluations of potential leaders in organizations may be skewed against women. Research has shown that women have to be more participative than men in order to be accepted as organizational leaders. In their meta-analysis, Eagly *et al.* (1992) found that female leaders received poorer evaluations than their male counterparts, especially when they exhibited an autocratic leadership style. Similarly, Brett *et al.* (2005) found that female supervisors experienced more negative repercussions than male supervisors did when they disciplined employees in an inconsiderate way.

Although the statistical effects of gender stereotypes on organizational outcomes are purportedly small (Bowen, Swim and Jacobs, 2000; Davison and Burke, 2000), even a small bias against women in organizational contexts can generate substantively significant discrepancies in career outcomes, due to the repeated and cumulative nature of personnel decisions in organizations (Agars, 2004). Furthermore, stereotypes and other heuristics are more likely to affect human decision processes under conditions of cognitive burden (Martell, 1996; Perry, Kulik and Bourhis 1996), for example where organizational decision makers consider very large amounts of complex and ambiguous information to make personnel decisions. Organizational decision processes can be structured to minimize the impact of gender biases by focusing decision makers on behavioural observations and objective accomplishments (Bauer and Baltes, 2002), but merely instructing decision makers to suppress stereotypes has the unintended effect of exacerbating their influence in memory (Kulik, Perry and Bourhis, 2000).

Stereotypes also affect the discourse surrounding the implementation of gender equity programmes in organizations, to the detriment of women's advancement opportunities. Because women and men are thought to be different, they are also thought to want different things in their work and in their lives. Meta-analytic research has shown that men do place greater importance on stereotypically masculine job attributes such as high earnings, freedom, promotion opportunities, and leadership, while women place greater importance on stereotypically feminine attributes such as intrinsically interesting work, relationships, working with people, and helping others (Konrad et al., 2000). Hakim (2000; 2002) suggests that changes in industrialized societies (i.e., equal employment opportunity laws, the availability of reliable contraceptives, and the expansion of part-time and white-collar jobs) have greatly increased the ability of women to fulfil

their personal preferences when conducting a job search.

Although women and men may differ somewhat in their career preferences, it does not logically follow that this difference implies women should be subordinated in the workplace. Yet, that is the conclusion drawn by some authors (e.g., Filer, 1985, 1986), particularly those individuals who attribute gender differences in preferences to innate, heritable traits (e.g., Browne, 2002, 2006). Such an argument ignores the question of why men's preferences are rewarded by organizations while women's are penalized. Such arguments also take the current form of organizing as a given and ask individual women to change if they desire to advance in their careers (Benschop, 2006).

## Objectification of women

The objectification of women adds to the difficulty of creating gender equity in organizations. The term 'objectification' refers to viewing a person as an object or 'sight' to be appreciated by others (Aubrey, 2006). The objectification of women is promulgated through the media, which depicts women's bare skin and body parts considerably more often than that of their male counterparts (Döring and Pöschl, 2006). Objectification has detrimental effects on women who, as a result of viewing themselves as objects and the desire to present a pleasing body image to others, engage in self-objectification. Self-objectification results in appearance anxiety, body shame and depression (Szymanski and Henning, 2007) and can lead to self-destructive behaviours such as smoking and eating disorders (Fiissel and Lafreniere, 2006; Harrell et al., 2006). Objectification also disrupts women's performance on cognitive tasks (Quinn et al., 2006). Indeed, in the 1990s, the body size and shape of males portrayed in the media became larger and more muscular while at the same time, the body size and shape of females became portrayed as smaller and thinner (Spitzer, Henderson and Zivizn, 1999). As a result, the discrepancy between the average young North American adult and the images portrayed in the media has increased substantially, with the result of an increasing prevalence of body dissatisfaction in both men and women (Spitzer *et al.*, 1999).

The propagation of an objectified view of women has an impact on their treatment in organizations in a number of ways. Most obviously, objectification facilitates the sexual harassment of women. Sexual harassment is defined as sexual behaviour toward a target person that is unwanted, repeated, and creates a coercive or hostile work environment (Bowes-Sperry and Tata, 1999). Sexually harassing behaviours include gender harassment, unwanted sexual attention, and sexual coercion (Fitzgerald, Gelfand and Drasgow, 1995). The objectification of women can be linked to all three of these types of sexually harassing behaviours. Gender harassment refers to a broad range of verbal and nonverbal behaviours that convey insulting, hostile, and degrading attitudes about women. The link to objectification results from the reduction of women from the status of people to the status of objects to be either admired or criticized, based on their physical appearance. Examples of gender harassment include sexual epithets, slurs, or taunts, the display or distribution of pornographic materials, and threatening, intimidating or hostile acts. Comments about women's bodies that are either complimentary or critical would fit this category.

Unwanted sexual attention includes a wide range of sexual behaviour, both verbal and nonverbal, that is offensive, unwanted, and unreciprocated; for example, repeated requests for dates, sexual comments or comments about a person's body or attire. Sexual coercion includes both bribery (e.g., being subtly bribed with some sort of preferential treatment to engage in sexual behaviour with a coworker) and coercion (e.g., experiencing negative consequences for refusing to engage in sexual activity with a coworker). Both of these categories of sexual harassment are related to objectification, as they both focus on women as sexual objects or sexual partners rather than workers or professionals brought into the organization for their skills and abilities.

A related detrimental effect of objectification on women in organizational settings is loss of status. Research has shown that 'sexiness' and 'status' are incompatible such that female managers who are dressed in a 'sexy way' receive more negative affect and are rated as less competent than counterparts dressed in a neutral way (Glick *et al.*, 2005). Given that sexiness and status are incompatible for women, the sexual harassment of women and the treatment of women as sex objects are ways of undermining their credibility as managers and professionals. A particularly heinous example of such behaviour occurred at the University of Pennsylvania, a prestigious school that appointed its first female President in 1994. Each year as Judith Rodin addressed the graduating classes of 1994 onwards, catcalls of 'Show us your tits!' rang out from the audience. Students justified this behaviour by calling it a 'tradition'.

Organizations attempt to deal with the objectification of women by instituting sexual harassment policies and training. The training is effective to the extent that it indemnifies the employer against later charges of failing to prevent the development of a sexually harassing work environment (Henneman, 2006). The effectiveness of the training for actually reducing sexual harassment is unknown (Roberson, Kulik and Pepper, 2003). However, the sincerity of attempts to reduce sexual harassment by business organizations that utilize images of women's naked skin and body parts to sell their products is questionable.

## Organizational responses and their limitations

Organizations have developed a variety of responses to try to enhance employment equity for women, including work-life flexibility, women's networks, and sexual harassment training programmes. Evidence suggests that these organizational initiatives can and do have positive effects but that their impact is limited. Micro-level processes such as continued gender stereotyping and interpersonal discrimination hinder progress and maintain barriers to gender equity. At a different analytical level macro factors contribute in important ways that form the focus of the next section.

## MACRO INTERFACE WITH ORGANIZATIONS

Despite commonalities in women's experiences, the historical, political and societal maps of each nation state differ, resulting in the need to consider implementation within a geographically and culturally contingent framework (Prasad, Konrad and Pringle, 2006). The differential power positioning of any particular disadvantaged group is determined by the local context. To understand how social identity groups are positioned and the relationships between them requires including historical influences that have moulded the contemporary landscape. The model suggested here for expanding decision making includes demography, specific historical and socio-political factors germane to the nation, legislation, and the labour market.

### Demography

Demographic analysis is at the foundation of attempts to create more equitable organizational conditions. Organizational demography is a well-established research area usually falling within a positivist paradigm (Riordan, 2000), providing information on the effects of the demography of organizational members. Relational demography is a variant, generally defined as 'the extent to which organizational members are similar or different in their demographic characteristics' (Linnehan, Chrobot-Mason and Konrad, 2006: 423), and examines the dynamics created by the proportions of majority and minority members. Most of the work in relational demography has the individual as the pivot point, accessing demographic comparisons with other group members, or a dyadic

partner such as a supervisor. It may be fruitful to apply the comparative principles of relational demography to population, as well as organizational, demographics.

Within Anglo-Western countries an increasing number of women have been included as a proportion of the paid workforce since the second wave of the feminist movement (Davidson and Burke, 2004). The proportion of women in management positions has slowly increased over past decades; however, as noted earlier, women are still generally under-represented in senior positions.

With the exception of women, the political power of marginalized groups loosely relates to representation and voice in population demography, e.g., Native Americans/Alaskans (1%) in the US, indigenous Aboriginals (2%) in Australia, indigenous Maori (15%)[1] in NZ. In the case of women, who usually constitute 50% of the population, patriarchy dominates democracy. There are other numeric exceptions too, where social and historical processes cut across simple demographic correlations resulting in the majority of demographic grouping being historically disadvantaged. For example, in both Malaysia and South Africa, the largest ethnic groups are the indigenous people who are disadvantaged in socio-economic terms. In post-apartheid South Africa, 50% representation by the majority population was seen as a desirable goal for employment equity even though Black South Africans constitute 79% of the population (Ratuva, 1999). In other nations, such as Malaysia and Fiji, there have been demarcations of power separating urban business enterprises (dominated by immigrants of Chinese and Indian origin) from land ownership and political control (Malay and Indo-Fijians respectively) (Yang et al., 2006).

The visibility of social identity markers is important for group members gaining a voice. Yet for many persons with disabilities and members of the gay/lesbian/bi-sexual/transsexual communities they are only visible because they are active. For these groups the absence of a visible social identity marker has both positive and negative aspects.

Invisibility means people who are most similar to the dominant group can 'pass' if they stay 'in the closet'. People who are most dissimilar to the dominant group cannot be invisible and cannot pass (e.g., person using a wheelchair, effeminate gay man, some transgendered women), and hence, are immediately stigmatized. Activism on the part of these communities has raised the issue of their inclusion to the level of government policy and organizational mandates. Some organizations also are coming up with voluntary programmes for inclusion, as the result of the activism of these groups.

From these somewhat disparate examples we argue that numbers alone are not enough, contextual information is needed to interpret the demographics and the power dynamics between the identity groups.

## *Historical and socio-political context*

Crucial to the interpretation of hierarchical workplace relations is the historical, socio-political context and the relative power positions amongst the social identity groups. Where government funding policy is based on 'need', indicators of relative poverty are created. Power positioning occurs, and access to resources is actively contested in every society, with shifts in the relative ranking of identity groups. The socio-political context is a combination of recent shifts in societal and political power intertwined with longer-term historical patterns.

Relationships between the disadvantaged groups and dominant groups are not fixed but change with shifts in societal discourses over time. For example in the US, Prasad (2001) analysed the dominant historical phases of equity and diversity discourses over the twentieth century; identifying three periods: a focus on class stratification; social identity groups of ethnicity, race, religion; the business case and the diversity industry. Compared to the historical mosaic of Canada, the US has carried the legacy of slavery (Prasad, 2001) which has overshadowed the struggles of indigenous peoples. Within Canada there have been and are parallel but separate struggles

for voice and sovereignty of the indigenous peoples, 'visible minorities'[2] as well as the Francophone identity within Quebec. In some countries, arguments of equality have been built on the legacy of a social movement for women's rights. In other countries, the evolution varies, for example, in the US, the women's movement built on the civil rights movement. In some cases, gender equity may blind a nation to other inequalities, for example, non-white immigrants in Sweden (Prasad *et al.*, 2006). Thus the positioning of historically disadvantaged groups and the development of equity arguments varies across nations.

Historical processes have been influential in the relative power positions of women and indigenous ethnic groups in society; for example, the suffrage movement, which gave both colonial and indigenous women the right to vote in 1893 in NZ. Within Australia and NZ (Prasad *et al.*, 2006) the place of indigenous peoples is partly attributable to the historical conditions of colonization, which has had a direct impact on their contemporary political influence. Unlike other comparable colonized countries, e.g., US, Australia, South Africa,[3] in New Zealand a founding Treaty was signed between Maori (indigenous people) and Pakeha (Anglo settlers), which on paper attempted to safeguard Maori sovereignty and/or guardianship[4] over their natural and cultural resources. The Treaty partnership in NZ began a discourse of biculturalism which, although contentious, sets a discursive frame for contemporary times (Jones, Pringle and Shepherd, 2000). In contrast, the similar discussions of ethnic relations in, for example, Australia, the US, Canada and EU are based on assumptions of multiculturalism and implicit assimilation. Multiculturalism positions one group as dominant, usually the descendants of the white colonists, resulting in minority ethnic groups becoming 'othered' (Prasad and Prasad, 2002).

The colonial legacy continues in acts of resistance by indigenous peoples, coupled with struggles by immigrant groups for greater political voice. Post-colonial tensions are also apparent in former colonizing nations such as the UK, The Netherlands and France, who are now receiving the descendents of the colonization process as migrants.

Another recent socio-political factor has been a shift towards a neo-liberal economic strategy, strengthening the hegemonic power of capitalist discourse globally as socialist-based economies have been undone. Within this socio-political mosaic, the role of the state is an important factor. It has the capacity to act as a force to counter inequalities and reinforce the democratic tenet that all people are equal before the law. In a myriad of ways social practices are supported by the law.

## Legislation

The nature of the government and the legislative framework creates and reinforces the normative conditions governing relationships between groups within society. Legislation both leads and reflects popular opinion and it is a guide for normative action in organizations. Legislation is affected by discussions transmitted through the tentacles of multinational corporations and shifts in blocs of politically similar countries. There are limits to the degree that the enactment of legislation can change behaviour, attitudes and values (Jain, Sloane and Horwitz, 2003), nevertheless, it provides a significant indicator of a society's aspirations.

Most developed countries, and many that are 'developing', have anti-discrimination legislation (Jain et al., 2003). Development into more proactive measures of employment equity appears to be an evolutionary process. This can be seen explicitly in the principles underlying the South African constitution, namely: all forms of discrimination must be eliminated; everyone is equal before the law, equality must be actively promoted (Ratuva, 1999). This evolutionary process was foreshadowed by the way that equal opportunities and affirmative action was introduced in the US, which became a leader in legislating for civil rights (Civil Rights Act of 1964) through anti-discrimination legislation and executive orders on affirmative action, as a result of direct action, rebellion and protest

by African-Americans. The process was a mutually reinforcing interchange between autocratic 'executive orders' (beginning with President Roosevelt's executive orders 8587 and 8802 prohibiting discrimination in federal employment) and following legislative acts covering the private sector (Konrad and Linnehan, 1999) that were not as prescriptive as the executive orders.

This action led the way for similar initiatives in, for example, UK, Canada, Australia, although recent UK legislation has been influenced more recently by the European Union (Kirton and Greene, 2005). Many Western countries have a system of annual reporting to a quasi-governmental body (e.g., Australia, Canada, US). In NZ, the equal employment legislative landscape most closely parallels the UK,[5] although a partially differentiating factor is that the public or governmental sector is bound by legislation, while the private sector can, and does, implement EEO policies and practices on a voluntary basis (Jones et al., 2000). This distinction has created a bifurcation in the labour market which potentially allows researchers a quasi-controlled research comparison of EEO implementation.

The effects of legislation on employment opportunities cannot be measured directly (Periton, Robinson and Lourdes, 2003) but the bipartite situation in NZ between the governmental and private business sector can provide an indication. An EEO Trust survey of members[6] (EEO Trust, 2001) demonstrated that although both sectors had relevant policy and similar opportunities for flexible work (80–90% of organizations), the public sector was significantly more active in developing plans and implementing relevant practices (although proportions were still low). The reasons for actions were not included in the survey but a likely influential factor is the annual reporting requirements by legislation for the governmental sector. Another indicator of socio-political and legislative pressures is that members of the historically disadvantaged groups are over-represented in the governmental sector compared to population demographics. For example, in

NZ (www.statistics.govt.nz) women make up over 60% of this workforce (compared to 47% in the total labour force). This feature appears in many Western countries, partly due to supportive legislation that provides a benchmark for more inclusive human resource practices.

While one should not overestimate what legal regulation can achieve (Dickens, 1999), it is clear that it can have an effective role, for example in helping change norms of unpaid care work (Appelbaum et al., 2002). In their comparative study of six countries, Jain et al. (2003, refer to Table, p. 42) found that legislative public policy measures have led to positive change in terms of workforce participation and importantly on employers' actions (e.g., broadening focus of employers to collect data on designated groups, encouraging employers to devise measures to attract, retain, and motivate particular workers and sensitizing employers to the effects of changing demographics). Sweden is the only country where an equal role for fathers and mothers has been a guiding principle of public policy on the family since the 1970s. Consequently, that country demonstrates significantly greater participation of women in paid work (90% of mothers with children under 5 years of age compared to 50% in UK) (Gustafsson, Kenjoh and Wetzels, 2002)

The legislative landscape varies by nation state. Within each country the government has the potential to act as a regulatory force affecting conditions of employment, the broad nature of the labour market and acceptable industrial relations.

### Labour market conditions

Contemporary labour market conditions are a strong driver in recruitment decisions. If the level of unemployment is high or the economy is in recession, then there is less pressure on organizations to hire members of historically disadvantaged groups. Conversely, if there are high levels of skill shortages in specific occupations, then the business imperative may take precedence over the desire for

homogeneity in the workplace. Emerging research (Perotin, Robinson and Loundes, 2003) has identified that SMEs (small and medium enterprises) are unlikely to rapidly take up equity initiatives, although they can be influenced by a strong regulatory environment, which can have strong effects where a country's economy has a high proportion of small businesses.

It might be expected that the expansion of female dominated areas of the economy (service sector, public sector) and extensions of flexible working in the public sector might mean increased advantages for women as traditional employment opportunities have been dominated by men. However in the EU case these changes have tended to reduce male privilege but not enhance women's position. Decreasing stability in core sectors has meant increasing insecurity in the periphery, therefore continuing to establish gender difference but at a lower level. For example government funding and assistance for large scale redundancies in traditional male areas, plus moves to privatization and flexibility in public sector employment has led to increases in sub-contracting and other conditions of employment vulnerability for women. There is a danger that men and women will compete for jobs based on which group is willing to accept the worst terms and conditions (Rubery, Smith and Fagen, 1999: 286).

Struggles for voice and greater power for some excluded groups, such as the working classes, have taken place through collective action by the union movement. Trade unions exist within a broader social context, particularly the political and industrial relations environments and consequently their role in the labour market and even the acceptance of collective bargaining varies widely. For example, 98% of the workforce in Austria is covered by collective negotiations compared to 15% in the US (Greene and Kirton, 2006). Although union activity is generally low, there is a litigious environment in the US which creates a pressure to act through fear of law suits. Union activity is moderately strong in NZ, partly due to the Labour Government's introduction of the Employment Relations Act in 2000, which reinstated a primary negotiating role for unions in workplaces. Unions have been strong in Australia but industrial relations are undergoing a shift with even the right of union membership and previously taken-for-granted employee conditions being questioned (ACTU, 2006). With equity issues coming under the responsibility of managers then 'unions are all but being written out of EO [equal opportunity] and MD [managing diversity] agendas' (Strachan, Burgess and Sullivan, 2004: 202). Overall, it could be expected that employment equity is more likely to flourish where there is a strong societal belief in collective bargaining as central to employment relations (Greene and Kirton, 2006).

### Decision framework

A decision-making model is suggested to provide scholars and practitioners implementing employment equity with a framework to consider the macro contextual factors that have been raised in this section (Figure 17.1).

Applying this structured framework to the case of New Zealand, various trends and tensions can be predicted within equity and diversity discourses: bifurcation in conditions between the public and private sectors; informal workplace negotiation in most small business, producing an ad hoc 'unmanaged diversity'; the strong presence of women in workplaces, especially the public sector; a strong presence of Maori in public discourse and in public sector employment; disharmony between minority groups due to a dominant discourse of biculturalism. These propositions all provided rich opportunities for further research and debate.

In summary macro contextual factors are a crucial part of organizational decision making to effectively implement employment equity. The interface of micro and macro influences will be discussed in the next section within meso-level organizational policies and practices.

## EMPLOYMENT EQUITY AT THE ORGANIZATIONAL LEVEL

There are obviously clear differences between countries in terms of the culture and structure of organizational practices and their relationship with broader legislative regimes and

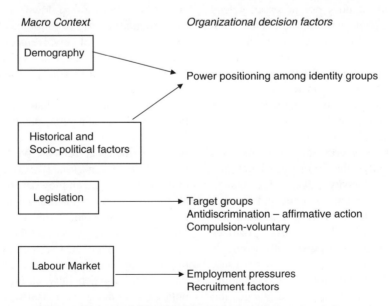

**Figure 17.1   Decision-making model for implementing employment equity.**

industrial relations climates. For example, where employer practices are tightly constrained by legal regulations or national collective regulations, changes in regulations will have a profound effect on organizational policies. Where the regulatory framework is looser, the pace of change depends much more on the individual initiatives of the organization (Rubery *et al.*, 1999). However the importance of what happens at the organizational level cannot be underestimated, as Rubery *et al.* comment: 'progress towards or retreat from gender equality ultimately depends on employment decisions and practices at the level of the organization' (1999: 62). As we have discussed before, the ability of organizational initiatives to achieve real progress in terms of gender equality is likely to be fairly limited, contained by the continued gendered nature of societies impacting on the efficacy of public policy and legislative regulatory regimes.

One of the key problems is the perennial gap between the rhetoric of policy and the reality of practice/outcomes. At the organizational level, why is it that, when it is accepted that there should be gender equality, and when most large organizations have EO policies, women still face disadvantage? It is clear that simply having a formal equality policy document does not necessarily lead to broader policy action. Using data from the large scale WERS survey in the UK, Hoque and Noon (2004) found that while EO practices are more likely to be found in workplaces where there is a formal EO policy, it does not guarantee action beyond that formal policy document. Indeed 16% of organizations with a gender policy did not have any corresponding practices. More generally, the evidence about the outcomes of diversity policies for women is contentious (Kossek, Lobel and Brown, 2006). Research in multiple countries has fairly consistently shown these practices to be positively associated with women's employment outcomes (e.g., Leonard, 1984, 1985, 1986; Leck and Saunders, 1992; Konrad and Linnehan, 1995; Leck, St. Onge and LaLancette, 1995; Holzer and Newmark,

2000; French, 2001); however, the amount of progress made continues to be disappointing (Benschop, 2006). In other words, EO policy action has had only weak positive equality outcomes.

The final section of the chapter focuses on the internal workings of the organization. It looks at three key areas as possible explanations for why interventions at the level of organizational practice have not been successful in generating more positive gender equality outcomes. First, the role of EO/diversity practitioners: those people with designated responsibilities for these areas within organizations. We argue that these people often face limited resources and difficult role conflicts which affect their ability to affect positive outcomes. Linked to this, we also discuss the conceptual confusion surrounding EO, and the potential impact that this has on the efficacy of policies. Second, we elucidate the problems of the predominance of the business case as a recent strategy for attending to EO issues within organizations, particularly when linked to wider macro-societal attitudes and behaviours. Third, we argue that the business case emphasis, coupled with the organizational position of EO practitioners within organizations, has meant that EO policies are most often a top-down intervention. Concomitantly, little attention has been paid to the views and involvement of non-managerial employees, which we see as a key weakness of effective equity implementation in organizations.

It should be noted that we recognize that there is an academic debate about the importance of terminology in this area, and on an international comparative basis, there are a variety of terms used (for example, equal opportunities, equal employment opportunity, affirmative action, equity, managing diversity or diversity management, Prasad *et al.*, 2006). For the sake of brevity, this chapter is not primarily concerned with elucidating the implications of the particular terms used, rather we look generally at organizational policy that is designed to deal with issues of equality and diversity, invoking the centrality of a power analysis to both concepts and thus using both terms interchangeably.

## The role of EO practitioners

Reflecting the shift from EO to diversity management, research suggests that in the US, Australia, New Zealand and UK diversity professionals have largely replaced former equality officers (Sinclair, 2000). Like its sister concept HRM, diversity management is positioned as a key business issue and therefore the literature usually emphasizes a pivotal role for all employees (line and senior managers) in policy implementation (Kossek and Lobel, 1996; Cornelius, Gooch and Todd, 2000). Writing about 'equality officers' based on research conducted in the UK in the late 1980s, Cockburn (1991) stated that the role attracted progressive people with a commitment to social justice. While diversity need not be synonymous with the business case, the question that we come back to later in this chapter is whether social justice aims can be, and are, pursued within the business case approach of the 2000s, and whether people with a strong commitment to business goals can also be committed to social justice.

While there is relatively little interrogation of this question, some authors do touch on the role of diversity professionals as agents of change. For example, based on research in the US, Litvin (2002) explores the compromises that 'diversity consultants' have to make in order to supply the 'product' their corporate clients want. She found dissonance between the diversity consultants' beliefs about what needed to be done and the more business focused objectives of their clients. Also in the US context, Meyerson and Scully's (1995) study of those they categorize as 'tempered radicals' outlines the state of ambiguity that those campaigning for equity-related action within organizations can face. They see these individuals as existing in a state of ambivalence, creating a dual identity, whereby they might act as critics of the status quo *and* also as critics of more radical change. In trying to speak to multiple constituencies,

tempered radicals might seek compromise, which might be seen as too conservative for some and too radical for others. Alternatively, the desire to belong might be so strong that a tempered radical might push away from the outsider dimension of his or her identity leading to co-optation, also creating feelings of isolation. Kirton, Greene and Dean (2007) also underline the applicability of this state of ambivalence to diversity practitioners in the UK, while Lorbiecki (2001) positions 'diversity vanguards' as 'outsiders-within'; people who feel compelled to speak out against discrimination and yet who also have to uphold the organization's business objectives. Such people practice something akin to what Jones and Stablein (2006: 160) call the '*dual agenda*' (see also Lawrence, 2000). Similarly, Sinclair (2000: 239) found that Australian 'diversity managers' were critical of the more 'palatable language' of diversity, which they accused of trivializing discrimination. In NZ 'Equal Employment Opportunity (EEO) practitioners' contested the individualistic approach of diversity and fought against its substitution for EEO (Jones, Pringle and Shepherd, 2000).

The little we know about diversity professionals indicates that they exist in a position of uneasy tension in their organizations and within diversity discourses. It is a position of uneasy tension exacerbated by the resource constraints experienced by EO practitioners. Evidence from recent research in the UK finds that EO/diversity practitioners are most often at middle management level, work only part-time on equality and diversity issues, and have relatively limited resources, indeed less than a third of respondent organizations had a budget (Mulholland, Ozbilgin and Worman, 2006). Given that the people who have to develop and implement policy have such limited access to legitimacy, resources and power, then it is perhaps not so surprising that highly successful policies are not necessarily forthcoming.

It should be noted that here are some indications that in the era of diversity management rather than that of EO, with the ascendance of the business case and the de-politicization of equality, diversity work may entail fewer costs than it did in the 1980s and early 1990s. Kirton, Greene and Dean (2006) find that diversity professionals in the UK context are now more mainstreamed in their organizations, often coming from a business background, and with clear commitment to a business case for EO/diversity action. Thus, diversity work may be less detrimental to individual careers than it was and, ironically, diversity practitioners might have more opportunity to accomplish equality and diversity objectives. The risk is that over-identification with management interests means that changes they drive are more likely to serve organizational objectives than necessarily improve working lives. This is an issue that is returned to in the next section.

### Conceptual confusion amongst EO practitioners

Prasad *et al.* (2006: 1) reflect on the difficulty of coming up with a definition of 'diversity': 'the language in the field is contentious and contested' (2006: 4) and such difficulty is also found when we look at the understandings of EO/diversity practitioners. Thinking about the ways that policy makers understand concepts and policy developments is important if talk and action are seen as related (Hamilton, 2001). An understanding of how different actors in organizations *understand* equity and diversity helps us to appreciate how and why actual policy and practice are formulated, implemented, resisted and challenged. Research findings indicate that there are clear conceptual misunderstandings and lack of clarity by academics and practitioners within organizations about what EO means.

A clear example of this confusion is whether gaining EO requires an approach premised on sameness or difference (Liff and Wajcman, 1996). Jewson and Mason (1986) found that individuals and groups frequently invoke various aspects of both conceptions, depending on the time, the circumstances, and their needs, often due to overall confusion and misunderstandings around conceptualizations

and practice of equality (see also Jones, 2004; Nentwich, 2006). Similarly, Cockburn (1989) finds that people interpret equality policies in workplaces differently depending on what is expected and desired from them, and their personal work demands and priorities. We could add here the perspectives of trade union practitioners (Kirton and Greene, 2006); there are significant national variations in the way in which diversity management has penetrated union thinking on equality policy making, regardless of the convergence of legislation in Europe (Greene, Kirton and Wrench, 2005; Wrench, 2005). Qualitative findings from a UK study (Kirton *et al.*, 2006) uncover real confusion amongst diversity practitioners about what equality and diversity mean and what organizational policies are actually striving to achieve. Similarly, Nentwich's (2006) study finds gender change agents in Switzerland using confusing and contradictory rationales for policy interventions.

The issue is that conceptual confusion can lead to policy confusion. Kirton and Greene (2005) outline a summary of mainstream policy in the UK and find a mixture of sameness and difference approaches. This means that it is not always clear what the overall policy aim is: To ensure women are treated equally, achieve equality of outcome, or recognize and value women's difference?

### The ascendance of the business case

Despite levels of conceptual confusion, there is no doubt that the business case strategy has provided the keystone for policy making and regulation in most countries in the equity area over the last 10 years and has attained a particularly strong hold in the US (Jones and Stablein, 2006; Kossek *et al.*, 2006; Litvin, 2006). Internationally there is much debate about whether moves towards diversity, rather than equal opportunity approaches, mean anything different in terms of policies or outcomes (Gagnon and Cornelius, 2000; Strachan *et al.*, 2004; Kirton and Greene, 2005; Litvin, 2006); however, it is doubtless that the business case for looking at diversity issues, (including gender as a category) has become more prominent.

The aims of the diversity approach and its emphasis on the 'business case' contrast in a number of significant ways with the 'equal opportunity' approach traditionally deployed by many organizations (particularly in the UK and US) that emphasized social justice and fairness (Miller, 1996). 'Managing diversity' aims to specifically meet organizational goals. In this sense the concept is business-driven, rather than being underpinned by broader notions of social justice (Kaler, 2001). Indeed Noon and Ogbonna (2001) argue that this is the key analytical differentiation between 'equal opportunities' and 'managing diversity': that they are underpinned by two different rationales: 'equal opportunities' by the social justice (or moral) case and 'managing diversity' by the business case. While 'equal opportunities' policies may utilize business rationales to achieve moral/ social justice ends, 'managing diversity' policies can be seen to have a more exclusive focus on business case (Kaler, 2001: 59). Thus, 'managing diversity' appeals to critics of traditional equality approaches, who have argued that the moral cause of 'equality' has little purchase in the competitive world of business (Linnehan and Konrad, 1999).

Herein is the problem. As Dickens (1999: 10) states: 'the privatised approach of leaving EO to individual organizations taking voluntary business case driven initiatives is an insecure foundation for general overall improvement in the position of women'. Business case arguments are inevitably 'contingent, variable, selective and partial' (Dickens, 2006: 299) and depend on economic premises, which means that such action is only encouraged when EO and business needs coincide. Moreover, there is always the danger that a business case can be articulated against EO action (Dickens, 1999).

Reflecting on discussions of the macro context, what is needed to affect positive equality outcomes, are policies that aim to change organizational (and broader societal) attitudes, behaviours and cultures. For example, Rubery *et al.* (1999: 287)

taking a cross EU perspective, make a call for organizational policies that recognize the need to reorganize both paid *and* unpaid work. In other words, it is crucial that there are not only policies targeted at women's equality, there needs to be a broad campaign that aims to make common cause with the interests of men as workers and as parents if real change is to be achieved. However, most research seems to indicate that policy programmes are usually based around traditional policy interventions, more designed to treat the symptoms of discrimination than affect culture and change attitudes (Liff, 1999; Kirton *et al.*, 2006). There is little evidence that UK, EU, Australian or NZ employers are abandoning traditional EO policies in favour of diversity ones (Kirton and Greene, 2005).

## The 'top-down' nature of policy approaches

It is important to recognize the weakness of stakeholder involvement in EO policy development and implementation. It has almost become a common sense notion that the broadest range of people within an organization should be involved in the development and implementation of EO related policies. Kirton *et al.* (2006) in the UK found that the majority of interviewees commented that 'leadership' of equality and diversity issues had to come from all levels of the organization, including crucially, line management and non-managerial employees. Lack of wider 'buy-in' to EO and ingrained negative attitudes were seen as serious barriers, particularly at line management levels. Despite this, the practice of EO saw only a very small group of organizations where there were integrated, multi-channel forms of communication and consultation that genuinely seemed to proactively engage employees. Most non-managerial employees had little idea about what policies existed, and importantly, did not understand the rationale for these policies. Similar findings emerged from a survey of 200 companies in four EU countries (EC, 2003). If conceptual confusion is obvious amongst diversity practitioners, this was even more the case for other stakeholders. Mulholland *et al.* (2006) found that around one third of organizations do not involve employees in the design and implementation of their diversity policies and practices. The danger is that this process then leads to managers speaking on behalf of women and other disadvantaged groups within organizations, or trying to 'double guess' their needs (Jones *et al.*, 2000).

In outlining her three pronged approach to EO action, Dickens (1999) not only includes business-led policies and legislative regulation but also what she terms social or joint regulation. The social/joint regulatory approach sees a significant role for representatives of lower level, non-managerial employees, and in particular for trade unions. For Dickens (1999), this strategy offers the potential to extend beyond employer-determined agendas depending primarily on the business case, and importantly, offers a 'voice mechanism' for non-managerial level employees, potentially enabling women to be involved in shaping equality agendas.

There are examples where a joint regulatory approach has appeared to have led to significant progress. For example, while we should be careful not to see the Swedish example as an equity paradise (Due, Billing and Sundin, 2006), in comparative terms it is evident that women do experience considerable advantages within this system. Of note is the tripartite nature of this social system, with Dehrenz, Delander and Niklasson (2002) seeing the involvement of trade unions as of central importance to its success. Similarly, Rasmussen, Lind and Visser (2004) comparing levels and experience of part-time work by women in New Zealand, Denmark and The Netherlands, point to the positive elements of the Danish and Dutch cases, which illustrate the strength of negotiated solutions, where government policy is developed in consultation with, and is supported by, trade unions and employers. In all three cases, the strength of trade unions is an important factor. For example, the decrease in collective bargaining coverage and union density in New Zealand coincided with an increase in involuntary part-time work, whereas the take up of the cause of part-time workers by Dutch trade unions is seen as crucial to workers' positive experiences through the 1990s.

Clearly, levels of unionization within countries are a problem. One aspect of difference between the US and EU contexts involves the role of unions within the employment relationship. Unsurprisingly, given the context of extremely low unionization in the US, the diversity management literature has tended to neglect the role of unions and instead the commitment of senior management is accorded pre-eminence. In addition, the narrow nature of the union bargaining agenda is explained in part by the fact that union decision making structures in Europe are generally unrepresentative of membership diversity (Greene and Kirton, 2006), particularly of women and minority ethnic members (ETUC, 2002), even in some of the more gender-egalitarian countries such as Sweden (Curtin and Higgins, 1998).

## CONCLUSION

In summarizing the situation outlined within this chapter, some strategy is needed that attempts to bring together the macro- and the micro-perspectives to interrogate conditions which optimize and impede the effective implementation of employment equity at the organizational level. Dickens' (1999) proposal for a three-pronged approach to achieve employment equity still retains salience. This approach recognizes the weaknesses of the business case, and legal regulation and social regulation in isolation, but sees more positive potential where they are complementary and reinforcing.

There are now many critiques of the business case which dominates in the US diversity literature. As Litvin (2006: 78) highlights there is a need to move beyond a 'mega discourse' towards one that retains politicized elements (2006), has a clear power analysis and is nuanced in terms of the local context. Such an approach emphasizes the macro elements but omits the crucial micro-analysis that commenced our chapter. It is through an understanding of the intrapersonal – processes of stereotyping and categorization – together with analysis of the interpersonal power-infused interactions between managers, employees, and between co-workers – that many of the factors hindering implementation can be understood. In conclusion, our argument is for a tripartite analytical approach to provide a more comprehensive and better understanding to an equity agenda that is all but stalled. Future research and argument needs to include macro and micro elements to unpack the complex tasks of creating and furthering employment equity in organizations.

## NOTES

1 U.S. http://factfinder.census.gov/servlet/Australia: www.une.edu.au/campus/chaplaincy/uniting/links/diversity. New Zealand: http://www.stats.govt.nz/census/2006-census-data/national-highlights/pdf

2 'Visible minorities' is ascribed to non-white ethnic groups, defined as 'persons, other than aboriginal persons who are non-Caucasian in race or non-white in colour' (Jain, Sloane and Horwitz, 2003: 113).

3 Canada, presents a similar but different situation, where treaties were signed between colonizers and the indigenous tribal groups resulting in multiple treaties. Yet consistent with the postcolonial story treaty rights have not been well honoured in Canada (Globe and Mail, February, 2007).

4 The two terms differed in the Maori (sovereignty) and English (guardianship) versions.

5 UK now has a significantly new approach to public sector mandatory duties going beyond gender to include race, disability and will have on gender equality (Dickens, 2006).

6 The organizations surveyed are all 'best practice' organizations and members of the Trust.

## REFERENCES

ACTU (2006) Government official confirms penalty rates and shift allowances axed under IR laws. Media Release 30 May. Retrieved from http://www.actu.asn.au/work_rights/news/1148962081_17469.html

An agency well pruned [Editorial]. (December 1, 2006). *The Globe and Mail*, p. A26.

Agars, M.D. (2004) 'Reconsidering the impact of gender stereotypes on the advancement of women in organizations', *Psychology of Women Quarterly*, 28: 103–111.

Appelbaum, E., Bailey, T., Berg, P. and Kalleberg, A. (2002) 'Shared work/valued care: New norms for organizing market work and unpaid care work', in H. Mosley, J. O'Reilly, and K. Schomann (eds) *Labour Markets, Gender and Institutional Change: Essays in Honour of Gunther Schmid*. Cheltenham: Edward Elgar, pp. 136–165.

Arai, A.B. (2000) 'Self-employment as a response to the double day for women and men in Canada', *Canadian Review of Sociology and Anthropology*, 37: 125–142.

Aubrey, J.S. (2006) 'Exposure to sexually objectifying media and body self-perceptions among college women: An examination of the selective exposure hypothesis and the role of moderating variables', *Sex Roles*, 55: 159–172.

Baltes, B.B., Briggs, T.E., Huff, J.W., Wright, J.A. and Neuman, G.A. (1999) 'Flexible and compressed workweek schedules: A meta-analysis of their effects on work-related criteria', *Journal of Applied Psychology*, 84: 496–513.

Bauer, C.C. and Baltes, B.B. (2002) 'Reducing the effects of gender stereotypes on performance evaluations', *Sex Roles*, 47: 465–476.

Benschop, Y. (2006) 'Of small steps and the longing for giant leaps: Research on the intersection of sex and gender within workplaces and organizations', in A.M. Konrad, P. Prasad and J.K. Pringle (eds) *Handbook of Workplace Diversity*. London: Sage.

Berry, M. (2006, June 20) 'Female presence in EU boardrooms shows little improvement', *Personnel Today*, 8–9.

Bianchi, S.M., Milkie, M.A., Sayer, L.C. and Robinson, J.P. (2000) 'Is anyone doing the housework? Trends in the gender division of household labor', *Social Forces*, 79: 191–228.

Bolzendahl, C.I. and Myers, D.J. (2004) 'Feminist attitudes and support for gender equality: Opinion change in women and men, 1974–1998', *Social Forces*, 83: 759–789.

Bowen, C.C., Swim, J.K. and Jacobs, R.R. (2000) 'Evaluating gender biases on actual job performance of real people: A meta-analysis', *Journal of Applied Social Psychology*, 30: 2195–2215.

Bowes-Sperry, L. and Tata, J. (1999) 'A multiperspective framework of sexual harassment: Reviewing two decades of research', in G.N. Powell (ed.) *Handbook of Women and Work*. Thousand Oaks, CA: Sage, pp. 263–280.

Brett, J.F., Atwater, L.E. and Waldman, D.A. (2005) 'Effective delivery of workplace discipline: Do women have to be more participatory than men?', *Group and Organization Management*, 30: 487–513.

Browne, K.R. (2002) *Biology at Work: Rethinking Sexual Equality*. New Brunswick, NJ: Rutgers University Press.

Browne, K.R. (2006) 'Evolved sex differences and occupational segregation', *Journal of Organizational Behavior*, 27: 143–162.

Cameron, A. and Massey, C. (1998) *Small and Medium-sized Enterprises: A New Zealand Perspective*. Auckland: Addison Wesley Longman NZ Ltd.

Casey, C. (2002) *Critical Analysis of Organizations: Theory, Practice, Revitalization*. London: Sage.

Catalyst (2005) *Beyond a Reasonable Doubt: Building the Business Case for Flexibility*. New York: Catalyst.

Catalyst (2006a) *2005 Catalyst Census of Women Board Directors of the Fortune 500: Ten Years Later, Limited Progress, Challenges Persist*. New York: Catalyst.

Catalyst (2006b) *2005 Catalyst Census of Women Board Directors of the FP500*. New York: Catalyst.

Cockburn, C. (1989) 'Equal opportunities: The short and the long agenda', *Industrial Relations Journal*, 20 (3): 213–225.

Cockburn, C. (1991) *In the Way of Women*. Basingstoke: Macmillan.

Cohen, P.N. and Bianchi, S.M. (1999) 'Marriage, children, and women's employment: What do we know?', *Monthly Labor Review*, 122 (12): 22–31.

Coltraine, S. (2000) 'Research on household labor: Modeling and measuring the social embeddedness of routine family work', *Journal of Marriage and the Family*, 62: 1208–1233.

Cornelius, N., Gooch, L. and Todd, S. (2000) 'Managers leading diversity for business excellence', *Journal of General Management*, 25 (3): 67–78.

Curtin, J. and Higgins, W. (1998) 'Feminism and unionism in Sweden', *Politics and Society*, 16 (1): 69–93.

Davidson, M.J. and Burke, R.J. (eds) (2004) *Women in Management Worldwide: Facts, Figures and Analysis*. Aldershot: Ashgate.

Davis, S.N. and Greenstein, T.N. (2004) 'Cross-national variations in the division of household labor', *Journal of Marriage and the Family*, 66: 1260–1271.

Davison, H.K. and Burke, M.J. (2000) 'Sex discrimination in simulated employment contexts: A meta-analytic investigation', *Journal of Vocational Behavior*, 56: 225–248.

Deckop, J., Konrad, A.M., Perlmutter, F.D. and Freely, J. (2006, Winter) 'The effect of human resource management practices on the job retention of former welfare clients', *Human Resource Management*, 45: 539–559.

Dehrenz, L., Delander, L. and Niklasson, H. (2002) 'Can Sweden's Rehn-Meidner model be put back on its feet?', in H. Mosley, J. O'Reilly and K. Schomann (eds) *Labour Markets, Gender and Institutional Change: Essays in Honour of Günther Schmid*. Cheltenham: Edward Elgar, pp. 36–62.

Dickens, L. (1999) 'Beyond the business case: A three-pronged approach to equality action', *Human Resource Management Journal*, 9 (1): 9–19.

Dickens, L. (2006) 'Re-regulation for gender equality: From either/or to both', *Industrial Relations Journal*, 37 (4): 299–309.

Diekman, A.B., Eagly, A.H., Mladinic, A. and Ferreira, M.C. (2005) 'Dynamic stereotypes about women and men in Latin America and the United States', *Journal of Cross-Cultural Psychology*, 36: 209–226.

Döring, N. and Pöschl, S. (2006) 'Images of men and women in mobile phone advertisements: A content analysis of advertisements for mobile communication systems in selected popular magazines', *Sex Roles*, 55: 173–185.

Dreher, G.F. (2003) 'Breaking the glass ceiling: The effects of sex ratios and work-life programs on female leadership at the top', *Human Relations*, 56: 541–562.

Due Billing, Y. and Sundin, E. (2006) 'From managing equality to managing diversity: A critical Scandinavian perspective on gender and workplace diversity', in A. Konrad, P. Prasad and J.K. Pringle (eds) *Handbook of Workplace Diversity*. London: Sage, pp. 95–120.

Eagly, A.H., Makhijani, M.G. and Klonsky, B.G. (1992) 'Gender and the evaluation of leaders: A meta-analysis', *Psychological Bulletin*, 111: 3–22.

EC (2003) *The costs and benefits of diversity: A study on methods and indicators to measure the cost effectiveness of diversity policies in enterprises: Executive summary*. Brussels: European Commission.

EEO Trust (2001) *Trust Diversity Index*. Auckland: EEO Trust.

ETUC (2002) *Women in Trade Unions: Making the Difference*. Brussels: ETUC.

European Professional Women's Network (2006) *Second Bi-annual European PWN Board Women Monitor*. Paris: European PWN.

Eurostat (2004) *How Europeans Spend their Time: Everyday Life of Women and Men*. Luxembourg: European Communities.

Fiissel, D.L. and Lafreniere, K.D. (2006) 'Weight control motives for cigarette smoking: Further consequences of the sexual objectification of women?', *Feminism and Psychology*, 16: 327.

Filer, R.K. (1985) 'Male–female wage differences: The importance of compensating differentials', *Industrial and Labor Relations Review*, 38: 426–437.

Filer, R.K. (1986) 'The role of personality and tastes in determining occupational structures', *Industrial and Labor Relations Review*, 39: 412–424.

Fitzgerald, L.F., Gelfand, M.J. and Drasgow, F. (1995) 'Measuring sexual harassment: Theoretical and psychometric advances', *Basic and Applied Social Psychology*, 17: 425–445.

French, E. (2001) 'Approaches to equity management and their relationship to women in management', *British Journal of Management*, 12: 267–285.

Fuwa, M. (2004) 'Macro-level gender inequality and the division of household labor in 22 countries', *American Sociological Review*, 69: 751–767.

Gagnon, S. and Cornelius, N. (2002) 'From equality to managing diversity to capabilities: A new theory of workplace diversity', in N. Cornelius (ed.) *Building Workplace Equality: Ethics, Diversity and Inclusion*. London: Thomson, pp. 13–58.

Geist, C. (2005) 'The welfare state and the home: Regime differences in the domestic division of labour', *European Sociological Review*, 21: 23–41.

Glick, P., Larsen, S., Johnson, C. and Branstiter, H. (2005) 'Evaluations of sexy women in low- and high-status jobs', *Psychology of Women Quarterly*, 29: 389–395.

Greene, A.-M. and Kirton, G. (2006) 'Trade unions and equality and diversity', in A.M. Konrad, P. Prasad and J.K. Pringle (eds) *Handbook of Workplace Diversity*. London: Sage, pp. 489–530.

Greene, A.M., Kirton, G. and Wrench, J. (2005) 'Trade union perspectives on diversity management: A comparison of the UK and Denmark', *European Journal of Industrial Relations*, 11 (2): 179–186.

Grover, S.L. and Crooker, K.J. (1995) 'Who appreciates family-responsive human resource policies: The impact of family-friendly policies on the organizational attachment of parents and non-parents', *Personnel Psychology*, 48: 271–288.

Gustafsson, S., Kenjoh, E. and Wetzels, C. (2002) 'The labour force transition of first time mothers in UK, Germany, the Netherlands and Sweden', in H. Mosley, J. O'Reilly and K. Schomann (eds) *Labour Markets, Gender and Institutional Change: Essays in Honour of Gunther Schmid*. Cheltenham: Edward Elgar, pp. 185–211.

Hakim, C. (2000) *Work-lifestyle Choices in the 21st Century: Preference Theory*. Oxford: Oxford University Press.

Hakim, C. (2002) 'Lifestyle preferences as determinants of women's differentiated labor market careers', *Work and Occupations*, 29: 428–459.

Halleröd, B. (2005) 'Sharing of housework and money among Swedish couples: Do they behave rationally?', *European Sociological Review*, 21: 273–288.

Hamilton, M.C., Anderson, D., Broaddus, M. and Young, K. (2006) 'Gender stereotyping and under-representation of female characters in 200 popular children's picture books: A twenty-first century update', *Sex Roles*, 55: 757–765.

Hamilton, P. (2001) 'Rhetoric and employment relations', *British Journal of Industrial Relations*, 39 (3): 433–449.

Harrell, Z.A.T., Fredrickson, B.L., Pomerleau, C.S. and Nolen-Hoeksema, S. (2006) 'The role of trait self-objectification in smoking among college women', *Sex Roles*, 54: 735–743.

Harrison, D.A., Kravitz, D.A., Mayer, D.M., Leslie, L.M. and Lev-Arey, D. (2006) 'Understanding attitudes toward affirmative action programs in employment: Summary and meta-analysis of 35 years of research', *Journal of Applied Psychology*, 91: 1013–1036.

Helfat, C.E., Harris, D. and Wolfson, P.J. (2006) 'The pipeline to the top: Women and men in the top executive ranks of U.S. corporations', *Academy of Management Perspectives*, 20 (4): 42–64.

Henneman, T. (2006, July 31) 'After high court ruling, firms may want to take long look at anti-harassment strategies', *Workforce Management*, 85 (14): 33–35.

Hewlitt, S.A. and Luce, C.B. (2006, December) 'Extreme jobs: The dangerous allure of the 70-hour workweek', *Harvard Business Review*, 84 (12): 49–59.

Holtzman, J. and Glass, J. (1999) 'Explaining changes in mothers' job satisfaction following childbirth', *Work and Occupations*, 26: 365–404.

Holzer, H.J. and Newmark, D. (2000) 'What does affirmative action do?', *Industrial and Labor Relations Review*, 53: 240–271.

Hoque, K. and Noon, M. (2004) 'Equal opportunities policy and practice in UK: Evaluating the "empty shell" hypothesis', *Work Employment and Society*, 18 (3): 481–506.

House, R., Rousseau, D. and Thomas-Hunt, M. (1995) 'The meso paradigm: A framework for the integration of micro- and macro-organizational behavior', in L.L. Cumings and B. Staw (eds) *Research in Organizational Behavior*. Greenwich, CT: JAI Press, 17: pp. 71–114.

Hymowitz, C. (2006) Women tell women: Life in the top jobs is worth the effort. *Wall Street Journal*, B1, 20 November.

Igbaria, M. and Guimaraes, T. (1999) 'Exploring differences in employee turnover intentions and its determinants among telecommuters and non-telecommuters', *Journal of Management Information Systems*, 16: 147–164.

Irman, L. (2006) 'Automatic activation and use of gender stereotypes', *Sex Roles*, 55: 435–444.

Jain, H.C., Sloane, P.J. and Horwitz, F.M. (2003) *Employment Equity and Affirmative Action*. Armonk: M.E. Sharpe, Inc.

Jewson, N. and Mason, D. (1986) 'The theory and practice of equal opportunities policies: Liberal and radical approaches', *Sociological Review*, 34 (2): 307–334.

Jones, D. (2004) 'Screwing diversity out of the workers? Three readings of the vocabulary of "diversity management"', *Journal of Organizational Change Management*, 17 (3): 281–291.

Jones, D. and Stablein, R. (2006) 'Diversity as resistance and recuperation: Critical theory, post-structuralist perspectives and workplace diversity', in A. Konrad, P. Prasad and J.K. Pringle (eds) *Handbook of Workplace Diversity*. London: Sage, pp. 145–166.

Jones, D., Pringle, J.K. and Shepherd, D. (2000) '"Managing diversity" meets Aotearoa/New Zealand', *Personnel Review*, 29 (3): 364–380.

Kaler, J. (2001) 'Diversity, equality, morality', in M. Noon and E. Ogbonna (eds) *Equality, Diversity and Disadvantage in Employment*. Basingstoke: Palgrave.

Kilbourne, J. (2005) 'What else does sex sell?', *International Journal of Advertising*, 24: 119–122.

Killeen, L.A., López-Zafra, E. and Eagly, A.H. (2006) 'Envisioning oneself as a leader: Comparisons of women and men in Spain and the United States', *Psychology of Women Quarterly*, 30: 312–322.

King, B. (2006, Jan/Feb) 'Orientalizing sexism: Hye Rim Lee's Toki', *Afterimage*, 33 (4): 25–29.

Kirton, G. and Greene, A.M. (2005) *The Dynamics of Managing Diversity: A Critical Approach* (2nd edn). Oxford: Butterworth Heinemann.

Kirton G. and Greene A.M. (2006) 'The discourse of diversity in unionised contexts: Views from trade union equality officers', *Personnel Review*, 34: 431–448.

Kirton, G., Greene, A.M. and Dean, D. (2006) 'The multi-dimensional nature of work in the "diversity industry"'. Paper presented at the *Industrial Relations in Europe Conference, IREC, Workshop on Industrial Relations and Diversity*, Ljubljana, Slovenia, 31 August–2 September 2006.

Kirton, G., Greene, A.M. and Dean, D. (2007) 'British diversity professionals as change agents – Radicals, tempered radicals or liberal reformers?', *International Journal of Human Resource Management*, 18 (11): 1979–1994.

Kirton, G., Greene, A.M., Dean, D. and Creegan, C. (2006) Findings from an ESF-funded project involvement of stakeholders in diversity management.

Retrieved from http://www2.warwick.ac.uk/fac/soc/wbs/research/irru/research/esfdiversity/professional_perspectives_report_01_06.pdf

Konrad, A.M. and Linnehan, F. (1995) 'Formalized HRM structures: Coordinating equal employment opportunity or concealing organizational practices?', *Academy of Management Journal*, 38: 787–820.

Konrad, A. and Linnehan, F. (1999) 'Affirmative action: History, effects and attitudes', in G.N. Powell (ed.) *Handbook of Gender and Work*. Thousand Oaks, CA: Sage, pp. 429–452.

Konrad, A.M. and Mangel, R. (2000) 'The impact of work-life programs on firm productivity', *Strategic Management Journal*, 21: 1225–1237.

Konrad, A.M., Ritchie, J.E., Jr., Lieb, P. and Corrigall, E. (2000) 'Sex differences and similarities in job attribute preferences: A meta-analysis', *Psychological Bulletin*, 126: 593–641.

Kossek, E. and Lobel, S. (1996) 'Introduction: Transforming human resource systems to manage diversity – an introduction and orienting framework', in E. Kossek and S. Lobel (eds) *Managing Diversity: Human Resource Strategies for Transforming the Workplace*. Cambridge, MA: Blackwell Business.

Kossek, E.E., Huber-Yoder, M., Castellino, D. and Lerner, J. (1997) 'The working poor: Locked out of careers and the organizational mainstream?', *Academy of Management Executive*, 11 (1): 76–92.

Kossek, E., Lobel, S. and Brown, J. (2006) 'Human resource strategies to manage work force diversity: Examining the "business case"', in A. Konrad, P. Prasad and J.K. Pringle (eds) *Handbook of Workplace Diversity*. London: Sage, pp. 53–74.

Kossek, E.E. and Nichol, V. (1992) 'The effects of on-site child care on employee attitudes and performance', *Personnel Psychology*, 45: 485–509.

Kulik, C.T., Perry, E.L. and Bourhis, A.C. (2000) 'Ironic evaluation processes: Effects of thought suppression on evaluations of older job applicants', *Journal of Organizational Behavior*, 21: 689–711.

Lawrence, B. (2004) 'Levels of analysis and the qualitative study of quantitative data', in F. Yammarino and F. Dansereau (eds) *Research in Multi-level Issues*, Vol. 3. Oxford: Elsevier Ltd., pp. 231–250.

Lawrence, E. (2000) 'Equal opportunities officers and managing equality changes', *Personnel Review*, 29 (3): 381–401.

Leck, J.D. and Saunders, D.M. (1992) 'Hiring women: The effects of Canada's Employment Equity Act', *Canadian Public Policy*, 18: 203–220.

Leck, J.D., St. Onge, S. and LaLancette, I. (1995) 'Wage gap changes among organizations subject to the

Employment Equity Act', *Canadian Public Policy*, 21: 387–400.

Lee, Y. and Waite, L.J. (2005) 'Husbands' and wives' time spent on housework: A comparison of measures', *Journal of Marriage and the Family*, 67: 328–336.

Leonard, J.S. (1984) 'Antidiscrimination or reverse discrimination: The impact of changing demographics, Title VII, and affirmative action on productivity', *Journal of Human Resources*, 19: 145–174.

Leonard, J.S. (1985) 'What promises are worth: The impact of affirmative action goals', *Journal of Human Resources*, 20: 3–20.

Leonard, J.S. (1986) 'The effectiveness of equal employment law and affirmative action regulation', in R.G. Ehrenberg (ed.) *Research in Labor Economics*, vol. 8, part B. Greenwich, CT: JAI Press, pp. 319–350.

Li, J. (2005) 'Women's status in a rural Chinese setting', *Rural Sociology*, 70: 229–252.

Liff, S. (1999) 'Diversity and equal opportunities: Room for a constructive compromise?', *Human Resource Management Journal*, 9 (1): 65–75.

Liff, S. and Wajcman, J. (1996) '"Sameness" and "difference" revisited: Which way forward for equal opportunity initiatives?', *Journal of Management Studies*, 33 (1): 79–95.

Linnehan, F. and Konrad, A. (1999) 'Diluting diversity: Implications for intergroup inequality in organizations', *Journal of Management Inquiry*, 8 (4): 399–414.

Linnehan, F., Chrobot-Mason, D. and Konrad, A.M. (2006) 'Diversity attitudes and norms: The role of ethnic identity and relational demography', *Journal of Organizational Behavior*, 27 (4): 419–442.

Litvin, D. (2002) 'The business case for diversity and the "iron cage" ', in B. Czarniawska and H. Höpfl (eds) *Casting the Other*. London: Routledge.

Litvin, D. (2006) 'Diversity: Making space for a better case', in A. Konrad, P. Prasad and J.K. Pringle (eds) *Handbook of Workplace Diversity*. London: Sage, pp. 75–94.

Lobel, S.A., Googins, B.K. and Bankert, E. (1999) 'The future of work and family: Critical trends for policy, practice and research', *Human Resource Management*, 38: 243–254.

Lorbiecki, A. (2001) 'Openings and burdens for women and minority ethnics being diversity vanguards in UK'. *Gender, Work and Organization*, Keele University, UK.

Lounsbury, M. and Ventresca, M. (2003) 'The new structuralism in organizational theory', *Organization*, 10 (3): 457–480.

Lyness, K.S., Thompson, C.A., Francesco, A.M. and Judiesch, M.K. (1999) 'Work and pregnancy: Individual and organizational factors influencing organizational commitment, timing of maternity leave, and return to work', *Sex Roles*, 41: 485–508.

Martell, R.F. (1996) 'What mediates gender bias in work behavior ratings?', *Sex Roles*, 35: 153–169.

Mathieu, J.E. and Taylor, S.R. (2007) 'A framework for testing meso-mediational relationships in organization behavior', *Journal of Organizational Behavior*, 28: 141–172.

McGregor, J. (2004) 'Women in management in New Zealand', in M. Davidson and R. Burke (eds) *Women in Management Worldwide: Facts, Figures and Analysis*. Aldershot: Ashgate Publishing, pp. 211–224.

McGregor, J. and Fountaine, S. (2006) *Census of Women's Participation in Governance and Professional Life*. Wellington: Human Rights Commission and NZ Centre for Women and Leadership.

Meyerson, D. and Scully, M. (1995) 'Tempered radicalism and the politics of ambivalence and change', *Organization Science*, 6 (6): 585–600.

Miller, D. (1996) 'Equality management: Towards a materialist approach', *Gender, Work and Organization*, 3 (4): 202–214.

Mintrom, M. and True, J. (2004) *Framework for the Future: Equal Employment Opportunities in New Zealand*. Wellington: Human Rights Commission Publication. Retrieved 13 Februrary, 2007 from www.hrc.co.nz/eeo

Moore, D.W. (2002) 'Americans more accepting of female bosses than ever', *The Gallup Poll Tuesday Briefing*, 5, May.

Mulholland, G., Ozbilgin, M. and Worman, D. (2006) *Diversity in business: How much progress have employers made? First Findings*. Survey Report, Chartered Institute of Personnel and Development (CIPD), London.

Nentwich, J. (2006) 'Changing gender: The discursive construction of equal opportunities', *Gender, Work and Organization*, 13 (6): 499–521.

Noon, M. and Ogbonna, E. (2001) *Equality, Diversity and Disadvantage in Employment*. Basingstoke: Palgrave.

Perotin, V., Robinson, A. and Loundes, J. (2003) 'Equal opportunities practices and enterprise performance: A comparative investigation on Australian and British data', *International Labor Review*, 142 (4): 471–506.

Perry, E.L., Kulik, C.T. and Bourhis, A.C. (1996) 'Moderating effects of personal and contextual factors in age discrimination', *Journal of Applied Psychology*, 81: 628–647.

Powell, G.N., Butterfield, D.A. and Parent, J.D. (2002) 'Gender and managerial stereotypes: Have the times changed?', *Journal of Management*, 28: 177–193.

Prasad, A. (2001) 'Understanding workplace empowerment as inclusion', *Journal of Applied Behavioral Science*, 37 (1): 51–69.

Prasad, A. and Prasad, P. (2002) 'Otherness at large: Identity and difference in the new globalized organizational landscape', in I. Aaltio and A. Mills (eds) *Gender, Identity and the Culture of Organizations*. London: Sage, pp. 57–71.

Prasad, P., Konrad, A.M. and Pringle, J.K. (2006) 'Examining workplace diversity', in A.M. Konrad, P. Prasad and J.K. Pringle (eds) *Handbook of Workplace Diversity*. London: Sage, pp. 1–22.

Prentice, D.A. and Carranza, E. (2002) 'What women and men should be, shouldn't be, are allowed to be, and don't have to be: The contents of prescriptive gender stereotypes', *Psychology of Women Quarterly*, 26: 269–281.

Quinn, D.M., Kallen, R.W., Twenge, J.M. and Fredrickson, B.L. (2006) 'The disruptive effect of self-objectification on performance', *Psychology of Women Quarterly*, 30: 59–64.

Rasmussen, E., Lind, J. and Visser, J. (2004) 'Divergence in part-time work in New Zealand, Netherlands and Denmark', *British Journal of Industrial Relations*, 42 (4): 637–658.

Ratuva, S. (1999) *Reconstruction, affirmative action and development in South Africa*. Working Paper 4/99, Suva: University of South Pacific.

Riordan, C. (2000) 'Relational demography within groups: Past developments, contradictions and new directions', *Research in Personnel and Human Resources Management*, 19: 131–173.

Roberson, L., Kulik, C.T. and Pepper, M.B. (2003) 'Using needs assessment to resolve controversies in diversity training design', *Group and Organization Management*, 28: 148–174.

Rubery, J., Smith, M. and Fagan, C. (1999) *Women's Employment in Europe: Trends and Prospects*. Routledge: London.

Schein, V.E. (2001) 'A global look at psychological barriers to women's progress in management', *Journal of Social Issues*, 57: 675–688.

Signorielli, N. and Bacue, A. (1999) 'Recognition and respect: A content analysis of prime-time television characters across three decades', *Sex Roles*, 40: 527–544.

Sinclair, A. (2000) 'Women within diversity: Risks and possibilities', *Women in Management Review*, 15 (5/6): 237–245.

Singh, V. and Vinnicombe, S. (2005). *The Female FTSE Index 2005*. Cranfield: Cranfield School of Management, Centre for Developing Women Business Leaders.

Singleton, J. (2000) 'Women caring for elderly family members: Shaping non-traditional work and family initiatives', *Journal of Comparative Family Studies*, 31: 367–375.

Spitzer, B.L., Henderson, K.A. and Zivizn, M.T. (1999) 'Gender differences in population versus media body sizes: A comparison over four decades', *Sex Roles*, 40: 545–565.

Strachan, G., Burgess, J. and Sullivan, A. (2004) 'Affirmative action or managing diversity: What is the future of equal opportunity policies in organizations?', *Women in Management Review*, 19 (4): 196–204.

Sümer, H.C. (2006) 'Women in management: Still waiting to be full members of the club', *Sex Roles*, 55: 63–72.

Szymanski, D.M. and Henning, S.L. (2007) 'The role of self-objectification in women's depression: A test of objectification theory', *Sex Roles*, 56: 45–53.

Thompson, C.A., Beauvais, L.L. and Lyness, K.S. (1999) 'When work-family benefits are not enough: The influence of work-family culture on benefit utilization, organizational attachment, and work-family conflict', *Journal of Vocational Behavior*, 54: 392–415.

Williams, J.E. and Best, D.L. (1990) *Sex and Psyche: Gender and Self-Viewed Cross-culturally*. Thousand Oaks, CA: Sage.

Wrench, J. (2005) 'Diversity management and unions in Europe: A comparison between the UK and Denmark', in L.N. Thisted and S. Nour (eds) *Moving the Frontiers of Diversity Management*. Copenhagen: Børsens Forlag.

Yammarino, F. and Dansereau, F. (eds) (2004) *Research in Multi-level Issues*, Vol. 3. Oxford: Elsevier Ltd.

Yang, C., D'Souza, G., Bapat, A. and Colarelli, S. (2006) 'A cross-national analysis of affirmative action', *Managerial and Decision Economics*, 27: 203–216.

Yi, C.-C. and Chien, W.-Y. (2002) 'The linkage between work and family: Female's employment patterns in three Chinese societies', *Journal of Comparative Family Studies*, 33: 451–474.

# 18

# Managing Multi-culturally in Organizations in a Diverse Society

Gill Kirton

## INTRODUCTION

Early research on diversity tended to be located in the mainstream management literature and typically had a prescriptive character, attempting to provide techniques and tools to help organizations to manage multi-culturally. Academics were accused of 'distant cheerleading', endorsing the importance of diversity management, but not treating it as a serious research area (Prasad and Mills, 1997: 5). The diversity literature is now far richer and is influenced by a variety of (sometimes overlapping) theoretical perspectives, including post-colonial theory, feminism, postmodernism, critical approaches, social identity theory. These perspectives are used to explore variously the underlying structures of inequalities (Humphries and Grice, 1995); the processes by which inequalities, marginalization and exclusion are produced and reproduced within organizations (Kersten, 2000; Kirton and Greene, 2006); the processes by

which resistance and challenges are generated and marshalled (Janssens and Zanoni, 2005; Kirton *et al.*, 2007); the effects of diversity on business performance (Kochan *et al.*, 2003; Strauss and Connerley, 2003); the success or failure of organizational diversity initiatives (D'Netto and Sohal, 1999; Maxwell *et al.*, 2001).

The increased academic interest in diversity reflects the burgeoning over the last decade of organizational policies seeking to 'manage' diversity. Such has been the spread of policies that diversity is often referred to as a new organizational paradigm (Gilbert *et al.*, 1999). Diversity management is said to refer to 'the systematic and planned commitment on the part of organizations to recruit and retain employees from diverse demographic backgrounds' (Thomas, 1990). The concern with how to manage diversity arose because of the increasing demographic complexity of the labour market, particularly in the USA where the management of diversity concept was born (Litvin 1997; Kelly and Dobbin, 1998). The now (in)famous *Workforce 2000* report (Johnston and Packer, 1987), alerted organizations in the US to the (allegedly) dramatic changes that were occurring in the American workforce. In particular the report highlighted that by 2000 white males would no longer be the dominant demographic group *entering* the US labour market. This prompted widespread discussion in the media, business and academic forums of the greater need for organizations to recognize the importance of managing a diverse or multi-cultural work-force. *Workforce 2000* talked about the impact of the increasing labour market participation of women and the ageing workforce, but it was the vision of increased racial/ethnic diversity that attracted most attention. Many of the most alarming predictions and discussions were the consequence of the researchers' errors or readers' misinterpretations; for example, the report was often (mis)read as stating that by 2000 white males would no longer be the dominant demographic group *within* the US labour market (Litvin, 2006). The widespread diffusion of the business case for diversity can be traced back to the *Workforce 2000* report, but certainly by the 2000s the diversity concept, with the business case at its core, has reached most, if not all, developed countries.

So, what is the business case for diversity? Exponents claim that in the context of an increasingly diverse society organizations benefit from having, utilizing and valuing a diverse workforce (Thomas, 1990; Ross and Schneider, 1992; Kandola and Fullerton, 1998). The four main organizational benefits are said to be: taking advantage of diversity in the labour market; maximizing employee potential; managing across borders and cultures; creating business opportunities and enhancing creativity (Cornelius *et al.*, 2001). However, the caveat offered by exponents is that the only hitherto 'proven' benefits relate largely to the rather obvious (and arguably not new) 'taking advantage of diversity in the labour market': specifically organization savings on recruitment, attrition and training; access to a wider pool of candidates; and

increased flexibility (Kandola and Fullerton, 1998: 36). The other supposed benefits are acknowledged as remaining highly debatable and unproven and arguably rather more fanciful.

The chapter identifies three major dilemmas of diversity that emerge from the critical literature on organizational diversity policies and initiatives. The first is the emphasis on the 'business case'. Prasad and Mills (1997: 17) suggest that this means that workforce diversity and multi-culturalism are being commodified and 'in danger of becoming trendy consumer items' within a diversity 'industry' with superficial policies that will not withstand the test of time or do anything to advance the equality project. Whether there is really a business case for all organizations at all times and in all places is also questionable (e.g., Kossek *et al.*, 2003). The second dilemma concerns how managers 'manage' diversity. Asymmetrical power relations (often based on gender and race/ethnicity) within organizations are glossed over by exponents, while diversity initiatives become something that is 'done' by rational, competent and prejudice-free managers to lower level employees (Blommaert and Verschueren, 1998; de los Reyes, 2000; Janssens and Zanoni, 2005). The third is the way that issues of resistance and challenge are downplayed by the upbeat language and rhetoric of the diversity discourse and the suggestion that everyone (even white men!) can and will benefit (Jones *et al.*, 2000; Kersten, 2000). Before engaging with these dilemmas, the chapter first outlines the main ways of theorizing diversity.

## THEORIZING DIVERSITY

Diversity is a highly problematic term. A question that is now frequently asked is what do organizations, policy makers and researchers, mean when they talk about diversity (Greene *et al.*, 2005; Prasad *et al.*, 2006)? On the one hand it might be argued that organizations cannot begin to develop strategies to 'manage' diversity or think about the challenges that might be encountered in doing so, until they have decided what is meant by the term. Echoing this, Cox (1994: 51) has asserted that 'conceptual clarity' is essential to advancing research on diversity in order to avoid confusion and ambiguity and to establish what might and might not be included in diversity research. On the other hand ambiguity and confusion are arguably inevitable, even desirable, especially when attempting to establish a universal definition of diversity. Various authors writing from beyond the Anglo-American context have rejected both the idea of a 'meta-language' of diversity that transcends or comprehends all differences and the idea of diversity as a 'global discourse' (Humphries and Grice, 1995; Kamp and Hagedorn-Rasmussen, 2004; Jones and Stablein, 2006). These authors have drawn attention to the inadequacies of US understandings of diversity for other national contexts – that is, the social, economic and political conditions that prompted the emergence of diversity in the US do not necessarily apply to all countries. In addition, the confusion and ambiguity that marks the diversity territory might actually be helpful to practitioners and policy makers as it might open up possibilities for broadening the organizational agenda beyond the rather more narrow focus of traditional 'equal opportunities' (EO) policies or for using diversity as a discursive tool to advance the interests of marginalized and disadvantaged groups (rather than organizational interests). The possibility of different national and organizational interpretations notwithstanding, it is worth outlining the main ways in which diversity is understood.

*First*, diversity can be used as a *descriptor* of employee differences (workforce diversity), but what differences are included? Some authors argue that diversity should be an inclusive description 'of the total workforce not a name for members of minority groups' (Cox, 1994: 51).This broad definition is intended to counter the fear that diversity research and policy might become a kind of code or smokescreen for a focus on gender and race/ethnicity (just as in

traditional EO and 'affirmative action' [AA] approaches) and therefore not a new paradigm at all. Potentially both individual and social group-based differences might be included in diversity; so while organizations might want to target policy initiatives at groups such as women, black workers, older workers, etc., they might also want to develop other initiatives to actively 'manage' individual differences such as personality characteristics or lifestyle choices (Kandola and Fullerton, 1998). The problem is that this implies an equivalence of dimensions of difference so that less obvious markers of difference (e.g., personality, work-style, life-style) are seen as having equivalent meaning and effects as the most visible and immutable markers (e.g., gender and race) (Sinclair, 2006). Further, if organizational policy is insensitive to the concept of group oppression, then the equality project is likely to be set back for 'minorities' because the reality is that although diversity has encouraged the spread of rhetoric of celebration of differences and multiculturalism, organizations are largely mono-cultural in terms of the norms, values and cultural preferences that underpin management practices and do not appear ready to accept differences on equal terms (Prasad and Mills, 1997).

Moreover, organizations are unlikely to dedicate the resources to deal with an infinite array of differences, so it is necessary for organizations to make decisions about what kinds of employee differences are relevant or legitimate and why? Obviously social, political and economic factors determine the nature of the labour supply (for example, more women, older people etc. than previously), forcing some employers to seek to attract as diverse a pool of employees as possible (as exponents of diversity suggest). However, it is management that decides the types of difference that are legitimate (probably the ones with an economic value) or relevant but in a negative way (perhaps because they are perceived as having a potentially detrimental effect in the organizational context) and only these legitimate and 'relevant' differences are likely to be actively 'managed' within a diversity approach (Janssens and Zanoni, 2005). In an analysis of mainstream organizational behaviour textbooks and their treatment of diversity, Litvin (1997) finds that, irrespective of the claim that diversity is about the entire workforce, it is usually defined in terms of demographic differences because it is characteristics such as gender, race/ethnicity, age that are seen as having the most bearing on business and hence on organizational policies and practices.

The *second* way of understanding diversity is as an *organizational policy approach* explicitly focused on utilizing and valuing employee differences – usually referred to as diversity management or managing diversity. As indicated earlier, diversity management has a longer history in the USA compared with the UK and other countries, but the precise relationship between this and the older EO and AA approaches is difficult to determine and has been widely debated (Liff, 1997; Kelly and Dobbin, 1998; de los Reyes, 2000; Kaler, 2001; Kirton and Greene, 2006). However, it is clear that organizations can and sometimes do use the label diversity management to symbolize a break away from these earlier approaches that were designed to tackle the discrimination and disadvantage experienced by 'minority groups' (usually women and black workers), rather than to fulfil organizational goals. From an organizational perspective, diversity has the advantage of being a more inclusive analytic category and is therefore potentially less contentious and divisive and therefore less likely to provoke the (white, male) backlash associated with earlier approaches (Litvin, 2006; Mir *et al.*, 2006). Thus, echoing the debate about the differences in practice between HRM and personnel management, while it is debatable whether or not the 'new' label really means any *deep* changes in the substantive content of organizational policies (Kirton and Greene, 2005), it can be useful (for researchers at least) to characterize the two approaches (EO/AA and diversity) as indicating competing emphases as this provides a conceptual map to locate organizational policies (Noon and Ogbonna, 2001).

So what distinguishes diversity management from the previous policy approaches (EO/AA)? Although there has been a lot written about what diversity is and is not and there are now a number of definitions that are not rehearsed here (see Lorbiecki and Jack, 2000), there is agreement about its central tenets and there are few differences between the US and UK (and other countries). Diversity management (i) advocates a systemic (or cultural) transformation of the organization, rather than a reliance on legal regulation and bureaucratic procedures; (ii) uses positive imagery and celebratory rhetoric, rather than highlighting discrimination and the penalties that organizations face under equality laws; (iii) efforts are justified by reference to the business case, rather than legal compulsion or the social justice case; (iv) includes a broad range of individual and social group based differences (Cox, 1994; Kandola and Fullerton, 1998; Kersten, 2000).

Although, as stated, it is useful to juxtapose EO with diversity management approaches, there is a danger that doing so fails to recognize the way that for many organizations diversity management is a shift, rather than a departure from EO or AA policies, not least because laws and regulations impose certain requirements on employers. Critical authors generally recognize the legacy of earlier approaches. For example, Liff (1997) proposes a multi-dimensional model of diversity management which highlights the degree of organizational commitment to social group equality as an objective and the perceived relevance of social group difference for policy making (the conventional EO and AA approaches).

*Third*, diversity can be seen as a *conceptual construct*. While diversity management in practice is related to the earlier policy approaches of EO and AA, diversity as a concept has philosophical origins that are different to concepts of equality. Concepts of equality rest on a belief in an ideal of universal humanity that involves treating everyone according to the same principles, rules and standards – what Young (1990) refers to as the 'assimilationist ideal'. Paradoxically, because any laws, rules or social practices that distribute benefits and rewards differentially according to group membership are perceived as unjust, this ideal will sometimes call for special or different treatment of marginalized groups (Young, 1990: 158) as in EO/AA. Young (1990: 159) states that the ideal of universal humanity, while now widely critiqued, has been extremely important in the struggle against exclusion and has made possible the assertion of the 'equal moral worth' of all persons. The diversity concept has its roots in a 'politics of difference', where social groups assert positive group differences and the vision of the 'good society' is one where there is equality among groups, who 'mutually respect one another and affirm one another in their differences' (Young, 1990: 163). According to Young (1990: 173) recognition of differences has emancipatory and transformational potential because asserting the value and specificity of the culture and attributes of oppressed groups is liberating and empowering for those groups and at the same time revitalizes the dominant culture. However, if this potential is to be realized it is necessary for differences to be respected in policy through initiatives that take notice of the specific situation of oppressed groups in order to offset any disadvantage they face.

Despite its emancipatory potential the diversity concept has been appropriated by managerialists. Indeed, one of the most striking features of diversity management is the managerialist language that infuses it (Lorbiecki and Jack, 2000). Lorbiecki and Jack (2000) claim that the diversity concept has evolved over time. They identify four 'critical turns' – demographic (mid-late 1980s), political (early 1990s), economic (mid-1990s) and critical (mid-late 1990s). The demographic turn explicitly recognized employee differences – the 'new' heterogeneity of the (US) workforce. Diversity management turned political when its inclusive philosophy (all individuals and groups should be equally valued) came to be seen as an attractive alternative to EO and AA approaches (with their special measures

to assist disadvantaged groups) that had provoked (white, male) backlash, particularly in the US. The economic turn came when articles in management and business magazines started to promulgate the business case for diversity and workforce diversity was positioned as an organizational resource. The diversity literature turned more critical once it became clear that despite the positive rhetoric, there were problems in implementing diversity initiatives within organizations.

*Fourth*, diversity can be regarded as a *discourse or a discursive practice* (taking the term 'discourse' to denote a 'representation of norms for accepted thinking and thereby as a model for the interpretation and understanding of society' [de los Reyes, 2000: 255]). The diversity discourse places the business case centre stage, making it appear incontestable common sense and logic that workforce diversity can only enhance organizational success (Litvin, 1997; Sinclair, 2006). Litvin (2006: 85) positions the business case for diversity as a 'normalized mega-discourse that enshrines the achievement of organizational economic goals as the ultimate guiding principle and explanatory device for people in organizations.' When organizations adopt the label 'diversity' to signal their acceptance of this guiding principle, this in itself can be regarded as a discursive strategy that has political consequences as it shifts the focus away from redressing inequalities to the achievement of economic goals.

The use of evocative, positive metaphors in the diversity (practitioner) literature (and reflected in the diversity statements of many organizations) is just one example of the discursive devices that are used to persuade and influence significant organizational actors about the supposed business benefits of diversity. For example, metaphors intended to conjure up images of the harmonious co-existence of differences such as the patchwork quilt, the cultural mosaic, the rainbow, the fruit/salad bowl, the tapestry, are often used by consultants-practitioners-trainers (Prasad and Mills, 1997; Litvin, 2006). Kirby and Harter (2002: 31) believe that metaphor analysis can yield 'fruitful understandings of the production and reproduction of social reality' in that metaphors function to argue for a particular attitude towards a subject. From this perspective, metaphors not only reflect thought, they guide it. Kirby and Harter (ibid.) characterize diversity management as a 'managerial metaphor' because it emphasizes the interests of management; it marginalizes the interests of those who are being 'managed'; it emphasizes economic benefits. Authors who take a discourse-based approach to analyzing diversity management do not argue that all organizations and managers uncritically absorb all the messages contained in the discourse and metaphors of diversity, but that these persistent messages do influence attitudes and practices (Kirby and Harter, 2002).

## DILEMMAS OF DIVERSITY

### Behind the business case for diversity

One fundamental criticism of the business case is that it need not necessarily lead to valuing people as individual human beings; employees might be 'valued' simply as factors of production, contributors to the bottom line (Litvin, 2006). Let us take one multi-national corporation as an example – Wal-Mart. Looking at Wal-Mart's web site (www.walmartstores.com) it appears that the company has devoted an impressive amount of resources to diversity. It states that 'thanks to several diversity-focused initiatives, we are a leading US employer of Hispanics, African Americans, women and seniors'. The company clearly states its affiliation to the business case when it says that one of its diversity goals is to have 'a workforce that's representative of our diverse customer base'. There is an 'Office of Diversity' which includes a 'Diversity Initiatives Department', a 'Human Resources and Diversity Insight Department' and a 'Diversity Relations Department', headed up by a senior vice-president and chief diversity officer. Over the last few years, Wal-Mart has

won various awards in the areas of diversity and inclusion. Yet in October 2005, *The Independent* newspaper in the UK reported in an article entitled 'Fat? Over 40? Don't bother applying for a Wal-Mart job' that a 'secret memo' had revealed a plan by the company to make it harder for older, 'less healthy people', to get a job in its stores. The strategy was allegedly designed to reduce the company's health care costs. Wal-Mart has also been accused of taking advantage of the precarious situation of illegal immigrants in the US to reduce its labour costs, employing them at sub-minimum wage levels with no benefits (Mir *et al.*, 2006). Wal-Mart is not alone in promoting a positive image of its diversity strategies and in using celebratory rhetoric to do so and yet apparently engaging in employment practices that point in a diametrically opposite direction.

Another example is soft drinks group Coca-Cola. In 2000 the company paid out $192 million to settle charges of race discrimination made by 2,000 African-American employees (*The Guardian*, 17 November, 2000), despite having a range of diversity initiatives in place. The disparity between the public face of diversity and actual employment practices is not confined to profit-making private sector companies. For example, in 2004 the UK Metropolitan Police Service was castigated for discriminating against minority ethnic officers and paying 'lip service' to diversity (*The Guardian*, 15 December, 2004). Examples could fill this chapter, if not this book, but what they demonstrate is the way that diversity policies founded on the business case all too often lack real substance and genuine commitment to valuing diversity, but, why do so many organizations bother even to pay 'lip service' to diversity when it is clear that doing so costs them money (in terms of the cost of training, communication, literature and any concrete initiatives)? From an institutional perspective it could be argued that the adoption of diversity statements and policies lends the organization legitimacy in the eyes of stakeholders and that such legitimacy is necessary for survival and prosperity

(DiMaggio and Powell, 1983). At a time when diversity is sweeping the developed world, there are powerful normative and isomorphic forces pushing organizations to jump on the 'diversity bandwagon'. Once on the 'bandwagon', the examples above demonstrate the difficulties of actually making diversity happen and lend support to the argument that the debate should not be about managing diversity as such, but about 'managing the negative side effects' of 'unaccepted diversity' (Blommaert and Verschueren, 1998: 14). Of course this sounds like a plea for a return to traditional EO and AA and is likely to prove unpopular with organizations.

One of the reasons for the gap between the rhetoric and reality of diversity management is that most organizations put forward generic business case arguments (summarized earlier). It is rare to see a specific business case tailored to the particular organization, its sector, markets, customers etc. This is intuitively erroneous. From a study of service sector companies Janssens and Zanoni (2005) are among a number of authors who make a convincing case for contexualized understandings of and approaches to diversity management. They find that organizations understand diversity in relation to the way that particular social group differences affect the organization of service delivery. In some organizations, while it might be necessary to hire a diverse workforce, differences might be seen as a potential problem hindering, rather than assisting, effective service delivery. In others, the customer might be the central actor in defining which dimensions of diversity are relevant and therefore valued by the organization (e.g., hospitals with diverse patients). In yet other organizations, the customer might be remote and invisible (e.g., call centres) and diversity management might be more concerned with internal employee relations matters (Janssens and Zanoni, 2005). This contextual variation will inevitably impact on the way that diversity is 'managed' and the 'types' of diversity that are sought and valued. There is also of course an inherently exploitative and opportunistic dimension to constructing employees simply

as organizational resources, which can only underscore the contingent (and therefore fragile) nature of business case justifications for diversity initiatives.

Furthermore, when the business case is the prime rationale for diversity initiatives, then diversity has to justify itself in financial terms (Sinclair, 2006). Indeed, academics have been accused of not providing practitioners with a method to 'numerically assess' diversity management within their organizations (Gilbert, et al., 1999: 72). A preoccupation with measuring the contribution of workforce diversity and diversity management to organizational success has filtered through to a segment of the literature (e.g., Ng and Tung, 1998; Gilbert and Ivancevich, 2000; Kochan et al., 2003; Wheeler, 2003). However, even though studies call for 'hard measures' (Gilbert and Ivancevich, 2000), they have not really properly answered how practitioners are to isolate the effects of other variables (such as state of the economy, labour supply etc.) on organizational performance and how they are to actually prove some of the more fanciful claims, for example the diversity contribution to innovation and creativity (see Ashton, 2003). The difficulties of evaluating diversity and of showing return on investment have been identified as major barriers to diversity initiatives (Wentling, 2004).

## Managers 'managing' diversity?

Diversity management is essentially a top-down managerial approach which places the emphasis on the role of senior and middle managers, but what is it that managers are meant to do? Senior managers are supposed to lead by example and primarily they symbolize the organization's commitment to diversity. They (e.g., chief executive officers) are often seen as catalysts of change and the 'success' of diversity management is often attributed to their involvement and leadership, particularly in the management literature (Gilbert et al., 1999; Gilbert and Ivancevich, 2000; Thomas, 2004). The rather optimistic assumption is made that the senior individual's widely communicated commitment to diversity filters down to individual managers, creates a climate of acceptance of diversity and modifies management and employee behaviour (Gilbert and Ivancevich, 2000). Accordingly the 'success' of diversity initiatives rests upon management rationality, rather than bureaucratic rationality (as in EO/AA approaches). While the stated commitment of senior managers might be regarded as laudable (e.g., Thomas, 2004), a cynic might argue that having reached the apex of the organization, lending one's name to a seemingly 'worthy cause' is a fairly easy thing to do.

In the case of middle managers, they seem to have a more challenging role – diversity has been described as the 'perfect litmus test for modern management capacity' (Schneider, 2001: 13). Diversity management puts a lot of faith not only in managers' commitment and interest, but in their ability actually to do something to effect the cultural transformation that is considered necessary if organizations are to be successful in their diversity efforts. The more prescriptive literature typically suggests that managers' competencies in dealing with diversity need to be and can be improved by attending training, using handbooks and by linking performance to appraisals and rewards (Kirby and Harter, 2002). For example, managers can be trained to identify 'tolerant' people and to act as role models of tolerance themselves (Strauss and Connerley, 2003). When put like this, the management role sounds perfectly straightforward – diversity management can be approached in a 'step-by-step' fashion with the aid of check lists (Dass and Parker, 1999). However, the 'do-ability' of diversity management is called into question in the more critical literature (Prasad and Mills, 1997; Lorbiecki and Jack, 2000; Zanoni and Janssens, 2003; Foster and Harris, 2005). To begin with, research has shown that the concept lacks clarity for managers both in terms of what it is and what they should be doing to implement it (Foster and Harris, 2005).

One significant issue is that the strong strand of individualism in diversity management implies that managers should be 'managing' individual differences (Liff, 1997). The idea of us all being unique individuals is appealing, if not seductive; yet fair treatment is widely held to mean being treated the same as everyone else. So should managers be treating everyone the same or differently if they want to be seen as competent and fair? The legal framework in most countries demands the former in order that 'fairness' and equal treatment can be demonstrated. If managers try to implement diversity policy by responding to individual differences, rather than treating everyone the same, then their practices are more likely to lead to feelings of unfairness and claims of unequal treatment (Foster and Harris, 2005). Foster and Harris' (2005) study situated in the UK retail industry indicates that managers are confused about whether to deliver sameness of treatment or to recognize and respond to individual differences.

Despite the emphasis on individual differences within diversity management, the business case might mean that certain groups are seen as making a special contribution to organizational goals. For example, women or minority ethnic employees are often held to bring different skills, values, ways of thinking and life experiences to the organization, which organizations could harness to enhance innovation and creativity (sometimes labelled the 'special contribution perspective') (Due Billing and Sundin, 2006). While special contribution arguments might be used to increase the employment and opportunities of certain under-represented social groups, there are also inherent dangers in doing so. When organizations start to highlight differences, there is a strong tendency to exoticize certain groups (who then become desirable and sought after 'others') and to pathologize others (who are stereotyped as having negative characteristics) (see Litvin, 1997, 2006; Lorbiecki and Jack, 2000; Mir et al., 2006). This is particularly problematic when it comes to race and ethnic difference. For example, Billing and Sundin (2006: 109) assert that while Scandinavian organizations seem to be able to appreciate some of the 'special contributions' of Scandinavian women, they appear less able to do so with many minority ethnic people, especially Muslim women.

Further, highlighting the special contribution of any social group tends to essentialize that group's characteristics in a way that is potentially constraining, if not damaging, for both individuals and the group as a whole. Some of the examples given of organizations' attempts to become more inclusive in the diversity literature do have essentialist undertones. For instance, Gilbert *et al.* (1999: 69) cite the US company Exxon Baytown which made special accommodations for an Asian woman 'whose culture dictated that she wait for silence before speaking'. So, instead of having to contribute during the course of group meetings (like everyone else) her team members apparently now provide her time to speak at the end. So, what might organizations and managers learn from these kinds of instances? There might be a temptation to assume that all Asian women need and welcome such special accommodations, but is this true? The problem is that some individuals might not be able or indeed want to live up to or play out their cultural stereotype whilst at work. To avoid casting all individuals in a group as the same (essentializing them) special accommodations would need to be invented anew for every single individual who felt marginalized or excluded. This seems like a tall order for hard pressed managers who are much more likely to prefer to operate within clearly defined rules and procedures (Foster and Harris, 2005). On the other hand if managers instead attempt to integrate or assimilate 'minorities' into the dominant culture of the organization (for example, in this case simply telling the Asian woman that she needs to be more assertive in meetings, just like her fellow team members) then their supposed ability to make a special contribution or be innovative and creative is likely to be stifled. The alternative is, of course, for the whole work group to question and possibly change their behaviour. However, managers may well ask whether all the effort involved in 'managing' diversity is really worth it?

## The dynamics of resistance and challenge

The idea that all organizational members will submit to diversity is undoubtedly naïve, but until fairly recently the literature neglected to explore resistance to diversity initiatives (Dick and Cassell, 2002). It is clear that because of or despite the fact that diversity has organizational interests at its core, there is a range of individuals and groups who might see it as in their interest to resist and challenge it. As Jones and Stablein (2006: 157) point out, resistance can come from different directions – from the bottom, middle or top of the organization. In itself resistance is neither 'right' nor 'wrong', as it really depends on the stake that individuals who resist and challenge have in the various initiatives within diversity management (Dick and Cassell, 2002). However, power inequalities within organizations mean that some groups and individuals are more able to impose their understanding of diversity on the strategies and practices that are used. For example, if senior people choose to highlight (stereotyped) differences, diversity management might paradoxically keep 'minorities' in subordinate positions (Billing and Sundin, 2006).

Jones and Stablein (2006: 145) propose that the rhetoric of diversity can be used to pursue goals other than business ones on behalf of those who have been denied power and opportunities in organizations. They argue that it 'can act like a Trojan horse, providing a vehicle to resist and transform relations of organizational power, while speaking of human resource management (HRM) and demographic change'. The idea of the 'Trojan horse' of diversity has resonance with the approach of UK trade unions who are highly suspicious of diversity management because of its business-driven nature, its focus on the individual and the fact that it is positioned as a top-down managerial activity. However, as pragmatic organizations, the unions are willing, with certain caveats (like keeping a focus on group-based discrimination and barriers to career advancement) to 'talk diversity' with employers in order to exert some influence on the evolving diversity agenda (Kirton and Greene, 2006). The response of trade unions to diversity, however, has been context-bound; for instance, it has been greeted with far more enthusiasm by Danish trade unions, where the promotion of diversity management is seen by unions to be a progressive development in the context of a negative public discourse on multiculturalism (Greene *et al.*, 2005).

One of the issues that the celebratory rhetoric of diversity conceals is the possible resistance of majority group members when organizations become more diverse. A substantial segment of the US diversity literature focuses on the effects of workforce diversity on work groups and teams, exploring the conflicts and tensions that can surface (particularly within racially mixed work groups) and their effects on performance (Jehn *et al.*, 1999; Pelled *et al.*, 1999; Kochan *et al.*, 2003; Bacharach *et al.*, 2005; Brief *et al.*, 2005). These are thought to be important considerations because conflict management takes up employees' time and reduces the ability of the work group to retain good employees. In addition it is argued that supportive peer relations foster trust, empathy and reciprocity, thus facilitating information and knowledge exchange (Bacharach *et al.*, 2005). The empirical research presents a mixed picture. For example, some studies show that social group (especially race) diversity impacts negatively upon work relations (Jehn *et al.*, 1999; Pelled *et al.*, 1999), while others find that it has a positive effect (Ng and Tung, 1998).

Kossek *et al.*'s (2003) study of the diversity strategy of a US university shows that gradually increasing the employment of previously under-represented women and 'minorities' does not necessarily lead to an improved climate in terms of perceptions of fairness of resource allocation, or good mixing in social interaction. Similarly, from their research Brief *et al.* (2005) state that people in more racially diverse organizations report

lower quality work relationships than those in less racially diverse organizations. However, Kochan *et al.* (2003) conclude that although racial and gender diversity does not have the positive effect on performance proposed by optimists, neither does it necessarily have a negative effect. Indeed, they state that there was some 'promising evidence' that under certain conditions 'racial diversity may even enhance performance' (ibid.: 17).

The extent to which these findings apply beyond the US context is difficult to determine. Although racial conflict is by no means a uniquely American phenomenon, it is particularly acute in the US and is rooted in the country's history of slavery and racial segregation (see for example, Bacharach *et al.*, 2005). For example, writing about the Australian context, which is becoming more ethnically diverse, D'Netto and Sohal (1999) describe migrant employees as compliant and not creating any problems for management. Therefore, they argue, the challenges that workforce diversity presents receives inadequate attention by organizations in Australia. If, however, a diverse workforce does create conflict, at least in the short term, then this might explain why some individual managers might behave in ways that resist diversity initiatives. While they might appreciate the possible long-term benefits of a diverse workforce, in the meantime there might be costs involved, such as selection/retention processes and cooperation processes. Thus, managers might face a dilemma of choosing between short-term costs and long-term benefits (Schneider and Northcraft, 1999).

## CONCLUSION: DIVERSITY – A PROGRESSIVE OR RETROGRADE TURN?

Diversity management emerged in a climate of backlash against established AA and EO policies. The business case for diversity was promulgated largely by the early practitioner-consultant-writers on diversity in both the US and UK (e.g., Kandola and Fullerton, 1998; Thomas, 1990). It was also enthusiastically adopted by the Society for Human Resource Management in the US (Litvin, 2006) and by the (now Chartered) Institute of Personnel and Development in the UK (Kirton, 2003). Practitioners had an inherent professional interest in re-invigorating equality initiatives and in (re-)igniting organizational commitment to such initiatives (Kelly and Dobbin, 2004). The now ubiquitous nature of the diversity concept in the UK and USA (and elsewhere) has spawned a multi-dimensional, multi-million pound/dollar 'diversity industry' in which diversity management has the status of a product (a management technique) that is sold to organizations and managers through consultants, trainers and 'how-to-do' books (Prasad and Mills, 1997; Kaler, 2001). However, the question of whether diversity management is a progressive or retrograde turn really depends on which standpoint is taken.

From the organizational or managerial perspective, the business focus of diversity management (if in some way it can be proven) is bound to be appealing. However, as discussed earlier, most of the supposed benefits of workforce diversity are unproven and it is difficult, if not impossible, to show return on investment for diversity initiatives. For example, Gilbert *et al.* (1999) claim that penetration of the glass ceiling, social integration, organizational attachment and positive attitudes towards diversity, will all increase, while psychological dissonance will diminish. It is argued that this will all lead to improved organizational performance, but are managers really convinced? Critical research would suggest not.

Optimists might argue that diversity can be used as a discursive device to renew a 'tired' EO or AA agenda and there does seem to be some purchase in this (Kirton and Greene, 2006). However, Jones and Stablein (2006) assert that the transformational potential of diversity can be resisted and taken back by the already powerful through strategies such as co-option, marginalization and tokenism enabling management to resist the progressive

potential of diversity management. Overall, diversity seemingly has little to offer the social justice case for equality because although a moral commitment is not entirely absent, it is supplementary rather than central. In contrast, organizational self-interest is a supplementary argument to justify initiatives within EO policies, which are more focused on employee rights and interests (Kaler, 2001). The rhetoric of diversity could also be used to conceal organizational 'non-action' on discrimination and inequalities and to convey the impression that 'there's no problem here'. If everyone is different and has different needs, aspirations etc., why does it matter if there are different outcomes? With this kind of neo-liberal thinking, unequal outcomes can easily be reconstructed as simply different. Thus the celebratory metaphors of diversity can be used to deny the existence of injustice, inequalities, discrimination and exploitation (Kersten, 2000). Further, diversity can be become so inclusive (of all types of individual and social group-based difference) as to become meaningless, both as a concept and as a policy approach. In the Swedish context, for example, it is argued that diversity has been used as an excuse for taking the gender perspective out of organizational agendas (Billing and Sundin, 2006).

So, is diversity redundant? Litvin (2006: 87) argues that 'thinking, talking and acting about diversity' needs to be 'liberated' from the 'mega-discourse' of the business case in order that a more effective discourse of diversity can be created, one that leads to organizational transformation, inclusion and opportunity for all. Even writers who seem 'pro-diversity' sometimes argue that the business case is insufficient. For example, Gilbert *et al.* (1999) claim that diversity management initiatives cannot succeed unless underpinned by ethical principles because management will simply not provide the necessary support and leadership. Reflecting this, there have been some attempts to reframe or even reclaim the business case for diversity, to argue that it should be broad, longer term, have an ethical basis and address social group-based disadvantage (Kirton, 2003). Others argue that business case rhetoric might have run its course, but that organizations still need to engage with the reality of workforce diversity and the societal expectation that diversity will be valued (Kochan *et al.*, 2003). Much of the critical literature asserts that workplace diversity and multiculturalism should be about inclusion (achieving adequate representation of 'minorities' at all levels of the organization and transforming organizational structures, values and discourses), rather than tolerance of the 'other' as implied by diversity (Prasad, 2006). Tolerance is like a gift bestowed by the powerful upon the marginalized; it can easily be taken away.

To conclude, the diversity concept symbolizes a shift away from the traditional EO and AA policy focus on the discrimination, under-representation and disadvantage that 'minority' groups experience, such that the underlying structures of inequalities, and the processes by which inequalities are reproduced at the organizational level, are likely to remain intact (Humphries and Grice, 1995). There is no evidence that the popularity of the concept is in decline (Cassell, 2000), but unless the tensions and dilemmas are exposed and confronted, there is little hope that diversity can deliver all that it promises either to organizations or to disadvantaged social groups (Kirton and Greene, 2006). Even then, whether the 'problems' presented by workforce diversity can be 'managed' out of existence is highly questionable (Kersten, 2000), as the chapter's discussion has shown.

# REFERENCES

Ashton, C. (2003) 'The importance of diversity in innovation', in M. Davidson and S. Fielden (eds) *Individual Diversity and Psychology in Organizations*. Chichester: John Wiley, pp. 19–40.

Bacharach, S., Bamberger, P. and Vashdi, D. (2005) 'Diversity and homphily at work: Supportive relations among white and African-American peers', *Academy of Management Journal*, 48 (4): 619–644.

Billing, Y.D. and Sundin, E. (2006) 'From managing equality to managing diversity: A critical Scandinavian perspective on gender and work place diversity', in A. Konrad, P. Prasad and J. Pringle (eds)

*Handbook of Workplace Diversity*. London: Sage, pp. 95–120.

Blommaert, J. and Verschueren, J. (1998) *Debating Diversity*. London: Routledge.

Brief, A., Umphress, E., Dietz, J., Burrows, J., Butz, R. and Scholten, L. (2005) 'Community matters: Realistic group conflict theory and the impact of diversity', *Academy of Management Journal*, 48 (5): 830–844.

Cassell, C. (2000) 'Managing diversity in the new millennium', *Personnel Review*, 29 (3): 268–273.

Cornelius, N., Gooch, L. *et al.* (2001) 'Managing difference fairly: An integrated "partnership" approach', in M. Noon and E. Ogbonna (eds) *Equality, Diversity and Disadvantage in Employment*. Basingstoke: Palgrave.

Cox, T. (1994) 'A comment on the language of diversity', *Organization*, 1 (1): 51–58.

D'Netto, B. and Sohal, A. (1999) 'Human resource practices and workforce diversity: An empirical assessment', *International Journal of Manpower*, 20 (8): 530–547.

Dass, P. and Parker, B. (1999) 'Strategies for managing human resource diversity: From resistance to learning', *Academy of Management Executive*, 13 (2): 68–80.

de los Reyes, P. (2000) 'Diversity at work: Paradoxes, possibilities and problems in the Swedish discourse on diversity', *Economic and Industrial Democracy*, 21: 253–266.

Dick, P. and Cassell, C. (2002) 'Barriers to managing diversity in a UK constabulary: The role of discourse', *Journal of Management Studies*, 39 (7): 953–976.

DiMaggio, P.J. and Powell, W.W. (1983) 'The iron cage revisited: Institutional isomorphism and collective rationality in organizational fields', *American Sociological Review*, 48 (2): 147–160.

Foster, C. and Harris, L. (2005) 'Easy to say, difficult to do: Diversity management in retail', *Human Resource Management Journal*, 15 (3): 4–17.

Gilbert, J. and Ivancevich, J. (2000) 'Valuing diversity: A tale of two organizations', *Academy of Management Executive*, 14 (1): 93–105.

Gilbert, J., Stead, B.A. and Ivancevich, J. (1999) 'Diversity management: A new organizational paradigm', *Journal of Business Ethics*, 21: 61–76.

Greene, A.M., Kirton, G. and Wrench, J. (2005) 'Trade union perspectives on diversity management: A comparison of the UK and Denmark', *European Journal of Industrial Relations*, 11 (2): 179–196.

Humphries, M. and Grice, S. (1995) 'Equal employment opportunity and the management of diversity', *Journal of Organizational Change Management*, 8 (5): 17–32.

Janssens, M. and Zanoni, P. (2005) 'Many diversities for many services: Theorizing diversity (management) in service companies', *Human Relations*, 58 (3): 311–340.

Jehn, K., Northcraft, G. and Neale, M. (1999) 'Why differences make a difference: A field study of diversity, conflict and performance in workgroups', *Administrative Science Quarterly*, 44: 741–763.

Johnston, W. and Packer, A. (1987) *Workforce 2000: Work and Workers for the 21st Century*. Indianapolis: Hudson Institute.

Jones, D., Pringle, J. *et al.* (2000) '"Managing diversity" meets Aotearoa/New Zealand', *Personnel Review*, 29 (3): 364–380.

Jones, D. and Stablein, R. (2006) 'Diversity as resistance and recuperation: Critical theory, post-structuralist perspectives and workplace diversity', in A. Konrad, P. Prasad and J. Pringle (eds) *Handbook of Workplace Diversity*. London: Sage, pp. 145–166.

Kaler, J. (2001) 'Diversity, equality, morality', in M. Noon and E. Ogbonna (eds) *Diversity, Equality and Disadvantage in Employment*. Basingstoke: Palgrave, pp. 51–64.

Kamp, A. and Hagedorn-Rasmussen, P. (2004) 'Diversity management in a Danish context: Towards a multicultural or segregated working life?', *Economic and Industrial Democracy*, 25 (4): 525–554.

Kandola, R. and Fullerton, J. (1998) *Managing the Mosaic: Diversity in Action*. London: Institute of Personnel and Development.

Kelly, E. and Dobbin, F. (1998) 'How affirmative action became diversity management', *The American Behavioral Scientist*, 41 (7): 960–984.

Kersten, A. (2000) 'Diversity management: Dialogue, dialectics and diversion', *Journal of Occupational Change Management*, 13 (3): 235–248.

Kirby, E. and Harter, L. (2002) 'Speaking the language of the bottom-line: The metaphor of "managing diversity"', *The Journal of Business Communication*, 40 (1): 28–49.

Kirton, G. (2003) 'Developing strategic approaches to diversity policy', in M. Davidson and S. Fielden (eds) *Individual Diversity and Psychology in Organizations*. Chichester: John Wiley, pp. 3–18.

Kirton, G. and Greene, A.M. (2005) *The Dynamics of Managing Diversity*. Oxford: Butterworth Heinemann.

Kirton, G. and Greene, A.M. (2006) 'The discourse of diversity in unionised contexts: Views from trade union equality officers', *Personnel Review*, 35 (4): 431–448.

Kirton, G., Greene, A.M. and Dean, D. (2007) 'British diversity professionals as change agents: Radicals, tempered radicals or liberal reformers?', *International Journal of Human Resource Management*, 18 (11): 1979–1994.

Kochan, T., Bezrukova, K. *et al.* (2003) 'The effects of diversity on business performance: Report of the diversity research network', *Human Resource Management*, 42 (1): 3–21.

Kossek, E., Markel, K. *et al.* (2003) 'Increasing diversity as an HRM change strategy', *Journal of Organizational Change Management*, 16 (3): 328–352.

Liff, S. (1997) 'Two routes to managing diversity: Individual differences or social group characteristics', *Employee Relations*, 19 (1): 11–26.

Litvin, D. (1997) 'The discourse of diversity: From biology to management', *Organization*, 4 (2): 187–209.

Litvin, D. (2006) 'Diversity: Making space for a better case', in P. Prasad, J. Pringle and A. Konrad (eds) *Handbook of Workplace Diversity*. London: Sage, pp. 75–94.

Lorbiecki, A. and Jack, G. (2000) 'Critical turns in the evolution of diversity management', *British Journal of Management*, 11 (Special Issue): S17–S31.

Maxwell, G., Blair, S. *et al.* (2001) 'Edging towards managing diversity in practice', *Employee Relations*, 23 (5): 468–482.

Mir, R., Mir, A. and Wong, D. (2006) 'Diversity: The cultural logic of global capital?', in P. Prasad, J. Pringle and A. Konrad (eds) *Handbook of Workplace Diversity*. London: Sage, pp. 167–188.

Ng, E. and Tung, R. (1998) 'Ethno-cultural diversity and organizational effectiveness: A field study', *The International Journal of Human Resource Management*, 9 (6): 980–995.

Noon, M. and Ogbonna, E. (2001) *Equality, Diversity and Disadvantage in Employment*. Basingstoke: Palgrave.

Pelled, L., Eisenhardt, K. and Xin, K. (1999) 'Exploring the black box: An analysis of work group diversity, conflict, and performance', *Administrative Science Quarterly*, 44: 1–28.

Prasad, P. (2006) 'The jewel in the crown: Postcolonial theory and workplace diversity', in A. Konrad, P. Prasad and J. Pringle (eds) *Handbook of Workplace Diversity*. London: Sage.

Prasad, P. and Mills, A. (1997) 'From showcase to shadow: Understanding the dilemmas of managing workplace diversity', in P. Prasad, A. Mills, E. Elmes and A. Prasad (eds) *Managing the Organizational Melting Pot. Dilemmas of Workplace Diversity*. Thousand Oaks, CA: Sage, pp. 3–30.

Prasad, P., Pringle, J. and Konrad, A. (2006) 'Examining the contours of workplace diversity: Concepts, contexts and challenges', in P. Prasad, J. Pringle and A. Konrad (eds) *The Handbook of Workplace Diversity*. London: Sage, pp. 1–22.

Ross, R. and Schneider, R. (1992) *From Equality to Diversity*. London: Pitman.

Schneider, R. (2001) 'Diversity now the ultimate test of management capacity', *Equal Opportunities Review*, 96: 11–17.

Schneider, S. and Northcraft, G. (1999) 'Three social dilemmas of workforce diversity in organizations: A social identity perspective', *Human Relations*, 52 (11): 1445–1467.

Sinclair, A. (2006) 'Critical diversity management practice in Australia: Romanced or co-opted?', in P. Prasad, J. Pringle and A. Konrad (eds) *Handbook of Workplace Diversity*. London: Sage, pp. 511–530.

Strauss, J. and Connerley, M. (2003) 'Demographics, personality, contact, and universal-diverse orientation: An exploratory examination', *Human Resource Management*, 42 (2): 159–174.

Thomas, D. (2004) 'Diversity as strategy', *Harvard Business Review*, (September): 98–108.

Thomas, R. (1990) 'From affirmative action to affirming diversity', *Harvard Business Review*, 68 (2): 107–117.

Wentling, R.M. (2004) 'Factors that assist and barriers that hinder the success of diversity initiatives in multinational corporations', *Human Resource Development International*, 7 (2): 165–180.

Wheeler, M. (2003) 'Managing diversity: Developing a strategy for measuring organizational effectiveness', in M. Davidson and S. Fielden (eds) *Individual Diversity and Psychology in Oranizations*. Chichester: John Wiley, pp. 57–78.

Young, I.M. (1990) *Justice and the Politics of Difference*. Princeton: Princeton University Press.

Zanoni, P. and Janssens, M. (2003) 'Deconstructing difference: The rhetoric of human resource managers' diversity discourses', *Organization Studies*, 25 (1): 55–74.

# 19

# The Organization of Human Resource Strategies: Narratives and Power in Understanding Labour Management in a Context of Change[1]

Miguel Martínez Lucio

## INTRODUCTION

Human resource management (HRM) is a major feature of organisational politics and of relationships within organisations. The chapter will aim to explain where human resource management is located in organisational and strategic terms. It addresses the question: What role does human resource management play in the organisational structures and strategies of firms? The chapter will focus on this broad question by assessing the argument that HRM is emerging as a crucial factor in the economic and social management of workers.

The argument has been advanced, at least at the level of rhetoric, that HRM has moved from reacting to changes in modern forms of labour management, and that it is now more strategic and integral to organisational politics and decision making. It will be argued in this chapter, therefore, that we need to go beyond debates about types of HRM which focus on binaries (e.g., soft/hard approaches). Instead, we need to focus on the ways in which HR professionals and related actors have attempted to develop a more central role for people management within organisations.

In order to develop this theme, the chapter will trace the development of five 'projects' that have emerged since the early 1980s, and that attempted to reposition HRM within the key activities and developments of management. First, there was the attempt to relocate HRM and 'push it down the line' in a context of decentralised organisations. Second, there was the project of creating the 'network firm' and developing the virtual structures of contemporary capitalism, in which the role of HRM was to be a link between internal and external providers and sub-units. These two projects have been central to the organisational reconfiguration of HRM.

The chapter will then focus on three more recent projects aimed at giving HRM a central role in the structure of organisations. The third project focused on the ethical dimension and the move to corporate social responsibility as ways to place HRM departments and considerations at the heart of an organisation's value system. Fourth, the emergence of the emphasis upon training and human resource development will be discussed. And finally, the current vogue for performance, and high performance in particular, will be surveyed as a way of illuminating HRM's role in achieving the effectiveness and quality of organisational outputs. In discussing each of the five projects, and related narratives, there will be an attempt to reflect on whether they have been successful in placing HRM in a strategic light and in a more pivotal organisational space.

In order to understand the organisational location of HRM, we need to move away from a fixation on management as a principal or isolated actor. On the contrary, we need to view the context within which HRM develops and the different actors and players that coalesce and drive some of the projects outlined above, and for what purpose. The chapter will conclude by presenting the argument that, for all the rhetoric and emphasis placed on HRM, it has not become as strategic a player or activity as one might have expected, and as many HRM professionals wanted. HRM is still in some ways marginal to the central processes of organisations and, even within the five projects there are tensions and dilemmas which pull HRM to the margins. Moreover, projects such as promoting the ethical dimension of business or the

concentration on performance measurement remain limited and contingent on external political and economic factors.

The chapter will focus on the US and UK contexts in particular, because there is a tendency for narratives of change (heroic discourses) of HRM to be prevalent in these, but it will cross-reference with the European context. The chapter will aim to present an understanding of the development of HRM not in terms of specific strategies and organisational dilemmas – the core of so many Anglo-Saxon interventions – but as political and institutional phenomena in its own right. HRM is not solely a strategy or array of practices for the management of the employment relation. HRM is a significant academic and knowledge based constituency located within business schools, consultancies and firms.

## ORIGINS, GENEALOGY AND CONTEXT

HRM now has an extensive literature. It has many dedicated journals and academic conferences. Many academics in the area of organisational and employment studies – especially within the Anglo-Saxon world – work within academic HRM Departments. However, the re-crafting of the language of personnel management and administration in the 1980s to include the term 'human resource management' was not without critical discussion. The relabelling of employees or workers as human resources, and the presumed Americanisation this entailed in terms of greater managerial prerogative, brought a significant set of responses. The central thrust of the process of relabelling HRM presumed a more proactive approach on the part of managers and represented a move away from an environment where outcomes were negotiated and there was a more pluralistic organisational culture and process (Keenoy, 1990; Martínez Lucio and Weston, 1992). The main reactions focused on the challenge that this unitarist move presented to the tapestry of internal organisational representation. The debate was often presented by listing the differences between personnel management and HRM in terms of their cultural, strategic and technical features (Guest, 1987; Storey, 1994). The main concern here was with the consistency of change (and in the case of British debates, the lack of it). HRM arrived as an Anglo-Saxon curiosity, i.e., an ideological mission in the US linked to the emergence of a New Right (Guest, 1990), that was also based on a steady undermining of regulatory cultures in the European context, e.g., collective bargaining. In fact, some viewed HRM as an attempt to internalise regulation, taking it out of the arena of industrial relations, and locate it within the boundaries of the firm and in terms of management prerogative rather than collective bargaining (Martínez Lucio and Simpson, 1992).

The discussion of HRM began to revolve around binaries. In the 1980s, there was much talk of competing perspectives between the Harvard (Beer *et al.*, 1984) and the Michigan Schools (Fombrun *et al.*, 1984). The first was more concerned with the impact on HRM of internal and external stakeholders, and saw HRM strategy as a pluralist negotiation between interests. Kochan's work continued this tradition by arguing that effective systems of HRM, in terms of the quality of labour and efficiency, are the outcome of a supportive and interventionist regulatory system combined with a dialogue between labour and management (Kochan and Osterman, 1994). The argument dovetails closely with the partnership tradition in industrial relations (Ackers and Payne, 1998; see Martínez Lucio and Stuart, 2004 for a discussion). However, the Michigan school was less concerned with external political fit and more concerned with cultural and strategic congruence between the different aspects of HRM within a firm based on fitting strategy to cultural aspects and the economic objectives of the firm.

For some this gave rise to a view that there was a soft and hard side to HRM. The argument initially hinged on the economic and social justification for these distinct approaches. With the coming of the late 1980s and early 1990s these binaries continued but in new forms. The question was whether

there were 'best practices' that were common to all firms and that should be adopted by all companies and their managers. This *universalistic* perspective was concerned with identifying transferable and superior HRM practices that could be mimicked and copied by firms (Pfeffer, 1994). The role of contingency and context was less important from this point of view: the Japanisation school of management and the emergence of Total Quality Management would be examples of this shift away from contingency and towards universalism. From this perspective, the role of HRM departments and strategists was to seek novel and innovative practices and then apply them. Within this context, the role of institutions such as business schools and consultants was to carry these messages of good fortune in an almost evangelical way. However, alternative positions argue that there are firm-specific characteristics and strategies that can mediate these practices, sometimes even enhancing them, leading to a moderating influence in terms of strategy (Fombrun *et al.*, 1984; Schuler and Jackson, 1987). Hence, the term *contingency* perspective is used. From this point of view, HRM professionals play a role in linking best practices with strategies, although who counts as an HRM strategist is normally a mystery. Questions concerning the internal organisational environment and context were enhanced in *configurational* approaches that pointed to the configuration and organisation of HRM practices and organisational functions as important to the emergence of HR strategy (Doty and Glick, 1994). This latter school is important for recent developments which are to be discussed later in terms of 'performance' and 'bundles'. However, it is sufficient to say at this point that in that early period the debate about HRM was constructed in terms of specific binaries: hard versus soft, universalistic versus contingency/configurational.

Indeed, in Europe this has led to a sharpening of views as to whether there was a European HRM that differed from American HRM (Brewster, 1993; Sparrow and Hiltrop, 1997). The idea of HRM being influenced by the degree and nature of employment and social regulation is at the heart of this European perspective. European HRM tends to have greater investment in training and development, stronger roles for external stakeholders such as trade unions, and HRM departments operate in a more political environment. The ability to produce a definitive analysis of such issues is always difficult, as Mayrhofer and Brewster (2006) have argued. However, political contingencies play a role in the HRM function in continental Europe to one degree or another (Almond and Ferner, 2006). Hence, we have seen another binary emerge – at least rhetorically – in terms of US/hard/universalistic/less industrial relations oriented approaches on the one hand and European/soft/configurational/more industrial relations perspectives on the other. Whether these are firm empirical realities or political desires is a matter for further discussion.

Why are these developments important to developing an understanding of our theme? These developments show that the arrival of HRM was contested from the start, and that if the philosophy and strategy is contested then the position of HRM itself is a matter of power relations both organisationally (internally) and socially (externally). In addition, such developments show that HRM represented an attempt to reinvigorate management's control of the employment relationship and to move competitiveness to the centre of business and labour agendas, although there appears to have been little consensus as to how this was to be done. However, at another level it needs to be recognised that there is a unifying theme behind all binaries, and in this case even those with opposing views wished to take HRM away from the role of 'reacting' to organised labour and dealing with conflict as it occurred (as it had done in the past). Although, historically, it had done more than this, stereotypes are a pervasive part of management education and learning (Grey, 2005). The 'aim' was, and is, to *locate* HRM as a central feature of management and business decision making and to link it to the broader economic and efficiency goals of the organisation. In effect, it was

being argued by all those involved that people matter now, but they matter as an asset – a 'strategic asset' within a highly competitive market. It is this rhetoric that has created a problem and not only because there is an absence of a corresponding reality; the last two decades have been dominated by a generic and hegemonic line of research which has explored the question of whether HRM makes a difference to the *bottom line* or not. In effect, a paradigm concerned with the centrality of HRM has emerged when it probably need not have. The question of rhetoric is therefore a significant feature of HRM as a practice, an academic discipline and as a profession (Legge, 1995).

There is one other factor that we need to consider before we can proceed to discuss the organisation of human resources and the location of relevant decision making, and before we can proceed to outline the unfolding of the discussion. Regardless of the tendency in US-inspired approaches to study HRM exclusively or mainly in terms of the internal environment of the firm and its link to the 'market', we need to appreciate the importance of organisation in terms of HRM functions themselves, their professional identity and their external organisational and regulatory context. Four implications follow from these points.

First, we must see the development of HRM not solely in terms of binary oppositions – A versus B – but as a series of discourses and narratives that develop and mutate (Thompson, 2007). The work by Grant and Oswick (1998) on the rhetorics of HRM pointed to deep division in the way HRM was understood by practitioners: there were those with an almost 'religious' approach, 'agnostics' and then 'atheists'. As their work has advanced they have concerned themselves with the way stories and narratives play a vital role in understanding organisational life and the development of HRM (see Grant *et al.*, 1998). The role of narratives, within the academic and professional constituencies of HRM, is an important feature of the protagonists' attempts to locate people management within a strategic context (ibid.). The question here is one of legitimacy – ensuring that HRM-related matters are important to the governmental structures of the firm and even society. That these are dependent on a range of external and internal regulatory and governance factors is becoming increasingly evident (Deakin *et al.*, 2004). Hence, any discussion of HRM must note how these narratives mutate and serve different purposes.

Second, there is a particular reason why narratives of HRM develop, rise and fall. In his seminal work on the views of people management held by different internal groups – engineers, accountants and personnel managers – Armstrong (1995) argued that we need to understand the way such issues are framed and prioritised. This introduces the importance of different professional interests and perspectives on the matter of HRM. HRM is an object of intervention where different professions may craft it to their own institutional ends and world views: it is not solely a discursive phenomena but a sociological one as well. HRM practitioners are therefore in competition with others to frame an approach to HRM that serves particular interests. The political dimension of the internal space of organisations is clear from the literature on the relationships between professional groups and their roles within organisations (Reed, 2006). The way professionals understand notions of service delivery, career development, and reward may vary and provide distinct narratives within the debate on HRM. In addition, HRM practitioners are themselves a professional group, constructing narratives that secure their role and influence within the firm and beyond. They may be less closed and consistent as a professional group, when compared with others, such as the stronger medical professions, but they indulge in forging narratives for the sake of their own legitimacy as well. To this extent narratives are, in the main, driven by interests.

Third, we need to locate these interests, actors and narratives in a broader context. In their discussion of transnational corporations and American HRM, Ferner and Tempel (2006: 32) argue within a neo-Gramscian analysis that whilst structural factors should never be discounted, questions of agency are important. In particular, 'institutions are subject to contestation, amendment, and defence by actors whose interest they engage'. Drawing on the work of Levy and Egan (2003) they conclude that organisational fields can be characterised by actors competing over the rules, institutions, and policies relation. In addition,

> At the micro level of the organisation, similar preoccupations are evident in the analysis of the 'mobilisation of bias' (Schattschneider, 1960) and in the study of rhetorics and symbolic systems deployed by interest groups within organisations to 'manage meaning' and to legitimate some courses of action while de-legitimating others (Pettigrew, 1973, 1985) (Ferner and Tempel, 2006: 22).

In effect, this trajectory of thinking remains inspired by the Harvard school's insistence that the role of organisational politics (the internal) and organisational environment (the external) remains important (Fombrun *et al.*, 1984). Moreover, to understand the array of actors such as different professional or functional groups in the organisation or different external stakeholders such as trade unions, business schools and customer groups means that we need to understand how such interactions operate. Circuits of power rest on established circuits which provide both material and ideological resources (Clegg, 1989), which draw on various cultural, economic and social forms of capital (Bourdieu, 1986) and which articulate discourses and meanings established in the economy and society (Laclau and Mouffe, 1985). So the political has to be added to our analysis as well.

Fourth, this means that the distinct narratives of HRM are not just loose, academically driven discourses. They are the outcome of competing interests, environmental factors, and strategic attempts to legitimate the role of people management around specific purposes and objectives. They are not clearly delineated projects with a start and sell-by date. They are not just fads and fashions, although management education and practice is full of these (Grey, 2005). These are narratives sustained by a range of actors with a range of interests and objectives. They attempt to relocate and reposition HRM in the real politics of the firm and in the outside world. The question is not just how HRM is organised, numerically staffed and positioned, but to see how HRM within an organisational environment is located within the functions and purposes of the firm. To understand this we need to appreciate that HRM is a process of political and ideological reinvention in the face of the tensions that emerge from managing labour in a context of greater competition and economic change. Thus, the remainder of the chapter will map the emergence of different schools of thought, and how they reflect shifts in the role of the state, capital, and other actors.

## WHERE IS HRM? THE ORGANISATIONAL ARCHITECTURE OF HRM IN A CHANGING CONTEXT

### 'It's about the individual now': flexibility and the individual in HRM

A primary narrative within HRM has been the flexibility and individualisation thesis. HRM was seen as a move away from collectivism and regulated systems of industrial relations and personnel administration with their reliance on bargaining. The new competitive environment of the 1980s required new organisational forms and greater recognition of the pressures of changing and ever-intensifying product markets. The emergence of the *flexibility* thesis and the discourse of the *individualisation* of HRM has been organised through a new range of players, such as business schools, consultancies, and even state bodies. The need to highlight and reward individuals in relation to their contribution and the ability to respond to change was seen as a cornerstone of the new HRM. The 1980s was an age when governments, in the UK and the USA, amongst other countries, formulated neo-liberal strategies and opposed collectivist approaches to the question of

employment in terms of welfare or trade union rights. The political dimension was complemented – although not quite evenly – with the vast growth of business schools and consultancies in the area of employment and work related issues (Martínez Lucio, 2007). The way forward was believed to rest on providing greater attention to the way people worked and contributed within their teams and their workplaces in general:

> Human resource management is a distinctive approach to employment management which seeks to achieve competitive advantage through the strategic deployment of a highly committed and capable workforce using an array of cultural, structural and personnel techniques (Storey, 1995:5).

Yet, regardless of these academic approaches, a prevalent narrative within early forays into HRM concerned the questions of marketisation, decentralisation and individualisation. Not only was the individualising of pay an increasing objective, but new forms of employment contracts and relations were proposed. The new worker was meant to be a flexible worker, i.e., sometimes working on a temporary basis with a looser organisational link with the firm. This was due to changing product markets, more easily deployed in relation to production and service delivery needs as they changed both within teams and within the firm generally, and working more flexibly by changing patterns of working hours. The nature of the flexible firm emerged, highlighting the relevance of different types of flexible arrangements within organisations (Atkinson and Meager, 1986; see Pollert, 1988 for a critique). The role of HRM in this instance was to facilitate such a development by ensuring payment systems and appraisal systems that could reflect the individual performance of an employee. In addition, HRM departments now had to map and survey the organisation in terms of its practices, its relationships and the link between organisational purpose and the manner in which people were managed. In one respect, HRM became relatively more strategic, adopting a role of *fine-tuning*. It was not a case of warding off conflict and fitting people to posts – there was a more strategic aspect emerging in relation to fitting staff to new objectives, new roles and new demands. There were meant to be 'levers' (Storey, 1994) that HRM professionals could use to ensure a more committed and effective workforce, such as communication systems and reward mechanisms. Whether this is what happened is the subject of great conjecture. (Sissons and Storey, 1993; Storey, 1994, Legge, 1995). Rhetorics and realities in HRM are never too far apart (Legge, 1995, 2007).

A major challenge to this new strategic location was not only related to the paucity of concrete results, but also to the challenge to HRM of decentralisation. The new HRM was meant to 'push decision making closer to the line'. Through teamworking, greater line and middle management discretion, and new forms of upward communication through individuals, HRM was meant to become the preserve of everybody in a firm. The argument was that the art of managing people would be part of a greater array of internal organisational stakeholders' skills. HRM represented the de-bureaucratisation of people management. The 1980s began to see a greater emphasis on the local, the immediate and the tangible in terms of how workers and local managers engaged with the challenge of change. Consultancies began to deal with this more directly; for example, this was especially so in terms of teamworking.

Yet where does HRM as a department fit here? Is the role one of ensuring consistency across departments and sections? Does it consist of setting ground rules for the local practice of HRM? Is it, ironically, in maintaining coherence bureaucratically? It becomes clear that this shift to a flexible and de-centred approach introduces tension into HRM. In terms of divisionalisation and decentralisation it is not uncommon for firms to decentralise HR practices or organisational structures only to recentralise and reinforce controls as a consequence of the contradictions, tensions and malpractices such developments can bring. The challenge of line manager competence and ability comes to the fore with greater decentralisation (Lowe, 1992;

Cunningham and Hyman, 1995). There are questions that emerge over the employee-oriented aspects of HRM as the strategic aspect is centralised and the operational, people-oriented aspect is left to unconvinced and unsupported line managers (Francis and Keegan, 2006). HRM's role becomes one that consists more of policing practices, especially when greater decentralisation occurred, from the late 1980s onwards, in an environment of greater sensitivity to individual employment rights on issues such as equality. What we find in relation to the location of HRM is an unresolved tension between the dispersal of HRM and the strategic, central monitoring role it is increasingly playing, which has implications for the boundaries of the profession, and where the core of its constituency is located.

## 'To be a networker': the network paradigm and HRM

Part of the problem with greater individualisation, flexibility and decentralisation is the potential engendering of a low trust and fragmented culture within employment and organisations generally. The idea of a fragmented and dualist organisation with HRM caught between greater complexity and the pressure for closer scrutiny challenged the coherence of HRM as an emergent project. What began to emerge within the narratives of HRM was an alternative view of the organisation based on changing organisational boundaries, greater subcontracting, and increased interest in the relations between organisational units. The emergence of *networking* or the *network firm* became a more mature version of the decentralisation thesis. The future of organisations rested in the way they worked between each other and created high trust relations around collaborative projects (Bahrami, 1992; Castells, 1996). Increasingly, we should view firms as a cluster of smaller business units – or smaller business units interacting with a larger one – having a greater emphasis on a decentralised approach in terms of structure, and using information technology and quality management to underpin change. There is a view that there should be greater flexibility within the organisation, and an ability to have a structure that covers various markets and shift emphasis between projects: central to this is the idea of the corporation without boundaries, with its complex supply chains and outsourcing.

HRM now speaks of a post-bureaucratic age – an age of networking and network management. There are various definitions of networks and networking. In effect, it is a half-way house between bureaucracy with its organisational structures and markets with their open transactions (see Powell, 1990). There are various points of coordination working together with a fair degree of autonomy. The degree of autonomy will vary. Cooperative networks are based on reciprocal relations, mutual interest and relations of trust. Networks lead to a network enterprise, linked to change through joint collaboration, which in turn influences social relations and the way individuals operate through networks as well. Functional networks perform a particular purpose. Networks are seen to be an alternative way of creating products and value. They are similar in some cases to co-operative networks, but they are driven by particular objectives and actors within the network (Ackroyd, 2002: 184–5)

Within this new organisational form, HRM's role is not clear. On the one hand, HRM can be seen as the solution to the problems with the immediate employment issues of each unit within a network. However, in order to add value it would have to develop a series of roles in terms of facilitating dialogue between units, training staff to work in new and more flexible ways, and in supporting strategic teams that straddle the networks. The support of mobile élite staff in management and in professional grades that work across networks and deal with the links between nodes requires a focused HR strategy, as seen with expatriate staff in transnational corporations. HRM becomes a link in and within corporate alliances and network structures – a cultural facilitator. HRM's future is in providing coherence to the external boundaries of the firm and its flexible strategists.

Once more there are tensions in the new HRM role. First, there can be tensions between the strategy and administration of HRM. The staff support function needs greater attention in the pursuit of new organisational forms. Second, there is a monitoring aspect that emerges in this new role, which does not clearly fit well with the rhetoric of high-trust in the network genre. MacKenzie and Forde (2006) highlight the extent to which the emergence of subcontracting and temporary employment agencies, as two pillars of the flexible firm and network age, emphasises the absence of decentralisation by the employer. On the contrary, they argue that we have witnessed a re-bureaucratisation of the firm through highly structured subcontracting and monitoring processes, based on dominant patron firms. As for temporary employment agencies, these have developed from facilitators to dominant employers and labour market coordinators in their own right. The myth of the re-emergence of the small firm and de-centred employer networks is challenged by the argument that sees a more dominant role and organised character to the firm through such highly structured and centralised forms of employment.

Third, this challenge to the role of HRM as the mechanism by which the network firm can be coordinated and the relationships across the network managed finds its most extreme expression in the fact that HRM may itself be subject to the logic of net-working and new organisational forms and be subcontracted. Many firms buy in their HRM function in terms of the administration of people management through dedicated specialist firms; and buy in core strategic support through consultants. Given this, HRM as a feature of the firm becomes part of the external community of stakeholders and players linked through contracts to the firm. What emerges is that the location of HRM may vary within this post-bureaucratic context. The tensions that emerge between a language of trust and a practice of contractual scrutiny may undermine the clear location of HRM. Increasingly HRM itself is not the subject of the network firm but its object as well.

## 'Managers have kids too': the ethical turn

The late 1990s brought a period of reflection as far as HRM was concerned. Various factors contributed to a concern with the aftermath of the 1980s. First, some people were aware that the position of HRM professionals and functions within the organisation was unclear, given the discourses and practices of dis-embedding traditional structures, creating uncertainty within organisations, and fetishising change. Second, in the UK and the USA new forms of HRM were not consistently achieving the flexible, high-commitment workplace many had anticipated. The idea of a workplace based on direct participation, autonomous teams, and dealing directly with HR issues was questionable. The decline – or apparent decline – of industrial relations institutions had not led to a coherent and cohesive alternative. Third, the political landscape was changing and employers had to anticipate the impact of new forms of regulation at work due to the re-emergence of social democratic agendas (Martínez Lucio and Stuart, 2004). That with hindsight the reality of such changes is subject to debate is another matter. Hence, we begin to see actors within HRM having to re-evaluate their position and narratives, or at least to complement the more market oriented approach with alternatives. In part, this is driven by the impact of a new consumer consciousness and a new type of workforce with new social demands.

The shift has two features. In this section, we focus on the ethical aspects, whilst in the next we discuss the question of training. There have been many companies that have had an ethical narrative as part of their portfolio of activities and branding. The desire to alleviate the negative consequences of a market economy and industrial work was apparent in some exceptional cases in the nineteenth century: Robert Owen in his Scottish workplaces and Titus Salt in Saltaire, Bradford, were two important reference points. Chocolate manufacturers such as Rowntree and Cadbury were influenced by the negative legacy of slavery and developed philanthropic approaches. However, these have normally been the exceptions.

More recently, the calls for corporate social responsibility have increased. Since the late 1990s, there have been a range of committees organised by entrepreneurs, government and trade unions in the UK (Fisher and Lovell, 2006: 302–310). The United Nations and the Organisation for Economic Cooperation and Development have involved themselves in providing standards and regulations for transnational corporations and for governments in their conduct of affairs, although many of these are voluntary regulations. Within HRM the notion of the 'good employer' has gained favour although for some this is a modest construct: the discussion of ethics in HRM and CSR has not quite kept pace with the broader business debates on this topic (Pinnington et al., 2007). However, as a narrative the notion of acting ethically and socially as an employer has slowly emerged. In many respects this is driven by a realisation that the workforce has changed in gender and ethnicity terms, family and care related issues appear to be more important, and the negative aspects of workplace burn-out have been exposed to some press coverage. The legal landscape has also changed. Whilst collective rights for trade unionists may be subject to change, individual rights are becoming increasingly significant. Employers are more frequently challenged by litigation. Increasingly, legal cases hinge not just on the details of any one problem but on whether an employer has systematic, ethical, and socially oriented procedures in place. The combination of social change and legal re-regulation means that organisations must be seen to have ethical and social procedures in place.

The change in the landscape of HRM issues, no matter how uneven its development, provides HR managers and professionals with a narrative that can be used to police the organisation in a more subtle and discreet manner. HRM departments can become internal moral auditors and sanction, or warn, wayward departments (Marchington and Wilkinson, 1996: 3). They can also provide crucial advice in navigating through the new ethical and social legal terrain (Beatty *et al.*, 2003). To this extent, HRM professionals can accumulate knowledge on social dimensions and concerns within a workplace through surveys and audits, establish criteria along ethical lines on such issues as recruitment or sickness procedures, and lead the crafting of ethical and social statements and declarations by an employer. In this respect, the equality and diversity narratives developed recently by HRM specialists would fit this logic. The future rests in the ethical 'rearmament' of HRM (Winstanly and Woodall, 2000). However, whether this is due to a genuine ethical concern or professional self-interest in the face of fragmentation needs to be studied. Concerns about consistency within ethical issues in HRM are quite common and references to hypocrisy are not uncommon (Foote, 2001).

The role of the main body representing HR managers in the UK – the Chartered Institute of Personnel and Development (CIPD) – has not been as committed to the ethical dimension as one would imagine (Watson, 2006). The independence and integrity of HR managers and professionals is considered to be less important than being professional and serving the employer (ibid.). In terms of business schools, as major players in management education, the question of CSR and business ethics remains in large part optional in terms of the curriculum. It is part of the soft option and seen not to fit masculine narratives and behaviours regarding the cult of change, with these masculine features pervading the culture of such educational institutions. However, the ethical and social can be a lever for individual clusters and networks of HR managers. As a narrative, it allows the marginalisation of HRM in the face of further fragmentation to be redressed to some degree. The outcomes, however, are another matter. Hence, dealing with the marginal status of the function has normally provoked a response through other avenues, as we will discuss below.

## 'Learning is good for the boss and for you': the training mantra in the politics of HRD

If there is one area where HRM has attempted to position itself with a view to contributing to the long-term benefit of employers and employees it is the area of training and learning. This particular narrative of the HR function is seen as balancing the interests of both sides of employment relations (Kochan and Osterman, 1994). Employees gain by developing their portfolio of skills and knowledge, and by developing their longer-term prospects through their labour market value. Employers gain because they have more skilled, flexible employees who in turn may exhibit indications that they are committed to the purpose of their employer in return for the provision of a training service. The idea is that this is a mutual gain for all. For HR managers this particular narrative balances the economic needs of employers with the broader social needs of the employee. It manages to encapsulate both dimensions of their relations at work.

The other reason why this could be such an attractive narrative is that it dovetails with the current grand narrative related to the knowledge economy (Castells, 1996). In future, or in the present, the basis of a successful competitive approach by an employer will be in their human assets and the knowledge base they develop. Innovation is in great part driven by knowledge workers (Reich, 1993). Moreover, even in low-level service delivery jobs there is a requirement for new, soft skills related to dealing with the customer and this creates a further need for a more focused training regime (Grugulis, 2007: 85–86). HR managers can, in effect, draw from this grand narrative – this more political and socially recognisable discourse – as a foundation for rethinking their role. The sphere of learning is important in political and policy terms: a regional competitive edge is perceived to be emerging from the quality and flexibility of labour (Room, 2005; Greenwood and Stuart, 2006: 77–106). Training for technical, soft, and political skills are not only part of the portfolio of HRM. HR managers can also cross-reference with other developments within managerialism. In the age of Knowledge Management, surveying, categorising, elaborating, copying and deploying knowledge is the key to an organisation's sustainability and development (von Krogh and Roos, 1996).

So the narrative of training and knowledge links HR specialists into the different areas of the firm, the daily practice of employees, the goals of the firm, and the broader, external, political and economic network of training providers and funding. This renewal through training is a central feature of current narratives. However, the benefits to the role of HRM are not so clear. There is no guarantee that training per se is a clear step towards a more capable and intelligent individual and towards a new knowledge economy (Grugulis, 2007). The first thing to note is that in the case of the USA and the UK there has not been a commensurate increase in training funds and commitment. Where they are strategically developed, as in the Nordic countries, it is in great part due to the role of the state and the provision of support from other actors such as trade unions (Payne and Keep, 2005). As a strategy for securing economic assets and resources it is therefore uncertain. Stuart (2007) argues that in the case of the UK – and one could apply this to the USA also – the problem with training is that trade unions have four problems when pushing for more investment. They lack members (and in non-union firms there are few voices apart from those of managers), they lack partners (a lack of strong, mutually supportive arrangements between management, unions and others), they lack a demand for skills (especially for high skill levels), and they lack employers (at least so far as legal obligations on employers for training are concerned). Trade unions face employers that may place the emphasis on symbols and gestures as opposed to systematic investment in resources and their transparent deployment (Grugulis, 2007). Learning and training can be a double-edged sword, with skills being redefined in order to create a

greater reliance on the employer or to diminish the strength and autonomy of employees (Stuart, 1996). The problem with training is that it is not so clearly an issue of mutual gain as one would have first imagined. This puts HR managers in an awkward position, partly because the independent stance that the training role supposedly provides is not so clear. What is more, a whole new 'industry' of learning and training has been spawned in some countries, such as the UK and the USA: there is a veritable array of institutions, consultants, independent trainers, coaching mentors, and others, who have generated a curious network and community related to training, but this training community is subject to market imperatives, trends, fashions and developments. Subcontracting is rife in this area and many providers of training are ex-HR managers and specialists who have been unable to influence core decisions about budgets and strategic direction in their area. In effect, steering a clear narrative and influential role through this dimension is difficult, given the diverse range of interests, actors and funding.

### 'Yes we are good for the bottom line': the cult of performance and HRM

By this stage, it is clear that HR practitioners deploy narratives in an attempt to reinvigorate their role and provide strategic influence in the conduct of businesses and employers. These narratives vary and provide different sources of legitimacy for their roles. The effectiveness of these roles, and of the narratives, is not clear because of the tensions that exist between the competing imperatives of control and co-operation central to the employment relation. In addition, HR professionals find that their own boundaries and positions are undermined by the developments in some of these issues, including networking and decentralisation, or that the narrative does not resonate with broader economic objectives. This is even the case when there has been an ethical turn in the business literature.

There is one particular narrative that has begun to emerge and that is central to the attempts of HR professionals and academic agendas in the quest for being taken seriously. The question of performance is essential to the progress of capitalist organisations but where the mystery lies is in the formulae and factors that give rise to enhanced performance and productivity. For Ulrich (1997) personnel managers can and must overcome their marginality by embracing competitiveness and the performance agenda. Performance is not a new topic of debate, being the subject of academic interventions in the industrial relations area and labour economic discipline for some time. However, there is now a burgeoning debate within HRM – especially in the USA – focused on using advanced quantitative research methods to uncover the 'bundles' of practices that contribute to better performance.

> ... there is a growing consensus that organisational human resource policies can, if properly configured, provide a direct and economically significant contribution to firm performance. The presumption is that the more effective systems of HRM practices, which simultaneously exploit the potential for complementarities or synergies among such practices and help to implement a firm's competitive strategy, are sources of sustained competitive advantage (Huselid, 1995: 634).

The challenge is to identify and correlate work practices with performance. Investment in particular work practices, such as teamworking for example, and their combination with other specific high performance work practices, can be associated with lower employee turnover and greater productivity amongst others (Huselid, 1995; Appelbaum et al., 2000). For many scholars this represented a way into the harder and more glamorous world of accounting and financial legitimacy. Even industrial relations academics feel that if they could prove that there were 'menus' of practices that included factors such as trade unionism, collective bargaining or collective forms of participation then it would show that high performance could be compatible with

a regulated environment that was predisposed to organised labour. All of a sudden, we could detect good practices that are efficient and not necessarily part of the 'hard' world of HRM in terms of performance measurement and surveillance of employees.

The problem is 'that many studies ... merely seek to demonstrate evidence of association between the use of high performance work systems and firm performance measures' (Danford et al., 2007). Many of the studies using the Workplace Employment Relations Surveys in the UK that seek to find a link to performance ignore the fact that positive employer perspectives do not resonate with employees who are more sanguine about such high performance practices (ibid.). In fact, as a consequence of not referencing the context of lean production, studies of such workplace practices fail to engage with the question of why outcomes may not be positive for workers even if they may be positive in financial terms for employers. Yet regardless of such deficiencies, and regardless of spurious understandings of causality, which do not map contextual and broader factors (Fleetwood and Hesketh, 2007), for some this debate about performance and the role of HRM strategy is a godsend. The debate begins to address the question of how calculated combinations or 'bundles' of practices are important to financial, performance and organisational outcomes. This places HR departments and strategists in a pivotal position within the firm. It also portrays HRM as being essential to corporate governance and financial strategy. Suddenly there is evidence of a link between the people element and the financial 'bottom line', without it necessarily being about savings from making staff redundant.[2]

The role of HRM here is as a matrix and articulator of practices and bundles – HRM as a link between accountancy and softer people-oriented values. So regardless of methodological and academic concerns (Thompson, 2007: 86–88), the buy-in from HRM specialists is a highly attractive proposition. It provides the fit and the fix between the harder performance dimension and the ethical-learning dimensions outlined earlier. However, some dilemmas remain. The first is that performance and the interpreting of performance by organisations may not see the link to softer and people-friendly HRM as important. The debate may prove that HRM is important in terms of practices that focus on appraisal, measurement, surveillance and work intensification (Danford *et al.*, 2007). If this is a possible outcome then HRM returns to the role of an accounting and calculative approach to people.

In its more idealistic terms, HRM posits work as liberating, as productive play and a route to a form of self-actualisation. Yet it also has a contradictory performative streak wherein play needs to be measured, controlled, manipulated, and if the player disagrees, then the HRM manager needs to enforce the rules of the game ... as Marx so forcefully pointed out, the employment relationship is fundamentally conflictual within capitalism (Hanlon, 2007: 276).

The second dilemma is that there are political contexts to this debate. The British state, for example, has entered into the performance narrative as an attempt to ensure industry and employers generally approach employment issues in a strategic manner. The idea has been that labour management must focus on quality and efficiency as well. This links to a whole set of narratives from the political structures of the European Union and a desire to see labour markets and labour skills deployed in more 'effective' terms to challenge the performance gap between the European Union and the USA and Japan (Greenwood and Stuart, 2006). The link to the ethical and the moral place of HRM is therefore not clear.

The third dilemma is how HR professionals are to evoke this narrative and for what purpose? The CIPD and similar bodies have conducted a lot of the research that shows a link between high performance workplace practices and performance – and less research that does not show the link – but this does not obviate the need for a clearer discussion of the type of HRM we are talking

about. Even if one agrees that key elements such as teamworking, problem solving teams and contingent pay are features of high performance work organisations (Becker and Gerhart, 1996) the question still remains as to how one implements these, how one links them to other practices, and what type should be implemented. It does not follow that HRM will oversee these practices as operational managers may play a much greater role. So, as a narrative to instil corporate and political enthusiasm for HRM it is unclear how it leads to the greater organisational centrality for HRM. Few studies appear to exist to date on how performance narratives are deployed within specific organisational contexts to enhance HRM issues.

## DISCUSSION

When we discuss the organisational role of HRM, we need to understand it in relation to the narratives and strategies that emerge. The consensus remains that HRM as a profession and as a function does not always occupy the central strategic dimensions of an organisation, even where labour management issues are not seen primarily as resolving industrial relations problems. In spite of the 'professionalisation' of HRM, through accreditation bodies and a dedicated knowledge stream, the reality of HRM in terms of its inability to refocus organisational politics is a curious continuity with past legacies. The position of the HR manager remains unclear (Gibb, 2000) and HR is rarely seen as a positive economic input (Becker and Gerhart, 1996). The continued secondary nature of HRM within the rubric of corporate governance and politics is a live issue.

The question of HRM's position in organisational terms cannot be separated from the contradictory pulls and pushes across various dimensions of the employment relation. The different trajectories of a changing employment system require different responses. This chapter has outlined how narratives have emerged that form the basis of the response to these changes. The challenge to HRM is that there is no clear location and space for managing the employment relation in an increasingly post-bureaucratic and globalised context. If anything, some of the literature suggests that some of the responses appear to be a reinvigoration of bureaucracy, based on an obsession with rule making (Church and Waclawski, 2001). This chapter has focused on five particular narratives or discourses. Each represents a way of managing the employment relation at a particular moment or in a particular context. It is clear many of these moments or contexts overlap. There have been narratives based on the decentralisation of HRM, the role of HRM in supporting the network firm, the role of ethical 'policing' within an organisation, the focus on employee development issues, and the mapping and support for practices that enhance organisational performance. These represent different roles for HRM.

One can see these narratives, in spite of the dilemmas such developments raise for the influence of HRM, as providing different platforms for making the case for HRM. They are part of the process of branding HRM and pointing to its relevance in a changing organisational context. Senior HR managers can roll out these narratives in their personal and strategic positioning within an organisation. Reference to the fear of fragmentation that comes with some approaches, the need to develop staff in

the wake of a post-bureaucratic context, and the need to monitor behaviour that can lead to litigation or negative branding is part of the politics of inter-departmental relations. Yet the question becomes whether such narratives are proactive and strategic – and consciously elaborated – or are they developed to sustaining a role for HRM in the wake of change and marginalisation? It is clear they play a dual role, but the internal political context should not be ignored.

There is a need to widen the remit of organisational analysis beyond the organisation itself. The discussion above shows how narratives related to HRM are subject to intervention from a range of other actors such as the state, trade unions, professional lobbyists, and consultancy networks. The ability of HR managers to lock into these spheres of interest is important. They provide legitimacy and alliances around themes that can strengthen their own internal lobbying and influence. Agency and politics is a fundamental part of HRM even if it is absent from many of the mainstream journals (Ferner and Tempel, 2006). A debate such as that on performance clearly involves a range of bodies, such as government departments, business schools, and even trade unions. Clusters of interests emerge that raise the profile of ethical or training issues, which produces a curious development. If one adds to these developments the fact that HRM is indeed fragmenting into different

**Table 19.1 Narratives, implications and realities of HRM**

| Narratives of HRM | Implications for HRM roles | Dilemmas for HRM roles (examples) |
| --- | --- | --- |
| Decentralisation of HRM | Supporting line management and establishing policy | Fragmentation and loss of control within the firm |
| The role of HRM in supporting the network firm | Developing network skills and regulating local suppliers | Being put out as a function: organisational exile |
| The role of ethical 'policing' within an organisation | Establishing and monitoring behaviour and values | Mainly monitoring and fad-driven |
| The focus on employee development issues | Focusing on skills and capacity generation amongst staff | Challenge of resource generation and external support (and the lack of these) |
| The support for practices that enhance organisational performance | Lobbying for particular practices – benchmarking on good practice | Unclear location and follow-through for arguing the case: potential lack of linkage between performance and HRM that undermines social and ethical agendas |

roles – monitoring, operational, and developmental – and different spaces – line management, the market through subcontracting and network nodes – then it may be through micro- and macro-political agency that HRM has a future. Within the firm, it means HRM acting as a body of knowledge around key strategists who in turn link into the external community of HR, employment and regulatory networks. The irony is that professional bodies and external standards become even more important within this context and this is visible in the way the CIPD lobbies – albeit idiosyncratically and in curious political terms – on the subject of HRM through research, consultancy, training and course accreditation and political links. The problem is that the 'outside' is about allies and there is a curious historical dimension in that traditional personnel management needed trade unions as 'allies' and 'competitors' to cement their role in the organisation. Perhaps a macro level of organisational behaviour and management needs to engage with the macro-political as well.

## NOTES

1 I would like to thank David Turner for assisting in the copy-editing of this chapter.

2 There is an argument that HRM departments became central to firms in terms of corporate decision-making and in terms of their relation to the boards of directors during the 1980s and 1990s as a consequence of greater restructuring, ongoing downsising, and periodic redundancies. HR departments had to manage these through selection procedures, retraining programmes, and communication systems aimed at softening the blow of change on employees at all levels of the company.

## REFERENCES

Ackers, P. and Payne, J. (1998) 'British trade unions and social partnership: Rhetoric, reality and strategy', *International Journal of Human Resource Management*, 9 (3): 529–550.

Ackroyd, S. (2002) *The Organisation of Business*. Oxford: Oxford University Press.

Almond, P. and Ferner, A. (2006) *American Multinationals in Europe: Managing Employment Relations Across National Borders*. Oxford: Oxford University Press.

Appelbaum, E., Bailey, T., Berg, P. and Kalleberg, A.L. (2000) *Manufacturing Advantage: Why High Performance Work Systems PayOff*, NY: Cornell University Press.

Armstrong, P. (1995) 'Accountancy and HRM', in J. Storey (ed.) *Human Resource Management: A Critical Text*. London: Routledge.

Atkinson, J. and Meager, N. (1986) *Changing Working Patterns*. London: NEDO.

Bahrami, H. (1992) 'The emerging flexible organization: Perspectives from Silicon Valley', *California Management Review*, (Summer): 33–52.

Beatty, R.W., Ewing, J.R. and Tharp, C.G. (2003) 'HR's role in corporate governance: Present and perspective', *Human Resource Management*, 42 (3): 257–269.

Becker, B. and Gerhart, B. (1996) 'The impact of human resource management on organizational performance: Progress and prospects', *Academy of Management Journal*, 39: 779–801.

Beer, M., Spector, B., Lawrence, P.R., Quinn Mills, D. and Walton, R.E. (1984) *Managing Human Assets*. New York: Simon and Schuster.

Bourdieu, P. (1986) 'The forms of capital', in J.G. Richardson (ed.) *Handbook of Theory and Research for the Sociology of Education*. New York: Greenwood Press.

Brewster, C. (1993) 'Developing a "European" model of human resource management', *International Journal of Human Resource Management*, 4 (4): 765–784.

Castells, M. (1996) *The Rise of the Network Society*. Oxford: Blackwell.

Church, A.H. and Waclawski, J. (2001) 'Hold the line: An examination of line vs staff differences', *Human Resource Management*, 40 (1): 21–34.

Clegg, S. (1989) *Frameworks of Power*. London: Sage.

Cunningham, I. and Hyman, J. (1995) 'Preparing managers for changes in employee relations', Occasional Paper Number 7, Strathclyde University.

Danford, A., Richardson, M. and Stewart, P. (2007) 'A labour-centred analysis of partnership and high performance work systems in high skills environments', Paper presented to ESEMK Seminar of High Performance Workplace, University of Stirling, Stirling, March.

Deakin, S., Hobbs, R., Konzelmann, S.J. and Wilkinson, F. (2004) 'Working corporations: Corporate governance and innovation in labour-management partnerships in Britain', in M. Stuart and M. Martínez Lucio (eds) *Modernisation and Partnership in Employment Relations*. London: Routledge.

Doty, D.H. and Glick, W.H. (1994) 'Typologies as a unique form of theory building: Toward improved understanding and modelling', *Academy of Management Review*, 19 (1): 230–251.

Ferner, A. and Tempel, A. (2006) 'Multinationals and national business systems: A power and "institutions" perspectives', in P. Almond and A. Ferner (eds) *American Multinationals in Europe: Managing Employment Relations Across National Borders*. Oxford: Oxford University Press.

Fisher, C. and Lovell, A. (2006) *Business Ethics and Values*. London: FT.

Fleetwood, S. and Hesketh, A. (2007) 'HRM performance research: Under-theorized and lacking explanatory power', *International Journal of Human Resource Management*, 17 (12): 1977–1994.

Fombrun, C.J., Tichy, N.M. and Devanna, M.A. (1984) *Strategic Human Resource Management*. New York: John Wiley and Sons.

Foote, D. (2001) 'The question of ethical hypocrisy in human resource management in the U.K. and Irish charity sectors', *Journal of Business Ethics*, 34 (1): 25–38.

Francis, H. and Keegan, A. (2006) 'The changing face of HRM: A changing balance', *Human Resource Management Journal*, 16 (3): 231–249.

Gibb, S. (2000) 'Evaluating HRM effectiveness: The stereotype connection', *Employee Relations*, 22 (1): 58–71.

Grant, D. and Oswick, C. (1998) 'Of believers, atheists and agnostics: Practitioners' views of HRM', *Industrial Relations Journal*, 29: 178–193.

Grant, D., Tom, K. and Oswick, C. (eds) (1998) *Discourse and Organizations*. London: Sage.

Greenwood, I. and Stuart, M. (2006) 'Employability and the flexible economy: Some considerations of the politics and contradictions of the European employment strategy', in L. Enrique Alonso and M. Martínez Lucio (eds) *Employment Relations in a Changing Society: Assessing the Post-Fordist Paradigm*. London: Palgrave Macmillan.

Grey, C. (2005) *Studying Organizations*. London: Sage.

Grugulis, I. (2007) *Skills, Training and Human Resource Development*. London: Palgrave.

Guest, D. (1987) 'Human resource management and industrial relations', *Journal of Management Studies*, 8 (3): 263–276.

Guest, D. (1990) 'Human resource management and the American dream', *Journal of Management Studies*, 27 (4): 377–397.

Hanlon, G. (2007) 'HRM is redundant?: Professions, immaterial labour and the future of work', in S.C. Bolton and M. Houlihan (eds) *Searching for the Human in Human Resource Management*. London: Palgrave.

Huselid, M.A. (1995) 'The impact of HRM practices on turnover, productivity and corporate financial performance', *Academy of Management Journal*, 38 (3): 635–672.

Keenoy, T. (1990) 'A wolf in sheep's clothing', *Personnel Review*, 19 (2): 3–9.

Kochan, T.A. and Osterman, P. (1994) *The Mutual Gains Enterprise: Forging a Winning Partnership among Labour, Management and Government*. Boston: Harvard University Press.

Laclau, E. and Mouffe, C. (1985) *Hegemony and Socialist Strategy*. London: Verso.

Legge, K. (1995) *Human Resource Management: Rhetoric and Realities*. London: Macmillan.

Legge, K. (2007) 'The ethics of HRM in dealing with individual employees without collective representation', in A. Pinnington, R. Macklin and T. Campbell (eds) *Human Resource Management: Ethics and Employment*. Oxford: Oxford University Press.

Levy, D. and Egan, D. (2003) 'A neo-Gramscian approach to corporate political strategy: Conflict and accommodation in the climate change negotiations', *Journal of Management Strategies*, 40 (4): 803–829.

Lowe, J. (1992) '"Locating the line": The front-line supervisor and human resource management', in P. Blyton and P. Turnbull (eds) *Reassessing HRM*. London: Sage.

MacKenzie, R. and Forde, C. (2006) 'The myth of decentralisation and the new labour market', in L. Enrique Alonso and M. Martínez Lucio (eds) *Employment Relations in a Changing Society: Assessing the Post-Fordist Paradigm*. London: Palgrave Macmillan.

Marchington, M. and Wilkinson, A. (1996) *Core Personnel and Development*. London: IPD.

Martínez Lucio, M. (2007) 'Neoliberalismo y neoconservadorismo interrumpido? El porqué de la existencia de una tradición crítica en las escuelas de dirección de empresas británicas', in C. Fernández Rodríguez (ed.) *Vigilar y Organizar: Una Introduccion a los Critical Management Studies*. Madrid: Siglo Veintiuno.

Martínez Lucio, M. and Simpson, D. (1992) 'Crisis and discontinuity in industrial relations: The rise of human resource management and the struggle over its social dimension,' *International Journal of Human Resource Management*, September *1992*: 173–190.

Martínez Lucio, M. and Stuart, M. (2004) 'Swimming against the tide: Social partnership, mutual gains and the revival of "tired" HRM', *International Journal of Human Resource Management*, 15 (2): 404–424.

Martínez Lucio, M. and Weston, S. (1992) 'Trade union responses to human resource management: Bringing the politics of the workplace back into the debate', in P. Blyton and P. Turnbull (eds) *Reassessing Human Resource Management*. London: Sage.

Mayrhofer, W. and Brewster, C. (2006) 'European human resource management: Researching developments over time', in R.S. Schuler and S.E. Jackson (eds) *Strategic Human Resource Management*. Oxford: Blackwell.

Payne, J. and Keep, E. (2005) 'Promoting workplace development: Lessons for UK policy from Nordic approaches to job redesign and the quality of working life', in B. Harley, J. Hyman and P. Thompson (eds) *Participation and Democracy at Work*. London: Macmillan.

Pettigrew, A. (1973) *The Politics of Organisational Decision-making*. London: Tavistock.

Pettigrew, A. (1985) *The Awakening Giant: Continuity and Change in ICI*. Oxford: Blackwell.

Pfeffer, J. (1994) *Competitive Advantage through People*. Boston: Harvard Business School.

Pinnington, A., Macklin, R. and Campbell T. (2007) 'Introduction', in A. Pinnington, R. Macklin and T. Campbell (eds) *Human Resource Management: Ethics and Employment*. Oxford: Oxford University Press.

Pollert, A. (1988) 'Dismantling flexibility', *Capital and Class*, 34: 42–75.

Powell, W.W. (1990) 'Neither market nor hierarchy: network forms of organization', *Research in Organizational Behavior*, 12: 295–336.

Reed, M. (2006) 'Engineers of human souls, faceless technocrats, or merchants of morality?: Changing professional forms and identities in the face of the neo-liberal challenge', in A. Pinnington, R. Macklin and T. Campbell (eds) *Human Resource Management: Ethics and Employment*. Oxford: Oxford University Press.

Reich, R. (1993) *The Work of Nations*. London: Simon and Schuster.

Room, G. (2005) *The European Challenge: Innovation, Policy Learning and Social Cohesion in the New Knowledge Economy*. Bristol: Pitman.

Schattschneider, E. (1960) *The Semi-sovereign People: A Realist's View of Democracy in America*. New York: Holt, Rinehart, and Wilson.

Schuler, R.S. and Jackson, S.E. (1987) 'Linking competitive strategy with human resource management practices', *Academy of Management Executive*, 3: 207–219.

Sissons, K. and Storey, J. (1993) *Managing HRM and Industrial Relations*. Milton Keynes: Open University Press.

Sparrow, P.R. and Hiltrop, J.M. (1997) 'Redefining the field of European HRM: A battle between mindsets and forces of business transition', *Human Resource Management*, 36 (2): 1–19.

Storey, J. (1994) *Developments in the Management of HRM*. Oxford: Blackwell.

Storey, J. (1995) 'Introduction', in J. Storey (ed.) *Human Resource Management: A Critical Text*. London: Routledge.

Stuart, M. (1996) 'The industrial relations of training: A reconsideration of training arrangements', *Industrial Relations Journal*, 27 (3): 253–266.

Stuart, M. (2007) 'United Kingdom – The Sound of one hand Clapping?', in L. Magnusson and J. Winterton (eds) *Trade Union Strategies for Developing Competence at Work: An Emerging Area for Social Dialogue*. Forthcoming.

Thompson, P. (2007) 'Making capital: Strategic dilemmas for HRM', in S.C. Bolton and M. Houlihan (eds) *Searching for the Human in Human Resource Management*. London: Palgrave.

Ulrich, D. (1997) *Human Resource Champions: The Next Agenda for Adding Value and Delivering Results*. Boston: Harvard University Press.

von Krogh, G. and Roos, J. (1996) 'The epistemological challenge: Managing knowledge and intellectual capital', *European Management Journal*, 14 (4): 333–337.

Watson, T. (2006) 'Progressive human resource management, HRM, ethical irrationality, and the limits of ethical action', in A. Pinnington, R. Macklin and T. Campbell (eds) *Human Resource Management: Ethics and Employment*. Oxford: Oxford University Press.

Winstanly, D. and Woodall, J. (2000) 'The ethical dimension of human resource management', *Human Resource Management Journal*, 10 (2): 5–20.

# 20

# Organizational Moral Responsibility

Carl Rhodes and Alison Pullen

## INTRODUCTION

This chapter provides a critical discussion of the notion of moral responsibility as it is relevant to the behaviour of contemporary organizations. Located within the broad domain of business ethics, such a notion of responsibility draws key attention to the relationship between organizations and the various people and institutions with which they interact and that register effects from their actions. In most general terms, the idea of being responsible immediately suggests a relation between persons – to be responsible in this sense is about being called to *respond* to others and to be held accountable to them for one's actions across the spread of space and in the unfolding of time. Considering macro-organizational behaviour in terms of moral responsibility places organizations within the ethical relationship between the organizational 'self' and its various others. This is a situation not restricted to those organizational practices that might be explicitly labelled 'ethical' but is a condition of all instances where organizational power is or can be exercised (Byers and Rhodes, 2007) – there is no organizational action that cannot be opened to ethical scrutiny. Responsibility requires the establishment and enactment of ethical relations that consider power in relation to the rights and needs of others. Further, responsibility requires rendering action as a form of 'decision' made under the burden of moral justification.

With the advent of practices associated with corporate social responsibility and the triple bottom line, for example, corporations are increasingly being held responsible, and propose to hold themselves responsible, for the effects of their actions on society, sustainability and the environment. Consumer pressure groups try to push organizations into taking responsibility for their actions in relation to customers. In the global political arena, organizations are held responsible for their significant effects on local economies and cultures. While the more traditional (yet still current) notion is that business organizations are primarily responsible to their shareholders, responsibility is now also mooted in relation to such diverse categories of persons as employees, cultural minority groups, the general public, political pressure groups and so forth. Such developments, *inter alia*, represent a shift regarding the social expectations of to whom organizations are responsible as well as what it is for which they are responsible.

Characterizing all these recent trends there is a diffusion of the rhetoric of organizational moral responsibility away from addressing the needs of the owners of capital as being primary, towards organizations as being increasingly held responsible to a wider group of people, concerns, and institutions, often labelled as 'stakeholders'. Concurrent with such developments, however, has been a politico-economic shift right towards a neo-liberal global economic agenda where the practical freedom of business corporations to exercise power has, in many domains, increased significantly in scope. In such an age of globalization, managerialism and corporate power, both organizational freedom and calls for organizational responsibility multiply. The resulting condition is one where organizational responsibility is both intensified *and* at stake. As a result of this, organizational responsibility has become increasingly complex and difficult:

In a global arena which is increasingly fragmented and in which myriad ethical traditions constantly come into contact with one another, sometimes violently so, and in which organizations of business and government are the major intermediaries between cultures, peoples and states, simple solutions to what have been made complex ethical problems are nowhere to be found (Clegg and Rhodes, 2006: p. 1).

While it is clear that the demands for organizational moral responsibility are widening, the efficacy and authenticity of the response from organizations is the subject of much more contestation – most saliently, in the growing debates over the meaning of what has come to be called 'corporate social responsibility' (CSR). CSR, as well as attracting academic attention, is subject to 'a growing interest amongst managers [...] especially for executives and

multi-national, multi-divisional companies' (McWilliams, Siegel and Wright, 2006: 2). Where organizational power has broadened globally and deepened practically, that for which organizations might be held responsible has massified in significance. It is in such a context that this chapter considers the character of moral responsibility as it can and has been understood in relation to business organizations. The chapter concerns itself with providing a critical discussion of the different ways that this responsibility has been researched and theorized.

The chapter begins with a discussion of the notion of moral responsibility as it has been treated in the organizational and management literature. This takes into account discussions of the meaning and ethics of capitalism, the notion of organizational stakeholders, and the idea of the socially responsible organizations. The chapter focuses on the different ways that organizations have been considered 'responsible' by sketching the different 'others' to whom organizations might be thought of as being beholden to respond to. The trajectory of this thinking traverses the liberal and neo-liberal valorization of the market where organizations are seen to be responsible only to shareholders. Also considered are various conceptions of stakeholder management, whether it be that addressing the demands of stakeholders is seen as the best way to achieve shareholder interests, or where organizations are called on to respond to the needs of others for the benefit of society at large. In interrogating these positions what is also considered are those writers who express a deep scepticism, or even disavowal, that organizations can ever be morally responsible on account of the profit motive that informs their very identity. In joining this critique, we note that self-other distinctions that dominate stakeholder based approaches commonly lack the form of proximity normally associated with responsibility – instead 'others' are packaged in neat categories (e.g., customers, employees, members of the public, and so forth) that escape reference to actual persons. The effect of this, we argue, is to create a divided responsibility not between persons but between abstract categories of persons – that is, no one in particular. The chapter ends with a discussion of the meaning of responsibility and how it might be formed in the gap between macro-organizational behaviour and individual conduct and decision making such that organizational moral responsibility remains alive in the undecidable unfolding of practice.

## SCANDALOUS RESPONSIBILITY

Public concern over the moral responsibility of business is an issue that is very much present in relation to contemporary business. In recent years this presence has been unavoidable through public debate over a range of high profile corporate collapses. Enron was castigated as a fraudulent and greedy corporation whose wrongdoings came to light in relation to its filing for bankruptcy in 2001. WorldCom was another organization that faced bankruptcy in 2002 in relation to fraudulent accountancy practices. Just one year later, Parmalat became a *cause célèbre* in the business world for fraud. Such 'corporate scandals', as they have come to be known, have caused a flurry of excitement amongst those who condemn corporations as lacking in moral fibre and responsibility. Nothing less than a 'new enthusiasm for the ethical' (Roberts, 2003: 250) has developed, and the 'business of business ethics' is booming. Tacitly, in these public debates the meaning of responsibility is commonly taken for granted, focusing on long-standing moralistic practice of passing judgement over organizations and their responsibility. Those who position themselves as the arbiters of morality are often quick to assign blame to corporations, aggressively pointing and wagging their fingers at what they see as corporate wrongdoing.

The 'corporate scandals' mentioned above are all clear examples of organizations that overtly broke both the law and contravened culturally accepted moralities concerning lying and stealing. What the scandals allowed,

in a somewhat effortless fashion, is for the organizations in question to be regarded as blameworthy for their actions. In other words these organizations were socially rebuked on the media stage for not having lived up to their moral responsibility. Such examples point to an extreme case of what it means to be morally irresponsible – where particular people are deliberately motivated by self-interest to use their powers for greedy self-gain at the expense of others, using fraudulent means. For some, this legal boundary *is* the boundary of organizational responsibility, such that there is no difference between legal responsibility and moral responsibility (see Banerjee, 2005). However, whereas responsibility concerns the relations between self and other, such a legalistic perspective suggests that one can pursue self-interest full tilt provided that the actions this entails do not exceed the limit of the law. This clearly seeks to provide a justification for the pursuit of self-interest within particular limits within which others should be considered. More generally, reference to moral responsibility in business is largely concerned with the relation between self-interest and the interest of others. More often than not critics concern themselves with the way that the pursuit of self-interest by business in the form of profitability and other measures of financial gain can and have had deleterious social outcomes. The issue of how self-interest might be understood forms a pivotal point in thinking about the moral responsibility of organizations.

What does it mean to be *responsible*? This is a question that immediately sets up a relation between entities such that one questions how one might *respond* to others. Cast in terms of moral responsibility this asks on what terms might one person's response to the other be justified as being 'good' or 'right'. And conversely under what conditions might it be unjustified – 'bad' or 'wrong'. In terms of distinctions, what we are referring to here is moral rather than causal responsibility. Causal responsibility is about determining the link between persons and actions – that is, that a particular person is said to have caused something to happen.

The relation here is simply between cause and effect. Moral responsibility, however, has a particularly social dimension to it in that it entails judgement as to the merit of how one person's acts affect other people. Moral responsibility is therefore to be considered in terms of how the free actions of one person effect other persons and how the goals and results of those actions can be evaluated as good or bad.

This question of responsibility between persons has long been a central consideration of moral philosophy that can be traced back to Aristotle's *Nichomachean Ethics*, written in approximately 350 BC, and its reflection on the conditions under which a person's actions can be judged as blameworthy or praiseworthy. For Aristotle, a person's free and voluntary actions are the ones for which s/he is responsible – such actions being voluntary to the extent that they involve decisions on the part of the person enacting them. By this account, moral responsibility requires a combination of deliberation and choice. That is, that the person who is responsible must have considered what actions might be taken and their possible effects on others, and on this basis chooses freely which decision s/he made by considering these potential effects. 'We deliberate about what is in our power' says Aristotle (2000: 42) and hence it is the exercise of this power that is in the purview of moral scrutiny.

While the scene for philosophical discussions of responsibility was set by Aristotle, it remains the case still that 'the issue of moral responsibility is arguably one of the most difficult questions moral philosophy has to deal with' (Zaborowski, 2000: 47). Similarly, it is a vexing question for organizations. Its consideration raises crucial questions about the relation between causality and freedom – that is, to what extent people can be regarded as being responsible for their free actions as opposed to those actions (and their effects) being beyond individual control or efficacy. It is notable here that the deterministic tendencies of modern science have increasingly relinquished the individual of moral responsibility. Doctrinaire approaches such as behaviourism, structuralism, and functionalism have overcome the idea of a person being responsible; persons are instead seen as being scientifically predictable and responsive (Zaborowski, 2000; see also Ghoshal, 2005). Despite such tendencies, however, the relation between determinism and causality on the one hand, and freedom and responsibility on the other, remain central to concerns about the behaviour of organizations and the people who represent them as managers and employees.

## ORGANIZATIONAL SELF-INTEREST

The pursuit of self-interest has long been an important focus in considerations of the meaning of business responsibility. A key point of departure in the discussion of self-interest is Adam Smith's (1776/1982, 1776/1986) *Wealth of Nations* – a work that embodies an explicitly moral theory about business conduct. As Smith famously stated: '[i]t is not from the benevolence of the butcher, the brewer or the baker that we expect our dinner, but from their regard to their own interest' (1776/1982: 119). For Smith the assumption is that the individual person 'neither intends to promote the public interest, nor knows how much he is promoting it' but is 'led by an invisible hand to promote an end which was no part of his intention' (1776/1986: 32). Here the intentions or virtues of the individual are not considered, inasmuch as the utility of the actions such that 'by pursuing his own interest he frequently promotes that of the society more effectually than when he really intends to promote it' (1776/1982: 32).

Smith's point is that while the butchers, brewers and bakers might pursue self-interest, collectively this pursuit is also, and unintentionally, of benefit to other members of society. Unlike Aristotle, it is not the deliberations of the individual, but the collective utility of individual actions, that accounts for responsibility. The market system, by this account, works under Smith's 'invisible hand' to translate self-interest into community interest without the intervention of any 'self'. Hence, social responsibility is met not by attending to it directly but by the unintended collective consequences of the pursuit of self-interest. Of note here is that Smith's attempt to 'write morality though self-interested competition in the marketplace forms much of the basis of our contemporary business ideology' (Goodpaster, 1983: 17). The implications of this are that the state is responsible for ensuring competitive markets such that in their pursuit of self-interest, economic resources will be used to the best collective advantage – meanwhile, for the corporation, 'morality is not its business' (Goodpaster, 1983: 17).

The view that business should pursue self-interest was articulated by Milton Friedman (1970) who famously stated that 'the social responsibility of business is to increase profits'. As with Smith, social responsibility and the pursuit of self-interest become conflated. The world of the post-war United States was, however, different to Smith's eighteenth century Britain, and Friedman's concerns were directed specifically at corporate organizations in which ownership and control are not in the same hands. Like with Smith, however, Friedman's dictum is not a call to be irresponsible or egocentric – quite the contrary; it is a particular understanding of responsibility that argues that pursuing self-interest (understood as profit) is *the* most responsible thing that a business can do.

Friedman was critically condemning of ideas concerning social responsibility circulating at the time, arguing that it is individual persons (in the form of corporate executives) that must be held responsible rather than an abstracted notion of the organization. Friedman's position was that the executive's responsibility was 'to conduct the business in accordance with [the employer's] desires, which generally will be to make as much money as possible while conforming to the basic rules of the society, both those embodied in law and embodied in ethical custom'. By this argument Enron, WorldCom and Parmalat would still be scandalized and judged socially irresponsible without contest. Friedman's 'businessman' is an agent of the employer and is thus responsible for pursuing the employer's interests. Friedman here locates the pursuit of this interest (analogously to Smith) with a faith in the market mechanism; for his businessman to do otherwise would be politically rather than commercially motivated and therefore not fitting for his vocation. Friedman (1962) is clear: 'there is one and only one social responsibility of business – to use its resources and engage in activities designed to increase its profits so long as it stays within the rules of the game, which is to say, engages in open and free competition without deception or fraud' (p. 133). We note here that Friedman is far from supporting amoral or immoral business conduct, it is just that he defends a particular normative moral theory – one that argues for what organizations and their agents *should* do. For Friedman, profit seeking is by its very nature moral as long as it remains within the bounds of law and custom. For the character known as the businessman, profit seeking is praiseworthy, self-interest is praiseworthy, and the market is praiseworthy.

## ENTER THE SOCIAL

When Friedman was associating responsibility with the pursuit of shareholder interests he was responding explicitly and directly to calls for organizational social responsibility that were current at the time. The views he opposed were those that encouraged managers to think of themselves as being directly responsible to a much broader group of constituents than the owners of capital. The historical antecedents of this trace back directly to Bowen's (1953) *The Social Responsibilities of the Businessman* where he explicitly asked the question: 'what responsibilities to society may businessmen reasonably be expected to assume?' (p. xi). Bowen's response was that business should 'pursue those policies, to make those decisions, or to follow those lines of action which are desirable in terms of the objectives and values of society' (p. 6). Similar concerns can be found when Davis (1960) asked the question: 'can business afford to ignore social responsibilities?' In addressing this question, Davis explicates his 'iron law of responsibility'. This law states that a business' social responsibilities should be commensurate with its power and, moreover, that businesses who avoid their social responsibilities will see their power erode. More generally, as Whetton, Rands and Godfrey (2001) summarize:

> The early advocates for CSR advanced many pragmatic arguments on behalf of CSR. These included the ideas that CSR activities: would help limit increases in government regulation; would develop a socially and economically stronger society more conducive to business success; would improve corporate reputation among existing and potential customers; would help attract and retain high quality employees; and had the potential to turn social problems into business opportunities. Arguments that business had a moral obligation to help society were also advanced, but were generally not articulated in as much detail (p. 380).

As is clear from this description, despite acknowledging the interests of others, from its advent the 'responsibility' in CSR was primarily a responsibility to the organization. So, while the 'social' is accounted for, what justifies business' need to respond to it is articulated primarily in the instrumental interests of the business. Put simply, the answer to the question of why business should be socially responsible, was because it was in business' best (self-)interest to do so.

In more recent years, as similar logic of self-interest on the part of business has developed in relation to the rubric of 'stakeholder management'. For Freeman (1984) strategic management should involve a consideration of the variety of constituents to whom the organization is related even though these are rarely explicit – predominantly this includes employees, customers, suppliers and community representatives. Such a focus, however, does not undermine the pursuit of self-interest on the part of business, it just extends its practice. The 'others' are to be considered by the stakeholder corporation precisely because they can impinge on the ability of that corporation to pursue and achieve the goals of its self-interest. Consideration of stakeholders is done in the self-defined interests of the organization, such that the purpose of stakeholder analysis is to help 'the firm identity its various stakeholders and their issues in order to understand what their stakes are and what powers they have to influence the firm' (Stead, Stead and Starek, 2003: 41). As McVea and Freeman (2005) note, this rests on the somewhat commonsense business view that

> value is created when entrepreneurs or managers put together a deal that simultaneously, and over time, satisfies the groups of stakeholders who play a critical role in the ongoing success of business: customers, suppliers, employees, communities and shareholder (p. 58).

So far, stakeholder theory appears just to be a footnote to Friedman but lacking the reflexive awareness of Friedman's moral theory. Indeed, it is most common for managerialist accounts of CSR to link such initiatives back to established business goals. In the 'market for virtue' (Vogel, 2005) the desire by business is for CSR to 'pay off' – often by integrating CSR with corporate strategy (Burke and Lodgson, 1996). As early as 1984 it was already the case that 'the relationship between a firm's corporate social responsibility (CSR) [...] and its financial performance has been [the] subject of lively debate since the 1960s' (Cochran and Wood, 1984: 42) – and the court is still out on whether CSR is good for financial performance (Margolis and Walsh, 2003; Vogel, 2005; cf. Orlitzky, Schmidt and Rynes, 2003). This debate has been articulated through a number of different positions – that there is a trade-off between financial performance and social responsibility; that the financial benefits of social responsibility outweigh the costs; and that the costs of social responsibility are off set by reductions in other costs (McGuire, Sundgren and Schneeweis, 1988). Adopting any of these positions seems to take the responsibility out of CSR when, despite the use of sophisticated analytical techniques, the unquestioned assumption of the inquiry is that: 'if certain actions (classified as socially responsible) tend to be negatively correlated with financial performance of firms, then managers might be advised to be cautious in this area' (Cochran and Wood, 1984: 42). In proceeding with such caution, managers have been advised to establish how 'CSR programmes can create strategic benefits for the organization' (Burke and Lodgson, 1996: 495). From such a perspective, any real deliberations over responsibility are blatantly absent such that the very idea of moral responsibility suffers intolerable abuse. For some, it seems, the vexing question of the irreducible conflict between economic objectives and social and humanitarian needs is answered with unreflective ease (Margolis and Walsh, 2003). Self-interest is alive and well, invigorated even.

## CARING ABOUT OTHERS?

As we have been discussing, stakeholder theory can be understood and practiced to aid the instrumental self-interest of business. Not all commentators agree however, with many people arguing an ethical case, rather than just a business case, for why business should be responsible to stakeholders. This expansion of stakeholder theory in the ethical domain is commonly associated with Donaldson and Preston's (1995) argument for a joint business and ethical case for stakeholder consideration (McWilliams, Siegel and Wright, 2006). Donaldson and Preston argue that stakeholder theory provides a normative basis for business and, moreover, bluntly stated, 'the plain truth is that the most prominent alternative to the stakeholder theory (i.e., the "management serving the shareowners" theory) is morally untenable' (Donaldson and Preston: 1995: 89). It is thus the case that although earlier debates on stakeholder theory (e.g., Freeman, 1984) 'argued that the stakeholder management approach lent itself to moral and normative analysis, it was only later, in the hands of business ethicists, that the normative branch of stakeholder theory began to emerge' (McVea and Freeman, 2005: 58). It is in

this sense that stakeholder theory has been developed as an overtly moral (and quite often moralizing) position.

Werhane and Freeman (1999) are explicit in staking the claim that stakeholder theory offers a normative ethics:

> Challenging the position that a manager's primary responsibility is to maximize profits or that the primary purpose of the firm is maximize the welfare of its stockholders, stakeholder theory argues that the goal of any firm and its management, is *or should be* the flourishing of the firm and *all* its primary stakeholders (p. 8, italics in original).

Such a view is based on a critique of what Freeman (1984) refers to as the 'separation thesis' – that is, what he sees as the mistaken, yet commonly held, view that business and ethics can be considered as separate domains. The ethical position taken up is that 'once the Separation Thesis is abandoned, it becomes crucial to see the actors in business as part of a common morality', and, moreover, that 'the stakeholder idea captures the basic idea of *responsibility* and applies it to business' (Werhane and Freeman, 1999: 7, italics added). The ethical position that is assumed is one where 'managers and others act (or should act) as if a stakeholder's interest has intrinsic value' (Donaldson and Preston, 1995: 74) – intrinsic in the sense that it is not seen merely as a means to and end for other (i.e., shareholder) interests.

The normative position that organizations should act in the greater good and beyond commercial self-interest is echoed in many discussions of corporate social responsibility. For McWilliams, Siegel and Wright (2006) CSR is defined as 'situations where a firm goes beyond compliance and engages in actions that appear to further some social good, beyond the interests of the firm and that which is required by law' (p. 1). The immediacy of this definition reinforces the division between two types of interests – those of the firm (legal interests and commercial interests) and those of society. This harks back to similar concerns raised by Frederick (1960) who asserted that 'social responsibility in the final analysis implies a public posture towards society's economic and human resources and a willingness to see that those resources are used for broad social ends and not simply for the narrowly circumscribed interests of private persons and firms' (p. 60). The key issue that was being raised here was directly oppositional to Friedman's (1962) legal boundaries around self-interest. In the early 1960s, for example, McGuire (1963) was specific in asserting that an organization's responsibilities to society exceed legal and economic obligations. It is clear here that self-interest is what is at stake, and the moral position is that part this self-interest should be sacrificed for the interest of others. Concurrently, such discourse immediately creates a bifurcation that informs its moral position: organizations are seen as different from, and other to, the society to which they are asked to be responsible. This categorization of difference is central in that it marks a division on which the organizational is set firmly on one side and the social firmly on the other. CSR activities further divide the social other into more particular categories. When such activities include environmentally friendly products, progressive human resources policies, pollution abatement, and helping community organizations (to use McWilliams *et al.*'s 2006 list) the social other is divided into the environment, employees, the eco-sphere and the community, respectively.

In terms of a moralistic turn-away from the pursuit of shareholder value, it is not uncommon for the ethical position taken in stakeholder theory and CSR to be self-righteous, simplistic and lacking in deliberation. Such a position is premised on the view that 'when major constituents of global society achieve the degree of sway that large businesses now have achieved, they create for themselves an increased responsibility to use their influence in a fashion that benefits their societies' (Gioia, 2003: 435). Although not explicit, this moral position is directly opposed to Smith and Friedman's morality of the market. So, Gioia surmises that the responsibility that is summoned by extensive and growing corporate power is one that is at odds with the assumption that 'the pre-eminent rule of corporate governance' is based on a primary corporate responsibility to stockholder property rights (p. 436). It would seem that what critics like Gioia are (too) quick to conclude as being the unethical rule is precisely the one that Friedman sees as ethical. What Gioia criticizes as 'the dominant right of shareholders to maximal return of their investments and the duty of executives to act in the service of that right' (p. 436) is precisely what Friedman was celebrating. The conventional conclusion that Gioia quickly arrives at is that organizations should be more socially responsible so as to regard themselves as 'instruments for creating common wealth' (p. 436). While such commentaries lend themselves to an easily appealing logic for responsibility and calls to arms to 'change the way we do business' (p. 437) the conflicting moralities embedded in such discussions are absent in the discussion. It is assumed that profit seeking is a form of self-interest at the expense of others (coagulated under the terms 'social') and therefore it is a blameworthy character trait.

## RESPONSIBILITY, RECIPROCITY AND RATIONALITY

While the positions on the responsibilities of business outlined above suggest different moral arguments and different practical trajectories, they all retain a belief in both the possibility and desirability of responsible business. Indeed such analyses foreclose on discussions of the legitimacy of business in general. This is achieved in that 'issues of corporate responsibility are of smaller scope than the ethical foundations of capitalism, since they presuppose to a great extent the fundamental legitimacy of capitalism – private property, for example, and free enterprise' (Goodpaster, 1983: 3). For those operating outside of such assumptions, however, 'the thought is that organizations, especially corporations, are essentially amoral entities – engines of profit or bureaucracies contrived for special purposes, driven by special interests' (Goodpaster, 1983: 16). From such a perspective the possibility that the character of the modern corporation can be considered morally responsible is questioned at its very core. It is on such a basis that Banerjee (2005), for example, argues that 'despite its emancipatory rhetoric, discourses of corporate social responsibility are defined by narrow business interests and serve to curtail the interests of external stakeholders' (p. 57). By this account organizational responses to calls for greater and broader responsibility are 'an ideological movement intended to legitimize the power of large corporations' (ibid.).

Of concern here is not just the moral justification of socially responsible business, but also the more practical matter of how organizations use discourses of social responsibility as a means to garner the appearance of ethicality when in the purview of external constituents. Roberts (2003), in exploring this issue, notes that 'responsibility and the desire to be seen as ethical are very different' (p. 251). He refers to this desire as an 'ethics of narcissus' where, rather than involving any real consideration of others, initiatives such as CSR merely fulfil a narcissistic urge to look good in the eyes of others (see Roberts, 2001, 2003). The point is that while increasing social and economic pressures on organizations can yield a response where organizations seek to position themselves superficially as being ethical, the result may well be the 'occluding of ethical sensibility' (Roberts, 2003: 255). Indeed, the irresponsibility of this occlusion is located in self-interest such that 'if ethical conduct is to be judged by its consequences, then the prime beneficiary of [corporate social responsibility] is the corporation itself' (p. 257). Here corporate endorsement of a discourse of responsibility is 'no more than the empty expression of pious wishes, which in practice amount to a flight from responsibility' (p. 263).

The position that Roberts articulates is that what goes by the name of responsibility in business is better regarded as a 'calculating ethics' (Jones, 2003) whose calculation is criticized precisely because of its thinly veiled self-interest. This is an ethics based on a 'calculus of advantage' that conflates responsibility with strategy, but where '[a]s soon as I become calculative or strategic about ethics, I am being ethical not out of respect for the Other, but out of respect for myself' (Jones, 2003: 235). Such thinking belies a deep-seated scepticism about the very possibility of an organizational moral responsibility, not the least because '[e]thics in business effectively rules out many ways of formulating decision-making and responsibility that are not amenable to some kind of organizational rationalization – an inner sense of duty, a concern for authenticity or desire for idiosyncratic ends, for example' (Parker, 1998b: S31).

The result of such considerations is less than optimistic: 'it is unlikely that any radical revision of corporate social responsibility will emerge from organizations' (Banerjee, 2005: 73). It has also been suggested that 'the means-end rationalization that ends in the practice now known as business ethics [...] seems to be destroying the very possibility of ethics itself' (Parker, 1998a: 289). An exposition of such an argument can also be found in Bauman's (1993) sociological account of ethics. As Bauman has argued, morality should not be regarded as a form of rationality, thought of in terms of a 'means-end scheme'. For Bauman in a 'moral order' that seeks to control ethics through various procedures that subsume the individual moral agent under an institutionalized ethical regime, the possibility of moral responsibility is squeezed out. At issue with such regimes, such as those of corporate social responsibility, is that they seek to resolve moral responsibility through the implementation of various institutionalized practices and codes that seek to guarantee ethics. As Roberts (2003) has argued, the organizational response to a call for responsibility 'has typically taken the form of the development of ethical codes, with associated internal communication and training, and, for some organizations, a move to the production of social and environmental reports as a complement to their financial accounts' (Roberts, 2003: 256). Following Bauman, however:

> Moral issues cannot be 'resolved', nor the moral life of humanity guaranteed, by the calculating and legislative efforts of reason. Morality is not safe in the hands of reason, though this is exactly what the spokesmen of reason promise. Reason cannot help the moral self without depriving the self of what makes the self moral: that unfounded, non-rational, un-arguable, no-excuses-given and non-calculable urge to stretch towards the other, to caress, to be for, to live for, happen what may. Reason is about making correct decisions, while moral responsibility precedes all thinking about decisions as it does not, and cannot care about any logic which would allow the approval of an action as correct (Bauman, 1993: 247–248).

The issue is that the technical rationality of organizing subsumes responsibility within its own calculating logic. It is in this way that '[t]he organization's answer to [the] autonomy of moral behaviour is the heteronomy of instrumental and procedural rationalities [...] actors are challenged to justify their conduct by reason as defined either by the approved goal or by the rules of behaviour' (Bauman, 1993: 124) – goals and rules that, in many contemporary organizations, are governed by the very practices named as corporate social responsibility. Moreover, when organizational action becomes routinized and accepted as 'normal' it is less and less open to moral scrutiny or contention such that organizational moral responsibility can be curtailed (Rhodes, Pullen and Clegg, 2007)

## GETTING CLOSE TO RESPONSIBILITY

Whether one is 'for' or 'against' corporate social responsibility and stakeholder management, one of the rationalities that defines the contours of the moral debate is the assumed distinctions between organizations on the one hand, and society its stakeholders on the other. In terms of considering organizational moral responsibility this is an important issue. Indeed, at its foundational level the very notion of responsibility can be located in

terms of the relations between self and other and in this case the 'self' is seen as the business organization and the 'other' is seen as the 'social'. In terms of stakeholder theories, this other to whom the organization is said to be responsible is understood in relation to major categories under which society is thought to be divided – as we saw earlier, most commonly, employees, customers, suppliers, and the public. Such categorization is both abstract and empirically questionable. Echoes of the familiar distinction between market and civil society can be heard. It is of note, however, that each of these categories is very problematic when it comes to considering real people. It is possible for a person who is an employee of an organization also to be a shareholder, for example, through an employee shareholding or stock option programme. That same person is clearly a member of the general public and may well purchase the products or services that the organization sells. In this example, we have one empirical person who quite easily and plausibly can be located in multiple stakeholder categories. The categorization of the 'others' of an organization into conventional groupings that make up the social is a convenient way to carve up the world for managerial purposes but this can only be achieved by violating the actual particularity of the persons who do have a stake in the corporation. The stakeholder is, by and large, a fictional entity socially constructed for the benefit of developing relatively easy and calculable moral positions, but ones that absent themselves from dealing with vexing moral questions that address the particularity of flesh and blood people.

Again following Bauman, consideration of the others to whom an organization might be responsible is achieved differently depending on the relative proximity with which those others are conceived. Indeed, to mass actual other people into broad stakeholder categories establishes a distance between organizations and people that only achieves a sense of responsibility through the blind-siding of the actuality of persons – settling instead for abstracting them in the anonymity of the category. Such issues have been addressed directly by Roberts (2001) who, following Lévinas, considers ethics to be located in the proximate relationship between self and other – not in terms of the 'fulfilment of the fantasy of being a sovereign individual' (Roberts, 2001: 119), but in the primary encounter with the other from which the self emerges. With Lévinas (1991/1978) this means that ethics and responsibility can only be found in relations where the other is seen as both particular and unknowable. The other is that to which we have ultimate responsibility – yet this includes 'all the others', 'the Others not present, and maybe not yet even living' (Byers and Rhodes, 2007: 247). This other is not to be reduced to the self as if s/he were merely a mirror for the self's reflection or a canvas for its projection but is sacred and unfathomable. Such a conception extends responsibility to its full possibilities. This is an 'infinite responsibility' to the other – a responsibility that exceeds reciprocity and self interest. Bauman, also reading Lévinas, places this relationship of responsibility in terms of how the moral self is 'constituted by responsibility ... [and] ... answerability to the Other and to moral self-conscience' (p. 11). Coming back to organizations, this raises the question of 'what place there is within the corporation for a "responsibility for" that is pursued despite, rather than because of, the self?' (Roberts, 2003: 257).

Can organizations answer to the other? In an ironic combination, it seems that Friedman and Roberts agree on the starting point for such an enquiry. Friedman (1970) states that '[w]hat does it mean to say that a "business" has responsibilities? Only people can have responsibilities [...] The first step toward clarity in examining the doctrine of social responsibility of business is to ask precisely what it implies for whom' (p. 32). For Roberts (2003) '[t]he corporate body is devoid of sensibility and, in this sense, is incapable of responsibility; ethics in business will always be a personal matter and the sensible corporation will always need to be built and grounded in individual conduct' (p. 251, see also Bevan and Corvellec, 2007).

In practical terms, this calls for responsibility to be practiced in 'moral proximity' (Bauman, 1993). As Bauman states '[p]roximity is the realm of intimacy and morality; distance is the realm of estrangement and the law' (p. 84).

This notion of proximity is not to be confused with physical proximity. As Bauman (1993) argues, proximity is to be understood in terms of one's conception of one's relations with others as positioned between the extremes of intimacy and anonymity. In intimacy, there is a great deal of knowledge of the other garnered through shared biography or ongoing interaction. In anonymity the other is outside of one's social space and is barely an object of one's knowledge. In between these poles we see people as not having personal identities but rather as being assigned to particular classes and categories (as is the case with 'stakeholders') – we do not know them, but rather know of them – they are types, not persons as such. With such a notion of proximity, the person who is one's neighbour can still be a stranger, yet one can share intimacy with people who are geographically quite dispersed. The point Bauman is making (following Lévinas) is that responsibility requires a relation that does not violate the particularity of the other by subsuming him or her under the generalization of the category (e.g., the category of stakeholder groupings). Such proximity relocates the other from the generalization of the organizational programme or rule back into 'the hard core of the moral self, back from the wasteland of calculated interests to which it had been exiled' (Bauman, 1993: 84). This is a moral proximity where the other is considered not from the far view of the categorization of the stakeholder but is thought of as a 'neighbour'. If we can agree that 'responsibility is silenced once proximity is eroded' (Bauman, 1989: 184) then corporate social responsibility is in trouble.

## DECIDING ON RESPONSIBILITY

Above we have tried to trouble the idea of organizational responsibility in relation to reciprocity, rationality and proximity. If responsibility in business is dominated by the notion of stakeholder management, then it would seem that responsibility is indeed in trouble – the notion of the stakeholder becoming so abstracted from any real people that it might actually distance organization's from their 'others'. This is the case when those others become defined in terms of the organization's own self-interest such that attention to the other (the very ground of ethics) is eroded. To consider others as stakeholders can easily become a glib excuse for *not* dealing with others as real and particular people – an easy way out of the very question responsibility. In the speedy pursuit of answers to questions of responsibility, the answers begin to take precedence over the questions and the questions forgotten. Moreover, in an age of global capitalism where the intricacy, velocity and plurality of the norms that come to bear on organizational life have escalated, these troubles of responsibility expand no matter how much hunger there is for tidy moral 'solutions' (such as CSR) to appease the moral anxieties of the harried executive. CSR and stakeholder management face the danger of becoming institutionalized to such an extent that debate about organizational responsibility and the horizon of its possibility becomes strangled by them. The status of responsibility in business might then become reduced to a situation where:

> Globalization processes of a more or less disruptive nature, the tremendous influence of the media, the agglomerated power of multinational corporations, the immense leverage applied by transnational lobbies together with recent financial scandals have meant that companies now *have to* conduct themselves in a more socially responsible manner (Galan, 2006: 1629–1630, italics added).

However, it is this notion of 'having to' comply, as if with no alternative, that is precisely antithetical to the whole idea of responsibility as requiring freedom, deliberation and choice in the face of conflicting demands from multiple others. The 'vexing reality' of the complex relationship between the financial, social and ethical concerns of

business are sidestepped through moralistic certainty (Margolis and Walsh, 2003). As we have seen in our review, there are numerous and varied perspectives on CSR and stakeholder management, but what is worth adding is that the dominance of these approaches as *the* discourse of responsibility for organizations means that responsibility itself gets reduced to that which is discursively institutionalized and taken for granted. When management knowledge becomes ideologized in practice what suffers is thinking and feeling; what suffers is responsibility itself.

The complexity of the global arena in which business increasingly operates is one that is manifest in a multitude of localized organizational settings. Contra to the idea of responsibility residing in incontrovertible imperatives enshrined in CSR discourse, in contemporary organizational life ethics is 'enacted in situations of ambiguity where dilemmas and problems will be dealt with without the comfort of consensus or certitude' (Clegg, Kornberger and Rhodes, 2007a: 3) even when that comfort is pursued with the utmost vigour. Responsibility is thus not located in a knowledge of how to go on, but in 'moral mazes' through which the individual manager must navigate (cf. Jackall, 1988). These are locations which require specifically that which contemporary approaches to business knowledge have so long sought to distance themselves – 'choice, actions, and the achievements of individuals' (Ghoshal, 2005: 77). We thus come to the end of this chapter with the question of how moving towards an understanding of organizational moral responsibility that accounts for this requires an acceptance of the 'undecidability' of moral action (Derrida, 1988, 1992, 1994, 1995).

Earlier in this chapter we drew attention to Aristotle's conception of responsibility as involving deliberation and decision. In approaching the end of the chapter, we now return to these themes in terms of Jacques Derrida's meditations on the character of responsibility, and relate them to organizations (see also, Jones, 2003; Clegg,

Kornberger and Rhodes, 2007b). Similarly to Aristotle, Derrida locates responsibility in relation to freedom. For him, however, the specificity of this relation is one where responsibility only emerges because free decision making must be considered beyond 'the programmable application or unfolding of a calculable process' (Derrida 1992: 24) such as a business calculation based on financially motivated self-interest. Derrida suggests that while responsible decisions are always preceded by 'juridico- or ethico- or politico-cognitive deliberation' (1992: 26) the moment of decision itself is always beyond such rationalities. If a responsible decision were just a matter of following a predetermined rule or process, it would involve no real choice and therefore would not be a decision characterized by moral responsibility. It is this moment of decision beyond the comfort of calculation that is the moment of undecidability necessary for responsibility. Such a notion of responsibility is neither entirely free nor anarchic – it is located within distinct possibilities for action. As Derrida (1988) describes it, '[u]ndecidability is always a *determinate* oscillation between possibilities (for example, of meaning, but also of acts). These possibilities are themselves highly *determined* in strictly *defined* situations' (Derrida 1988: 148, italics in original). While responsibility is regarded in relation to individual decisions, it is not a matter that is divorced from organizations or organizing, nor is it separate from those organizational schemes that talk in the language of ethics and responsibility – all of these are part of the 'defined situations' to which Derrida refers. If responsibility is to be carried out within and on behalf of organizations, we can surely expect that the determinate possibilities around which ethical deliberation will occur will involve the organization and its various political and normative positions as they are legalistically prescribed or culturally sedimented (including, of course, CSR and stakeholder management).

In terms of organizational responsibility such considerations are able to link back the relation between the individual and the organization in terms of responsibility. True, the ultimate responsibility comes back to the person who decides and who endures the ordeal of undecidability, but that does not mean that organizations are irrelevant – they are the very context of legal frameworks, ethical norms and political concerns in which the decisions are framed and made. In terms of practices associated with, for example, corporate social responsibility, it is false to assume that responsibility can be 'organized' for the many or guaranteed for the organization but that does not render those practices irrelevant to moral responsibility – they are pressures under which that responsibility is acted. This is not to suggest per se that organizations should or should not embrace such practices, but rather that they are best regarded not in terms of responsibility, but prior to responsibility and in terms of power – they are attempts, both direct and cultural, to modify the behaviour of others around various particular notions of responsibility. Their normativity, however, is such that, much as any other practices of power, they function to get other people to do, say and think things that they would otherwise not do, say or think. While this may be important it is not responsibility. As Bennington (2000) describes:

> Simply following one's duty, looking up the appropriate action in a book of laws or rules, as it were, is anything but ethical – at best this is an *administration* of rights and duties, a *bureaucracy* of ethics. In this sense an ethical act worthy of its name is *inventive*, and inventive not at all in expressing the 'subjective' freedom of the agent, but in response and responsibility to the other (p. 68, italics in original).

The point we wish to make is first that, following Derrida, responsibility requires *undecidability*, and second that this undecidability can never be pre-empted by organization. This attests to the view that responsibility is a personal rather than organizational matter (Roberts, 2003); personal responsibility, however, is conducted in an organizational setting that, at least in part, determines the possibilities of how that responsibility can be taken up. Indeed, it is the case that in organizational settings:

> ethical responsibilities attendant on relations of power always involve decisions; so, when the author of some organizational action seeks to pass them off as structurally determined, then the abdication of ethical responsibility is usually a trick to deceive just consideration of the choices that have, in fact, implicitly been made (Clegg, Kornberger and Rhodes, 2007b).

Responsibility is always at play within politico-organizational contexts where the politics are such that the presence of responsibility might be buried under the cloak of the determining rule that seeks to rule out choice and rule out any original response to others – and this is both a choice of what to do, and a choice of who to be. Conversely, by embracing undecidability, responsibility might still account for power and govern its exercise but would never be subsumed by it. The issue of responsibility, once understood in terms of undecidability is one where:

> However careful one is in the theoretical preparation of a decision, the instant of the decision, if there is to be a decision, must be heterogeneous to the accumulation of knowledge. Otherwise, there is no responsibility. In this sense not only must the person taking the decision not know everything [...] the decision, if there is to be one, must advance towards a future which is not known, which cannot be anticipated (Derrida, 1994: 37).

In these terms CSR and the knowledge of stakeholders are best regarded as such an 'accumulation of knowledge'. This does not mean that they are neither important nor powerful – the evidence clearly says that they are. What it does mean, however, is that they by no means exhaust the meaning of responsibility. Indeed, organizational moral responsibility cannot be prefigured in organization or knowledge about it – such responsibility is not rational, it is not reciprocal, and it is not subject to pre-given categories. In Derrida's terms, it is always something that will be 'to come', something that is located in the future based

on decisions whose consequences remain unknown at the time that the decision is made. For responsibility to be present 'the future must be understood not as pre-ordained [...] the future must be open and uncontained by the past and present, even though it is conditioned by them' (Grosz, 2005: 75)

## CONCLUSION

In both reviewing and problematizing the way that responsibility has been understood in relation to organizations, the point we have been trying to get to is in line with Derrida's argument that there is never a guarantee of responsibility in advance – after all, the future remains an 'alterity that cannot be anticipated' (Derrida, 1994: 64). Responsibility demands constant attention; it does not quit. As we have seen, while some offer tidy normative theories of how business can be responsible, there is some deep scepticism about the very possibility that business might be thinkable in such terms. What is possible, however, is that a concern for responsibility might be brought to life in organizations rather than shut down with finalizing 'solutions' that seek its guarantee. In the case of the practices and discourses associated with Corporate Social Responsibility and stakeholder management, when these things become taken-for-granted roads to morality their capacity to inform moral responsibility diminishes. Instead, responsibility can be considered as a horizon of possibility that, while demanding vigilant attention, is not something that can be achieved once and for all in the administrative arrangements of the here and now. This means that ethics and responsibility are not things that can ever be governed by organizational programmes, rules or codes and, moreover, they might be diminished by such arrangements should they serve to inhibit the exercise of freedom and decision, and, of course, it is such a freedom that is the very condition of responsibility. The quality of organizational moral responsibility is to be located in the manner and extent to which this freedom is exercised and the kind of character that this builds for individual persons.

# REFERENCES

Aristotle (2000) *Nichomachean Ethics*. London: Penguin.

Banerjee, S.B. (2005) 'The ethics of corporate social responsibility', in S.R. Clegg and C. Rhodes (eds) *Management Ethics: Contemporary Contexts*. London: Routledge, pp. 55–76.

Bauman, Z. (1989) *Modernity and the Holocaust*. Cambridge: Polity Press.

Bauman, Z. (1993) *Postmodern Ethics*. Oxford: Blackwell.

Bennington, G. (2000) 'Deconstruction and ethics', in N. Royle (ed.) *Deconstructions: A User's Guide*. Houndmills: Palgrave, pp. 64–82.

Bevan, D. and Corvellec, H. (2007) 'The impossibility of corporate ethics: For a Levinasian approach to managerial ethics', *Business Ethics: A European Review*, 16 (3): 208–219.

Bowen, R.H. (1953) *The Social Responsibilities of the Businessman*. New York: Harper and Row.

Burke, L. and Lodgson, J.M. (1996) 'How corporate social responsibility pays off', *Long Range Planning*, 29 (4): 495–502.

Byers, D. and Rhodes, C. (2007) 'Ethics, alterity and organizational justice', *Business Ethics: A European Review*, 16 (3): 239–250.

Clegg, S.R. and Rhodes, C. (2006) 'Questioning the ethics of management practice', in S.R. Clegg and C. Rhodes (eds) *Management Ethics: Contemporary Contexts*. London: Routledge, pp. 1–10.

Clegg, S.R., Kornberger, M. and Rhodes, C. (2007a) 'Business ethics as practice', *British Journal of Management*, 18 (2): 107–122.

Clegg, S.R., Kornberger, M. and Rhodes, C. (2007b) 'Organizational ethics, decision making, undecidability', *The Sociological Review*, 52 (2): 393–409.

Cochran, P.L. and Wood, R.A. (1984) 'Corporate social responsibility and firm performance', *Academy of Management Journal*, 27 (1): 42–56.

Davis, K. (1960) 'Can business afford to ignore social responsibilities?', *California Management Review*, 2: 70–76.

Derrida, J. (1988) 'Afterword: Toward and ethic of discussion', in G. Graf (ed.) *Limited Inc*. Evaston IL: Northwestern University Press, pp. 111–154.

Derrida, J. (1992) 'Force of law: The 'mystical foundation of authority', in D. Cornell, M. Rosenfeld and D.G. Carlson (eds) *Deconstruction and the Possibility of Justice*. London: Routledge, pp. 3–67.

Derrida, J. (1994) 'Nietzsche and the machine: Interview with Jacques Derrida', *Journal of Nietzsche Studies*, Issue 7, Spring 1994.

Derrida, J. (1995) *The Gift of Death*. Chicago: University of Chicago Press.

Donaldson, T. and Preston, L. (1995) 'A stakeholder theory of the corporation: Concepts, evidence and implications', *Academy of Management Review*, 20 (1): 65–91.

Frederick, W.C. (1960) 'The growing concern over business responsibility', *California Management Review*, 2: 54–61.

Freeman, R.E. (1984) *Strategic Management: A Stakeholder Perspective*. Englewood Cliffs, NJ: Prentice Hall.

Friedman, M. (1962) *Capitalism and Freedom*. Chicago: University of Chicago Press.

Friedman, M. (1970) 'The social responsibility of business is to increase its profits', *The New York Times*, September: pp. 32–33.

Galan, J.I. (2006) 'Corporate social responsibility and strategic management', *Journal of Management Studies*, 43 (7): 1629–1641.

Ghoshal, S. (2005) 'Bad management theories are destroying good management practices', *Academy of Management Learning and Education*, 4 (1): 75–91.

Gioia, D.A. (2003) 'Business organizations as instrument of societal responsibility', *Organization*, 10 (3): 435–438.

Goodpaster, K.E. (1983) 'The concept of corporate responsibility', *Journal of Business Ethics*, 2: 1–22.

Jackall, R. (1998) *Moral Mazes: The World of Corporate Managers*. New York: Oxford University Press.

Jones, C. (2003) 'As if business ethics were possible, "within such limits" ...', *Organization*, 10 (2): 223–248.

Lévinas, E. (1991/1978) *Otherwise Than Being or Beyond Essence*. Dordrecht: Kluwer.

Margolis, J.D. and Walsh, J.P. (2003) 'Misery loves companies: Rethinking social initiatives by business', *Administrative Science Quarterly*, 48: 268–305.

McGuire, J.B. (1963) *Business and Society*. New York: McGraw-Hill.

McGuire, J.B., Sundgren, A. and Schneeweis, T. (1988) 'Corporate social responsibility and firm financial performance', *Academy of Management Journal*, 31 (4): 854–872.

McVea, J.H. and Freeman, R.E. (2005) 'A names-and-faces approach to stakeholder management: How focusing on stakeholders as individuals can bring ethics and entrepreneurial strategy together', *Journal of Management Inquiry*, 14: 57–69.

McWilliams, A., Siegel, D.S. and Wright, P.M. (2006) 'Corporate social responsibility: Strategic implications', *Journal of Management Studies*, 43 (1): 1–18.

Orlitzky, M., Schmidt, F.L. and Rynes, S.L. (2003) 'Corporate social and financial performance: A meta-analysis', *Organization Studies*, 24 (3): 403–441.

Parker, M. (ed.) (1998a) *Ethics and Organizations*. London: Sage.

Parker, M. (1998b) 'Business ethics and social theory: Postmodernizing the ethical', *British Journal of Management*, 9 (Special Issue): S27–S36.

Rhodes, C., Pullen, A. and Clegg, S.R. (2007) *Narrative ethics and organizational downsizing*, School of Management Working Paper, University of Technology, Sydney [available at: http://www.business.uts.edu.au/management/workingpapers/files/RhodesPullenClegg2007.pdf].

Roberts, J. (2001) 'Corporate governance and the ethics of Narcissus', *Business Ethics Quarterly*, 11 (1): 109–127.

Roberts, J. (2003) 'The manufacture of corporate social responsibility: Constructing corporate sensibility', *Organization*, 10 (2): 249–265.

Smith, A. (1776/1982) *The Wealth of Nations: Books I–III*. New York: Penguin.

Smith, A. (1776/1986) *The Wealth of Nations: Books IV–V*. New York: Penguin.

Stead, W.E., Stead, J. and Starek, M. (2003) *Sustainable Strategic Management*. New York: M.E. Sharpe.

Vogel, D. (2005) *The Market for Virtue: The Potential Limits of Corporate Social Responsibility*. Washington: Brooking Institution Press.

Werhane, P.H. and Freeman, E.R. (1999) 'Business ethics: The state of the art', *International Journal of Business Reviews*, 2 (1): 1–16.

Whetton, D.A., Rands, G. and Godfrey, P. (2001) 'What are the responsibilities of business to society?', in A. Pettigrew, H. Thomas and R. Whittington (eds) *Handbook of Strategy and Management*. London: Sage, pp. 373–408.

Zaborowski, H. (2000) 'On freedom and responsibility: Remarks on Sartre, Lévinas and Derrida', *The Heythrop Journal*, 41 (1): 47–65.

# 21

# Deconstructing Sustainability: Organizations in Society

Suzanne Benn

## INTRODUCTION

In recent years, a series of major reviews and reports by leading economists (Stern, 2006), environmentalist groups (Ayukawa, Naoyuki *et al.*, 2007), scientists (IPCC, 2007) and organizational theorists (Jermier *et al.*, 2006) alike have highlighted the need for a global response to the destructive impacts of industrial development on the planet. To turn the situation around means the demise of some existing industries and the rise of new industries which are environmentally sustainable. It means a new way of doing business and a new way of working within business organizations. There will be new demands on employees – more emphasis on creativity and innovation, more emphasis on services rather than on products, more accountable relationships with suppliers and new ways of marketing into new markets. All have implications for the theory and practice of organizational behaviour (OB).

This chapter is a critical review of sustainability as it has been presented to date in the OB literature. I develop a framework that could assist OB theory and practice in working more effectively within a worldview that prioritizes a sustainable future. The principles underpinning the framework are then applied to an exemplar design for a sustainable business community.

## DEFINITIONS

Sustainability came to prominence in the 1980s as an attempt to resolve increasingly evident tensions between economic growth, social equity and the limits to natural resources. O'Riordan's (1985) aphorism of more than two decades ago still well describes the vexed task of defining the term as an 'exploration into a tangled conceptual jungle where watchful eyes lurk at every bend'. It is a concept at once lauded as the guiding principle of our time and damned as so fuzzy and readily politicized as to be almost meaningless.

Sustainable development remains the most significant body of theory on how to achieve sustainability. Although new understandings continue to emerge, sustainable development is still most widely defined as 'development that meets the needs of the present without compromising the ability of future generations to meet their own needs' (World Commission on Environment and Development, 1987). The term encompasses a wide range of value judgements on the future of society and the planet. It entails the integration of environmental protection, social advancement and economic prosperity and requires juggling three highly evaluative objectives: intergenerational equity, intragenerational equity and the precautionary principle. These three principles are summarized below:

- Intergenerational equity: that the present generation should ensure that the health, diversity and productivity of the environment is maintained or enhanced for the benefit of future generations
- Intragenerational equity: the development of social and economic policies that promote equity concerning distribution of wealth, access to facilities and environment or the distribution of negative environmental impacts
- The precautionary principle: if there are threats of serious or irreversible environmental damage, lack of full scientific certainty should not be used as a reason for postponing measures to prevent environmental degradation (Australian Government, 2003).

Although sustainable development applies at global, regional and local levels (Bressers and Kuks, 2004), it is strongly associated with global organizations and inter-organizational structures such as the United Nations and the World Business Council for Sustainable Development. It is a systems-based approach, incorporating both social and ecological systems and draws on the fields of politics, economics, development and environmental studies, as well as a host of other sub-disciplinary areas. Dryzek's point is well made: sustainable development and sustainability are better understood as

discourses rather than as precise definitional terms (Dryzek, 1990; 2000; Dryzek *et al.*, 2003).

Given the problems of lack of universally endorsed definition, breadth of application and highly political post-colonial associations (Banerjee, 2003), it is not surprising that sustainable development, like sustainability, is the subject of wide and ongoing debate. Its influence on the global stage is such that some scholars (e.g., Castro, 2004) rate it with democracy and globalization as one of the most ubiquitous and contested concepts of our time. Critics argue that the looseness of sustainable development terminology enables the discourse to be determined by international élites, led by the United Nations and the World Bank, intent on promoting free trade and continuing the capitalist and Western dominated agenda of business expansion and the rational management of resources (Banerjee, 2003; Berlin and Berlin, 2004). Others see sustainable development as a management discourse that legitimizes markets and capitalism (Shiva, 1993), and serves the interests of technological and economic entrepreneurs (Christoff, 1996), rather than providing a serious attempt to accord any intrinsic value to the natural environment and maintain intergenerational equity in terms of access to natural resources. Yet for many eminent scholars, sustainable development remains the only serious theoretical attempt to integrate social, environmental and economic considerations so as to reduce the resource intensity of production and levels of consumption and change what is consumed (e.g., Baker, 2006). For example, Stuart Hart, a leading researcher in the area, argues that the ladder of sustainability moves through more technical approaches to a pinnacle of sustainable development (see Hart and Milstein, 2003).

In this chapter I shall explore how organization theory and behaviour can more directly address the question of sustainable development – as distinct from the sustainability of the individual organization. I agree with Dryzek *et al.*'s (2003) point that meeting these core objectives requires organizational decision makers to balance relationships in terms of prioritizing across three sets of boundaries between:

- Humans and the rest of the biosphere
- Present and future generations
- Developing and developed worlds.

A recent model proposed by Ebner and Baumgartner (2006: p. 13) is useful for the task set for this chapter. It distinguishes between sustainable development, corporate sustainability and corporate social responsibility. According to this model, sustainable development, as defined by Brundtland, offers ideas concerning sustainable orientation on a *macro* level. Corporate sustainability also rests on the pillars of economic, ecological and social issues but applies at the *meso* level of the organization. The social dimension of corporate sustainability is corporate social responsibility (CSR). The three pillars of corporate sustainability are often referred to as the Triple Bottom Line, a business model described as creating value for stakeholders by preserving or enhancing economic, environmental and social capital (Rosebro, 2006).

## SUSTAINABILITY DISCOURSE IN ORGANIZATIONAL BEHAVIOUR

Given its widespread influence it is not surprising that in the last decade sustainability has surfaced in the study of OB. In this field, however, its messy contestation is reduced predominantly to the assumptions and constructions of two leading discourses: the win-win and the moral imperative.

### The discourse of win-win

On the one hand we have the discourse of the rational actor, in which the self-interest of employees, and of the firm, is of paramount importance (Australian Government, 2003). The win-win argument privileges the economic sustainability of the firm, justified through resource-based or

strategic management perceptions concerning the economic benefits of the triple bottom line (e.g., Bansal and Roth, 2000; Holliday, Schmidheiny and Watts, 2002; Branco and Rodrigues, 2006). Environmental priorities are seen as just making good sense, from the point of competition in the market.

Tensions between conflicting commitments within organizations to social, environmental and economic elements of sustainability are minimized in this discourse. The rational actor viewpoint is also supported by an economistic view of the natural environment as theorized in the natural resource based view of the firm (Chan, 2005) and links to the instrumental school within stakeholder theory, which recommend the establishment of trust-based ties between businesses and their stakeholders (Heugens, Van den Bosch and Van Riel, 2002: 36). While the major emphasis is on the for-profit sector, not-for-profits are also drawn in through rational consideration of the strategic benefits of social entrepreneurship and CSR (e.g., Rondinelli and London, 2003; Aalders, 2002; Dunphy, Griffiths and Benn, 2007).

Relatively early influences on the field came from business strategy specialists such as Porter and van der Linde (1995) and Hart (1995). Porter and van der Linde (1995) argued on behalf of the readily achieved benefits, the win-win solutions obtained from managers picking the 'low-hanging fruit' of environmental efficiencies. Hart continues to argue that the firm gains competitive advantage by managers moving strategically through the hierarchy of pollution control, pollution prevention, product stewardship and sustainable development (Hart, 1995; Hart and Milstein, 2003). Other leading writers (Hoffman and Bazerman, 2007) argue that the sustainability discourse has largely halted at product stewardship. Overall, the major focus has remained on the firm's leaders as rational actors, only engaging in sustainability to avoid fines or because of the competitive advantage associated with exploiting various green characteristics (e.g., reviewed in Jermier *et al.*, 2006). As Jermier and Forbes point out (2003), the dominating theme in the academic literature presents being green as just rational: the win-win solution of the business case for sustainability.

In Avery's classification, this approach typifies leadership behaviour in Anglo-US capitalism. The purpose of business is to maximize shareholder value, an aim supported by management prioritizing strictly in accordance with the short term interests of shareholders and themselves (Avery, 2005).

## The discourse of the moral imperative

The other leading discourse is normative, drawing on business ethics principles to advocate sustainability as ethical practice in employee decision making. In contrast to the rational self-interest of the business case, the actor is ethical and the leader morally transformed (e.g., Dyllick and Hockerts, 2002; Desjardins, 2006). Its scholars pose a critique of the business case rhetoric, calling on themes such as holistic and 'eco-centric management' (e.g., Shrivastava, 1995), a range of post-materialist concepts (e.g., Giacalone, Jurkiewicz and Dunn, 2005; Doyle and Doherty, 2006) as well as value-based management techniques and transformational change (Dunphy, Griffiths and Benn, 2007). With sustainability seen as essentially an ethical issue, a key theme is that different value systems and ethical beliefs of individuals or groups within the firm underpin different understandings of sustainability with differing implications for the behaviour of organizations (e.g., Marrewijk and Werre, 2003). On this view, economics is not regarded as value-neutral. As Desjardins (2006: 4) puts it: 'economic, ecological and ethical concerns are all directed at the same question: what are the best ways for human beings to live and flourish within the biosphere which is their only home?'

Critics of this discourse note a highly evangelical tone that downplays the difficulties in improving sustainability performance or moving to a new 'ecological order' (Newton and Harte, 1997; Newton, 2002). According to Welford (1998) for instance,

corporations must be cajoled or persuaded or even forced to change, implying the need for a green or eco culture. As pointed out by Newton (2002), research by Crane (2000) and Green (2000) challenges the view that moralized employees, managers or leaders are necessary for sustainability to be implemented in organizations.

## Factors shaping the discourses

While each discourse has its proponents and its critics, the conceptual development of each discourse is increasingly influenced by the expanding niche consultancy area of corporate ethics, sustainability and social responsibility (Windell, 2007), operating at the *meso* level. To illustrate, roughly one-third of hits on Google for 'corporate sustainability' include the term 'consultancy'.

While the win-win and moral imperative discourses compete for interpretative support they share a key characteristic. Each focuses on the behaviour of individuals and groups within the individual firm or as the centrepiece of its stakeholder relations. This is not altogether surprising given the domain of OB as it has been interpreted in the Academy of Management Organizational Behaviour Division's Domain Statement:

> Specific domain: the study of individuals and groups within an organizational context, and the study of internal processes and practices as they affect individuals and groups (Academy of Management, 2007).

This domain statement does not direct the attention of OB researchers to wider responsibilities involving contemporary human communities. Nor does it refer in any significant sense to the future generations or other species of the biosphere which feature in sustainable development discourse. Perhaps these omissions are those alluded to by the editor of a leading OB journal in his editorial, noting the importance of international and humanist topics for OB research (Ashkanasy, 2007). As this editor points out, no doubt this statement is useful for the AoM to delineate one Division or Interest Group from another. It is not helpful in encouraging the OB researcher to investigate the impact of leadership or employee attributes, for instance, on the ability of organizations to work within a framework which can address boundary issues characterizing sustainable development. A search within this particular journal under 'sustain*' yielded no articles with reference to sustainable development or even corporate sustainability as defined above.

The result of the rapid spread of corporate consultancies, mentoring and coaching services built onto an existing OB tradition of preoccupation with the behaviour within the individual organization is that the wider discourse of sustainable development is comparatively neglected as a topic of interest in OB. Policy discourse typically prescribes sustainable development as working across boundaries (for example the UK 2006, *Securing our Future Report* argues for working across organizational, departmental, cultural, political boundaries). However, this challenge has not been taken up as a topic of interest or review in OB. While considerable attention is given to the 'boundaryless organization' (e.g., Rousseau, 1997), characterized by flexible membership, departmental identity and responsibilities or the cross-functional and process-based approach to competitive business (Zairi, 1997), there is little attention given to how this might translate to a commitment to sustainable development.

The positive psychology approach proposes correcting the over-negative approach of OB and its history of fixing problems with employees, teams and leaders. The aim is said to be to address the 'need for a positive search for and understanding of the good in people, not only at work, but also in life' (Luthans, 2002: 704). I would add that not only has OB been overly focused on finding the problems, but problems within the context of the individual organization – with little heed for its impact on the wider biosphere. The debate remains at the *micro* level and does not engage at the *macro* level of the nested

social and ecological systems featuring in sustainable development discourse. To further illustrate my argument, the next part of the chapter looks at one of the most important areas of OB: leadership.

## Leadership and sustainability

Leadership is one of the most written about areas of management studies, and in particular, exemplifies one of the core concerns of OB. The highly influential GLOBE project involving 127 country co-investigators representing 62 nations has defined leadership as the ability to motivate, influence and enable individuals to contribute to the objectives of organizations of which they are members (House, 1998). In a recent review, Jackson (2005) argues that despite the stated aim of GLOBE scholars to take leadership study out of the American business school and into a more interdisciplinary and critical perspective, it retains a strongly individualized and North American flavour (Jackson, 2005). In a similar vein, arguing from the contrary perspective to that of the Anglo-Saxon axis, Avery (2005) has argued that what she calls Rhineland leaders have a comparatively more long-term perspective and a higher focus on employee welfare and stakeholder groups. As a result, these organizations show a greater capacity to engage with sustainable development, a perspective that is ignored by their Anglo/US counterparts.

The critical study of leadership is a crucial aspect of OB. As Jackson (2005) points out, leadership is a source of inspiration but may equally be turned to exploitative ends. This highlights the failure of leading leadership journals to address the key issues of sustainable development, such as intergenerational and intragenerational equity. It is disappointing that the most respected journal in the field of leadership contains only one reference to 'sustainable' and that is in the context of authentic leadership and sustained performance (Gardner *et al.*, 2005). According to a recent review in this journal, even the much broader concept of ethical leadership remains relatively unexplored (Brown and Treviño, 2006). If there is little in the scholarly specialist OB journals which links leadership and sustainable development, there is even less linking gender, leadership and sustainability or sustainable development. This is despite a long history of ecofeminist thought and wide recognition by scholars of sustainable development that capitalist systems of production impact more negatively on women and that women today make up the majority of the world's poor (Baker, 2006).

There is some interest at the micro level of CSR and corporate environmental sustainability. Egri and Herman's (2000) well known study shows successful leaders in environmental sustainability have personal values that are ecocentric and open to change. They are transformational leaders with personality characteristics which tend to include a need for achievement, affiliation and power while also exhibiting a high degree of emotional maturity and self-confidence. The GLOBE project has recently related aspects of neo-charismatic leadership on the part of CEO's to the social responsibility performance of their firms (Waldman *et al.*, 2006). Recent GLOBE findings are that CSR is a multidimensional construct, whose dimensions include concern for shareholder/owners, stakeholders and state/community. This research indicates that CSR, just as other values, drives the actions of managers. From the perspective of institutional theory, the future implication is that organizations will increasingly adopt such societal-level values as a way of gaining legitimacy (Waldman *et al.*, 2006). However, there has been little research to date on how CSR values might relate to the sustainable development principles of intergenerational equity and the precautionary principle.

Working from a critique with what she labels as the leadership literature's preoccupation with identity, individualized norms and expectations, and performance measurement, Sinclair (2007) has developed a framework with two dimensions: high/low

voice and inside/outside the organization. The high voice/outside (discursive activism) and low voice/outside (collaboration and networking) areas of the framework are relevant to leadership on the boundary issues that I have argued underpin sustainable development. As Jermier *et al.* (2006) have argued, encouraging the creation of *discursive spaces*, collaboration across sectors and organizational types and between individual actors is one way that business can be stimulated to reflect on its purpose and role in the biosphere. To do this, leadership needs not only vision and integrity (Waldman *et al.*, 2006) but to demonstrate preparedness to revise its value proposition to give accord to the cultures, traditions, species and generations that lie outside the accepted corporate boundaries of action. Recent reviews highlight the emergence of versions of dispersed leadership, acknowledging that leaders act across the organization (Parry and Bryman, 2006). Yet even this more participative approach to leadership does not address the *boundary issues* that I have identified as underpinning sustainable development.

## Making the links between OB and sustainable development

In the next section, I explore how organization theory and behaviour can more directly address the question of sustainable development that requires organizational decision makers to reflect on, review and balance their priorities within three sets of relationships: between humans and the rest of the biosphere; between present and future generations and between the developing and developed worlds.

My initial exploration suggests that the *macro* perspective of sustainable development lies outside the dominating worldview of OB theory and practice. In their critique of OB as it applies to sustainable development, Bazerman and Hoffman (1999) argue that profound cognitive and cultural changes in individual attitudes and beliefs are required if sustainable development is to be accepted. These scholars point out that cognitive and organizational bias, such as overconfidence, the tendency to discount the future, and an over-reliance on compliance, may be restricting any profound shift (Hoffman and Bazerman, 2007). Employee and leader perceptions of their rights and responsibilities are another key limiting factor in corporations embracing sustainable development. For instance, it can be argued that individual managers have no obligation to move to sustainability – if firms collectively cause impact, then it is up to legislators to change policies (Bowie, quoted in Desjardins, 2006: 44).

Leading scholars have recently mounted a strong argument that designing products and services to target the Bottom of the Pyramid market – the 4 billion people living on less than $2 per day – can overcome such barriers to private sector organizations working to address the challenges of sustainable development (Hart, 2007; Prahalad, 2005). Addressing the requirements of this market would require business to engage with civil society organizations and local governments, and to stimulate local innovations and entrepreneurship. Prahalad (2005) argues that the building blocks for developing such products and services include that they be scaleable and transportable across countries and cultures and that the products be eco-friendly. Such a strategy could potentially facilitate an expression of OB that could address issues of intragenerational equity, although it is less clear that it would minimize environmental problems to the extent its proponents claim.

As some scholars have noted (e.g., Stormer, 2003; Fergus and Rowney, 2005a), if the OB discourse is to address sustainable development, then it must encompass a *boundary-spanning*, inter-systems approach, with the business organization or corporation no longer the central focus but interconnected with other aspects of society and the ecosystem. What is needed is an OB discourse that prioritizes an integrated inclusive process of celebrating diversity in all its forms and values

in order to encourage such interconnectivity (Fergus and Rowney, 2005a, 2005b).

## A FRAMEWORK FOR CHANGE: REFLEXIVE ECOLOGICAL MODERNIZATION

### Competing discourses within environmental sociology

In *Leading Beyond the Walls*, Drucker (1999) and his colleagues have argued that OB must move beyond its preoccupation with the group and the organization and consider the 'common good'. The discourse of sustainable development conceptualizes this wider 'community' as spanning both generation and species. I believe that if these concerns are to be addressed, the study and practices of OB should be informed by concepts drawn from environmental sociology, a field of study in which society-environment interactions are the key focus.

Here, too, however, the scholarly writings are polarized around two competing discourses:

- The theory of the treadmill of production
- The contrasting perspectives of ecological modernization.

The treadmill of production discourse, led by Schnaiberg and his associates, has its roots in neo-Marxist thinking (e.g., Schnaiberg and Gould, 1994; Schnaiberg, Pellow and Weinberg, 2002). The model of the treadmill is used to convey a politico-economic context in which relations between the state and the capitalist market system compel an ongoing expansionism, resulting in unsustainable impacts and withdrawals from the ecosystem.

Ecological modernization theory, on the other hand, argues that the capitalist economy can be restructured to deliver environmentally responsible systems of production and consumption. One of its key assumptions is that capitalism is a system undergoing constant change. Increasingly, its theorists argue, the source of change is environmental degradation (Hajer, 1995; Mol and Sonnenfeld, 2000; Mol and Spaargaren, 2002). As Mol (2001: 59) puts it:

The basic premise of ecological modernization theory is the centripetal movement of ecological interests, ideas and considerations within the social practices and institutional developments of modern societies.

Examples include the widespread adoption of environmental management and reporting systems, the various incentives for load-based licensing and other institutional arrangements now prevalent in the developed world, particularly those emerging to deal with climate change. Ecological modernization has been theorized as occurring in a number of forms (Christoff, 1996). 'Weak' ecological modernization, for instance, focuses strongly on technoscientific approaches to sustainable development, seeking political and social solutions in the developed world. Stronger versions look to broad changes in economies and polities at the international level and thus intragenerational aspects of sustainable development. 'Reflexive' ecological modernisation (Hajer, 1995; Dryzek, 1997) is a strong version that incorporates elements of reflexive modernization and 'risk society' theory, largely derived from the work of Ulrich Beck (1992, 1995, 1997a, 1997b, Beck et al., 2003).

Debate on the comparative virtues of the treadmill and ecological modernization approaches to sustainability dilemmas has been extensive and has crossed into organization studies as well as policy, law and government discourses. Both discourses sit within the modernist perspective, and are normative in that they assert the reality of environmental problems associated with capitalism, and the need for certain standards if the negative impact is to be addressed. Yet the prescriptions they offer for OB differ markedly. With the treadmill model, OB must change in line with de-industrialization; for ecological modernists, leadership and other elements of OB study and research must generate a form of hyperindustrialization,

requiring a certain reliance upon techno-logical innovation (Buttel, 2000; Mol and Spaargaren, 2002). Because of the weight it places on technological advancement, ecological modernization is also dependent upon implementation of the precautionary principle.

In selecting one of the discourses over the other, I have opted for ecological mod-ernization, but in the reflexive ecological modernization form. This is not the 'mild' form of ecological modernization criticized in association with the win-win discourse described previously, but a version linked to the highly influential theory of 'risk society', the German sociologist Ulrich Beck's (1992) conceptualization that issues of environ-mental and social risk are challenging the legitimacy of the foundational organizations of industrial society. A core principle of 'risk society' is that many of the negative effects of industrialization, such as the effects of toxic chemicals and carbon emissions, cannot be contained within organizational, political or geographic boundaries (Beck, 1992). They therefore raise major questions for assigning and administering accountabilities.

Reflexive ecological modernization, to my mind, incorporates key theoretical elements that address the requirements I have set out for sustainable development. While I recognize its emphasis on economy and technology may 'preempt(s) any ideological conflict' (Bluhdorn, 2000: 211), in the reflexive version described below it offers some suggestion as to how reflexivity and reflection can have an impact on organizational decision making and OB, with the result of reducing ecological impacts and addressing issues of intergenerational equity. Second, it is international in scope and addresses the need to consider international dimensions of development. With major development now occurring in China and India, it does not seem possible to argue along the lines of the treadmill. Intragenerational equity principles require consideration of the right for the countries of the South to develop. Third, technology and innovation are crucial to sustainable development, but only if the precautionary principle is applied simultaneously.

As mentioned, reflexive ecological modernization flows from the linked theories of 'risk society' and reflexive modernization (Beck, Giddens and Lash, 1994; Giddens, 1994). In the 'risk society' the sustainability issues impacting on contemporary organizational and individual life are reflexive risks that enlightenment rationality has itself produced (Beck, 1992; Goldblatt, 1996). These risks are unintended, emerge as consequences of industrial development and are distinct from the natural disasters of pre-industrial society. They include global warming, competition and conflict over increasingly scarce natural resources such as water, toxic environments, and weapons of terrorism. On this argument, the post-industrial era is characterized by the uncertainties and generalized feelings of distrust relating to the incalculability and unpredictability of risks that can be minimized but not removed. Key to the argument is how Beck (1994) distinguishes *reflexivity* from *reflection*. Whereas reflection refers to a subject's more or less conscious knowledge, reflexivity refers to 'unintentional self-dissolution, self-endangerment' the 'self-confrontation of modernity' (Beck, 1994: 5). The *reflexive* or structural component of reflexive modernization refers to this resulting calling of traditional systems and organizations to question (Buttel, 2000). As a result of the loss of legitimacy of traditional sources of authority, and the search for solutions to address these conditions of risk, new 'sub-political' decision making arenas, composed of local, decentralized and temporary collections of individual citizens and various types of individual organizations, emerge. Whatever the outcome of decision making in such arenas, these 'decentralized centres of sub-politics', comprising media publics, employers organizations, individual actors, community groups, government and corporate bodies, have the potential to further challenge the authority of traditional institutions of industrial society (Beck, 1995: 73). Interactions within this arena generate more

critical self-awareness that has the potential to alter the trajectory of capitalist development towards a more sustainable position (Giddens, 1991; Beck, 1992; Beck et al., 1994; Beck, Bonss, and Lau, 2002; Beck et al., 2003; Adams, 2004). Actors are freed from preoccupation with class, empowered by new roles and identities. This is the *reflection* component of reflexive modernization that its theorists argue will enable societies to address sustainability challenges through progressively modernizing. In short, reflexive ecological modernization theory posits that the emergence of new actors and institutions on the political stage of environmental reform will improve on the state-led regulatory strategies of the 1970s and 1980s (Mol and Spaargaren, 2002). In reflexive ecological modernity, boundaries of organizations, markets, cultures, and nations are shattered by a critical mass of unintended side effects, or 'tipping points' associated with market expansion, and technical development. Boundaries reform, but in the context of 'sub-politics': decentred and temporary multiple stakeholder ways of collectively agreeing on the path forward.

## IMPLICATIONS FOR OB THEORY AND PRACTICE

The dynamics of individualization, globalization and environmental and social risk are confronting business organizations with new forms of risk such as managing a new and more demanding set of stakeholders. Individual citizens and employees of all levels are faced with new and critical responsibilities as they attempt to deal with the legacy of industrial society. Post-industrial risks and threats are hybrid in nature:

> [T]hey are produced by civilization, abolish fundamental dichotomies and offer a complex, difficult-to-decode ethical and cultural dynamic' (Beck, 1997b: 21).

The overall question is how to shift organizations into more reflexive patterns so that all decision makers at every level are confronted with the inability of our existing institutions to forestall or manage these complexities (Eckersley, 2004); such a move is required to address the *macro* questions of sustainable development. According to reflexive ecological modernization theory, this task requires multifaceted consideration of organizational fields at a range of scales from global to local. The approach is decentred and multidisciplinary rather than a search for an overarching approach. To deal with the levels of uncertainty apparent in 'risk society', what is needed is a *discursive space* (Dryzek, 1997) that allows for flexibility and choice, the ability of organizations to dissolve or reform links with other organizations and to re-route decision making in rapidly changing conditions of social and environmental risk.

The key issue for OB hinges around the prescriptions for reflexive behaviour such as the development of critical self-awareness (Hajer, 1995) and hence learning through: 'authentic and competent communication about environmental issues among a broad variety of participants' (Dryzek, 1997: 148); embracing the key role of technology while giving regard to precaution; ensuring concern with the international dimensions of development, and giving consideration to the multiple and interdisciplinary possibilities for environmental and social solutions to negative impacts of development (Christoff, 1996). This, I would argue, needs to be coupled with recognition of the role of a range of new, or different actors, employing new or different disciplines for evaluation. These strategies could result in the emergence of *flexible, choice-laden discursive spaces* that lead to fundamentally different and innovative, but better-informed, decision-making processes.

To address these issues, OB research could usefully adopt methodologies designed to uncover our taken for granted assumptions and ways of leading and managing organizations. Gephart (2006), for instance, argues that deploying methodologies such as ethnostatistics, or the study of the social production and use of statistics, could facilitate our understanding of how managers, leaders,

employees, make sense of risks facing them, their organization, society and the planet. They would provide a radically reflexive viewpoint on the quantitative data underpinning much work in OB. Such methods would probe the worldviews that have inhibited our addressing of the problematic represented by sustainable development.

I have argued that confining the 'sustainable development' discourse to the 'business case' and the 'normative case' of the individual actor and the individual organization limits its reach. If we are to expand the scope of the discourse and analyse the activities of transnationals in terms of their power relations and their relationship to the key challenges of sustainability, such as global and local distribution of resources and values, across communities, organizations and individuals, then we need to think about the process in new ways. I have argued that reflexive modernization theory gives us a lens through which to explore how organizations might open themselves up to the multilevel and decentring demands of sustainable development. What does it mean for the sustainable development process?

Research on organization behaviour as it relates to sustainable development is limited by an individualized approach common to both the win-win, market-based and the ethical practice, values-based discourses. This approach fails to adequately appreciate the value of management frameworks that may be inappropriate to the sub-political arrangements and uncertainties and complexities characterizing reflexive modernization. As Orssatto and Clegg's (1999) case of the automobile system illustrates, a shift away from a focus on the individual organization to an analysis of the power relations of wider organizational fields can expand the understanding of how to transform macro-systems of production and consumption according to sustainable development.

Benn and Nelson (2006) have pointed to the principles of situated learning (Lave and Wenger, 1991; Wenger, 1999) as a way of rethinking how OB practice may move towards engaging with sustainable development. Reviews such as Ballard's highlight the wide agreement in the scholarly literature across a number of disciplines on the centrality of learning and reflection to attaining sustainable development (Ballard, 2005). There is wider empirical evidence supporting this. For instance Hobson (2003) showed in her review of Global Action Plan Eco-Teams that success depends on individuals bringing habitual actions into *'discursive consciousness'*, thereby opening them up to change. Turcotte's research has highlighted the role of processes of *constructive confrontation* within partnerships and collaborations between stakeholders as a means of encouraging learning (e.g., Turcotte and Pasquero, 2001) and problem-solving.

In concrete terms this means engaging as a flexible community of practice in sustainability projects and consciously establishing 'sub-political' arrangements that foster reflexive review through interaction between locally focused multiple stakeholder arrangements.

I have three suggestions to facilitate business organizations entering into such arrangements. My first suggestion rests on corporate leaders accepting the precautionary principle. Implementing a precautionary approach to the impact of its operations on local communities through reversing the onus of proof would expand discursive space and support radical reflexivity (Pollner, 1991) by including diverse actors in decisive discussions, uninfluenced by authority or undue expert status (Kelly, 2004). Taking such an approach to policymaking would encourage critical engagement and contestation between players such as corporations, public interest groups, and environmentalists, encouraging more explicit rendition of stakeholder interests (Maguire and Ellis, 2003).

My second suggestion is to link the decentred organization into non-hierarchical networks such as the grass-roots networks, which encompasses many different understandings and experiences with risk (Schlosberg, 1999), with the aim of forging local, 'subpolitical' arenas of decision making

(Beck, 1997b). The diverse nature of the network and its lack of bureaucratic structure (Dryzek, 1997; Schlosberg, 1999) would provide the multiple less-ordered interactions between diverse actors that encourage reflexivity and learning (Vaughan, 1999).

My third suggestion would have business and industry working within the context of a more active civil society, which would also entail a new role for state organizations. Rather than appeasing interest groups (Davidson and Frickel, 2004), government organizations would actively support less resourced actors with knowledge and other tools and facilities in order to ensure a more inclusive political community (Eckersley, 2004).

I argue that each of these measures would challenge a current system which allows the burden of risk to be shifted across the boundaries of nations, cultures, species and generations. The problem still remains, however, of reducing consumption. How can OB theory and practice encourage the reduction in consumption necessary if the developed world is to reduce its spending on unnecessary or frivolous items and thus model further unsustainable consumption patterns in the developing world? Unsustainable consumption patterns are underpinned by structural features of consumerism, such as the cycle of work and spend (Desjardins, 2006). If OB writers focused more on how to reduce work hours, and support the creative development of employees so as to add to, rather than to diminish their autonomous selection of a better work life balance, perhaps they would be contributing to sustainable development more than is currently obvious.

### A case for the future: the eco-city of Dongtan

These reflections on consumption lead to the obvious question. Is there any concrete evidence that the theory and practice of reflexive ecological modernization can shape the future according to the principles of sustainable development? To my mind, this means evidence of smart growth, enabled because communities are planned and designed around the holistic needs of the biosphere (Desjardins, 2006) and thus playing out a form of reflexive ecological modernization. Such a concept of planned emergence is on the drawing board in an unlikely space – in the People's Republic of China. Although ecological modernization theory was initially developed by scholars in the North, recent studies (e.g., in Mol, 2006) indicate that China is undergoing a process of political modernization, where new structures for decision making are emerging in response to the evident environmental crisis, as has happened in the European context. Such development can be taken as some evidence of the nascent application of the ecological modernization framework and should be the basis for ongoing in-depth empirical observation. As Mol and Carter say, concerning recent initiatives in China: 'the direction of those reforms is similar (to previous examples in Europe): greater decentralization and flexibility, and a shift away from a rigid, hierarchical, command-and-control system of environmental governance' (Mol and Carter, 2006: 40). Environmental laws and programmes have increased greatly since the 1980s. Most importantly however, in terms of playing out the theory of ecological modernization, China's economic system is beginning to include environmental and health dimensions, such as polluter pays and higher charges for resources. These moves, albeit still weak, demonstrate some recognition of the interdependence of economic, environmental and social systems.

The oft-heard phrase 'The future belongs to China' nowhere confronts one more than in cities such as Shanghai, the ultimate fantasy of consumerism, reflecting in its night time kaleidoscope the aspirations of rapid development. Shanghai exemplifies the treadmill. Yet it also promises an alternative model for a sustainable future, theorized according to reflexive ecological modernization. Given a political system of strong central control, a role for non-state actors engaging at the sub-political level is not what one would expect in China. However, as Mol argues, there

are three key exceptions where sub-political arrangements are emerging: joint venture or internationally operating firms, research organizations and the environment industry itself. In Shanghai, these three arenas of non-state activity are being brought together as work has commenced on the development of a futuristic business community, interconnected with its ecology and with its local community, to be constructed on the Ramsar wetland island of Chongming, in the Yangtze near Shanghai.

In August 2005, Arup, the renowned engineering and consultancy firm, was contracted by Shanghai Industrial Investment Corporation (SIIC) to design and masterplan the world's first eco-city, Dongtan. Dongtan will be a city of three villages that meet to form a city centre. The first phase of development aims to be completed by 2010, in time for the World Expo in Shanghai, and will accommodate a population of up to 10,000. There is expected to be a population of 500,000 by 2050. Plans include: to construct buffer zones to protect the Ramsar wetlands from pollutants; to maximize access to all facilities and workplaces through public transport; to utilize local farmlands and carbon dioxide from energy generation to grow organic crops for sale in the city; to reduce consumption of water by 50%; to reduce waste water by 84% and both to increase energy efficiency and develop enough renewable energy for all needs, by producing energy from biomass such as rice husks from the local rice mills (Arup, 2006).

Our interview with the senior architect and engineer on the Dongtan project was a conversation designed to cross a number of disciplinary areas.[1] In addition to my involvement, from a Faculty of Business, other parties to the conversation included my research colleague, Andrew Martin, an environmental lawyer, specializing in water law, Shanfeng Dong, the senior architect, and Liu Qiang, a project engineer, from the Dongtan project. The aim of the conversation was to explore the multilevel and cross-boundary approach that, as I have argued, underpins sustainable development. This chapter concludes with a brief analysis of this initial interview in what we hope will be an ongoing research project into an innovative and sustainably-oriented form of organization development at a community, indeed, a city level.

Shanfeng Dong and Liu Qiang placed a strong emphasis in the design and planning on holistic, interconnected social, environmental and economic systems, underpinned by systematic and ongoing feedback and learning systems, supported by highly sophisticated IT technologies and leading edge engineering. They described business development as subsumed into a city system that would be defined by local needs such as local employment, the rice farmers and the Ramsar Wetland upon which the city is to be situated.

Shanfeng describes their holistic approach:

> We look at Dongtan as an eco-city and that means the whole city system. Within this city system we look at the sustainable development in each aspect. What does that mean? Within a city, everything is connected. So when you are talking about employment and people living and working nearby, this is linked with another business question – for example, how investors come or industries can grow – they are all connected.

Liu Qiang described the integrated and progressive monitoring and learning process using a specific integrated resource management tool developed by Arup:

> The key point on this is that we have all disciplines and a hub. This hub is a software tool to connect all the disciplines together. And every discipline we will have to input the data manually, and to suit for different cities. Within the model if you change one parameter, then all the others will be changed at the same time.

Shanfeng Dong and Liu Qiang each described a business strategy with three phases of business development: tourism and leisure, R&D and innovation industries including the health sector and related clusters, and education. To implement its integrated strategy the planners and designers and business strategists for Dongtan will need to establish relationships with local communities, with all levels of government and with a number of business sector organizations, resource service companies. NGOs such as the Ramsar Wetland Bird Protection Bureau would also be called on to provide expertise.

In the passage below, Shanfeng describes the interconnected learning processes envisaged and his recognition of the challenges in bringing together different types of knowledge, including a range of experts and local information:

> That is the very difficult part of it. However once you get this right you will get the 'sustainable design'. It is not a fixed proposal, but it will be the same methodology we adopt. If you go to different places the solutions would be quite different, because the sustainability framework concluded by a sustainable workshop always vary. Meanwhile, in order to get it right, during working process we need input not only from within Arup globally, but also from local experts as well as local residents who are living there, and very importantly, from a mixed income backgrounds. Only in this way can we make sure that this will reflect more or less everyone's desire, because everyone needs to improve rather than only one group of people getting improvement but the other doesn't.

In a discussion on the importance of community facilities, Shanfeng gives his interpretation of the creation of what I have called '*discursive spaces*'.

> The brief is very simple – just for us to build an eco-city, but it is included within our integrated design, many of the community facilities – the social infrastructure; they are part of our socio-economic team's work. They are identifying that and looking at all the hospitals and the community facilities in terms of the population structure and the incomes to make sure those social-infrastructures are easily accessible by people. The museums and the cultural facilities are part of our cultural planning team's work. In our work world we do more than that actually – we create spaces … places for people to emotionally get connected to, and museums can be part of that. But many of the cultural elements are not that directly money-related. It is more like an open space – so the feeling of the space, and how that responds to the literature, philosophy, education, sociology and psychology – all those that matters. So it is, in our view, a more completed set … more than just physical things I would say.

## DISCUSSION

It is interesting to consider the eco-city of Dongtan in light of the processes of reflexivity. I suggest the staged approach to the emergence of the interconnected community at Dongtan could allow for interplay between reflection and reflexivity that could lead to more ecologically rational outcomes. The real test for the reflexive ecological modernization framework will be if the models offered by Dongtan and the string of eco-villages and cities planned across China serve to undermine the dominant paradigm of development in China.

The definition of sustainable development outlined earlier referred to the importance of organizational decision makers reflecting on and addressing the issue of how to prioritize relationships across the boundaries between species, generations and the developed/developing world. In this chapter, I have argued that a focus on sustainability as an integrated learning process has the capacity to provide new insight into the practical component of the 'sustainable development' programme in conditions of reflexive ecological modernity. I have made some suggestions as to how OB research and practice might contribute.

Dongtan provides an illustration of how this might work. Our observations, drawn from very initial research into a project of groundbreaking potential, support some key conceptualizations of reflexive ecological modernization and offer a positive means of enabling organizations to move beyond the micro-preoccupations of individualized corporate sustainability to work within the macro-principles of sustainable development. Our respondents described the planning for Dongtan as the creation of *flexible, choice-laden discursive* spaces, incorporating *sub-political or decentred arenas of decision making* that allowed for *decentred learning and continuous dialogue* across its various parts. In short, I argue that if OB research and practice heeded recent work in environmental sociology and took an interest in *building the reflective learning process onto the ongoing reflexivity and critique* now evident in association with the emerging ecological crisis in both developing and developed world then it could assist in preventing the development of this crisis.

In other words, our understandings, expectations and worldviews (Gephart, 1996) of what is effective OB need to be challenged in light of the precautionary actions required to diminish the negative impacts of global capitalism. This will only be done if managers and leaders, groomed by the often out-dated and institutionalized practices of business schools, re-invent their roles and responsibilities and engage at the inter-organizational and interdisciplinary level, surfacing and confronting the complex demands of sustainability and sustainable development. In this chapter I have underlined the issues of multiple boundaries across and within generations and species that exemplify the complexity inherent in sustainable development. Hence it seems to me that recent scholarly work exploring the non-linearity and unpredictability of organizations as complex systems and the implications for leadership (Plowman *et al.*, 2007) could offer a means of bridging the field of OB into sustainable development. If leadership and management can enable reflection and develop meaning around the multiple non-linear interactions characterizing an engagement with sustainable development then OB will have moved forward to the new millennium.

## NOTE

1 S. Benn and A. Martin, interview with Dong Shanfeng and Liu Qiang, Office of Arup, Shanghai, 20 January 2007.

## REFERENCES

Aalders, M. (2002) Drivers and drawbacks: Regulation and environmental risk management systems. Centre for Analysis of Risk and Regulation, London School of Economics. Available online at: http://www.lse.ac.uk/

collections/CARR/documents/discussionPapers.htm (accessed on 2 July 2005).

Academy of Management (2007) Domain Statement for Organizational Behaviour Division, at http://www.aomonline.org/aom.asp?id=18# (accessed 18 August 2007).

Adams, M. (2004) 'Conversations with Ulrich Beck', *The British Journal of Sociology*, 55 (4): 587–588.

Arup China (2006) Dongtan Backgrounder, provided by Ove Aarup, London.

Ashkanasy, N. (2007) 'Revisiting JOB's mission', *Journal of Organizational Behaviour*, 28: 353–355.

Australian Government (2003) Corporate Sustainability – an Investor Perspective: The Mays Report, Department of Environment and Heritage, Canberra at http://www.environment.gov.au/settlements/industry/finance/publications/mays-report/index.html (accessed 16 August 2007).

Avery, G. (2005) *Leadership for Sustainable Futures*. Cheltenham/Northampton, MA: Edward Elgar.

Ayukawa, Y., Naoyuki, Y. *et al.* (2007) *Climate Solutions, WWF's Vision for 2050*. Gland, Switzerland: WWF International.

Baker, S. (2006) *Sustainable Development*. Abingdon and New York: Routledge.

Ballard, D. (2005) 'Using learning processes to stimulate change for sustainable development', *Action Research*, 3: 135–156.

Banerjee, B. (2003) 'Who sustains whose development? Sustainable development and the reinvention of nature', *Organization Studies*, 24: 143–180.

Bansal, P. and Roth, K. (2000) 'Why companies go green: A model of ecological responsiveness', *Academy of Management Journal*, 43: 717–736.

Bazerman, M. and Hoffman, A. (1999) 'Sources of environmentally destructive behavior: Individual, organizational and institutional perspectives', *Research in Organizational Behavior*, 21: 39–79.

Beck, U. (1992) *The Risk Society*. (trans. Mark Ritter). London: Sage Publications.

Beck, U. (1994) 'The Reinvention of politics: Towards a theory of reflexive modernization', in U. Beck, A. Giddens and S. Lash (eds) *Reflexive Modernisation*. Cambridge: Polity Press, pp. 1–55.

Beck, U. (1995) *Ecological Enlightenment – Essays on the Politics of the Risk Society*. Atlantic City, NJ: Humanities Press.

Beck, U. (1997a) 'Global risk politics', in M. Jacobs (ed.) *Greening the Millennium? The New Politics of the Environment*. Oxford: Blackwell Publishers, The Political Quarterly.

Beck, U. (1997b) 'Subpolitics, ecology and environment', *Organization and Environment*, 10 (1): 52–65.

Beck, U. (1998) *Democracy without Enemies*. Cambridge: Polity Press.

Beck, U., Giddens, A. and Lash, S. (eds) (1994) *Reflexive Modernization: Politics, Tradition and Aesthetics in the Modern Social Order*. Cambridge: Polity Press.

Beck, U., Bonss, W. and Lau, C. (2003) 'The theory of reflexive modernisation', *Theory, Culture and Society*, 20: 1–33.

Benn, S. and Nelson, C. (2006) 'Sustainable Development as Organisational Learning', Paper presentation. Business as an Agent of World Benefit Conference, Academy of Management and UN Global Compact, Cleveland, OH.

Berlin, B. and Berlin, E. (2004) 'Community autonomy and the Maya ICBG project in Chiapas, Mexico: How a bioprospecting project that should have succeeded failed', *Human Organization*, 63: 472–86.

Bluhdorn, I. (2000) 'Ecological modernization and post-ecologist politics', in G. Spaargaren, A.P.J. Mol and F.H. Buttel (eds) *Environment and Global Modernity*, London: Sage, pp. 209–228.

Branco, M. and Rodrigues, L. (2006) 'Corporate social responsibility and resource-based perspectives', *Journal of Business Ethics*, 69: 111–132.

Bressers, H. and Kuks, S. (eds) (2004) *Integrated Governance and Water Basin Management: Conditions for Regime Change Towards Sustainability*. Dordrecht/Boston/London: Kluwer Academic Publishers.

Brown, M.E. and Treviño, L.K. (2006) 'Ethical leadership: A review and future directions', *The Leadership Quarterly*, 17: 595–616.

Brown, M., Treviño, L. and Harrison, D. (2005) 'Ethical leadership: A social learning perspective for construct development and testing', *Organizational Behavior and Human Decision Processes*, 97: 117–134.

Buttel, F.H. (2000) 'Ecological modernization as social theory', *GeoForum*, 31: 57–65.

Castro, C. (2004) 'Sustainable development', *Organization and Environment*, 17: 195–225.

Chan, R. (2005) 'Does the Natural-Resource-Based view of the firm apply in an Emerging Economy? A survey of foreign invested enterprises in China', *Journal of Management Studies*, 42: 625–672.

Christoff, P. (1996) 'Ecological modernisation, ecological modernities', *Environmental Politics*, 5: 476–500.

Crane, A. (2000) 'Corporate greening as amoralization', *Organization Studies*, 21 (4): 673–697.

Davidson, D. and Frickel, S. (2004) 'Understanding environmental governance', *Organization and Environment*, 17: 471–492.

Desjardins, J. (2006) *Business, Ethics and the Environment*. Upper Saddle River, NJ: Prentice Hall.

Doyle, T. and Doherty, T. (2006) 'Green public spheres and the green governance state: The politics of emancipation and ecological conditionality', *Environmental Politics*, 15: 881–892.

Drucker, P.F. (1999) 'The new pluralism', in F. Hesselbein, M. Goldsmith and I. Somerville (eds) *Leading Beyond the Walls*. San Francisco, CA: Jossey-Bass Publishers, pp. 9–17.

Dryzek, J. (1990) *Discursive Democracy*. Cambridge: Cambridge University Press.

Dryzek, J. (1997) *The Politics of the Earth*. Oxford: Oxford University Press.

Dryzek, J. (2000) *Deliberative Democracy and Beyond*. Oxford: Oxford University Press.

Dryzek, J., Downes, D., Hunold, C., Schlosberg, D. and Hernes, H. (2003) Green states and social movements. Oxford Scholarship Online. Available at: http://www.oxfordscholarship.com/oso/public/content/politicalscience/0199249024/toc.html (accessed on 25 June 2005).

Dunphy, D., Griffiths, A. and Benn, S. (2007) *Organisational Change for Corporate Sustainability*, 2nd edn. London and New York: Routledge.

Dyllick, T. and Hockerts, K. (2002) 'Beyond the business case for corporate sustainability', *Business Strategy and the Environment*, 11: 130–141.

Ebner, D. and Baumgartner, R. (2006) 'The Relationship between sustainable development and corporate social responsibility', Corporate Responsibility Research Conference, 4–5 September, Dublin, at http://www.crrconference.org/downloads/2006ebnerbaumgartner.pdf (accessed 10 March 2007).

Eckersley, R. (2004) *The Green State: Rethinking Democracy and Sovereignty*. Cambridge, MA: MIT Press.

Egri, C. and Herman, S. (2000) 'Leadership in the environmental sector: An examination of values, leadership styles, and organizational contexts', *Academy of Management Journal*, 43: 571–604.

Fergus, H. and Rowney, J. (2005a) 'Sustainable development: Lost meaning and opportunity?' *Journal of Business Ethics*, 60: 17–27.

Fergus, H. and Rowney, J. (2005b) 'Sustainable development: Epistemological frameworks and an ethic of choice', *Journal of Business Ethics*, 57: 197–207.

Gardner, W., Avolio, B., Luthans, F., May, D. and Walumbwa, F. (2005) 'Can you see the real me? A self-based model of authentic leader and follower development', *Leadership Quarterly*, 16: 343–372.

Gephart, R. (1996) 'Simulacral environments: Reflexivity and the natural ecology of organizations', In D. Boje, R. Gephart and T. Thatchenkery (eds) *Postmodern Management and Organization Theory, Vol. 45–59*. Thousand Oaks, CA: Sage, pp. 202–222.

Gephart, R. (2006) 'Ethnostatistics and Organizational Research Methods', *Organizational Research Methods*, 9: 417–431.

Giacalone, R.A., Jurkiewicz, C. and Dunn, C. (eds) (2005) *Positive Psychology in Business Ethics and Corporate Responsibility*. Greenwich, CT: Information Age Publishing.

Giddens, A. (1991) *Modernity and Self-identity. Self and Society in the Late Modern Age*. Cambridge: Polity Press.

Giddens, A. (1994) *Beyond Left and Right – the Future of Radical Politics*. Cambridge: Polity Press.

Goldblatt, D. (1996) *Social Theory and the Environment*. Cambridge: Polity Press.

Green, K. (2000) 'Greening organizations: Purchasing, consumption and innovation', *Organization & Environment*, 13: 206–225.

Hajer, M.A. (1995) *The Politics of Environmental Discourse: Ecological Modernization and the Policy Process*. Oxford: Oxford University Press.

Hart, S.L. (1995) 'A natural resource-based view of the firm', *Academy of Management Review*, 20: 986–1014.

Hart, S.L. (2007) *Capitalism at the Crossroads: The Unlimited Business Opportunities in Solving the World's Most Difficult Problems*. Upper Saddle River, NJ: Wharton School.

Hart, S.L. and Milstein, M. (2003) 'Creating sustainable value', *Academy of Management Executive*, 17: 56–69.

Heugens, P., Van den Bosch, F. and Van Riel, C. (2002) 'Stakeholder integration', *Business & Society*, 41: 36–60.

Hobson, K. (2003) 'Thinking habits into action: The role of knowledge and process in questioning household consumption practices', *Local Environment*, 8: 95–112.

Hoffman, A.J. and Bazerman, M.H. (2007) 'Changing practice on sustainability: Understanding and overcoming the organizational and psychological barriers to Action', in S. Sharma, M. Starik and B. Husted (eds) *Organizations and the Sustainability Mosaic: Crafting Long-term Ecological and Societal Solutions*. Northampton, MA: Edward Elgar, pp. 84–105.

Holliday, C., Schmidheiny, S. and Watts, P. (2002) *Walking the Talk: The Business Case for Sustainable Development*. Sheffield: Greenleaf Publications.

House, R. (1998) 'A brief history of GLOBE', *Journal of Managerial Psychology*, 13: 230–240.

Intergovernmental Panel on Climate Change (2007) Climate Change 2007. Working Group 1 IPCC Fourth Assessment Report, at http://ipcc-wg1.

ucar.edu/wg1/wg1-report.htm (accessed 16 August, 2007).

Jackson, B. (2005) 'The enduring romance of leadership studies', *Journal of Management Studies*, 42: 1311.

Jermier, J.M. and Forbes, L.C. (2003) 'Greening organizations: Critical issues', in M. Alvesson and H. Willmott (eds) *Studying Management Critically*. London: Sage, pp. 157–176.

Jermier, J., Forbes, L., Benn, S. and Orsato, R. (2006) 'The new corporate environmentalism and green politics', in S. Clegg, C. Hardy, T. Lawrence and W. Nord (eds) *Handbook of Organisational Studies*. London: Sage Publications, pp. 618–650.

Kelly, T. (2004) 'Unlocking the iron cage: Public administration in the deliberative democracy theory of Jurgen Habermas', *Administration and Society*, 36: 38–61.

Lave, J. and Wenger, E. (1991) *Situated Learning: Legitimate Peripheral Participation*. Cambridge/New York: Cambridge University Press.

Luthans, F. (2002) 'The need for and meaning of positive organizational behaviour', *Journal of Organizational Behaviour*, 23: 695–706.

Maguire, S. and Ellis, J. (2003) 'The precautionary principle and global chemical risk management', *Greener Management International*, 41: 33–47.

Marrewijk, M. and Werre, M. (2003) 'Multiple levels of corporate sustainability', *Journal of Business Ethics*, 44: 107–119.

Mol, A. (2001) *Globalisation and Environmental Reform*. Cambridge, MA: MIT Press.

Mol, A.P.J. (2006) 'Environment and modernity in transitional China: Frontiers of ecological modernization', *Development and Change*, 37: 29–56.

Mol, A.P.J and Carter, N. (2006) 'China's environmental governance in transition', *Environmental Politics*, 15: 149–170.

Mol, A. and Sonnenfeld, D. (2000) *Ecological Modernisation around the World*. London: Routledge.

Mol, A.P.J. and Spaargaren, G. (2002) 'Ecological modernisation and the environmental state', in A.P.J. Mol and F.H. Buttel (eds) *The Environmental State under Pressure*. Oxford: Elsevier Science Ltd. (Research in Social Problems and Public Policy; 10). pp. 33–53.

Newton, T. (2002) 'Creating the New Ecological Order?', *Academy of Management Review*, 27: 523–540.

Newton, T. and Harte, G. (1997) 'Green business: Technicist Kitsch?', *Journal of Management Studies*, 34: 75–98.

O'Riordan, T. (1985) 'What does sustainability really mean? Theory and development of concepts of sustainability', in *Sustainable Development in an Industrial Economy*, Proceedings of a Conference, Queen's College, Cambridge: Centre for Economic and Environmental Development.

Orssatto, R.J. and Clegg, S.R. (1999) 'The political ecology of organizations: Towards a business-environment analytical framework', *Organization and Environment*, 12 (3): 263–279.

Parry, K. and Bryman, A. (2006) 'Leadership in Organisations', in S. Clegg, C. Hardy, T. Lawrence and W. Nord (eds) *Handbook of Organisational Studies*. London: Sage Publications, pp. 447–465.

Plowman, D., Solansky, S., Beck, T., LaKami, B., Kulkarni, M. and Travis, D. (2007) 'The role of leadership in emergent self-organization', *The Leadership Quarterly*, 18: 341–356.

Pollner, M. (1991) 'Left of ethnomethodology: The rise and decline of radical reflexivity', *American Sociological Review*, 56: 370–380.

Porter, M.E. and van der Linde, C. (1995) 'Toward a new conception of the environment-competitiveness relationship', *Journal of Economic Perspectives*, 9: 97–118.

Prahalad, C.K. (2005) *The Fortune at the Bottom of the Pyramid*. Upper Saddle River, NJ: Pearson Education Publishing as Wharton School Publishing.

Rondinelli, D. and London, T. (2003) 'How corporations and environmental groups collaborate: Assessing cross-sector alliances and collaborations', *Academy of Management Executive*, 17: 61–76.

Rosebro, J. (2006) 'Does Ford have a better idea about sustainability (ii)?', Green Car Congress, at http://www.greencarcongress.com/2006/03/does_ford_have_.html (accessed 10 March 2007).

Rousseau, D. (1997) 'Organizational behavior in the new organizational era', *Annual Review of Psychology*, 48: 515–546.

Schlosberg, D. (1999) *Environmental Justice and the New Pluralism*. Oxford: Oxford University Press.

Schnaiberg, A. and Gould, K. (1994) *Environment and Society*. New York: St Martin's Press.

Schnaiberg, A., Pellow, D. and Weinberg, A. (2002) 'The treadmill of production and the environmental state', in A. Mol and F. Buttel (eds) *The Environmental State Under Pressure*. Oxford: Elsevier Science, pp. 15–32.

Shiva, V. (1993) 'The greening of the global reach', in W. Sachs (ed.) *Global Ecology*. London: Zed Books, pp. 149–56.

Shrivastava, P. (1995) 'Ecocentric management in a risk society', *The Academy of Management Review*, 20: 118–138.

Sinclair, A. (2007) *Leadership for the Disillusioned*. Crows Nest, NSW: Allen and Unwin.

Stern, N. (2006) *Stern Review on the Economics of Climate Change*, HM Treasury, at http://www.

hm-treasury.gov.uk/independent_reviews/stern_ review_economics_climate_change/stern_review_ report.cfm (accessed 16 August 2007).

Stormer, F.L. (2003) 'Making the shift: Moving from "ethics pays" to an inter-systems model of business', *Journal of Business Ethics*, 44: 279–289.

Turcotte, M. and Pasquero, J. (2001) 'The paradox of multistakeholder collaborative roundtables', *Journal of Applied Behavioral Science*, 37: 447–464.

Vaughan, D. (1999) 'The role of the organization in the production of techno-scientific knowledge', *Social Studies of Science*, 31: 913–943.

Waldman, D. *et al.* (2006) 'Cultural and leadership predictors of corporate social responsibility values of top management: A GLOBE study of 15 countries', *Journal of International Business Studies*, 37: 823–837.

Welford, R. (1998) 'Essential matter: Corporate environmental management means business as usual', *United Nations Research Institute for Sustainable Development*, http://www.unrisd.org/unrisd/website/newsview. nsf/0/CD86A72B352CB86B80256B7B0040CA43? OpenDocument (accessed 14 March 2007).

Wenger, E. (1999) *Communities of Practice: Learning, Meaning, and Identity*. Cambridge: Cambridge University Press.

Windell, K. (2007) 'The commercialisation of CSR: Consultants selling responsibility', in F. den Hind, F. de Bakker and P. Neergaard (eds) *Managing Corporate Social Responsibility in Action*. Aldershot/Burlington, VT: Ashgate Publishing, pp. 33–52.

World Commission on Environment and Development and Commission for the Future (1987) *Our Common Future*. Oxford: Oxford University Press.

Zairi, M. (1997) 'Business process and management: A boundaryless approach to modern competitiveness', *Business Process Management Journal*, 3: 64–80.

# 22

# Managing Organizational Expression

Majken Schultz and Mary Jo Hatch

## INTRODUCTION

This chapter focuses on how organizations express who they are and what they stand for to all of their internal and external stakeholders. As opposed to some of the other topics reviewed in this Handbook, 'organization expression' is not a well-established academic field with either a clear set of core concepts or any well-established perspectives. On the contrary, inclusion of this topic in the Handbook is based on the observation that academics increasingly use concepts such as identity, values, vision, mission, corporate branding and corporate reputation to study the forms that organizational expression takes and the practices and processes companies engage in order to express themselves. Furthermore, consultants and managers are showing interest in managing organizational expressions for the purposes of adding value to their brands or muscle to their reputations, and this produces pressures to integrate across the full range of different business functions, making this topic particularly appropriate for macro OB.

There are many reasons why organizations are devoting more and more energy and resources to expressive organizational practices. One is that companies face increasing difficulty sustaining competitive advantage based on product differentiation alone. Stand alone products and services are easy targets for imitation and companies search for renewed uniqueness by turning to the organization itself. Another reason is that numerous stakeholders, ranging from NGOs to institutional investors, pressure organizations for greater transparency and openness about their affairs, governance and citizenship practices. Last, but not least, employees and customers have developed expectations about what organizations should offer them in return for their commitment and loyalty. Increasingly, employees do not just look for a place to work, they also search out a source of identification that enhances their self-esteem and provides a sense of belonging. Similarly, customers today do not only consume products and services, they also consume the attributes of personal identity that association with an organization brings. Together these developments require organizations to become more explicit about the premises for their business strategy and the values that lie behind them.

In order to serve as a destination in this search for meaning among internal and external stakeholders, organizations must be able to offer expressions that invite sense-making and offer markers of identity. However, not all organizational expressions are deliberate or intentional, and some expressions are easier to manage than others. For example, the Nike Swoosh and the iconic Apple logo are examples of intentional expressions that become relatively straightforward to manage once they are created; but the behaviour of a Nike supplier towards the media, or the attitude of an employee interacting with customers in the local Apple store are also important organizational expressions that, compared with a corporate logo, are much harder to control and more complex to manage. Nonetheless, organizational behaviours as well as the symbolism they uphold constitute the organizational expressions that determine stakeholders' perceptions of the organization.

The problem of managerial control has several implications for the management of organizational expressions. First organization expression cannot be fully conceived or managed within the boundaries of any single academic discipline. Thus, managing organizational expression entails a multidisciplinary and multi functional approach. Second, most disciplines have defined their core constructs and related managerial practices within their own internal framework without considering how the same phenomenon or practice is defined within other disciplines. This implies that organizational expression demands a broader perception of individual constructs than found within individual disciplines. The combined interplay between the many different forms of expression creates what Schultz, Hatch and Larsen (2000) labelled 'The Expressive Organization' arguing that the symbolic and emotional dimensions are becoming central to doing business. In this chapter we address basic concerns related

to how and why organizations express themselves and then provide an overview of what we consider to be the main theories and approaches relevant to managing organizational expression. Although we stress the cross-disciplinary origins of organizational expression, we ground the many conceptual voices within organization theory. The ambition to manage organizational expression raises several questions concerning the authenticity of expression, the involvement of stakeholders in creating and consuming expressions, and the illusion of managerial control of the expressive process. These questions are examined in the third section of the chapter, while the last section points to some of the ways in which expressive organizations can enrich and expand our understanding of management.

## ANTECEDENTS OF THE FIELD

There are two main reasons why organizations seek to express themselves. One reason is the aspiration to make a *difference* in the marketplace by distinguishing the organization from its competitors by creating products and experiences that are unique to the company (Aaker, 1996; Albert and Whetten, 1985). Being seen and heard is the first step to being noticed by stakeholders and thus basic awareness is the foundation for creating an image or reputation, but being regarded as a preferred supplier, partner or employer and earning the emotional attachments this brings from stakeholders requires more than simple awareness and in this regard organizations increasingly turn to processes of self-expression via developing their style or voice. For example, the preference for an Apple computer not only depends upon a purchase, it also means buying into an attitude towards computing that differentiates Apple and pc users. Understanding such a dynamic led Apple marketers to an ingenious advertising campaign featuring two people who represented these differences: the stodgy older pc user, and the cooler if geekier Apple user. Associations to commercials such as these encourage Apple users to express their felt differences by using their computer to signify belonging to the Apple World.

Many scholars will argue that organizational expressions along with organizational forms are the victims of institutionalization and imitation processes across different organizations (Meyer and Rowan, 1977; Scott and Meyer, 1994). This implies that organizations tend to become more similar in their values, symbols and various identity markers and as a consequence it becomes harder to tell companies operating in the same business area apart. For example, banks, airlines and mobile phones can all look remarkably alike. However, the focus of managing organizational expression is to keep searching for new ways to make a difference that are relevant and meaningful to stakeholders in spite of institutional pressure to conform. Southwest Airlines is a notable example of creating an emotional difference that is relevant to employees and customers alike. The Southwest difference is based in fun and unique customer service. The new cell phone 'Serene', created in collaboration between Bang and Olufsen and Samsung, is another attempt to make a difference based in product design, aesthetics and user interface.

The second important reason organizations express themselves is to attract stakeholders to the organizations by creating a sense of *belonging* among them. This is most obvious in relation to employees. Many employees do not just choose a place to work – they join a company because of the values, ideas and activities with which they will be asked to identify. Furthermore, the perceived uniqueness of the organization often provides a source of pride and esteem that creates a feeling of commitment among employees and other organizational stakeholders. The people working for Southwest Airlines are not just working for an airline to receive a pay-check. They are part of a group that expresses care and respect for one another, which gives employees reason to connect with the belief that their warmth and creativity are foundations for the company they serve.

The importance of making employees feel that they belong to the organization has been emphasized in the literature on organizational identification. Leading scholars within this field claim that how employees experience themselves as members of an organization and whether they are able to identify with organizational values and beliefs are central to understanding the engagement and satisfaction that they reap from their organizational membership (Ashforth and Mael, 1989; Pratt, 2003). According to Ashforth and Mael, the ability of management to get employees to identify with the organization opens onto new kinds of symbolic leadership in the areas of socialization, role conflict and inter-group relations. The main argument in this literature is that strong identification with the organization overshadows the multiple and sometimes conflicting roles and relationships that people must maintain inside and outside the organization. Employees of Southwest Airlines may have different roles and individual attitudes depending on whether they serve customers in the air or provide administrative services on the ground, yet they have the chance to share a strong feeling of belonging to Southwest and their 'customer service commitment' (see www.southwest.com) helps them to transcend potential conflicts.

By the same token, dedicated customers or suppliers also feel that they belong to the organization and use organizational expressions as evidence that confirms (or denies) their sense of belonging. As stated by researchers such as Du Gay (2000) and Kozinets (2002), customers consume the organization for their own purpose and engage in sense-making of their individual consumption. Such enthusiastic customers may even appropriate the organization's expressions for their own purposes, such as when members of Harley-Davidson fan clubs tattoo the Harley logo on their arms and go on a 'ride' with other Harley owners and employees, or when kids join the LEGO Club to share 'My Own Construction' (individual LEGO constructions) with other users (see www.lugnet.com).

Many managers and consultants have long held the mistaken belief that organizations own the meanings of their expressions. Meaning necessarily belongs to those who provide it – that is to the internal and external stakeholders who value organizational expressions and determine their worth via their own perceptions (e.g., firm reputation) and actions (e.g., regarding purchases and loyalty). This belief in managements' ability to 'give sense' to organizational expressions (Gioia and Chittipeddi, 1991) coined the phrase 'sense-giving' has dominated the areas of identity management and corporate branding (e.g., Olins, 1989; 2004; Schmitt & Simonson; 1997). Here the evocative design of corporate symbols and the orchestration of large-scale marketing campaigns and other communication efforts have seduced management into assuming that their intentions will be echoed in stakeholder perceptions.

In more recent work the focus has shifted to how stakeholders make sense of organizational expressions and construct what often turns out to be a cacophony of multiple meanings for each of them. The managerial challenge is thus transformed from one of controlling and centralizing corporate expressions to one of engaging and listening to stakeholders, forging new expressions in response to stakeholder perceptions, concerns and interests. Nissan learned to do this during their massive turnaround in which they redefined not only their beliefs and values, but learned to interact with customers in new and what the company called more 'authentic ways'. Local Nissan dealers moved into new physical settings designed to express the renewed energy of their brand, while the Nissan Shift advertising campaign reflected the numerous ways in which their customers responded to the brand, which the company discovered via psychographic marketing research. At the same time the company expanded involvement in the local community and started to build 'authentic' customer relations, which in the words of Nissan 'embodies boundary-pushing passion as part of everyday life'.

## CENTRAL APPROACHES AND MAIN THEORIES

As stated above, 'organizational expression' is not an established academic field, but is rather a theme that can be found in many different disciplines and that ranges across several theoretical terrains. The book, *The Expressive Organization: Linking Identity, Reputation and the Corporate Brand* (Schultz, Hatch and Larsen, 2000), grew out of this cross-disciplinarity. In this book a group of leading scholars with different disciplinary backgrounds and interests were asked to write about how organizations express themselves through organizational identity, image, culture, reputation and corporate branding. While the group of authors experienced high agreement that all these constructs were important and interrelated, you can see a myriad of disciplinary differences in the ways they use terms such as identity, image and brand. Thus, our overview of organizational expressions will reflect cross-disciplinary differences as well as the cross-functional difficulties managers face when they engage in managing organizational expression.

### The symbolic foundation

While some complications emerge from differences between conceptual definitions, a more fundamental challenge is that almost all behaviour that occurs in an organization becomes an organizational expression for someone, from employee actions and even the silent gestures of top management during a meeting, to statements made by customers and the stockholding behaviour of investors. For that reason it is impossible to point at specific artefacts, forms or types of behaviour that will always be interpreted as expressions of the organization. Expressiveness depends on context as well as the uses made and meanings given to them by their audiences. Thus, in order to become a full-blown and recognized organizational expression any artefact, claim or set of behaviours must be associated with some meaning by one or more individuals. This symbolic dimension of organizational expressions is prominent within each of the multiple disciplines that study organizational expressions (Pondy *et al.*, 1983; Cohen, 1985; Gioia, 1986; Gagliardi, 1992). However, because a single expression can be associated with multiple and even contradictory meanings constructed by different stakeholders, the symbolic meaning and importance of an expression can change over time, sometimes fading out of everyone's consciousness. For example, a very large office stuffed with high class designer furniture is most likely perceived as an expression of power and status among managers, whereas employees may find that it represents the oppression and greed of top management. Fifteen years ago, walking around with a big laptop was seen as an expression of status and importance by many people, as this device was only accessible to the most valued employees in most companies. Today a big laptop has the opposite symbolic meaning, as it shows that you are not keeping up with the latest gadgetry.

One implication for management is that the symbolic meaning of organizational expressions cannot be taken for granted. Associated meanings often differ between stakeholders, just as the messages symbols communicate may change over time. As a first step in managing organizational expressions managers must sensitize themselves to symbolic multiplicity and seek to understand the cultural contexts and myths that influence how meaning is embedded and constructed (Holt, 2004). This will not only give managers a better understanding of the role of current expressions, but also enable them to tap into the tensions and desires that activate their stakeholders in the construction of new expressions. When Nike chose to market their new golden football shoe using a video clip with Brazilian star Ronaldihno doing incredible things with a ball, they were not only marketing an expression of sports in the vein of their 'Just Do It' slogan. Nike also tapped into the style and rich mythology of Brazilian football, which millions of people relate to the Brazilian team's global reputation for playing elegant and spirited football.

With that basic understanding of the symbolic nature of organizational expression in mind there are some forms of organizational expression that, while not interpretable without input from multiple audiences, are likely to become meaningful to stakeholders and thus are worthy of management attention. These are depicted in Figure 22.1 where we locate them in terms of the disciplines that have traditionally taken responsibility for their management.

## Organizational culture and identity

Within the field of organizational behaviour, the concern for organizational expression is most often found in organization culture studies and more recently in the focus on organizational identity. Organizational culture studies have generated awareness of the importance of symbols and artefacts as expressions, but also as objects to be used by managers for influence (see Martin, this volume). In the framework proposed by Edgar Schein, artifacts are the most visible and immediate of organizational expressions, including objects, words and deeds. Artifacts provide both symbolic and physical material to organizational members who use them to express their culture's deeper layers – espoused values, values in use and assumptions (Schein, 2004). The importance of artifacts to management is elaborated by Schein in his distinction between primary and secondary mechanisms by which leaders embed and transmit organizational culture to organizational members and other stakeholders. While the primary mechanism focus on how leaders express their values and attitudes, the secondary mechanism refer to significant organizational expressions (Schein, 2004: 246):

Primary Embedding Mechanisms:

- Managerial reactions in crisis situations
- Criteria for management's distribution of scarce resources
- Criteria for management's distribution of power and status
- Criteria for management's recruiting, promoting and firing of employees

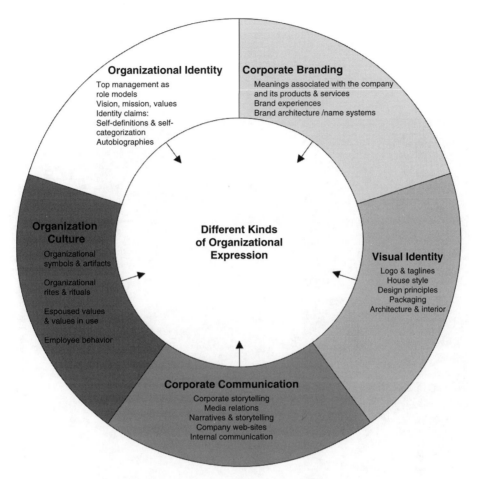

**Figure 22.1    Organizational expressions from different disciplines.**

Secondary Embedding Mechanisms:

- Organizational design and structure
- Organizational systems and procedures
- Rites and rituals of the organization
- Design of physical space, façades and buildings
- Stories about important events and people
- Formal statements about organizational philosophy, creeds and charters

The embedding of culture happens, for example, when managers tell organizational stories, create and use objects and images that represent the organization, and employ metaphors, nicknames and other figures of speech to express to stakeholders which values are treasured in the organization.

For example, in their efforts to transform the organization, top managers often repeat the same phrase over and over again in order to create a 'burning platform', such as 'Must-Win-Battles' or 'The Will to Win'. In some cases management can deliberately use artifacts to engage employees in expressing their interpretation of the organizational culture. This has happened, for example in the toy company LEGO Group during their crisis in 2003–2004, where employees were invited to use the LEGO bricks to express their interpretation of the problems that faced the company at the time. Figure 22.2 shows examples of how people can use LEGO bricks to express their perceptions about corporate problems (see also Schultz *et al.*, 2006).

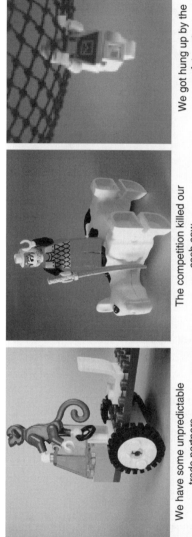

We have some unpredictable trade partners

The competition killed our cash cow

We got hung up by the safety net

Misunderstanding the customers' needs

Too much income from one source?

There are too many skeletons in the closet

**Figure 22.2    Examples of how people can express perceptions about corporate problems using LEGO play materials. Reprinted with permission.**

In similar ways, organizational rites and rituals, such as meeting patterns, management traditions and celebrations may be invoked to express the attitude and aspirations of top management. Also, organizations are increasingly using their physical space to express their cultural core values and remind occupants what the organization stands for. Some of the most compelling examples in Europe are the new headquarters buildings by ING Group in The Netherlands and Agbar in Barcelona. At ING the buildings are designed to be transparent, bold and sustainable in order to express the values of freshness and openness that management wanted to nurture in the culture by the open spaces, lightness and bright colours. In Spain water provider Agbar chose French architect Jean Nouvel to design their new and very phallic Torre Agbar, which changed the Barcelona skyline. Torre Agbar was not only a remarkable and highly visible manifestation of the vision of the company; it has become a symbol of the New Spain and the business potential in the formerly public monopolies. Figure 22.3 shows the new headquarters building and its influence on Barcelona.

As explained by Martin (2002), the symbolic meaning attached to organizational expressions may differ radically between different subcultures within the organization, just as artifacts may take on ambiguous meanings invoking simultaneous contradictory emotions. For example, expressions of the proud cultural heritage of a company may simultaneously invoke romantic sentiment and deep irrelevance. The multiplicity in the interpreted expressions becomes even more diverse in relation to external stakeholders, where customers from different national cultures and social lifestyles may interpret the same expression in radically different ways. This was the case, for example, when American consumers perceived LEGO's world famous bricks as generic plastic construction blocks by American consumers, whereas European consumers associated LEGO bricks with children's development and playful learning (Schultz *et al.*, 2006). Intriguingly, artists who use LEGO bricks, parents of LEGO users, and many other subcultures within the LEGO network harbour more subtle variants on these various meanings.

The concept of organizational identity addresses how organizational members define and construct themselves as an organizational collective (see Brown this volume). Compared with the concept of culture, organizational identity has a stronger focus on the textual, reflexive and narrative dimensions of how organizational members express

**Figure 22.3   The new headquarters of Agbar by Jean Nouvel, Barcelona.**
First image © 2006 Lluis Ribes, reprinted with permission. Second image © 2007 Andy Stuart, reprinted with permission.

who they are (Hatch and Schultz, 2000). Organizational identity researchers have also been concerned with how symbolic expressions are used to represent identity, as in the case of Pratt and Rafaeli showing how the meanings of dress (uniforms versus one's own clothes) were negotiated among organizational members in the construction of their identity as nurses and members of specific working units/subcultures (1997).

Other researchers attend to the role of organizational discourse in self-representations and the communication of organizational beliefs to both internal and external stakeholders (e.g., Cheney and Christensen, 2001). Related to Schein's distinction between espoused values and values in use, this critical perspective on identity treats the concept like espoused values in the sense that most of this work is concerned with identity claims and organizational autobiographies. Some of this work focuses on the organization as a social actor that states and explains itself in ways that indicate concern for legitimacy, while other work is more in line with organizational culture theory in that it emphasizes collective beliefs and understandings of 'who we are as an organization' held by organizational members (Whetten and Mackey, 2002; Ravasi and Schultz, 2006).

Within organizational culture studies there has been a fierce debate regarding whether or not cultural expressions can and should be managed. The sceptics point at the difficulties of managing subjective meaning and sense-making processes or point to the oppressive side of using 'soft power'. By the same token others have been optimistic regarding the managerial possibilities of 'engineering' organizational culture, typically defined as values based management. Nevertheless, insights from both organizational culture and identity theory have inspired management practices by providing tools and processes for managerial influence (i.e., managing values, artifacts and other symbolic expressions) and pointing at the symbolic dimensions of managerial action, such as paying attention to the expressive dimensions of organizational structure.

## Corporate identity, branding and communication

Researchers working on corporate identity, corporate branding and corporate communication have examined expressions from the point of view of how to construct and manage organizational expressions targeted to both internal and external stakeholders. The most pronounced attempts to create and control organizational expression are found within the field of corporate identity, which originated in graphic-visual traditions dedicated to the design of corporate logos, symbols and house style (Olins, 1989). Here, the use of corporate heritage as well as the design of names and shapes and the use of colour has resulted in a whole industry dedicated to creating visible, recognizable and distinct expressions for companies. Wally Olins, one of the leading thinkers in this area, founded the company behind the creation of the Orange brand, the first lifestyle driven provider of mobile telephony in the UK. The square of bold Orange colour was intended by the designers to symbolize the fresh and free spirit of Orange, while in reality it might have been associated with a range of different meanings by other stakeholders. Other companies have been keen to preserve their rich heritage through their entire range of corporate signalling. For example Johnson and Johnson always seek to enhance the longevity and trust people have in their brand by relying on the set of core expressions they have used since 1943 when their Credo was first written down (see www.jnj.com about the Credos history).

Many of the practices developed in relation to corporate identity drifted into corporate branding making it difficult to distinguish the concepts of organizational expressions used by marketing, strategy and organizational theory. As opposed to branding individual products, which has a long tradition within marketing, corporate branding focuses on how companies use a range of different resources based in the organization itself to express their uniqueness and to differentiate their brand (Hatch and Schultz, 2001;

Balmer and Greyser, 2003; Schultz, 2005). Compared to corporate identity, corporate branding is also more concerned with how employees and customers interpret and act towards corporate expressions. Organizations as brands have been labelled a 'branded house' opposed to a 'house of brands' (Aaker, 1996) implying that there is a set of central ideas, belief and symbols that are connected to everything the organization does. No matter whether they operate within music, airlines, books, health clubs, games, and so on, Virgin companies clearly belong to the same corporation led by British icon Richard Branson. All companies use Virgin's red and white street-style to express their central ideas of 'fun, value for money, innovation, competitive challenge and brilliant customer service' (see www.virgin.com/about us). In addition Richard Branson has not held back in exposing himself as a symbolic expression of his company, whether dressed as a bride at the opening of Virgin's first Bridal Store in London, or demonstrating the importance of standing up to challenges by flying his hot-air balloon around the world (or nearly so).

Expressions of corporate identity and corporate brands tend to be more coherent across different businesses and markets as they serve as markers of recognition and trust in a global marketplace. However, the growing nationalism and awareness of local cultures constantly raise questions about how organizational expressions should be adapted to local and regional cultures, while still being recognized as part of the same brand. One of the brands that successfully tapped into local cultural expressions is Swedish Absolut Vodka which, through their playful and evocative marketing campaigns, combined the shape of their bottle with a range of different, but related cultural expressions, such as different local cities.

Corporate communication has focused mainly on how organizations tell stories to internal and external stakeholders about who they are, what they are doing and how they are doing it. They use a range of different internal and external communication channels to tell these stories (see Cheney

and Christensen, 2001; Cornelissen, 2004). Corporate communication grew out of public relations, which concerns how organizations express themselves through the media and how they learn to improve their corporate reputation by interacting with journalists and the business press. Increasingly, organizations also use corporate web-sites, weblogs and other kinds of on-line presence to communicate about themselves and to invite stakeholders into a dialogue with them. In these regards more and more companies are turning to the formation of on-line communities, customer clubs or other types of on-line/off-line events where stakeholders can engage more regularly with the company and each other by expressing their opinions, beliefs and experiences with the company's products and service. Although the digital dimension is very important in seeking to involve external stakeholders, they also offer expanding opportunities for employees to engage directly with external stakeholders, such as the annual Brick Feast held in the US, where managers and employees from LEGO Company are invited by the LEGO Fans to join the celebration of people's individual and collective constructions (see www.brickfest.com).

## Towards cross-disciplinary frameworks

One of the implications of the increasing overlap between stakeholder audiences is that the same organizational expression will be interpreted from different perspectives at the same time. For example, a lot of the corporate descriptions on web-sites about core values, company history and dedication to citizenship are equally relevant for employees scrutinizing corporate values, customers searching for interaction (to complain or to praise), students exploring job opportunities, journalists looking for historical information and investors requesting detailed data. Another implication is that expressions intended for one audience may have significant impact on other audiences. Cheney and Christensen (2001) demonstrated how organizational marketing efforts speak more to organizational members than its customers, just as citizens put great emphasis on how organizations treat and communicate with their employees in their judgement of corporate reputations (Fombrun and Van Riel, 2003). This more comprehensive and ambiguous role of organizational expressions is reflected in the development of more integrated conceptual frameworks including several of the core concepts relevant to organizational expressions that emerge from a multiplicity of academic disciplines (Hatch and Schultz, 2000, 2001, 2003; Balmer and Greyser, 2003). One example of such an integrated framework is the conceptualization of corporate branding by Hatch and Schultz pointing at the alignments between the everyday practices of the organization (organizational culture); where the organization aspires to go (strategic vision) and how the organization is perceived by external stakeholders (images). The corporate branding framework shows how managers can use the full range of expressions related to culture, identity, vision and image in creating both distinctiveness and a feeling of belonging in the eyes of all stakeholder audiences. Thus, a more integrated approach to organizational expression has significant implications to management practice, pushing management in a much more cross-functional and less turf-focused direction. The ability of management to overcome cross-functional boundaries, which have been institutionalized for decades in theory and in practice points at one of the most critical issues in managing organizational expressions.

## CRITICAL ISSUES FOR THE PRESENT

There are several critical issues in the management of organizational expressions.

### *The need for cross-functional collaboration*

The ability to overcome cross-functional boundaries in managing organizational

expressions is one of the most critical challenges to management, as organizational expressions not only emerge from different academic disciplines, but also have been developed within different professional subcultures in organizations, most often between human resources, marketing, corporate communication and investor relations. Some of the functions most often involved in managing organizational expressions are summarized in Figure 22.4.

The challenge in managing organizational expressions is to create cross-functional collaboration between these different business functions, and blend their different competencies and affiliations with various stakeholder groups. If the organization is dominated by isolated subcultures, the risk is that each function brings along its own set of pitfalls reflecting the limitations of any specialized competence. For example, marketing and sales functions learn what consumers want and how to create marketing campaigns, promotion material, sales initiatives, training etc. that help their companies respond to customer demands. Human resource functions focus on recruiting new employees through ads, web-sites and events and developing and retaining those they already have, for example by creating individual rewards that celebrate organizational values. Meanwhile, corporate communication disseminates information internally using channels such as intranets, corporate magazines and events, and externally to media and special interests via all kinds of press releases, interaction with media, information material, specialized reports (e.g., reports related to corporate social responsibility, media training of managers). These activities, in turn, cause the company to develop functional distinctiveness among advertising and sales groups that, in their own ways grow dissimilar from each of the others due to their responsibility for customers.

More and more companies have started to establish specific functions dedicated to the bigger picture of corporate brand or reputation management (Fombrun and Van Riel, 2003). These functions often have a dual role of

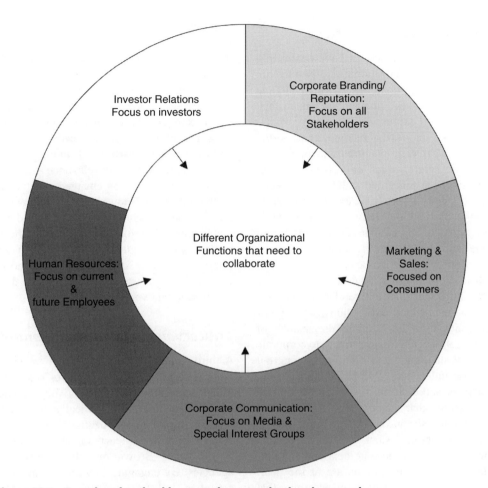

**Figure 22.4   Functions involved in managing organizational expressions.**

initiating cross-functional collaboration and spearheading the overall identity of the corporate expressions. For example in Danish pharmaceutical company Novo Nordisk the corporate branding function has been responsible for creating and translating the central idea of 'Changing Diabetes' into the multiple needs of specific markets and business areas involving pretty much all staff functions in the organization.

Turf wars are deadly to the management of organizational expressions, as organizational expressions rely on cross-fertilization of competencies, knowledge and perspectives among a range of different professional disciplines and business functions. The risks can best be seen in cases where silos allow

a single business function to hijack the brand management process. For example, if marketing takes over corporate expressions, they are often restricted to marketing campaigns that do not resonate throughout the organization or extend beyond customers to touch other stakeholders. The risk of corporate communication hijacking the expressions is that they become little other than a platform for media relations and corporate social responsibility programmes. Or, if human resources stage the dominating expressions they may focus so intently on internal issues such as values-based management or the use of expressions for recruiting purposes that customer impact and external stakeholder relevance are lost from sight

## The limitations of consistency

In general many managers have mistakenly believed that organizational expressions are amenable to the techniques by which tangible corporate assets are managed when, in fact, organizational expressions require new management techniques that recognize and use the added value of their intangible and much more symbolic nature. Much expressive management has been concerned with the consistency and regularity of symbolic expressions based on the assumption that it is the tangible dimension of representations such as logos, style and stories that requires managerial attention. Also, the managerial concern with consistency assumes that stakeholders are more attracted to repetitive clarity than they are to open-ended expressions. This focus on controlling the tangible dimensions of organizational expressions traces to corporate identity, marketing and brand managers, but has also influenced value-based management practices and numerous variants of culture and identity management (e.g. Aaker, 1996; Schmitt and Simonson, 1997; Schein, 2004).

When scholars such as Dave Whetten (2006) argue that the statement and communication of identity claims are at the heart of identity management, he is assuming that official and explicit self-presentations are the most central expressions of organizational identity for stakeholders. This stance shows bias towards consistent self-proclamations opposed to scholars who argue that shared understandings and beliefs among organizational stakeholders are the foundations for identity, even with their multiple meanings and symbolic ambiguity (Ravasi and Schultz, 2006). Other scholars have argued that the belief in consistency will not stand the test of time as it is downright counterproductive to stick to one expression in the face of dynamic movements in the economy. In his work on iconic brands, Douglas Holt showed that it is the ability to change modes of expression that keeps companies relevant in their local context, and claimed that the ability to change defines iconic brands (Holt, 2004). He offered the examples of several iconic American brands, such as Budweiser and Harley-Davidson which have changed their marketing and symbolic expressions radically over time in response to the shifting issues of importance to their customers. He presented the Budweiser campaign 'This Bud's For You' as an example of a company tying working class masculinity to the popularity of Reagan and Rambo in the early 1980s in the US, and how this approach lost its relevance at the end of the decade and was changed completely by the self-ironic Budweiser Frog Campaign. His argument is that management should pay much more attention to the macro-cultural context and the identity conflicts that are important to their key audiences instead of insisting on consistency and clarity in their organizational expressions.

## Critical voices of power and control

A third issue concerns the extent to which organizations are able to control organizational expression and whether they should. Many companies systematically track and then fine-tune their organizational expressions using marketing impact studies conducted by Millward Brown or other advertising agencies. By engaging in various marketing activities and tracking stakeholders' reactions, they are left with the impression that expressions can be controlled for intended consequences, but critical voices from both inside (employees) and outside (customers) these companies challenge this presumption of control by taking matters of organizational change into their own hands. For instance, consumers have forced McDonalds to adapt to local cultures and traditions making it now possible to buy a decent espresso at McDonalds in Milan, while other countries have demanded and received healthy options on local McDonalds' menus.

Consumer driven brand communities provide more evidence that organizational expressions are part of a wider conversation. This evidence can be found, for example, in consumer communities dedicated to Jeep, Mini and Saab automobiles or those comprised of devotees to Harley-Davidson or

Triumph motorcycles (Muniz and O'Guinn, 2001; Antorini and Andersen, 2005). Consumers who join such communities create their own experiences of products sometimes transforming the tangible product (e.g., by customizing the vehicle in their own way) as well as its associated meanings (e.g., by connecting the car with specific kinds of activities or experiences). One foreseeable consequence of this aspect of organizational expressiveness is that organizations will proactively involve internal and external stakeholders in acts of co-creation. This could lead to more democratic and dispersed ways of managing organizations, but could also be seen as new forms of co-optation, where the creativity of consumers are exploited by corporations.

According to another group of observers, organizational expressions are increasingly taking over both public and in some cases private domains of communication. Naomi Klein (2000) and others have argued that, as a form of corporate expression, brands invade our lives leaving little opportunity to avoid their manipulative and seductive power, even if we wanted to. This is, for example, the case of companies sponsoring everything from school materials to sporting events in the hope of making us associate their own corporate logo with our personal interests. Klein claims that within the last 10 years, many public organizations, NGOs and individuals have been turned into brands by being forced to develop and sometimes even leverage the marketing value of their expressions in order to survive. Consider how competition over resources and attention has pushed some NGOs to join forces with companies in cause related marketing and other kinds of corporate citizenship. As a result, NGOs like the Cancer Foundation and the Red Cross lend legitimacy and respect to companies while receiving money and – according to Klein – surrender to the global capitalism in return. Within critical culture studies other scholars have argued that organizational expressions themselves are dominated by consumerism, transforming what were once meaningful expressions originating in the organization's culture into empty speech cluttering the marketplace (Alvesson, 1990; Du Gay, 2000).

Acknowledging the limitations of control is not restricted to critics. For example, recent marketing studies have focused on how consumers embrace, change and customize products and services to fit their individual needs and values. One such example is the on-line bookstore Amazon. Based on your purchase history, this company can offer a unique set of books to you using a personal tone of voice. Other companies are seeking similarly involving means to create organizational expressions personalized to your interests and desires on their web-sites. For example BP's 'On the Street Campaign' invited consumers all over the world to post home-made video clips describing their opinion about the world's energy situation. Thus, the insistence upon full managerial control over organizational expressions that dominated the early days of corporate branding is being replaced by appreciation for more flexible and customized expressions. Critics may argue that corporate domination is receding from view, yet remains a powerful force under the surface, while optimists argue that never before have people had so many opportunities to reject brands and expressions that they do not like (e.g., Olins, 2001).

## New directions

There are several pertinent issues pertaining to the future management of organizational expressions. One set of issues relates to organization's ability to develop new forms of management that acknowledge the cross-functional nature of organizational expression. This implies that organizational expressions be 'led from the middle' in order to create connections between employees as they construct and deliver expressions to stakeholders who, in turn, interpret, transform and bounce back to organizational members impressions of what these expressions mean to them. The development of cross-functional management practices becomes even more complex as organizations expect managers to involve both internal and external stakeholders proactively in the co-creation of expressions. In this sense the management of organizational expressions will require the ability to listen to stakeholders as well as creativity in taking the multitude of their different meanings and perceptions.

Another set of issues relate to the question of authenticity. As organizations become ever more professional and evocative in the way they construct and communicate organizational expressions, it becomes increasingly important for both employees and customers to tell the difference between an authentic expression and those expressions that are fakes. At the most tangible level, this is, for example, found in the area of luxury goods, where companies such as Louis Vuitton, Prada and Bulgari are struggling to maintain their authenticity in the face of abundant fakery. In their struggle to fight back these organizations have added still more meaning and heritage to their products using a full range of organizational expressions to protect and nurture their authenticity. As part of this process of expanding their sources of authenticity organizations become aware of the historical development of their organizations and engage in a process of connecting past design language and historical markers with the creation of current expressions that reinterpret and twist their past heritage.

As organizations increasingly seek to customize their expressions and invite stakeholders to join in, it becomes increasingly more difficult to tell who is making the promises and who is responsible for the performance. This raises another issue with respect to authenticity. When Wal-Mart employees dressed in a company jacket with 'How can I help you?' emblazoned on the back, walk in the other direction when they see you approaching, are they denying corporate authenticity or expressing their own? What is an authentic expression of a customer-focused and service-oriented culture when employees are trained to deal with customers

in particular ways that may be a far cry from what they or their customers want from the organization? Thus, on the one hand we predict that stakeholders will be even more concerned with honesty and trust in the ways organizations express themselves, and on the other hand each stakeholder him/herself will increasingly take an active part in assuming responsibility for creating authentic expressions. We predict that this conundrum will make it much more difficult to claim the critical outsider position found in the work of Naomi Klein and others.

Taken together, we believe the future challenges posed by organizational expressions require a paradoxical approach to management. Managers will have to learn to become skilful and sophisticated in balancing the many simultaneous different pressures and trends that will be brought to bear on and through organizational expressiveness. On the one hand, new forms of stakeholder involvement will emerge and turn the organization into a facilitator for the co-creation of expressions with stakeholders rather than an independent producer. By the same token each stakeholder will seek to combine and individualize expressions to suit his or her personal identity. Organizations will have to construct expressions that are adaptable to local cultures, styles and tastes in order to engage stakeholders and create a sense of belonging. On the other hand, organizations must be recognized and perceived as distinctive by multiple stakeholders in a marketplace saturated with symbols. Organizational expressions will need to be somewhat coherent making it clear that they refer to the same organization in order to reap the benefits from their brand. In their search for ways to balance coherence and adaptation, managers will have to remain true to both past values expressed by the organization while creating relevance for the future. Managers will engage in new forms of practices that blend functions, competencies and mindsets in less predictable ways than in the past, while at the same time keeping a strong focus on the central ideas of the organizations' identity.

# REFERENCES

Aaker, D.A. (1996) *Building Strong Brands.* New York: The Free Press.

Albert, S. and Whetten, D.A. (1985) 'Organizational identity', in L.L. Cummings and B.M. Staw (eds) *Research in Organizational Behavior, vol. 7.* Greenwich, CT: JAI Press, pp. 263–295.

Alvesson, M. (1990) 'Organization: From substance to image', *Organization Studies*, 11: 373–394.

Antorini, Y.M. and Andersen, K. (2005) 'A communal approach to corporate branding', in M. Schultz, Y.M. Antorini and F. Csaba (eds) *Corporate Branding. Purpose/People/Process.* Copenhagen: Copenhagen Business School Press, pp. 79–103.

Ashforth, B.E. and Mael, F. (1989) 'Social identity theory and the organization', *Academy of Management Review*, 14: 20–39.

Balmer, J.M.T. and Greyser, S. (2003) *Revealing the Corporation.* London: Routledge.

Cheney, G. and Christensen, L.T. (2001) 'Organizational identity: Linkages between internal and external communication', in F.M. Jablin and L.L. Putnam (eds) *New Handbook of Organizational Communication.* London: Sage Publications, pp. 231–269.

Cohen, A. (1985) *The Symbolic Construction of Community.* London: Tavistock Publications.

Cornelissen, J. (2004) *Corporate Communication. Theory and Practice.* London: Sage Publications.

Du Gay, P. (2000) 'Markets and meanings. Re-imagining organizational life', in M. Schultz, M.J. Hatch and M.H. Larsen (eds) *The Expressive Organization – Linking Identity, Reputation, and the Corporate Brand.* Oxford: Oxford University Press, pp. 66–77.

Fombrun, C. and Van Riel, C. (2003) *Fame and Fortune: How Successful Companies Build Winning Reputation.* London: FT-Prentice Hall.

Gagliardi, P. (ed.) (1992) *Symbols and Artefacts: View of the Corporate Landscape.* Berlin: de Gruyter.

Gioia, D.A. (1986) 'Symbols, scripts, and sensemaking', in H.P. Sims (ed.) *The Thinking Organization.* San Francisco: Jossey-Bass, pp. 49–74.

Gioia, D.A. and Chittipeddi, K. (1991) 'Sensemaking and sensegiving in strategic change initiation', *Strategic Management Journal,* 12: 443–448.

Hatch, M.J. and Schultz, M. (2000) 'Scaling the tower of Babel: Relational differences between identity, image and culture in organizations', in M. Schultz, M.J. Hatch and M.H. Larsen (eds) *The Expressive Organization.* Oxford: Oxford University Press, pp. 11–36.

Hatch, M.J. and Schultz, M. (2001) 'Are the strategic stars aligned for your corporate brand?', *Harvard Business Review*, 78/2: 128–134.

Hatch, M.J. and Schultz, M. (2003) 'Bringing the corporation into corporate branding', *European Journal of Marketing*, 7/8: 1041–1064.

Holt, D.B. (2004) *How Brands Become Icons: The Principles of Cultural Branding.* Boston: Harvard Business School Press.

Klein, N. (2000) *No Logo.* London: HarperCollinsBusiness.

Kozinets, R.V. (2002) 'Can consumers escape the market? Emancipatory illuminations from burning man', *Journal of Consumer Research*, 29: 20–39.

Martin, J. (2002) *Organizational Culture: Mapping the Terrain.* Thousand Oaks, CA: Sage.

Meyer, J. and Rowan, B. (1977) 'Institutionalized organizations: Formal structure as myth and ceremony', *American Journal of Sociology*, 83/2: 340–363.

Muniz, A. and O'Guinn, T. (2001) 'Brand community', *Journal of Consumer Research,* 27: 412–432.

Olins, W. (1989) *Corporate Identity.* London: Thames & Hudson.

Olins, W. (2001) 'The case for brand', *Economist* September 8, viewpoint.

Olins, W. (2004) *On Brand.* London: Thames & Hudson.

Pondy, L., Frost, P., Morgan, G. and Dandridge, T. (eds) (1983) *Organizational Symbolism.* Greenwich/London: JAI Press.

Pratt, M.G. (2003) 'Disentangling collective identity', in J. Polzer, E. Mannix and M. Neale (eds) *Identity Issues in Groups: Research in Managing Groups and Teams.* Stamford, CT: Elsevier Science Ltd., pp. 161–188.

Ravasi, D. and Schultz, M. (2006) 'Responding to organizational identity threats: Exploring the role of organizational culture', *The Academy of Management Journal*, 49 (3): 433–458.

Schein, E.H. (2004) *Organizational Culture and Leadership* (3rd edn). San Francisco: Jossey-Bass.

Schmitt, B. and Simonsen, A. (1997) *Marketing Aesthetics – The Strategic Management of Brands, Identity, and Image.* New York: The Free Press.

Schultz, M. (2005) 'A cross-disciplinary perspective on corporate branding', in M. Schultz, Y.M. Antorini and F.C. Csaba (eds) *Corporate Branding Purpose/People/Process.* Copenhagen: Copenhagen Business School Press, pp. 23–57.

Schultz, M., Hatch, M.J. and Ciccolella, F. (2006) 'Brand life in symbols and artifacts: The LEGO company', in A. Rafaeli and M.G. Pratt (eds) *Artifacts and Organizations: Beyond Mere Symbolism.* New Jersey: Lawrence Erlbaum, pp. 141–160.

Schultz, M., Hatch, M.J. and Larsen, H. (eds) (2000) *The Expressive Organization: Linking Identity, Reputation and the Corporate Brand.* Oxford: Oxford University Press.

Scott, R.W. and Meyer, J. (1994) *Institutionalized Environments and Organizations: Structural Complexity and Individualism*. Thousands Oaks, CA: Sage Publications.

Whetten, D.A. (2006) 'Albert and Whetten revisited: Strengthening the concept of organizational identity', *Journal of Management Inquiry*, 15 (3): 219–234.

Whetten, D.A. and Mackey, A. (2002) 'A social actor conception of organizational identity and its implications for the study of organizational reputation', *Business and Society*, 41: 393–414.

# 23

# Management Fashion and Organizational Behaviour

René ten Bos and Stefan Heusinkveld

## ANTECEDENTS OF THE FIELD

The history of management fashion can be traced back to the nineteenth century. Of course, during these early stages of capitalism there were no managers, but there were entrepreneurs and workers. These people – who all struggled to survive in the unruly circumstances that were the result of early industrialization and capitalism – were addressed by an amazing array of writers who claimed to boost morale and spirits among those who were considered to be in need of it. These writers can be seen as the predecessors of those who produce what nowadays is routinely referred to as 'self-help literature'. Indeed, the very concept of 'self-help' has its origins in the nineteenth century. It was coined by the eminent Victorian author, journalist, and reformer Samuel Smiles (1812–1904) who published a book under the same title in 1859. Extolling bourgeois virtues such as diligence, humility, and obedience, Smiles produced an instant bestseller in the United Kingdom.

The most conspicuous figure addressed by self-help writers in America was 'the self-made man'. As authors such as Wyllie (1954) and Hofstadter (1962) have shown, this all-American concept of the self-made man was coined by Kentucky senator Henry Clay (1777–1852) during a speech in 1832:

> In Kentucky, almost every manufactory known to me is in the hands of enterprising and self-made men, who have acquired whatever wealth they process by patient and diligent labor (Clay, cited in: Hofstadter, 1962: 255).

Soon after these legendary words, the self-made man became not only a recognizable but indeed a 'spiritual dominant' figure in American life. Following Wyllie (1954), Hofstadter hastens to add that the word 'spiritual' is very apt here. The literature of self-help, after all, was not meant to be about the recommendation of business methods or business techniques. On the contrary, concepts such as 'self-help' and 'self-made man' can be seen as 'an outgrowth of Puritan preachings and the Protestant doctrine of the calling' (Hofstadter, 1962: 254). Wyllie (1954) points out that prominent self-help writers were often congregational clergymen. Central in this discourse was also the concept of 'character': personality was deemed to matter much more than talent or intelligence. A robust character not hindered too much by intelligence and wit was regarded as vital for the prosperity of entrepreneurs and workers under capitalistic circumstances. Indeed, insofar as the gurus of that time – from Clay and Smiles to people like Andrew Carnegie – were emphasizing the importance of academic education, they were clearly not in agreement with the prevailing spirit of the times. Business people have usually treated intellect with scorn (Veblen, 1918; Whyte, 1956). In a recent survey, Rimke has described self-help literature as follows:

> Self-help literature describes the self as a unified centre of personal agency which can act upon itself, other, and the world. This conception presents the individual as the sole ontological pivot of experience. Further, the self is conceived as possessing an inner reservoir of power that can be assessed (Rimke, 2001: 64).

In her review of the literature, Rimke takes issue with the contemporary dominance of psychology-based efforts to govern people while using notions such as 'self-help'. Writing about the nineteenth century, Wyllie and Hofstadter address the religious rather than psychological contexts that fostered concepts such as the 'self-made man'. This suggests that the overly religious undertones that were present in earlier texts about self-help were increasingly being replaced by an emphasis on self-reliance and self-pride. Whereas the distinction between service to God and service to the self broke down in the nineteenth century, something which has enabled the upsurge of a most 'curious cult of religious practicality' (Hoftstadter, 1962: 264), God virtually disappeared in the twentieth century. What was left was a variety of secularized forms of self-therapy. Titles such as Siimon Reynolds' *How to Become Happy in 8 Minutes* (1996) are perhaps the epitome of this

development. This bizarre best-selling book can be seen as the logical outcome of a process that Hofstadter has described in terms of a secularization of religion. Discussing Henry Link's best-selling *The Return to Religion* (1936), Hofstadter (1962: 269) infers that this book is, in spite of its title, 'in no sense a religious or devotional work'. Link was not a clergyman, but a business consultant and psychologist who carefully constructed his career by working for nearly all large business corporations in America. Link understands religion as 'an aggressive mode of life by which the individual becomes the master of his environment, not its complacent victim' (cited in: Hofstadter, 1962: 269). For the contemporary worker, God has become an aid rather than a judge and a redeemer. Indeed, God has become a consultant.

Hofstadter is not able to suppress his worries about the influence of people like Link:

> On the surface, this [apparent return to religion] may seem to indicate a turning away from the secular goals of the older self-help books, but it actually represents a turning away from their grasp of reality, for it embodies a blurring of the distinction between the realms of the world and the spirit. (…) The process represents, I believe, not a victory for religion but a fundamental, if largely unconscious, secularization of the American middle-class mind. Religion has been supplanted, not, to be sure, by a consciously secular philosophy, but by mental self-manipulation (Hofstadter, 1962: 266–267).

Perhaps, one might understand this otherworldly *Weltanschauung* as a result of the kind of spiritual transformation needed to make people fit to work in what meanwhile had become an inevitable phenomenon in the organizational landscape: the bureaucracy. From the early twentieth century onwards, we witness an entirely new kind of consulting discourse which not only focuses on the allegedly 'spiritual' dimension of work under capitalistic conditions but also on its more 'organizational' aspects (Galambos, 1970; Barley and Kunda, 1992; Kipping, 1999). A few decades before Link published his book about the alleged return to religion within organizations, Frederic Taylor (1911) introduced his idea about the principles of Scientific Management. At face value, these principles excluded any consideration for emotion, spirituality or religion. Taylor's message seemed to be 'a durned mean one' (Taylor, cited in: Liu, 2004: 90) in the sense that the worker under the circumstances he planned for was expected to suppress any emotion or belief whatsoever. Liu, however, is keen to point out that the real meanness of Taylor's message was that the modern workplace as he saw it should not be a place where meanness is a possibility: the essence of scientific management is that the goal becomes to create a system where the inevitable emotions – love, hate, mourn, belief – had no practical effect at all and were smoothed down by the system.

How does this relate to the discourse of self-help that already existed well before scientific management became accepted? Liu (2004: 96) surmises that Taylorism in fact became one of the first systems of 'emotional labor management'. In order to make it feasible that everyone would abide by the new system rules, an entirely new kind of worker was envisaged. No longer was it the dirty, stupid, and hostile worker, let alone the independent self-made man who worked in order to serve the lord, but a worker who could be seen as a friend of management. Liu points out that 'friendship' is an absolute crucial notion in the work of Frederic Taylor. It is not the self that takes centre stage in the Taylorist universe but rather the other who is no longer seen as a natural fiend or adversary. It is well known that Taylor imagined his system to be in total sympathy with the demands of the unions: any antagonism between the owners of capital and the workers was deemed to be illusory. Harmony rather than discord should be the rule (Shenhav, 1999). Friendship became a keyword to achieve this harmony, but friendship is clearly not to be taken as the rather insecure and personal emotion that it oftentimes is in the relationship between two or more people. Henry Ford was very clear about this:

I pity the poor fellow who is so soft and flabby that he must always have 'an atmosphere of good feeling' around him before he can do his work. Unless they obtain enough mental and moral hardiness to lift them out of their soft reliance on 'feeling' they are failures (Ford, cited in: Jardim, 1970: 120–121).

So, friendship was in fact being in harmony with the prevailing system (Liu, 2004: 98). All emotional excitement should be kept at bay. The ideal worker is friendly *and* impersonal, committed *and* cool, mature *and* uncritical. The result of these ideas – which were, needless to say, not only related to Taylor but also to people like Harrington (1913) and Leffingwell (1917) who wrote about efficiency and scientific office management – can best be summarized in one word: boredom. An overwhelmingly rigid orderliness began to held sway in the bureaucracies that became to dominate the corporate landscape. As one business historian explains:

At General Electric, AT&T, Procter & Gamble, and nearly every other large company, encyclopedic manuals dictated every aspect of workplace practice, from the layout of stamping machines to the format of quarterly reports to the placement of pencils on a secretary's desk (Kleiner, 1996: 10).

This orderliness was considered as a prerequisite for the emotional control that was required. The obsession with this kind of control became also a hallmark of later, perhaps somewhat more subtle efforts to reduce any conceivable antagonism or other kinds of emotional upheaval within the organization. Most notably, one might think here of Human Resource Management. In Liu's terms, HRM is about enforcing 'a norm of low affect through cultural means designed to secure not just the "harmonization" but the *identification* of the manager, professional, supervisor, and (as much as possible) the clerical workers with the technological/technical system' (Liu, 2004: 96). If Liu is right in his analysis, concepts such as Human Resource Management can be understood as a kind of Taylorism-in-disguise: no longer is the compliance of blue-collar workers the main goal but the compliance of higher-ups in the organization.

In the last decades, it was the concept of 'corporate culture' (Barley, Meyer and Gash, 1988) which played a crucial role in the process of engendering this compliance: it is based on the fantasy of a 'unitary system of friendship' which was to be designed in order to 'channel, mold, enhance, sustain, challenge and otherwise influence the feeling of organizational members – toward the organization itself, others in the organization, customers of the organization, and, crucially, themselves' (van Maanen and Kunda, 1989: 43; see also: Liu, 2004: 124). Corporate culture is perhaps the synthesis of emotion management and system management.

What we have suggested so far is that, long before talk about management fashion came fashionable itself, there were already two sets of strangely interrelated discourses popular in organization, consultancy, or even academia. One set focuses on the self-help of the working man and the other on his organizational adaptability. In the first set, a focus on religion is unmistakable: religion fosters the kind of robust characters that can help entire nations to prosper economically. In the second set, the focus is instead on organizational aspects as well as on the emotional posture of the workman. Unlike religion, emotion is regarded to be an ambivalent phenomenon: a threat that only with proper control and channelling might be transformed into an opportunity. In what follows, we will maintain that both these sets of discourses have become more and more interrelated into what we nowadays call management fashion. Notions such as self-help, spirituality, emotion, harmony, and many more are still prevalent in the work of consultants, gurus, and others who have the wish to appeal to contemporary managerial taste.

## CENTRAL APPROACHES

In this section, we will discuss some central contemporary views on management gurus and management fashion. First of all, we should point out that much of this literature did not resist the temptation to evaluate or condemn gurus and fashion in the name of what Toulmin once dubbed 'The Dream of High Science', that is, a conception of science which is general, timeless, abstract, objective, and axiomatic (Toulmin, 1996: 205). This 'rationalist criticism' of the production and consumption of management ideas is the first approach that can be distinguished in the literature on this issue. The second approach that might be distinguished is less rationally and more politically inspired in that its adherents argue that popular management ideas can have and often do have hideous consequences for people at work and should therefore be condemned. The 'humanistic-political approach', as we prefer to call it, shares a desire to debunk the managerial 'hypes' and 'fads' with the rational approach but, contrary to the latter, it does not resort to overly rationalist or scientific explanations to express its displeasure with fashion. It is only the third approach to be distinguished here that is prepared to abandon the strongly normative stance typical of the other two approaches. Its adherents accept that fashion in general is an unmistakable part of current developments in our society. According to its adherents, there are no reasons to dream about special areas such as management science or business administration where people are supposed to be blissfully immune to the sordid temptations of fashion. Indeed, the concepts introduced above – self-help, spirituality, emotion, or harmony – still beguile many people in and outside working organizations. Having arrived at this conclusion, the third approach studies the way the setters of fashion, most notably management gurus, express themselves. We will label this approach the 'explanatory approach' since it does not condemn management fashion as such, but from a variety of different perspectives seeks to provide explanations how and why these ideas have become so attractive.

### The rationalist approach

Management fashion has been defined as 'a relatively transitory collective belief, disseminated by management fashion setters, that a management technique leads to rational management progress' (Abrahamson, 1996a: 255; see also: Abrahamson, 1996b: 117). This definition is, we suggest, so provocative because it rather bluntly stipulates the adherence of management fashion setters and followers to managerial rationalism as if this were not a controversial issue. After all, many commentators on the subject have stressed the irrational or even anti-managerial aspects of what they can only see as dangerous fads and hypes (Donaldson, 1996; Hilmer and Donaldson, 1996; Micklethwait and Wooldridge, 1996; Ramsey, 1996; Du Gay, 2000; Hoopes, 2003; Sorge and van Witteloostuijn, 2004). Such irrationality, they go on to argue, exemplifies a lack of professionalism on behalf of managers and undermines a more accurate (read: academic or scientific) understanding of what is going on in our organizations. The recipes offered are seen as 'ineffective' and 'counter-productive' and therefore cannot but unavoidably produce failure in organizational praxis (Sorge and van Witteloostuijn, 2004). Micklethwait and Wooldridge, to mention just one example, claim that due to the fascination for fashion among both practitioners and scholars management thinking has become, 'more than any other branch of academia', infested with 'fear and greed' (1996: 11). To underscore this claim, they argue that in management thinking 'marketing is more interesting than the product' (1996: 346) and that the end result is 'enormous profits for the gurus but confusion for their clients' (1996: 68).

So, Abrahamson's claim that management fashion is generally committed to rational managerial goals does not necessarily imply that such goals are actually achieved. In an earlier article, Abrahamson (1991) has indeed suggested that the ideas of fashion setters may do more harm than good in organizations. This suggestion was by no means outrageous or exceptional. Fashionable organization concepts such as organizational development (OD), matrix management, T-groups, cultural management, core competencies, learning organizations, total quality

management, or business process redesign have always seduced academics to cast doubt on the validity or applicability of all these ideas (Anthony, 1977; Carroll, 1983; Mayer, 1983; McGill, 1988). Writers such as Hilmer and Donaldson (1996), Micklethwait and Wooldridge (1996) or, to mention one more example, Eccles, Nohria and Berkley (1992) can be seen as observers who have continued this tradition of rationally-motivated scepticism with respect to managerial fashion. They argue that fashionable management ideas have a poor empirical basis, are presented in an informal way, and do not meet scientific standards.

In a book called *American Business and the Quick Fix*, McGill has complained that fashionable management myths often consist of hopelessly simplistic solutions that undermine managers' understanding of the real complexities that pertain to their work. McGill argues that these myths have 'drawn managers away from the realities of modern management and fixed them in patterns of feeling and thought that are inappropriate to contemporary organizational life' (1988: 202). In McGill's view these management ideas are simply 'wrong'. Other rationalists (e.g., Hilmer and Donaldson, 1996; Micklethwait and Wooldridge, 1996; Hoopes, 2003; Sorge and van Witteloostuijn, 2004) have resorted to even more drastic language and argued that these ideas are 'dangerous', 'amoral', 'conceited', 'sick' or 'idiotic'. Instead of using these 'sick' management ideas Sorge and van Witteloostuijn (2004) argue for the application of 'healthy organization theories' to guide organizational change. The language used by the critics is sometimes so strong that one cannot help feeling that its users also think it applies equally well to the management practitioners who are willing to listen to and enact the 'nonsense' they hear.

## The humanistic-political approach

The humanistic-political approach questions fashionable concepts not because of their unclear relationship with the formal-rational goals of the organization but because of their alleged tendency both to privilege the interests of certain groups within and outside the organization (e.g., top managers, stockholders, consultants, or even cultural norms of American religious fundamentalists and nationalists [Grint, 1994; Grint and Case, 1998]) and to undermine the 'quality of life' of those who are subjected to the implementation of fashionable concept, for example, because it renders working conditions 'more stressful' (Knights and McCabe, 1998: 184). The accusation that guru-led management ideas endorse the hidden political agenda of managers (e.g., Barley and Kunda, 1992; Boje and Winsor, 1993; Knights and Murray, 1994; Willmott, 1994; Grint, 1995; Alvesson and Willmott, 1996; ten Bos, 1997) has even tempted some of the critics to suggest that totalitarian or 'Orwellian' motives pervade fashionable trends such as cultural management (Kunda, 1992; Willmott, 1993). Underlying these seemingly far-fetched suggestions is a deep concern about the emancipation of workers and employees.

Discussing the 'excellence' literature spawned by people like Peters and Waterman (1982), Alvesson and Willmott (1996: 98) argue that 'the individual employee is free to do what he or she wishes as long as this is what the boss wants the employee to wish'. Indeed, in many management fashions, only lip-service is paid to concepts like empowerment and diversity. What we mean by this is that these concepts are well entrenched outside the business literature, for example in feminism, black activism and grassroots practices. Nevertheless, these terms have been made palatable to managerial audiences, a process during which many shifts in the meaning of such concepts occurred. The practice of empowerment is not necessarily related to participation of all members of the organization as might be expected in a democracy, but to the participation of only those who are acknowledged as experts (ten Bos, 2000). Empowerment therefore fosters meritocracy rather than bureaucracy. Similar arguments can be made against the management of diversity. As Liu (2004: 57)

argues, diversity in the management mould is 'multicultural, because it is not cultural in any customary sense. It is constructed not so much out of men and women as from cultural-bare "atoms"'. These atoms – which are, part and parcel of the politics of low affect so customary in contemporary organization – can be easily programmed into post-cultural and quasi-empowered teams. In sum, where empowerment implies an erasure of democracy, diversity management implies an erasure of culture. These are the harsh consequences of what Alvesson and Willmott refer to as 'nascent technocratic totalitarianism' (1996: 99).

A similar point is made by the Canadian philosopher Mark Kingwell (1996: 313–317) when he, following Benjamin DeMott (1993), describes leadership fashion as a highly dangerous combination of fantasy, populism, technocracy, and cliquism that is bad for democracy and freedom since it disparages the ability of American citizens to cope with conflict and disagreement. Carter and Jackson (1998: 156–157) follow this line of thinking and argue that the messages of management gurus are only 'ostensibly democratic'. Gurus are pilgrims who use 'techno-media' to bring 'evangelical' messages about the betterment of production processes in organizations rather than about a better quality of the lives of those who work there (see for an example of the evangelic theatrics of the re-engineering gurus, Boje et al., 1997). In a similar way, theorists have developed critical work on more recent guruesque ideas about change management (Collins, 1998), organizational culture (Chan, 2000) and knowledge management (Styhre, 2003).

All these authors seem to agree that management ideas may help managers to replace open argument, debate and polyphony by socially manipulated consent (Clegg et al., 2006; Boje, 2008). It is, however, important to keep in mind that this kind of criticism to the guruesque ideas differs from the rationalist approach discussed above in that it concedes that some fashions at least seem to recognize employees as fully-fledged individuals with higher-order or even spiritual needs. In this sense the humanistic-political approach displays more awareness of the history of management thought than the rational approach discussed above. Although Alvesson and Willmott warn against 'ideologically polluted versions of emancipation' and argue that emancipation is *'not a gift to be bestowed upon employees but rather an existentially painful process'*, they suggest that some fashionable concepts, especially the ones they describe as 'humanistic management theory' (empowerment, teamwork, human relations, etc.), might receive a *'carefully qualified* welcome' (1996: 162; emphasis in original). Such qualified welcomes for management fashions can also be found in Parker (1998) or in Eccles, Nohria and Berkley (1992). Parker points out that he feels 'uneasy about attempts to manipulate the identity of organizational members' and yet has to admit that he feels attracted 'by the idea of working for an organization that I/we can believe in' (1998: 89–90). Eccles *et al.* go off on a somewhat different tack when they argue that although much in management fashion amounts to mere rhetoric, it is always the kind of rhetoric that is able 'to coax, inspire, demand, or otherwise produce action in organization' (1992: 26).

The refusal of the humanistic-political approach to downright condemn the management ideas is, we suggest, a strategic move that serves to encourage a more open discussion between academic and popular branches of management thinking. As Alvesson and Willmott (1996: 160) point out, '[o]ur concern is to encourage greater dialogue between the "mainstream" and "critical" wings of management [thinking]....' For instance, next to offering a fundamental critique of the current theorizing on knowledge management by stressing that it ignores: 'the ontological, epistemological and political qualities of knowledge' (Styhre, 2003: 8), Styhre's work intends at the same time to: 'further refine and improve the knowledge management literature' (2003: 11). This willingness to engage in a dialogue, however, should not lead academics to become infected or polluted by wrong-minded ideologies. It is this intellectual and moral purity that allows Alvesson and Willmott to warn their readers not to harbour 'any illusions about the philosophical and political differences that distinguish their respective positions' (ibid.). We may note here that it is not easy to see how this normative and suspicious remark might contribute to a more fruitful dialogue between different strands in management thinking. It can be seen as a token of the authors' pessimism about the very possibility of such a dialogue.

## The explanatory approach

Already quite a long time ago, Wren suggested that the ideas of well-known management gurus such as Herzberg, Argyris or McGregor should not be condemned because they are wrong or inadequate but that they deserve to be studied in relation to the local and historical context in which they did occur (Wren, 1973: 490; cited in: Huczynski, 1993: 116). This stream of research abandons the normative stance and, from a variety of different perspectives, seeks to provide explanations of how many fashionable ideas have attracted the managerial masses and are widely appreciated in the contemporary society (Sturdy, 2004). We can distinguish between (1) deterministic and (2) more voluntaristic views.

The more deterministic explanations focus on broader cultural, economic or scientific patterns in the environment of the organization: a successful company will attract imitators, ecological awareness in society at large may create an eco-hype in companies, or the very existence of management fashion depends on the strength of a nation's economy (Grint, 1997: 48). Such explanations often assume an environment which determines, at least to an important extent, what fashion producers and fashion consumers do. It might be argued that in this line of thinking it is the role of the 'knowledge entrepreneur' to miraculously capture the *Zeitgeist* of a particular period and to make its essentials available to the managerial masses (Grint, 1994: 193; Grint, 1997: 55). Elements such as individual choice and taste are generally ignored or downplayed. As a consequence, many analyses of why particular fashions come into being do not refer to a particular set of skills on behalf of the 'knowledge entrepreneur' but to a broader environment that is assumed to produce them. It is argued, for example, that the religious or nationalist character of a particular society (most notably, the Protestant-American society) is conducive to the fashion phenomenon (Grint, 1995, 1997; Jacques, 1996); it is also argued that our culture is a consumerist and entrepreneurial one which is beneficial to management fashion (Keat, 1990; Du Gay, 1996, 2000; Grint, 1997); others have pointed out that the 'knowledge entrepreneurs' echo developments in science (e.g., the rise of the genetic sciences will inevitably lead to management books on organizational DNA; see: Grint, 1997; Furusten, 1999); finally, some scholars deploy biological or ecological terms such as 'life-cycles', 'variation', or 'selection' in order to explain the popularity of fashions (Abrahamson and Fairchild, 1999; Carson *et al.*, 1999; Heusinkveld and Benders, 2001).

Barley and Kunda (1992) have captured this line of thinking by arguing that fashionable ideas are always a reflection of broader changes in our society. They even suggest, in line with Kondratieff, that there have been four or five 'long waves' of economical and technological development and that this is reflected in managerial ideologies and fashions of the corresponding period (1992: 391). More specifically, they argue that these ideologies are answers to the cultural contradictions inhering in a particular period and suggest that they are either rational (generally at the beginning of a period) or normative (at the end of it). Barley and Kunda have been criticized for maintaining an untenable fact-value dichotomy, and for their apparent determinist assumptions (Eastman and Bailey, 1998), but Grint (1997: 52) points out...

... that the message is actually not as deterministic as it sounds. It may be that what is required is for managers to understand the structural forces that impinge upon them and alter their methods and ideologies so that they are symmetrical with, and aligned to the current state of affairs. For example, if we assume that [Barley and Kunda's] model is accurate then we should soon start to see an increase in capital investment, technological advancement, and economic growth, along with a gradual switch from normative to rational ideologies.

Many explanatory approaches of fashion, however, do not focus on such structural patterns but stress the highly complicated interchange between the various actors who are held responsible for the constitution of what might be called the fashion system. It is argued that fashions are the product of a management knowledge industry that include 'knowledge entrepreneurs' such as, management consultants (Clark, 1995; Benders *et al.*, 1998), business schools, business media (Furusten, 1999), politicians and professional interest groups (editors, publishers, conference organizers, etc.) who play a crucial role in the production and transfer of management ideas to management practitioners (Kieser, 1997; ten Bos, 2000; Suddaby and Greenwood, 2001; Sahlin-Andersson and Engwall, 2002). Arguably, the role of the management guru has by far attracted the most attention.

It is believed that particularly the management gurus – academics, consultants or former business leaders (Huczynski, 1993: 40) – have a special talent that allows them to recognize and cater to the needs of managers (Jackson, 1996: 572). They can do this because they are 'virtuosos in symbolic management' (Jackall, 1988: 134) or 'master rhetoricians' (Jackson, 1996; see also: Kieser, 1997: 56; Jackson, 1999; Clark and Greatbatch, 2002b). Particularly their 'powerful preaching skills' allows them to create a receptive climate for new ideas among a management audience (Huczynski, 1993; Greatbatch and Clark, 2005). Others, however, downplay this virtuosity and argue that gurus simply use the same labels, metaphors, and platitudes as managers are allegedly inclined to do (Czarniawska-Joerges, 1990). Another telling example of guru language is provided by Gary Hamel in his book about a new panacea called 'business concept innovation'. In order to persuade his readers that it is utterly senseless to try to improve 'the efficiency of worn-out strategies', he provides the following 'argument':

> Dakota tribal wisdom says that when you discover you are on a dead horse, the best strategy is to dismount. Of course, there are other strategies. You can change riders. You can get a committee to study the dead horse. You can benchmark how other companies ride dead horses. You can declare that it is cheaper to feed a dead horse. You can harness several dead horses together. But after you've tried all these things, you're still going to have to dismount (Hamel, 2000: 54).

Whether one sees this passage as exemplifying symbolic virtuosity or not is, we suggest, a matter of *taste* (see for a more elaborate discussion of taste in management fashion, ten Bos and Heusinkveld, 2007). Here, it suffices to note that management gurus apparently have the ability to write in languages that resonate with the managerial tongue, but they are also able to utilize even more persuasive forms of communication. Greatbatch and Clark (2005) and Clark and Salaman (1996: 6), for example, argue that not only written language plays a key role, but also oral language and the way it is presented during so-called guru-performances or on videotapes. These performances, they point out, always carry 'a risk of total and public failure' (Clark and Salaman, 1996: 12) and therefore require enormous skills in risk management. As Huczynski (1993: 263) stated, there is not any magic formula for catching the mood of the management audience in the hope that the performance becomes a success.

However, as Stuart Crainer (1999: 178–179) points out with respect to one important guru, Tom Peters is not really a risk manager (although he admits to be nervous for performances) but an 'artist', a 'rock star' or a 'natural performer' who knows how to manipulate people's minds because he feels he has 'a common cause with people in his audiences', even though he is earning more dollars a day than most members of his

audience in a year. The point, of course made by the current literature, is that the guru has the gift of making his audience believe that there is such a common cause. Peters himself has suggested what unites him with his clients:

> All of life, be it giving a seminar, being a chief executive officer or reporting, is acting. If you are intent on convincing somebody of something, there is an element of showmanship. And showmanship has both seedy and legitimate connotations (Peters, cited in: Crainer, 1999: 180).

The central role of guru's public performances in the production and consumption of their ideas has not escaped notice among academics (e.g., Huczynski, 1993: 243–267; Grint, 1997: 39–40; Kieser, 1997: 65; Clark and Greatbatch, 2002a; Fincham, 2002; Collins, 2003). Clark and Salaman (1996) have even suggested that the guru's performance resembles that of a witchdoctor who knows only too well that the quality of his or her magic depends on the quality of the staging. Using metaphors developed by Mangham and Overington (1986), Jackson (1996: 585) has suggested that the guru is not only a performer but also 'a "playwright" to the organization that chooses to participate in his or her "play"'. Mangham (1990) has suggested that gurus can become successful performers because they have an audience of managers who are constantly performing themselves. Vaill has gone so far as to suggest his readers – presumably managers – to abandon what he calls the 'list-of-functions approach' and to embrace the metaphor of 'management as a performing art' because managerial action…

> … is a concrete process performed by a whole person in relation to a whole environment populated by other whole persons (that is, not other lists of functions). This whole process is embedded in time and is subject in the real time of its operation to all turbulence and change that surround it, that indeed suffuse it, because the turbulence and change are within action takers as much as they surround them. Simply to name the function to be performed as though it were the action ignores all of this richness of the actual action-taking process and, worst of all, ultimately masks the richness and leads to an

empty model of what the action taking *process* is (Vaill, 1989: 114–115).

Vaill argues that people in organizations are not simply function holders but whole persons whose behaviour can best be understood in terms of 'performing arts'. They use all sorts of tactics to enhance their images at work (Bolino, 1999: 82–83). Gurus perfectly relate to the performance quality of organizational life in the sense that they are seen by managers as experts in the creation of images and impressions.

## CRITICAL ISSUES AND FUTURE DIRECTIONS

We expect that overly normative approaches of management fashion will not dominate future research in the field. Management fashion has been, as we have shown, on the stage since the early days of capitalism and we expect its role will remain important in the near future. Management fashion is a complicated phenomenon that belies simple normative judging. It is not simply a for/against matter. We will end by listing a few critical issues that will also determine future research.

### The role of knowledge entrepreneurs

Much interest has been paid to the relationship between the producers of fashion and their clients. More specifically, the peculiar relationship between the consultant or guru on the one hand and managers, professionals, and other consumers of fashion has stirred and will continue to stir scholarly attention. The central question will be how 'knowledge entrepreneurs' interact with their consumers in the dissemination of management ideas (Sturdy, 1997; Fincham, 1999; Wright, 2002; Wright and Kitay, 2004). As Clark and Salaman (1998: 155) have noted, management gurus do not so much resolve the problems of their clients as construct, in close interaction with their audiences, a managerial

reality which is replete with meaning and expectations management practitioners are able to recognize. As a result, the production and consumption of guruesque ideas are not separate processes (Collins, 2003) but are engendered in an atmosphere in which both the producers – most notably the gurus among them – and consumers of fashionable management ideas are thriving. The guru-client relationship involves a constant interaction between the two parties in which clients should be seen as co-creators (Huczynski 1993: 258). For instance, one famous management guru, Eliyahu Goldratt, explained to his audience that they in fact 'sold' his 'Theory of Constraints' to themselves (Oliver 1990: 25, cited in Huczynski 1993).

Is this to say that consumers of management fashion engage in acts of self-deceit? Or is there something else going on? Clark and Greatbatch (2002b and 2004) have stressed the importance of studying the highly complicated 'backstage' interchange between the different actors in understanding the production of ideas. It is clear that gurus do not operate in isolation and enjoy the assistance of many other people, most notably, the editors of well-known publishers. However, it is pointed out that producing fashionable ideas is not a homogeneous and straightforward process. Specifically, knowledge entrepreneurs may deploy different forms of fashion development (Heusinkveld and Benders, 2002) and experience that developing new fashions does not necessarily fit with established practices and do not automatically enjoy the support within their agencies (Heusinkveld and Benders, 2005). Other recent studies showed how the knowledge entrepreneurs' service offerings are subject to notable changes as well. For instance Giroux (2006) showed how some quality gurus adapted their views in the process. And David and Strang (2006) demonstrated how consultancies went into the market for TQM when this concept was becoming fashionable in the early 1980s. General consultancies entered the initially specialist TQM-market when the TQM-business was on the rise. After the boom, they withdrew from the market on a large scale, thereby leaving TQM once again to the specialists.

## The social-cultural context of fashion

As we have argued elsewhere, management fashion also needs to be studied as part of a social-cultural context (ten Bos and Heusinkveld, 2007). More specifically, in late-capitalistic society we witness a situation in which traditionally respected distinctions between private and public, fact and value, or objectivity and subjectivity are no longer taken for granted. This also entails that science no longer is a stronghold of indisputable truths. The idea that organizations can be managed on the basis of sound scientific or rational principles has become more and more exceptional. There are always many more – ethical, religious, new age – principles that inspire people in organizations and people do not feel ashamed for that. Wolfe (2000: 69, 73) suggests that we live in a period where shame for one's convictions has disappeared because room is given to 'all possible interpretations'. What Wolfe is up to here is that knowledge is no longer a prerogative of the academic, but everybody is allowed to have a say (see also Liu, 2004).

It is in this domain, we suggest, that, for example, the management guru feels at home. He or she has understood that one of the consequences of the pluralism Wolfe has in mind is that 'tastemaking' through presentation and performance has become central. Perhaps it might be added that this is why gurus are on equal footing with radio and television evangelists who are also excellent and successful tastemakers. Should we follow rationalists such as Sorge and van Witteloostuijn (2004) in bemoaning this pluralist state of affairs? Well, if we choose to do so, we run the risk of 'selective perception': we only hear and see what we want to hear and see (Rollin, 1994: 15). We will fail to understand, for example, that the current development of our society is so that it is highly unlikely that societal and organizational changes are not influenced by aesthetic, religious, or otherwise

non-objective judgements. The fact that these judgements are notoriously difficult to pin down in scientific terms (Lieberson, 2000) does not warrant their methodological denial.

## The consumption of fashion

The focus of much research into management fashion continues to be on the creation and promotion on it. The 'consumption' of management fashion is still a poorly understood element in the current research, beyond an assumption that organizations have adopted the popular rhetoric (Clark, 2004; Benders *et al.*, 2007). The fashionability of many ideas are at odds with managers' mindfulness, and suggest that these are never adopted for their intrinsic potential of improving organizational affairs, yet only because of impulsive and ill-considered actions. Recently, the study of Staw and Epstein (2000) indicated that the adoption of fashion does not necessarily lead to enhanced performance but contributes to a favourable reputation (see also Beck and Walgenbach, 2005). As a result, the image of gullible imitators prevails over active practitioners with critical and self-reflexive attitudes (Watson, 1994; Benders and van Veen, 2001).

What do we know about the actual impact of management fashion on organizational praxis and management practitioners? Increasingly, fashion theorists focus on the highly complicated interplay between a fashion's discourse and the practices that are associated with this discourse (Zbaracki, 1998; Cole, 1999; Kelemen, 2000; Benders and Verlaar, 2003; Sturdy and Fleming, 2003; Fincham and Roslender, 2004). Moreover, a fashion's ambiguity is considered a vital aspect to become widely accepted among a large group of different organizations (Kelemen, 2000; Benders and van Veen, 2001). This 'interpretative viability' makes a concept easily applicable in different situations and allows for the possibility to be interpreted in different ways. While a concept may reduce the variety of available solutions, it cannot determine *a priori* how practices are shaped in organizations during an implementation phase (DeCock and Hipkin, 1997; Kelemen, 2000). In addition, Boiral (2003) even showed that contrasting attitudes of organizational members are the normal response to fashions within management praxis (see also Noon *et al.*, 2000).

## The question of ethics

Many management fashions have an ethical import and this will in the near future become a more and more important area of research in two respects. In the first place, scholars will develop an interest in the ethical or moral impact of particular fashions. For example, what are the consequences of personnel appraisals or audits in organizations? Is delayering or re-engineering morally acceptable? In the second place, we witness the fashionability of ethics itself. Business ethics, sustainability, trust, or social corporate responsibility can all be seen as management hypes (Jones, Parker and ten Bos, 2006) even though their advocates would empathically deny this. Critical and philosophical analyses of these 'moral' hypes are still relatively scarce but will proliferate in the near future.

## The world of 'cool'

The study of management fashion will not be confined to organizational scholars. Indeed, in this chapter we have also used resources from the area of literary theory (e.g., Liu, 2004), cultural theory (e.g., Frank, 1997), and history (Hofstadter, 1962). A truly multi-disciplinary perspective will yield new insights in a highly complicated field. Frank (1997) and Liu (2004), for example, have described management fashion in terms of 'hip', 'cool', and 'hot'. One of the things that drive the producers of fashion is to make clear that organizations do not necessarily need to be the dull and ashen places of orderliness that the gurus of scientific management had in mind when they were dreaming about the possibilities to calm down emotion and effect. Frank (1997: 86) writes about a 'new capitalism' that is hip, sexy, satirist, scoffing, and so forth, but in his study he clearly focuses

on the world of advertisement. Advertisement business all over the world has long ago conquered the world of 'cool'. There is no reason, however, not to apply the concept of 'cool' to organizational fashion. When managers dream of flow, creativity, innovation, knowledge-intensive work, cultural management, and so on, they clearly fancy something 'cool'. What does this indicate? In our view, it indicates that over the years management work has constantly changed its ethos, its character, its style, its feeling, and its politics. There is no doubt that this ever-changing field will remain a topic of interest for many organizational and not so organizational scholars.

## REFERENCES

Abrahamson, E. (1991) 'Management fads and fashion: The diffusion and rejection of innovations', *Academy of Management Review*, 16 (3): 586–612.

Abrahamson, E. (1996a) 'Management fashion', *Academy of Management Review*, 21 (1): 254–285.

Abrahamson, E. (1996b) 'Technical and aesthetic fashion', in B. Czarniawska and G. Sevon (eds) *Translating Organizational Change*. Berlin: De Gruyter, pp. 117–137.

Abrahamson, E. and Fairchild, G. (1999) 'Management fashion: Lifecycles, triggers and collective learning processes', *Administrative Science Quarterly*, 44 (4): 708–740.

Alvesson, M. and Willmott, H. (1996) *Making Sense of Management: A Critical Introduction*. London: Sage.

Anthony, P. (1977) *The Ideology of Work*. London: Tavistock.

Barley, S. and Kunda, G. (1992) 'Design and devotion: Surges of rational and normative ideologies of control in managerial discourse', *Administrative Science Quarterly*, 37 (3): 363–399.

Barley, S., Meyer, G. and Gash, D. (1988) 'Cultures of culture: Academics, practitioners and the pragmatics of normative control', *Administrative Science Quarterly*, 33 (1): 24–60.

Beck, N. and Walgenbach, P. (2005) 'Technical efficiency or adaptation to institutionalized expectations? The adoption of ISO 9000 standards in the German mechanical engineering industry', *Organization Studies*, 26 (6): 841–866.

Benders, J. and van Veen, K. (2001) 'What's in a fashion? Interpretative viability and management fashion', *Organization*, 8 (1): 33–53.

Benders, J. and Verlaar, S. (2003) 'Lifting parts: Putting conceptual insights into practice', *International Journal of Operations and Production Management*, 23 (7): 757–774.

Benders, J., Nijholt, J. and Heusinkveld, S. (2007) 'Using print media indicators in researching organization concepts', *Quality and Quantity*, 41 (6): 815–829.

Benders, J., van den Berg, R.-J. and van Bijsterveld, M. (1998) 'Hitch-hiking on a hype: Dutch consultants engineering re-engineering', *Journal of Organizational Change Management*, 11 (3): 201–215.

Boiral, O. (2003) 'ISO 9000: Outside the iron cage', *Organization Science*, 14 (6): 720–737.

Boje, D. (2008) *Storytelling Organizations*. London: Sage.

Boje, D. and Winsor, R. (1993) 'The resurrection of Taylorism: Total quality management's hidden agenda', *Journal of Organizational Change Management*, 6 (4): 57–70.

Boje, D., Rosile, G., Dennehy, R. and Summers, D. (1997) 'Restorying reengineering: Some deconstructions and postmodern alternatives', *Communication Research*, 24(6): 631–668.

Bolino, M. (1999) 'Citizenship and impression management: Good soldiers or good actors?' *Academy of Management Review*, 24 (1): 82–99.

Carroll, D. (1983) 'A disappointing search for excellence', *Harvard Business Review*, 61 (6): 78–88.

Carson, P., Lanier, P., Carson, K. and Guidry, B. (1999) 'Clearing a path through the management fashion jungle: Some preliminary trailblazing', *Academy of Management Journal*, 43 (6): 1143–1158.

Carter, P. and Jackson, N. (1998) 'Management gurus: What are we to make of them?', in J. Hassard and R. Holliday (eds) *Organization/Representation: Work and Organization in Popular Culture*. London: Sage, pp. 154–172.

Chan, A. (2000) *Critically Constituting Organization*. Amsterdam/Philadelphia: John Benjamins.

Clark, T. (1995) *Managing Consultants*. Buckingham: Open University Press.

Clark, T. (2004) 'The fashion of management fashion: A surge too far?', *Organization*, 11 (2): 297–306.

Clark, T. and Greatbatch, D. (2002a) 'Collaborative relationships in the creation and fashioning of management ideas: Gurus, editors and managers', in M. Kipping and L. Engwall (eds) *Management Consulting*. Oxford: Oxford University Press, pp. 129–145.

Clark, T. and Greatbatch, D. (2002b) 'Knowledge legitimation and audience affiliation through storytelling: The example of management gurus', in T. Clark and R. Fincham (eds) *Critical Consulting: New Perspectives on the Management Advice Industry*, Oxford: Blackwell Publishers, pp. 152–171.

Clark, T. and Greatbatch, D. (2004) 'Management fashion as image spectacle: The production of best-selling management books', *Management Communications Quarterly*, 17 (3), 396–424.

Clark, T. and Salaman, G. (1996) 'The management guru as organizational witch doctor', *Organization*, 3 (1): 85–108.

Clark, T. and Salaman, G. (1998) 'Telling tales: Management gurus' narratives and the construction of managerial identity', *Journal of Management Studies*, 35 (2): 127–161.

Clegg, S., Kornberger, M., Carter, C. and Rhodes, C. (2006) 'For management?', *Management Learning*, 37 (1): 7–27.

Cole, R. (1999) *Managing Quality Fads: How American Business Learned to Play the Quality Game*. New York: Oxford University Press.

Collins, D. (1998) *Organizational Charge: Sociological Perspectives*. London: Routledge.

Collins, D. (2003) 'The branding of management knowledge: Rethinking management fads', *Journal of Organizational Change Management*, 16 (2): 186–204.

Crainer, S. (1999) *The Tom Peters Phenomenon. Corporate Man to Corporate Skunk*. Oxford: Capstone.

Czarniawska-Joerges, B. (1990) 'Merchants of meaning: Managing consulting in the Swedish public sector', in B. Turner (ed.) *Organizational Symbolism*. New York: De Gruyter, pp. 139–150.

David, R. and Strang, D. (2006) 'When fashion is fleeting: Transitory collective beliefs and the dynamics of TQM consulting', *Academy of Management Journal*, 49 (2): 215–233.

DeCock, C. and Hipkin, I. (1997) 'TQM and BPR: Beyond the beyond myth', *Journal of Management Studies*, 34 (5): 659–675.

DeMott, B. (1993) 'Choice academic pork: Inside the leadership studies racket', *Harper's*, 12: 61–77.

Donaldson, L. (1996) *For Positivist Organization Theory: Proving the Hard Core*. London: Sage.

Du Gay, P. (1996) *Consumption and Identity at Work*. London: Sage.

Du Gay, P. (2000) *In Defense of Bureaucracy*. London: Sage.

Eastman, W. and Bailey, J. (1998) 'Mediating the fact-value antinomy: Patterns in managerial and legal rhetoric, 1890–1990', *Organization Science*, 9 (2): 232–245.

Eccles, R., Nohria, N. and Berkley, J. (1992) *Beyond the Hype: Rediscovering the Essence of Management*. Boston: Harvard Business School Press.

Fincham, R. (1999) 'The consultant-client relationship: Critical perspectives on the management of organizational change', *Journal of Management Studies*, 36 (3): 335–351.

Fincham, R. (2002) 'Charisma versus technique: Differentiating the expertise of management gurus and management consultants', in T. Clark and R. Fincham (eds) *Critical Consulting: New Perspectives on the Management Advice Industry*. Oxford: Blackwell Publishers, pp. 191–205.

Fincham, R. and Roslender, R. (2004) 'Rethinking the dissemination of management fashion: Accounting for intellectual capital in UK case firms', *Management Learning*, 35 (3): 321–336.

Frank, T. (1997) *The Conquest of Cool: Business Culture, Counterculture, and the Rise of Hip Consumerism*. Chicago: University of Chicago Press.

Furusten, S. (1999) *Popular Management Books. How They are Made and What They Mean for Organizations*. London: Routledge.

Galambos, L. (1970) 'The emerging organizational synthesis in modern American history', *The Business History Review*, 44 (3): 279–290.

Giroux, H. (2006) 'It was such a handy term; Management fashions and pragmatic ambiguity', *Journal of Management Studies*, 43 (6): 1227–1260.

Greatbatch, D. and Clark, T. (2005) *Management Speak: Why We Listen to What Management Gurus Tell Us*. London: Routledge.

Grint, K. (1994) 'Reengineering history: Social resonances and business process reengineering', *Organization*, 1(1): 179–202.

Grint, K. (1995) *Management: A Sociological Introduction*. Oxford: Polity.

Grint, K. (1997) *Fuzzy Management. Contemporary Ideas and Practices and Work*. London: Blackwell.

Grint, K. and Case, P. (1998) 'The violent rhetoric of re-engineering: Management consultancy on the offensive', *Journal of Management Studies*, 35 (5): 557–577.

Hamel, G. (2000) *Leading the Revolution*. Boston, MA: Harvard Business School Press.

Harrington, E. (1993/1913) *The Twelve Principles of Management*. London: Routledge/Thoemmes.

Heusinkveld, S. and Benders, J. (2001) 'Surges and sediments; Shaping the reception of reengineering', *Information & Management*, 38 (4): 241–253.

Heusinkveld, S. and Benders, J. (2002) 'Between professional dedication and corporate design: Exploring forms of new concept development in consultancies', *International Studies of Management and Organization*, 32 (4): 104–122.

Heusinkveld, S. and Benders, J. (2005) 'Contested commodification: Consultancies and their struggle with new concept development', *Human Relations*, 58 (3): 283–310.

Hilmer, F. and Donaldson, L. (1996) *Management Redeemed: Rebuking the Fads that Undermine Our Corporations*. New York: The Free Press.

Hofstadter, R. (1962) *Anti-intellectualism in American Life*. New York: Vintage.

Hoopes, J. (2003) *False Prophets: The Gurus Who Created Modern Management and Why their Ideas are Bad for Business Today*. Cambridge, MA: Perseus Publishing.

Huczynski, A. (1993) *Management Gurus: What Makes Them and How to Become One*. London: Thomson Business Press.

Jackall, R. (1988) *Moral Mazes. The World of Corporate Managers*. New York: Oxford University Press.

Jackson, B. (1996) 'Re-engineering the sense of self: The manager and the manager guru', *Journal of Management Studies*, 33 (5): 371–390.

Jackson, B. (1999) 'The goose that laid the golden egg? A rhetorical critique of Stephen Covey and the effectiveness movement', *Journal of Management Studies*, 36 (3): 353–377.

Jacques, R. (1996) *Manufacturing the Employee. Management Knowledge from the 19th to the 21st Century*. London: Sage.

Jardim, A. (1970) *The First Henry Ford: A Study in Personality and Business Leadership*. Cambridge, MA: MIT Press.

Jones, C., Parker, M. and ten Bos, R. (2006) *For Business Ethics*. London: Routledge.

Kelemen, M. (2000) 'Too much or too little ambiguity: The language of total quality management', *Journal of Management Studies*, 37 (4): 483–498.

Kieser, A. (1997) 'Rhetoric and myth in management fashion', *Organization*, 4 (1): 49–74.

Kingwell, M. (1996) *Dreams of Millennium. Report from a Culture on the Brink*. New York: Viking.

Kipping, M. (1999) 'American management consulting companies in western Europe, 1920 to 1990: Products, reputations, and relationships', *The Business History Review*, 73 (2): 190–220.

Kleiner, A. (1996) *The Age of Heretics: Heroes, Outlaws, and the Forerunners of Corporate Change*. London: Nicholas Brealey.

Knights, D. and McCabe, D. (1998) 'What happens when the phone goes wild? Staff, stress and spaces for escape in a BPR telephone banking work regime', *Journal of Management Studies*, 35 (2): 163–194.

Knights, D. and Murray, F. (1994) *Managers Divided: Organizational Politics and Information Management Technology*. Chichester: Wiley.

Kunda, G. (1992) *Engineering Culture: Control and Commitment in a High-tech Corporation*. Philadelphia: Temple University Press.

Leffingwell, W. (1917) *Scientific Office Management*. Chicago: Shaw.

Lieberson, S. (2000) *A Matter of Taste: How Names, Fashion, and Culture Change*. Yale: Yale University Press.

Link, H. (1936) *The Return to Religion*. New York: MacMillan.

Liu, A. (2004) *The Laws of Cool: Knowledge Work and the Culture of Information*. Chicago: University of Chicago Press.

Mangham, I. (1990) 'Managing as a performing art', *British Journal of Management*, 1 (2): 105–115.

Mangham, I. and Overington, M. (1986) *Organizations as Theatre*. Chichester: Wiley.

Mayer, R. (1983) 'Don't be hoodwinked by the panacean conspiracy', *Management Review*, June: 23–25.

McGill, M. (1988) *American Business and the Quick Fix*. New York: Henry Holt.

Micklethwait, J. and Wooldridge, A. (1996) *The Witch Doctors: What the Management Gurus Are Saying, Why It Matters and How to Make Sense of It*. London: Heinemann.

Noon, M., Jenkins, S. and Martínez Lucio, M. (2000) 'Fads, techniques and control: Competing agendas of TPM and Tecex at the Royal Mail', *Journal of Management Studies*, 37 (4): 499–520.

Parker, M. (1998) 'Organization, community, and utopia', *Studies in Cultures, Organizations, and Societies*, 4: 71–91.

Peters, T. and Waterman, R. (1982) *In Search of Excellence: Lessons from America's Best-run Companies*. New York: Harper and Row.

Ramsey, H. (1996) 'Managing sceptically: A critique of organizational fashion', in S. Clegg and G. Palmer (eds) *The Politics of Management Knowledge*. London: Sage, pp. 155–172.

Reynolds, S. (1996) *How to Become Happy in 8 Minutes*. New York: Plume.

Rimke, H.M. (2001) 'Governing citizens through self-help literature', *Cultural Studies*, 14 (1): 61–78.

Rollin, R. (1994) 'Popular culture and the death of "good taste" ', *National Forum*, 74 (4): 13–17.

Sahlin-Andersson, K. and Engwall, L. (2002) *The Expansion of Management Knowledge: Carriers, Flows and Sources*. Stanford: Stanford University Press.

Shenhav, Y. (1999) *Manufacturing Rationality: The Engineering Foundations of the Managerial Revolution*. Oxford: Oxford University Press.

Smiles, S. (1859) *Self-help*. London: Murray (also available at: http://www.gutenberg.org/etext/935).

Sorge, A. and van Witteloostuijn, A. (2004) 'The (non)sense of organizational change: An essay about universal management hypes, sick consultancy metaphors, and healthy organization theories', *Organization Studies*, 25 (8): 1205–1231.

Staw, B. and Epstein, L. (2000) 'What bandwagon may bring: Effects of popular Management techniques on corporate performance, reputation and CEO pay', *Administrative Science Quarterly*, 45 (3): 523–556.

Sturdy, A. (1997) 'The consultancy process – An insecure business?', *Journal of Management Studies*, 34 (3): 389–413.

Sturdy, A. (2004) 'The adoption of management ideas and practices: Theoretical perspectives and possibilities', *Management Learning*, 35 (2): 155–179.

Sturdy, A. and Fleming, P. (2003) 'Talk as technique: A critique of the words and deeds distinction in the diffusion of customer service cultures in call centers', *Journal of Management Studies*, 40 (4): 753–773.

Styhre, A. (2003) *Understanding Knowledge Management: Critical and Postmodern Perspectives*. Malmo: Liber.

Suddaby, R. and Greenwood, R. (2001) 'Colonizing knowledge: Commodification as a dynamic of jurisdictional expansion in professional service firms', *Human Relations*, 54 (7): 933–953.

Taylor, F. (1911) *The Principles of Scientific Management*. New York: Harper & Brothers.

ten Bos, R. (1997) 'Business process redesign: The wheel of Ixion', *Employee Relations*, 19 (3): 248–264.

ten Bos, R. (2000) *Fashion and Utopia in Management Thinking*. Amsterdam: John Benjamins.

ten Bos, R. and Heusinkveld, S. (2007) 'The guru's gusto: Management fashion, performance and taste', *Journal of Organizational Change Management*, 20 (3): 304–325.

Toulmin, S. (1996) 'Concluding methodological reflections. Élitism and democracy among the sciences', in S. Toulmin and B. Gustavson (eds) *Beyond Theory. Changing Organizations through Participation*. Amsterdam: John Benjamins, pp. 203–225.

Vaill, P. (1989) *Managing as a Performing Art. New Ideas for a World of Chaotic Change*. San Francisco, CA: Jossey-Bass.

van Maanen, J. and Kunda, G. (1989) 'Real feelings: Emotional expression and organizational culture', *Research in Organizational Behaviour*, 11: 43–103.

Veblen, T. (1918) *The Higher Learning in America. A Memorandum on the Conduct of Universities*. New York: Huebsch. Also available at: http://socserv2.mcmaster.ca/%7Eecon/ugcm/3ll3/veblen/higher.

Watson, T. (1994) 'Management flavours of the month: Their role in managers' lives', *International Journal of Human Resource Management*, 5 (4): 892–909.

Whyte, W. (1956) *The Organization Man*. New York: Penguin.

Willmott, H. (1993) 'Strength is ignorance; Slavery is freedom: Managing culture in modern organizations', *Journal of Management Studies*, 30 (4): 515–552.

Willmott, H. (1994) 'Business process re-engineering and human resource management', *Personnel Review*, 23 (3): 34–46.

Wolfe, A. (2000) 'The opening of the evangelical mind', *The Atlantic Monthly*, 286 (4): 55–76.

Wren, D. (1973) *The Evolution of Management Thought*. New York: Wiley.

Wright, C. (2002) 'Promoting demand, gaining legitimacy and broadening expertise: The evolution of consultancy-client relationships in Australia', in M. Kipping and L. Engwall (eds) *Management Consulting: Emergence and Dynamics of a Knowledge Industry*. Oxford: Oxford University Press, pp. 184–202.

Wright, C. and Kitay, J. (2004) 'Spreading the word: Gurus, consultants and the diffusion of the employee relations paradigm in Australia', *Management Learning*, 35 (3): 271–286.

Wyllie, I. (1954) *The Self-made Man in America*. New Brunswick, NJ: Rutgers.

Zbaracki, M. (1998) 'The rhetoric and reality of total quality management', *Administrative Science Quarterly*, 43 (3): 602–636.

# PART FOUR

# Organizing on a Macro Scale

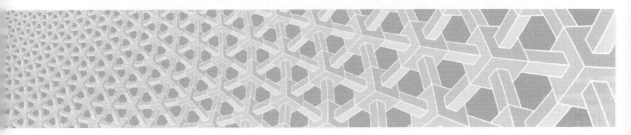

# 24

# Organizational Change Management

David C. Wilson

## ANTECEDENTS OF THE FIELD

The topic of change has been centre stage in organization theory for many years. It continues to be a central theme, exercising the minds of scholars in many disciplines as well as practitioners to try and explain both the how and the why of organizational change. To try and seek an original theory of change as a starting point for the multiple perspectives we currently embrace is something of a false trail. Each theory of change we now draw upon (see following section) is inextricably embedded in its own assumptions, constructs and contexts. Ever since humans have organized themselves into even rudimentary social groups, there have arisen concerns and debates over how to carry out tasks more effectively and efficiently. For example, early hunters experimented with different ways of trapping animals for food and tribes changed their migration patterns as new terrain, food and water supplies were discovered or heard about. Even these seemingly 'obvious' changes would have been, at the time, considered major organizational changes for the tribe as new or different ways of doing things (and thinking about the world) were suggested or were assimilated into the social group. Changing hunting grounds would likely have been considered to be what we call today a 'strategic change' (Wilson, 1999); that is, a big change, organization-wide in its consequences and ramifications, with associated high levels of risk if things went wrong. The varying range of levels and extent of change is summarized in Table 24.1.

What if the new hunting grounds are not plentiful? This would have been a stereotypically high stakes (revolutionary transition) decision (get it wrong and the tribe will die). One can imagine the debates amongst the group's decision makers which might have preceded any such decision to change (or not). Alongside those suggesting the move, there would have been those arguing to keep to the old hunting grounds. Despite reduced numbers of animals, they might argue, there are still some to hunt, and a new hunting ground has no hard evidence that it will be as plentiful as the protagonists argue. Why should we change?

**Table 24.1 Levels and degrees of operational and strategic change**

| Degree of change | Level of change | Characteristics |
|---|---|---|
| Status quo | Can be both operational and strategic | No change in current practices. A decision *not* to do something can be strategic as well as operational |
| Expanded reproduction | Mainly operational | Change involves producing 'more of the same' (for example, goods and services) |
| Evolutionary transition | Mainly strategic | Sometimes radical changes occur but they do so within the existing parameters of the organization (for example, existing structures or technologies are retained) |
| Revolutionary transition | Predominantly strategic | Change involves shifting or redefining existing parameters. Structures, processes and/or technologies likely to change |

*Source*: Wilson, 1999: 20.

To analyse and make sense of these discussions and what eventually happened (new hunting grounds or not) we would have to examine not only the context of the tribe (where it was situated and when, how long it had been together) but also the social features of the group (the rituals, symbols and values the tribe sustains) and its constituent members (language, identity, interpretation) before we could untangle the complexities of simply describing the change and what happened. To analyse such changes, rather than describe them, brings additional complexities. As Wensley (2003) argues, such an analysis requires, at least, both intention and anticipation to be fully explored. Organizations and individuals exhibit dual aspects of *intention* – the purpose or the goal of an action and *anticipation* – the action of looking forward to something however ill-defined. A profit-making organization, for example, may state in its strategic reports that it *intends* to increase market share by five per cent in one year. A public service organization may have a statement about making the world a better place or *anticipating* a future where (for example) education is somehow 'better' and more accessible to individuals. As Das (1986) notes, subjective futures (individual imaginings of the future) can only show how we might think about or project futures, but these may have little to do with the happenings of the future which do occur or emerge. We will revisit this issue of temporality in later sections of the chapter. For

the time being, the point is that the temporal projection of futures which exist in the minds of individuals (or the collective minds of groups) may have very little congruence with what actually happens in some future state. Thus intention and anticipation are interwoven amongst subjective projections and what might be described as more objective events (e.g., the tribe does move to a new hunting ground, but to a different one to that originally proposed and is one which does not correspond to the future desired state descriptions of those who wanted to move). How do we make sense of that?

Answering such a question is difficult because the antecedents to change are to be found in a wide range of (arguably incommensurable) disciplines ranging from philosophy and the understanding of human nature, through psychology and the analysis of motives, personality and the like, to the socio-cultural aspects of organizing and organization. Economists also provide their own rationales for change. These range from those generated within *microeconomics* which examines markets and the behaviours of organizations and individuals; those that arise in *macroeconomics*, which examines national income and growth and theories of *international economics*, which examines international trade based upon the exchange of goods and services by people in different national economies. Each approach has a distinctive account of drivers for, and explanations of, change. For example, microeconomists argue that individuals will seek to maximize utility out of various situations. They will assess what they gain and lose from a situation or a change, and make a rational choice to embrace the option or the outcome which most closely maximizes individual gain, elevating self interest to a priority. Macroeconomists and international economists argue that the drivers of change can be found in the economic and competitive infrastructure of national economies (see Porter, 1986, 1998) where the exploitation of inequalities such as the costs of production or raw materials provide a stimulus for organizational changes. In this way, economists provide an explanation for the apparent paradox that some countries will import goods that, domestically, they are demonstrably capable of producing for themselves (e.g., textiles, coal). The drivers of change thus become resources, cost minimization and profit maximization. Porter's concept of 'clusters', or groups of interconnected firms, suppliers, related industries, and institutions that arise in particular locations, became a strong argument for companies and governments to think about economies, to assess the competitive advantage of locations and, as a result, often instigate changes in private and public sector policies to support or discourage domestic production.

The antecedents of the field, therefore, span a wide range of levels of analysis from the macro-socio-economic to the subjectively constructed world of the individual. Table 24.2 outlines the range of levels of analysis and attempts to describe their key features, disciplines and orientations.

In addition, previous theorists of change have identified key factors of the change process itself, which may permeate a variety of levels of analysis (Pettigrew, 1985; Pettigrew and Whipp, 1991; Wilson, 1999). These include the importance of context (primarily an assessment of where change takes place such as the type of organization or society); content (meaning what the change is about, such as the adoption of a new technology) and process (describing the characteristics of the change journey from first idea

to implementation). These three constructs were postulated by Pettigrew (1985). Wilson (1999) emphasized the importance of clarifying the scale of change (see Table 24.1). However, the scope of change also varies. Therefore, change can:

- Be slow, gradual, incremental, and evolutionary. It may be barely noticeable by individuals or societies (e.g., changes in societal values, theological tolerances; society gradually accepting new trends such as the contraceptive pill, African-American/women's voting rights, and greater tolerance and acceptance of homosexuality);
- Be fast, radical, sudden and revolutionary. It might contain elements of surprise or unexpectedness to those involved or affected by the change (e.g., new forms of music such as punk, techno, new technologies such as the iPod or iPhone, or the declaration of military hostilities);
- Affect almost all people in a society (e.g., new viruses, genetic modification, the threat of terrorism, human-caused climate change, the build-up of toxic chemicals in the environment, energy shortages and full human utilization of the Earth's photosynthetic capacity) (Diamond, 2005);
- Affect only a selection of the population (e.g., changes in pension, incapacity, social or sickness benefits and provision, the pricing policies of Ferrari cars);
- Be cyclical – a pattern of recurring phases of growth and decline (e.g., the fashion industry, life-cycle models of products, services and organizations).

The external (to the organization or the individual) context of change has also been a concern to theorists of change, since this context is argued to shape and influence specific change efforts. For example, the world's population has become more concentrated in the less developed world and in cities. There has been, for example, a huge growth in internet use, a decline in infant mortality rates and illiteracy. More people are living in freedom, GDP per capita has increased, and poverty has declined worldwide. Organizations operate in the context of these macro-level changes which, in turn, organizations may influence and shape by the decisions they take and the actions they embark upon (see Giddens, 1984

**Table 24.2  Levels of analysis and orientations towards organizational change**

| Level of analysis | Key features (examples) | Key disciplines |
|---|---|---|
| Socio-cultural | • Examines changes in the nature, the social institutions, the social behaviour or the social relations of a society, community of people, or other social structures.<br>• Includes any event or action that affects a group of individuals that have share values or characteristics.<br>• Can be seen in acts of advocacy for the cause of changing society in a normative way. | History, Politics, Anthropology and Sociology. |
| Socio-economic | • Examines the economic bases of societies and the changes produced as a result.<br>• Includes world trade, capital transfers, foreign direct investment and the economic role of the multi-national enterprise<br>• Can be seen in advocacy for the globalization of goods and services and striving for national advantage | Macro-economics and International Business. |
| Socio-organizational | • Examines the socio-cultural aspects of organizations and groups<br>• Includes culture, structure, power, conflict and social theories of decision making<br>• Can be seen in advocacy for looking at organizations as social groups where the understanding of social behaviours can underpin and inform an understanding of change. | Organization Theory, Organizational Behaviour, Social Psychology, Sociology of Organization. |
| Economic organizational | • Examines the competitive or efficiency bases of organization<br>• Includes resources, the economic power of suppliers, customers, competitors and the impact and influence of government regulations.<br>• Can be seen in market-based models of organization (e.g., apply economic yardsticks of performance against all organizations, including voluntary and public sector; or economic booms and slumps as drivers of change | Economics, Politics (especially government regulation) and Political History |
| Individual | • Examines the psychological characteristics and/or the subjective interpretive world of the individual<br>• Includes personality, identity, values, and norms.<br>• Can be seen in discursive accounts and in individual interpretations and accounts of change. | Psychology, Sociology of Social Construction, Discourse Analysis and Sense-making |

on 'structuration'). Giddens argues that practices are continued and enduring, so that social reproduction of familiar systems and structures occurs. Social action and interaction as 'tacitly enacted practices' become 'institutions or routines' and 'reproduce familiar forms of social life'.

These contextual changes (and hence organizational actions and responses) do not, however, happen equally throughout the world. For example, in 1960, infant mortality rates were more than 4.5 times higher in developing countries than among industrialized countries. In 2000, infant mortality rates in developing countries were around 10 times greater than in industrialized countries. That is, infant mortality rates declined faster in the more developed countries. There were similar disparities in illiteracy and political freedom. Conditions did improve among less developed countries, but not as much as they did among more developed countries. Some countries (e.g., many in Africa) experienced a worsening of conditions, such as increases in infant mortality rates, increases in illiteracy, and less freedom for individuals (Shackman, et al., 2004; Rajan, 2006). Therefore, depending upon where an organization is located, such external contextual influences will shape (to an extent) any change process in any organization. Change is therefore not totally voluntaristic. It is not wholly in the remit of managerial agency.

However, some antecedents of change research have been coloured by an abiding faith in managerial agency, where change is viewed as a rational, linear and top-down process conceived, driven and implemented by senior managers. The antecedents of this managerialist perspective, which became increasingly popular as management research developed as a key discipline, (see, for example, Lewin, 1951; Bennis et al., 1976; Peters and Waterman, 1982; Porras and Collins, 2002) can be found in much earlier philosophical writings. For example, ancient Greeks such as Callicles and Thrasymachus (coevals of Plato) embraced a view of change, later expressed in Athenian political circles, and subsequently most cogently expressed by Machiavelli, as predominantly the privilege of those in senior positions. For example, Machiavelli assumed almost total managerial control when he described change as likely to 'do injuries' to lower orders and that those in senior positions should 'do injuries all together, they will hurt less; bestow benefits little by little, so they will be felt more strongly' (Adams, 1977: 180).

Resistance to change was seen by Machiavelli (and others) as a kind of collective selfishness of the lower orders. Those in senior positions, therefore, should become what have more recently been termed 'troubleshooters' since 'when you see the trouble in advance, it is easily remedied, but when you wait until it is on top of you, the antidote is useless, the disease has become incurable' (Adams, 1977: 9).

Thus, the role of those in senior positions (senior managers) was to be constantly vigilant, ascertain well in advance, of the need for change, formulating a plan and implementing it, overcoming what many authors viewed as the inevitable resistance to change, mostly from the lower orders (Lewin, 1951). Such a view has had a long innings and is still a feature of much normative change literature especially in practitioner management journals, but as we shall see in the next section, there is a wide range of current theories not all of which adhere so strongly to the potency of managerial agency.

## CENTRAL APPROACHES AND MAIN THEORIES

The previous section attempts to convey the pervasiveness and centrality of change in organizational discourse. Making theoretical sense out of often contradictory theories means that, inevitably, this chapter will focus to a greater extent on some theories (which are thus held here to be primary) and to a lesser extent on others. Accordingly, much research which lies at the individual or small group levels of analysis is not discussed, the logic being that this is a Handbook whose focus is on macro- rather than micro-organizational behaviour. Consequently, large areas of more micro-focused research, such as individual perceptions of change (see for example, Isabella, 1990) and organizational development (OD) (see Cummings and Worley, 1993) are not covered.

Typically, OD approaches are those anchored in a logic or sequence of activities which involves creating a vision (as senior managers outline the outcomes of the change), developing commitment and motivation throughout the organization to this end, achieved not so much by direct managerial agency but by a more complex process of capturing and developing political and behavioural support from various stakeholders within and outside the organization. Some authors argue that such OD processes would include the implementation of change programmes such as Total Quality Management or Business Process Re-engineering and that these rightly fall under the aegis of macro-organizational theory, however.

Programmatic changes are usually expensive packages designed and created as generic solutions to a myriad of organizational change problems. Many authors have pointed to the unintended consequences of installing such programmes in organizations. For example, Wilson (1999) noted that the adoption of total quality programmes in the 1980s and 1990s in many organizations could easily result in the programme causing more disruptions than solutions by a number of processes which include the implementation of the programme becoming an end in itself rather than as a means to an end (to increase customer satisfaction for example). The considerable increased use of and reliance upon computers in organizations has resulted in a wide range of computer-based programmes sold by commercial vendors (often consultants) as panacea-like solutions to organizational problems. One example would be ERP (Enterprise Resource Planning) systems, which are designed to provide a technological backbone to integrate all parts of an organization such as purchasing, manufacturing, logistics, service and support, order administration, sales and marketing, human resources and finance.

Hall (2002) and Grant *et al.* (2002) argue that the broad scope and scale of potential applications of systems such as ERP (ranging from downsizing through job redesign to the introduction of team structures) have two essential dynamics: first, they are very attractive to managers since they offer seemingly easy (if expensive) solutions to complex problems; and, second, they involve organizations in complex, strategic change processes. These authors argue that such changes are characteristically unidirectional. That is, they involve organizational structures

and processes being changed to accommodate the programmed package and not the other way around (i.e., customize or tailor the package to suit or accommodate specific characteristics of the organization). Such changes, according to Grant *et al.* (2002) often display common characteristics whereby ERP is implemented as a generic package; it fails to achieve what was claimed by senior managers and vendors; managers then revise their projections for successful implementation but persist with it, arguing that employees will get used to it in time and that they often don't like change and hence resist implementation of the programme.

Beyond change programmes we can find a host of theoretical approaches to change, summarized in the next paragraphs. The broad conceptual dimensions used to map this variety of approaches can first be orientated around to what extent change is seen as a *planned* or *emergent* process and the extent to which the course of change might be seen as a *voluntaristic* or *determined* activity. Planned change describes a sequence of steps or stages which prescribe what managers should do and has been summarized by Pettigrew and Whipp (1991) as 'leading change'. Briefly this means a process by which managers develop concerns (creating an agenda to change); foster an understanding of the problem throughout the organization; plan, act and eventually stabilize the change, locking it into place in the organization. Emergent perspectives view change as a process which is almost never planned, but is one which emerges from a host of organizational and individual activities. Such processes are visible as patterns in streams of activities (Mintzberg and Waters, 1985). Change, therefore can only be characterized after it has happened. Voluntarism and determinism are also opposite ends of the dimension of social action (Parsons, 1937). The term voluntarism is applied to those theories of change that are based upon the intentions or motives of actors who are assumed to act 'voluntarily' and not as 'determined' by social or organizational structures.

By using these constructs, we can begin to map some of the key theoretical approaches to change. As Van de Ven and Poole (1995) discovered, there are over one million articles published on the subject of change in pure and social science disciplines. Since that search (conducted in 1994) the number is now closer to two million articles. Nevertheless the ideal-type classification system used by Van de Ven and Poole (1995: 514) helps begin to make sense of the major epistemological approaches, at least as a starting point for classifying theories or change. They distinguish four main categories: life-cycle, teleological, dialectic and evolutionary approaches.

## Life-cycle theories

These conceptualize change as a process which follows the 'natural' life-cycle of entities such as products, projects and organizations themselves from birth through maturity to old age and death. The key underlying premise of such approaches is that of deterministic development. Change has a logic to it which can be pre-figured by reference to the present state. Youth will progress to maturity and old age and the change process will begin and end deterministically withstanding environmental changes and even shocks. Change is a pre-programmed series of events of phases.

## Teleological theories

These conceptualize change as planned, or as emanating from purpose, and these theories have found considerable support in many management theories, including Lewin's (1947) force field analogy in which planned change progresses through three stages which he termed unfreezing (from the old state), moving and refreezing (to the new state). These three simple phases or steps provided the foundations for a whole raft of approaches describing and advising steps to be taken by those leading change. These include approaches by Judson (1991), Kotter (1996) and Armenakis, Harris and Field (1999).

## Dialectic theories

These conceptualize change as a process of conflicting interests which struggle against one another to try and influence both the processes and the outcomes of change. Change depends upon, and is shaped by, clashes of contradictory interests (individual, organizational or societal) and the outcome represents a synthesis of these conflicting struggles. Rooted in the dialectical process of thesis, antithesis and synthesis (see Hegel, 1937; Kolakowski, 1978), change emanates from innate political tensions in organization and organizing (Wilson, 1999).

## Evolutionary theories

These conceptualist change as cumulative processes that occur at the level of populations of organizations, communities or societies. Derived from biological metaphors concerning the survival and development of species, typical theories would include the population ecology approach in organization theory (Hannan and Freeman, 1977). Organizations, like biological species, survive only if they can adapt to environmental shocks or stimuli which can be unforeseen (Aldrich, 1979). These shocks create variation in an otherwise stable system. Survival depends on an organization's ability to compete for scarce resources and to adapt to new circumstances. In many ways, such theories are similar to life-cycle theories in that they are open to analysis as recurrent and probabilistic shifts in environmental conditions (for example demographic changes are predictable). Survival of the population of organizations overall depends upon their ability to adapt, although it is never possible to determine precisely which individual organizations will survive.

Broad as they are, these different epistemologies reveal significant variation in how the change process might be conceptualized as planned, emergent, voluntaristic or deterministic in nature. However, such theories tell us little about the characteristics of the process itself. This is developed in the next section.

## Change processes: the temporal dimension

We have established that change is a theoretically complex process, but it is also temporal in nature and is not necessarily linear or continuous (Whelan-Berry *et al.*, 2003). Virtually all of the epistemologies described above have an inherent assumption of equilibrium/change/equilibrium in which periods of change emanate out of periods of stability and are followed by periods of activities (transitions) to a new future state (new equilibrium).

However, there is a tension between continuity and discontinuity as well as the epistemology of change (Greiner 1972; Gersick 1991; Weick and Quinn, 1999). Continuous change assumes each change effort seamlessly builds upon the previous phase of change activity. Before examining these temporal aspects in more depth, it is worth noting that many management theorists (and consultants) have supported the view of continuous change as a positive step toward ensuring organizational survival and growth As de Wit and Meyer (1999: 144) point out, the well-known tortoise of Aesop's fable keeps moving slowly, but surely and continuously. It wins the race. The hare, on the other hand, shows off its ability to sprint and takes great leaps forward, but eventually loses the race. Endurance, persistence and small, continuous improvements to the ways in which we organize are argued to be more effective than discontinuous leaps. There are some strong voices in favour of continuous change which cluster around three basic principles:

- Continuous improvement
- Continuous learning
- Constant adaptation to changing conditions.

Continuous improvement implies that all individuals in an organization should always be driven to change, which will be anchored in their dissatisfaction with the status quo. This attitude needs to be constructive so that changes can be suggested, designed and put in place. The overall philosophy is that things can always be done better (Stacey, 1993).

Continuous learning means that all individuals in an organization should continually update or increase their knowledge base.

This means acquiring new knowledge and techniques as well as acquiring knowledge sufficient for decision makers to say 'no' to what might seem reasonable proposals at first sight and to be able to challenge taken-for-granted behaviours and attitudes in the organization. Crises can thus be avoided as far as possible since they inhibit longer-term thinking and promote short-term reactions and decisions (Senge, 1990). Constant adaptation to changing conditions means that organizational design must be such that it avoids becoming inflexible and hence a barrier to further change. Flexible structures and systems, coupled with open and change-receptive cultures, provide sufficient motivation, security and curiosity for individuals to tolerate the inevitable uncertainty and insecurity associated with change (Kagono *et al.*, 1985).

A counterpoint to continuous change and the dangers of assuming it is possible (and under the full control of managerial agency) can be found amongst scholars who argue change is unlikely to be continuous and instead will be characterized by stochastic, discontinuous episodes, not necessarily interconnected by any logic of continuity. The main arguments for this view can be found amongst intuitionalist organization theory (see DiMaggio and Powell, 1983). These authors argue in favour of organizational inertia where most organizations develop routines over time (institutionalized ways of organizing). Not only are these embedded routines a feature of organizations and organizing (Granovetter, 1985), but also individuals feel comfortable in such rather predictable structures and hence also are likely to resist change at the individual level of analysis.

Zukin and DiMaggio (1990) identify four types of embeddedness:

- *Structural*: the relational quality of inter-actor exchanges and the architecture of network ties between actors
- *Cognitive*: structured mental processes which direct social and economic logics
- *Cultural*: shared beliefs and values which shape social and economic aims

- *Political*: the institutional limits on economic power and incentives.

Embeddedness refers to the process by which social relations shape organizational actions (Granovetter, 1985). If arm's-length ties become embedded as firms engage in coordination and adaptation with other firms, then firms in the network may begin to trade only with a confined set of network partners. The flow of new or innovative information into the network begins to decrease; eventually it is closed off in highly embedded networks because there are few non-redundant links to outside members who potentially could introduce new ideas into the network. Over time, isomorphic processes can also decrease network diversity and increase organizational inertia so that change is difficult and costly for network partners (Hannan and Freeman, 1989). Examples of such inertia through inter-firm social relations can be found in Grabher's (1993) study of the decline of the Ruhr Steel industry and Glasmeier's (2000) research on the failure of the Swiss watch-making industry. Both authors argued that a closed network structure in each of these industries limited the recognition of new and innovative processes and contributed to the decline of firms in these industries.

In addition, in highly embedded networks, feelings of obligation, friendship, or betrayal may also be so intense that emotions in favour of retaining the status quo triumph over any concerns to change. Either process is likely to lead to a network which is out of fit with its environment, and is likely to lead to organization or industry failure.

Organizational success which, like failure, accrues over time, also presents a conundrum identified by Miller (1990) as the 'Icarus paradox'. This Greek myth describes how Icarus is said to have flown so close to the sun that his artificial wax wings melted and he plunged to his death in the Aegean Sea. His greatest asset (his wings which had brought him many successes) led to his downfall when he tried to reach the sun. Complacency and hubris can be close bedfellows of success. However, success can breed the seeds of its own destruction beyond managerial hubris, since it also further embeds and reinforces routines and practices in organizations which run deep and are resistant to change (see Greenwood and Hinings, 1993).

These stabilities can be found in formal and informal systems, standard operating procedures, the distribution of power, and the strong ties of organizational culture. They can also be found in factors such as long-term contracts and commitments, fixed investments and inflexible financial and accounting procedures (Ghemawat, 1991; Arthur, 1996). If significant change is to happen then crises (real or constructed) need to be created. In this way, the organization becomes jolted into action. This kick-start effect is known as the punctuated equilibrium view of change (Gersick, 1991). Change happens in bursts of activity (followed by further periods of consolidation). These discontinuities can be analysed at different levels of analysis. At the individual level, reluctance to change and settled ways of doing things makes individuals predisposed to maintain the status quo and only embark upon change when things become too tough to remain as they are. Groups (social or work) will also exhibit the same behaviours.

Organizations have structural and cultural – institutional – arrangements which act as barriers to change unless significant and threatening events spur action. Industries, too, will exhibit inertia until a crisis point means the equilibrium is punctured and radical change occurs. The airline industry is a good example of discontinuous change. Only two of the top eight US airlines are profitable (Jet Blue and SouthWest) and the remaining six are making huge losses with two under bankruptcy protection from their creditors. These two profitable airlines are low-cost carriers just like many of the Internet-based airlines which service European destinations (e.g., easyJet, Ryanair and Thompson). The challenge of low-cost carriers and greater price transparency via the Internet has created crisis and discontinuous change amongst full-cost airlines (McGee, Thomas and Wilson, 2005).

In addition to examining the continuity or discontinuity of change processes, the size, scale and scope of change over time relates to the likelihood of success in implementing change. Work by Hannan, Polos and Carroll (2003) uncovered some revealing (if representationally mathematically complex) relationships. Using the collapse of Barings Brothers (a British Bank) in 1995 as an example, Hannan, Polos and Carroll (2003) argue that reorganization in the bank had created an infrastructure (organizational architecture) which allowed Nick Leeson (the so-called 'rogue trader') to operate in a way which sealed the demise of the bank. The organizational conditions under which these activities took place allowed his actions to go undetected. In a different firm with a different architecture, Leeson would likely have been identified early on in the process and prevented from trading.

The organizational context of Barings allowed a number of activities to take place which amounted to significant changes in its size, scale, scope and eventual disaster for the organization. According to Hannan, Polos and Carroll (2003: 428):

- The structure of the organization was porous with no clear lines of responsibility and accountability. This allowed Leeson to operate undetected for at least two years.
- Confusion of the reporting lines in the organization could be traced to the recent reorganization of the bank.
- The matrix structure which resulted from reorganization failed to work in practice. It was never clear who Leeson's product managers were (a common problem of ambiguous responsibility in matrix structures) and they had little knowledge of his trading activities.
- Leeson was in charge of both the front and back office functions of the bank and was therefore in a position to override any internal controls.
- The organizational sub-units (departments) which dealt with Leeson's activities were very poor at communicating with one another and this allowed Leeson to trade in the now infamous account 88888, of which senior managers of the Baring Group claimed no knowledge.

The conclusion drawn from the above example is that changes can go badly wrong when organizations change their architectures. The new design of the organization can allow large changes to sweep through the organization, with often few or no controls to keep them in check. Hannan, Polos and Carroll (2003: 428) identify two pertinent concepts from their mathematical model. These are:

- *Opacity*: low opacity occurs when there is limited foresight about how different units in the organization are interconnected and work together. The lower the opacity, the higher the likelihood of changes becoming out of control and beyond the capacity of the organization to deal with them when things go wrong.
- *Asperity*: high asperity indicates an organizational culture which will not readily accept changes and which will cling to the 'old' ways of working. The higher the asperity, the greater the likelihood that changes will fail.

Key explanations for failure lie in the scale and scope aspects of change processes. For example, high opacity leads to individuals underestimating the time reorganization will take as well as the associated costs of change, thereby prompting them to undertake changes with adverse consequences. Complex, opaque organizations which have a high level of cultural asperity will tend to get themselves into trouble by implementing changes that cost far more than was foreseen. In the worst cases, these can be costs that cannot be covered by whatever new organizational form or circumstances the change has brought about. Like Barings, the organization may well go bankrupt. The Barings example also illustrates the impact one person, or a small group, can have on the fortunes of an organization and the speed with which changes (mostly discontinuous) can occur.

There is little doubt that such changes occur over time but it worth noting that Purser and Petranker (2005: 182) argue that little attention has been paid to considering the temporal dimension which underlies these change processes. As Burrell (1992: 165) argues: 'the whole notion of change relies heavily upon a conception of temporality (but it is) remarkable that the philosophy of time has been a neglected issue'.

Temporal assumptions abound in virtually all theories of change. Since change, especially planned change, implies a temporal dimension with an assumed future different from the current state of affairs, we have neglected an adequate conceptualization of temporality in our examination and discussion of change processes. Specifically, models of change which involve phases (such as freeze, rebalance, unfreeze) assume that analysts can take a position which is both external to continuous change and stands outside time itself, recomposing artificial phases in the change process as if they really existed (Bergson, 1944). To summarize these complex arguments is beyond the scope of this chapter, but the essence of the Bergsonian critique, echoed by Purser and Petranker (2005) is that all change is emergent; the 'future' arrives without taking a form we can isolate and categorize, since the future is always becoming (rather than become). Change theorists have ignored the dynamic of time itself and instead utilized it as an abstraction or an index to denote a process. Such an index allows the freeze framing of time (as in taking a photograph for example) but time itself does not stop and hence the future arrives continuously, rendering any conceptions drawn from the still frame outdated and possibly irrelevant. The implications of such a view appear to be abandonment of any conceptions of future states (visions, goals, ambitions) and instead to see change processes as akin to experimentation with the unknown and as improvised rather than planned actions. The debate will continue amongst scholars interested in drilling deep into conceptions of time; only the future will tell if these theoretical approaches to time establish resonance with theories of change.

## Change processes and technologies

Just as the temporal dimension of change can be isolated for study in its own right, so too can the relationships between technologies and change, particularly since one of the founding fathers of systemic change, Kurt Lewin, singled out technology as a key 'driving force' in helping 'unfreeze' the current situation and as a key aspect of 'refreezing' the system in a changed context. We will not deal here with the intricacies of different technologies. That is beyond the scope of this chapter, but we will examine some of the key assumptions surrounding technology and change in an attempt to make sense of a burgeoning field of research.

Despite the sometimes breathless discussion of new technologies, such as the development of the Internet, the rise of genetic modification and nanotechnologies (where measurements are commonly at the level of one billionth of a metre – or 1/75000 of a human hair), technology and change have a long historical association as the following example demonstrates. Relatively simple technological changes are firmly embedded in social organization and have proved historically quite difficult to implement. The organization of bell-ringing in churches is an example. Initially, there were three ways to ring a church bell – hit it on the outside; push the bell so the bell moves but the clapper doesn't, or pull the clapper but not the bell. At first, bells were rung by a number of men pulling on a lever. The three-ton bell at Canterbury Cathedral in England needed some 20 men who would all strain and pull and raise it a little, and then let go. For greater control, a wooden half-circle with a rope was attached to the headstock. The pull of the rope turned the half-wheel, and the bell swung with the half-wheel. Control was minimal, but the bells could be rung in order. Eight bells for example could be rung in either 12345678 or reverse order. The technological change that allowed greater control was when a full wheel was attached to the headstock. Now, the order of bell-ringing could be changed almost infinitely, rather than be in a fixed sequence (ascending or descending). The alteration of the sequence, however, depended upon the skill (rather than the strength) of the bell-ringer. The skill was to swing the bell through 360 degrees and balance it mouth up. Different strengths of rope pull would then determine which bell sounded and in which sequence. This technological change demanded a new kind of bell-ringer who could demonstrate different and additional skills to sheer strength and the social organization of bell-ringing changed irrevocably.

Modern technologies have the same inter-woven characteristics with social organization as this early example of bell-ringing. For example, discussions abound over the use of the Internet and information technologies in higher education. Barone *et al.* (2001) argue that these technologies will transform higher education for the better, whereas Tenner (1996) argues that the same technologies are 'destroying' higher education. These views are diametrically opposed and are influenced by deeply felt values about what higher education is, what is best for higher education, and what new technologies can do. Technologies can be argued to destroy the good work of teaching and research, or they can be argued to stimulate failing or poor performing institutions into new life and development. Similar arguments prevail (grounded largely on deeply held values rather than precise information) in recent discourse over genetic modification (it will enrich us all, versus it will do more harm than good); nanotechnologies (they will help make things smaller, lighter, tougher and have direct medical applications such as targeting only cancer cells, versus views that these are meddling with nature and we will live to regret their application) and global warming (it is important versus it is not).

New technologies in particular, are polar-ized as good or evil. Maguire (2004), for example, shows how new technologies become categorized in public and scientific discourse as 'problems' or 'solutions' as DDT was developed as an effective insecticide, then was outlawed as dangerous in marketing, technical, popular and scientific policy dis-courses. While disputed claims and discourse are a feature of new technologies (what used to be good is now described as bad; what was claimed to be true now no longer holds) a key assumption embedded into many texts is that technology is a change agent. It stimulates change in a similar way to that described by Lewin (1951). More recent studies (e.g., Ball and Wilson, 2000) argue that technologies cannot simply be seen as objective agents or drivers of change. What matters most is how they are incorporated and used in organizations. It is this variation in how the same technology (in this case computer-based monitoring systems) is used in a range of organizations which reveals how changes are perceived and implemented. Like the bell-ringers of old, it is not the technology per se, it is how it is used and implemented in organizations that helps the understanding of different change trajectories.

## CRITICAL ISSUES AND NEW DIRECTIONS FOR THE FUTURE

Untangling different levels of analysis, different disciplinary perspectives and the complex and non-linear aspects of change presents an array of substantial theoretical and empirical challenges. New directions would seem to beckon both intra- and inter-organizationally. Looking intra-organizationally, Whelan-Berry *et al.* (2003) have argued for an increased understanding of change across levels of analysis and emphasized that the interplay of organization, group and individual levels is ill-understood. Purser and Petranker (2005) favour a renewed emphasis on the subjective interpretation of change by individuals accompanied by action-based methods to uncover the dynamics of human interactions and how they make sense of their temporal existence. Collinson and Wilson (2006) argued that the neo-institutionalist perspectives which portray organizational routines as barriers to change may be turned on their respective heads and that routines can, in some cases, be generators of change as well as barriers.

The majority of existing empirical analysis on organizational change tends to be located in a restricted range of organizational types. There is very little evidence, for example, whether change processes and analytical models which seem to apply to large commercial enterprises (such as those studied by Pettigrew and Whipp, 1991), yield equal analytical strength when applied to small and medium-sized firms or entrepreneurial start-ups. These organizations are likely to present different challenges to understanding and implementing change. For example, the relatively reduced resource base of small firms may mean that cyclical hire-and-fire decisions take priority (as environments change from munificent to scarce) over the subjective interpretations of individuals anticipating change. Equally, managing temporary project groups and contracting short-term staff may also be strategic issues for these kinds of organizations, whereas the same issues may be relegated to the administrative margins of larger enterprises.

Both the public and the non-profit sectors have been relatively neglected as empirical sites for researching change and research still resides in the dominant logic outlined by Wilson (1999), which assumes that what works in a commercial enterprise can be implemented (without translation for context) in public and non-profit organizations. A greater range of change theories and models which are sensitive to the different politic and social contexts of public and non-profit organizations seem well overdue.

Inter-organizationally, the challenges for analysts of change lie in the complexity of modern, networked, highly visible constellation of relationships between organizations of all types. Business-government relationships and clusters of high technology firms, for example, present the change analyst with sets of different questions from the mainstream knowledge base of change. Equally, researchers of change from an inter-organizational perspective will also have to be mindful that they do not become embroiled in the increasingly powerful discourse (and perhaps hype) of change. We have seen how researchers in the social sciences have revealed the arguably biased nature of scientific discourse. For example, pharmaceutical companies have been accused of creating new illnesses (such as 'social anxiety' disease) and then selling the cure. This 'pill for an ill' discourse permeates our everyday organizational lives and embeds emotive constructs (it's good for us; it's bad for us) in changes such as globalization, new technological futures, nanotechnologies and genetic modification. Separating the hype from the established knowledge base may be the first step for researchers wanting to understand the dynamics of change processes from an inter-organizational perspective.

Overall, there certainly seems a need for dynamic theoretical models in which variables can be portrayed as temporal (one can be part of another in different time frames) and in which feedback loops and connections can be revealed to see how they vary, interrelate and operate in a nonlinear fashion. Such dynamic, non-linear models are a key set of challenges for future researchers of change, whether from an intra- or an inter-organizational perspective. The development of such models, furnished with a greater range and variety of organizational types and examples, may enable researchers to establish new patterns as well as uncover previously hidden patterns and may help develop the field from its current context of analytical debates to one of predictive utility and applicability to some degree.

## REFERENCES

Adams, R.M. (1977) *The Prince: A New Translation, Backgrounds, Interpretations, Peripherica.* New York: Norton and Co.

Aldrich, H. (1979) *Organizations and Environments.* Englewood Cliffs, NJ: Prentice-Hall.

Armenakis, A.A., Harris, S. and Field, H. (1999) 'Paradigms in organizational change: Change agent and change target perspectives', in R. Golembiewski (ed.) *Handbook of Organizational Behaviour.* New York: Marcel Dekker.

Arthur, W.B. (1996) 'Increasing returns and the new world of business', *Harvard Business Review,* July/August: 100–109.

Ball, K. and Wilson, D.C. (2000) 'Power, control and computer-based performance monitoring: Repertoires, resistance and subjectivities', *Organization Studies*, 21 (3): 539–565.

Barone, C.A. and Hagner, P.R. (eds) (2001) *Technology-enhanced Teaching and Learning. EDUCAUSE Leadership Strategies No. 5.* San Francisco, CA: Jossey-Bass.

Bennis, W., Benne, K.D., Chin, R. and Corey, K.E. (1976) *The Planning of Change* (3rd edn). New York: Holt, Rinehart and Winston.

Bergson, H. (1944) *Creative Evolution.* New York: Modern Library.

Burrell, W.G. (1992) 'Back to the future', in M. Reed and M. Hughes (eds) *Rethinking Organizations.* London: Sage, pp. 165–183.

Collinson, S. and Wilson, D.C. (2006) 'Inertia in Japanese organizations: Knowledge management routines and failure to innovate', *Organization Studies*, 27 (9): 1359–1387.

Cummings, T.G. and Worley, C.G. (1993) *Organizational Development and Change.* St Paul, MN: West.

Das, T.K. (1986) *The Subjective Side of Strategy Making; Future Orientations and Perceptions of Executives.* New York: Praeger.

de Wit, B. and Meyer, R. (1999) *Strategy Synthesis: Resolving Strategy Paradoxes to Create Competitive Advantage.* London: International Thomson Press.

DiMaggio, P. and Powell, W.W. (1983) 'The iron cage revisited', *American Sociological Review*, 48: 147–160.

Gersick, C.J.G. (1991) 'Revolutionary change theories: A multi-level exploration of the punctuated equilibrium paradigm', *Academy of Management Review*, 6: 10–36.

Ghemawat, P. (1991) *Commitment: The Dynamics of Strategy.* New York: Free Press.

Giddens, A. (1984) *The Constitution of Society: Outline of the Theory of Structuration.* Berkeley: University of California Press.

Glasmeier, A.K. (2000) *Manufacturing Time: Global Competition in the Watch Industry 1795–2000.* New York: Guilford Press.

Grabher, G. (1993) 'The weakness of strong ties. The lock-in of regional development in the Ruhr Area', in G. Grabher (ed.) *The Embedded Firm. On the Socio-economics of Industrial Networks.* London/New York: Routledge: pp. 255–277.

Granovetter, M.S. (1985) 'Economic action and social structure: The problem of embeddedness,' *American Journal of Sociology*, 91: 481–510.

Grant, D., Wailes, N., Michelson, G., Brewer, A. and Hall, R. (2002) 'Rethinking organizational change' (special issue), *Strategic Change*, 11: 5.

Greenwood, R. and Hinings, C.R. (Bob) (1993) 'Understanding strategic change: The contribution of archetypes', *Academy of Management Journal*, 3: 1052–1083.

Greiner, L.E. (1972) 'Evolution and revolution as organizations grow', *Harvard Business Review*, July/August: 37–46.

Hall, R. (2002) 'Enterprise resource planning systems and organizational change: Transforming work organization?', *Strategic Change*, 11 (5): 263–270.

Hannan, M., Polos, L. and Carroll, G.R. (2003) 'Fog of change', *Administrative Science Quarterly*, 48 (3): 399–432.

Hannan, M.T. and Freeman, F. (1977) 'The population ecology of organizations', *American Journal of Sociology*, 82: 929–964.

Hannan, M.T. and Freeman, J. (1989) *Organizational Ecology.* Cambridge, MA: Harvard University Press.

Hegel, G.W.F. (1937) *The Philosophy of History.* New York: Dover.

Isabella, L. (1990) 'Evolving interpretations as a change unfolds: How managers construe key organizational events', *Academy of Management Journal*, 33: 7–41.

Judson, A. (1991) *Changing Behaviour in Organizations: Minimising Resistance to Change.* Cambridge, MA: Blackwell.

Kagono, T., Nonaka, I., Sakakibara, K. and Okumara, A. (1985) *Strategic Versus Evolutionary Management: A US-Japan Comparison of Strategy and Organization.* Amsterdam: North Holland Press.

Kolakowski, L. (1978) *Main Currents of Marxism, Volume 1.* Oxford: Oxford University Press.

Kotter, J. (1996) 'Leading change: Why transformation efforts fail', *Harvard Business Review*, 73 (2): 59–67.

Lewin, K. (1947) 'Frontiers in group dynamics', *Human Relations*, 1: 5–41.

Lewin, K. (1951) *Field Theory in Social Science.* New York: Harper & Row.

Maguire, S. (2004) 'The co-evolution of technology and discourse: A study of substitution processes for the insecticide DDT', *Organization Studies*, 25 (1): 113–134.

McGee, J., Thomas, H. and Wilson, D.C. (2005) *Strategy: Analysis and Practice.* Maidenhead: McGraw-Hill.

Miller, D. (1990) *The Icarus Paradox: How Excellent Companies Bring about Their Own Downfall.* New York: Harper Business.

Mintzberg, H. and Waters, J.A. (1985) 'Of strategies deliberate and emergent,' *Strategic Management Journal*, July/Sept: 257–272.

Parsons, T. (1937) *The Structure of Social Action.* New York: McGraw-Hill.

Peters, T. and Waterman, R. Jr. (1982) *In Search of Excellence: Lessons from America's Best-run Companies*. New York: Harper & Row.

Pettigrew, A.M. (1985) *The Awakening Giant: Continuity and Change in ICI*. Oxford: Blackwell.

Pettigrew, A.M. and Whipp, R. (1991) *Managing Change for Competitive Success*. Oxford: Blackwell.

Porras, J.I. and Collins, J. (2002) *Built to Last*. New York: Harper Business.

Porter, M.E. (1986) *Competition in Global Industries*. Boston, MA: Harvard Business School Press.

Porter, M.E. (1998) *The Competitive Advantage of Nations*. New York: Free Press.

Purser, R.E. and J. Petranker (2005) 'Unfreezing the future: Exploring the dynamic of time in organizational change', *Journal of Applied Behavioral Science*, 41 (2): 182–203.

Rajan, C. (2006) *Global Politics and Institutions: Frontiers of a Great Transition* (*vol. 3*). Boston, MA: Tellus Institute.

Senge, P. (1990) 'The leader's new work: Building learning organizations', *Sloan Management Review*, Fall: 7–23.

Shackman, G., Liu, Y.-L. and Wang G. (Xun) (2004) 'Global Social Change Reports', http://gsociology.icaap.org/reports.html.

Stacey, R. (1993) 'Strategy as order emerging from chaos', *Long Range Planning*, 26 (1): 10–17.

Tenner, E. (1996) *Why Things Bite Back*. New York: Vintage Books.

Van de Ven A.H. and Poole, M.S. (1995) 'Explaining development and change in organizations', *Academy of Management Review*, 20 (3): 510–540.

Weick, K.E. and Quinn, R. (1999) 'Organizational change and development', *Annual Review of Psychology*, 50: 361–386.

Wensley, R. (2003) 'Strategy as intention and anticipation', in S. Cummings and D.C. Wilson (eds) *Images of Strategy*. Oxford: Blackwell.

Whelan-Berry, K.S., Gordon, J. and Hinings, C.R. (Bob) (2003) 'Strengthening organizational change processes: Recommendations and implications from a multi-level analysis', *Journal of Applied Behavioral Science*, 39 (2): 186–207.

Wilson, D.C. (1999) *A Strategy of Change*. New York: International Thompson.

# 25

# 'We Have Always Been Oligarchs': Business Elite in Polyarchy

David Courpasson

## INTRODUCTION

Fifty years after Mill's (1957) masterpiece, *The Power Elite*, substantial transformations have largely reshaped the political regimes and structures of power in business organizations. Several elements are particularly interesting to highlight when analysing power élites in business.

First, business organizations are no longer founded on a 'bureaucratic order'. Their modalities and forms of functioning are marked by [some] of the features of post-bureaucratic or post-entrepreneurial models of organizations: rule-governed contexts have been progressively replaced/completed by project-governed or dialogue-and-network-governed contexts. Second, business organizations are confronted by increasingly diverse sets of constituencies which, both externally and internally, constrain the political decisions of business leaders. Without going so far as to suggest that business leaders have

lost their 'political power' and gained more 'administrative power', to use Tocquevillean categories, it is possible that they are no longer the exclusive and omnipotent 'Masters of Business' that they used to be in earlier, more patriarchal, times. However true or exaggerated these features might be, we can suggest that the plasticity of the political realm in today's business organizations contrasts sharply with the well-ordered and vertical world of business described by Mills, and from which he and his successors depicted the corporate élite as relatively stable and socially produced by relatively clear cut class and network processes (Useem, 1984; Davis *et al.,* 2003).

We shall argue in this chapter that the fundamental social and ideological structure of business élites has not really changed over the last decades, while the empirical contexts within which they operate have evolved. Put differently, we shall see why business élites should still be analysed as *oligarchs* in an otherwise more pluralist organizational context. The objective of this chapter is therefore to develop a political vision of corporate élites, in which we shall not focus on the élite's features, modes of reproduction and backgrounds but on the relationships between current political regimes of organizations and corporate élite forms of action.

Thinking about corporate élite dynamics implies seeing the relationship between élite perpetuation (oligarchy) and resistance/contestation in the workplace as different from a mere antagonistic interplay; theories of protest have a 'frictional' relationship with concepts surrounding formal organizations (Gamson and Schmeidler, 1984). However, simultaneously, the confrontation between these perspectives should not lead one to obscure systems of domination. On the contrary, we shall suggest in this chapter that what is likely to emerge in what we shall term polyarchic regimes could foster élite perpetuation and structures of dominancy, under the auspices of 'orchestrated mobilizations' (Strang and Jung, 2005) and protest absorption processes (Leeds, 1964).

Two major questions are addressed in this chapter. First, we will strive to better understand why, while a sort of common-sense views corporate élites (and obviously, élites in general) as having an objective and subjective significant influence over the course of nations and organizations (see Samuels, 2003), social science theories (and more singularly, management theories, where they even address the issue) still regard élites as mostly constrained, and fail to see élite members as capable of making moral, strategic, tactical and, so to speak, political choices, without necessarily being forced to lead the way in such or such direction. Marx is among the most famous defenders of this idea when he proposes that 'Men make their own history, but they do not make it as they please' (Marx, 1972: 8, in Samuels, 2003: x). The always excessive and sometimes illegitimate power of élites is largely given by contextual cues; it contrasts with the fact that they mostly 'read scripts' rather than actually write them. Second, the argument will suggest a better account of the relationships between élite legitimacy and political structures based on the toleration, even the encouragement, of patterns of contestation within the polity. Thus, a sort of new 'political profile' of corporate élite will be sketched, underlying the necessary new vision that organizational leaders must have of contestation in the workplace.

In this chapter we will adopt a moderate vision of élite power. The corporate context is extremely constraining, probably more so than many other social contexts. The reality of leadership in business organizations is a reality of accommodation and compromise building with a multitude of exogenous and endogenous factors and constituencies, but it is also a reality of extreme concentration of power in the hands of small circles of a 'chosen few': the very relevance of èlitism in the business realm comes from the fact that, if they are sometimes powerless, élite members are nevertheless the repositories of inter-generational forms of oligarchic power resilience (McLean and Harvey, 2006) and of inter-organizational circles of socialization and learning, often called 'interlocks' (Mizruchi, 1996). Thus, this chapter is fundamentally about a dilemma: analysing corporate élites sheds light both on the capacity of specific individuals to tip the balance in favour of chosen directions and also on how and why they admit their powerlessness and use it politically. We describe this dilemma in terms of 'hybridization' between diverse ingredients of managerial and political action such as:

- Business organizations have both oligarchic and democratic features with respect to their power structures
- The social structures of the élite (backgrounds and careers) are both evolving and resilient
- Corporate élites might be relatively powerless, but this powerlessness is in itself a political capacity to 'do what they want'
- Business leaders reproduce themselves through a complex compromise between domination and contestation: polyarchy (Dahl, 1971), it will be argued, best defines this approximate political regime.

The chapter is organized as follows. First, we consider the much-debated question of the actual power of leaders: asking the question 'Do leaders matter?' is the underlying fulcrum of this chapter. Without understanding why leadership matters, why certain actors do have the power to orient the fate of collectives, those whom Aron (1960) termed 'Men of great Destinies' (and they are mostly men), we are unable to grasp the particular combinations between structural forces constraining élites and the transformative agency of individuals which shapes the interplay between the reproduction of institutional power and 'transgressive contentions' (McAdam, Tarrow and Tilly, 2000) and other change efforts that require the mobilization of diverse actors. Second, we set up the scene of élite political action, a scene characterized today by a controversy whether organizational 'new' regimes are democratically oriented or 'oligarchically' oriented. We suggest going beyond this classical opposition to move toward a more 'hybrid' context we call *polyarchy*. In the concluding section, we strive to suggest what sort of leaders fit those polyarchic and more contentious working places that we depict. We shall offer some reflections about the co-transformation of élite patterns of action and of political regimes of organization, which are likely to change profoundly the vision of power and contestation in the workplace.

## WHY BUSINESS LEADERS MATTER

The vision of élite power that most share is that leaders are 'embedded agents operating within relational structural fields that distinguish the possible from the impossible and the likely from the less likely' (Katznelson, 1997: 82). Another taken for granted assumption is that élite power is mostly contingent, that is, that it is mostly bequeathed and sometimes built and legitimized, but that its very effects are dependent on the diversity of political situations. The notion of an élite is encumbered by this sort of prejudice: èlitism is founded on strategies of reproduction and

self-perpetuation, and these strategies are the only stable feature of élite power. While they devote their energy, capacities and social networks to their own reproduction, élite groups do not have much time and energy to take care of changing and caring for the polity. Therefore, they tend to rely on the rhetoric of the 'Great Forces' which constrain them and hamper the creation of new forms and rules of the game. It is useless to seek for other explanations as to why business leaders are not creative and rely so much on consulting firms, although such a vision may be selling things a bit short as far as the business world is concerned.

It is right to admit that the border between business organizations and politics is highly permeable. As business issues shape the 'global world', the great forces of structures and power relations are more and more intertwined: when business leaders misbehave, when they make illegitimate decisions, when they decide to close factories and dismiss thousands of people, they can claim that their preferences are constrained or transformed by 'power relations'. Still, to follow Samuels (2003), if much power is actually contingent (accidental and event-dependent), there is something missing in most stories of power and change: the influence of specific leaders over the course of events. In other words, as Samuels puts it, 'Leaders such as Gandhi and Lenin may have become colossal figures not only because they seized opportunities presented by shifting global forces but also because they constructed the most consequential "contingencies" of their age' (2003: 4). Building power requires builders, so to speak. Some historical decisions (such as Churchill refusing to yield to the Nazis, see Betts, 2000) are simply not predictable because they are founded on the agency of leaders. Studies of 'policy entrepreneurs' (Kingdon, 1995), institutional entrepreneurs (Rao, Morrill and Zald, 2000), or social movement leaders (Morris and Staggenborg, 2004) show how ingredients such as luck, constraint and professional/individual capacities always work in parallel, leading, as perfectly theorized by Emirbayer and Mische's (1997) framework, to constant combinations between structural forces and agency.

If we take the example of the creation of new organizational forms, there is an interplay between a political project involving collective action, and the role of specific 'élites' in enhancing and supporting change. Collective action is necessary to de-institutionalize existing beliefs and values and to generate and instantiate new ones (Rao, Morrill and Zald, 2002). Institutional leaders are necessary in their capacity to identify political opportunities, mobilize constituencies. Leaders are also critical to social movements: 'they inspire commitment, mobilize resources, create and recognize opportunities, devise strategies, frame demands, and influence outcomes' (Morris and Stagenborg, 2004). In business organizations, change is brought both by the action of leaders and by the myriad of interpretive actions coming from grassroots actors themselves (Vallas, 2006). Any analysis of why and how leaders matter must therefore encompass the analysis of the interactions between leaders' actions and subordinate interpretations, in line with a Weberian focus on the nature of leadership as social action.

To sum up, the idea is that a relational and action vision of corporate élites is necessary when we situate corporate élites in a polyarchic political environment (on which more below). We think that élite action in the business realm should be based neither in the rather excessive vision of Michels, according to which followers willingly and gratefully cede agency to their leaders, nor in the entrepreneurial version of resource mobilization theory. The problem with resource mobilization theory is that it overemphasizes agency, arguing in a similar way to Burawoy's 'manufacturing consent', that grievances might also be manufactured (McCarthy and Zald, 2002). Instead, we should see élite action as being embedded in organizational and political characteristics (Zald and Ash, 1966). Different types of élite members come out of different types of pre-existing organizational features. For example, in the American women's movement, 'older branch' leaders came out of backgrounds in traditional voluntary organizations and unions, while 'younger branch leaders' emerged from experiences in more participatory and 'New Left' kinds of organizations (Freeman, 1975 in Morris and Stagenborg, 2004).

Leaders matter when they recognize the need for structural strain and conduciveness and 'precipitating factors' in order to create adequate conditions for change, that is to say, to destabilize the previous order, of which their own perpetuation is a part. Leaders emerge not only out of class and educational processes, but through the very process of change itself, during which they also contribute to shaping the conditions for the agency of other [non-élite] participants. As Vallas aptly puts it (2006), organizational transformation has to be thought of in a *relational* way because it is the outcome of interactions between managerial imperatives and subordinates' interpretations and adoption decisions when confronted to actual restructurings of their jobs. In other words, our argument here is that both oligarchic and democratic élite theories miss the structure/agency linkages, exaggerating, in a different manner and for different purposes, the efficacy and exclusive influence of leadership, while underestimating the agency of subordinates in the generation, design and implementation of change. We thus need what we call an *intermediate élite theory* (*polyarchic* élite theory) that is capable of grasping the more complex relationships between what conditions élite preferences and actions and what shapes employees' orientations and their influence on the change outcomes.

Recent studies demonstrates that élite resilience is striking (Davis *et al.*, 2003); however, we shall suggest that where élite power resilience is likely to be established upon the basis of political regimes that are more open to contestation, more complex political structures have to be designed and legitimized. In other words, we propose that élite resilience, in an era of rapid social change, cannot be based exclusively on the cohesiveness and closure of inner circles and social networks of competence and acquaintance: it needs to deal with the question of organizationally endogenous contestation and with the power structures that can allow this contestation to flourish and to produce change.

## Corporate élites in their political context: democracy, oligarchy, or which pluralism are we talking about?

The first section of this chapter suggested that talking about [corporate] élites means talking about the political regimes through which business organizations are ruled and transformed. From this question derives the 'nature' of the élite holding corporate power: are they pluralist-fragmented élites or concentrated élites?

Roughly speaking, there are two opposite views of élite patterns and dynamics within democratic contexts in the classical socio-logical and political literature. The first is the classical 'èlitist' view (Michels, 1915; Pareto, 1935; Mosca, 1939; Mills, 1957). The classical view defends the idea that, despite the democratic character of a given institution or a given organization, power is systematically and really concentrated in the hands of a small group of individuals, the 'ruling few'. The second is the more recent 'pluralistic' view (Dahl, 1957, 1971; Aron, 1960; Parsons, 1969). It defends the idea that the power structure is funda-mentally characterized by a diversification and a dissociation of power, giving rise to a plurality of élite groups ensuring competition and the dynamics of rivalries necessary to the sustainability of democratic regimes.

When dealing with business organizations the opposition between èlitist and pluralist views is in large part sterile because the organizational context is, in fact, paradoxical: in contemporary organizations, oligarchic regimes need élite diversification to be sus-tained and perpetuated. It is the contestation and the competition arising from internal fragmentation which provides resources to the oligarchs to establish 'contested oligarchic' forms of governance, as we will call *polyarchies* (Dahl, 1971). The peculiar polit-ical dynamic stems from the multiplication over the last decades of new professional groups within organizations, often gathered under the expression 'knowledge workers' (Alvesson, 1995). These sub-élites are mostly used as providers of 'would-be oligarchs', via the creation of leadership nurseries, breeding grounds for élites in which the vectors of rivalries between aspirants are monitored from the top. It is by analysing the interactions between central oligarchs and these intermediate bodies that we might better understand the contemporary political dynamics of business organizations and their élites.

The mutual exclusivity drawn between oligarchy and democracy in most analyses of power and governance does not account for the intimate forms of hybridization existing between these two extreme political struc-tures. Particularly, the managerial literature on new organizational forms assumes that the question of authority could be addressed either through the decision-making process[1] (more or less decentralized) or through the nature of authority (either hierarchical or collegial: see Waters 1989, 1993). In the same vein, the opposition made between models of institutionalization of power and models of circulation of power (Ocasio 1994; Ocasio and Kim, 1999) renders the institu-tionalizing and the circulating mechanisms mutually exclusive, which oversimplifies the intimate corporate political dynamics involved.

When we return to classical political writers, we find that institutionalizing and circulating principles are not opposite features but complementary traits of the political structure of organizations. The persistence of an oligarchic political regime is the consequence of the circulation of oligarchs: likewise, the circulation of oligarchs may be the consequence of mechanisms of power's entrenchment. Therefore, examining corporate élite implies seeing organizations as contested oligarchies, i.e., places where underlying political mechanisms and the controlled circulation of different élites and key people within and/or outside the firm leads to the perpetuation of the principal oligarchy (CEOs and major directors). Does that mean that business organizations are *fatally* inegalitarian, lacking original infusions of vitality in the longer run?

The question of egalitarianism has proven to be one of the most controversial issues in the political and organizational field because it is about the issue of equality. It is addressed best in various theories of democracy. At the outset, we should acknowledge that, of course, business organizations are not nor do they aspire to be democracies. However, they have to have some egalitarian elements if the next generation of leaders is to emerge as those best suited for rule. There have to be elements of internal democracy between contenders. Dahl points out that political equality is a crucial issue

> not only as a means of self-protection, but also as a necessary condition for many other important values, including one of the most fundamental of all human freedoms, the freedom to help determine, in cooperation with others, the laws and rules that one must obey (…) differences in ownership and control of enterprises (…) are deeply implicated in inequalities of many kinds: in esteem, respect, and status, in control over one's daily life, in income and wealth (…) in life chances for adults and children alike (1985: 5–6).

Hinings and Greenwood (2002) similarly argue that the issue of the distribution of power and privileges within organizations that is, the question of why power structures are fundamentally concentrated, is one which has been addressed too fitfully by organizational scholars these past two or three decades. We suggest it is partly because of an inability to think about the simultaneous dynamics of opposite political regimes, that is, to think about power in *hybrid* instead of in *exclusive* terms. As far as the social production of oligarchy is concerned, these hybrid views derive from the work of Tocqueville and Michels.

## Corporate *élites* in the maze of democratic regimes

Before connecting back to the argument concerning corporate élites, a brief excursus on democratic theory is necessary, which entails looking at Dahl's engagement with Tocqueville. Dahl (1985: 8–9) summarizes Tocqueville's argument in four sets of propositions:

(1) Equality is increasing and inevitable
(2) Liberty is 'a good of supreme importance (…) but the love of equality is stronger than the love of fidelity', which may be threatened
(3) A condition for liberty to be true is the existence of mechanisms restricting the concentration of power
(4) There is, nonetheless, a paradoxical dynamic toward despotic forms of government.

Reflecting on democracy, Dahl confirms Tocqueville's view that democratic regimes are prone to self-destruction and that the dynamics of equality might turn democracy into a new form of tyranny (Dahl, 1985: 31). At best, the fragility of democratic regimes forces them to use a 'partly democratized oligarchy' (Dahl, 1985: 41), an 'oligarchical democracy' in Wilde's terms (1978). Thus, it is the combination of opposite forms of government that is likely to help democratic regimes survive within oligarchic structures of power. Taking the case of US corporations, Dahl asserts, 'the internal governments of economic enterprises are flatly undemocratic both *de jure* and *de facto*' (1985: 55). More specifically, he considers that the government of US large corporations could be seen in term of guardianship: 'Although managers are nominally selected by a board of directors, which in turn is nominally chosen by and legally accountable to stockholders, in reality new managers are typically co-opted by existing management which also, in practice, chooses and controls its own board of directors' (Dahl, 1985: 117: see also Herman 1981; Mizruchi, 1983). In this perspective, organizations are, politically speaking, ruled by a co-optive guardianship, creating barriers around a restricted group of individuals holding major power resources and governing their allocation. Corporate élite formation is therefore consubstantial with organizational settings.

In his book on Tocqueville, Poggi (1972) insists on four factors which, tied together, oblige democratic regimes to combine with oligarchic tendencies. The first factor is the *status insecurity deriving from democratic rules*. Poggi reminds us that for Tocqueville individuals in a democratic society display an amazing similarity of concerns and patterns of actions; democratic rules offer abstract and general commands, which discipline those individuals who might otherwise think that they are 'unique'. The desire for advancement and security is therefore stronger than the drive to develop individual aspects of one's own personality. Individuals, being supposedly 'equals' and sharing rights of 'citizenship', focus their attention 'on the advantages that they do not share with all' (Poggi 1972: 35). Indeed, discrepancies between individuals, according to the diversity of the dimensions of status (income, prestige...), render the democratic individual uncertain, worrying about the immediate future, under constant pressure to evaluate and compare his/her position, and resentful and fearsome that they might be overtaken by others. Most people expect to improve their situation by their own effort more than by solidary actions or through cooperation with 'equals'. A mass of equal and atomized individuals needs an oligarchy to avoid being permanently threatened by anarchy, according to Tocqueville. The pervasiveness and strength of central government produces contrary condition to those of anarchy. Under a tutelary oligarchy, people enter into compulsory relationships of cooperation, partly because they have similar concerns, fears and weaknesses.

The second factor is what Poggi terms the *privatization of individual concerns* (1972: 43). As Tocqueville argues: 'everybody shuts himself tightly into himself, and from there claims the right to judge the world' (1969: 550). Democratic social relations lead individuals to see themselves, and others

constituted as being either alike, or different to them, as the only point of reference, emphasizing constantly their capacities and performances rather than their membership of orders with social bonds. Every individual is a potential threat in the race for status and reward. Therein resides the democratic paradox pointed out by Poggi, one that is likely to produce oligarchic tendencies: in democracy, membership in the political sphere should be extended to the larger society rather than restricted to élites. At the same time, however, such openness encourages those who, in Weber's memorable phrase, live neither for nor off politics to develop an apolitical outlook and political apathy – which comprises the third factor. *Participation in public affairs is actually weak*: few, other than the élites, really invest much effort in political decisions (such as the choice of leaders), and thus an oligarchic minority tends to dominate, reinforcing what Poggi calls the 'consumerist view of politics' (1972: 45). The fourth factor concerns the *non-existence and lack of power of intermediate groups* in the democratic system. For Tocqueville, individuals, weakened by their isolation, are all the more powerless the more the governing body is overwhelmingly more powerful: the disintegration of social ties is thus followed by temporary and transitory relationships which do not provide space for strong intermediate bodies of influential actors.

For Tocqueville, the best way to assure that individuals should be treated as equals in the same way is by having one single government for all people. The idea of unique authority stems from the belief in the fundamental equality of all individuals. If all people are equal, each individual should be able and obliged to take care of their self, without the assistance of others; alone, however, their ability to self-govern proves to be limited. Thus, the demand for enlarged and centralized governments is the result of the democratic principle of individual rights and freedom (Zuckert, 1983). As Zuckert reminds us, following Tocqueville's insights, decentralized political institutions do not restrict the powers of the central government, at least because of this constant request for 'superior' instances coming from people. Efficient despotism partly results from the deficiencies of people in assuring the concrete achievement of the self-government principle of democracy.

For all the reasons evoked above, political leaders tend to favour the development of intermediate groupings, intensifying individual commitments and limiting the prerogatives of the central power to a restricted set of issues. Thus, they try to enhance the construction of strong and efficient internal élites, owing much to the leader, and eventually, aspiring to become leaders. That this is the case is as true of business as political leaders: business oligarchy also reproduces itself through these processes of internal centrally coordinated democratization.

As individual concerns are 'privatized' in Tocqueville's terms, the leaders must make purposeful decisions if they are to move away from despotic tendencies. Therefore, oligarchs sustain their power by developing democratic principles and peculiar intermediate groups of 'political' actors, but it is still the central oligarchic power which determines and delineates the type of groups, their prerogatives and who, in these groups, is likely to compose the 'inner circle' (Useem, 1984). The *circular nature of [business] oligarchy* is what makes it different from a despotic regime; as Poggi puts it, despotism is a degeneration of the inertial tendencies of democracy (1972: 49). Oligarchy may paradoxically hinder despotic tendencies by engineering a 'constitutional and organizational design' which creates space for intermediate political bodies (Poggi, 1972), thus enhancing institutional differentiation within the organization. As such, the major differentiation deals with the political agenda: oligarchy centralizes governmental issues and decisions, while intermediate bodies deal with administrative decisions, within a delimited sphere of competence. They do not make general laws but they constitute familiar settings for individuals who rely on them,[2] because they are more meaningful than organizational political structures and also

because they are 'nurseries that develop future leaders' (Poggi, 1972: 52).

Tocqueville's insight is that oligarchy may combine with institutional differentiation and fragmentation.[3] The relatively composite nature of the political structure is likely to place boundaries on governmental action, boundaries deemed all the more legitimate as the oligarchs themselves maintain them. The fragmentation of the organization in different intermediate bodies selectively aims also to diffuse political ambitions within people. Thus, we argue there is a mutual conditioning between oligarchy and democracy within business organizations, leading to the perpetuation of the corporate oligarchy.

## Michels and the professional oligarch

Michels defined the famous iron law of oligarchy in the following terms: 'It is organization which gives birth to the dominion of the elected over the electors, of the mandataries over the mandators, of the delegates over the delegators. Who says organization, says oligarchy' (Michels, 1915: 401). Lipset *et al.* (1956) following in Michel's path, recognized that 'at the head of most organizations stand a small group of people (…) whose tenure and control is rarely threatened by a serious internal organized opposition' (Lipset *et al.*, 1956: 4). In Lipset's view, the link between oligarchic forms of government and the overwhelming power of the incumbent leaders is mainly explained by monopolies over the resources of politics: effective channels of communication to the membership, skills of leadership, financial resources, status and prestige; in that sense, an organization that would be in some respects democratic has to break these monopolies one way or another, especially by offering members the opportunity to acquire organizational and political skills, at least for those aspiring members of the sub-élite.

The idea underlying Michels' iron law of oligarchy is that administrative and political demands lead to bureaucratization, as a set of rules centralizing authority, even in organizations whose rule is to promote equality, namely social democratic political parties. If we follow May (1965), Michel's basic reasoning could be contained in three apparently contradictory propositions: that organization precludes democracy, can destroy democracy, and can facilitate democratization (May, 1965: 418). According to Michels,

> Organization implies the tendency to oligarchy... Immanent oligarchical tendencies [exist] in every kind of human organization which strives for the attainment of definite ends...Oligarchy is...a preordained form of the common life of great social aggregates...The majority of human beings, in a condition of eternal tutelage, are predestined...to submit to the dominion of a small minority, and must...constitute a pedestal of an oligarchy...leadership is a necessary phenomenon in every form of social life [and] every system of leadership is incompatible with the most essential postulates of democracy...All order and civilization must exhibit aristocratic features (Michels, 1915: 11, 32: 390–400, 402).

Despite these 'radical' declarations, Michels tends to define oligarchy as an intermediate form between pure democracy and pure autocracy. To him, organization necessitates oligarchy as a set of arrangements that are neither absolutely democratic nor absolutely autocratic (May, 1965: 419), but, more crucially, Michels argues

> Democracy leads to oligarchy, and necessarily contains an oligarchical nucleus. When democracies have gained a certain stage of development, they undergo a gradual transformation, adopting the aristocratic spirit, and in many cases also the aristocratic forms, against which at the outset they struggled so fiercely...[organization] is the source from which the conservative currents flow over the plain of democracy (Michels 1915: 22, 168, 408).

The emergence of the iron law of oligarchy is what happens to groups that initially are democracies. Such an aristocratic tendency is manifest, for Michels, in any kind of association, which becomes more or less rapidly 'divided into a minority of directors and a majority of directed' (1915: 32). To him, what is crucial in this dynamic is that 'the first appearance of professional leadership' marks 'the beginning of the end' for democracy (1915: 36). Thus, democracy also ends 'by undergoing transformation into a form of government by the best, into an aristocracy' (1915: 89). People attaining bureaucratic eminence are those considered the most talented and precious individuals: as for Tocqueville, Michels sees democracy as, rather than being based on a 'simple equality', a way of giving to each individual 'the possibility of ascending to the top of the social scale ... annulling ... all privileges of birth ... the struggle for preeminence should be decided in accordance with individual capacity'. It is an agenda common with Weberian bureaucracy even if, according to Michels, 'the bureaucratic spirit corrupts character and engenders moral poverty' (1915: 189). Oligarchy, based on the advent of professional leadership, creates a struggle between leaders striving in competition to solidify their own positions. For Lipset et al. the existence of democracy implies permanent insecurity for those in governing positions (1956: 10). For Michels professional leaders have a fundamental interest in yearning for status-maintenance. Moreover, this interest seems to converge with the political apathy of the masses. Michels evokes the 'general immobility and passivity of the masses' and sees it 'as a major source of oligarchy' because 'the leaders ... constitute a more stable and constant element' (1915). As a result, it is this 'technical indispensability of leadership' (1915: 400) which renders the leaders stable and the followers obedient: people 'cannot dispense with the qualities he [the leader] has acquired in virtue of the very position to which they have themselves elevated him, and because they do not see their way to find an adequate substitute' (1915: 86). In other words, people's need for strong points of reference and stability takes the shape of the fragmented oligarchies being scattered cautiously and purposefully by business leaders within the organization, thanks to the policies of mobility.[4]

Let us, in the next section, switch focus to current organizational preoccupations. In the maze of new emerging organizational and political forms, one thing remains constant: all alternative forms of organization and power that have been invented over say, the last 30 years, share something in common – they are all supposed to replace, banish and to end the iconic but despised form of bureaucracy. New organizational forms proliferate everywhere as alternatives to bureaucracy in the literature.

## CORPORATE ELITES IN A POLYARCHIC WORLD

Precisely because most alternative forms have sought to loosen bureaucratic controls and procedures (Clegg *et al.*, 2006), they are increasingly likely to encourage contestation and participation because they are not relying on clear cut hierarchical structures. As Vallas puts it, 'conflict and instability, rather than simple or passive consent, may thus be inherent features of the new managerial regimes' (2006: 1710) which obliges corporate élite and their local 'servants' to constantly negotiate and tolerate contentious behaviours they would not have tolerated previously.

Oligarchy, to be perpetuated, needs to enhance and encourage potential contestation and rivalries, as well as political ambitions among the sub-oligarchs, the Tocquevillean paradox sketched above. Debates among members should be monitored and their scope relatively defined but contestation must be viewed as possible by the members of the organization. A political structure allowing people to contest, selectively rewarding contestation, and at the same time utterly ruled by a small and self-perpetuating circle of corporate leaders is what we call polyarchy, deriving from the initial framework developed by Dahl (1971). Polyarchy draws its features both from oligarchic and democratic forms of government. To define this model, we need first to compare it to three other political models: the bureaucratic (Weber, 1968), the collegial (Waters, 1989, 1993; Lazega, 2000), and the democratic-collectivist (Rothschild-Whitt, 1979; Rothschild and Whitt, 1986).

These are also models of power (Waters 1993).

## Three alternative political models of organizations

For the purpose of this chapter, we will succinctly describe these models in order to provide some insights into the 'fourth' model, polyarchy, as the contemporary political structure produced by and producing the continuing perpetuation of corporate oligarchies.

Bureaucracy is evidently the cornerstone of organization studies, and a central icon of contemporary sociological and organizational thought. Basically, since Weber, bureaucracy has been defined according to three major criteria: '(1) The regular activities required for the purposes of the bureaucratically governed structure are assigned as official duties. (2) The authority to give commands required for the discharge of these duties is distributed in a stable way and is strictly delimited by rules concerning the coercive means, physical, sacerdotal, or otherwise, which may be placed at the disposal of officials. (3) Methodical provision is made for the regular and continuous fulfillment of these duties and for the exercise of the corresponding rights; only persons who qualify under general rules are employed' (Weber, 1968: 956). Bureaucracy signifies the concentration of the means of administration and of control over these means, under the tutelage of a rule-governed system of government.[5] To achieve these goals, Weber stipulates that 'Bureaucratic domination means fundamentally domination through knowledge (…). This consists on the one hand in technical knowledge which, by itself, is sufficient to ensure it a position of extraordinary power. But, in addition to this, bureaucratic organizations, or the holders of power who make use of them, have the tendency to increase their power still further by the knowledge growing out of experience in the service' (Weber, 1968: 225). Bureaucracy, from this point of view, precludes the possibility that organizations might be governed as 'polities'. In other words, it tends to indirectly hampering discussion, deliberation and decision among the members of the organization. Bureaucracy is ruled by legitimate oligarchic systems founded on the concentration of knowledge in the hands of the 'ruling few'. Thus, at first sight, bureaucracy is not open to contestation; it might even be designed as a way to practically 'discourage' contestation, while not forbidding it officially.

The difficulty in creating organizations as 'open polities' (Davis *et al.*, 2005), such as polyarchic models, contributes to interest in the research directions offered by the so-called *collectivist organization* (Rothschild-Whitt 1979; Rothschild and Whitt, 1986). The construction of this model aims to counter the political inevitability of bureaucratic oligarchies, that is, to uncover the conditions which impede or facilitate participative collective decision-making processes. What Rothschild and Whitt call these 'alternative institutions' (1986: 12) represent 'rejection of mainstream organization and an attempt by members to live out other values' (ibid.). Collectivist organizations are based on a certain idea of participative democracy, arguing for 'self-governance in the workplace' (1986: 13). Collectivism means that 'obedience is given to ideology: that is to ideological norms rather than formal laws or rules' (Satow, 1975: 527–528). Central oligarchic domination is erased so that legitimate authority resides in the whole collectivity, a true 'community' in Tönnies' terms, where individuals are incorporated into the polity. Contrary to oligarchic kinds of political structures, collectivist decisions are morally binding only if they reflect the collective will and if they are taken after a process of democratic deliberation supposed to help in achieving a consensus (1986: 50). Egalitarianism is the central feature of such settings where social stratification and differentiation are minimized, to eliminate rivalries and the division of labour. Collective deliberation rather than true contestation therefore constitute this political type. Put differently, collectivist organizations shape closed political structures under the auspices

of the 'tyranny of the collective', instead of the tyranny of the inner circle, so to speak.

The problem with the two previous models is that they both tend to close the polity and therefore, to foster a non-genuine pluralist perspective. In bureaucratic power structures, discussion is simply not included in the package; in collectivist power structures, deliberation of the collective/within the collective might prevent specific individuals taking risks and formulating personal grievances. Collective organizations are often shaped strongly by collectivist ideologies that make it difficult to challenge the conventions of their belief.

Some scholars suggest that collegial forms might offer a hybrid between both models. Waters defines collegial organizations as 'those in which there is dominant orientation to a consensus achieved between the members of a body of experts who are theoretically equals in their levels of expertise but who are specialized by area of expertise' (1989: 956). In other words, a mix between élite knowledge (the professionals) and consensus seeking behaviours is likely to be established. Such forms of power may become more important as a growing number of firms are involved in knowledge-intensive production (Alvesson, 1995; Lazega, 2000; Adler, 2001) founded on the permanent creation of new professions. Those knowledge-intensive firms are often accompanied by a decrease in rational and concentrated systems of power, through both the reduction of hierarchical levels and the political involvement of a growing number of people. Formal egalitarianism, collective decision making via collective forums and diverse committees, selection of official positions through elections among professionals, institute the democratic body regulating contentions, and therefore, encourage contention between peers, because consensus is obtained systematically in relation to knowledge (Waters, 1993: 75). Collegiality is a way of limiting central authorities by organizing special social relationships between comparable groups of individuals. Power here is both the object of contention (for example when it comes to evaluating which group is superior in the internal scales of status and prestige) and serves to regulate contention.

Do these alternative models offer clear political alternatives to oligarchic tendencies, or do they just widen the diversity of legitimate forms of oligarchy: rule-based oligarchy, communitarian oligarchy or knowledge-based oligarchy? Do corporate and professional élites spread their wings over actual power distribution mechanisms and continue to exercise more or less obtrusive control over the emergence of contesting and resisting actors? Let us finish with our argument. If élites strive to keep on self perpetuating, they need to give a new impetus to patterns of contestation within the organizational polity. The question has mainly been addressed in organizational literature through the connection between organization theory and social movement theory (Davis, *et al*., 2005). We suggest now an alternative founded on the creation of *polyarchic élite*.

## Polyarchies

Dahl (1971) has already identified the potentiality of the polyarchic model. To him, 'Polyarchies (…) are political regimes that have been substantially popularized and liberalized, that is, highly inclusive and extensively open to public contestation' (1971: 8). Dahl suggests locating political regimes theoretically in a space bounded by two dimensions: public contestation and the right to participate. Polyarchy appears to be an 'imperfect approximation' of the democratic model. It arises when the mutual security of the governors and the governed is preserved. In other terms, the chances of public contestation are greater when governmental actors are not impeded in acting according to the values and principles of the basis on which they hold office. However, once fragments of the polity have understood and interpreted the rules of the game, their contestation is likely to be welcomed, accepted and potentially, 'absorbed' by the organization (Leeds, 1964).

We therefore define polyarchic organizations as mainly characterized by a tension between the official recognition of the political plurality of members and of their right to disagree with the leaders, and the simultaneous concentration of political power.

In polyarchic organizations, contestation is no doubt higher than participation and inclusiveness, to follow Dahl's categories. But what differs from mere 'competitive oligarchies' (Dahl 1971: 8) is that the low inclusiveness results from individual choices rather than from the political structure itself. Nothing really impedes the political participation and voicing of individuals, particularly at local and sub-group levels. People have the official right to contest, but they mostly don't. The weakness of contestation within corporations is a problem for corporate oligarchs, we suggest. It is more and more difficult to convince the polity that business is ruled by entrepreneurial systems and behaviours, when obedience to procedures and official codes is the fulcrum of management models. Therefore, oligarchs strive to develop new sub-élites based on corporate professions or quasi-professions to enhance participation. It is through these types of intermediary political groupings that oligarchies can coexist with political pluralism and therefore encourage contestation.

We posit a theory of political pluralism, based on the idea that 'in a large complex society, the body of the citizenry is unable to affect the policies of the state' (Lipset *et al*., 1956: 15). According to Lipset and his colleagues it is therefore necessary to fragment the political body: 'democracy is most likely to become institutionalized in organizations whose members form organized or structured sub-groups which while maintaining a basic loyalty to the larger organization, constitute relatively independent and autonomous centers of power within the organization … democracy is strengthened when members are not only related to the larger organization but are also affiliated with or loyal to sub-groups within the organization' (1956: 15).

Polyarchies encourage the development of powerful internal professions, as we noted above. There is also a political purpose behind such models, because 'the stability of any democracy depends not on imposing a single unitary loyalty and viewpoint but on maintaining conflicting loyalties and viewpoints in a state of tension' (Crossman, 1954: 66). Polyarchic oligarchs try to build a democratic plurality while reinforcing the power of the inner circle. Social fragmentation striving towards mere individualization generates a particular nature of social relationships: the polyarchic organization is composed of a manifold of 'loosened communities' (Courpasson and Dany, 2003; Courpasson, 2006), i.e., groups where binding solidarities are weak, but where temporary cohesiveness may be strong, as in the case of project teams or sub-units confronted with stiff internal competition for resources and performance rankings. Weak and short-lived solidarity among members is also part of the hybridization process of polyarchy. The explicit mixing of concentrated oligarchic power and of open systems of contestation and participation are likely to give birth to an uncertain solidarity, where short lived cohesions replace long run belongings and identities.

The *contentious* culture of polyarchies is nourished while giving to central managerial oligarchs the legitimacy to close the discussion and to take decisions, in the name of the collective good, since, as Lipset puts it, democracy 'rests on the fact that no one group is able to secure such a basis of power and command over the total allegiance of a majority of the population that it can effectively suppress or deny the claims of groups it opposes' (1956: 411). Oligarchs are not really threatened by being open to the possibility of opposing arguments.

### 'We have always been oligarchs': élite resilience and transformative élite

Beyond Putnam's remark that 'power has always been confined to a ruling few' (1976), the debate relative to the appropriate level of élite production, and of the degree of élite fragmentation remains open. We have suggested analysis of the polyarchic political regime within which corporate élite set up the rules of the organizational game. To sum up, we propose that élite fragmentation is a reality of organizations but it is monitored by inner circles which have the power to create or enhance the creation of new internal sub-élites that are socially controlled as 'would-be leaders' nurseries'.

The question of the exogenous and/or endogenous production of élites is relative to the opposition between analysis in terms of inter-organizational élite production (Mizruchi, 1996) and intra-organizational élite production. There is an extended literature on patterns of élite production (Putnam, 1976) whose findings are still equivocal. From internal modes of executives' careers (either sponsored or contested to take Turner's [1960]) categories to the social dynamics of interlocking directorates (Mizruchi, 1996), through the role of specific social networks in the simultaneous production of élite and of perpetuation of élite structure (Davis, *et al.*, 2003), little definite resolution of patterning exists. In the following table (Table 25.1), we nevertheless draw from Useem's initial classification of the three bases of élite production to better understand the principles of élite production, before striving to see whether those very principles are changing or persisting today.

The most classic categorization of élite production systems is that of Useem (1984). Three major modes are highlighted (see also Pettigrew, 1992): inter-organizational élite cohesion and social/professional learning through governance systems (the interlock effect); condensation and sedimentation of class-based principles, which are founded on the existence of an aristocracy and of all its social devices (the upper-class effect); organizational mechanisms of career management, enabling the corporation to select the people and to define the criteria of corporate ascent (the organization effect). It is interesting to note that each of these social mechanisms rely upon political foundations and significations.

**Table 25.1 Some functions of the principles of élite production (From Useem, 1984)**

| Functions/Principles | Class-based | Network-based | Company-based |
|---|---|---|---|
| Typical mechanism of production | Boarding Schools | Interlocks | Fast-tracks |
| | 'Ivy League' kinds of educational system | | Internal education programmes |
| Typical leadership profile | Heirs | Political managers | Corporate professionals |
| Values bolstered | Business leaders as aristocracy and defenders of tradition | Business leaders as political representatives | Business leaders as parochial defenders |
| Political purpose | Social perpetuation and élite unity | Cohesive ties and business as a whole power structure | Endogenous stratification monitored from the top |

In other words, the prevalence of one or another of these principles allows us to shed light on a specific *cultural cognition* associated with the very notion of élites, namely, upper-class mechanisms that stipulate that élite production is constantly intermingled with élite perpetuation, and this principle of perpetuation implies that élites keep a significant distance with the mass of the governed. Such distance is the essential principle of legitimacy of the élites; it is by being different, it is by signalling that getting to the top is not possible for everybody, irrespective of their merits, that the élite persuades people that there are impervious worlds and that these worlds are necessary to the balance of societies – and the organization.

The interlock effect has a different meaning. There is an economic perspective that proposes that the exchange of resources between board members and the fact that these exchanges are likely to improve governance decisions and therefore, organizational performance, is what is important. Because corporate élite members are 'professionals', as Michels would put it, their cooperation will surely reduce the uncertainties of business decisions. Second, there is a class perspective on interlocks (Zeitlin, 1974) which stresses the social cohesiveness produced through the interlocking directorates: in this view, élite power might well shift from individual companies to transcorporate networks where the actual location and identity of power holders is fuzzier and less controllable by external actors. Finally, the organization effect

puts the stress on the capacity of individual organizations to choose and design their own models of authority and legitimacy. By career mechanisms, companies strive to differentiate themselves so as, for example, to be perceived as more attractive for highly qualified workers. The élite production system aims therefore to shape a particular organizational identity.

That being said, as Mills reminds us, the common objective of all these principles is to decide to what extent and for what political reasons the élite should be socially and culturally homogenous (Mills, 1957: 19) or should transform and control this transformation by choosing the new characteristics of the new members.

## CONCLUSION: POLYARCHIC ELITISM

Periods of change can be extremely fruitful for reconsidering certain foundations, both in social and organization theory and in the shaping of new political regimes. Particularly, in this chapter we have argued that current upheavals in the business world should lead us to rethink entirely the organizational and sociological foundations of élite legitimacy and action via the official inclusion of contestation within political regimes. From the perspective developed here, every kind of managerial decision should be considered as an object of contention by the polity, which does not mean that contestation is going to be systematized and utilize the productive energies and efforts of polyarchic polities.

It means that corporate élite should accept that their very prominence implies that they are more and more becoming subject to forms of 'organizational activism' previously hosted by states and governments, and orchestrated by unions and clearly organized movements. In polyarchies, however, business leaders are more and more subject to challenges from within. To follow Tilly (2006), new *repertoires of contention* are progressively going to affect the structures of organizational power and therefore, some ingredients of élite power. Some are linked to global movements (Davis and Zald, 2005), others to internal 'opt-out revolts' (Mainero and Sullivan, 2006), or to the multiplication of overlapping 'team arrangements' allowed by transnational cooperation straddling several organizations and countries. It turns out that classical oligarchic structures *à la Michels* or *à la Weber* are probably unable to fully understand and take advantage of the new forms of contention that emerge from the maze of hybrid democratic regimes.

In this chapter, we have tried to address the eternal question of corporate élite power through defining a possible type of political structure which might be more conducive to democratic leadership and the agency of the polities through contestation. We have even suggested that the long-lasting oligarchic political strategy of self perpetuation might be reinforced by the creation of hybrid political models simultaneously enhancing contestation and power concentration. Elite resilience is shaped by social structures and clear cut class effects. It is also guided by the capacity of élite members to go beyond their status as oligarchs so as to create conditions for developing the agency of participants. If they understand all the innovative potency of new forms of mobilization and resistance, contemporary organizational leaders should devise strategies of power entrenchment and of openings for contestation. Exploring this tension is probably one of the most promising directions for connecting organization studies and political analysis. Clemens (2005) clearly defines how feminist contributions have demonstrated the ways through which

'second wave feminism' has generated a rich array of new organizational forms; in other words, contestation is likely to result in the celebration of organization as a key to success. It is through organization that contestation is likely to be productive. Polyarchy entails that 'activists' are allowed to create alternative forms of mobilization and entrepreneurship so that they contribute to change. In polyarchies, contestation does not equate with protest against routine politics and established élite. It is through the creation of new organizational forms that contestation is likely to be different from mere evanescent and temporary rebellions (Clemens, 1996).

Put differently, contestation might well be the fundamental principle of corporate élite power: contested mobility and careers, contested decisions, contested principles of action – these are the norms. Future oligarchs must accept that the diversity of constituencies, as well as what is more important, the soundness of these constituencies on certain topics, should lead them to adopt cooperative and contested forms of management instead of relying on extremely concentrated and falsely empowered polities. The polyarchic framework opens new ways of thinking about the co-evolution of élite resilience processes and of organizational transformation: we need to understand that élite self perpetuation may be conditioned by the capacity of some organizations to comply with internal contestation and requests, to accept that they might be wrong, to listen to the agency of actors, to use this agency for accurate and timely workplace transformation. Such insights shed a new light on pluralist perspectives on élite power.

Understanding how élite perpetuation is dependent on accepting resistance to change would perhaps simply confirm that hegemonies are, more or less, established on the connivance of the polities, but that this connivance does not rest upon the rationales of indifference, laziness, lack of time, or lack of genuine interest in improving the workplace. On the contrary, polyarchic leaders must develop their understanding of those sorts of social complexities if they want still to 'be oligarchs' in the future. Paradoxically, maybe, being an oligarch today means getting rid of a basic theoretical imagery leading one to think of èlitism in terms of oppression and domination, and to conceive of contestation in terms of opposition. Other imageries of social ordering are needed to move towards èlitist polyarchies.

## NOTES

1 This tendency reminds us of what Lukes (1974) termed the uni-dimensional view of power, exclusively focused on observable decision and issues placed on the explicit political agenda (see Dahl, 1957). However, numerous writers, including Lukes (1974), have since recognized how a two- and three-dimensional view, which includes concealed agendas and non-decisions may be useful to understand the multiplex actions and inactions involved in the 'circuits of power' (Clegg, 1989) constituting the political structure of organizations.

2 Typically this is the purpose of sub-units, teamwork and professional bodies to assure this intermediate function within contemporary organizations, as we will suggest later in this chapter.

3 To Tocqueville, addressing more specifically the question of democracy in the entire society, this fragmentation goes hand in hand with the existence of politically significant rights, such as taking part in the elections, freedom of association or freedom of expression: 'every citizen, vested with rights, takes part within his own sphere in the process of government' (1969: 383). Obviously, the question of knowing under which conditions individuals will exercise their rights is beyond the scope of this chapter. According to Tocqueville, it is likely that the exercise of rights could turn into the expression of selfish demands.

4 As we will suggest, project management is part of these political means of enhancing both the creation of a specific nursery of potential leaders and the atomization of individual futures by the temporary alliances made around a project theme. We have termed these phenomena 'loosened communities' (Courpasson and Dany, 2003; Courpasson, 2006).

5 From a political point of view, bureaucracies are according to Weber monocratic forms, i.e., where 'power is concentrated in the position of a single individual leader and which is distributed down a bureaucratic hierarchy to a group of officials who in turn execute the policies of the leader in relation to a non-official group of followers constituted as clients, workers, or citizens' (Waters, 1993: 56); an administrative corresponding model of oligarchy at first glance.

## REFERENCES

Adler, P. (2001) 'Market, hierarchy and trust: The knowledge economy and the future of capitalism', *Organization Science*, 12 (2): 215–234.

Alvesson, M. (1995) *The Management of Knowledge-intensive Companies*. Berlin/New York: De Gruyter.

Armstrong, E.A. (2002) 'Crisis, collective creativity, and the generation of new organizational forms: The transformation of lesbian/gay organizations in San Francisco', in M. Lounsbury and M. Ventresca (eds) *Social Structure and Organizations Revisited. Research in the Sociology of Organizations*. Amsterdam: JAI, pp. 361–397.

Aron, R. (1960) 'Social class, political class, ruling class', *European Journal of Sociology*, 1: 260–281.

Betts, R.K. (2000) 'Is strategy an illusion?', *International Security*, fall: 5–50.

Clegg, S. (1989) *Frameworks of Power*. London: Sage.

Clegg, S., Courpasson, D. and Phillips, N. (2006) *Power and Organizations*. London: Sage.

Clemens, E. (1996) 'Organizational form as frame: Collective identity and political strategy in the American labor movement', in G.F. Davis, D. McAdam, R.W. Scott and M.N. Zald (eds) *Comparative Perspectives on Social Movements: Opportunities, Mobilizing Structures, and Cultural Framings*. New York: Cambridge University Press, pp. 205–226.

Clemens, E. (2005) 'Two kinds of stuff: The current encounter of social movements and organizations', in G.F. Davis, D. McAdam, R.W. Scott and M.N. Zald (eds) *Social Movements and Organization Theory*. Cambridge: Cambridge University Press, pp. 351–367.

Courpasson, D. (2006) *Soft Coercion. Liberal Organizations and Domination*. Copenhagen: Copenhagen Business School Press/Liber.

Courpasson, D. and Francoise D. (2003) 'Indifference or obedience? Business firms as democratic hybrids', *Organization Studies*, 24 (8): 1231–1260.

Crossman, R.H.S. (1954) 'On political neuroses', *Encounter*, 2: 66.

Dahl, R. (1957) 'The concept of power', *Behavioral Science*, 2: 201–215.

Dahl, R. (1971) *Polyarchy. Participation and Opposition*. New Haven: Yale University Press.

Dahl, R. (1985) *A Preface to Economic Democracy*. Berkeley: University of California Press.

Davis, G. F., Yoo, M. and Baker, W.E. (2003) 'The small world of the American corporate elite, 1982–2001', *Strategic Organization*, 1 (3): 301–326.

Davis, G.F., McAdam, D., Scott, W.R. and M.N. Zald (2005) *Social Movements and Organizational Theory*. Cambridge: Cambridge University Press.

Davis, G.F. and M.N. Zald (2005) 'Social change and social theory and the convergence of movements and organizations', in G.F. Davis, D. McAdam, W.R. Scott and M.N. Zald (eds) *Social Movements and Organization Theory*. Cambridge: Cambridge University Press.

Emirbayer, M. and Mische, A. (1997) 'What is agency?', *American Journal of Sociology*, 103 (4): 962–1023.

Freeman, J. (1975) *The Politics of Women's Liberation*. New York: Longman.

Gamson, W.A. and Schmeidler, E. (1984) 'Organizing the poor', *Theory and Society*, 13: 567–584.

Herman, E.S. (1981) *Corporate Control, Corporate Power*. Cambridge: Cambridge University Press.

Hinings, C.R. and Greenwood, R. (2002) 'Disconnects and consequences in organization theory', *Administrative Science Quarterly*, 47: 411–421.

Katznelson, I. (1997) 'Structure and configuration in comparative politics', in M.I. Lichbach and A.S. Zuckerman (eds) *Comparative Politics: Rationality, Culture, and Structure*. Cambridge: Cambridge University Press, pp. 81–112.

Kingdon, J.W. (1995) *Agendas, Alternatives, and Public Policies*, 2nd edn. Boston: Little, Brown.

Lazega, E. (2000) *The Collegial Phenomenon*. Oxford: Oxford University Press.

Leeds, R. (1964) 'The absorption of protest: A working paper', in W.W. Cooper, H.J. Leavitt and M.W. Shelly II (eds) *New Perspectives in Organizational Research*. New York: Wiley.

Lipset, S.M., Trow, M.A. and Coleman, J.S. (1956) *Union Democracy. The Internal Politics of the International Typographical Union*. Glencoe, IL: The Free Press.

Lukes, S. (1974) *Power. A Radical View*. London: Macmillan.

McAdam, D., Tarrow, S. and Tilly, C. (2000) *Dynamics of Contention*. Cambridge: Cambridge University Press.

Mainero, L.A. and Sullivan, S.E. (2006) *The Opt-Out Revolt. Why People are Leaving Companies to Create Kaleidoscope Careers*. Mountain View, CA: Davies-Black Publishing.

Marx, K. (1972) *The Eighteenth Brumaire of Louis Napoleon*. New York: International Publishers.

May, J.D. (1965) 'Democracy, organization, Michels', *The American Political Science Review*, 59 (2): 417–429.

McCarthy, J.D. and Zald, M.N. (2002) 'The enduring vitality of the resource mobilization theory of social movements', in J.H. Turner (ed.) *Handbook of Sociological Theory*. New York: Kluwer Academic/Plenum Publishers, pp. 533–565.

McLean, M. and Harvey, C. (2006) *Business Elites and Corporate Governance in France and the UK*. London: Palgrave Mcmillan.

Michels, R. (1915) *Political Parties. A Sociological Study of the Oligarchical Tendencies of Modern Democracy*. New York: Hearst's International Library Co.

Mills, C.W. (1957) *The Power Elite*. New York: Oxford University Press.

Mizruchi, M.S. (1983) 'Who controls whom? An examination of the relation between management and boards of directors in large American corporations', *Academy of Management Review*, 8 (3): 426–435.

Mizruchi, M.S. (1996) 'What do interlocks do? An analysis, critique, and reassessment of research on interlocking directorates', *Annual Review of Sociology*, 22: 271–298.

Morris, A. and Staggenborg, S. (2004) 'Leadership in social movements', in D.A. Snow, S.A. Soule and H. Kriesi (eds) *The Blackwell Companion to Social Movements*. Malden, MA: Blackwell, pp. 171–196.

Mosca, G. (1939) *The Ruling Class*. New York: McGraw.

Ocasio, W. (1994) 'Political dynamics and the circulation of power: CEO succession in U.S. industrial corporations, 1960–1990', *Administrative Science Quarterly*, 39: 285–312.

Ocasio, W. and Hyosun K. (1999) 'The circulation of corporate control: Selection of functional backgrounds of new CEOs in large U.S. manufacturing firms, 1981–1992', *Administrative Science Quarterly*, 44: 532–562.

Pareto, V. (1935) *The Mind and Society: A Treatise on General Sociology*. New York: Harcourt, Brace and Co.

Parsons, T. (1969) *Politics and Social Structure*. New York: Free Press.

Pettigrew, A. (1992) 'On studying managerial elites', *Strategic Management Journal*, 13: 163–182.

Poggi, G. (1972) *Images of Society. Essays on the Sociological Theories of Tocqueville, Marx and Durkheim*. Stanford: Stanford University Press.

Putnam, R. (1976) *The Comparative Study of Political Elites*. Englewood Cliffs, NJ: Prentice Hall.

Rao, H., Morrill, C. and Zald, M.N. (2000) 'Power plays: How social movements and collective action create new organizational forms', *Research in Organizational Behavior*, 22: 237–281.

Rotschild, J. and Allen Whitt, J. (1986) *The Cooperative Workplace. Potentials and Dilemmas of Organizational Democracy and Participation*. Cambridge: Cambridge University Press.

Rotschild-Whitt, J. (1979) 'The collectivist organization: An alternative to rational-bureaucratic models', *American Sociological Review*, 44: 509–527.

Samuels, R.J. (2003) *Machiavelli's Children*. Cornell: Cornell University Press.

Satow, R.L. (1975) 'Value-rational authority and professional organizations: Weber's missing type', *Administrative Science Quarterly*, 20: 526–531.

Strang, D. and Jung, D. (2005) 'Organizational change as an orchestrated social movement: Recruitment to a corporate quality initiative', in G.F. Davis, D. McAdam, R.W. Scott and M.N. Zald (eds) *Social Movements and Organization Theory*. Cambridge: Cambridge University Press, pp. 280–310.

Tilly, C. (2006) *Regimes and Repertoires*. Chicago: The University of Chicago Press.

Tocqueville, Alexis de (1969) *Democracy in America*. (Trans. Lawrence, G. and JP Meyer). New York: Harper and Row.

Turner, R.H. (1960) 'Sponsored and contest mobility and the school system', *American Sociological Review*, 25 (6): 855–867.

Useem, M. (1984) *The Inner Circle*. New York: Oxford University Press.

Vallas, S.P. (2006) 'Empowerment redux: Structure, agency, and the remaking of managerial authority', *American Journal of Sociology*, 111 (6): 1677–1717.

Waters, M. (1989) 'Collegiality, bureaucratization and professionalization: A Weberian analysis', *American Journal of Sociology*, 94 (5): 945–972.

Waters, M. (1993) 'Alternative organizational formations: A neo weberian typology of polycratic administrative systems', *The Sociological Review*, 54–81.

Weber, M. (1968) in R. Guenther and C. Wittich (eds) *Economy and Society. An Outline of Interpretive Sociology*. New York: Bedminster Press.

Wilde, A.W. (1978) 'Conversations among gentlemen: Oligarchical democracy in Columbia', in J.J. Linz and A. Stepan (eds) *The Breakdown of Democratic Regimes: Crisis, Breakdown, and Requialibrium*. Baltimore: Johns Hopkins University Press.

Zald, M.N. and Ash, R. (1966) 'Social movements organizations: Growth, decay, and change', *Social Forces*, 44 (3): 327–341.

Zeitlin, M. (1974) 'Corporate ownership and control: The large cooperation and the capitalist class', *American Journal of Sociology*, 79 (5): 1073–1119.

Zuckert, C.H. (1983) 'Reagan and that unnamed Frenchman (De Tocqueville): On the rationale for the new (old) federalism', *The Review of Politics*, 45: 421–442.

# 26

# Organizational Design

Gerard Fairtlough and Rosemary Beckham

## INTRODUCTION

Structured organizations have existed for thousands of years. However, the systematic study of organizational design is generally considered to have come into its own in eighteenth century Europe, focused at first on political and military organizations, as a part of the state building that occurred after the signing of the Treaty of Westphalia. The explicit focus was initially on states and their organizations, and some of the most famous work in the genre – Max Weber's theory of bureaucracy – drew its inspiration from the example of states. In Weber's case the state in question was Germany, which at the turn of the nineteenth century had become both the most admired modern state in Europe as well as an economic powerhouse of commerce. Max Weber studied the structure and operation of government, church and, to a lesser extent, business organizations. Weber's elaboration of the concept of bureaucracy has been extremely influential on theoretical understanding of organization design, and remains so today (Weber, 1964, 1920). At about the time that Weber was developing his ideas work-study was initiated by Frederick

Taylor in the United States early in the twentieth century and was an important influence on organization design at the micro level. Of equal influence to Taylorism was Fordism – the alignment of organizations with their dominant technology. Today, the design of new organizations and the redesign of existing ones is a widespread practice within business, government and civil society. The assumption is that the right design can improve the effectiveness of an organization.

## THE PURPOSES OF ORGANIZATION DESIGN

When you ask why it is necessary to design organizations, the reason usually given is the need to define which tasks are assigned to which individuals or groups, which can be referred to as the 'task-definition' purpose of organization design. While it is indeed important to be clear about who is doing what, task-definition is often straightforward or obvious. The main reason why organization design can be contentious or emotional is rather its connection with power and status. These are depicted in the lines and boxes of an organization chart that define who has power over whom and how big someone's job apparently is. We can refer to this as the 'power-definition' purpose of organization design.

In our view the key concept for organization design is that there are three, but only three, ways to organize. The three ways differ in their treatment of power, so this concept relates particularly to the power-definition purpose of organization design.

## POWER

Power is a necessary part of getting things done but a display of power may provoke resistance and thus concealed power is less likely to be questioned. There are exceptions. In a *mafia*, for example, power is displayed because the *capo* wants to be seen by his followers and his rivals as capable of anything. The ultimate source of power may be violence, as in the *mafia* example. Violence is also important for the power of the state, which always has recourse to the police and the army. States seek a monopoly of violence in their territories – and sometimes beyond. Power also derives from the control of resources, particularly money. Those who have their own money, or control the use of resources, usually have power to get others to do what they want.

In many organizations, power may take quite a mild form. And it can be legitimate – for instance when elected politicians act with the consent of the governed. On these occasions a different name may be more appropriate – that of 'authority'. The power of the better argument, and power derived from experience or expertise, are also legitimate – and in these cases may be called 'influence'. The charisma of the power-holder is important, too, and power can operate at an impersonal level. Thus, when belief systems and ideologies are internalized they become controlling. This form of power is grounded in the human need to belong. Behind impersonal power are actual people. Somewhere in the process, individuals are making the rules, doing the indoctrination, granting

membership, or organizing the discipline. So it is never a single person using the power to enforce hierarchy. Even though power distribution is uneven, people are involved and most have *some* power.

Stewart Clegg (1989) has shown that power is not static but dynamic, in constant flux. On this view, if power is not used, it dies. Its use provokes resistance between opposing power-plays in a series of shifting alliances and stratagems, contestation and struggle. Hardy and Clegg (1996) have written that in most discourse about organizations, talk about power is suppressed, and the natural order of hierarchy tacitly accepted. When hierarchy is taken for granted, its condition is reinforced and the connection between power and hierarchy goes unquestioned. Power is not discussed unless it is seen either as corrupt or rebellious. The power-definition purpose of organization design requires attention to two areas of power in organizations: the first is its complex dynamic process. The second is the hegemony of hierarchy.

Hegemonic practice means the dominance of one or other way of looking at the world, where the intellectual, political and cultural combine to make that way of looking at the world feel as if it is the only way. Unquestioned hegemonies favour dominant groups and allow things to go unchallenged for centuries. Even when communists created revolution in Czarist Russia, many traditions continued unchallenged, including a continued acceptance of the inevitability of hierarchy in organization. Despite the breakdown of communism in the late 1980s, hierarchy still holds sway in Russia.

Gerard Fairtlough (2005) has suggested that the grip hierarchy has on organizational participants may be akin to addiction and that, as with all addictions, it leads the addicts to believe there is no real alternative. He describes this addiction as the hegemony of hierarchy, attributable to a combination of genetic inheritance, cultural influences from childhood onwards, and the interest those at the top of a hierarchy have in making hierarchy seem inevitable. When writers on organizations treat hierarchy as unavoidable, the connection between power and hierarchy goes unexamined. Power is legitimately required to achieve organizational aims, but it is also used merely to reinforce hierarchy. The connection between these two uses of power is generally obscure, with bad effects on organizational performance, sometimes via ineffective organizational design. Thus the widespread concealment of power in organizations both obscures the operation of hierarchy and reinforces its hegemony. Therefore clarity about the nature of power and the nature of hierarchy should be fundamental to rational organization design.

## TRIARCHY THEORY

The concept that there are just three ways of organizing has been given the slightly pretentious title of 'Triarchy Theory'. It was first elaborated in Fairtlough's book, *The Three Ways of Getting Things Done: Hierarchy, Heterarchy and Responsible Autonomy* (2005). There are, according to Fairtlough, two fundamental alternatives to hierarchy. The first is heterarchy, which involves multiple sources of rule rather than the single rule of hierarchy. An organizational example is the relationship between the partners in a traditional law firm, where all partners are of roughly equal status, sharing decision making, risks and rewards. A further example is the balance of powers between the executive, legislature and judiciary in the US political system.

The second alternative is responsible autonomy, under which an individual or a group has autonomy to decide what to do, but is accountable for the outcome of the decision. It might be called 'no rule', or rather, no external rule. The existence of accountability distinguishes responsible autonomy from anarchy. Examples are: privately-owned businesses that operate autonomously, providing they satisfy their creditors, and basic scientific research, in which principal investigators are free to choose their line of enquiry, providing it leads to results judged valuable by peer-review.

Heterarchy and responsible autonomy are similar in being non-hierarchical but otherwise are completely distinct. Heterarchy involves intensive interaction leading to coordinated action. Responsible autonomy has less interaction and greater self-sufficiency. Both have their place and organizational designers should make full use of them, rather than being lured into thinking that only hierarchy is legitimate or simply unavoidable. Cloke and Goldsmith (2002) have written of the need to transform 'processes that support hierarchy into those that support heterarchy': their argument is that managers need to relinquish the luxury of prestige and employees need to surrender the luxury of irresponsibility. Cloke and Goldsmith distinguish between 'natural' and 'organizational' hierarchies, with the implication that some people may be born to have superior status, a distinction that has a long pedigree in organization and management theories, from Taylor to the present day. However, the proposition is dubious, because context is so important to the leadership qualities that are useful and necessary; hence the position is one that the present authors cannot accept.

There are many possible explanations for why hierarchy holds us in its grip. A genetic disposition may be a critical factor. Most primates demonstrate a bias to hierarchy. If humans are genetically predisposed to hierarchy, with their alpha and beta patterns of dominance and submission and their lines of order and social dominance, then it would be natural that hierarchy became hegemonic. An associated reason for the persistence of the hegemony of hierarchy may also be belief in the 'great man'. When something goes wrong in an organization – downward profits, political party losses or lowering standards in a school – the first impulse is to blame the CEO, party leader, or head teacher, but as Tolstoy commented 'the connection between these men and the nations has not been discovered' and the transference of the collective will of a people to particular historical leaders is a hypothesis not supported by history. Yet the theory persists. Good leaders depend on the preparedness of others to follow, but in a hierarchy, we have to place our trust in the hands of a few people. In deciding to do so, we risk losing sight of collective responsibility and the part each individual plays in allowing something to happen.

Tradition is another reason for the continuing hold of hierarchy as the dominant way to get things done. Thomas Hobbes and Max Weber both believed that without a single person in authority an organization could not exist, thrive and survive. For thinkers like these, and the many influenced by their thought, an absence of hierarchy means only the absence of order, discipline, system, motivation and leadership.

## CULTURAL THEORY

To better understand the interaction between hierarchy, heterarchy and responsible autonomy in organizations, Fairtlough turns to aspects of Cultural Theory (Thompson *et al.*, 1990), which developed out of the work of Mary Douglas (1973). This theory states that there is no single organizing principle, only ways of organizing and dis-organizing:

> Since … no single way of life ever has things all its own way, there can be no such thing as an organisation. Instead there are just four ways of organising, each of which is also a way of disorganising the other three (Thompson *et al.*, 1990: 187).

Cultural Theory models social control as forms of power through which individuals are manipulated and try to manipulate others. The theory also shows how the dynamic interaction between an individual and their social environment, constantly changes by negotiation and through choice – forming and reforming the individual's worldview. Douglas' (1973) original work in Cultural Theory distinguished between two basic forms or dimensions of social control. These are called 'grid' and 'group'. Grid refers to the structure of rules, laws and mores that all members of a society feel bound by and can be seen as a rational dimension. Group refers to the mutual control that members of

a bounded group, often a small group, exert on each other. It is a social dimension, which provides a flexible, adaptive form of control.

To Douglas's two dimensions 'group' and 'grid', Thompson *et al.* (1990) add two further 'discriminators' – equality and competition and thereby produces five archetypes: insular; hierarchical; entrepreneurial; sectarian; and hermitic. Each type possesses its own mutually exclusive logic; two are passive but three are active. Rationalities and environment affect the activity of change as an individual, a part of, or all of a group shifts between types.

Applying the dimensions of equality and competition onto the group-grid framework, four/five types of community are mapped out, but only three are proactive:[1]

| | |
|---|---|
| HIGH GRID/LOW GROUP: | Isolated individuals/Fatalism |
| HIGH GRID/HIGH GROUP: | Hierarchies |
| LOW GRID/HIGH GROUP: | Communes/Egalitarianism |
| LOW GRID/LOW GROUP: | Entrepreneurial Individuals/Individualism |

The three active groups match closely those of Triarchy Theory: hierarchy/hierarchy; egalitarianism/heterarchy; and entrepreneurial individualism/responsible autonomy. As in Triarchy Theory, the mutually exclusive types demonstrate that choice is substantial but finite. Overlap, particularly between the three active groups, makes cooperation, movement and communication between types possible: the limit to the number of types enhances its probability whilst 'straining' towards 'consistency'. Because the active categories of each approach are based on common criteria they are simultaneously mutually exclusive and 'jointly exhaustive': it is this paradox that enables classification. Cultural Theory presents a realistic picture of the 'unity in diversity of human experience' that matches that of Triarchy Theory – a competitive dynamic that plays itself out through power (Thompson *et al.*, 1990).

Individuals tend to 'shun' incompatible views as they search for relationships that are compatible with their value system in a process that can be described as one of 'elective affinity', to use Weber's adaptation of one of Goethe's play titles. For example, a hierarchist will tend to reject the consensual or democratic. Paradoxically, s/he often simultaneously compartmentalizes behaviours from other types and groups. Such a person may be consensual at work and patriarchal at home, or be politically democratic, but exclude blacks, women and Muslims from voting. Similarly, in organizations, there may be the same compartmentalization of behaviour.

All three active ways may interact successfully but only if 'creative leadership' is in place. The model is never static because people change their worldviews whenever surprises intervene to disrupt preferred patterns of relationship. Thus, change is essential to stability as the constant tipping from one group into other marks out instability in the parts and coherence in the whole. Each needs the others to maintain stability whilst allowing for contingent change.

First, the correspondence between the theories explains why there are three and only three active ways of getting things done. Second, Cultural Theory models the dynamic interaction between the three ways of getting things done that Triarchy Theory espouses. The correspondence between three active ways not only allows analysis of existing organizations but also the projection of what may happen if the degree of hierarchy is decreased to allow for greater dispersal of power and responsible autonomy.

Cultural Theory confirms social control as power; the grid-group framework demonstrates the dynamic interaction between manipulated and manipulating individuals and different forms of power (Douglas, 1973). Triarchy Theory marks the importance of critique and argument to good organization to balance between equality and competition. People tend to follow one particular type of the three active ways of life do so, on the presumption that these ways of doing things will produce particular outcomes – at least until these outcomes fail to materialize. At this point, adherents begin to doubt their way of life and shift towards another mode

of rationality: individuals, for example, may shift their support to a different political party or read a different newspaper: in organizations, such changes occur by changing the mix between hierarchy, heterarchy and responsible autonomy.

In today's organizations, frequent redesign may not just be the whim of those in charge of the hierarchy but result from dissatisfaction, due to an organization's failure to live up to stated promises. Triarchy Theory suggests that it is possible to envisage more fundamental shifts taking place when the hegemony of hierarchy is relaxed (Fairtlough, 2005). It claims that the three active ways of organizing combine to get things done describe a complex, interconnected plurality in a coherent overall system, which conforms to Cultural Theory's 'constrained relativism' of overlap, communication and integration (Thompson *et al.*, 1990: 269). In both, a constant series of actions and reactions are, at best, complementary and convergent.

Triarchy Theory's additional claim that the hegemony of hierarchy is the main stumbling block to greater integration of the three ways – with more low grid/low group or low grid/high group – recognizes that for all three active ways to operate successfully together, 'creative leadership' is essential at all levels of the operating systems. This is affirmed in Cultural Theory.

## CONTINGENCY THEORY

Weber's model for organizational design is remarkably systematic and prescriptive and it was highly influential for 30 years or so after World War II. It depends on hierarchy, on the separation of line and staff functions, on established rules and on clear lines of authority. Members of the bureaucracy are to be selected impersonally, on the basis of professional merit, and are generally meant to have lifetime careers with one organization. Bureaucracy was a great advance on earlier organizational designs that were dependent on the whim of the patron at the top and the fawning of clients below.

Large bureaucratic organizations often have scale-invariant features, meaning that the structure of an organization is replicated within its sub-units. For example, an army division has a certain pattern of line and staff elements, and the division's sub-units, brigades, have a similar pattern on a smaller scale. Such a scalar design made the system easy to understand and implement. The historical success of Weberian bureaucracies in the military, political and business spheres, combined with its intellectual rigour and comprehensiveness, gave Weber's formulation an authority that was seldom questioned. An important result of this was to reinforce the hegemony of hierarchy as the way to organize. The dominant thinking of Weber and Taylor emphasizes 'one best way' of doing things. However, in the early 1960s, the idea that there was one right way began to be increasingly challenged.

Burns and Stalker (1961) identified two distinct organizational designs, which they termed 'mechanistic' and 'organic': each, they said, were suitable to organizations of different kinds. Mechanistic design gives people specialized tasks, and has formalized procedures and centralized decision making. Organic design is flexible and decentralized, and gives people wider responsibilities. When tasks are repetitive, the mechanistic style was claimed to be best. When tasks are variable, the organic style was best. Examples are the automobile production line (mechanistic) and the research laboratory (organic). Thus the preferred design depended on the task of the organization and the kind of environment in which it operates. Where the environment is highly predictable then a mechanistic design works well; however, in highly uncertain environments it is not appropriate – the organic model works much better.

Contemporaneously with Burns and Stalker, Chandler proposed that organization design should depend on the organization's strategy (Chandler, 1962). His slogan was: 'Structure Follows Strategy'. Again, the emphasis was on different designs for different purposes. Thus, there was opposition to what was taken to be Weber's view – that there is one right way to organize – which was the bureaucratic way. Following this stream of thought, Lex Donaldson (2001) has assembled persuasive evidence that organizational design should be adjusted to the contingency of strategy or of task. The general term for these approaches is that they are contingency models – how you design the organization depends on the contingencies it has to deal with.

All these contingency approaches are highly rationalistic. They assume designing an organization is like designing an airplane – careful engineering will produce the best structure and the best operating processes. The assumption is that human needs and behaviours can largely be ignored, because human beings can be selected, trained and disciplined to behave as the organizational structure requires them. The contingency views that gathered pace from the 1960s onwards were most obviously antithetical to one earlier current in organization and management theory. The human relations school of organization studies was initially driven by insights from individual psychology, but by the 1980s group dynamics had become the predominant approach. Human relations, generally, was regarded as something separate from organizational design, as an add-on needed to sort out messy human problems. From the 1980s onwards, the concept of organizational culture, which first surfaced in anthropologically inclined human relations work in the 1930s, has become influential, making a closer connection between organizational design and the people who have to live with and within it. Thus John Roberts (2004) uses the acronym PARC to define organizations: People, Architecture, Routines and Culture.

A strictly hierarchical system misuses power and refuses a culture of openness, trust and creativity, thus reducing an organization's ability to adapt. Triarchy Theory claims that hierarchy is not the only design for an organization. The two other ways to design an organization are heterarchy and responsible autonomy. We cannot choose only one of the three ways. For one thing, organizational styles are contextually contingent.

Whilst useful, the contingency model fails to demonstrate the necessary power dynamic for changes in order – and why there has to be a movement between the three ways of getting things done.

## THE LEARNING ORGANIZATION

Arie de Geus (1997) maintains that the essential capability for any organization is its ability to learn and therefore to be able to adapt to changing circumstances. If this is so, organization design should be designed for learning. For de Geus, the learning organization is one whose success derives from its skill and awareness in the development of a strong knowledge base through complex human interaction. It thus prioritizes people. Four components mark the difference between short-term success and longevity in organizations: 'sensitivity to the environment'; a clear, cohesive identity; tolerance and decentralization, and conservative financing. The first describes a company's 'ability to learn and adapt' (de Geus, 1997: 16) and is the key to the other three.

Two design principles have been identified that promote learning. The first of these is a concept introduced by the Brazilian legal theorist and philosopher, Roberto Unger, who has produced a series of works that analyse the nature of modern society and explore possibilities for radical social change. Some of Unger's concepts may be valuable in organization studies as well as in the study of society in general. In his book *Plasticity into Power*, Unger (1987) uses the concept of plasticity as a key way of understanding the different economic and military success of these societies. By 'plasticity' Unger means the ease with which work relations between participants in a societal institution (including an organization of any kind) can be 'constantly shifted in order to suit changing circumstances' (Unger, 1987). He says that plasticity provides the opportunity to innovate in the way production, administration, or warfare is conducted. Plasticity allows for variation in ways of getting things done, and Unger particularly emphasizes the importance of facilitating movement away from hierarchy, and of experimenting with alternative ways of getting things done. Innovations should include occasional large-scale reforms but should also be cumulative aggregations of smaller-scale moves. Unger believes that there is no predetermined set of institutions that promote plasticity, although the copying of institutions that have proved successful in different circumstances is a sensible way to proceed, if the copying is experimental and is conducted in the spirit of plasticity.

Unger (1987) finds that two factors increase plasticity: the first of these is a reduction in the distinction between the roles of task-definition and task-execution, which is, roughly speaking, the distinction between those who manage and those who do the work. Allied to this is a reduction in the distinctions between different work-roles, between those of the specialist and the generalist, between those of the expert and the enthusiast, between staff and line. The second factor is not part of the immediate organizational setting (whether of production, administration or warfare) but concerns the larger framework of institutions (public and private) within which organizations have to function. According to Unger, the softening of established social roles and of hierarchies in the wider society promotes plasticity within that society's organizations. Unger's arguments for plasticity as the basis for societal success are based on numerous historical examples. The breadth of Unger's examples and the clarity of his analysis are compelling. In short, along with openness, mutual trust and skill in interpersonal process, a dedication to increasing plasticity in organizational arrangements is also a key factor in promoting organizational learning.

The other key concept derives from evolutionary thinking. Complex Evolving Systems (CESs) can include human beings, as for instance in the example of a market, but they can also be non-human. A prime example of a mainly non-human CES is Darwinian evolution, where the operation of natural selection enables organisms to evolve over time. Even a non-living CES is possible, for example a computer programme that evolves fantastic structures by following a few simple rules. A key feature of a CES is the emergence of order, sometimes intricate and innovative, as a result of the operation of relatively simple principles. To take a further example, in a natural eco-system there is interaction between predators and their prey, between the elements of a food chain, or between generalist organisms which range widely and specialist ones which find their own niches to exploit. As time goes by, identifiable patterns emerge in the eco-system from a huge variety of interactions and order appears from randomness. Thus CESs are natural or human systems that exhibit self-organization, emergent properties and the generation of new order.

Complexity thinking has given us the concept of co-evolution. Two or more entities interact over time, each adapting itself to the behaviour of the other or others. All of the entities change through this co-evolutionary process. Contrast co-evolution with adaptation – for example an organization adapting to its environment; here, the organization is seen to change but the environment doesn't. Adaptation is one way only. Co-evolution is different. Co-evolution happens in a network of elements, all of which change as they interact and thereby influence each other. The idea of a separate environment is set aside. Adaptation (a one-way process) is hierarchical; co-evolution (a mutual process) is heterarchical. Co-evolution is a process of learning for all involved. In such heterarchical situations organizational actors have to pay close attention to others' language and behaviour and to the unfolding relationships with others. Such learning might be the result of a formal negotiation or of a trust-building exercise, or it could be the result of time spent working together. Thus, heterarchical interaction encourages continuing learning about getting things done, including the learning of interactive skills such as negotiation, facilitation and diplomacy. The interaction promotes adaptation and development.

## DESIGNS FOR HETERARCHY

In this section we describe a number of organizational arrangements that promote heterarchy as a means of getting things done. These include organizational democracy, enabling infrastructures and decision-making structures. We also present two examples of successful heterarchical practice. Organizational democracy helps organizations move towards heterarchy. Democratic practices in professional partnerships, such as legal and accounting firms, demonstrate that these practices are fully compatible with business success, on a small or a large scale. Of course, democratic practices can be more or less inclusive and many of these firms are characterized by a high degree of non-inclusivity of members. They are democratic amongst those at the apex of the partnership. Thus, there is a valid objection that many such partnerships are highly hierarchical and that employees in them often find them far from democratic. However, we are not suggesting that these firms are, in general, ideal role models for heterarchy, even though some of the practices in particular firms may be worth copying. While role models are of limited use, since each organizational situation has its own demands and copying what has worked somewhere else will not necessarily be useful, they are useful as guides and we will present two rather different organizations with this aim in view. Examples of this kind often become out-dated quite rapidly but are still informative.

### The BP example

The major oil company BP is one of the largest organizations in the world, at least in financial terms. As well as on personal knowledge of the company gained from informal contact with its staff and with others in the oil and chemical industries and on the work of Hansen and Von Oetinger (2001), in writing about BP we draw on John Roberts's excellent book *The Modern Firm* (Roberts, 2004). Roberts agrees with other observers in giving much of the credit for BP having a successful organizational form to John Browne, who became CEO of BP in 1995. However, Roberts recognizes the contributions of other BP executives, so his is not simply a 'great man' story. At the end of the 1990s, Browne was responsible for the exploration and production activities (E&P) of BP. He and others had seen that smaller, entrepreneurial firms were better at finding new sources of oil and getting them into production than were the major companies. The majors had superior financial and technical resources, but were not able to deploy them as effectively as their entrepreneurial competitors.

Browne looked for a way of organizing a large company that could capture some of this entrepreneurial spirit. The old BP E&P organization had numerous committees and complex systems for approval of expenditure and of other decisions. The new organization that was redesigned had a small executive committee (Browne and two others) to which 20 or so 'asset managers' reported. 'Assets', and their management, was a term with a far less bureaucratic feel than the more conventional 'business unit'. An asset might be a single oil field. Binding the Executive Committee and each asset manager was an explicit contract, under which the manager undertook to deliver a well-defined performance. Providing the contract was fulfilled, the asset manager had great freedom to operate without interference from central staff. Managers could hire and fire their own staff and use external resources rather than BP departments, if they wished. The central BP staff was nearly reduced to nil, partly by redeployment into the assets and their management.

The new organization started to deliver good results within a few years. However, it was clear that improvements could still be made. The slimming down of central staffs meant that asset managers could not easily gain assistance when faced with business or technical problems. To fill this gap 'peer groups' of asset managers were created. Four or five managers formed a group, the members of which gave each other help when asked. The groups were formed with members who faced similar tasks, for example, there was a group of assets where the main task was to find new oil. Peer groups shared examples of good practice and later on the method of 'peer challenge' was introduced in which peers scrutinized the contracts between managers and the executive committee. Peers were able to point out areas in which more demanding targets might be possible, thus 'raising the game' of the whole peer group. Later still, peer groups took on responsibility for allocating their capital spending, a structural redesign that affected the whole organizational culture in E&P. There was great emphasis on performance, on mutual trust and mutual help, and on admitting to mistakes and difficulties at an early stage. The peer groups utilize what is called 'T-shaped management', in which managers share knowledge freely across an organization while remaining committed to their individual business unit (Hansen and Von Oetinger, 2001).

John Browne is a forceful personality which, together with his hierarchical position, enabled him to introduce a novel, and possibly risky, organizational structure quite rapidly. Browne was the boss and his ideas were followed. He was probably helped by the professionalism of BP's E&P staff and their recognition that his ideas were sound. Having successfully climbed the corporate ladder, Browne may have believed that hierarchy was the way to get things done, but the performance of BP's smaller competitors had to be explained and their reliance on responsible autonomy, rather than hierarchy, was one explanation. So Browne decided to reconstruct power relations so that the asset managers were more central. They would be held accountable for performance, but they had freedom to decide how they would perform. Hierarchy gave way to responsible autonomy as the most important organizing principle in BP's E&P arm.

Hierarchy may have helped at the start, but once responsible autonomy took over as the guiding principle the 'assets' were given operating freedom and explicit contracts. A few years later, the emphasis shifted to heterarchy, as the peer groups were formed.

A good deal of power and responsibility was devolved to these groups, and their mutual trust was a key feature of their successful heterarchical interaction. Asset Managers were effectively responsible to the peer group of which they were members – a genuine heterarchy.

When Browne became CEO of BP as a whole, he introduced across the company the structure that had worked so well in E&P. BP had previously been a cumbersome bureaucracy, with a complex matrix structure, albeit simplified under successive CEOs. Giving radical autonomy to the assets (then called 'business units') was a big change. In his book, Roberts (2004) uses the term 'desegregation' to describe the process of 'creating relatively small sub-units within the organization in which significant decision rights are lodged'. Routines and processes are such as to hold the sub-units responsible for delivering performance. Financial reporting was switched to make the assets similar to an independent company. Other management information was disaggregated so that asset performance was highlighted.

In the late 1990s BP made several large acquisitions, most notably the US oil companies Amoco and Arco. Large mergers often fail to meet the objectives set when the deal is done, but BP's deals have all worked well. Roberts (2004) writes: 'It is arguable that the value created in BP's acquisitions of Amoco and Arco came from applying BP's superior management systems to the physical and human resources of the acquired firms'.

### The Gore example

W.L. Gore is the company making Gore-Tex waterproof fabric products. In the BP example the most interesting feature is the progress from hierarchy to responsible autonomy and then to a synergistic combination of responsible autonomy and heterarchy. In the Gore example, the key feature is the beneficial separation of leadership from hierarchy. The company's success depends on distributed leadership and the culture of the company is such that this leadership is respected and followed. There are no job titles and organization charts but leadership is thoroughly professional. Projects are well thought out and well presented: self-selected project champions cannot gather support from co-workers unless this is the case. As support accumulates for a project, it becomes better and better defined, for instance as people skilled in project accounting join the team, as well as those with relevant marketing or technical experience. Projects inevitably compete for key people and other resources, and there is rivalry between them. However, priority choices are made heterarchically. The long-established culture of the company helps this work. People are reasonable when pushing their own projects since they hope others will be reasonable in future. Also, heterarchical negotiation over resources is a skill that has developed over the years. Alan Deutschman (2004) writes: 'Bill Gore [the company's founder] threw out the rules. He created a place with hardly any hierarchy and few ranks and titles. He insisted on direct, one-to-one communication; anyone in the company could speak to anyone else. In essence, he organized the company as though it were a bunch of small task forces'.

As effective heterarchies partly depend on a supporting culture in the organization, it takes some time to get them established. This is why a strong and determined leader, like John Browne at BP, can be important in moving to heterarchy. Or a small, well-motivated executive group could play this part. Either way, there is something of a paradox. The use of hierarchical power can, at first, impose the dispersed power of heterarchy.

## ENABLING INFRASTRUCTURE

Eve Mitleton-Kelly's essay 'Ten Principles of Complexity and Enabling Infrastructures' (2003) provides an excellent summary of the principles of complexity thinking and their application to organizations. She shows how self-organization (for example, in a largely autonomous project team) can produce novel solutions to problems, develop new concepts and give rise to emergent organizational forms. One of Mitleton-Kelly's contributions to complexity thinking is the concept of enabling infrastructure (which can also be called enabling environment or enabling conditions). An enabling environment has various aspects that all support self-organization: socio-cultural, system-technical, and leadership-power aspects. An enabling infrastructure facilitates learning and the generation and sharing of knowledge. It is fairly similar to Malone's coordinate-and-cultivate style of management (Malone, 2004). Mitleton-Kelly (2003) writes: 'Risk-taking is meant to help find new solutions... It is in the nature of exploration that some solutions will work and some will not...' A good leader provides psychological space for people to learn, but also physical space and resources for that learning to take place. Skills and mechanisms also form part of an enabling infrastructure for heterarchical and autonomously responsible ways of getting things done. A further part of the infrastructure is a culture with an understanding of and commitment to the long-term interests of the whole organization, rather than to any sectional interests. With a culture of this kind it is quite easy to avoid the self-indulgent anarchy and endless debate that hierarchy-addicts fear will be the result of any move away from their ways of getting things done. It is also quite easy to develop respect for others' self-discipline and professional pride. A widespread willingness to exercise constructive leadership can also be developed. These are aspects of an enabling infrastructure.

## STRUCTURED DECISION MAKING

### Ringi and forums

With heterarchy, everyone is able to get involved, which provides potential for endless talking. So how do things get done? First, it must be recognized that in a heterarchy, participation brings not only power but also responsibility. It is no good playing at participation, expecting that eventually a hierarch will stop the game and imperatively command people what to do. In a heterarchy, that won't happen. Second, decision making must be structured, into a minimum of three phases. Phase 1 is setting the agenda: deciding which subjects should be tackled, which decisions should be made, and when. Phase 2 is setting up small groups to make detailed studies of the chosen subjects, made up either of experts, or of people representative of the organization, or of both. Phase 3 involves implementation, something that is done in a quite deliberative fashion in Japanese organizations. A feature of Japanese organizations has been the *Ringi* system, in which key decisions must have the approval of all the senior staff of the organization. Approval is given by a signature, indicating that the person whose signature it is has seen the case and considers it sound. To collect 100 or more signatures for a decision might seem cumbersome, but as part of an established practice, with familiar arrangements, it can be quite straightforward, and the time needed to get approval is well known in advance. The organization concerned is often strongly hierarchical and there may be pressure from the top on those whose agreement is sought. Nevertheless the system does make for collective responsibility and provides an opportunity for individuals to stage a divergent view, in a serious context.

A similar practice to the *Ringi* system, which can be used in conjunction with it, or independently, is to have a Forum, or regular meeting of a group of people from an organization. These can be chosen by seniority, or to represent a cross-section of the organization's staff. Up to 25 people might be involved, but a group of 8 to 12 will usually be more effective. The forum discusses key issues, sometimes at an 'away day', and can be used to approve key decisions. Discussion in a forum should be open, constructive and free from domination by the powerful. Discussion can be facilitated by a member of the group or by an Organization Development specialist. Careful listening is one of the norms that should become established for the working of the group.

# DESIGNS FOR RESPONSIBLE AUTONOMY

## Explicit internal contracts

Connectivity (meaning interaction between organizational participants) is something that cannot be increased indefinitely, without breakdown (Mitleton-Kelly, 2003). Heterarchy must stop somewhere. The boundary of the organization is one obvious limit, but in large organizations there will have to be other boundaries, which is where responsible autonomy comes in – ways have to be found to divide the organization up into chunks, which have as much natural autonomy as possible. Decisions about the boundaries of autonomous sub-units, and about the encapsulation of the sub-units, can be hierarchical or heterarchical, but once autonomous units have been established, and their responsibilities agreed, they have to operate under the encapsulating rules. Moving towards greater autonomy is in most ways simpler than moving towards greater heterarchy.

There are guidelines for moving to responsible autonomy: Initially, ask the question: is autonomy the right way to go, rather than seeking better heterarchy? Autonomy may be simpler, but will it get things done in the way the organization needs? If, indeed, responsible autonomy seems appropriate, then look at scale. Is it right to give autonomy to a small, self-organizing team? Or would a few hundred people be the right size? Or is a still larger sub-unit a better size for the tasks involved, in spite of the dangers of too much interaction? Are there limits to growth for the autonomous unit, or could small turn into large without causing problems? Whatever the scale, the next thing to work out is the mode of encapsulation. The boundaries of the autonomous unit's field of action and responsibilities need to be carefully defined before it sets off on its self-organizing path.

Of course, as time goes by these boundaries can be renegotiated but the clearer are the boundaries, the easier any renegotiation will be. For autonomy to be genuine, renegotiation must be a heterarchical process. Critique must be put in place from the start. The autonomous unit has to know how it will be held to account. What information will it have to provide regularly to the wider world? What are the criteria for success and failure? When will audits or reviews be held, how will these be organized, and who will be involved? It is careful thought at the beginning that makes autonomy succeed. Finally, a procedure for resolution of disputes should be set up, which does not have to be anything complicated – it might be agreed that a single trusted individual should adjudicate.

# EXTERNAL FORCES/INSTITUTIONAL THEORY

Since the late 1970s, the insight that organizations are profoundly influenced by their wider institutional environment has been elaborated into Institutional Theory. Scott *et al.* (1994) write that this environment has a direct influence on organizational design due both to 'hard' external regulation and 'soft' concepts that provide meaning to participants. Another key idea is that, because formal design is patterned in accordance with the wider environment, the actual functioning of an organization is only loosely coupled to its formal design.

External meaning systems and related behavioural patterns, including those picked up by organizational participants during their education and in other employment, infuse every organization. Symbols, stories, myths and ceremonies are copied from other organizations, particularly from those in the same field. Legal, regulatory and professional requirements are imposed on the organization. These infusions and impositions mainly affect the formal design of the organization. Its informal design is mainly generated internally, by innovation and by adaptation to local circumstances and to the capabilities and personalities of participants.

Greenwood and Hinings (1993) suggest that people involved in a field of activity share 'interpretive schemes' derived from shared ideas, beliefs and values. For example, those involved in the law, including judges, partners in law firms, professors in law schools and state regulators of the legal system, develop a number of shared interpretive schemes that make sense of what happens in their legal system. A particular interpretive scheme produces a set of structures and routines called an 'archetype'. Thus, the formal organizational design of a law firm may be expected to follow one of a limited number of archetypes. Institutional theory leads to the conclusion that formal organizational design usually isn't rationally chosen by the organization concerned, or at least is only chosen from a few predetermined archetypes. The conclusion might seem overblown, but it does question the extent to which *organizational* design is in fact *institutional* design.

## THEORIES IN PRACTICE

'There is nothing so practical as a good theory', as Kurt Lewin (1951) states. Why should this be so? One answer is that theories are generalizations from practice, which means they can pack in a vast amount of experience. There is an equally powerful reason why theories work: a good theory must be based on good conceptualization. Well-thought-out concepts are clear and precise, giving them a wide appeal. Because widely appealing concepts become broadly shared terminology, this makes for effective communication between lots of people. A further advantage of theory is that it usually postulates a social mechanism of some kind. A mechanism often suggests where an intervention would be valuable and what kind of intervention is needed.

In this chapter, we wished to describe the value of theories in general, rather than to provide a comprehensive account of the theories that are useful in organizational practice, so we are sorry if your favourite theory is not included. A further aim is to be useful to all organizational participants, not just to those at the top of a hierarchy or to people (such as consultants) who are paid to find solutions to organizational problems. If a theory is simple, easily understood and quick to use it will be particularly useful to participants. We have therefore concentrated on theories that meet these criteria.

In conclusion, the picture of an organizational designer, a manager or a consultant prescribing an organization's structure and function, now needs to change. A more accurate picture needs to include organizational learning, adaptation and evolution. A variety of theories are available to help organizational participants during this process. These include Contingency Theory, Power Theory, Triarchy Theory, Institutional Theory and Complexity Theory.

## ACKNOWLEDGEMENT

We acknowledge the help of Stewart Clegg, Andrew Trickett and Imogen Fallows in preparing this article.

## NOTE

1 In Cultural Theory, the hermit has been excluded as it floats between the other four groups.

## REFERENCES

Burns, T. and Stalker, G.M. (1961) *The Management of Innovation*. London: Tavistock.

Chandler, A.D., Jr. (1962) *Chapters in the History of the American Industrial Enterprise*. Cambridge, MA: MIT Press.

Clegg, S. (1989) *Frameworks of Power*. London: Sage.

Cloke, K. and Goldsmith, J. (2002) *The End of Management and the Rise of Organizational Democracy*. San Francisco: Jossey-Bass.

de Geus, A. (1997) *The Living Company*. Boston, MA: Harvard Business School Press.

Deutschman, A. (2004) 'The fabric of creativity', Fast Company, no. 89, viewed 4 May 2007, <http://www.fastcompany.com/magazine/89/open_gore.html>.

Donaldson, L. (2001) *The Contingency Theory of Organizations*. London: Sage.

Douglas, M. (1973) *Natural Symbols*. New York: Vintage Books.

Fairtlough, G.H. (2005) *The Three Ways of Getting Things Done: Hierarchy, Heterarchy and Responsible Autonomy in Organizations*. Axminster: Triarchy Press.

Greenwood, R. and Hinings, C.K. (1993) 'Understanding strategic change: The contribution of archetypes', *Academy of Management Journal*, 36 (5): 1052–1081.

Hansen, M. and Von Oetinger, B. (2001) 'Are you managing to a "T"? Time to break with tradition'. Harvard Business School Working Knowledge for Business Leaders, viewed 4 May 2007, <http://hbswk.hbs.edu/cgi-bin/print>.

Hardy, C. and Clegg, S. (1996) 'Some dare call it power', in S.R. Clegg, C. Hardy and W.R. Nord (eds) *The Handbook of Organization Studies*. London: Sage, pp. 622–641.

Lewin, K. (1951) *Field Theory in Social Science: Selected Theoretical Papers*. New York: Harper & Row.

Malone, T. (2004) *The Future of Work: How the New Order of Business Will Shape Your Organization, Your Management Style, and Your Life*. Boston, MA: Harvard Business School Press.

Mitleton-Kelly, E. (2003) 'Ten Principles of Complexity and Enabling Infrastructures', in E. Mitleton-Kelly (ed.) *Complex Systems and Evolutionary Perspectives of Organisations: The Application of Complexity Theory to Organisations*. Oxford: Elsevier Science.

Mitleton-Kelly, E. (2004) 'The information systems: professional as a hermit', *Innovation: The European Journal of Social Science Research*, 17 (4): 289.

Roberts, J. (2004) *The Modern Firm*. Oxford: Oxford University Press.

Scott, W.R., Meyer, J.W. *et al.* (1994) *Institutional Environments and Organizations: Structural Complexity and Individualism*. London: Sage.

Thompson, M., Ellis, R. and Wildavsky, A. (1990) *Cultural Theory*. Boulder: Westview Press.

Unger, R. (1987) *Plasticity into Power: Comparative-historical Studies of the Institutional Foundations of Economic and Military Success: Variations on Themes of Politics, a Work in Constructive Social Theory*. Cambridge: Cambridge University Press.

Weber, M. (1964, 1920) *The Theory of Social and Economic Organization* (Trans. A.M. Henderson and T. Parsons). New York: Simon & Schuster.

# 27

# Projects for Life: Building Narrative Capital for Positive Organizational Change[1]

Arne Carlsen and Tyrone Pitsis

The striking feature for the appearance of life is that the process that constitutes the reality of a living being is one that extends beyond the form itself and involves for its expression the world in which this form lives. George Herbert Mead, *The Philosophy of the Present* (1932/2002: 66).

In this chapter we explore a domain of macro-organizational behavior that we believe intensifies the complexities and tensions of life at work – that of projects, and how projects are made for life. Projects are a form of organizing in which individuals are temporarily but interdependently linked to achieve a specific outcome or set of outcomes. These outcomes can include the production of ideas or products, solutions to problems, provision of a service, or the construction of public or private infrastructure (Clegg, Kornberger and Pitsis, 2008). Projects can take on many forms, varying from a small team within single organizations, all the way through to a collection of organizations working closely together in the form of an alliance.

Irrespective of the size or type of project, all projects are unique organizational endeavor because they span organizational boundaries, occur in complex and uncertain contexts, and are typically underpinned by a range of overt and covert control and governance mechanisms. Many projects involve sets of key performance indicators that often are intended to provide the actors in projects a sense of certainty. As such most project actors adhere to the belief that all outcomes are achievable and pre-defined. Ironically, they do so in environments that are anything but certain, or even achievable for that matter. Indeed, if several researchers of projects are to be believed, typically no less than 80% of projects fail to meet their objectives – and almost no project meets all of its stated objectives (Flyvbjerg, Bruzelius and Rothengatter, 2003; van Marrewijk *et al.*, 2008). Flyvbjerg and his colleagues ask the pertinent question that if so many projects fail, why do so many projects continue to be approved and funded?

While we agree that most projects fail in terms of their stated objectives, we argue that people continue to invest time, effort and even their own lives in projects for reasons that go beyond rational notions of the past history or projected future of success and failure. To investigate this, we take issue with the dualist notion of success and failure and argue that projects, even ones that fail in the traditional sense of failure, can be ideal arenas of positive personal and organizational change. Of course, if we do take issue with terms such as success and failure, we must also take issue with the distinction between macro- and micro-organizational behavior as artificial distinctions, necessitated by the dominant discourses of so-called micro-organizational behaviour. In reality, it is impossible to demarcate the line where the micro ends and the macro begins – as humans we can never separate ourselves from our contexts, context is not just macro or micro, context is everything. To paraphrase Alfred Schütz (1967), we only attend to those things that fit our perception of reality, or that complies with what we already know.

Transformational projects enact change at multiple level of analysis (Hackman, 2003), and it is increasingly becoming less clear where projects begin and any other form of organizing ends, so much so that projects now are believed to be the 'default' mode of being (Lundin and Hartman, 2000). Many change efforts transcend organizational borders through a plurality of direct and indirect stakeholders. The project increasingly becomes the focus for change processes that are simultaneously local in a variety of individual contexts and organizational environments and extra-organizational in the sense that their teleo-affective structures may be predicated upon tensions, movements and causes well beyond any one of the participating organizations. Projects are thus ideally suited contexts for studying organizational change processes in their temporal-relational contexts.

In this paper we show how some projects build narrative capital that is repeatedly drawn upon for future oriented purposes long after they have formally elapsed. The building of narrative capital takes place through four interrelated processes: 1) *creating deviance* (how project experiences are assigned weight as being novelties that open up for change), 2) *instantiating* (how deviances are appropriated and charged with status as desired exemplars of future experiences), 3) *extending* (how successful experiences are replicated and made formative of development trajectories, and 4) *expansive connecting* (how development efforts are strengthened by being linked to stories unfolding outside the organization). Through these four processes, project experiences may be made for life.

## THE TIME OF YOUR LIFE

To construct our own narrative of how projects enable the generation of positive organizational change we will incorporate three seemingly disparate projects: 1) the development of an IT-application for collecting dependency allowance debt, 2) oil exploration in a peripheral license in the Norwegian Sea, and 3) a major construction project for cleaning up Sydney's waterways. The projects are widely different in size, duration, ambitions, outcomes, and the types of knowledge domains being central – could they possibly have anything in common? We argue that these three projects are typified by the production of narrative capital that generates positive organizational change.

The three projects were chosen from a number of research projects being conducted within our respective research centers (Arne Carlsen is at SINTEF Technology and Society in Norway, and Tyrone Pitsis is at The Centre for Management and Organization Studies in Australia). The selected projects stood out not because of their size, monetary gains or competency development alone but because they have been flagged as being highly generative additions to the life stories of their parental organizations and instrumental in creating positive organizational change. Through these cases we conduct a comparative analysis of the generative dynamics of positive change from project experiences. We evoke the concept of *narrative capital* to explain how some pivotal experiences are made significant and acted upon by key stakeholders. Narrative capital gains its significance not only through mere acts of celebration of past affairs, and how these past affairs relate to the present, but because it is repeatedly drawn upon, and used for future oriented purposive action.

Before we continue we should be clear that if we are to say that 'projects are for life,' then we must also address temporal-relational issues of projects and how they enact change for both organizations (macro) and individuals (micro). As such, our analysis responds to a plea for empirical research on temporal-relational contexts of organizational change processes (Boden, 1994; McLaughlin, 2001; Carroll, 2002; Cunliffe, Luhman and Boje, 2004; Mutch, Delbridge and Ventresca, 2006). The individual, organizational, spatial, relational, and temporal aspects of change are not as easy to compartmentalize as we would like to believe. To do so requires being attuned to how change processes unfold in multiple contexts and with blurred boundaries between levels of analysis (Pettigrew, 1992; Langley, 1999; Pentland, 1999; Pettigrew, Woodman and Cameron, 2001; Van de Ven and Poole, 2005).

What kind of temporality, then, is involved in the experiencing of positive change? Temporality not only addresses how change processes evolve over historical time and in context but involves increased sensitivity to 'inner time,' as temporal existence attains its meaning through recollection of the past and expectation of the future in light of the present (Crites, 1971; Polkinghorne, 1988; Bruner, 1990). Experiencing in the present is always a social present (Schütz, 1967) in which the knowledge with which we

understand our past, our present and our futures is socially experienced, understood and shared – it is intersubjective (Pitsis and Clegg, 2007). Both the relational and the temporal dimension need consideration if we are to understand the forms of human agency that underpin positive change efforts (Emirbayer and Mische, 1998). Both dimensions also point towards a narrative approach.

The remainder of the chapter proceeds as follows. First, we qualify why a focus on projects and projection may be considered particularly valuable in studying processes of positive organizational change and their temporal-relational contexts. Second, we outline the methods we used in studying the change processes instigated by the three projects. Third, we discuss major findings in terms of how building narrative capital may generate positive change. Fourth, we move on to some implications.

## PROJECTS AND PROJECTING

… it is not surprising that some would have us stay where we are a little longer to rest, to wait … this country of the United States was not built by those who waited and rested and wished to look behind them. This country was conquered by those who moved forward – and so will space. … Those who came before us made certain that this country rode the first waves of the industrial revolutions, the first waves of modern invention, and the first wave of nuclear power, and this generation does not intend to founder in the backwash of the coming age of space. We mean to be a part of it – we mean to lead it. For the eyes of the world now look into space, to the moon and to the planets beyond, and we have vowed that we shall not see it governed by a hostile flag of conquest, but by a banner of freedom and peace. John F. Kennedy – 1962, Address to Rice University on the Space Effort.

Once upon a time projects were typified by visions of grandeur. Integral to the project outcomes was the desire to create something memorable; an iconic legacy that will demonstrate to present and future generations, societies, kingdoms and empires the superiority, power and might of the individuals and societies enacting these projects. Sometimes these projects were offered to lovers, neighbors and friends as signs of goodwill and the building of relational capital. The Taj-Mahal is a symbol of love; the great pyramids of Egypt are shrines and conduits within which kings and queens travel on to eternity – and people's lives were devoted and also sacrificed to construct them, often unwillingly, for they were mostly slave labor; the Statue of Liberty, a gift from the French indelibly etched on the minds of new immigrants, reminding them about what they left behind and the wonderful possibilities that the future promises; the stirring speech on the plan to put people on the moon delivered by John F. Kennedy in 1962, and the subsequent moon walk, are all transformational events, all histories in the narrative of generations of the past. All these projects just mentioned are *for life* in the sense that they continue to capture the imagination of people irrespective of generation or nationality.

Everyday projects in organizations may seem a long way from building pyramids and embarking upon space quests, far from being transformational events. Indeed, if we go to the project management literature, the emphasis continue to be overly rational, fixated on technical aspects of projects that are believed to be measurable (Pitsis, Clegg, Marosszeky and Rura-Polley, 2003; Pitsis, Kornberger and Clegg, 2004; Hodgson and Cicmil, 2006), and therefore manageable, despite research suggesting that few major projects meet budgets, schedule and many other key performance indicators (Flyvbjerg, Bruzelius and Rothengatter, 2003; Hodgson and Cicmil, 2006). In addition, much of the project literature has tended to overlook the role that projects play in enacting change in people beyond that of how peoples' resistance to change can effect the bottom line, the adoption of technology, or the success of company restructuring upon share price (see Dunphy, Griffiths and Benn, 2007).

By invoking projects as the unit of analysis for understanding positive organizational change, we need to move well beyond an understanding of projects as well managed time-bound activities to meet predetermined and measurable aims. Understanding projects as vehicles of change require reorienting towards contexts of inspiration and transition. Not only do projects result in many non-measured outcomes such as cultural change, learning, creativity and innovation (Huxham, 1996; Hardy, Phillips and Lawrence, 2003; Pitsis *et al.*, 2004; van Marrewijk, 2004). Project experiences can also constitute personal project pursuits (Little, Salmela-Aro, and Phillips, 2007), self-adventures (Carlsen, 2008) or episodes in larger life projects (McAdams *et al.*, 1997; McAdams, 1999). In this sense, projects are arenas where people satisfy fundamental needs of experiencing drama, purpose and generating legacies for future generations. Projects can thus be powerful manifestations of human agency and underpin human growth. Accordingly, the study of projects has direct appeal for a study of life in organizations (Dutton, 2003) and organizational lives (Grant, Little and Phillips, 2006).

More principally, and as indicated earlier, a study of how projects are vehicles for positive change must seek to understand how projects constitute *moving horizons of collective engagement and meaning* that flow beyond the boundaries of the project as a micro-managed time-bound event. It means seeing how project experiences stretch beyond clock time into inner time as interpretive resources to be shared, questioned, reinterpreted and drawn upon for the purposes at hand. In this sense, phenomenology has much to offer the field of Positive Organizational Scholarship (POS) in terms of researching how people come to experience their social world and how they act upon it in everyday life. Most importantly for our argument, a phenomenological perspective avoids normative assumptions about what a person should or should not experience as positive (Pitsis, 2007b; Pitsis and Clegg, 2007) – something that POS (and Positive Psychology) critics perceive as a major flaw with the evolving field of positive psychology (Lazarus, 2003; Fineman, 2006). Phenomenology – and narrative inquiry specifically – underpins our approach in this chapter because it nullifies such criticism by allowing room for the actors to narrate what is experienced as positive or negative, rather than the objective scientist attributing such values upon people. Moreover, phenomenology's emphasis on temporality also addresses how experiences change and transform over time – what seems positive or negative one day, may be experienced as negative or positive in the future. The very essence of phenomenology, therefore, assumes experience transcends space and time and that what we experience never occurs in a vacuum devoid of past, present and future.

## BUILDING NARRATIVES

Given our discussion above on phenomenology, the work of Alfred Schütz is particularly relevant to this chapter. For Schütz (1967; 1970) the most critical aspect of sense-making is that interpretation of life events involved selecting an experience out of one's stream of experiences and highlighting how the meaning of an action to an actor depended upon the project guiding the extended temporal process of the sub-acts leading to its realization. In other words, people make sense of life around their projects, and it is our projects that create meaningful experiences in our lives and helps us interpret and make sense of our social world (Schütz, 1967: 61): 'the meaning of any action is its corresponding projected act'.

What Schütz conceived of as an act in its project(s), others have emphasized as acts in their narratives. Narratives may be defined as sequences of human actions and intentions through time (Sarbin, 1986), and acts may be seen intelligible only insofar as they find their place in one or more enacted narratives (MacIntyre, 1981). MacIntyre argues that we identify a particular action by placing it in two types of context; the history of its agent(s) and the history of the settings to which the intentions of the agent(s) belong. Indeed we may say that the emergent negotiation of

temporal-relational contexts from experience is the specialty of the narrative (Polkinghorne, 1988; Bruner, 1990; Sarbin, 1998). Every act of doing something may be located within the history of its doer, his/her context and traditions of social practice, and every thrown projection into the future is an act of narrative imagining that may or may not be assigned weight (Sarbin, 1998). The function of narrative in the creation of meaning is *not* to produce chronologies of distant and true experiences or to establish stable scenarios of the future. Rather, narration amounts to the continuous construction of reality in times present, past and future. The act of narrating is situated in the succession of uniquely passing presents, bathed in the naked immediacy of lived experience (Cunliffe, Luhman and Boje, 2004). Projects can never be free of social context and while they contain elements of projecting past experience into the future, they also contain elements of improvisation to the here and now – or the acting on the present.

So far we have highlighted that projects can be complex arenas of positive organizational change. We have qualified that a study of projects as vehicles of change will span several levels of analysis. We have also argued that for projects to invoke positive change, project experiences need to somehow escape the limited context of the project as a time-bound event itself and enter larger contexts by enlisting the imagination of people into new horizons of meaning. Such horizons of meaning have an inherent narrative form. They are temporal-relational fields of meaning and engagement – stories in the making – that range from personal projects to collectively formed projections – and so ideally suited to phenomenological approaches. The overall questions for our study are: Which kinds of project-in-context development trajectories bring about positive organizational change and what does that tell us about positive change? How do project experiences constitute resources for organizational change after the projects have elapsed? To answer these questions we present a comparative analysis of three cases.

## RESEARCH SETTING AND METHOD

The cases offered here are not three projects as such but three sets of 'project-in-organizational change-context' experiences. Our focus is thus more on the consequences of the projects rather than the projects in and of themselves. The three cases have been selected from multi-year research sites where the authors have followed three organizational settings through a period of three to six years. See Table 27.1.

Our basis for selection of the cases is twofold. First, we have used a positive deviance approach in the sense described by Dutton (2003) and Quinn (1996). While relatively new to organizational behavior theory and research, the positive deviance approach has been popular in medicine, community health, education, and cultural studies (Cooperrider and Whitney, 1995; Heckert and Heckert, 2004; Marsh et al., 2004). By collecting the narratives of positive deviance as experienced by the actors involved in their contexts, the assumption is that those positive deviant acts can be shared and transferred to other contexts and situations (Marsh et al., 2004: 1178). In line with the positive deviance approach we thus have selected projects that stand out in terms of organizational stakeholders asserting positive development trajectories having been experienced that have been in some way decisive for the overall history of the organization – be it a single entity or a temporary interorganizational project. They also stand out in the sense that they are *still* actively remembered for utilitarian everyday purposes.

The second basis for sampling is more pragmatic. Through prior studies we have had unusual access to the research sites over many years and thus been able to gain a rich understanding of the contexts of the change processes. Case 1 is sampled from an interpretive study on the relationship between identity formation and organizational development in an IT consulting firm and a communication agency (Carlsen, 2005; 2006). Case 2 is sampled from an ongoing multi-year (2003–) action research project

on matters of creativity and organizational development in the exploration units of a major oil company. Case 3 is sampled from a longitudinal case study of a project for cleaning up Sydney harbor for geopolitical reasons, followed by additional studies of other projects conducted by the same organization; Sydney Water Corporation. All three cases are thus sampled from within other studies because they stood out as being positive, based on the above mentioned criteria; they are taken from diverse industries, and are contrasting or comparative in terms of project size, type and role of external stakeholders in the change processes taking place.

Our case studies are informed by narrative inquiry (Kohler-Riessman, 1993; Czarniawska, 1998; Clandinin, 2007). A narrative lens is particularly well suited to span multiple levels of analysis and can capture the complexities of meaning making across dimensions of temporality. As such, we do however recognize the inevitable dilemma of prioritizing multiple cases versus one or two. Slimming the case descriptions to the chosen dimensions of comparative analysis will always incur a loss in thickness and interpretive space (see Stake, 2005). On the other hand, multiple case studies enhance possibilities for theory building (Eisenhardt, 1989; 1991; 2007), and analytical generalizations (Yin, 1994)

All the cases reported here were part of separate studies in which rich ethnographic methodologies were used, including in-depth interviews of a broad range of direct and indirect stakeholders, observation of people as they worked and related, as well as various archival data and sensemaking events. See Table 27.1. Upon sampling the project-in-organizational-change-processes as cases for this study, we have: 1) re-examined previous case records (interview material, archives, field notes and paper drafts) during several steps of analysis; and, 2) conducted minor follow-up data collection where deemed necessary. The follow-up studies centered on how the chosen three projects are referred to, understood and used in the organizational change processes in the three organizational settings.

**Table 27.1   Overview of cases, positive outcomes and data collection**

| Case projects | Case organizations | Main positive change outcomes | Data collection |
|---|---|---|---|
| Helene; development of a system for dependency allowance debt; 3 years, around 4 man-years | Calculus; a Scandinavian IT consulting firm, established 1985, 150–200 employees | Demonstrated feasibility of proprietary concepts, opened the door to new projects and markets, re-established faith in vision | Interpretive study 2001–2004, 35 interviews, archives, observations (around 150+ hours), plus background from three action research projects 1999–2002. |
| Norne; oil exploration in a license in the Norwegian Sea; 1986–1991; around 25 man-years, plus drilling | StatoilHydro (mainly the exploration units); a Norwegian based integrated oil and gas company, ~29,000 employees | Resulted in a 25 bn US$, 17 bn € (based on an oil price of 50 US$ per barrel) discovery that paved the way for further exploration and offshore industrialization in northern Norway | Action research project 2003 – in exploration units; at the time of writing: 36 interviews, archives, participant observation on three sets of workshops; 2+1 days. Four follow-up interviews and media search for the Norne project. |
| Olympia; a major Sydney Olympics infrastructure project conducted by Sydney Water Corporation (SWC) in alliance with 4 private firms between 1997 and 2000. | The alliance was the case, with Sydney Water Corporation (SWC) as the main organization studied; SWC is one of Australia's oldest publicly owned bureaucracies responsible for managing and innovating the provision of clean water, waterways and treatment of sewerage in the greater Sydney region | Transformation of organization from bureaucracy to project alliances structures; introduction of new modes of managing projects, and transition. Resulted in major technological and knowledge-based innovations that were adopted in Australia and internationally by private and public organizations. | Rich longitudinal ethnography over 3 years (1997–2000) that included 40 in-depth interviews with direct and indirect stakeholders, 400 hours of participant observation of people at work, observational analysis, attendance of all alliance governance team meetings, and analysis of media and other archival data. |

The analysis of the data has proceeded as an ethnographically informed systematic comparison within and between cases (Eisenhardt, 1989; 1991) with iterations of open and selective coding (Strauss and Corbin, 1990) and subsequent matching of empirical observations to the emergent theoretical categories (Miles and Huberman, 1994). The open coding was based on a re-examination of original case records (for all cases as well as a re-reading of previous analysis with relevance for Case 1 (Carlsen, 2005; 2006) and Case 3 (Pitsis *et al.*, 2004; 2003; Pitsis, 2007a). To aid analysis, we wrote several versions of slimmed down case stories (see Appendix 1) for all cases. These condensed narratives have been integral in mediating our movement from larger narratives of the cases to the analytical scheme of matching observations to categories (see Table 27.2). The condensed narratives also serve the purpose of broadening the basis for member checks from key interviewees and reviews by peers knowledgeable of the history of the case organizations. Finally, we hope these stories will aid readers in attaining a good understanding of each of the three cases.

## BUILDING NARRATIVE CAPITAL

The three projects in this study share features of generating positive organizational change through the building of *narrative capital*.

**Table 27.2  Key case observations mapped against the four processes of building narrative capital**

| | Creating deviance | Instantiating | Extending | Expansive connecting |
|---|---|---|---|---|
| Helene in Calculus | (1) First delivery of a 'technology support system for casework that spanned an entire business process'; (2) first use of in-house technology platforms; (3) first 'knowledge representation' (the specifics of rules, heuristics etc.) in a domain model held separate from the process engine (the model of the work process)' | Talked of internally and externally as an exemplar of superior abilities and 'the kind of work we really would like to do'; thus construed as an 'identity exemplar'; re-established faith in industrial dreams of the founders | The project experiences are extended into several parallel trajectories of practice: (1) a series of new projects and a new market focus towards the public sector; (2) development of a proprietary framework for work process modeling with re-use software libraries; (3) the separation of the process engine and domain model became a design principle | *Connecting to knowledge tradition:* The project was seen as re-establishing the original mission of the firm by reconnecting to the promises of expert systems technologies.<br>*Metaphorical connecting:* At the industry level the project was used to mark the conception of proprietary framework later considered 'magic potions' in recurrent battles with larger competitors. |
| Norne in StatoilHydro | Northernmost successful exploration effort in the Norwegian Sea at that time, finding oil where many had given up; first validation of new theory for hydrocarbon migration and faults in the geological area; first offshore field on the Norwegian shelf developed with a production and storage ship tied to sub sea templates | Held up as a faith bound discovery on which the further successful extension of the offshore adventure to northern Norway would turn; re-established hope and willingness to take risks both in northern Norway and in small fields | A series of discoveries followed in the region based upon the same geological theory for migration and traps; Norne fortified the Harstad office as regional stronghold and strengthened regional exploration activities; the technological solutions for the development of the field were also replicated into a series of other similar projects | *Connecting to regional development:* The project was talked of internally and externally as being key in establishing northern Norway as a new offshore province.<br>*Metaphorical connecting:* Adoption of mythological name of goddess of faith and use of story to underline the value of faith itself |
| Olympia in Sydney Water Corporation | First (The Project Alliance) Mega-Project that sought to transform bureaucratic major public organization, better enabling it to deal with uncertainty and ambiguity. The project was acknowledged as the first of its kind in the world in which both private and public organizations formed a temporary legally recognized organization where risk, reward, knowledge and resources would be shared and a transparent open-book management approach was used. | Held up as an ideal exemplar for public/private partner alliances that operate under ambiguous and complex contexts. The project gained political mileage as an exemplar of successful government policy and expenditure. All parent organizations highlighted the innovation and creativity that resulted directly from the project. Case studies of the project are now used as training resource for new alliance projects. | Alliancing as a dominant mode of practice was extended to other parts of SWC. A series of innovations in project management, including for example community stakeholder management, were transferred onto separate but concurrent projects conducted by partner organizations. Related applications of innovations in technology, human resource management, safety, and risk minimization were extended into new projects as they unfolded. | *Connecting to local community:* Successful handling of demanding high-price real estate stakeholders in immediate surroundings transformed community perception.<br>*Connecting to the 2000 Olympics:* The dramatic frame of getting ready for the eyes of the world was regularly invoked in project meetings.<br>*Connecting to outsourcing trend:* Occurred in context of widespread government spending cuts and downsizing, and so benefited in the sense that aspects of the organization were outsourced to private industry through Olympia. |

By narrative capital we understand the value of adding chapters to organizational life stories in terms of sustaining positive legacies and generating new possibilities for development and growth. The term is borrowed from the work of the narrative psychologist Karl Scheibe (1986; 2000), who uses it to denounce the value of chapters added to individual life stories, largely a retrospective phenomenon of stock-taking. To Scheibe, narrative capital results from embarking upon dramas; time-bound and goal directed adventures where challenges are met and risks are handled. Narrative capital is conceived as an individual resource, stories that people dine out on and that form sources of meaning and a sense of excitement in life. Extending this lead from Scheibe, we suggest narrative capital might be best understood as (also) a collective and prospective phenomenon, as implied by our inspiration from Schütz (1970; 1967). In comparison to related organization theory constructs, such as social capital (Adler and Kwon, 2002), positive social capital (Baker and Dutton, 2007) intellectual and human capital (Nahapiet and Ghoshal, 1998; Van de Ven, 1999), and positive psychological capital (Luthans and Youssef, 2004), narrative capital is a *temporal-relational* construct that includes teleo-affective fields of meaning. The prospective dimension of agency is the key here. The value of experiences that build narrative capital is partly that they constitute resources that strengthen development trajectories and open up new landscapes of possibilities, and partly the fortifying of expectation for the future in itself, not necessarily directed towards clearly conceived ends. Narrative capital is indeed narrative in form, a perspective either absent or largely underplayed in the conceptions of social capital referred to. As we shall show, projects for life gain their significance first and foremost because they generate or strengthen stories of what could be. In this regard, four key constructs emanate from the data, all explaining how projects are vehicles for positive organizational change through building narrative capital: 1) creating deviance, 2) instantiating, 3) extending, and 4) expansive connecting. See Table 27.2 for a mapping of key empirical observations in each project-in-change case against these constructs. The appendix includes a detailed account of each project.

## Creating deviance

*Creating deviance* refers to the combination of doing a particular set of acts and the subsequent perception and construction of these acts as representing a novelty; some kind of breach from previous experience. The three case projects are noted by organizational members and external stakeholders for representing a variety of such breaches. The 'Helene' system was presented internally and externally as a pioneering feat on several dimensions of organizational practice, see Table 27.2. The Norne project was held up – much helped by media attention – as the northernmost successful offshore oil exploration effort in the Norwegian Sea at the time. To the exploration groups the discovery confirmed a theory of hydrocarbon distribution that broke with the local geological models underpinning previous exploration efforts in that area. The Olympia project was sold as the first interorganizational alliance of its kind in the world, delivered as a temporary project-based organization that includes the customer as an integral part of the project-based organization, where risks and rewards were shared and tendering would not be based on price, but on cultural fit.

Key to all the three projects is that they are both *experienced* and *noticed*. They are not so much novelties, waiting to be discovered as they are actively construed, as breaches from previous experiences. One may say that creating deviance hinges on the use of selective attention in noticing something from the stream of experiences and bracketing it as new (James, 1890/1950). In all four cases the process of creating deviance functions as a narrative opener. As argued by Bruner (1990: 47), the narrative 'specializes in forging a link between the exceptional and the ordinary,' and breaches from normality are chief stimulants of construction of meaning. One may say, still following Bruner (1990), that a breach in experience sets up an interpretive deficit that invites social creation of meaning. Whether this meaning making is primarily oriented towards the past or towards the future is a crucial point here. We suggest that the *opening-up function* of the project experiences stem from a certain incompleteness brought about by new expectations for their future implications. They invoke or fortify broader fields of possibilities and aspirations. Initially, such expectations may not have a very clear direction as the full plurality of experiences undergone has not yet been taken out of its ambiguous cradle and connected to successive experiences. Retrospectively one might say that the projects represent experiences that opened up new paths of practice (e.g., new forms of projects or new ways of handling projects), new territories for action (e.g., new markets for Calculus, new local exploration opportunities for StatoilHydro) or new avenues of interpretation (e.g., conjuring entirely new geological models, technology frameworks and relationships for Sydney Water Corp.). However, there is no determinism in this, no *a priori* set direction for development, a point Weick (1979) consistently makes.

The narrative opening function of the deviances noticed and made from the three projects has a parallel set of explanation. Schütz borrowed from James and Husserl to argue for multiple realities co-existing in the social world. It is through the experience of what Schütz (1967) terms *shock* that alternative realities become noticed. In later works, Schütz (1973) expanded on this and defined 'finite provinces of meaning', as a set of experiences belonging to a specific cognitive style that are – with respect to that style – not only consistent within themselves, but also compatible with one another. Creating deviance may be considered a shock in experience potentially powerful enough to break through the limits or boundedness of one's *finite province of meaning* thus shifting ones view of reality to another province of meaning. Schütz reminds us that the world

of working in 'standard' time is not the sole finite province of meaning, but merely one of several available to our intentional lives. Assigning this kind of radical shift in meaning to a project is a difficult claim to make, as all interpretations of such experience are inclined to be retrospectively smoothed (Bruner, 1990). The point still remains though that the cognitive opening brought about by the project experience may vary from seeing new turns in already established provinces of meaning to embarking upon entirely new ones. The intensity of expectations following these cognitive shifts, thus the overall strength of the deviant experiences in being story openers depend on their emotional charging through a process of instantiating.

## Instantiating

Of all the perceived breaches in experience, some are made more central than others. The jolts that are assigned the most meaning achieve their significance through *instantiating*. By instantiating we refer to the process of selectively appropriating accounts of deviant past experience and charging these accounts with status as an anticipatory and/or desired exemplar of future experiences.

At Calculus, the Helene application was talked of internally and externally as a demonstrator of superior capabilities. The project was used as a veridical identity exemplar of past and future practice in internal training sessions and in sales presentations for prospective clients. It signified the kinds of work organizational members 'really wanted to do' and restored faith in the initial mission of the firm – to commercialize expert systems technologies. Instantiating may also take place in a public field where outside stakeholders are active co-authors. This is the case for Norne. Here, both internal and external stakeholders emphasized the discovery as a Destiny carrier on which the further successful extension of the offshore adventure to Northern Norway would turn. Internally it was also used as an exemplar of the importance of faith in itself: the exploration efforts had prevailed through setbacks of dry wells and much resistance.

In Sydney Water Corporation (SWC) instantiating took place in a contested terrain as the organization was polarized between the 'converts' and the 'black-hats.' The converts refer to the people who were pro-alliance and believed the experience of Olympia could add great value to SWC if the knowledge and innovations were captured and shared. The black hats were a collective term used to describe anyone not positive about the project. To this group, empowerment, open-book management, openness to risk and practicing self-leadership with an emphasis on 'soft' human relations with private industry, was perceived with great skepticism. The 'convert' voices became the dominant ones as the project progressed. Olympia was increasingly referred to as an ideal exemplar for public/private partner alliances that operate under ambiguous and complex contexts. Case studies of the project are now used as training and development resources for new alliance projects.

Anticipatory exemplars may be regarded as parallel to the puzzles Kuhn (1962/1996) identified as constitutive of scientific paradigms. In our context, the word constitutive refers more to spanning out futures, or acts of *becoming*, than to questions of marking boundaries, belonging. Instantiating is a past-future typification (Schütz, 1967) of experience where one predicts or hopes for some kind of recurrence. Instantiating is done for future-oriented purposes and can mean intense emotional charging as a field of desire is invoked: *This is what we truly want to do. This is what we would like to become.* Conceived as such, instantiating represents a type of inductive learning from one or very few samples (March, Sproull and Tamuz, 1991). The principle movement is from concrete instances to more generalized stories of what could be or what we could become. In this way the stories of the projects become exemplary narratives (Durand and Calori, 2006) that are told and retold in anticipation of future experiences and that in doing so set up the field for positive

organizational change. Moving along those hoped-for trajectories calls for a process of extending the project experiences.

## Extending

By extending we mean a process by which one seeks to replicate some aspect of past successful experience and follow up on the trajectories for development that are opened up or can be inferred from these experiences. Principally, extending results from a form of agency where one draws upon the successful past in reflective and creative use of prior experience in accordance with evolving desires and purposes (Emirbayer and Mische, 1998). Extending is multi-leveled and may take place along a large variety of directions.

At Calculus, the presentation of the applications in front of new clients led to several new projects of the same kind. The use of in-house technology platforms in the work with Helene proved a starting point for the full development of a proprietary framework for work process modeling with re-use software libraries. And the discovery that the work process engine (the model of the work process) and domain model (the specifics of rules, heuristics and so forth) should be separated, was later reinforced as a central design principle. The Helene project thus represented an experience where the four sets of novelties provided starting points for three parallel trajectories of practice. The same pattern can be seen for Olympia. SWC was able to transfer the exemplary results on community and stakeholder consultation to all its projects, it was able to introduce alliancing as a mode of operation within SWC, and was also able to offer its advice to other government bodies who were seeking to establish alliances. The project came as SWC was still suffering from a number of public relations nightmares: water contamination, customer billing problems, negative media, and corporate downsizing. Years of poor stakeholder relationship management across many government bodies meant any change to the norms was quickly attended to – stakeholder expectations therefore were also transferred to other public organizations. As one community member said: 'if Sydney Water can do this [community consultation], and do it so [expletive] well, then I think the RTA [Roads and Traffic Authority], StateRail and all those other [expletives] can do it too!'.

For exploration in StatoilHydro, the Norne discovery had direct consequences in a series of new (though smaller) discoveries in the same region, based upon the same set of geological theories for migration and traps, a so-called fill-spill model (briefly, that oil resources migrating to a sealed structure will fill it before spilling over to a neighboring structure, fill this and then spill further until exhausted). This is not as much an extension of ways of working as it is extending an interpretive scheme.

Extending includes visioning and imaginative *search* from particularly successful experiences: 'How can we sell a second or third project using such technologies? Can the design principle be used for other types of applications? Can we generate more business within the same market segment? What are the best new exploration targets given the validation of our model? Which new project opportunities follow from the media attention and favorable attribution of superior capabilities?' Following Cyert and March (1963), we may see such search processes as contingent upon previous experiences, accumulative and 'local.' What one searches for is concentrated on territories close to the current one. It is a search both enabled and constrained by clients and competitive organizations. It is also – and in contrast to the conception of Cyert and March – an agentic process with active forethought, imagination of alternative scenarios and reflexive distancing from the original experiences. Successful project experiences attract interpretive interest and immediately trigger a series of thrown projections for possible extensions.

It is also important to note here that the many possible levels of extending means that the resulting path dependencies are *not* unitarily determined by prior experiences

(as with instantiating). Each unique visit to experiences may branch out in a multiplicity of suggestions of what could, ultimately, be a form of *play* with the plurality of experience (Barthes, 1986; 1981) through a serial movement of dislocations and associations. It follows from this that extensions may be delayed by many years. For example, the experience of making the Norne discovery was later recognized by StatoilHydro personnel to fall within an overall pattern of exploration where significant discoveries typically emerge from many years of failures. It seems that many success stories in exploration share a plot with a breakthrough interpretation in the wake of a series of costly geological interpretations later found invalid. The notification of this pattern has a number of consequences for exploration, amongst them the importance of dry-well analysis, the role of faith and being able to handle alternative interpretations in parallel. Each of these implications means a possible extension of practice. Each may open up new discursive space. To see which processes of extending that is assigned the most weight for organizational change, one needs to go beyond the organization.

## Expansive connecting

By expansive connecting we mean the process by which organizational change efforts are strengthened by being linked to stories unfolding outside the organizations. Seemingly paradoxically, the three sets of narrative capital in the positive spirals of organizational change do not only occur in organizations. They always form part of extra-organizational development trajectories, be they disciplinary traditions, mythical structures, regional development or other larger social wholes.

There are three forms of expansive connecting evident in the case stories. The first is a direct contextual relationship made or used by stakeholders to enhance the importance of the projects themselves. The success of the Helene project at Calculus is underlined by placing it in the context of the artificial intelligence tradition. Likewise, the importance of the Olympia project for cleaning up the harbor is enhanced by it taking place surrounded by some of the world's most expensive real estate and at a time where organizational identity was damaged by public relations disasters such as water contamination.

The second form of expansive connecting goes beyond a mere emphasis on context to a strong framing of the project as being directly part of a distinct larger *Project*. A chief example of this is the strong connecting of the Norne discovery to the regional development story of Northern Norway. The connecting is performed both internally by geologists, pursuing a vision of contributing to regional development, and externally, by the domestic press, local politicians, industry spokespersons and other commentators. Virtually all the media accounts dealing with the discovery connect it to regional development of Northern Norway. One might safely say that most of the public significance of the discovery is linked to this larger development story. A directly parallel case occurs with the Olympia project occurring in the contexts of the Sydney Olympics in 2000. Winning the Olympic Games meant that the New South Wales Government had to ensure the cleanliness of Sydney Harbor – possibly not so much for public health reasons as for potential tourism and the overall success of the Olympics. Project management repeatedly invoked the dramatic frame of the eyes of the world being upon Australia and Sydney as a means to connect the project of cleaning up the harbor to the *Project* of getting ready for the Olympics. For both these two examples, the significance of expansive connecting is not that of an outside context, separated from the daily work of the geologists and construction workers. Rather it works in and through their daily work – prior to the success itself – as an invoked frame of why their work is important. In this sense, it forms the very horizon of their expectation.

The third form of expansive connecting is subtler as it involves the use of metaphors and plot-borrowings that to varying degrees may resonate in myths and more or less tacit narrative structures (Crites, 1971; Carlsen, 2006). The Norne project is linked to Norse mythology and may be seen as achieving its faith status partly by its naming. The Helene project forms part of a growth trajectory that is mediated by the use of the metaphor of the Indomitable Gauls, borrowed from a cartoon series, and is later assigned weight as being the cradle of 'magic potions' – the role that the development of the re-use libraries was assigned. Olympia was inevitably tied to the genesis of a shared democracy, and would as such be bathed in idealistic undertones.

Principally, what expansive connecting does is to place projects within temporal-relational fields of meaning that stretch beyond the organization, as acts within larger narrative structures (MacIntyre, 1981). It is a process that expands the meaning of work in general (cf. Gardner, 1996; O'Connor, 2000) and projects in particular. Furthermore, the stories the projects animate are composite; a kind of narrative heteroglossia (Bakhtin, 1991; Holland *et al*., 1998) that allow for many forms of identifications and sources of engagement. Expansive connecting thus ultimately answers the question: which larger stories or development trajectories outside the organization does this project form part of or brush up against?

## SPIRALS OF POSITIVE ORGANIZATIONAL CHANGE

We opened this chapter by arguing that projects in many ways represent ideal contexts for studying positive organizational change and that for projects to generate such change, project experiences need to transcend their immediate time-bound contexts and enter larger temporal-relational fields of meaning; to be 'made for life.' What then have we learned about how projects are made for life and what are the implications of this learning for theories of positive organizational change?

Our comparative analysis of four deviant projects-in-organization change cases has

**Figure 27.1 The four processes building narrative capital and spirals of positive organizational change.**

identified four interrelated processes of building narrative capital where upward spirals of positive organizational change are generated or fortified: creating deviance, instantiating, extending and expansive connecting, see Figure 27.1. The overall thrust of these processes is reminiscent of appreciative inquiry (Cooperrider and Sekerka, 2003) in the sense of expanding from the local positive core to a larger whole. However, the four processes should be understood as mutually reinforcing rather than a sequence that starts with creating deviance and ends with expansive connecting. Each process remains active throughout the spiral of change. Indeed, expansive connecting may, for example, contribute to instantiating by placing experiences in a narrative structure that enhances their importance. Likewise, creating deviance may also take place through repeated visits to past experience that take on new meanings in light of new circumstances. In each of their distinct ways, the four processes all provide (temporary) answers to the lingering question: *Which project(s) is this particular project an act of?*

Narrative capital refers to collectively construed stories in the making that are assigned social weight as belonging to the organizational life histories of key stakeholders inside or outside the organization. It should be understood more as a dynamic development resource than as a fixed asset. It is a generative resource that stretches out in times past and times future, that does not exist outside its constitutive processes, and that does not diminish with use. The prospective dimension of potentiality is the key in relation to organizational change. Two sets of implications for theories of positive organizational change follow from this.

First, with a heritage from pragmatism (see James, 1890/1950, chap. 9), the three cases show that the deviant experiences underpinning positive organizational change are plural and equivocal. Deviant experiences do not come prepackaged into neat categories of strategy, identity or learning, nor do the processes they instigate. Rather, change experiences unfold as intertwined movements where processes that have identity relevant, strategy relevant and learning relevant moments occur in confluence (Carlsen, 2006). Jolts or shocks in experience are more like a mixed stew of last night's leftovers than a fine consume. The spirals of positive change are multidimensional and support a confluence theory of change. What seems key is to understand how dynamic relationships between some form of positive experiences and socio-cognitive-emotional resources may result in positive cycles of change. Instantiating seems to be a clear conceptual macro-OB parallel to building Reflected Best Self Portraits (Roberts *et al.*, 2005) on the micro-OB individual level.

There are also interesting micro to macro parallels between Fredrickson's (2001; 2006) theory of how positive experiences broaden and build people's thought-action repertoires and the building of narrative capital. The appreciative and opening up functions of creating deviance and instantiating, point towards the importance of positive emotions associated with pride and hope, *and* their narrative character. Pride seems to be associated with stories of past achievements. Hope seems lit by the rays of possibilities and moving horizons of expectations in the stories of what could be. Perhaps we can think of the repeated remembering of successful project experiences as producers of combined pride-hope emotions that in turn enable change? In this sense, narrative capital is a form of emotional capital to be repeatedly constituted and drawn upon.

Second, our analysis shows a pattern of positive change being driven by expanding temporal-relational fields of meaning and engagement. Expanding here means both orientations towards a future and a progression from the local towards a wider inclusion of stakeholders and/or wider development trajectories outside the organizations. Forms of projecting are central here. All the four processes of building narrative capital identified – creating deviance, instantiating, extending and expansive connecting – have undeniable prospective elements. The addition of these qualities to theories of sensemaking is certainly needed. Weick (1979; 1995) presents sensemaking as a retrospective phenomenon in which meaning is created and understanding occurs by looking back on one's actions. Sensemaking, according to Weick (1995), may be viewed as an act of reflection such as a (p. 26) 'cone of light that spreads backwards from a particular present' and is driven by a feeling of 'order, clarity, and rationality' (p. 29). Weick acknowledges a role for expectation or faith (referring to James' *Will to Believe*), but insists that the creation of meaning in general is an attential process directed backwards (pp. 25–26) and that strategies are best conceived retrospectively from an imagined future position (p. 29); future perfect thinking. Weick's lead has been followed by, for example, Gioia, Corley and Fabbri (2002) who explicitly exclude prospective components in identity formation (p. 623): '*Only* via retrospective interpretation can organizations articulate their identity' [emphasis added]. It is only relatively recently that Weick has explicitly stated a prospective component to sensemaking (Weick, Sutcliffe and Obstfeld, 2005). Weick *et al.* (2005: 419)

argue that sensemaking provides a balance between prospect in the form of anticipation, and retrospect in the form of resilience. However, what appears to be missing is the generative, inspirational and transformative nature of prospective sensemaking in the Weick *et al.* discussion.

While such classic works on sensemaking have contributed greatly to the management and organizational theory landscape they still underplay the prospective aspect so central in Alfred Schütz's conceptions of meaning and action – for Schütz (1967) these two concepts cannot be separated. Action is spontaneous behavior and cognition self-consciously projected and always (also) oriented towards the future. Making sense of project experiences is indeed retrospective in the sense that it is a response to a previous act; a present-past interpretation, but this response can never be brought out of its threefold present (Carlsen, 2006; Pitsis and Clegg, 2007: 402–404). Sensemaking is also a present-past-future meaning making process, as recollection never takes place outside the scope of one's interest in the future (Crites, 1971; 1986; Bruner, 1990). Project experiences are remembered because they form a sequence with the present in a way that extends forward. Projects are *for life* because people remember and act upon project experiences in ways that opens up new landscapes of possibilities for actions, facilitate belief in trajectories of development and gives a shaped and shared sense of where one wants to go. The limiting of forward-looking imagination to future perfect thinking assumes that all anticipation is oriented towards clear end positions from which one may look backwards. It is not. The cone of light also spread forwards. The overall discursive function of building narrative capital may be likened to what the historian Koselleck (1979) has coined as describing 'spaces of experience' in such a way that they open up new 'horizons of expectations.' Indeed, the positive organizational change outcomes we have discussed do not end with end of the projects; they are always filled with possibilities growth, change, and new beginnings.

## NEW BEGINNINGS

Transforming rocks into pyramids, materials into space rockets to land on the moon, prospecting an oil field into a dream of new regional development, a small IT application that restored faith, a clean harbor for the Olympics into transformation of public-private alliancing: all projects setting up stories of what could be. These are adventures that occur in space and time, they transform with time, can alter pre-existing knowledge and the way we experience life as it unfolds before us and as we act upon it. Projects are yearnings for something beyond the self; like a child they constitute both evolving legacies of work and horizons of expectations for the future. Our projects span the boundaries of the Others' projects. Each and everyone of us are part of someone's project – be it another individual, a company, a government department, or so on. Sometimes our involvement in Other's projects is intentional, other times it is not. Positive organizational change is never only organizational, never just macro or micro, and derives its momentum for that very reason. Projects for life are made for life because they are assigned social weight as stretching beyond the protagonists, beyond the project, beyond the organization, beyond the foreseeable future, beyond our sense of self.

## NOTE

1 This chapter has benefited from discussion at the conference 'Empirical Currents of Positive Organizational Scholarship' at the University of Michigan in December 2006. We are also thankful for inputs to earlier version of the chapter from Stewart Clegg, Saku Mantere, Kjersti Bjørkeng, Tord F. Mortensen, Reidar Gjersvik and Kim Cameron. We would especially like to acknowledge and thank our industry partners for their openness and honesty, and also the Australian Research Council's support through the ARC Linkage grant LP0348816.

## REFERENCES

Adler, P.S. and Kwon, S. (2002) 'Social capital: Prospects for a new concept', *Academy of Management Review*, 27 (1): 17–40.

Baker, W.E. and Dutton, J.E. (2007) 'Enabling positive social capital in organizations', in J.E. Dutton and B.R. Ragins (eds) *Exploring Positive Relationships at Work*. Mahwah, NJ: Lawrence Erlbaum Associates.

Bakhtin, M. (1991) *The Dialogic Imagination*. Austin: University of Texas Press.

Barthes, R. (1981) 'Theory of the text', in R. Young (ed.) *Untying the Text: A Post-structuralist Reader*. London: Routledge, pp. 31–47.

Barthes, R. (1986) 'From work to text' (R. Howard, Trans.) *The Rustle of Language*. New York: Hill & Wang, pp. 56–64.

Boden, M. (1994) *The Business of Talk*. Cambridge: Polity Press.

Bruner, J. (1990) *Acts of Meaning*. Cambridge, MA: Harvard University Press.

Carlsen, A. (2005) *Acts of becoming. On the dialogic imagination of practice in organizations*. Doctoral dissertation. Trondheim: Norwegian University of Science and Technology.

Carlsen, A. (2006) 'Organizational becoming as dialogic imagination of practice. The case of the Indomitable Gauls', *Organization Science*, 17 (1): 132–149.

Carlsen, A. (2008) 'Positive dramas. Enacting self-adventures in organizations', *Journal of Positive Psychology*, 3 (1): 55–75.

Carroll, C. (2002) 'The strategic use of the past and future in organizational change', *Journal of Organizational Change Management*, 15 (6): 556–552.

Clandinin, D.J. (ed.) (2007) *Handbook of Narrative Inquiry. Mapping a Methodology*. Thousand Oaks, CA: Sage.

Clegg, S.R., Kornberger, M. and Pitsis, T.S. (2008) *Managing and Organizations: An Introduction to Theory and Practice*. London: Sage.

Cooperrider, D.L. and Sekerka, L.E. (2003) 'Toward a theory of positive organizational change', in K.S. Cameron, J.E. Dutton and R.E. Quinn (eds) *Positive Organizational Scholarship: Foundations of a New Discipline*. San Francisco: Berrett-Koehler, pp. 225–240.

Cooperrider, D. and Whitney, D. (1995) *Appreciative Inquiry: A Constructive Approach to Organizational Development and Social Change*. Cleveland, OH: Case Western Reserve University.

Crites, S. (1971) 'The narrative quality of experience', *Journal of the American Academy of Religion*, 39 (3): 291–311.

Crites, S. (1986) 'Storytime. Recollecting the past and projecting the future', in T. Sarbin, (ed.) *Narrative Psychology: The Storied Nature of Human Conduct*. New York: Praeger, pp. 152–173.

Cunliffe, A.L., Luhman, J.T. and Boje, D. (2004) 'Narrative temporality: Implications for organizational research', *Organization Studies*, 25 (2): 261–286.

Cyert, R.M. and March, J.G. (1963) *A Behavioral Theory of the Firm*. Englewood Cliffs, NJ: Prentice Hall.

Czarniawska, B. (1998) *A Narrative Approach to Organization Studies*. Qualitative Research Methods Series 43. Thousand Oaks, CA: Sage.

Dunphy, D., Griffiths, A. and Benn, S. (2007) *Organizational Change for Corporate Sustainability: A Guide for Leaders and Change Agents of the Future*. New York: Routledge.

Durand, R. and Calori, R. (2006) 'Sameness, otherness? Enriching organizational change theories with philosophical considerations on the same and the other', *Academy of Management Review*, 31 (1): 93–114.

Dutton, J.E. (2003) 'Breathing life into organizational studies', *Journal of Management Inquiry*, 12 (1): 5–19.

Eisenhardt, K.E. (1989) 'Building theories from case study research', *Academy of Management Review*, 14 (4): 532–550.

Eisenhardt, K.E. (1991) 'Better stories and better constructs: The case for rigor and comparative logic', *Academy of Management Review*, 16 (3): 620–627.

Eisenhardt, K.E. (2007) 'Theory building from cases: Opportunities and challenges', *Academy of Management Journal*, 50 (1): 25–32.

Emirbayer, M. and Mische, A. (1998) 'What is agency?', *American Journal of Sociology*, 103 (4): 962–1023.

Fineman, S. (2006) 'Accentuating the positive', *Academy of Management Review*, 31 (2): 306–308.

Flyvbjerg, B., Bruzelius, N. and Rothengatter, W. (2003) *Megaprojects and Risk: An Anatomy of Ambition*. Cambridge: Cambridge University Press.

Fredrickson, B.L. (2001) 'The role of positive emotions in positive psychology – The broaden-and-build theory of positive emotions', *American Psychologist*, 56 (3): 218–226.

Fredrickson, B.L. (2006) 'Unpacking positive emotions: Investigating the seeds of human flourishing', *The Journal of Positive Psychology*, 1 (2): 57–59.

Gardner, H. (1996) *Leading Minds. An Anatomy of Leadership*. (In collaboration with E. Laskin.) London: HarperCollins.

Gioia, D.A., Corley, K.G. and Fabbri, T. (2002) 'Revising the past (while thinking in the future perfect tense)', *Journal of Organizational Change Management*, 15 (6): 622–634.

Grant, A.M., Little, B.R. and Phillips, S.D. (2006) 'Personal projects and organizational lives: When personal projects are not merely personal', in B.R. Little, K. Salmela-Aro and S.D. Phillips (eds) *Personal Project Pursuit: Goals, Action, and Human Flourishing*. Mahwah, NJ: Erlbaum Associates, pp. 221–246.

Hackman, J.R. (2003) 'Learning more by crossing levels: Evidence from airplanes, orchestras, and hospitals', *Journal of Organizational Behavior*, 24 (8): 1–18.

Hardy, C., Phillips, N. and Lawrence, T.B. (2003) 'Resources, knowledge and influence. The organizational effects of interorganizational collaboration', *Journal of Management Studies*, 40 (2): 321–347.

Heckert, A. and Heckert, D.M. (2004) 'Using an integrated typology of deviance to analyze ten common norms of the U.S. middle class', *Sociological Quarterly*, 45 (2): 209–228.

Hodgson, D. and Cicmil, S. (2006) *Making Projects Critical*. New York: Palgrave.

Holland, D., Lachiotte, W. Jr., Skinner, D. and Cain, C. (1998) *Identity and Agency in Cultural Worlds*. Cambridge, MA: Harvard University Press.

Huxham, C. (1996) 'On the theory and practice of transformational collaboration: From social service to social justice', in C. Huxham (ed.) *Collaboration and Collaborative Advantage*: Vol. 8. *Creating Collaborative Advantage*. London: Sage.

James, W. (1890/1950) *Principles of Psychology*. New York: Dover.

Kohler-Riessman, C. (1993) *Narrative Analysis*. Qualitative Research Method Series 30. Thousand Oaks, CA: Sage.

Koselleck, R. (1979) *Futures Past. On the Semantics of Historical Time*. Cambridge, MA: MIT Press.

Kuhn, T.S. (1962/1996) *The Structure of Scientific Revolutions*. 3rd edn. Chicago: The University of Chicago Press.

Langley, A. (1999) 'Strategies for theorizing from process data', *Academy of Management Review*, 24 (4): 691–710.

Lazarus, R.S. (2003) 'Does the positive psychology movement have legs?', *Psychological Inquiry*, 14 (2): 93–109.

Little, B.R., Salmela-Aro, K. and Phillips, S.D. (2007) *Personal Project Pursuit. Goals, Action and Human Flourishing*. London: Lawrence Erlbaum.

Lundin, R. and Hartman, F. (2000) 'Pervasiveness of projects in business', in R. Lundin and F. Hartman (eds) *Projects as Business Constituents and Guiding Motives*. Boston, MA: Kluwer-Academic Press.

Luthans, F. and Youssef, C. (2004) 'Human, social, and now positive psychological capital management: Investing in people for competitive advantage', *Organizational Dynamics*, 33 (2): 143–160.

MacIntyre, A. (1981) *After Virtue*. London: Duckworth Press.

March, J.G., Sproull, L.S. and Tamuz, M. (1991) 'Learning from samples of one or fewer', *Organization Science*, 2 (1): 1–14.

Marsh, D.R., Schroeder, D.G., Dearden, K.A., Sternin, J. and Sternin, M. (2004) 'The power of positive deviance', *British Medical Journal*, 329 (7): 1177–1199.

McAdams, D.P. (1999) 'Personal narratives and the life story', in A. Pervin and O.P. John (eds) *Handbook of Personality. Theory and Research*, 2nd edn. New York: Guilford Press, pp. 478–500.

McAdams, D.P., Diamond, A., de St. Aubin, E. and Mansfield, E. (1997) 'Stories of commitment: The psychosocial construction of generative lives', *Journal of Personality and Social Psychology*, 72 (3): 678–694.

McLaughlin, P. (2001) 'Toward an ecology of social action: Merging the ecological and constructivist traditions', *Human Ecology Review*, 8 (2): 12–28.

Mead, G.H. (1932/2002) *The Philosophy of the Present*. New York: Prometheus Books.

Miles, M.B. and Huberman, A.M. (1994) *Qualitative Data Analysis. An Expanded Sourcebook*, 2nd edn. Thousand Oaks, CA: Sage.

Mutch, A., Delbridge, R. and Ventresca, M. (2006) 'Situating organizational action: The relational sociology of organizations', *Organization*, 13 (6): 607–625.

Nahapiet, J. and Ghoshal, S. (1998) 'Social capital, intellectual capital, and the organizational advantage', *Academy of Management Review*, 23 (2): 242–266.

O'Connor, E. (2000) 'Plotting the organization. The embedded narrative as a construct for studying change', *Journal of Applied Behavioral Science*, 36 (2): 174–192.

Pentland, B.T. (1999) 'Building process theory with narrative: From description to explanation', *Academy of Management Review*, 24 (4): 711–725.

Pettigrew, A.M. (1992) 'The character and significance of strategy process research', *Strategic Management Journal*, 13 (8): 5–16.

Pettigrew, A.M., Woodman, R.W. and Cameron, K.S. (2001) 'Studying organizational change and development: Challenges for future research', *Academy of Management Journal*, 44 (4): 697–713.

Pitsis, T.S. (2007a) *My Life as a Project: The Phenomenology of Project-based Organizing*, Doctoral dissertation, University of Technology, Sydney, Australia.

Pitsis, T.S. (2007b) 'Positive psychology', in S.R. Clegg and J. Bailey (eds) *International Encyclopedia of Organizational Studies*. Thousand Oaks, CA: Sage.

Pitsis, T.S. and Clegg, S.R. (2007) 'We live in a political world: The paradox of managerial wisdom', in E. Kessler and J. Bailey (eds) *Handbook of Managerial*

*and Organizational Wisdom*. Thousand Oaks, CA: Sage, pp. 399–422.

Pitsis, T.S., Clegg, S., Marosszeky, M. and Rura-Polley, T. (2003) 'Constructing the Olympic dream: A future perfect strategy of project management', *Organization Science*, 14 (5): 574–590.

Pitsis, T.S., Kornberger M. and Clegg, S.R. (2004) 'The art of managing relationships in interorganizational collaboration', *Management Journal*, 7 (3): 47–67.

Polkinghorne, D.E. (1988) *Narrative Knowing and the Human Sciences*. Albany: State University of New York Press.

Quinn, R.E. (1996) *Deep Change. Discovering the Leader Within*. San Francisco: Jossey-Bass.

Roberts, L.M., Dutton, J.E., Spreitzer, G., Heaphy, E. and Quinn, R.E. (2005) 'Composing the reflected best self-portrait. Building pathways for becoming extraordinary in organizations', *Academy of Management Review*, 30 (4): 712–736.

Sarbin, T.R. (1986) 'The narrative as a root metaphor for psychology', in T.R. Sarbin (ed.) *Narrative Psychology*. Westport: Praeger Publishers, pp. 3–21.

Sarbin, T.R. (1998) 'Believed-in imaginings. A narrative approach', in J. De Rivera and T.R. Sarbin (eds) *Believed-in Imaginings. The Narrative Construction of Reality*. Washington, DC: American Psychological Association, pp. 15–30.

Scheibe, K.E. (1986) 'Self-narratives and adventure', in T.R. Sarbin (ed.) *Narrative Psychology*. Westport: Praeger Publishers, pp. 129–151.

Scheibe, K.E. (2000) *The Drama of Everyday Life*. Boston: Harvard University Press.

Schütz, A. (1967) *The Phenomenology of the Social World*. Chicago: Northwestern University Press.

Schütz, A. (1970) *On Phenomenology and Social Relations*. Chicago: The University of Chicago Press.

Schütz, A. (1973) in M. Natanson (ed.) *The Problem of Social Reality: Collected Papers*. (4th edn). The Hague: Martinus Nijhoff.

Strauss, A. and Corbin, J. (1990) *Basics of Qualitative Research*. Newbury Park, CA: Sage.

Van de Ven, A.H. (1999) *The Innovation Journey*. Oxford: Oxford University Press.

Van de Ven, A.H. and Poole, M.S. (2005) 'Alternative approaches for studying organizational change', *Organization Studies*, 26 (9): 1377–1404.

van Marrewijk, A.H. (2004) 'Crisis in the transition of Telecom Alliance Unisource', *Journal of Managerial Psychology*, 19 (3): 235–251.

van Marrewijk A.H., Clegg, S., Pitsis, T.S. and Veenswijk, M. (2008) 'Managing public-private megaprojects: Paradoxes, complexity and project design', *International Journal of Project Management*, Projected for 26 (6) August 2008.

Weick, K.E. (1979) *The Social Psychology of Organizing*, 2nd edn. New York: McGraw-Hill.

Weick, K.E. (1995) *Sensemaking in Organizations*. Thousand Oaks, CA: Sage.

Weick, K.E., Sutcliffe, K.M. and Obstfeld, D. (2005) 'Organizing and the process of sensemaking', *Organization Science*, 16 (4): 409–421.

Yin, R.K. (1994) *Case Study Research*, 2nd edn. Beverly Hills: Sage.

## APPENDIX 1: CASE STORIES

### Helene at Calculus

Calculus was established in 1985 as an offspring of an international maritime corporation. The firm grew from a dozen to 180 persons during the mid-1990s. The dominant work activities of the firm have been development work on 'knowledge-based systems,' IT system deliveries to the public sector and product development of a high-end modeling tool. Calculus was founded with a mission to build an international corporation for applied artificial intelligence (AI) technology. This was in the middle of a worldwide wave of euphoria about the prospects of AI. A dozen persons were soon employed to work on client projects, mostly within the offshore and process industries. After a promising start, they experienced mixed results. Most projects were development of prototypes or concept studies, often with high research content and limited potentials for widespread use in client organizations. Implementing the systems could incur large up-front investments in what many held as unproven technology. The company soon scrambled by without any noticeable expansion.

Then a series of events caused a turnaround and the company embarked upon a strong growth period. Two relatively small projects are invariably emphasized by the long-timers of the firm as being decisive in this growth. During the time of data collection they were still regularly brought up in everyday conversations and external presentations. The first project was initiated in 1991: *CompAns*, a project to develop a system for competence analysis and determination of schoolteacher seniority. The system incorporated a wide range of rules and legislative practices and is claimed to be the first use of rule-based reasoning in an IT application for the public sector in Scandinavia. In 1994, CompAns led to *Helene*, a project to develop a system for collecting dependency allowance debt. Helene is affectionately remembered for demonstrating a number of firsts: A) delivery of a 'expert technology support system for casework that spanned an entire business process,' B) use of in-house technology platforms, and C) 'explicit knowledge representation in a domain model held separate from the process engine.'

From these seeds, the Helene project represented an experience that allowed the practice of Calculus to broaden into several parallel trajectories. In the training of newcomers and in presentations at conferences or during client visits, Helene was presented as a veridical exemplar of past *and* future practice. The presentation of the application in front of new clients led to several new projects of the same kind and opened the way for further entry into the public sector market. The use of in-house technology platforms in the work with Helene proved a starting point for the full development of a proprietary framework for work process modeling with re-use libraries. Likewise, discovery that the work process engine (the model of the work process) and domain model (the specifics of rules, heuristics and so forth) should be separated, was later reinforced as a central design principle. In this way, the experiences from the project generated new activity by a form of replicating.

The project experiences also had effects on self-confidence and faith. All founders and long-time informants describe Helene as representing one of the major turning points in the development of Calculus and instrumental in bringing the organization out of many years of standstill. The employees of Calculus had for a long time struggled with what many outsiders saw as obscure technologies and with little success. Here were finally some confirmations that proved their efforts worthwhile. Positive client reactions affirmed confidence in specialized practices and revitalized collectively held aspirations for commercializing front-end technology of expert systems and artificial intelligence. As stated by one of the long-timers of the firm:

> For the first time we had some applications that actually fulfilled and demonstrated our vision. Not only were they useful and quite unique at that time, but they represented just the kind of work we really wanted to do. This gave an enormous boost to our confidence.

## Norne in StatoilHydro

Norne is the name of the goddesses of destiny in Norse mythology. It is also the name of a field of hydrocarbons in the Norwegian Sea. Like many other discoveries, this one followed after a series of dry wells. What was special about Norne was that it was located on the border of Northern Norway, further north than any previous discovery. Also, the 9–10 dry wells (each costing 20 to 50 million dollars) in this region during the 1980s had made many geologists and other stakeholders doubtful that there would be any exploitable oil reserves this far north. Combined with low oil prices, signs of resignation had begun to set in with increasing risk aversion towards the 1990s.

Magnar Larsen was part of a group of geologists at the Statoil (now StatoilHydro) Harstad office that were responsible for exploration north of the 65°30" latitude on license PL128 (1986–1991), which included the area where Norne was eventually found. Said he:

> We saw the analogies with areas further south and maintained belief in the region. Today this is obvious to anyone. It was not at that time. … Many said that outside Nordland, it is dry. That made us extra eager to find oil. … We were convinced there had to be oil in this region, we *wanted* it to be oil outside Northern Norway.

The exploration license would soon expire. There had been two dry wells, and the area would have to be turned back to the authorities if no discovery was confirmed.

Magnar's group gained hope for a discovery by studying the results from a dry reservoir level in a neighboring field; Alve, at the time a non-commercial gas discovery. It was apparently another disappointment; only 2–3 deciliters of oil in addition to the non-exploitable amounts of gas. The interesting part was that this oil was movable. Encouraged by the proved existence of movable oil in the area, the group sat down in a series of informal discussions to analyze the geological explanations for all the dry wells, despite the many promising structures. Previous dry wells had all been drilled on structural highs. Could the oil have been trapped in faults closer to the source rock? During one such discussion, Magnar made a sketch on the backside of a napkin indicating that the oil proved to be once in place at Alve might have migrated to a fault structure with a better closure. This was the structure that is called Norne today. Much effort followed to elaborate upon and qualify the prospect. It was the group's last chance to drill in this license, and they took extra care to make the prospect look good. Against much resistance, they managed to convince their own management, their peers in quality assurance, and the partners, and the well was drilled in 1991. It was a significant discovery; estimated to be around 500 million barrels of oil (appr. 25 bn US\$, 17 bn €, assuming an oil price of 50 US\$ per barrel).

The discovery was initially received by a mix of skepticism and unbound optimism, all linked to development of offshore industry and workplaces in northern Norway. Some commentators cautioned against building false expectations again. Others thrived on the news. Up the coast, local mayors began campaigning to locate the various land-based parts of the field operations of Norne in their region, a debate that was to continue for many years. When the name 'Norne' was assigned in 1993, the symbolical significance of the 'goddess of faith' was immediately picked up by the press and assigned to the further exploration adventures in northern Norway.

The geological model validated by the discovery of Norne broke with previous assumption and spurred further exploration activities in the same region. Based on the new theory of hydrocarbon migration in the area – a so-called fill-spill model – a series of smaller discoveries was made throughout the next years. The discoveries further bolstered faith in the geological provinces outside northern Norway and stimulated more interest in exploration there from many oil companies. Norne also became a prototype for development of medium-sized and small offshore fields as it was the first offshore field on the Norwegian shelf developed with a production and storage ship tied to sub-sea templates. Flexible risers carry the wellstream to the ship, which rotates around a cylindrical turret moored to the seabed. Production from Norne began in 1997. The land-based operations organization was located in Harstad which since then has been the stronghold for exploration outside northern Norway and the Barents Sea.

The consequences of the project were also many for Magnar Larsen personally:

> Afterwards there was a lot of furor. You were pushed forward, they wanted to interview me, not my style really... But it did not exactly hurt my professional reputation as a geologist. I was invited to give my opinion about oil discoveries elsewhere... The biggest event for me as a geologist was Norne. I have been part of other discoveries, but this was the peak, it had so many spillover effects... It is important for me to have been part of something that mattered. I am a political person, so the societal significance of this of great concern to me... I remember a person who had just become my leader said: 'This is going to stay with you'. He was right.

## Olympia in Sydney Water Corporation

Olympia was a temporary project-based alliance between a large public and four private organizations. The stated aim of Olympia was to deliver 20 km of tunnel to channel stormwater away from Sydney Harbor for the 2000 Olympics. The project had to be constructed within two years of the time of commission, and many expert consultants believed this would be impossible

because an equivalent project in California took seven years to construct. Olympia was envisioned in 1997 by Sydney Water Corporation (SWC), because it was believed only an alliance chosen, not on best price, but on shared cultural principles could conduct such a complex and time demanding project. The project was the first of its kind in the world where private and public organizations formed a temporary project-based organization where risk, reward, knowledge and resources would be shared and open-book management approaches used. SWC had the unique role of being both a client and a partner organization. A covert aim of Olympia was to transform – and for some in SWC, revolutionize – how projects were governed and delivered, an ambitious expectation given its history.

Established in 1888, SWC is one of the oldest and largest publicly owned bureaucracies in Australia. Prior to major change, SWC designed, built, owned and operated its entire infrastructure. In the 1970s SWC had over 17,000 staff, 1994 under 14,000 and 2007 it had approximately 3,300 staff and assets worth over $12 billion. With downsizing, SWC relied on private industry to build infrastructure and provide consulting services. Until 1997 SWC allocated almost its entire capital works expenditure to traditional price-competitive contract-based projects, Olympia was the first trust-based mega-project alliance conducted. Today almost 40% of SWC capital works budget is allocated to alliance projects.

Olympia had four transformational affects upon SWC. First, Olympia offered insight into how bureaucracies can rationalize their workforce and achieve a more nimble organizational design. Olympia was used as an exemplar within SWC to argue that it had a lot to offer as a knowledge intensive firm, especially given internal resistance towards alliancing because it is perceived as enabling rationalization of the workforce:

> We are not the recalcitrant bureaucracy that the public, and the private sector, perceive us to be. We have so much to offer by way of expertise and

knowledge in a whole range of areas. ... and it took Olympia Alliance to show me, well us, that ... a lot of people are still blind to this ... which is disappointing. If they worked on Olympia ... I think their commitment to alliancing would be very different. (Project Director, interview 11 July, 2000).

Second, Olympia allowed the partners to enhance the benefits of loosely coupled ties that occurred through five organizations collaborating to solve problems. Not only did each organization apply its own knowledge and expertise to Olympia problems, they also took learning from Olympia and incorporated it into other projects. Each parent organization had knowledge about both 'good' and 'bad' performing subcontractors, suppliers, systems and processes and all partners were able to improve the way they did things.

A third benefit accruing from Olympia was positive organizational identity. SWC had been tarnished by a giardia/cryptospiridium water contamination. Sydney residents had to boil their water before it could be consumed causing anger towards SWC. The Olympia project required construction in some of the world's most expensive real estate, and had the potential for major resistance.

However, the project was delivered as the Olympia project, and not the SWC project. Olympia allocated a large amount of resources towards building community psychological capital via community site visits, visits down tunnels to see construction, community involvement in project decisions. One key story is best told by a community member from a construction entry site:

[Olympia staff] came by and talked to us, we then had a meeting ... We were rather angry at the eyesore that was the construction site, the massive mounds of dirt and holes ... they brought us together, got a leading architect and all together we designed a building that would cover the site. It's quite amazing, we are used to people coming in and digging our roads up, and the only time you hear about it is when the jackhammers go off first thing in the morning. It makes a real difference.

Finally, Olympia won awards in Australia, USA and Europe for its innovations in tunneling and project management, opening the door to future SWC alliancing projects. Olympia has enabled SWC to position itself as the exemplar public organization in mega-project alliances.

# 28

# Corporate Governance

Rob Watson

## INTRODUCTION

What is Corporate Governance and why should it matter? Corporate governance has attracted researchers from many academic disciplines and the resulting literature encompasses studies using a wide variety of theoretical frameworks and research methods. Perhaps not surprisingly, this diversity has also spawned many definitions of our field of inquiry. Rather than trying to detail and reconcile some of the more popular definitions of corporate governance, it is perhaps more useful to start by briefly considering each of its two components. The term *corporate* clearly restricts the subject matter to this particular form of business organisation; it implies that the corporate form has some distinctive features that are worthy of special attention. The *governance* term indicates that the focus is upon the organisational and political processes involved in resolving disputes and conflicts of interest between participants. As will become apparent, the corporate form allows changes in corporate strategy and financial policy to substantially alter the payoffs and financial risks to which different corporate participants are exposed. Hence, the exercise of executive discretion

and its organisational and financial consequences for corporate participants are the primary focus of much corporate governance research.

In the US and UK, the institutional and legal framework has always supported the principle that, in the absence of financial distress, executive discretion ought to be exercised in accordance with the financial interests of the company's shareholders. The rationale for this is that, as the suppliers of risk capital and entitled only to the residual value of the business after all other claims have been satisfied, shareholders are the group least able to protect their interests via contractual, regulatory or behavioural means. For these reasons, definitions of corporate governance used by practitioners, regulators and corporate governance reformers and activists in these countries have tended to exclude non-shareholder participants such as creditors, employees or customers. For example, Monks and Minnow (2001), two well-known shareholder activists, define corporate governance as:

... relationship among various participants in determining the direction and performance of corporations. The primary participants are (1) the shareholders, (2) the management (led by the chief executive officer), and (3) the board of directors. Monks and Minnow (2001: 1).

As the primary focus of this chapter is the corporate governance systems of the US and UK, this provides a good definition for structuring an overview of the evolution, recent developments and current challenges facing these shareholder-oriented corporate governance systems.

As mentioned above, a basic premise of corporate law for both countries has always been that managerial discretion ought to be very much focused on furthering the interests of the shareholders as a whole. This premise holds irrespective of whether or not the enterprise is a widely-held, publicly listed, company or a small and closely-held (i.e., is owned and managed by a small group of, often family-related, investors) entity. This Anglo-US shareholder orientation is not, however, a universal view, at least in relation to large and/or otherwise economically significant incorporated businesses. Many commentators have suggested that the shareholder focus and other supposed 'deficiencies' of the Anglo-US corporate governance system could be remedied by requiring executives to consider the interests of a broader range of 'stakeholders'. Such critics often draw attention to the many successful European and developed Asian economies, where the notion that managerial discretion ought to be exercised in ways that further the interests of some other stakeholder group such as employees, the State or managers themselves, is often embedded in their corporate and labour law systems (Rajan and Zingales, 2003). These alternative corporate governance models do, however, tend to be associated with economies with relatively few widely held firms and underdeveloped financial systems which suggests that these arrangements reflect and reinforce the preferences of the incumbent corporate owners and controllers in the counties concerned (Roe, 2005). As corporate law and governance practices in the UK and US are equally deeply embedded in their respective national systems of corporate ownership and liquid capital

markets, it is unlikely that the importation of stakeholder notions would be either politically feasible or economically desirable. Equally, in the absence of incumbent support for fundamental change, other national corporate law and governance practices can be expected to be highly resistant to external pressures stemming from international harmonisation initiatives that seek to impose common codes of practice irrespective of differences in national, political, institutional or ownership characteristics (Hansmann and Kraakman, 2001).

The reminder of the chapter is organised as follows. Section 2 begins with a discussion of the corporation, its major advantages over the business partnership model and the unique governance problems associated with this organisational structure. The distinctive and novel feature of this organisational form is that it has a separate legal status completely independent from that of its owners (i.e., the shareholders that provide the firms' risk capital) and/or its senior executives (i.e., the employees responsible for corporate strategy and operational management). This legal fiction, the product of eighteenth and nineteenth century legislators in the UK and US, implies that the company, not its owner-managers, is the contracting party with respect to all business dealings and that, as a consequence, the owner-managers ought not to be held personally responsible should the company at some stage be unable to honour its financial obligations. That is to say, unlike a business partnership where each of the partners remain both jointly and individually responsible for any partnership debts, incorporation limited the owner-managers' liability to their ownership claims (the value of their individual shareholdings).

The risk diversification and investment opportunities of incorporation over the traditional business partnership model were substantial and, by the turn of the twentieth century the familiar 'standard model' of the closely held company, and the legal framework required to support it was in place in all the developed economies of the time (Hansmann and Kraakman, 2001).

It is also noteworthy that, regardless of political and legal context, it has rarely if ever been seriously doubted that the primary duty of the owner-managers of closely held companies was simply to use their decision-making discretion to further the interests of shareholders, i.e., themselves and any minority investors. Moreover, irrespective of the legal jurisdiction of the countries concerned, it is apparent that similar workable legal and behavioural solutions were fairly quickly enacted to deal with the two primary governance problems associated with the closely held company form, namely the protection of minority shareholders and, due to the 'limited liability' of the owner-managers in relation to the corporation's debts, creditor protection (La Porta *et al.*, 1998).

In Section 3, the additional governance issues associated with the widely held corporation and the separation of ownership from control are discussed. The corporate form did not merely provide new investment and risk diversification opportunities for owner-managers. With the possibility of total financial ruin removed and investors no longer needing to monitor each other's behaviour (or, indeed, even to be aware of the identity of other investors), limited liability rendered it feasible for anyone with surplus funds to invest in company shares. This has encouraged the development of companies entirely controlled by professional managers where there is clearly no requirement or expectation for the vast majority of shareholders to become involved in the management of the enterprise. Indeed, by creating a separation of ownership (risk bearing) from control (managerial skills), the corporate form facilitated both specialisation (division of labour) and, when allowed to sell shares to the general public, effectively removed any constraints on the potential size of the firm. The growth in the size and widely held ownership structures of corporations was naturally greatly encouraged in the US and UK where well functioning public markets (Stock Exchanges) provided both new and existing firms with opportunities to raise capital from the general public through the issuing of new shares. Through the trading of already issued shares, stock markets also provided additional benefits to investors in the form of pricing information, liquidity (the ability to quickly and easily sell their shares without causing adverse price effects) and the ability to initiate or vote for radical changes in corporate ownership and management.

In terms of wealth generation, primarily through its ability to access and efficiently exploit huge economies of scale, and the creation of many new savings and investment opportunities, the widely held, publicly listed corporation has proved to be one of mankind's greatest organisational innovations and, not surprisingly, such firms now dominate most economic sectors. However, the fact that corporate strategy and the control of its resources lies with the professional managers, clearly implies that shareholders have to rely upon the decision-making discretion of senior executives to use the firms' resources in ways that generate an acceptable return on their investments. The basic problem is that executives may have different interests from those of shareholders but, because they control corporate strategy and resources, they may be tempted to use their discretion in ways that damage their shareholder's wealth. The effectiveness of the various legal, organisational and market-based incentives and constraints upon managerial discretion have, therefore, constituted the primary corporate governance concern associated with the widely held corporation.

The discussion indicates that though the vast majority of widely held firms are well managed and governed, a spate of high profile corporate governance scandals in the UK and US have shown that these traditional solutions to the 'control problem' are sometimes inadequate. This section includes brief reviews of some of the governance problems that have surfaced and the rationale and likely effectiveness of the subsequent reforms introduced to remedy the situation. The chapter concludes with a brief review of alternative 'stakeholder' views regarding the objectives of corporate decision making and the corporate governance systems found in other developed and developing economies that appear to embody in their systems of corporate law and practice similar stakeholder notions. This includes an analysis of how these alternatives differ from the Anglo-US model and an assessment of whether they appear to have any advantages that could usefully be incorporated into the current shareholder oriented systems of the UK and US.

## THE DEVELOPMENT AND GOVERNANCE OF THE CLOSELY HELD COMPANY

By the onset of the industrial revolution in the latter part of the eighteenth century, the UK already had a long history of international trade, the trading of shares in Chartered and Regulated companies and experimentation with different forms of business organisation. As the industrial revolution progressed and the risks, financial investments and size of the average firm all increased significantly, the disadvantages of the available legal business organisations had become all too evident. Partnerships and the relatively few examples of Chartered and Regulated companies all discouraged potential investors from investing in businesses that they did not also control and have detailed knowledge of the wealth and behaviour of fellow investors. This was because these business organisations exposed investors to potentially unlimited liability for the organisation's and other investor's debts. This naturally limited the number of investors, the size of the business and the number of businesses with which even the most wealthy of individuals could become involved.

Given the leading role played by the UK in the industrialisation process it ought not to be a surprise to learn that the UK was also the first country to create the legal and institutional framework for the development of a new form of business organisation that overcame the problems associated with previous arrangements. The development of the now familiar 'standard model' of the corporation can best be viewed

as the culmination of a series of incremental changes to existing organisational forms from the fourteenth to the early nineteenth century. However, once all the essential elements of this 'standard model' were in place in the UK (and the US) by the mid-nineteenth century, the corporate form was rapidly adopted by many other countries so that by the turn of the twentieth century virtually all businesses of any size in all the developed economies were corporations. So, what are the essential elements of the corporation that made it so appealing to so many business people and legislators around the developed world?

Briefly, the distinctive, i.e., innovative, characteristics of a corporation are:

(1) The corporation is a legal entity, entirely distinct from its investors (i.e., members or shareholders) and the individuals that direct and control the business (i.e., its managers).

(2) This legal status provides the corporation with rights and duties, including the right to sue and to be sued on its own account, independent from its members. Moreover, its independent existence provides a firm legal distinction to be made between property of the corporation and the property of its members.

(3) The corporate form therefore sweeps away any legal responsibilities of the corporation in respect of any financial obligations of its members. Even more importantly, incorporation also puts clearly defined limits on the liability of members (and managers) for the debts and other obligations of the corporation. The liability of members is restricted to the value of their share capital.

(4) Because the corporation is independent of its members, unlike a partnership which would have to be dissolved if one or more of its members died or wished to leave, it exists in perpetuity – or until such time as a court or a majority of its members agree to wind-up the company.

(5) Limited liability and perpetual succession allowed both existing issued shares (ownership claims) and any new share issues by the corporation to be freely traded without this having any implications in respect of the corporation's legal status, activities or management.

The most economically beneficial innovation arising from incorporation was, and remains, the limiting of owner-manager financial risks in relation to the corporation's debts and the freeing of both the company and individual investors from any legal responsibility for the business-related debts of other members and business associates (partners). Even for the smallest of businesses, the corporate form of organisation therefore provided owner-managers and outside investors with many new financing and investment opportunities, including the ability to effectively diversify their wealth and to avoid total financial ruin in the event of business failure.

The obvious and substantial benefits to owner-managers of the corporate form over the alternative partnership arrangements quickly led everywhere to the creation of many small and closely held companies owned and controlled by a few, usually related, individuals. The closely held company, a proportion of which may be far from small in terms of output or employment, remains by far the most common form of company today across all developed economies (Keasey and Watson, 1994). However, from the outset, the closely held company structure was seen to generate two main governance problems; namely, the need to protect the interests of minority (non-controlling) shareholders and creditors.

## THE PROTECTION OF MINORITY (NON-CONTROLLING) SHAREHOLDERS

Unlike a partnership where any of the participants can force the dissolution of the partnership irrespective of the size of their financial interest, due to perpetual succession, forced dissolution is no longer possible for the minority shareholders of companies. Moreover, as the shares of closely held firms are not traded in public stock markets and corporate charters frequently place restrictions on the transfer of shares, minority shareholders are uniquely exposed to the risk that the controlling shareholder-managers may act contrary to their financial interests. For example,

the controlling shareholder-managers could be motivated to engage in behaviours that reduce other shareholder's wealth, such as introducing excessive managerial pay and perquisites packages for themselves or the selling of corporate assets below market value to related parties. The traditional corporate law solution to this governance problem has been to make management accountable to shareholders via an independent board of directors, with the latter having a fiduciary duty to act on behalf of all the company's members (Ezzamel and Watson, 1997). In addition, prior to investing funds in a business any minority shareholder has the option of negotiating whatever contract they think will best protect their interests, for example, by making the purchase of the shares dependent upon having a guaranteed place on the board. Just as importantly, financial information disclosure and audit requirements and the existence of independent and well functioning court systems in the UK and US also allowed minority shareholders to monitor and evaluate the performance of the management and board of directors and, when judged necessary, exercise these legal rights.

Even though the large majority of closely held companies are small family-owned businesses and partnerships, the protection afforded to minority shareholders has an importance far beyond simply helping to resolve quarrels between closely related business partners. These protections applied to any investor and, by allowing entrepreneurs and innovators to access a large pool of potential outside investors, greatly enhanced competitive pressures on existing firms by increasing the likelihood that new entrants could emerge and challenge incumbents (Rajan and Zingales, 2003). The flexibility of the closely held company in terms of allowing investors to come to whatever agreements they think best serves their interests continues today to provide the legal framework by which the majority of new enterprises with high growth prospects are able to secure the funding and managerial resources necessary to realise their potential. The most obvious manifestation of this is the high levels of new enterprise formation rates in the US and UK and the substantial numbers of closely held companies owned and controlled by coalitions of professional managers and outside investors, such as venture capitalists, other corporate entities and financial institutions, for the purpose of exploiting growth or corporate restructuring opportunities. Of course, the involvement of active professional investors has also been greatly influenced by the availability of investment exit options such as a public listing and hence it is no accident that both countries also have deep and liquid stock markets and high levels of new firms listing on the market (see Roe, 2004).

## THE PROTECTION OF CREDITORS

An important corollary of limiting the liability of owners for the debts of the business is that creditors require additional protection to discourage owner-managers from taking excessive risks with their borrowed funds. As noted above, this issue constitutes the second of the two main corporate governance problems associated with the corporate form. In the UK and most other jurisdictions the primary solution to this problem has consisted of developing an institutional infrastructure that includes accessible and independent civil law courts to enforce contractual agreements, the overturning of the protection of limited liability when fraudulent intent has been established, greater disclosure and audit of financial information to outside creditors and, in the event of default, corporate bankruptcy laws that give creditors the right to take over the business and sell its assets to satisfy their outstanding financial claims (Watson and Ezzamel, 2005).

It is perhaps worth emphasising that an inescapable aspect of any business venture is that it has to undertake risky projects in order to prosper. Trade creditors and financial institutions that provide financing to any business enterprise know that this exposes them to some risk of default because, by definition, not all risky projects are likely to be successful. This implies that the majority of business failures tend to be the result of misconceived business strategies and poorer than expected outcomes (i.e., entrepreneurial 'over-confidence') rather than representing any attempt by the owners to defraud creditors (Keasey and Watson, 1994). However, business risk, i.e., the variance of a firm's operating cashflows, can be greatly increased by corporate financial policies, that is, debt creates additional risk via financial leverage and the higher the debt relative to equity finance, the greater is this financial leverage. Due to 'limited liability', however, the owner-managers potential downside risks from taking on too much debt may be minimal because bankrupt companies cease to have any responsibility for satisfying creditor claims beyond what can be raised from selling its assets. Thus, the corporate form has required creditors to develop lending and trade credit policies that minimise their exposure to uncompensated business and financial risks.

To demonstrate both the basic problem and some of the governance solutions to deal with it, consider the following illustrative example (adapted from Watson and Ezzamel, 2005). Figure 28.1 shows the respective payoff functions to shareholders (i.e., Max[0, V-D]) and debtholders (i.e., Min[D, V]), where V = the value of the firms' assets and D = the firms' total debt obligations.[1]

We can examine the effect upon shareholder and debtholder pay-offs of a pure leverage decision involving paying the shareholders a dividend using borrowed funds, i.e., neither the assets of the firm nor its anticipated operational cashflows are affected by the decision. For the sake of simplicity, suppose we assume no transactions or information costs and that both parties have perfect knowledge regarding expected future cashflows and their variance. Let us also assume that the firm's initial (pre-dividend) outstanding debt obligations, $D_0$, are £50. The expected value of the firm (E[V]) is £100, and the symmetrically distributed range of possible firm value outcomes is $E(V) \pm X$, where $X = £20$. The initial value of the firm's

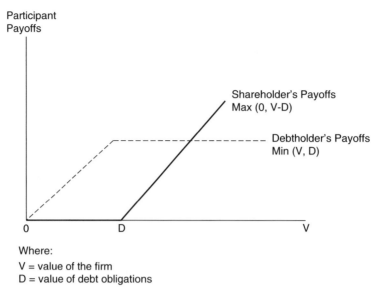

**Figure 28.1   Corporate payoffs with limited liability.**

equity ($S_0$ = E[V]-D), which we require in order to calculate shareholder returns, is therefore £50. Though the expected return in terms of both total firm value and shareholder rewards is 0%, because debt constitutes 50% of the total finance used by the firm, the actual minimum and maximum possible returns to shareholders (−40% and +40%) are exactly twice as great as the minimum and maximum percentage changes in firm value, i.e., −20% and +20%. The debtholders will however probably be unconcerned at this level of leverage since whatever outcome occurs there will always be sufficient value in the firm to fully satisfy their financial claim of £50.

If we now assume that the firm decides to borrow a further £30 (i.e., $D_1$ = £80) in order to pay a further dividend. Given our assumptions, this will also not impact on firm value or operating risks. It will however further increase financial leverage and hence the variability in shareholder outcomes since their minimum and maximum possible payoffs will now be respectively £0 (i.e., S = 100 − 80 − 20 = 0) and £40 (100 − 80 + 20 = 40) which, given a new equity base of £20 (i.e., 100 − 80), represent returns to

shareholders of −100% and +100%. Once, again however the debtholder's claims can be honoured irrespective of the cashflow outcome for the firm.

Though in the above case, the debtholders claims can be satisfied even if firm value is at its minimum value of £80, any further debt financed dividend payments will necessarily be at the expense of the debtholders. Clearly, if presented with the above information, the debtholders would refuse to fund any additional dividend payments. However, shareholders can increase their potential returns if they can persuade the debtholders to lend the firm further funds, say by convincing the debtholders that the cashflow distribution is less variable than it really is. We can drop the assumption that debtholders have accurate information regarding the cashflow distribution and assume instead that the firm's managers have convinced them that the minimum and maximum deviations from the expected firm value of £100 are +/− £10 rather than £20. If this induces the debtholders to lend the firm an additional £10, then the debtholders will be exposed to the possibility of bearing some of the business risk without sharing any of the upside potential.

To illustrate, the minimum and maximum payoffs for the shareholders now become 0 and £30 which, given their equity investment of £10, generates shareholder returns of −100% and +200% respectively. If the minimum outcome occurs (with firm value at £80, i.e., £100 − £20), not all of the debtholders £90 can be honoured, i.e., the firm will exercise its option to default and the debtholders will be left with the firm's assets – which in this case are worth £80. The truncated downside payoff profiles to equity holders of firms with high debt levels may therefore encourage managers to mislead outside investors regarding actual business risks since if the firm defaults some or all of these downside losses will be borne by the debtholders. Conversely, all upside gains will still accrue to the shareholders which, due to their smaller equity investment, will earn them proportionately higher percentage returns than the same firm value outcome would generate for the shareholders of low or no debt firms. In addition, high leverage and limited liability may also encourage owner-managers to alter the composition of the firm's assets and/or the riskiness of its cashflows.[2]

What the above numerical illustrations make plain is that owner-manager incentives to engage in opportunistic behaviour at the expense of their creditors only occurs when corporate equity is insufficient to absorb business and financial risks. Debtholders and other outside creditors can therefore avoid the possibility of exposure to uncompensated risk simply by restricting their lending to companies with low debt ratios and high equity relative to business risks. The high value of the owner-managers' equity ensures that they have no incentives to shift business risk onto outsider creditors. Moreover, a wide variety of business policies (e.g., credit checking and control policies) and contractual and legal safeguards are generally available at low cost to creditors to protect their interests. For example, the simple expedient of securing business loans on the personal assets of owner-managers (e.g., their family home) effectively dismantles some of the limited liability protection of shareholders by increasing the size of the equity buffer that protects creditors – and significantly reducing the interest rate premium the business is charged (Keasey and Watson, 2000). Conversely, creditors should clearly avoid supplying credit to companies that are already highly indebted and/or otherwise financially vulnerable since the combination of high business risk and the distorted incentives arising from having 'little to lose' greatly increase the probability of creditor losses.

The main point to take away from the above analysis is that it produces some very obvious and relatively easy to implement business strategies that enable creditors to avoid losses arising from dealing with limited liability customers. Indeed, the dominance of the corporate form today and the fact that in over 100 years only fairly minimal changes to company law in this area have been required, indicates that creditors have not experienced major difficulties in finding satisfactory contractual and behavioural ways by which to effectively limit the financial risks that the corporate structure exposes them to. Banks and other creditors have generally not been reluctant to lend to closely held companies and, when failure rates have caused significant creditor losses, this has rarely been as a result of owner-manager opportunism or fraud (Keasey and Watson, 1991). Rather, creditor losses occur when an unexpected economic downturn falsifies the (now all too apparent) optimistic assumptions upon which previous lending decisions had been based. Clearly, creditor protection arrangements are not meant to protect creditors from the consequences of their own poor forecasting abilities and risky lending and credit policies.

## THE GOVERNANCE OF THE WIDELY HELD PUBLIC COMPANY

The undoubted advantages of incorporation for both entrepreneurs and potential investors, along with the successful development of legal and behavioural solutions to deal with its two main governance problems, has led to the closely held company becoming the most numerous type of business organisation to be found throughout both developed and emerging economies. Of course, the benefits of the corporate form in terms of providing limited risk investment opportunities could also be enjoyed by anyone with the available funds when firms were able to register as public limited companies and to raise substantial investment funds by offering shares to the general public. In the US and UK, the development of large and widely held corporations run by professional managers, was greatly facilitated by their 'developed financial systems' which included:

(1) respect for property rights, (2) an accounting and disclosure system that promotes transparency, (3) a legal system that enforces arm's length contracts cheaply, and (4) a regulatory infrastructure that protects consumers, promotes competition, and controls egregious risk taking (Rajan and Zingales (2003: 18).

As the experience of many other countries shows, without these underlying developed financial system characteristics, it is almost impossible for a country to be able to successfully develop and operate well functioning stock exchanges that allow new and existing firms with good prospects to raise new capital and previously issued shares to be efficiently priced and cheaply traded in liquid markets (Roe, 2004).

## THE SEPARATION OF OWNERSHIP FROM CONTROL

The growth of the widely held corporation which is able to obtain investment funds from a much larger number of shareholders creates an additional corporate governance problem that is more-or-less absent from the closely held company; because the majority of shareholders do not participate in the management of the business, i.e., there is a separation of ownership from control, their wealth depends to a large extent on the

actions of corporate executives over whom they necessarily have limited control. Limited control is inevitable since, in order to fulfil their duties, executives require a large degree of discretion over the day-to-day use of the firm's assets and in regard to the formulation and implementation of corporate strategies. That is to say, executive employment contracts are necessarily 'incomplete' because 'complete contracting', i.e., fully specifying *ex ante* the precise actions the executives should take in all possible circumstances, is an impossibility due to bounded rationality,[3] asymmetric information and the costs associated with becoming informed (Hart, 1995).

In the case of widely held firms characterised by a significant degree of separation of ownership from control, there is an ever-present danger that executives may develop priorities and/or preferences that differ from those of shareholders. Berle and Means (1932) first drew attention to this possibility and these concerns were later developed by Jensen and Meckling (1976) into what has subsequently become known as 'agency theory'. The central problem that agency theory addresses has two dimensions. First, due to their high firm-specific risk exposure, executives may be more risk averse than diversified shareholders with respect to firm investment decisions. Hence, executives may prefer not to undertake risky but worthwhile (i.e., positive 'net present value' [NPV]) projects. This is what agency theorists call the 'under-investment' hazard. Alternatively, the executives of firms with poor investment options may wish to use corporate free cash flows to invest in low or negative NPV projects, waste resources on ill-founded mergers or pursue unprofitable growth strategies (the 'over-investment' problem) rather than returning surplus cash to shareholders.

Second, even though monitoring executive performance is clearly in shareholder's collective interests, if the shareholders consist of many diversified individual investors, each of whom will have only a small proportion of their portfolio invested in any one firm, then it is unlikely that any individual shareholder will find it in their interests to actually incur the costs associated with adequately monitoring and influencing executive discretion. Thus, incomplete contracts, monitoring and information costs in relation to evaluating performance and effectively disciplining poorly performing executives, creates an important role for both internal (e.g., the board of directors and performance related pay packages) and external corporate governance mechanisms (product market competition, and corporate control contests) to ensure that executives use their discretion to enhance shareholder value.

## SHAREHOLDERS, MARKETS AND CORPORATE SCANDALS

Before examining the control functions of board of directors, it is perhaps worth examining the assumption that corporate governance failings amongst large and widely held, publicly listed firms occur because no individual shareholder holds a sufficiently high equity stake in the business to find it worthwhile to monitor executives. The first point to note is that firms with purely widely held ownership structures where there is no significant shareholder, were not particularly common even amongst the largest US firms when Berle and Means first published their work (see, for example, Holderness, 2003). This remains the case in the US today and international comparisons suggest also that it is in fact a comparatively rare organisational form even amongst the largest of businesses of many developed economies (see La Porta et al., 1999). Though it is true that the vast majority of individual shareholders are neither involved in the management of the business nor hold a controlling stake, most firms do in fact have one or more significant blockholders that participate in the management of the enterprise. Typically in the UK and US, controlling blockholders consist of a controlling family, executives and other board members or other corporate entities, whilst the controlling blockholders in many other countries will also often include the State and banking institutions. In the UK and US, venture capital investors and private equity firms may also be significant controlling blockholders, but financial institutional involvement, though large in terms of total share ownership, consists largely of pension funds, mutual funds and insurance companies that are restricted to holding non-controlling blocks of shares.

The empirical evidence suggests such institutional investors tend to be knowledgeable and diligent monitors that are increasingly willing to intervene to change either the direction or management of underperforming companies (see the contributions in Watson, 2005). The more recent rise in the number and importance of blocks of shares held by hedge funds and private equity groups has also created a new class of active and often very effective shareholders that help keep corporate managers very much focused on shareholder value creation.

The existence of one or more blockholders with a controlling interest in the firm and the likelihood of one or more knowledgeable and/or active non-controlling shareholder blocks requires the original agency model to be extended to include the possibility of conflicts of interests between different classes of shareholder. In some recent theoretical models (e.g., Shleifer and Vishny, 1986; Jensen, 1993), the owners of large equity blocks are assumed to have sufficient incentive to monitor executives since by definition they have a large non-diversified financial interest in ensuring that executives pursue only value increasing opportunities. As the benefits associated with this monitoring are also shared with other shareholders (the so-called 'shared benefits of control'), the existence of such a blockholder can be viewed as being in all shareholders interests. Blockholders do not, of course, necessarily have identical interests and some types of controlling blockholders may be primarily motivated by the prospect of obtaining benefits not shared with other shareholders (the 'private benefits of control'). In the vast majority of cases, however, a combination of competitive pressures, monitoring by other shareholders and the legal protections available to all minority shareholders may be sufficient to keep such private benefits to a minimum. Holderness (2003), for example, summarised the findings of the extensive (US-based) empirical research on this topic as follows:

> surprisingly few major corporate decisions have been shown to be different in the presence of a blockholder. One exception is that external blockholders appear to monitor the form and level of managerial compensation. Conversely, there is little evidence that blockholders affect leverage. Ownership concentration appears to have little impact on firm value. If one wants a single 'take-away' point from the rapidly growing literature on ownership concentration, it is that small shareholders and regulators have little reason to fear large percentage shareholders in general, especially when a large shareholder is active in firm management. (p. 60).

It is fairly clear that in relation to widely held publicly listed companies, UK and US corporate governance has always relied heavily upon the openness and efficiency of competitive product and capital markets to ensure that managers remain focused on shareholder wealth concerns. The above conclusion by Holderness, suggests that these competitive pressures are *usually* sufficient to keep even deeply entrenched controlling blockholders from taking advantage of minority shareholders. However, even the most competitive and efficient market mechanisms occasionally fail to work and, as recent corporate scandals illustrate, the chief perpetrators involved were usually controlling blockholders – indeed, precisely the type of 'large shareholder … active in firm management' that Holderness claims 'small shareholders and regulators have little reason to fear'.

As regards the circumstances of these corporate governance failings and the role played by the controlling blockholders, a remarkably similar sequence of events was evident. Indeed, the anatomy of a typical corporate scandal seems remarkably stable irrespective of time, location or size of enterprise (see Keasey and Watson, 1991). An unexpected corporate failure generally

begins with excessively risky projects, in combination with highly leveraged capital structures (but often not transparently so to outsiders) being initiated by an entrenched and unaccountable CEO-blockholder (autocrat) at the height of an economic and share price boom. When the boom is followed by an economic downturn, what marks out these CEOs from the many others that had been similarly overconfident during the recent good times is that they opt to take advantage of complacent auditors and insufficiently motivated and ill-informed boards to produce misleading and/or fraudulent information regarding the firms' financial condition and prospects to outside shareholders and market regulators. This then enables these, by now delinquent, CEOs to hide the true situation from outsiders for some time but which, upon eventual discovery, generally results in even larger losses to shareholders and unsecured creditors.

As the above account suggests, corporate governance failings tend to come to light during economic and share price downturns and, though directly involving only a tiny proportion of all firms, a cluster of such cases has the potential to undermine investor confidence in the system as a whole. Major changes to corporate and securities laws, Stock Exchange listing and reporting requirements and the market for corporate control have therefore tended to be introduced subsequent to obvious market failures coming to light and clear evidence of serious and widespread managerial misconduct (corporate scandals). Recent corporate governance reforms in these countries fit this well-worn historical pattern. It was only in 1992 in the UK and after 2000 in the US after each country's respective cluster of high-profile unexpected business failures and corporate scandals, perpetrated by entrenched CEO-blockholders, that significant corporate governance reforms to reduce the likelihood of such events reoccurring were introduced.

In both the UK and US, the corporate governance reforms introduced after these episodes have concentrated upon strengthening shareholder information and control rights, increasing the independence and duties of the board, particularly non-executive board members, and encouraging the introduction of incentive mechanisms designed to realign manager and shareholder interests.

## THE BOARD OF DIRECTORS

The legal responsibilities of boards of directors in the UK and US are to collectively manage the business in accordance with its constitution for the benefit of its shareholders and to comply with the financial reporting and other disclosure requirements stipulated by Company Law and securities legislation. The board of directors is legally responsible for formulating and implementing business strategy on behalf of shareholders but it is also the primary institutional mechanism by which the shareholders render the executives appointed to manage the assets on their behalf accountable for their stewardship.

Traditionally, these two, somewhat contradictory, functions have been reconciled in UK Company Law by relying upon the system of 'accountability through disclosure' based upon shareholder rights and information disclosure. Shareholder rights include voting at the annual general meeting (AGM) to appoint and/or dismiss from office directors and to determine the conditions of employment, terms of office and remuneration of the board. These shareholder rights require the board to produce and make available to shareholders prior to the AGM 'independently' audited financial statements to enable shareholders to assess the adequacy or otherwise of the board's stewardship over the period.

As discussed earlier, in 1990, with investor confidence at a low ebb and concerns that the government may impose their own reforms if the financial and corporate sector did not come up with their own proposals, the Committee on the Financial Aspects of Corporate Governance (the Cadbury Committee) was set up jointly by the Stock Exchange Council and the Financial Reporting Council to make recommendations for improving the UK's system of corporate governance.

The Cadbury (1992), and subsequent corporate governance reports, made recommendations that focused on the composition of the unitary board and emphasised the monitoring role of non-executive directors (NEDs) in relation to the executive board members. The Cadbury report viewed NEDs as having a major role in improving the accountability of executives to their shareholders and recommended that each public company should employ a minimum of three independent NEDs. The notion of 'independence' is somewhat formal since the report simply defines this in terms of having no pre-existing business relationship with the firm (paragraph 2.2). Nevertheless, as Ezzamel and Watson (1997) noted, 'the dual roles required of NEDs can be expected to undermine any initial "independence of judgement" before too long, particularly since the proposals do not increase either the power or incentives to oppose executives when the latter appear to be acting contrary to shareholder interests'.

The influence and independence of NEDs was, however, strengthened through the establishment of three board sub-committees: the nominations committee (to advise on the appointment of new directors), the audit committee (to advise on the audit and to have free access to company financial information and its auditors) and the remuneration committee (to advise on directors emoluments and service contracts). The establishment of these board sub-committees clearly offered more scope for NEDs to discuss financial disclosure and remuneration policy options and to collectively influence management than was previously the case. The main problem that the reforms have not addressed is that, whilst the independence of NEDs from management is a necessary condition for them to ensure that management are focused on shareholder interests, this is a far from sufficient condition. NEDs probably also need to be made more dependent upon shareholders, i.e., ensuring that they have sufficient incentives to effectively monitor and control executives. The lack of strong NED incentives to safeguard shareholder interests is perhaps best illustrated by the decisions and practices of the remuneration committees introduced in the UK in 1993.

## EXECUTIVE PAY AND REMUNERATION COMMITTEES

There has undoubtedly been a great deal of media and public interest in the apparently 'excessive' and 'unjustified' pay increases enjoyed by senior executives in both the US and the UK over the past 15 years or so and this phenomenon has frequently been attributed to poor corporate governance. The notions of 'excessive' or 'unjustified' pay awards are, of course, highly value laden and in much media reporting appear to be synonymous with CEOs and other senior executives receiving high pay awards relative to either (1) other employees and/or (2) irrespective of any obvious improvements in the performance of their organisations. Certainly, the average pay of senior executives, particularly the CEO, in the US and UK has increased at a much faster rate than that of other employees (Conyon and Murphy, 2000) and many empirical studies have failed to produce convincing evidence that CEO pay increases have been related to improvements in firm performance (Barkema and Gomez-Mejia, 1998). Some academics have attributed these results to managerial power, or simply greed. Bebchuk and Fried (2003), for example, contend that managerial entrenchment and poor independent director monitoring and control are endemic in the US due to its explicitly manager-friendly corporate laws and limited shareholder rights. To these authors, managerial entrenchment and control over the board of directors, coupled with diversified (and hence largely acquiescent) shareholders, are the primarily factors responsible for recent hikes in executive pay because they allow managers to effectively determine their own pay. Bebchuk and Fried (2003) argue that the only constraints upon pay are disclosure rules that make it more difficult to disguise and/or avoid reporting the real costs to shareholders and the increased risk of provoking shareholder revolts and public 'outrage'.

The managerial power framework is of course useful in focusing attention on the ever-present possibility that entrenched executives may be able to extract substantial economic rents from their positions. However, this framework does not fit well with the observation that when CEOs move firms, i.e., when by definition they are not entrenched, they appear to experience few difficulties in being able to negotiate even more generous pay packages for themselves than they had with their previous employer. Also, managerial power does not appear to provide a convincing explanation as to why CEO pay has increased in similar ways throughout the developed world irrespective of the significant differences between countries in terms of managerial entrenchment and the presence of alternative corporate governance control mechanisms. For example, UK corporate law and governance, though similar to the US in terms of legal origins, disclosure and financial reporting, unitary boards, remuneration committees and an apparently identical shareholder focus, provides much more extensive shareholder voting rights and powers to control and dismiss the board of directors. These stronger shareholder rights, along with higher levels of institutional ownership and fewer constraints on the market for corporate control, have not produced significant managerial entrenchment problems for the UK. Even so, the UK has experienced much the same pattern of rapidly rising CEO pay unrelated to firm performance improvements as has the US (Conyon and Murphy, 2000).

Many financial economists (for a review, see Conyon, 2006) have taken the more plausible view that the general increase in executive pay reflects changes in the price firms are willing to pay for scarce executive and other specialist human capital. It has frequently been argued that firms have been willing to pay senior executives more due to the increasing size, complexity and profit-making opportunities of firms. The theoretical literature suggests that greater competition for scarce human capital will generate internal promotion and pay outcomes that have all the attributes of competitive 'tournaments' (e.g., Lazear and Rosen, 1981; Lazear, 1989). Tournaments necessarily produce much more diverse pay outcomes as the value of the winner's 'trophy' (the wage increase from the promotion and the opportunity to progress to the next hierarchical level) increases dispro-portionately in order to motivate the requisite degree of competition for key positions within the organisation. Another implication of tournament theory is that greater compe-tition and higher rewards lower down the organisational hierarchy will necessarily lead to proportionately larger pay increases for more senior organisational members.

In both the US and UK, remuneration committees, consisting of part-time, non-executive directors that meet on average only twice per year, are now the institutional mechanism by which these internal and external labour market pressures have been translated into senior executive pay awards (for a review, see Stiles and Taylor, 2002). In the UK, every corporate governance code from Cadbury (1992) to the current 'Combined Code' (2002) has recommended that remuneration committees take account of labour market pressures by basing pay awards primarily upon what 'comparable' companies were paying their executives and, for incentive alignment purposes, to make pay more closely related to improvements in firm performance.[4] In practice, this encouragement of remuneration committees to focus on pay comparisons and performance related pay has tended to increase CEO pay levels as risk averse and resource constrained remuneration committees have sought to avoid being perceived as under-valuing their senior executives. The evidence (e.g. Ezzamel and Watson, 1998 and 2000) suggests that remuneration committees have realised that they can minimise the possibility of board-room conflict, recruitment and retention

problems and inadvertently signalling low managerial quality to outsiders, simply by paying their CEO somewhat more than the apparent market rate. Though, from the perspective of each individual remuneration committee, being relatively generous to the CEO is a reasonable strategy, the statistical impossibility for all CEOs to be paid more than average implies that their average pay levels will necessarily be 'bid-up' over time.[5]

Remuneration committees' apparent 'bidding-up' of executive pay has not, however, gone unnoticed by the business world. For example, the Institute of Directors (1995: 4) felt obliged to advise its members that remuneration committees 'should avoid setting packages which are generous in relation to market levels and beware of pressure always to be in the "upper quartile"'. In a similar fashion, the Combined Code has also highlighted this same problem:

> B.1.2 Remuneration committees should judge where to position their company relative to other companies. They should be aware what comparable companies are paying and should take account of relative performance. But they should use such comparisons with caution, in view of the risk that they can result in an upward ratchet of remuneration levels with no corresponding improvement in performance....

It will be noted that though they were both able to recognise the tendency for remuneration committees to raise pay levels, neither the Institute of Directors nor the drafters of the Combined Code felt able to offer any suggestions as to how to reduce the problem.

## ALTERNATIVE MODELS OF CORPORATE GOVERNANCE

As we have seen, the Anglo-US system of corporate governance is highly success-ful in that the corporate sector generates great wealth and investment opportunities for a wide range of investors and only a tiny minority of companies ever give their investors or regulators any serious cause for concern. This is a remarkable achievement, particularly given that the Anglo-US system relies predominantly upon a combination of:

i.  open and competitive product markets that encourage innovators to challenge incumbent firms;
ii. deep and liquid financial markets that provide a wide range of investment opportunities (either directly or via a collective savings institution such as a pension fund) for anyone with funds to invest and which facilitates efficient pricing and corporate restructuring to occur through control contests;
iii. strong legal rights and information disclosures to shareholders, and at least some significant shareholders that monitor corporate performance;
iv. the recruitment and rewarding of suitably qualified and appropriately incentivised managers; and,
v.  boards of directors focused on ensuring that corporate strategy and policies and the composition of the current management team remain consistent with shareholder interests.

Several of the above characteristics, for example, open and competitive product markets and corporate restructuring, greatly increase business uncertainty and though the shareholders remain the primary residual risk bearers, other stakeholders such as suppliers and employees will also necessarily be exposed to uncompensated business and financial risk. This inescapable risk bearing issue has led several writers to conclude that these groups should also be given formal decision rights and that shareholder interests should no longer dominate corporate decision making. Some of these writers (e.g., Armour et al., 2003; Plender, 2003) have even claimed that recent developments in the UK have significantly reduced the centrality of shareholder interests. It is suggested that due to the implementation of EU Directives, the UK's system of corporate governance has been moved much closer to that of Germany where debtholders

and employees already have a variety of formal decision rights that limit managerial discretion in several important areas relating to investment, financing and restructuring strategies.

An analysis of the developments that Armour et al. (2003) and others (e.g., Kay and Silberson, 1995; Parkinson, 2003) are referring to do not actually provide any additional formal decision rights – merely rights to be consulted, which of course, require no changes to be made to UK corporate governance. However, would granting additional decision rights to UK corporate stakeholders actually be a good thing in terms of efficient risk bearing, value creation and governance? As in Germany where employees of large firms control 50% of the seats on supervisory boards, effective control rights for non-shareholders would require formal involvement in decision processes – including having a veto on decisions that have an adverse impact on their situation. For a market-oriented economy and system of governance such as the UK, formally entrenching debtholder and/or employee representatives into corporate decision making would be a radical and unwelcome departure from existing practice. Neither debtholders, employees nor State officials appear likely to have any particular expertise in evaluating corporate strategies or ensuring efficient and appropriately focused management. The widely held public company has prospered precisely because it has been able to provide suitably skilled and motivated management teams with the resources and direction necessary to successfully compete in the product and financial markets. This shareholder focus has clearly never implied that the interests of other corporate stakeholders are of no concern to corporate management. Rather, the interests of these other stakeholders are protected, not by corporate law, but by other areas of law and regulation, e.g., health and safety and consumer protection legislation, competition law, labour and trade union laws.

It is apparent that many of the European and Asian countries with these alternative systems of corporate governance also tend to lack deep and liquid securities markets since their corporate ownership patterns are generally characterised by large and rarely traded controlling blocks of shares held by family groups, the State or other corporate entities (Roe, 2003; Hansmann and Kraakman, 2001). Typically, the controlling blockholders maintain control through dual class shares and control pyramids that provide them with voting rights far in excess of their cash-flow rights (e.g., their share of dividends). The desirability of these alternative models is questionable since the empirical evidence suggests that the main consequence has been to further entrench 'privileged insiders' (incumbent management and, as in Germany, core employees) and to discourage the development of financial markets and the flow of new firms and innovators that might have endangered these incumbent's positions. Thus, despite the views of some commentators that the Anglo-US model ought to become less shareholder focused, neither the necessity nor the desirability of adopting a more inclusive stakeholder system have been established. Indeed, in practice, contrary processes driven by global competition and the relative success of the Anglo-US corporate model, appear to be pressuring these alternative corporate governance systems into adopting (possibly inappropriate but more recognisably) Anglo-US shareholder focused characteristics (Hansmann and Kraakman, 2001).

## NOTES

1 For the financially inclined, the respective payoffs for shareholders and debtholders are analogous to that of a 'call option' holder and the writer of a 'put option' on the underlying value of the firm and with strike prices equivalent to the value of the outstanding debt obligations.

2 The proposition that managers always act in shareholder interests and that the convexity in shareholder payoffs at high debt levels may result in the expropriation of debtholders, is one of the major insights to be derived from the application of option pricing ideas to corporate securities (for a review, see Harris and Raviv, 1991).

3 The concept of bounded rationality was first coined by Herbert Simon (1955) and it refers to the limitations of human cognitive capabilities and our reliance upon simplified cognitive processes and decision criteria (heuristics). These cognitive processes result in judgemental biases and decisions based on inappropriate anchoring, stereotypes, frame dependencies, overconfidence and the escalation of commitment (see the original contributions to this literature in Kahneman *et al.*, 1982). Recent reviews of the research into the judgmental biases of agents in economics, investment and managerial decision making can be found respectively in Conlisk (1996), Shefrin (2000) and Bazerman (2002).

4 It is worth stressing that none of the UK corporate governance reports (i.e., Cadbury, 1992; Greenbury, 1995; Hampel, 1998; Higgs, 2003) have suggested that remuneration committee ought to control or attempt to hold down executive pay.

5 Even prior to their widespread introduction in 1993, it was apparent that firms with remuneration committees tended to award relatively generous pay increases to their CEOs and were largely reliant upon the information and recommendations supplied by outside 'pay consultants' regarding 'comparable' market pay rates and the complexities of performance-related pay schemes (see Main and Johnson, 1993 and Forbes and Watson, 1993 for reviews of the evidence).

## REFERENCES

Armour, J., Deakin, S. and Konzelmann, S. (2003) 'Shareholder primacy and the trajectory of UK corporate governance', *British Journal of Industrial Relations*, 41: 531–555.

Barkema, H.G. and Gomez-Mejia, L.R. (1998) 'Managerial compensation and firm performance: A general research framework', *Academy of Management Journal*, 41 (2), April: 135–145.

Bazerman, M. (2002) *Judgement in Managerial Decision Making* (5th edn). New York: John Wiley Publishers.

Bebchuk and Fried (2003) 'Executive Compensation as an Agency Problem', Working Paper 9813, National Bureau of Economic Research.

Berle, A. and Means, G.C. (1932) *The Modern Corporation and Private Property*. New York: MacMillan Publishers.

Cadbury Report (1992) Committee on the Financial Aspects of Corporate Governance: Financial Reporting Council, London.

Combined Code (2002) *The Combined Code on Corporate Governance, London Stock Exchange*. London: Gee & Co.

Conlisk, J. (1996) 'Why bounded rationality?', *Journal of Economic Literature*, 34: 669–700.

Conyon, M.J. (2006) 'Executive compensation and incentives', *Academy of Management Perspectives*, 20 (1) February: 25–44.

Conyon, M.J. and Murphy, K. (2000) 'The prince and the pauper? CEO pay in the United States and United Kingdom', *The Economic Journal*, 110, November, 2000: 640–671.

Ezzamel, M. and Watson, R. (1997) 'Wearing two hats: An analysis of the monitoring and control functions of non-executive directors', in K. Keasey, S. Thompson, and M. Wright (eds) *Corporate Governance: Economic, Management and Financial Issues*. Oxford: Oxford University Press, pp. 54–79.

Ezzamel, M. and Watson, R. (1998) 'Market comparison earnings and the bidding-up of executive cash compensation: Evidence from the UK', *Academy of Management Journal*, 41: 135–145.

Ezzamel, M. and Watson, R. (2002) 'Pay comparability across and within UK boards: An empirical analysis of the cash pay awards to CEO and other board members', *Journal of Management Studies*, 39: 207–232.

Forbes, W. and Watson, R. (1993) 'Managerial remuneration and corporate governance: A review of the issues, evidence and Cadbury Committee proposals', *Accounting and Business Research*, 23: 331–338.

Greenbury Report (1995) *Directors' Remuneration – Report of a Study Group Chaired by Sir Richard Greenbury*. London: Gee & Co.

Hampel Report (1998) *The Committee on Corporate Governance – Final Report of the Study Group Chaired by Sir Ronald Hampel*. London: Gee & Co.

Hansmann, H. and Kraakman, R. (2001) 'The end of history for corporate law', *Georgetown Law Journal*, 89: 439–468.

Harris, M. and Raviv, A. (1991) 'The theory of capital structure', *Journal of Finance*, 46: 297–355.

Hart, O. (1995) 'Corporate governance: Some theory and implications', *Economic Journal*, 105: 678–689.

Higgs, D. (2003) *Review of the Role and Effectiveness of Non-executive Directors*, London: Department of Trade and Industry, January (available: www.dti.gov.uk/cld/non_exec_review).

Holderness, C.G. (2003) *A Survey of Blockholders and Corporate Control, Economic Policy Review*. New York: Federal Reserve Bank of New York, pp. 51–64.

Institute of Directors (1995) *The Remuneration of Directors: A Framework for Remuneration Committees*. London: Institute of Directors.

Jensen, M.C. (1993) 'The modern industrial revolution. Exit and the failure of internal control mechanisms', *Journal of Finance*, 48: 831–880.

Jensen, M.C. and Meckling, W.H. (1976) 'Theory of the firm: Managerial behaviour, agency costs and ownership structure', *Journal of Financial Economics*, 3: 305–360.

Kahneman, D., Slovic, P. and Tversky, A. (eds) (1982) *Judgement under Uncertainty: Heuristics and Biases*. Cambridge: Cambridge University Press.

Kay, J. and Silberston, A. (1995) 'Corporate Governance', *National Institute Economic Review*, August: 84–97.

Keasey, K. and Watson R. (1991) 'Financial distress prediction models: A review of their usefulness', *British Journal of Management*, 2 (2) July: 89–102.

Keasey, K. and Watson, R. (1994) 'The 1986 Insolvency and Company Directors Disqualification Acts: An evaluation of their impact upon small firm financing decisions', *Small Business Economics*, 6 (4): 257–266.

Keasey, K. and Watson, R. (2000) 'Small firm bank borrowings: An empirical analysis of interest rate premia in the UK', *Journal of Business Finance and Accounting*, 27: 247–259.

La Porta, R., Lopez-de-Silanes, F. and Shleifer, A. (1999) 'Corporate ownership around the world', *Journal of Finance*, LIV (2): 471–517.

Lazear, E.D. (1989) 'Pay equality and industrial politics', *Journal of Political Economy*, 97, June: 561–580.

Lazear, E.D. and Rosen, S. (1981) 'Rank order tournaments as optimum labor contracts', *Journal of Political Economy*, 89: 841–864.

Main, B.G.M. and Johnston, J. (1993) 'Remuneration committees and corporate governance', *Accounting and Business Research*, 23: 351–362.

Monks, R. and Minnow, R. (2001) *Corporate Governance*. Oxford: John Wiley Publishers.

Parkinson, J. (2003) 'Models of the company and the employment relationship', *British Journal of Industrial Relations*, 41: 481–509.

Plender, J. (2003) *Going off the Rails*. London: John Wiley Publishers.

Rajan, R. and Zingales, L. (2003) 'The great reversals: The politics of financial development in the twentieth century', *Journal of Financial Economics*, 69: 5–50.

Roe, M. (2003) *Political Determinants of Corporate Governance: Political Context, Corporate Impact*. Oxford: Oxford University Press.

Roe, M. (2004) 'Explaining western securities markets', in A. Grandori (ed.) *Corporate Governance and Firm Organisation*. Oxford: Oxford University Press.

Roe, M. (2005) *Corporate Governance: Political and Legal Perspectives*. London: Edward Elgar.

Shefrin, H. (2000) *Beyond Greed and Fear*. Boston, MA: Harvard University Business School Press.

Shleifer, A. and Vishny, R.W. (1986) 'Large shareholders and corporate control', *Journal of Political Economy*, 94: 461–488.

Simon, H.A. (1955) 'A behavioural model of rational choice', *Quarterly Journal of Economics*, 69: 99–118.

Stiles, P. and Taylor, B. (2002) *Boards at Work*. Oxford: Oxford University Press.

Watson, R. (2005) *Corporate Governance and Ownership*. London: Edward Elgar.

Watson, R. and Ezzamel, M. (2005) 'Financial structure and corporate governance', in K. Keasey, S. Thompson and M. Wright (eds) *Corporate Governance: Accountability, Enterprise and International Comparisons*. London: John Wiley Publishers, pp. 45–59.

# 29

# Globalization and Organizational Behavior

Stewart Clegg and Chris Carter

## INTRODUCING GLOBALIZATION

The last 20 years have witnessed an unprecedented intensification of political, financial and informational connectivity. Events once deemed virtually unimaginable have come to pass and globalization – likened by Antony Giddens (1999), in his Reith lectures, to an out of control juggernaut – is the major story of our times. While the present manifestations of globalization may be novel, the experience of being a part of a globally interconnected world is nothing new: if we look back a century to the high water mark of imperialism, it is worth reminding ourselves that the Edwardian era was one in which global capital had become highly internationalized. World War I ended the first wave of modern globalization (1870–1914) and it took a further six or seven decades for it to re-emerge, following years of protectionism, war, and ideological conflict between the Soviet Bloc and the USA and its allies.

During the twentieth century there were numerous failed attempts to create a world

system – be they through the expansion of Nazi fascism to create a European-wide empire linked to other fascist spheres of interests elsewhere or through the ideas of the Soviet bloc, created in part through the key role of the Soviet Union in defeating fascism, as the vanguard of international socialism. The internal implosion of the Soviet Union, and the rapid disintegration of its empire, was enthusiastically cheered by neo-conservative commentators, as the end of ideological struggle. Political figures such as Margaret Thatcher and Ronald Reagan were icons of the time celebrating a new market-based era. Politics, it was presumed, would give way to markets and as markets opened up even more of the global economy to trade, authors such as Francis Fukuyama (1989) went as far as trumpeting the end of history, signaling liberal democracy to be the ultimate culmination of the human condition. In many important respects Fukuyama's ideas now seem absurd although the 'Washington consensus,' which he represents, arguably remains the most powerful ideational body in the world. The work of Thomas Friedman (1999, 2005) is perhaps the best contemporary example of this mode of thought. Friedman regards the fall of the Berlin Wall as signaling the genesis of the third era of globalization, or globalization 3.0 as he puts it. Seeing globalization as a golden straitjacket, Friedman argues in his best selling 'the world is flat' that the globalized era has, *inter alia*, ushered in a level playing field for international commerce. Friedman identifies 10 flatteners which have changed the world and that are bringing about the level playing field. They are:

(1)  The fall of the Berlin Wall
(2)  The development of the Web and netscape
(3)  Supply Chain Management
(4)  Opening sourcing – such as web blogs
(5)  Workflow software that allows computers to talk to one another
(6)  Personal mobile devices – such as mobile phones, laptops, blackberries etc.
(7)  Informing devices – search engines such as Google
(8)  Offshoring – corporations switching operations between continents
(9)  Insourcing – where a company performs an important function for another company
(10) Outsourcing – corporations contracting out key operations, often to different continents from the corporation's homebase.

For Friedman these flatteners are dismantling barriers to unfettered capitalism. According to his analysis, we are witnessing an unstoppable integration of markets, nation states, and technologies, one which is constitutive of an epochal shift in capitalism. He characterizes the new epoch as the 'flat world,' to which he argues there is no alternative (which is, of course, reminiscent of Margaret Thatcher's arguments about monetarism in the 1980s). The Washington consensus, expressed through the policies of the US Government, World Bank and International Monetary Fund, has profound and often devastating effects on the rest of the world. In the absence of a political economic alternative, capitalism is touted as inevitable, unstoppable and desirable. In Friedman's hagiography of 'flat world' capitalism, its capacity to bolster de-regulation, and its

centrality to the knowledge economy are listed as among its virtues. For Friedman, flat world capitalism creates a level playing field, unleashing new forms of capitalism consigning the concerns and policies of European social democratic governments to historical anachronisms. Friedman (2005) fails to countenance that free markets can be injurious to people and that 'flat world' economics can be environmentally disastrous.

The semiology of globalization opens up a violent hierarchy that privileges markets over government, the private over the public sector, and, individuals over collective interests. The dominant ideas of our age are configured around an economically liberal consensus that writes out collectives, minorities, the poor, and notions of public service. In its place is the triumph of big business and entrepreneurialism regarded as almost a cargo cult – something that will save us from poverty and ignorance if we just lie back and wait for the future benefits it will bestow. The 'Third Way' politics of Bill Clinton and Tony Blair were symptomatic of these shifts; while cloaked in social democratic sentiment they proved to be enthusiastic supporters of a neo-liberal agenda. Joseph Stiglitz (2003), the Nobel prize winning economist, in his analysis of the Clinton Administration highlights that the guiding logic consisted of 'what is good for Goldman Sachs, or Wall Street, is good for America and the world' (Stiglitz, 2003: xiv–xv; 24–6). The Clinton years, dubbed the 'Roaring Nineties' by Stiglitz, witnessed a boom in the financial markets. This boom paved the way for talk of the 'New Economy' associated with the dot com boom, deregulation and financialization. The new economy lasted as long as most new waves do: not very long at all. If it can be dated as beginning about the time that the World Wide Web took off commercially from about 1996 its demise can clearly be signaled in events that gathered speed in 2007. It was fun while it lasted: jobs grew, spending increased, and consumption of ever-cheaper Chinese and Asian goods flooded into the ports of the developed world in a cargo-cult of consumption. The downside of the cargo cult, fueled by easy money, low interest, and credit-funded consumption, became evident in 2007 with the 'credit crunch' caused by a decade of low global interest rates in the West and cheapening consumption due to the shift of consumer-goods production eastwards to Asia, especially China. When the loans turned sour and the full extent of bad debts becomes known, together with the inflationary consequences of the doubling of oil prices in twelve months, this caused a rapid decline in real disposable income and threatened widespread recession. Under such circumstances central banks reduce the availability of credit and increase the cost of accessing credit by raising interest rates. Such monetary regimes have predictable effects on consumer and organizational behavior: consumers consume less and organizations begin to lay off members or diminish their propensity for new hires.

The ideological nature of globalization has been examined by Manfred Steger. His argument is that 'globalism consists of a *set of six core claims* that play crucial semantic and political roles' (2007: 369, italics in original). The six claims, according to Steger, serve to decontest globalization. In other words, the six claims attempt to transform globalization from being a controversial phenomenon, necessitating critical inquiry and resistance, into a self-evident and natural order of things.

Steger (2007) sees the promotion of globalization as an ideological project. We agree with him. It is useful to remember that categories are the means through which we routinely, albeit largely unconsciously, observe and classify events and experiences as we understand them to be in the languages that we ordinarily use. They are ontologically prior to both discourse and rhetoric, one more fundamental or philosophically primitive, as it were. The inevitability and desirability of globalization is fast becoming one such category, such that it is difficult to think of a world without globalization, or, a different form of globalization. Lakoff (1987: 5–6) suggests that 'There is nothing more basic than categorization to our thought, perception,

action, and speech. Every time we see something as a kind of thing, for example, a tree, we are categorizing. Whenever we reason about kinds of things – chairs, nations, illnesses, emotions, any kind of thing at all – we are employing categories.' And these categories are necessarily experiential and empirical; they are grounded in our ways of being in the world. Globalization has now become a fundamental category for relating to the world. For some, it is a process to be resisted as anti-social; for others it justifies almost any kind of adaptation to changing circumstances as necessary. For instance, in Olivier Torrès' (2006) fascinating account of *The Wine Wars*, the attempt by Californian-based Robert Mondavi to establish a vineyard in the French region of Languedoc escalates into what is represented as a war on the very essence of *la belle France* itself, by an anti-globalization rebellion of communists, ecologists, hippies, local business people and wild boar hunters. The globalizers lost; the disparate and opportunist coalition won. The chance for innovation to enter into the enterprises making and marketing wine in Languedoc was lost and tradition won out. In essence, this is what is at stake in globalization: either people committed to traditional local ways of doing things resist or people who are not prepared to resist accept whatever it brings.

## UNDERSTANDING THE CONTOURS OF GLOBALIZATION

This chapter introduces some of the debates from within the social sciences and argues that macro-organization behavior needs to engage with globalization as the most urgent phenomenon shaping society because it represents the worldwide integration of virtually every sphere of life, touching consumption, savings, production and the rise and fall of organizations (Parker, 2003: 234).

The key features of globalization are not clearly demarcated across the social sciences: Roland Robertson and Kathleen White remind us that globalization is 'an essentially

**Table 29.1   Manfred Steger's six claims of globalism (summary of Steger 2007: 370–376)**

| Claim | Argument |
|---|---|
| Claim 1: Globalization is about the liberalization and global integration of markets. | Globalization is treated as an economic phenomenon. Economic liberalization is seen as synonymous with liberty, which should therefore be spread throughout the world. |
| Claim 2: Globalization is inevitable and irreversible. | Globalization is 'saturated with adjectives like "irresistable", "inevitable", "inexorable" and "irreversible"' (Steger 2007: 371). Globalization is represented as a natural phenomenon that has to be adapted to rather than resisted. As Steger notes, this serves the function of delegitimating alternative discourses about globalization. |
| Claim 3: Nobody is in charge of globalization. | Globalization, it is claimed, is about organic, self-regulating markets. Consequently, globalization is cast as leaderless and not captured by a single national or corporate interest. In the wake of America's actions in the post 9/11 world this is a more difficult argument to sustain. |
| Claim 4: Globalization benefits everyone (…in the long run). | In a rhetorical gambit reminiscent of some of the monetarist 'trickle down' theorists from the 1980s, advocates of globalization argue that everyone benefits from globalization eventually. |
| Claim 5: Globalization furthers the spread of democracy in the world. | Globalization theorists argue that increases in economic development are synonymous with higher degrees of democracy. The corollary, according to advocates of globalization, is that globalization is a good thing *per se*. |
| Claim 6: Globalization requires a global war on terror. | Steger (2007) notes that while the absence of a 'War on Terror' would not cause globalization to collapse, it is an important facet of contemporary globalization. Of course, if war continues it will become an increasingly important part of globalization's make-up. |

contested concept' (2007: 54). They argue that while it is virtually impossible to provide a definitive answer to the question of 'what is globalization?', nonetheless it is important not to reify it as a 'thing' but see it as 'two major directional tendencies, increasing global connectivity and increasing global consciousness' (2007: 64). George Ritzer (2007: 1) defines globalization as:

> an accelerating set of processes involving flows that encompass ever-greater numbers of the world's spaces and that lead to increasing integration and interconnectivity among those spaces.

Bob Jessop (2000) has pointed out that restructuring and rescaling are the two prime effects of globalization. By restructuring he refers to the way in which there are changes in the relations between different spheres of life. An example of this would be the way in which economic rationalism has penetrated numerous spheres of the public sector. Things that were once taken for granted in social democracies as essentially public services such as water supply or electricity and gas provision are now subject to market forces. It is now considered routine for bodies such as hospitals, councils and schools to be subject to quasi-market logics. Rescaling is the process through which different scales of social life are changed. Globalization can be thought of as worldwide integration in virtually every sphere achieved principally through markets, a process whereby the world becomes more interconnected and the fates of those people and organizations in it become more intertwined. In business terms, globalization means business without frontiers, people and enterprises crossing national boundaries and dealing with the world, not just the home base. The global juggernaut is often seen as the United States economy; some analysts view globalization as being, in essence, an Americanization of the world, even though many of the icons of globalization are of course non-American: Prada, Gucci and BMW, for instance. George Ritzer (1993) has argued persuasively that what is overwhelmingly being posited as the global is, in large part, American: American products, designs and politics dominate the global world – even when they are being manufactured by Chinese, Mexican or Brazilian companies. American corporations such as Gap, McDonalds and Starbucks are a commonplace feature of cities across the world. Friedman (2005) also sees globalization as quintessentially American. The US plays a dominant role in the world; it is the only military capable of global power projection. American consumption, especially of energy, drains natural resources from this world. America is not only hugely globalized, it is also massively indebted, with much of that debt held in Chinese and Japanese banks. The global world floats on a sea of oil and other energy resources that, according to some analysts, are at a tipping point in terms of exploitable reserves and existing price mechanisms. Future reserves will only be had at historically much higher prices. Thus, what increasingly is being globalized are North American values, products, force and debt, and unsustainable modes of production and consumption. North America is showing classic signs of the hubris of empire. While the rhetorical power of the Washington consensus is at its zenith, the shaky foundations on which American power is based are all too clear to see. We will now turn to the financial crisis of 2007/2008 to explore some of these issues.

## FINANCIALIZATION AND THE CREDIT CRUNCH

One striking illustration is the evident weaknesses of the US financial system manifested in the ongoing credit crunch crisis. In late 2007 the financial world was thrown into turmoil by American indebtedness as the sub-prime mortgage crisis unfolded. While the ramifications of the crisis are far from clear, the interconnected nature of the global financial system was evident. American banks were for a number of years pursuing a strategy of growth by providing mortgages to so-called 'sub-prime' borrowers. Sub-prime (as opposed to prime or near prime) borrowing is a category that refers to those with poor credit histories and/or marginal employment status. The banks offered mortgages to hundreds of thousands of sub-prime Americans, who were now able to enter the housing market. American banks then securitized this debt by packaging it and selling it off to other banks and investors, from America and overseas. The mortgages offered to sub-prime lenders generally offered discounted interest rates for the first few years of the loan. When the discounted rates came off the mortgages and were accompanied by a general interest rate rise, hundreds of thousands of sub-prime borrowers were unable to meet the repayments and eventually their homes were repossessed. Boarded up, repossessed but largely unsaleable homes are a commonplace feature of marginal suburban areas in American cities. The repossessions contributed to a drop in American real estate prices and a liquidity crisis as banks encountered cash flow problems. Normally banks borrow on the money markets when they require liquidity. The money markets shuddered to a halt as banks – short of cash – were unwilling to lend to each other and set about hoarding any monies they could obtain.

The crisis went global when it crossed the Atlantic and hit Northern Rock – a bank from Newcastle, England. Northern Rock, which had sourced most of its capital from the money markets, was unable to raise the funds that it required which, in turn, led to a run on the bank. Within a few days, thousands of customers withdrew billions of pounds of their savings for fear of losing their money. Despite the British government standing as guarantor to Northern Rock, the withdrawals continued and led to a massive bail-out and eventual nationalization of the bank by the British Government. More recently, the American Bear Stearns Bank lurched into crisis. The Bank of England, European Central

Bank and the Federal Reserve Bank have been pumping huge amounts of money into the banking system to try and prevent a complete freezing up of the financial sector. Large international banks have been forced to raise money through rights issues of shares, while the viability of smaller banks, such as Bradford and Bingley (which specialized in loans to 'buy and let' investors and real estate speculators), are in question.

Northern Rock is an illustrative case of the globalization of finance. It was an old style British Building Society serving the north-east of England which demutualized, in the late 1980s following the liberalization of financial services and sought to become one of the leading mortgage providers in the UK. It pursued an aggressive strategy of growth backed up by a business model which relied on raising monies from the money markets, which were then lent out as mortgages. When the money markets froze Northern Rock was unable to access the funds it needed. Consequently, it was forced to go to the Bank of England who acted as a lender of last resort. In the aftermath of the crisis there were no suitors for Northern Rock, which led to the British Government becoming the reluctant new owners of the failed bank. While nationalization has become a pejorative term – a catch-all phrase used to capture the supposed inefficiencies, incompetence and bureaucracy that have ideologically become 'fixed' to the idea of state run organizations – the Northern Rock débâcle is a striking reminder that there are serious limits placed on the ability of markets to deal with such situations. The banking crisis has thrown up the bizarre specter of wild gambles made by retail banks being underwritten by the taxpayer. Such is the ideological stranglehold on the collective imagination that the private sector is still venerated in spite of a litany of corporate failures. The Orwellian style mantra of 'private good, public bad' points to the importance accorded large corporations and financial markets when looking for solutions to global problems. While the past decade has seen a global privatization of organizational behavior – more and more employment has been moved into the private sector – the diminution in value that has accompanied the end of this decade has seen the relatively new specter of Sovereign Wealth Funds haunting the graveyards of failed and failing firms. In an exquisite irony the decade of rip-roaring capitalism has prepared the way for wealthy state-backed funds from oil states, not only in the Gulf but also in social democratic Norway, to takeover this private capital. In addition, cashed-up funds from the Gulf, China and India are taking over the assets of the old imperial centers in a reverse of earlier patterns of globalization while states such as the US seek to block them doing so in a subvention of the free-market ideologies proclaimed so long and loud in the recent past.

## PROCESSES OF GLOBALIZATION

According to Peter Dicken (2007: 8), we live in a globalizing rather than globalized world. Dicken suggests that there is an interpenetration of four parallel processes creating globalization.

(1) *Localizing processes*: where geographically concentrated activities with varying degrees of functional integration occur, playing a key role in the global economy. Key ports such as Rotterdam, Singapore and Hong Kong or airports such as Heathrow and Frankfurt would be obvious examples.

(2) *Internationalizing processes*: this is where there is a simple spread of economic activities across national borders but with low levels of functional integration. The *maquiladora* plants of Monterrey, in Northern Mexico, which use cheap land and labor to service goods or produce components and goods for the US economy, would be a case in point. For instance, GE has a plant that services all of its North American radiological equipment there.

(3) *Globalizing processes*: characterized by a both extensive geographical spread and a high degree of functional integration. The global auto industry would be a case in point, where new models may come from any of a number of countries, despite that we might think of them as 'national' cars. German cars, which many people prefer because of the perceived quality of

German workmanship, might come from Brazil, The United States, South Africa or the Czech Republic, for instance.

(4) *Regionalizing process*: characterized by globalizing processes that take place at a regionally supranational scale such as the EU or EFTA, or other similar common markets.

Corporations sometimes have considerable potential to shape policy within nation-states. In countries that are competing with one another for foreign direct investment from these global entities, then, in a process more akin to a beauty contest than any economic planning model, less developed nations will sometimes compete against each other in terms of tax incentives, grants, and other inducements to attract firms to their country. Within countries, regional policies operate to try and bring investment to particular regions.

Globalization has a technical core, which is organized in terms of flows of inputs, their distribution globally, transformation, and outputs, organized through global supply chains. These in turn, are embedded in technological and logistical systems, which, in turn, are coupled with financial and governance systems. The key actors, without doubt, are transnational firms, whose ability to move facilities and resources globally sets in play the dynamic flows through global circuits, at the core of which is a production complex, incorporating material inputs, transformation processes, distribution networks and channels to market for the consumption of goods. Each of these is reciprocally interconnected. Supporting the core are technological and logistical systems, which in turn are contained within a financial system and a governance system of regulation, coordination and control. Financial systems are extremely important: they control the supply and value of the underlying key commodity, which of course is capital. The section above on the credit crunch highlights the interconnected nature of the world financial system. Financial markets and complex financial products – such as securitized debt – have compressed the financial system such

that a local difficulty in one part of the world can soon escalate into a global crisis. Donald MacKenzie (2006), a sociologist of finance, has highlighted the way in which financial models play a performative role in actively making markets rather than reflecting them. MacKenzie charts the growth of futures contracts which grew from virtually nothing to a $300 trillion market by the middle of this decade. His argument is that this would not have been possible without the finance theories that were developed in the 1970s and 1980s.

Circuits of global production have an impact in four ways:

(1) *On the global relations between states*, as we see some states flourish as a result of globalization, such as China and India in recent times. Others – particularly in sub-Saharan Africa – face parlous economic and political circumstances as their economies, often as a result of IMF interventions, are opened up to the market.

(2) *On issues of sustainability*, as places such as China and India industrialize on the back of a fossil fuel industry which is ecologically most damaging. The levels of pollution in the Pearl River Delta, for instance, which is China's main export route, are calamitous. China is currently making huge investments in Africa and Latin America – buying up natural resources to fuel the copper, zinc and coal needs of their rapidly expanding industries.

(3) *On people's conceptions of who they are*: it reaches into societies and enables people to migrate and move from one society to another – the millions of 'guest workers' in the Middle East Oil Rich countries of the Gulf, for instance – or the people who become illegal migrants from Africa and Asia in search of a better life, so it has a considerable impact on hanging conceptions of personal identity. People only develop a sense of self in relation to others. For most of human history, these others were framed by what was available at the local, often village, level. Today, even the most remote villager can see themselves against the mirror that the media projects into their communities.

(4) *On the multi-cultural diversity of organizations and communities*: in almost any of the world's great cities today there are people working with each other, competing with each other, and

playing with each other whose ancestors come from villages all over the globe. Multi-cultural society is normal.

## GLOBALIZATION'S MAJOR PLAYERS

Globalization is a complex set of ideas and processes that have increasingly been cleverly and simply packaged. It is important in order to try and understand who the major actors are in driving the globalization package. In the post-war period it was popular to talk of the military–industrial complex, a term coined by President Dwight Eisenhower in his valedictory address. The military–industrial complex referred to the link between big business and the military in dictating policy. This concept was resonant with the critique of American Society, by C. Wright Mills (1956), the eminent sociologist, who argued that a milieu of politicians, military leaders and business executives set the agenda for the country, according to their own shared interests. The military–industrial complex was arguably at its zenith during the Vietnam War where the escalation of the conflict was driven by military chiefs and big business. We argue that the military–industrial complex while still important – one only has to think of the arms sales made by the West to other regimes or the role the Halliburton corporation is playing in the largely privatized theater of war that is Iraq – is now overshadowed by the business-consulting complex. One of the key distinctions between the military–industrial complex and its successor, the business-consulting complex, is that the latter comes replete with a set of powerful ideas about how organizations should be structured and managed. The business-consulting complex is a way of characterizing the close relationship between big business, large management consultancy firms, large accountancy firms, IT firms, business schools and government. The degree, for example, to which MBA style management thinking permeates American and British government policies is quite remarkable.

Transnational corporations are central figures in packaging globalization. That they exert massive influence over governments and peoples' lives is beyond dispute. The annual turnover of some corporations exceeds the gross domestic product of some nation states. As Thomas (2007: 85) points out that the behavior of 'transnational corporations are both competitive and collusive.' Corporations aim to secure a competitive advantage for themselves – often with the help of government (Thomas, 2007) – while at other times acting together as a group to promote their shared interests. One of the ways in which their shared interests has been organized and promulgated has been through the emergence of a powerful management ideas industry over the last 25 years. The management ideas industry has successfully packaged, communicated and commodified organizational change programs as a cultural ideal and a desirable good. A management-ideas industry has been fueled by the rise of business schools, especially through the provision of MBA degrees, the growth in management consultancies, and the emergence of self-styled management gurus. Taken together this amounts to an actor-network that has successfully packaged and commoditized managerial initiatives. These models of 'best practice' have been disseminated throughout the organizational world. These create blueprints of what organizations 'should' look like and what managers 'should' do. Collectively the key players of the management ideas industry have helped produce management fashions. Interestingly, the management-ideas industry has been successful in taking ideas from the private sector and transferring them to the public sector, a process of translation that has changed the nature of the public sector.

Important actors in the management ideas industry have been the major IT companies, such as SAP and Cap Gemini. The changes in IT have been one of the major enabling factors behind globalization. IT firms have played an important role in the development of the management ideas industry. Recent initiatives such as Enterprise Resource Planning and Knowledge Management rely very heavily on IT practices. Matthias Kipping (2002) has argued that consultancies go through waves of development. According to his analysis large IT firms are riding the most recent wave and are becoming the dominant players in the consulting industry.

The emergence of a global management project is, in part, a phenomenon spread through hugely influential 'guru' books. There is now a huge commercial market in popular management books and a circuit of celebrity for those who write them. They are the gurus of the modern age, the 'management gurus.' Tom Peters is the most celebrated and, at the same time, infamous of the management gurus. Gurus are generally self-styled and known for their image and rhetoric intensity. Producing airport lounge best-sellers and conducting world lecture tours, gurus hawk their homespun nostrums throughout the corporate world. Analysts of gurus have argued – in a McLuhan (1964) fashion – that the medium is the message. Evangelical-style exhortations to change accompanied by convincing stories and snappy sound bites characterize the genre. The books follow a similar vein and, as we suggested above, are often taken to task for their theoretical and methodological failings, which is, perhaps, to miss the point. Even more managers are likely to listen to a guru presentation or perhaps read a guru book than are likely to attend business school (Clegg and Palmer, 1996). Many of the gurus have enjoyed glittering corporate careers and their ideas on management are lent a credibility by this corporate experience – such texts have elsewhere been characterized as 'karaoke texts,' in a reference to their 'I did it my way' quality (Clegg and Palmer, 1996). Often, key texts will anchor key management consultancy products.

Large-scale management consultancy has grown exponentially and consultants have become major actors in the creation and trans-mission of management ideas. Management consultants simultaneously instill a sense of security and anxiety in their clients: security, because they imbue managers with a sense of certainty and control over the future or whatever organizational problem it is that the consulting is concerned with; anxiety, because the managers are in a sense emasculated – unable to manage without the guidance of consultants (Sturdy, 2006). It is not just corporations that are subject to consultancy nostrums – their influence has long been felt in the public sector, including the inner sanctum of Western governments.

While many US consultancies had been in existence for much of the last century – coming out of the systematic management movement of Taylor's day – it is over the last 20 or so years that demand for their services has boomed. Organizations such as McKinseys and the Boston Consulting Group have become high-status brands in their own right. Other consultancies emerged out of the large accountancy partnerships. Uniquely placed as the auditors to large firms, most large accountancy firms commercialized to the extent that their consultancy operations became at least as important as the core auditing business, which was notably the case with Arthur Andersen and their most infamous client, Enron. In 2001, the last year of Enron's existence, they spent $100 million (2001 prices) on audit and consultancy services from Arthur Andersen. In the account outlined by Hanlon (1994) it was these processes, inte-gral to Arthur Andersen's commercialization, which subverted the professional duty of the auditors to certify that Arthur Andersen had not been provided with *true* and *fair* accounts.

The role of the large accounting firms is pivotal to understanding the story of the rise of consultancies. By the mid-1980s the market for financial audit was mature and had stagnated. In any case, outside of a few accounting firms in a few geographical locations, competition between these firms was frowned upon and for the most part regarded as being somewhat aggressive and ungentlemanly. What the large accounting firms possessed was a monopoly over the provision of audits to large firms. The 'full professional jurisdiction' (Abbott, 1988) was protected by law. The large accounting firms developed a number of capabilities, one of which was the ability to cultivate and sustain long-term relationships with clients.

These connections were often cemented by their own accountants going to work in client firms after a number of years with the accounting partnership. Accounting partnerships also possessed highly sophisticated means of charging for audits and managing large-scale interventions into organizations.

The shifting context of accounting firms in the 1980s allowed them to diversify outside of audit activities, though their clients were generally those that they also sold audit services to. Audit became the wedge that opened the corporate door to the on-selling of additional services. Hanlon (1994) has demonstrated the way in which the large accounting firms commercialized themselves – pursuing capital accumulation strategies; also Greenwood et al. (1999) have written extensively on the unique characteristics of accounting firms that allowed them to globalize so successfully.

Power (1994) has argued that we increasingly live in an *audit society*, one in which the principles of verification and calculability underpin society. During this time accountants and management consultants have risen to powerful positions within civil society. In the UK, for instance, large accounting firms played an important role in drafting privatization and private finance initiatives. They were simultaneously to profit from the implementation of such policies. Government work, that was once the sole preserve of mandarins, is now often carried out by accountants and management consultants. It is noteworthy that management consultants played a substantial role in drafting policy for the Blair Government. While Blair and many of his cabinet ministers were lawyers by training, his government could *de facto* be regarded as the first MBA government in Britain; likewise the George W. Bush administration had the highest number of MBAs seen in US government. What marks out a mandarin from a management consultant or an accountant is a different type of intellectual capital: the mandarin was most likely to be a classicist, schooled in a classical discipline, educated at a socially élite university, and drawn from a wealthy family background.

The moral sentiments of the knowledge borne by a management consultant are more technocratic and democratic, and are likely to be premised on less concern with social origins, and education in a business school, usually in an MBA.

In our discussion of the business-consulting complex, aside from mentioning the creeping managerialization of governments, we have fallen silent on the state. States also package and resist globalization. Why they might sometimes resist is clear: Globalization poses major challenges to the nation state. It is clearly impossible for governments to manage their economies in the way in which they once did: capital and corporations are simply too footloose; equally, industrial production has shifted predominantly to China, India, Mexico and parts of south-east Asia. In spite of such changes the state remains a crucial actor in the globalizing world. One has only to look at the pivotal role played by the, nominally communist, Chinese State in developing export capitalism in China, or, to the role played by the US government in prosecuting war in Iraq. Similarly, the links between the Russian government and their energy corporations, such as Gazprom, shows the pivotal role of a nation state in globalization. While supra-national bodies, of which the European Union is the exemplar *par excellence*, exist and have gradually accrued more influence, they remain a pale imitation of the power of a nation state – lacking democratic accountability, a monopoly on violence, and, in many powerful quarters, moral legitimacy. States do still matter and some will be more, or less, opposed to different conceptions of what is globalization.

## RHETORIC FOR AND AGAINST GLOBALIZATION

Let us return to states once more; this time the United States, which as we have seen is regarded by many as being the country that above any other is driving globalization. George W. Bush's intervention immediately post-9/11 was a moment of undecidability, decided by strategic action according to the principles of oppositional logic. The attack on the Twin Towers was without doubt one of the key moments of the last decade. The attack could have been described in many ways. As events transpired we got a 'war on terror' waged by 'terrorists bent on destroying our freedoms,' a description that was particularly impoverished and only made sense to a particularly unsubtle, binary, black-and-white way of thinking: Globalization + Americanization = Modernization = Good; Globalization + Islamicization = Traditional-ization = Bad. Our point is that the simplistic rhetorical repertoires, that accompany much of the discourse on globalization, encourage us to simple binaries in which one is either for or against abstract processes that can lead us to abstract nouns such as a 'War' on 'Terror.' From the organizational behavior perspective of combatants – whichever side they are on – the implications of simple rhetoric can be profound and sometimes fatal.

From an organizational perspective, the important issue is to try and understand motivation relative to constructions of reality and structured context. Needless to say, as Weber observed, understanding is not equivalent to identifying with or legitimating. A deliberate avoidance of binary logic would have meant that the proper response of the US government would have been to send anthropologists, organization theorists and sociologists to the Middle East, rather than soldiers! Or, at least, seek the advice of such specialists at home. Of course, that would have been hard to sell but it would have been the more intellectually sophisticated response.

The binaries that you use depend on the categories that you attend to. It is clear from analysis of the evidence collected by the Commission that enquired into 9/11 that the President, George W. Bush, and Condoleezza Rice, the National Security Adviser, had received at least 40 briefings from the CIA alerting them to Osama bin Laden specifically, as well as the threat of a terrorist attack in the months of 2001 preceding the attack. However, these were not the categories that were policy concerns before 9/11 dictated.

They were not institutionalized. Instead, as a speech that Condoleeza Rice was due to give on 9/11 indicates, which was canceled because of the attacks, the focus was on big $ defense, not the security of the state. The speech, which was intended to outline her broad focus on the Bush Administration's plans for a missile defense system included only passing reference to terrorism and the threat of radical Islam. One may be justified in assuming that for the top management team of the United States at that time, the categories with which they dealt were those that were widely promoted by the business–consulting complex rather than the daily briefings received from George Tenet, head of the CIA. Indeed, the effect of this disavowal of the CIA-inspired advice, which one would assume did benefit from anthropological, organiza-tional, sociological and political science input, given the organization's resources, was to leave the administration in an essentially untutored position immediately after 9/11. Indeed, Bush's first statements after 9/11 called for a 'crusade' against the enemies of America who had launched the attack. One would not think that culturally sensitive social scientists would have advised such a binary positioning. Organizational behavior that constitutes categories such as 'Crusaders' should not be surprised if, at the same time, opposite identities such as Jihadist, are also legitimated. Motives are not made up purely of intentional states of being but are composed of available categories with which to assemble sense and attribute motive. The game of motive in organizational behavior sometimes has high and escalatory stakes.

Manfred Steger's work outlined in Table 29.1 above highlights globalization rep-resented as an unstoppable phenomenon. Such images are difficult to shake off. Of course, as Foucault (1977) teaches us where there is power there will be resistance. Resistance to globalization often has a carnivalesque quality, such as in the large protests that take place on every occasion the G8 finance ministers or world trade organization meet. After chaos at meetings in Prague and Seattle, the finance élites now convene in more secure and remote locations. There is of course a delicious irony to the fact that democratically elected foreign ministers can only meet under a blanket of heavy security. Yet while the protestors' rhythmic drumming, partying and leftist sloganeering confronting police in full riot gear makes for striking imagery, it is not clear that anything is changed by such protests. Similarly, acts of resistance against the pace of globalization, such as those by the wonderfully titled Slow Food movement, do not strike at the heart of globalization but they are a reminder that life can be different.

In Michael Hardt and Antonio Negri's (2000, 2004) seminal analysis of globalization, they introduce the idea of an emerging global empire which *inter alia* is unleashing what they term the 'multitude,' to resist empire. According to Hardt and Negri, resistance will take on novel and varied forms. The Zapatista uprising in Chiapas, Southern Mexico is often cited as an example of this. On January 1, 1994, Zapatistas – composed primarily of the dispossessed and marginalized rural poor – stormed into a number of major towns in Chiapas. They quickly withdrew but had made their point. Over the years to come, Subcommandante Marcos, the enigmatic leader of the Zapatistas, used the internet to organize on a global scale. Similarly, labor unions have used the web effectively in organizing disputes (Carter et al., 2003).

## CONCLUSION

Globalization is a complex assemblage of processes to which it is hard to do justice to in a book chapter. Nonetheless this chapter points to the importance of understanding globalization and its consequences. For us, a key motor of globalization is the business-consulting complex – spreading ideas across the organizational world. These ideas come at a cost for they write out other possibilities, other ways of being.

Increasingly, the Washington consensus that saturates globalization, as it is currently configured, while impeccably *economically* liberal is dangerously *politically* illiberal.

The twentieth century gave us new forms of totalitarianism of which Fascist, Stalinist and Maoist regimes were examples. Globalization, and its rhetoric of necessity, offers a new form of illiberal liberalism: liberal markets and illiberal antitheses to entrenched ways of doing things, to traditions. One of the traditions under threat in the sophisticated states of Western Europe are the traditional social democratic terms of equality, egalitarianism and justice. Discourses of globalization often elevate simplicity and banality at the expense of more sophisticated understandings of the world. Our vignette on Bush and the War on Terror illustrates this point.

Macro-organizational behavior generally falls silent on issues of politics and globalization. To continue to ignore issues of globalization and power will render macro-organizational behavior as little more than a technicist irrelevance: an interesting parlor game for those attending élite Business Schools, before they enter employment with large multi-nationals or consultancies. We think macro-organizational behavior should be more ambitious than it currently is and engage with the major issues of our times, many of which can be subsumed under the general category of globalization.

The key questions all have a global component: for instance, how is global warming to be tackled? How can global inequalities be tackled? How can organizations help contribute to everyday social democracy and the civility of society in those places where they globally nest, especially where it is the reliance on the local illiberalities with regard to wages and labor conditions that encourage that nesting? Macro-organizational behavior has developed a canon of powerful insights into the organizational condition – it is time for these to be put to work on important issues facing humanity.

## REFERENCES

Abbott, A. (1988) *The System of Professions: An Essay on the Division of Expert Labour.* Chicago: Chicago University Press.

Carter, C., Clegg, S., Hogan, J. and Kornberger, M. (2003) 'The polyphonic spree: The case of the Liverpool dockers', *Industrial Relations*, 34 (4): 290–304.

Clegg, S. and Palmer, G. (1996) *The Politics of Management Knowledge*. London: Sage.

Dicken, P. (2007) 'Economic globalization: Corporations', in G. Ritzer (ed.) *The Blackwell Companion to Globalization*. Oxford: Blackwell, pp. 291–306.

Foucault, M. (1977) *Discipline and Punish*. London: Allen Lane.

Friedman, T. (1999) *The Lexus and the Olive Tree*. New York: Anchor Books.

Friedman, T. (2005) *The World Is Flat*. New York: Farrar, Strauss and Giroux.

Fukuyama, F. (1989) *The End of History*. London: Hamish Hamilton.

Giddens, A. (1999) Runaway World. *Reith Lectures*. BBC.

Greenwood, R., Rose, T., Brown, J., Cooper, D. and Hinings, C. (1999) 'The global management of professional services: the example of accounting', in S. Clegg, E. Ibara and L. Bueno (eds) *Global Management: Universal Theories and Local Realities*. London: Sage Publications.

Hanlon, G. (1994) *Commercialisation of the Service Class*. London: Macmillan.

Hardt, M. and Negri, A. (2000) *Empire*. Cambridge, MA: Harvard University Press.

Hardt, M. and Negri, A. (2004) *Multitude*. New York: The Penguin Press.

Jessop, B. (2000) 'The crisis of the national spatio-temporal fix and the tendential ecological dominance of globalizing capitalism', *International Journal of Urban and Regional Research*, 24 (2): 323–360 (38).

Kipping, M. (2002) 'Trapped in their wave: The evolution of management consultancies', in T. Clark and R. Fincham (eds) *Critical Consulting: New Perspectives on the Management Advice Industry*. Oxford: Blackwell, pp. 28–49.

Lakoff, G. (1987) *Women, Fire, and Dangerous Things: What Categories Reveal about the Mind*. Chicago: University of Chicago.

MacKenzie, D. (2006) *An Engine, Not a Camera: How Financial Models Shape Markets*. Cambridge, MA: MIT Press.

McLuhan, M. (1964) *Understanding Media: The Extensions of Man*. New York: McGraw-Hill.

Parker, B. (2003) 'The disorganization of inclusion: Globalization as process', in R. Westwood and S.R. Clegg (eds) *Debating Organizations: Point-counterpoint in Organization Studies*. Oxford: Blackwell, pp. 234–251.

Power, M. (1994) *The Audit Explosion*. London: Demos.

Ritzer, G. (1993) *The McDonaldization of Society*. Thousand Oaks, CA: Pine Forge Press.

Ritzer, G. (2007) 'Introduction', in G. Ritzer (ed.) *The Blackwell Companion to Globalization*. Oxford: Blackwell, pp. 1–13.

Robertson, R. and White, K. (2007) 'What is globalization?', in G. Ritzer (ed.) *The Blackwell Companion to Globalization*. Oxford: Blackwell, pp. 54–66.

Steger, M. (2007) 'Globalization and ideology', in G. Ritzer (ed.) *The Blackwell Companion to Globalization*. Oxford: Blackwell, pp. 367–382.

Stiglitz, J. (2003) *Globalization and its Discontents*. New York: W.W. Norton.

Sturdy, A. (2006) 'Management Education', in G. Ritzer (ed.) *Encyclopaedia of Sociology*, Oxford: Blackwell.

Thomas, G. (2007) 'Globalization: The major players', in G. Ritzer (ed.) *The Blackwell Companion to Globalization*. Oxford: Blackwell, pp. 84–102.

Torrès, O. (2006) *The Wine Wars*. London: Palgrave.

Wright Mills, C. (1956) *The Power Elite*. Oxford: Oxford University Press.

# Index